Masters, servants, and
  magistrates in Britain and

Masters, Servants, and Magistrates in Britain
and the Empire, 1562–1955

STUDIES IN LEGAL HISTORY

Published by the University of North Carolina Press
in association with the American Society for Legal History

Thomas A. Green and Hendrik Hartog, editors

Masters, Servants, and Magistrates in Britain and the Empire, 1562–1955

Edited by

Douglas Hay and Paul Craven

The University of North Carolina Press

Chapel Hill and London

Publication of this work was supported by a generous grant
from the William Nelson Cromwell Foundation.

Paul Craven and Douglas Hay codirect the Master and Servant Project
at York University (Toronto), an equal collaboration reflected in
the alternating order of their names on joint publications.

Set in Janson Types
by Tseng Information Systems, Inc.
Manufactured in the United States of America

⊗ The paper in this book meets the guidelines for permanence
and durability of the Committee on Production Guidelines
for Book Longevity of the Council on Library Resources.

Library of Congress Cataloging-in-Publication Data
Masters, servants, and magistrates in Britain and the
Empire, 1562–1955 / edited by Douglas Hay and Paul Craven.
    p. cm. — (Studies in legal history)
Includes bibliographical references and index.
ISBN 978-0-8078-2877-9 (cloth : alk. paper)
    1. Master and servant—Great Britain—History.
2. Labor contract—Great Britain—History.
3. Master and servant—Great Britain—Colonies—History.
4. Labor contract—Great Britain—Colonies—History.
I. Hay, Douglas. II. Craven, Paul, 1950- III. Series.
    KD1634.A75M37 2004
    346.4102′4—dc22
                2004000731

Portions of Chapters 10 and 16 have appeared previously, in somewhat
different form, in, respectively, Martin Chanock, *The Making of
South African Legal Culture, 1902–1936: Fear, Favour and Prejudice*
(Cambridge, 2001), and David M. Anderson, "Master and Servant
in Colonial Kenya, 1895-1939," *Journal of African History* 41,
no. 3 (2000): 459-85, and are both reprinted here with the
permission of Cambridge University Press.

11 10 09 08 07   6 5 4 3 2

Contents

v

Tables and Figures

FIGURES

Acknowledgments

The planning for this volume took place more than a decade ago. Since then, the editors have incurred a host of debts, and they hope that they have remembered most of those to whom thanks are particularly owed. The database of imperial statutes that underlies this volume (and will be explored in another) took far longer to assemble than we had imagined at the outset, and its creation would have been impossible without the assistance of our coauthors and many librarians and research assistants. All the contributors supplied statutes from manuscript and printed sources, but we owe particular thanks to Chris Tomlins and Michael Quinlan, for material from many jurisdictions of colonial America and Australia, and above all to Mandy Banton, who provided exhaustive lists of African materials and over the years has followed up questions about literally hundreds of other statutes and ordinances. The project, and this volume, would have been impossible without her unfailingly generous assistance.

Among the librarians and archivists who greatly assisted us, we thank Balfour Halevy, Judy Ginsberg, Marianne Rogers, Louise Tsang, and Maureen Boyce of Osgoode Hall Law School; Kathy Drake of the South African Library, Cape Town; Ian Pearce, Chief Archivist of Tasmania; and the staffs of the Public Record Office, the British Library, the Institute of Advanced Legal Studies and the School of Oriental and African Studies (London), the Foreign and Commonwealth Office Library, the Law Library of the University of Oxford, the libraries of Griffith University and the Queensland Parliament, and many other collections in Canada, the United States, the United Kingdom, and elsewhere. We are also grateful to Deanna Jubas, Elaine Glossop, Ross Irwin, and many others at Osgoode and York, and to everyone at the UNC Press, for their assistance in preparing the volume for publication.

Research assistants, graduate students, and postdoctoral colleagues were responsible for a large part of the location and collection of statutory materials and their coding and full-text entry for computer analysis at York University, as well as other research assignments. In Canada, we had the help of

Tom Archibald, Sheryl Beckford, Jeff Bookbinder, Jane Burton, Dan Condon, Patrick Connor, Janice Cook, Karen Cunningham, Fred Ernst, Magda Fahrni, Chris Frank, Cara Fraser, Denise Guthrie, Courtney Harris, Doug Harris, Kathryn Harvey, Rose Hutchens, In Ha Jang, Orion Jhaj, Martha Kanya-Forstner, Seann McAleese, Siobhan McClelland, Sam Marr, Craig Morrison, Vicki Majerovich, James Muir, Claire Mummé, Cary Nieuhoff, Adele Perry, Stuart Swartz, Will Traves, Craig Wilson, and Tracy Wynn. Overseas, we received crucial help from Mark Harding (London), Tonia Novitz (Oxford), Ruth Paley (London), Sanjay Sharma (London), and James Sutton (Stafford).

Among the many colleagues who have advised and assisted and contributed materials over many years, we thank David Arnold, Harry Arthurs, Dale Brawn, Elizabeth Elbourne, Jean-Marie Fecteau, Don Fyson, Harry Glasbeek, Tom Green, Dirk Hartog, Greg Kealey, Shula Marks, Greg Marquis, Ruth Paley, Diana Paton, Jim Phillips, Allen Robertson, Robert Ross, David Sugarman, Robert Tignor, and Jeremy Webber.

Finally, we gratefully acknowledge the financial support of the Social Sciences and Humanities Research Council of Canada and the research support of York University (Toronto) and Osgoode Hall Law School.

Note on Citations

All references to the British Parliamentary Papers series of sessional and command papers, which included colonial "Blue Books," an informal designation for statistical, financial, and other reports returned to London by colonial governments, are indicated either by "PP" or the command number or both. The form of citation used for Parliamentary Papers before 1870 is "PP" followed by the year of the annual series, the paper or command number(s) in parentheses, the volume number within the year, and the page number separated by a colon—for example, PP 1856 (441) 50:633. Each Parliamentary Paper from 1870 onward has its unique command number. By convention, from 1877 to 1899, the command number is prefaced by "C," from 1900 to 1918 by "Cd," and from 1919 to 1956 by "Cmd." For these years we have not consistently supplied volume numbers, as the sequential command number system provides ready access to the particular document.

Statutes (including ordinances, proclamations, and orders-in-council) are cited in the footnotes and Index of Statutes by the name of the enacting jurisdiction (in parentheses), the date, regnal year, or statute number of the enactment (following the form in use at the time and place), and the year of enactment. English, British, and United Kingdom Statutes are cited in the form given in the *Chronological Table of the Statutes Covering the Period from 1235 to the End of 1965* (London, 1966). In the text, statutes are often identified by title and year.

Masters, Servants, and Magistrates in Britain

and the Empire, 1562–1955

ONE

Introduction

Douglas Hay and Paul Craven

. . . all the statutes heretofore made, and every branch of them, as touch or concern the hiring, keeping, departing, working, wages, or order of servants, workmen, artificers, apprentices and labourers, or any of them, and the penalties and forfeitures concerning the same . . .

—(Engl.) 5 Eliz. c.4 (1562)[1]

For more than 500 years, the law of master and servant fixed the boundaries of "free labor" in Britain and throughout the British Empire. Compounded of statutory enactments, judicial doctrine, and social practice, it defined and controlled employment relations for almost a quarter of the world's population in more than 100 colonial and postcolonial jurisdictions.[2] Variant forms governed servants and masters in Tudor England, seventeenth-century Virginia, eighteenth-century Barbados, nineteenth-century Assam, and twentieth-century Kenya. Immensely varied, it was also often strikingly similar in different times and places, and always had three defining characteristics. The first was the idea that the employment relation was a matter of *private contract* or agreement for work and wages[3] between an employer who thereby acquired the right to command and an employee who undertook to obey. The second was the provision for *summary enforcement* of these private agreements by lay justices of the peace or other magistrates, largely unsupervised by the senior courts. The third was *punishment* of the uncoopera-

1. Enacted (and often cited) 1563; English, Scottish, British, and United Kingdom citations are standardized on *Chronological Table of the Statutes* (London: HMSO, many editions), which gives 1562.

2. This volume is concerned almost entirely with jurisdictions within the formal constitutional empire, rather than those within the "informal empire" of British economic and political influence.

3. In the case of apprenticeship to a trade, maintenance and instruction replaced wages entirely or in part.

tive worker: not damages to remedy the breach of contract, but whipping, imprisonment, forced labor, fines, the forfeit of all wages earned. This distinctive conjuncture of civil contract, informal justice, and effective criminalization of the worker's breach was enacted in thousands of statutes, enforced around the globe in a web of closely related language, doctrine, and social practice.[4] Its commands and particularly its penalties provoked resistance, political conflict, and ultimately repeal.

This book considers together both British and colonial master and servant law to explore its commonalities and differences and, in particular, to consider how it was used and enforced.[5] Master and servant was one of the many legal ligaments that helped make the British Empire a thinkable whole by the eighteenth century. To the limited degree that it has been described by historians and lawyers, rather than simply evoked, the general law of empire usually has been treated as the common law.[6] Yet master and servant was in its essentials statute law. Because it was the business of lay justices and other magistrates at the lowest level of the judicial hierarchy, whose decisions were not matters of formal record, the law and its enforcement remained largely unexamined by the senior courts, especially before the nineteenth century. Master and servant preoccupied the legislatures.[7] An enormous volume of employment legislation was produced by 100-odd imperial jurisdictions. The

4. Convict labor was also very important in many parts of the British Empire, often as a precursor or coexisting system, but it is not our subject. Although master and servant law provided penal sanctions, workers under such contracts were not convict labor.

5. Several of the chapters also examine the case law. Paul Craven and Douglas Hay are preparing a second volume, dealing with the spread of legislation throughout the empire, the borrowing and elaboration of both language and concepts of master and servant law in the statutes, and their relationship to the economic and political structures of each colony. By the nineteenth century all British jurisdictions—England and Wales, Scotland, and Ireland—participated in a common body of statute law. In earlier centuries, however, the law of master and servant in Scotland and Ireland was distinctively different from that of England. Master and servant statutes of the Irish Parliament, while based on English models, contained distinctive provisions and penalties. Scotland, an increasingly civilian jurisdiction from the Middle Ages until the nineteenth century, had its own law of employment relations both statutory and judicial, enforced not only by justices but also in sheriff and burgh courts and (before 1746) in courts of hereditary jurisdiction. Research on Scotland and Ireland is in progress. In this book, for the most part, "British law" refers to the law of England to 1707, of Great Britain to 1801, and of the United Kingdom thereafter.

6. For the emergence of concepts of empire and the remarkable disjunction between imperial and British histories (a disjunction seen also in the history of law), see Armitage, *Ideological Origins*, especially ch. 1; for the general and specialized literature, see Winks, *Historiography*. Among the small number of comparative studies of statutory law in the empire are MacKenzie, *Empire of Nature*; Fletcher et al., *Women's Suffrage*. On control from London, see Swinfen, *Imperial Control*. A recent finding-aid to sources is Dupont, *Common Law Abroad*.

7. Preyer, "Crime, Criminal Law, and Reform," 54.

sheer bulk of these statutes, together with the deliberate exclusion of master and servant from the lawcourts (by privative provisions, judicial deference, and other means),[8] forces us to reconsider the characterization of imperial legal regimes as simply common-law or mixed common-law-with-civilian-or-other regimes (Quebec, South Africa, Mauritius, Scotland, Sri Lanka, etc.). Instead, we argue here, the law of master and servant existed in large measure as a separate body of imperial law that had remarkably little contact, over long periods, with the high legal regimes in which it was everywhere nested.[9]

Master and servant law emerged in an immense diversity of settings: in rural and industrial Britain; in the tobacco fields of colonial America and the sugar plantations of the West Indies; in Canadian forests and Australian sheep stations; in African diamond mines and Indian tea gardens; in merchant ships on the high seas, and in the warehouses and workshops of a thousand towns. The details of its variation in these different settings, including huge differences in the rate and severity of enforcement, invite us to examine how law changes, how it is adapted, and how it shapes and is shaped by the societies in which it is embedded. This volume examines the law and particularly its enforcement after 1600 in Britain, colonial America, Newfoundland, Canada, Australia, the British Caribbean, Africa, India, and Hong Kong, in fourteen case studies. This introduction and a chapter on the Colonial Office explore the economic, ideological, and political dimensions, and the regional differences and distinct chronologies, of what became an immense structure of imperial law. The use or disuse of the law in any given jurisdiction, and its specific terms, illuminate the experience of labor and the profitability of capital. Comparisons among these many jurisdictions, over several centuries, raise important questions about the nature of high and low law, about freedom, about markets, about empire.

While there has been considerable historical writing about particular employment regimes—master and servant in England, indentured labor in early America, postslavery "apprenticeship,"[10] nineteenth-century industrial immigration, among the most familiar—these areas of scholarship have remained largely insulated within their regional or national histories. The main

8. The insulation of master and servant disputes from the high courts was increased by the fact that although both parties could sue there, in most jurisdictions this almost never happened: servants could not afford to do so, and masters could not expect to get damages of any significance. The latter fact was frequently held to justify penal sanctions.

9. See the later section on Master and Servant as Imperial Law.

10. In this Introduction, we use quotation marks to distinguish the "apprenticeship" of the 1830s, used to manage the transition from enslaved to contracted labor, from the traditional usage of apprenticeship as an instrument for training and guardianship of young people. Both are forms of master and servant law.

exceptions have been literatures on "apprenticeship" and on the massive nineteenth-century migration of Indian, Chinese, and Melanesian labor under indenture, both of which have had to come to terms with direct imperial regulation of these regimes. Yet the details of the statutes, their significance, and their enforcement have been insufficiently explored. Little attention has been paid to their similarities to English master and servant law, or even to the other earlier or coincident employment law regimes in the same colonies.

For example, in the Caribbean white indentured servitude preceded slavery. Following abolition, freed slaves were subject to the compulsory bound labor of "apprenticeship." When it ended in 1838, new penal statutes were enacted to govern the ex-apprentices. But these laws failed to keep ex-slaves and their descendants on the plantations, so British Guiana and Trinidad (and, to a much lesser extent, Jamaica) began in the mid-nineteenth century to import indentured Indian labor, generating in the process a thick statute book and stunningly high rates of penal enforcement.[11] Moreover, Jamaica continued to legislate for masters and servants during the period of slavery,[12] while British Guiana enacted regulations governing casual laborers in Georgetown during the period of indentured Indian plantation labor.[13] In these jurisdictions there were as many as four or five distinct and partially overlapping regimes, each based in its own set of statutes. All were variations on the larger theme of master and servant law, sharing in its common characteristics. Other colonies that experienced neither "apprenticeship" nor industrial immigration nevertheless had coincident varieties of employment contracts regulated by different statutes, with the same common characteristics, as did England itself.

Here we explore some of the issues raised by the large existing literature and by the contributors to the volume, who have shared a comprehensive database of some 2,000 master and servant statutes. This chapter summarizes the origins and proliferation of statutory master and servant law, considers the importance of the statutes themselves as evidence, and gives an abbre-

11. The weight of the evidence suggests rather that it was not the presence or absence of an indenture (considered in the older literature to be a mark of unfreedom), but the nature of all the legal terms of a contract express or implied, and the specific details of enforcement, that determined the nature of the employment relationship, and the relative freedom of action of the parties. Indenture is treated here as an important and varied form of the sociolegal relation of master and servant, rather than as a singularity.

12. For example, (Jamaica) 55 Geo.III c.19 (1814), providing for the adjudication of disputes "between masters or mistresses and servants, hired, contracted, or indented (overseers of sugar and coffee plantations, and pens, and other servants, receiving wages at a rate exceeding one hundred pounds per annum, excepted)."

13. De Barros in this volume.

viated chronology of the spread of their provisions throughout the empire. Analysis of these provisions undermines the conventional categories of "free" and "unfree" labor found in most of the economic and historical literature. This introduction also demonstrates the immense range of uses of master and servant law; summarizes the ways in which it interacted with vagrancy laws, dispossession, and policing through the example of southern Africa; compares enforcement levels in different economies and societies; and suggests an approach to the large question of what constitutes an imperial system of law.

English Origins

From the beginnings of the common law, but especially from the Ordinance of Labourers and Statute of Labourers, England's central state took a sharp interest in the terms of employment.[14] The fourteenth-century legislation was a response to demands for and by labor attributed to the enormous demographic consequences of the Black Death. In the words of the Statute of Cambridge (1388), "Servants and labourers will not, nor by a long season would, serve and labour without outrageous and excessive hire."[15] The magistrate, often a layman, first appears as the rural justice of the peace in fourteenth-century England; indeed, it has been argued that the master and servant law, the justices of the peace, and the gentry class from which they were drawn were three aspects of one momentous transformation.[16] From that point until the twentieth century the enforcement of employment contracts was almost entirely in the hands of these men and their urban counterparts. They were only on rare occasions required to account for their actions to high-court judges, who in most periods before the mid-nineteenth century rarely questioned their decisions.[17] Unlike the high courts and quarter sessions, the magistrate's summary hearing was not a court of record. Often his actions were

---

14. (Engl.) 23 Edw.III cc.1–8 (1349), (Engl.) 25 Edw.III st.2 (1350; usually usually dated 1351: see note 1 above.) The English state's interest in the terms of service from at least the fourteenth century is well known. Yet because the most common forum was a hearing before one or two magistrates or a local bench of them, more has been written about the genesis of the statutes than about enforcement. An exception is the medieval period: see Putnam, *Enforcement*, and Poos, "Social Context," who notes the emphasis on social control as well as economic interest, on the part of local employers as well as the central state. On these statutes, see R. Palmer, *Black Death*; for the literature on the 1562 statute, see the works cited in the chapter by Hay.

15. (Engl.) 12 Ric.II cc.3–9 (1388).

16. R. Palmer, *Black Death*; see the chapter by Hay for further discussion.

17. For the eighteenth century, see Hay, "Dread of the Crown Office"; for the nineteenth century, see Frank, "Warrington Cases," and Frank, "Constitutional Law," and his chapter in this volume.

not recorded in any sense.[18] As a result, there was often a triple disjuncture between the law as enacted by statute, the law as applied by magistrates, and the law as interpreted by the high courts.

Almost all the elements of the early legislation (compulsory service, apprenticeship, penalties for leaving work, attempts to tie workers to particular status and employers) were recapitulated in the forty-eight sections of the Statute of Artificers (1562), whose categories dominated the law until the nineteenth century. Over the next four centuries, legislation and judicial decisions elaborated these statuses, rights, and duties, in several distinct models of nonslave labor. Although their exact contours changed over time, these were the elements that colonial governments adopted, modified, or rejected in creating labor regimes throughout the empire. Quite different models of coercion and remedy from those of England were invented in colonies that relied extensively on imported or indigenous workers who were not of European origin, but even there the English (and probably some Scottish) models provided crucial elements, and invite comparisons.

The English hierarchy of employment statuses was based on age, terms of engagement, financial standing, and often specific occupation, for different trades were subject (by statute and case law) to different obligations. There were also some geographically and occupationally distinctive forms of contracts. In this sense there was no one law of employment common to most or all workers in early modern England: there were important common elements, but much difference in detail. Abstraction and innovative generalization took place only in the nineteenth century, when the project of theorizing the English law of contract included descriptions of the principles of employment (which nonetheless retained its distinctive character within the larger body of contract law).[19] From the mid-nineteenth century, a general theory of contract informed new legislative activity, which quickly drew nearly all workers into a common legal regime. The statutes in Britain, and in some parts of the empire, were partly purged of penal sanctions and recast in neutral language that purported to balance the duties and remedies of both parties.

Until then, the law provided most of the content for a large and diverse set of employment relations. For young people, mainly boys but also a very few girls, *apprenticeship* took several forms, from carefully drawn agreements for

18. The archival records of superior courts vary in their extent but vastly exceed the surviving records of individual magisterial activity for earlier centuries, although the latter dealt with an immensely greater number of cases.

19. For an argument that contracts of employment affected the formation of general contract doctrine, see Orth, "Contract and the Common Law."

the children of wealthy parents to the coercive parish apprenticeships of the poor. This status rested on medieval and Tudor law that required apprenticeship to practice enumerated trades, but it was eroding badly by the eighteenth century, and its compulsory clauses were repealed in 1814. Among adults, the medieval and Tudor law distinguished several kinds of workers, all generically termed *servants*. There were *servants in husbandry* (agriculture), hired by the year; *artificers* and *workmen* (who in towns were also subject to the rules of their guilds or companies), who might be hired by the year, for other periods, or for specific tasks; and *day laborers*, whose muscle power was called upon in every area of agricultural and artisanal practice. All are mentioned in medieval legislation, and by 1600 the contracts of these groups, comprising most adult workers, fell within the jurisdiction of the magistrates. Confusingly, from the late eighteenth century *domestic servants* were excluded by judicial decision from the scope of master and servant statutes in England, although they usually were included in the colonies. There was also the legal category of *covenant servant*, often a highly skilled worker who had entered into articles of agreement to serve under specified conditions for a specified term, which might be longer than a year. Special varieties of written contracts existed in a number of trades, particularly mining, where an annual "bond" was in use in some coalfields by the early eighteenth century, and in merchant shipping, where seamen's labor agreements embodied in written articles were found throughout the empire as a matter of imperial policy. Indentured servants for labor in the colonies also entered into written articles with elements drawn from apprenticeship and/or adult covenant agreements.

The balance of this body of law, the degree to which it favored employer or worker, shifted over the centuries, sometimes between decades, trades, places. Its coexistence with other changing legal provisions was also important. Besides master and servant law in the sense discussed here (the individual contract and its summary enforcement), a large number of civil and criminal statutes and doctrines governed collective labor relations and labor standards. Best known are combination acts and criminal conspiracy (making trade unions and strikes illegal), fixing of maximum and occasionally minimum wages (medieval and Tudor provisions still enforced at least occasionally as late as the eighteenth century), and, increasingly in the nineteenth century, new civil and criminal liabilities of trade unions and the growth of protective legislation around mines and factory employment. These are not our subjects. However, the law of master and servant also was used against strikers, who almost always offended against the laws governing the individual contract by stopping work or by persuading others to leave or refuse employment.

By the 1830s and 1840s many elements of master and servant law, but notably imprisonment of workers for breach, and the use of the law to crush trade union activity, had become contentious in England and Scotland, probably because it was being administered more harshly by less disinterested magistrates, in a state with increased capacity for imprisonment, hostile to the protections found in the older law, and committed to freedom-of-contract ideology. Litigation underwritten by trade unions, and their well-organized 1844 campaign against the extension of master and servant penalties to new trades, coincided with popular political protest, including the democratic demands of the Chartist movement of 1838–48.[20] When the English statistics began to be collected, in the mid-1850s, they showed some 1,500 workers imprisoned most years, and many more thousands who lost some or all of their wages, suffered dismissal, and very occasionally were whipped. New protests led to 1867 legislation that greatly reduced the penal sanctions; in 1875 one of the founding campaigns of the united modern trade-union movement succeeded in erasing them from the statute law.

The scholarship on early modern and modern England has expanded greatly in the past decade, but it is still not extensive. Simon's pioneering article half a century ago dealt mostly with the years 1850–75, the last 5 percent of the period that penal sanctions were used in England since their introduction in the fourteenth-century statutes.[21] She asked who used master and servant law, noted its (unexplored) roots in an eighteenth-century and earlier past, and showed how a theory of freedom of contract made for new arguments against the criminal penalties, leading to their abolition. But the article only touched on the much larger history, parts of which have recently begun to emerge in detailed studies of other periods.

For the postmedieval period, local studies have noticed the law as it was applied to industrial workers and apprentices in different parts of England.[22] Some recent work assesses its use in the eighteenth and early nineteenth centuries, marking the significance of increased rates of imprisonment to the role of justices of the peace, the heart of English local government.[23] The special legislation enacted for seamen has merited separate study, given its distinctive characteristics, and one scholar has also considered the degree to which English law in the nineteenth century offers a contrast to enforcement of labor contracts in Germany, as an approach to assessing the larger characteristics

20. For the 1844 campaign, see the chapter by Frank in this volume.
21. Simon, "Master and Servant."
22. Woods, "Master and Servants"; Rushton, "Matter in Variance"; J. Lane, *Apprenticeship*; see the chapter by Hay for these and the following works.
23. Hay, "Patronage, Paternalism, and Welfare"; Hay, "Master and Servant in England."

of each national system.[24] More has been written on the doctrine of master and servant, mainly for the nineteenth century, than on enforcement or political significance, until recently.[25] Two books published in 1991 reconsidered the nature of American and English employment law in the nineteenth century, with emphasis on its longer roots and coercive nature, and the distinctive abandonment[26] in the United States of penal sanctions.[27] A full treatment of the law in the period originally covered by Simon, circa 1850–75, is centered on refuting the myth (peculiar to American legal scholars, misled equally by constitutional doctrine and sociological theory) that "free labor" in the United States and England had fully emerged by the eighteenth century; the legal basis of the coercive mechanisms of forfeited wages in the first, and imprisonment and fine in the second, is explored in detail.[28] Other recent work on England explores in detail the crucial role of trade-union agitation and litigation in delegitimating the penal sanctions in the 1840s and 1850s, and incidentally helping shape the law for many other summary offenses, as well as master and servant, for the future.[29]

Yet at almost exactly the same historical moment there was a great reinvigoration of penal sanctions in old and more recent colonial acquisitions, particularly in the West Indies and in parts of Africa. Such projects were not new. From the subjugation of Britain's first colony (Ireland, acquired piecemeal from 1169 to 1606) governors at home and abroad had been intensely interested in the organization, through law, of labor in the territories of the empire. In the seventeenth century there began a vast extension of master and servant law, often with harsher terms than in England, first in colonial America (the earliest statutes appeared in 1631–32 in Virginia) and the new Caribbean colonies such as Barbados (acquired in 1625), where a full master

24. Dixon, "Seamen and the Law" (which has little on enforcement); Steinmetz, "Dejuridification."

25. Napier, "Contract of Service"; Freedland, *Contract of Employment*; Deakin, "Contract, Labour Law"; Deakin, "Contract of Employment."

26. American exceptionalism appeared early in the thirteen colonies, particularly with respect to the penal sanctions, which were already greatly attenuated before the Revolution: see Tomlins in this volume. In this book we do not consider United States employment law after independence.

27. Orren, *Belated Feudalism*, focuses on the coercive elements that remained embedded in American employment law; Steinfeld, *Invention*, suggests that coercion largely receded with the end of penal sanctions by the early nineteenth century, under the political pressure of a constituency of white workers determined to distinguish their status from that of slaves.

28. Steinfeld, *Coercion*, emphasizes legislation and especially judicial doctrine, rather than enforcement. Steinberg, "Capitalist Development," is an important study of local enforcement.

29. Frank in this volume; Frank, "Constitutional Law," chs. 2–3; Frank, "Warrington Cases."

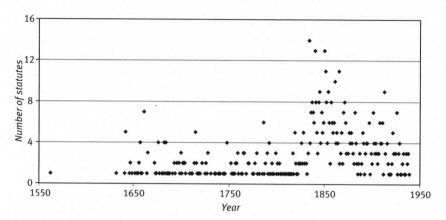

and servant statute was enacted in 1661.[30] Over three centuries almost 2,000 statutes and ordinances made their appearance in more than 100 colonies, developing a colonial master and servant law that drew upon, elaborated, and often subverted the metropolitan models. About 700 of these can be considered "core" enactments (rather than amendments or restatements), and it is a formidable corpus of legislation, some 1.2 million words, girdling the globe (Figure 1.1).[31] The colonial law developed distinctive structures of its own, including the sanctions and remedies provided for employers and workers. It was also often administered in highly oppressive and exploitative ways, particularly where workers were not of British or European origin.

Taking Statutes Seriously

In this book, and the larger project of which it is a part, we take the statutes seriously.[32] Employment law—penal and regulatory employment law in par-

30. (Virginia) 7 Car.I n.30 (1631), (Virginia) 8 Car.I n.28 (1632); (Barbados) n.30 of 1661.

31. Statutes, ordinances, and orders-in-council held by the York Master and Servant Project, include amendments and reenactments; the core statutes are also held in full text and coded form for computer analysis. The collection is imperfect for some colonies (we know of some enactments for which we could not find an original and unamended text) but is substantially complete for core statutes. The evolution of methods, and findings to date, from this part of the project are reported in Hay and Craven, "Master and Servant in England and the Empire"; Craven and Hay, "Criminalization"; Craven, "Clustering Engine"; Craven, "Automatic Detection and Visualization"; and see below.

32. Karsten, *Between Law and Custom*, 326–60, does not take statutes seriously enough. In his account of the "informal law" of labor contracts in the white dominions, Karsten acknowl-

ticular—is a creature of statute. The formal policy of the law is in the statutes, and so too is much of the history of the law and indeed of the empire as a legal and political entity. Taking the statutes seriously is not to hold them out as mirrors of what masters, servants, and magistrates were doing on the ground. As the chapters that follow amply demonstrate, the statute law was sometimes ignored, sometimes willfully misapplied, and often stated in terms so broad as to allow the justices an almost infinite discretion. The ultimate historical test of the lived experience of employment law lies in the detailed recovery of the justices' transactions and, beyond that, in the choices made by individual masters and servants, the ways in which their understanding of the law influenced their practice. But justices' chambers were not courts of record; moreover, few masters and still fewer servants have left us direct evidence of their calculations. The chapters that follow reconstruct a narrative about the summary enforcement of master and servant law from the sources that remain, bringing those fragments of lived experience into dialogue with the statutes.

Taking the statutes seriously has profound implications for a comparative history of employment law. It requires us to search for explanations of similarities or differences in enforcement across time or geography, not only in political economy or the discourse of doctrine but in the language and policy of the statutes in force. The comparative investigation of the statutes raises questions about the organization of empire. How consistent was this body of law throughout the empire? To what extent were colonial enactments mere transcripts of the metropolitan statutes? What control did the imperial center exercise over colonial law? How were statutory provisions and policies transmitted? Did colonial enactments influence metropolitan law? Did the master and servant law of the colonies at any time more closely reflect the idiosyncrasies of their local political economies or legislative trends in the metropolis?

There was never one single enactment that applied to all employment relations throughout the empire. The great Statute of Artificers purported to repeal and replace "all the statutes heretofore made, and every branch of them" affecting the employment relationship, but even in England a lengthy series of new acts, many of them applying to particular trades and occupations, emerged to complicate the picture. To the extent that any colony simply received English statutes, the initial state of its lawbook depended on the date

---

edges but does not discuss the differences among the master and servant acts in force in the various jurisdictions, differences that often had large consequences in law and practice.

of its foundation.[33] This alone would generate much diversity given the pace of legislative change in England in the eighteenth and nineteenth centuries, and the long march of imperial formation. But simple reception was a convenient fiction. Local authority determined which acts were suitable to be received—an Upper Canada judge rejected the Statute of Artificers as "a local act which was probably adapted to the state of society in England three hundred years ago, but is not now, and never was adapted to the population of a colony"[34]—and even the effective date, sometimes years after the fact.[35] Governors and colonial legislatures were empowered to enact local legislation, "as near as may be amenable to the laws of England," and it was for them to decide (at least at first instance and, in practice, often finally) what that requirement meant. Indeed, governors of new possessions might be directed to model their legislation not on the British acts, but on those of established colonies.[36] Even in colonies with express reception dates, local legislatures might declare there to be no act in force regulating the relations of master and servant, thereby effectively removing notionally received British enactments from the colonial statute book. Elsewhere, however, British master and servant law might be received by implication via the controlling common law rather than by reception of particular statutes.[37] A few colonies expressly provided for aspects of British employment law (especially apprenticeship) to take effect, usually with the proviso, "except insofar as the same are inapplicable to the circumstances of this Colony."[38] By contrast, many jurisdictions provided for the enforcement of employment contracts made outside the colony so long as they were consistent with local enactments.

With rare exceptions, the imperial parliament did not make employment legislation for the colonies. In the early 1820s British acts for the administration of justice in New South Wales and Van Diemen's Land, and for the incorporation of land and colonization companies there, gave local justices

33. The doctrine of reception (as opposed to legislative copying) applied to English statutes before 1707, British statutes from 1707 to 1800, and United Kingdom statutes from 1801. Some statutes of the Irish Parliament (before it disappeared at the formation of the United Kingdom in 1801) were copied elsewhere. So far we have not identified any Scots statutes from before the union of 1707 (which created Great Britain) subsequently used as models.

34. *Dillingham v. Wilson* (1841), 6 UCQB (O.S.) 85, per Sherwood J.

35. See, for example, Bell, "Reception."

36. Thus Virginia was the model for early Nova Scotia: see Craven in this volume.

37. While colonies notionally received the British statutes at the date of their foundation, they received (again, notionally) British common law continuously. As much of the common law of employment developed by way of judicial interpretation of master and servant statutes, a colony might acquire legal principles founded in the British statutes indirectly, through the case law.

38. For example, (W. Australia) 37 Vict. n.12 of 1873.

jurisdiction over disputes between masters and indentured servants. When the Canada Company was reestablished in 1824, its (British) act was based on these models, despite the insistence of its directors that their circumstances were not at all similar, not least because Upper Canada had a local legislature whereas the Australian colonies (at the time) did not.[39] The Australian companies made some use of the indenture provisions of these statutes,[40] but their Canadian counterpart did not, and there is no evidence that what would likely have been seen as unwarranted metropolitan interference ever came to the attention of the local Assembly or the courts.

The imperial government took a pronounced and continuing interest in three particular aspects of colonial employment relations: the merchant marine, the abolition of slavery, and the export of indentured labor from India. Before 1762, when the British merchant shipping act was made perpetual and applied to the American colonies,[41] there appears to have been limited metropolitan supervision of colonial legislation affecting seamen's employment relations.[42] From early in the nineteenth century, though, British merchant shipping legislation was drafted to apply on the high seas and in the ports of all colonies without legislatures (and to British ships in foreign ports with consular representation). Colonial shipping legislation was scrutinized for compliance with the imperial model to regularize sailors' working conditions and protect British shipping interests in the imperial labor market. In consequence, these acts were much more nearly the image and transcript of their metropolitan models than other employment legislation.[43] For many

39. The British acts are: (U.K.) 4 Geo.IV c.96 (1823); 5 Geo.IV c.86 (1824); 6 Geo.IV c.39 (1825); 9 Geo.IV c.51 (1828); 9 Geo.IV c.83 (1828); and 11 Geo.IV & 1 Wm.IV c. 24 (1830). In 1824, the Canada Company directors expressed themselves "rather surprised to observe that after having submitted the draft of a charter drawn up with great care . . . no notice whatever has been taken of that document but a transcript has been made of the Australian Company's published Act." Archives of Ontario, F-129 (hereafter Canada Company), Series A-3, v.1, Canada Company Records, Minutes of Committees, 20 Oct. 1824. The Australian indenture provisions were not copied in the 1825 Canada Company act but were inserted in the 1828 amendment: see Canada Company, series A-6-4, v.1, Simon McGillivray to Hon. William Huskisson, 19 Apr. 1828.

40. The Australian Agricultural Company planned to employ British indentured servants as "constables and floggers" to supervise convict labor but they were soon replaced by convict trustees: J. Perkins, "Convict Labour," 170, and see the chapter by Quinlan in this volume.

41. (G.B.) 2 Geo.III c.31 (1762), extending and making perpetual (G.B.) 2 Geo.II c.36 (1728) as continued temporarily by several intervening enactments.

42. Several eighteenth-century acts of West Indian colonies made it an offense for visiting ships' masters to abandon sick sailors there: for example, (Bahamas) n.194 (1790); (Barbados) Ordinance of 30 Oct. 1754. Fines and fees provided for by the eighteenth-century British legislation and its nineteenth-century colonial successors were directed to the support of sailors' hospitals.

43. For example, (Newfoundland) 1 Vict. c.9 (1837); (India) n.1 of 1859. The imperial power

colonies, the transition from slavery to master and servant via "apprentice-ship" was accomplished by imperial legislation and orders in council, and again the compliance of the legislative colonies was closely (although incompletely) supervised.[44] The imperial regulation of Indian labor migration was addressed in part by elaborate colonial enactments giving effect to standardized conditions of passage and employment conditions. But in most other respects, particularly later in the history of master and servant, colonies were left to their own devices in legislating for employment relations. Moments of intervention — for example, to regulate the style of cane that could be used to chastise African servants[45] — were exceptions to the norm of inattention and inactivity.[46]

Master and servant statutes were everywhere the same, and everywhere different. This somewhat paradoxical statement is true at every level — applied, conceptual, even linguistic. As the chapters that follow demonstrate, the uses of the law were constantly reinvented in the changing circumstances of different political economies. Similar ideas recur over great spans of time and geography, but often in novel combinations. The statutes drew on a common stock of words and phrases but arranged them so diversely that few can be said to be simple transcripts of earlier models.

For an example of similarity and diversity in the statutory lexicon, consider the scope clauses of the acts, which set out the trades, occupations, and other categories of workers to which they applied. Reading the legislation, some broad distinctions are readily apparent.[47] Many British acts named specific occupations — tailors, pitmen, potters — "and others," thereby affording the judges ample opportunity to extend or narrow their application depending on how they chose to crack the nut.[48] Few colonial statutes were so particular, although the 1847 South Australia list, including *artificers, sawyers, splitters, sheep-shearers, and persons engaged in mowing, reaping or getting in of hay or corn or in sheep-washing and other labourers*, stands comparison with the 1823 British

---

of disallowance was used inter alia to remove colonial legislation enabling the arrest of articled seamen for debt. See Quinlan, "Balancing Trade with Labour Control," and the chapter by Craven in this volume.

44. See the chapters by Turner and Banton in this volume, and the discussion below.

45. For example, (S. Rhodesia) n.10 of 1926; (N. Rhodesia) n.56 of 1929.

46. For a detailed discussion of Colonial Office supervision of employment legislation, see the chapter by Banton in this volume.

47. This discussion is based on a collection of 695 core master and servant statutes from ninety-six jurisdictions: see Figure 1.1. A slightly expanded and refined core statute collection underlies the York Master and Servant Project's dissemination and distribution analyses (forthcoming).

48. Willis, "Statutory Interpretation." For judicial interpretation of the scope provisions, see the chapters by Hay and Frank in this volume.

list of *servants, artificers, handicraftsmen, miners, colliers, keelmen, pitmen, glass-men, potters, labourers or other persons or apprentices.*[49] Some colonial statutes listed occupations unknown to their British counterparts, and vice versa. Un-like Britain, many colonial statutes defined their scope in racial rather than expressly occupational terms, although seafarers, porters, and other long-distance transport workers were commonly distinguished from other labor.

Taking a closer look, we find some 140 distinct occupation words in the texts of the statutes. Some occur in just one act—*amah, coachbuilder, farrier, hunter, plumber, sealer,* among others—while a few are much more common. *Servant* appears in 411 statutes, *labourer* in 301, *apprentice* in 259.[50] These and other terms occur in various combinations: the Statute of Artificers' formula, *servants, workmen, artificers, apprentices, labourers,* recurs in an Australian stat-ute as late as 1935.[51] Among the more common combinations (measured as greatest co-occurrence within a single sentence) are *apprentice* and *servant* (66 statutes), *labourer* and *servant* (64 statutes), *artificer, labourer,* and *servant* (55 statutes). Combinations of occupational terms are more common than indi-vidual appearances: of the 411 statutes in which *servant* (or *servants*) appears, it co-occurs with one or more of *apprentice, labourer, artificer,* or *workman* in all but 153 cases. The result is a broad diversity of statutory language built on a relatively narrow foundation. Nor are these distinctions without a dif-ference—they had consequences for whether particular contracts could be enforced, and how.

In the real world of the statutes, of course, occupation words occur not only in various combinations that define the scope of the legislation, but in a much wider variety of substantive contexts. Thus, *servant* might be found not only in association with *apprentice* or *seaman* but also with *runaway* or *disobe-dient* or *mistreated,* with *imprisoned* or *whipped* or *unpaid.* To identify and com-pare significant terms in their lexical habitat, we have developed a technique we call "domain word in context," or DWIC. A domain word is a term of art in the subject area of master and servant law. To compare statutory language, we extract all the contexts within which such a term appears, for example,

49. (S. Australia) n.9 of 1847; (U.K.) 4 Geo.IV c.34 (1823).

50. There are 267 occupational terms (i.e., as apart from racial, ethnic, or national distinc-tions), nearly half of them plural forms of terms that also appear in the singular. Text analy-sis commonly distinguishes between unique words, called *types,* and their occurrences, called *tokens.* The 695 statutes considered here contain 8,324 types and 1,205,275 tokens. In the dis-cussion below, we emphasize the number of *statutes* in which a type appears, rather than the number of tokens, and we generally equate singular and plural forms. Thus, "servant" appears as a token 5,569 times, and "servants" 1,543 times. "Servant" occurs in 350 statutes, and "ser-vants" in 316. Because both forms frequently occur together, the number of statutes in which either appears (the number of greatest interest here) is not 666, but 411.

51. (S. Australia) n.112 of 1878 as am. (1935) adds the term "clerk."

twenty-one-word extracts consisting of the domain word and the ten words on either side of it.[52] Using the computer, we compare each of these contexts (dwics) with all of the others, counting the number of words each pair has in common.[53] By repeating the technique with a large number of domain words, we can identify similarities in language that suggest compelling hypotheses about patterns of statutory borrowing and adaptation, and about the extent of direct metropolitan influence on the language of colonial legislation.

Staying with the example of occupational scope, there are more than 20,000 contexts centered on the fifteen most common occupation types. Table 1.1 lists the domain words and summarizes their occurrences. Even at this most abstract level, the truism about similarity and difference is clearly apparent. Only 38 of the 695 statutes do not contain at least one of these fifteen terms, but fewer than 1 in 750 comparisons is successful.[54] However, among the successful comparisons, 5,542 are between *identical* dwics, and another 5,040 have 19 or 20 words in common.

To make practical sense of these results, some further analysis is necessary. Assume that a provision from statute A, the earliest in date, appears in identical language in statutes B and C, the latest. There will be three successful comparisons: A→B, A→C, B→C. It is unlikely that the drafters of statute C borrowed from both A and B. To develop an hypothetical model of this provision's dissemination, we can make some simplifying assumptions. For example, where A and C are from the same jurisdiction, but B is from a different one, we can assume A→C and A→B but discard B→C. Where they are all from the same jurisdiction, we can assume A→B and B→C but discard A→C. Applying these and similar heuristics, we can reduce the 60,000 successful comparisons in Table 1.1 to about 12,000.

This has two consequences. First, it eliminates some of the more weakly linked statutes from the analysis. In the occupational scopes example, it elimi-

---

52. Each context is the same length, and extracted from a single sentence. Where the domain word occurs close to the beginning or end of the sentence, its position in the context is adjusted accordingly.

53. We have experimented with various word-frequency-based weighting schemes. Our experience to date is that substantial overlap in the number of words is a better indicator of similarity than frequency-based scoring. In the results reported here, we compare twenty-one-word contexts, with a minimum of twelve words (57 percent) in common. For a close examination of the statistical peculiarities of written language, see Baayen, *Word Frequency Distributions*.

54. This is not an especially good index of dissimilarity, though, because it also reflects the fact that the same domain word is often used in different contexts in a single statute. A comparison of two *identical* statutes, each with five substantially different dwics for a particular domain word, would have just 20 percent in common (five of twenty-five pairwise comparisons). One way of compensating for this is to count only the single strongest comparison for each domain word for each pair of statutes toward the success rate.

TABLE I.I.
Occupational-Scope dwics, or Domain Word in Context

Domain Word	Statutes	Contexts (DWICs)	Pairwise Comparisons[a]	Successful Comparisons[b]
Servant/s	411	6,858	23,512,653	22,771
Laborer/s	301	4,963	12,313,203	11,666
Apprentice/s	259	3,990	7,958,055	12,741
Domestic/s	147	336	56,280	603
Artificer/s	112	720	258,840	3,385
Seaman/men	92	1,770	1,565,565	3,662
Workman/men	76	337	56,616	359
Journeyman/men	62	367	67,161	661
Handicraftsman/men	55	303	45,753	2,550
Sailor/s	41	171	14,535	137
Boatman/men	40	97	4,656	169
Mechanic/s	38	171	14,535	289
Mariner/s	34	403	162,006	1,006
Porter/s	29	63	1,953	67
Coolie/s	22	293	42,778	104
Total	657	20,842	46,074,589	60,170

[a]Calculated as $n*(n-1)/2$. In practice the number of comparisons is somewhat less, as we do not compare dwics within a statute.

[b]Here the threshold for success is defined as 57 percent overlap, where two 21-word dwics have at least 12 words in common. Later in the discussion below, a 90 percent threshold (at least 19 words in common) is used.

nates 55 of them, reducing the number of candidate statutes to 602. Second, it permits us to treat the remaining pairs as links in various chains, so that we can construct a more complex model of the dissemination of statutory language. Figure 1.2 is a segment of such a model tracing a *servant* dwic from the Statute of Artificers to late nineteenth-century British Guiana.[55] The weights of the connecting lines indicate the extent of the overlap. Where there is a series of intervening weak links, the model is quite unreliable; it resembles nothing more closely than the game of "broken telephone" in which a whispered message is distorted beyond recognition through repeated transmissions. The chain on the left of Figure 1.2 is a good example. The original dwic, *. . . such master mistress or dame shall not put away any such servant at the end of*

55. The figure is a visualization of the pairwise linkages data. Each node (box) represents one dwic (identified in this simplified illustration by abbreviated jurisdiction and year). The edges (lines connecting the boxes) vary in weight to indicate the strength of the overlap. Figure 1.1 is drawn from a detail of a much larger graph of *servant* dwics, with 6,859 nodes and 4,238 edges, in which the longest chain (at the 57 percent threshold) is sixteen statutes deep.

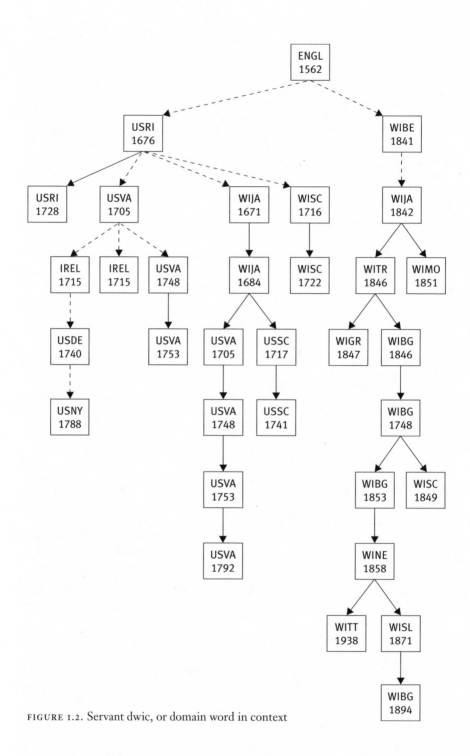

FIGURE 1.2. Servant dwic, or domain word in context

his term or that any such . . . has become . . . *in the said master or mistress or clerk apprentice or servant the said justice of the peace or mayor recorder or* . . . in the New York statute of 1788 at the end of the chain. But where most of the intervening links are stronger, the message survives remarkably well: employers are to care for their sick servants and not abandon them to be a burden on the community. The Rhode Island excerpt of 1676, . . . *mistress dwells and if any master or mistress of any servant or servants shall put away any such servant before the* . . . clearly resembles the 1562 passage, and the basic idea is still recognizable after the transmission via Jamaica[56] to Virginia in 1792: . . . *any master or owner shall put away lame or sick servant under pretence of freedom and such servant becomes chargeable to* . . . The long chain on the right of the figure begins with a Bermuda statute of 1841, . . . *artificer, handicraftsman or labourer shall not put away such servant artificer handicraftsman or labourer before the end of his term under* . . . and ends in British Guiana a half century later with . . . *of any particular work puts away dismisses or discharges such servant before the completion of his contract such employer unless he* . . . Once again, the similarities are palpable despite the obvious differences.

Of course, we do not suggest that by demonstrating that two statutes have a sequence of twenty-one words in common, or mostly in common, we have proved the one to have been borrowed or adapted from the other. We do suggest that the accumulation of such similarities is strong internal evidence for such transmission, and in many cases is the only accessible evidence, especially for large-scale comparisons. If this is accepted, we can interrogate our collection of about 12,000 occupational scope links to suggest some generalizations about the dissemination process.

There are two alternative null hypotheses. One is that colonial legislation is a transcript of British legislation. The other is that each colony's legislation is sui generis. We have already seen enough to know that neither of these is tenable. This leaves a huge middle ground: just how influential were the metropolitan statutes, as distinct from intercolonial borrowing, in shaping the specific provisions of the colonial laws?[57]

One sort of answer is suggested by examining the occupational dwic data.[58]

56. The graph is drawn this way because the Virginia excerpt has more words in common with the Jamaica excerpt than it has with the Rhode Island one.

57. The domain word method can also be used in reverse, as it were, to find the antecedents of particular statutes of interest. For example, a close study of the language of Nova Scotia's first master and servant statute (1765) shows substantial parts to have been copied from Virginia statutes, although Chief Justice Jonathon Belcher, who prepared it, cited only British and Irish precedents. Other such applications of dwic analysis have informed some of the accounts elsewhere in this volume about the origins of important local statutes.

58. But *only* suggested: framing such a hypothesis will require the analysis and integration

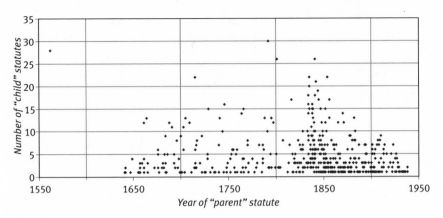

FIGURE 1.3. "Child" statutes by year of "parent" (57 percent overlap)

For ease of reference, let us call the earlier of a linked pair of statutes the "parent," and the later the "child." One way of framing the metropolitan influence question is to ask whether British statutes have significantly more "children" than colonial ones. The occupational scope analysis includes 500 "parent" statutes after simplification. Most of them have only a few "children." But there is a small handful of unusually prolific "parents," distributed, as Figure 1.3 indicates, fairly evenly across the period of this study. Of the nine "parents" with twenty or more children, four are British, one Irish, one American, one West Indian, and two African.

If we restrict the comparison to nearly identical twenty-one-word dwics (at least nineteen words in common), there are 5,860 context pairs after simplification, and 309 "parent" statutes, of which just 26 (shown in the upper half of Figure 1.4) have five or more "children." They fall into three temporal groupings: 1562–1792 (five "parents"); 1834–59 (twelve); 1893–1926 (nine).[59] Four of the five "parents" in the first group are British; just two (one of them an imperial order-in-council) in the second group; and none in the third. Eight of the thirteen "parents" in the second group are from the West Indies (reflecting the regional surge in legislative activity produced by "apprenticeship" and Indian indentured immigration); four of the nine in the last group

---

of a much more extensive and varied range of domain words than the fifteen occupational scope terms considered here. This work is ongoing. In the following, we speak of "statutes" being linked. The reader must keep in mind that a relatively sparse subset of linked word sequences is standing in for the statutes in this discussion. The findings set out here are therefore tentative and incomplete; the more systematic analysis is currently in preparation.

59. A single data point in the chart represents one or more "parent" statutes at that intersection of the X and Y axes. There are twenty-four data points in the upper half of the figure, representing twenty-six statutes (as there are two statutes in each of two years).

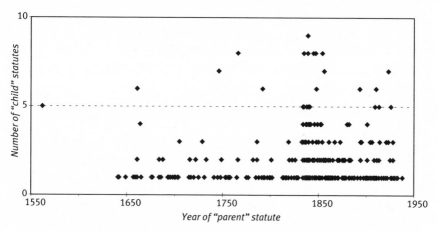

FIGURE 1.4. "Child" statutes by year of "parent" (90+ percent overlap)

are African, and four others from the Far East. This suggests a receding direct influence of British on colonial statutes over time, and a greater propensity for local legislatures to model their enactments on those of other colonies (with or without imperial encouragement.)

Table 1.2 lists, for each of these twenty-six prolific, high-similarity "parent" statutes, the regional distribution of their "children." The figures in italics show the numbers of "children" within the same broad geographical region as their "parents." For example, the 1746 British statute has seven "children" in all, two from within Britain, three from Australia, and one each from North America and the West Indies. The "parent" statutes fall into two distinct groups according to the geographic dispersion of their offspring. By and large, the earlier and the British statutes have broader impact than the later and non-British ones. The last three British statutes include two merchant shipping acts and an imperial order relating to the end of colonial slavery. We can distinguish between statutes that are important regional hubs and those which are influential models beyond their own region. (Some of these statutes are discussed in more detail later.)

Labor and the Law in the Older and Newer British Empires: An Outline

The employment law of the empire began evolving first in the mainland American colonies and the West Indies in the early and mid-seventeenth century. In the seventeenth and eighteenth centuries half the migrants to the mainland colonies were indentured or convict laborers, whose passage was

TABLE I.2.
Regional Influence by "Parent"'s Jurisdiction and Year[a]

"Parent" Statute Jurisdiction	Year	Britain	North America	West Indies	Australia	Africa	India and Far East
Britain							
England	1562		1	4			
Great Britain	1746	*2*	1	1	3		
Great Britain	1766	*1*	1	3	3		
Great Britain	1792	*1*			3	2	
United Kingdom (shipping)	1835	*1*	5	2	1		
Imperial order	1838			3		1	1
United Kingdom (shipping)	1854	*1*	4	2			1
West Indies							
Barbados	1661		1	5			
Barbados	1834			4		1	
Antigua	1835			5			
British Guiana	1838			4	1		
Saint Vincent	1839			5		2	1
Bahamas	1839			7		2	
Bermuda	1841			2	3		
Grenada	1847			7			1
British Guiana	1848			6			
Australia							
Tasmania	1840			1	4		
New South Wales	1845			2	6		
Africa							
Cape Colony	1856					7	
Gold Coast	1893					6	
Kenya	1910					6	
Uganda	1913					5	
India and the Far East							
Johore	1909						5
Fed. Malaya	1923						7
Kelantan	1926						5
Straits Settlement	1926					1	4

[a] 15 scope types; 21-word dwics; 90 percent overlap.
[b] Numbers in italics indicate "children" within the same broad geographical region as their "parents."

advanced against future service, whether contracted for voluntarily or imposed by the courts in accordance with local legislation. Indentured servitude became further differentiated as it continued to develop in the presence of other, less coercive kinds of labor contracts for American-born whites and slavery for blacks. Ultimately the racial distinction in slavery dissolved the divide between free and indentured white laborers: whites were free, blacks were slaves, and indentured laborers disappeared from America. The association of whips and chains with slave status contributed to the emergence of a master and servant law largely purged of the penal sanctions found in England and the rest of the empire. In nonplantation colonies, such as Massachusetts, the notion of bound service came to be associated almost exclusively with young persons.[60]

The West Indian legislation had also come to differentiate slaves and servants clearly by the mid-seventeenth century, as slavery began its ascendancy over European indentured labor. Thus in 1664 Jamaica had both an act "For the better ordering and governing of Negro slaves," and another, "For the good governing of servants," with very different terms.[61] As racial distinctions transformed the society, creole white servants remained subject to a body of law similar in many ways to the English forms, including some varieties of apprenticeship, but the social and economic significance of imported non-slave indentured labor disappeared. Slavery dominated the island economies for the next 100 years; by 1807 the trade was illegal, and in the last decades of slavery the system was under the surveillance of officials appointed by the imperial government, and intense scrutiny by abolitionist organizations in Britain. The compulsory emancipation of slaves by act of the imperial Parliament in 1834 involved the creation of a new transitional status, confusingly called "apprenticeship," in most of the former slave colonies in the Caribbean (and elsewhere). In 1838 it was superseded by new master and servant laws to govern what was now officially designated as fully free labor. Freedom of contract was accompanied by new police and prison establishments and stringent vagrancy legislation. These instruments were to be crucially important in determining how oppressive penal sanctions were to non-European workers in many other colonies in the nineteenth and twentieth centuries.[62]

Meanwhile the number of colonial jurisdictions with master and servant acts had increased immensely, despite the loss of the thirteen mainland American colonies in 1783. Under British rule, Nova Scotia (acquired in 1713; British settlement from 1749) and Quebec (acquired by conquest in

---

60. Tomlins in this volume.
61. (Jamaica) Acts of 20 Oct. and 2 Nov. 1664.
62. Turner in this volume; see also below.

1763) adapted both British (including Irish) and American legislation; subsequently, newly established colonies in what is now Canada based their master and servant acts largely on those of other colonies in the region, with an eye to a generalized British model.[63] In Australia, opened to white settlement as a convict colony in 1787, master and servant legislation was at first imposed by British acts for the administration of justice.[64] New South Wales enacted the continent's first local master and servant act in 1828.[65] Cape Colony proclamations of 1809 and 1812 were designed to draw natives into the labor force, in part by compelling the apprenticeship of their children.[66] Sierra Leone, Gambia, and the island of St. Helena enacted legislation to enforce labor contracts, sometimes with labor-protective clauses.[67] In early nineteenth-century Madras and Bengal, company and municipal labor regulations hewed fairly closely to the policy of the eighteenth-century English statutes. They were soon followed by state and then India-wide legislation, some of it with unique local features.[68] The tiny but immensely valuable plantation economy of Mauritius began an intensive and ultimately controversial development of highly coercive master and servant law after the end of "apprenticeship" in 1838.

To these regimes were added, later in the nineteenth century, many others in Africa and Asia, where master and servant acts were coupled with vagrancy, pass, police, prison, and other legislation to attract, control, and direct flows of labor. The usual object was to supply labor to territories where capital investment in mines and plantations could not be profitable (or as profitable) without penal coercion. The use of penal contracts (and powers of private arrest) was crucial to proprietors of the tea "gardens," or plantations, of Assam, to hold to their contracts the large numbers of migrant laborers from other parts of India.[69] The end of "apprenticeship" in the Cape produced new master and servant statutes in 1841 and 1856, widely copied in the region, that were part of a spreading African legislative project of extraordinarily detailed employment, vagrant, and pass law provisions.[70] Always, master and servant

63. Craven in this volume.

64. (U.K.) 4 Geo.IV c.96 (1823); (U.K.) 9 Geo.IV c.83 (1828).

65. (New South Wales) 9 Geo.IV n.9 of 1828; see Quinlan in this volume.

66. Described in more detail below.

67. (Sierra Leone) 1 Geo.IV n.25 (1820); (Sierra Leone) 3 Geo.IV n.28 (1822); (Gambia) Act of 29 July 1825; (St. Helena) Bylaw of 1825. See Banton in this volume.

68. On the early municipal legislation and its enforcement, see Ahuja, "Origins"; on the later development of statute law and its enforcement, see in this volume the chapter by Michael Anderson, and for Assam in particular, that of Mohapatra.

69. Mohapatra in this volume.

70. See the chapters by Banton, Chanock, David Anderson, and Rathbone in this volume, and discussion below.

legislation was also used to establish, mark, and reinforce racial and cultural boundaries between the English and European colonial elites, and indigenous peoples. In Hong Kong, acquired in 1841, the regulations took account of the simultaneous cultural distance and daily intimacy of Europeans and the Chinese servants on whom they were so dependent, while marking further distances from the unknown and feared millions who lay outside their compounds and beyond the borders of the small colony.[71]

By the middle of the nineteenth century, the imperial organization of Indian (and some Chinese) labor for long-distance migration under indentures was well established. The governors of the empire, despite disagreements about ways and means, channeled 1.2 million of their subjects from British India to Mauritius, Ceylon, Natal, the Transvaal, East Africa, and, over much greater distances, to Fiji, and especially the British Caribbean. In the Caribbean, more than 400,000 indentured Indians worked the plantations, replacing the slaves and "apprentices" who shunned plantation labor once freed in 1838. This immense tropical experiment in "industrial immigration," beginning in the 1840s, was mediated by new statutes in India and the colonies receiving indentured immigrants, and additional legislation to manage the intake (under different contractual terms) of indentured workers from China and elsewhere, based loosely on the Indian migrant model. In the Pacific, almost 90,000 Melanesians were imported under indenture in Fiji and Queensland.[72] This vast international migration, and its statutory expression, recapitulated many of the legal forms, the modes of enforcement, the economic purposes, and the coercive character of the indentured labor of two centuries earlier. There were some significant differences, notably the racial distinctions, the distances traveled, and the close oversight by the competing bureaucracies of the imperial government's Colonial Office and (for Indian labor) the India Office.[73]

Indentured labor migration, long the subject of concern and protest among some British, Indian and other colonial politicians (among them Gandhi), and long-standing tension between the India and Colonial Offices, ended with the First World War.[74] Penal master and servant legislation nonetheless

71. Munn in this volume.

72. On Natal, where the system was modeled on Mauritius, see Metcalf, "Hard Hands," and below. On Pacific islanders, see Munro, "Labor Trade in Melanesians," and Munro, "Historiography"; and for both Queensland and Fiji, the literature cited in Munro, "Patterns of Resistance." Much of the literature on Fiji emphasizes a labor policy protective of Fijians themselves, a view contested by Bain, "A Protective Labour Policy?," discussing illicit but effective use of master and servant legislation.

73. See the chapter by Banton in this volume.

74. Tinker, *New System of Slavery*; Northrup, *Indentured Labor*.

continued to be enacted, amended, and enforced in dozens of imperial jurisdictions long after it had been repealed in the United Kingdom: in Malaya,
North Borneo, the British Caribbean, many African jurisdictions, Kedah, the
Straits Settlements, and elsewhere. By the 1930s it was Colonial Office policy
to have these statutes repealed (in response to International Labour Organization standards and domestic political pressure) but internal division, political complications, and inanition meant that much of the legislation did not
disappear until colonial independence in the 1950s and 1960s, and sometimes
not even then.[75]

Free and Unfree Labor

The nature and purposes of indentured labor have been much debated in the
literature, reflecting in part the different approaches of economic and social
historians. Economic historians have seen long-distance migration as the expression of choice by economically rational sellers and buyers of labor. Social
historians, in contrast, have emphasized the structures of power that determined conditions of work, directed workers toward the indentured sector,
and held them there through very long-term contracts enforced by penal
sanctions. Yet these questions about indentured labor regimes are special instances of a more general problem of master and servant law. For in all these
regimes, with or without "apprenticeship" and indentured migration, law and
its enforcement shaped both markets and social experience. Markets are always constituted by the law that enforces the bargains made in them. Whether
and how the state intervenes or abstains is expressed largely through legal
rules and their enforcement (or deliberate nonenforcement) and so rests ultimately on its coercive power. Law is always coercive, even when it is also
simultaneously facilitative and enabling of social organization. Nor is the law
neutral: its rules, at any particular time, tend to favor to a greater or lesser
degree one or the other party in any given labor relation. Freedom of contract does not mean freedom to abandon the contract. The "security interest"
in maintaining a contract disadvantageous to the other party is particularly
striking when corporal punishment and imprisonment are part of the security apparatus.[76] The clear aim of much master and servant legislation was to
make labor supply and performance more reliable and, especially in the case
of migrant labor, cheaper than it could be obtained otherwise, if it could be
obtained at all.

75. Banton in this volume.
76. Mensch, "Freedom of Contract as Ideology."

The meaning of "free labor" has come under close interrogation in the recent literature about many colonial jurisdictions, and so by implication (and occasionally explicitly) has the place of law and its enforcement. Formerly, the literature emphasized the nature of economic development and labor markets in the early modern world and rather neglected law as an element in both. Thus the extensive and theoretically informed economic literature on indentured labor in early colonial America dealt in large measure with such issues as the sources and price of indentured labor, the exercise of choice by those coming to America (e.g., choosing Virginia rather than Antigua), and the manner in which the terms of nonconvict indentures reflected the bargaining that produced them.[77] The emphasis in such accounts was not on sanctions but on markets, and indeed most of the literature had remarkably little to say about enforcement. The contrast with slavery was often cast largely in terms of relative economic advantage to employers and workers; the characterization of three kinds of labor—"unfree" slavery, "unfree" indenture, "free" labor without penal coercion—sometimes repeated hypostatized ideal types originating in an older sociological literature.

More recently, accounts of societies with both indentured white labor and slavery have taken a more subtle approach to issues of freedom and coercion. Research on slavery has generated new comparisons of slave and nonslave labor, including the role of law in constituting regimes of labor in the early Atlantic world, especially colonial America and the West Indies in the seventeenth and eighteenth centuries, the period in which the rise of racial slavery was accompanied by the decline of white indentured labor.[78] The early regime of white indentured labor in plantation economies provides helpful comparisons.[79] It is now recognized that legal coercion including physical and other punishments was used in both slavery and employment. What is not as well known is that penal sanctions not only persisted but increased in much English and colonial master and servant law in the eighteenth century, and enforcement rates increased significantly in Britain in the nineteenth century, and massively in many colonies.[80] Coercion is a complex continuum of forms and practices.

77. The classic account is Galenson, *White Servitude* (see the appendix for English magisterial oversight of indentures); see also Galenson, "Labor Market Behavior," and such studies as Grubb, "Long-Run Trend." A recent review and critique is Salinger, "Labor, Markets, and Opportunity." In general, and especially on enforcement, see the chapter by Tomlins in this volume.

78. For a recent summary and critique, see Lucassen, "Brief Overview."

79. On Barbados and other islands, see Beckles, *White Servitude*; Beckles, "Black Men in White Skins"; Beckles, "Rebels and Reactionaries"; Beckles, "Irish Indentured Servants."

80. Contrast Eltis, "Labour and Coercion"; Eltis, "Slavery and Freedom"; Eltis, "Euro-

Although this book is not about slavery, the law discussed here had close connections with slavery, and with its abolition and aftermath, in at least two important ways. First, it is important to recognize that the dichotomous bright line between freedom and coercion, found in American constitutional jurisprudence and enshrined in a long sociological literature, misleads about the realities of both slavery and employment. "Freedom" included in many jurisdictions the forced labor of children under involuntary contracts imposed without parental consent, imprisonment and whipping for breach of contract well into the nineteenth century and beyond, and the determined undermining of alternative means of subsistence (common rights, the old poor law, indigenous and other traditional economies) to force people into the labor market and to suppress wage rates. On the other hand, as recent studies have shown, under the right conditions slavery could accommodate slave wages and private property, forms of individual and collective bargaining, and even work stoppages, notwithstanding the system's ultimate reliance on the constant threat of violence and the brutal suppression of slave revolts.[81] The conclusion seems inescapable that arguments about "free" and "unfree" labor, especially those based on broad juridical and social categories rather than detailed examination of law, are not illuminating. The devil is in the details, of law and social practice, repression and bargaining.[82] The balance of coercion and market bargaining advantage was always contested, and the law and especially its enforcement, not only in slavery and employment but also in vagrancy, public order, taxation, and access to land and other forms of property, were crucial in constructing masters' coercion or strengthening workers' resistance to it. Workers also had their own forms of coercion, in riot or sabotage, but these were exceptional punctuations of the constant pressure of legal coercion that shaped the terms of labor bargaining.

The second connection between slavery and employment is diachronic: the fact that slavery replaced indentured labor in the sixteenth century in the

---

peans." Thus Eltis, *Rise*, 7: "Indeed, while free labor in the modern sense scarcely existed before the nineteenth century, by 1800 the coercive element in the master-servant, employer-employee relationship [in Western Europe] had been in decline for a better part of a millennium." See the chapter by Hay for the argument that in England it had been increasing between 1700 (or earlier) and 1850; and the chapters by Chanock, Mohapatra, Banton, Turner, and David Anderson for evidence that in many parts of the empire it continued to increase thereafter.

81. See in particular M. Turner, *Chattel Slaves*.

82. The need for research on the wider range of legal mechanisms is also noted in Steinfeld and Engerman, "Labor—Free or Coerced?"; in the introduction to the same volume (Brass and van der Linden, *Free and Unfree Labour*), Brass criticizes accounts of law that neglect enactment and enforcement (including theirs) for "fetishizing legality." The importance of other kinds of law is also emphasized in the introduction of Steinfeld, *Coercion*.

West Indies, and that indentured labor replaced slavery there and elsewhere in the empire after abolition in 1834. The details of enforcement of the servant and slave laws before the 1820s are still imperfectly known, given the informality of many proceedings before magistrates, and the fact that what records survive are only beginning to be explored fully.[83] Abolition prompted the rapid extension and elaboration of scores of statutes defining the law of master and servant for populations formerly subject to the law of slavery (see Figure 1.1). Postslavery "apprenticeship" had a precursor in arrangements for the disposition of "liberated Africans" after the imperial abolition of the slave trade in 1807. Africans rescued from slave ships by the Royal Navy were collected at St. Helena and Sierra Leone, then induced or pressured into indentures and transferred to long periods of servitude in the British Caribbean colonies and Mauritius.[84] On Mauritius, the spectacularly productive sugar colony acquired by the British from the French in 1814, their servitude could be as long as fourteen years; they were employed in public works and hired out to private employers, including some of the principal merchants and government officials. A commission that investigated their fate reported in 1828 that when assigned to slave owners, such "liberated apprentices" were often more badly treated than slaves, a claim that appears to be substantiated by death rates on plantations.[85]

When abolition of slavery itself everywhere in the empire became British government policy, the nature of the ensuing labor regime was of intense concern to Parliament and also to the (compensated) slave owners. As many scholars have observed, abolitionists expected or at least argued that freedom would bring economic growth: they said slavery was incompatible with economic prosperity. These arguments had powerful resonance in early and mid-Victorian England.[86] But "free labor" emphatically was not understood to be labor free of penal coercion in the colonies, as it was not in England itself. "Apprenticeship" was defended as both an education in contractual, market relations for ex-slaves and an absolute necessity to prevent the withdrawal of labor from plantations. It has been the subject of a large literature in the history of the West Indies, and its history in other jurisdictions affected by the

83. For an account of the enforcement of the slave laws by magistrates in Jamaica, and citations to much of the relevant literature, see Paton, "Punishment."

84. Schuler, *"Alas, Alas Kongo"*; Schuler, "Recruitment."

85. A. Barker, *Slavery and Antislavery*, 41. The policy of indenturing liberated slaves appeared again following abolition, although this time with extensive protective provisions. Statutes to this effect were adopted in Trinidad in 1835, 1850, and 1861, St. Lucia in 1849, Grenada and Jamaica in 1850, British Guiana in 1850 and 1864, and the Bahamas in 1861 and 1862. Nova Scotia adopted legislation in 1834 prohibiting the landing of liberated slaves on its shores.

86. Drescher, "Free Labor vs. Slave Labor."

Imperial Abolition Act of 1833[87] has recently grown rapidly.[88] It was repealed in 1838, several years earlier than planned, in the face of unrest and the fear of a general uprising by West Indian "apprentices."

"Apprenticeship" bore heavily on workers, especially when compared to the ameliorative reforms imposed by the British Parliament in the final decades of slavery.[89] A recent study of Mauritius finds that rates of absenteeism were very similar before and after emancipation, and that there were important continuities in coercion.[90] In this book, Mary Turner argues for the British Caribbean that the improvements in the condition of slaves insisted upon by the British Parliament and public opinion in the 1820s and 1830s in fact mandated a higher standard of living, greater security, and less punishment than was to be the case under "apprenticeship."

The link to indentured or "apprentice" labor at both the inception and abolition of racial slavery challenged the received wisdom about "free" labor and "free" markets. There has been an increasing tendency to put the word "voluntary" in quotation marks when discussing the contractual arrangements in plantation settings and to recommend closer examination of the compulsions of penal law.[91] Divergent economic experiences with emancipation in the British West Indies formerly tended to privilege explanations based on ex-slaves' ability to acquire land, thereby allowing escape from the plantation sector. Where they could not (Leewards and Barbados), they remained on the plantations; where they could, either indentured immigration supplied the need for labor (British Guiana and Trinidad) or the sugar industry never recovered (Jamaica). Later versions of the argument gave less prominence to the land:labor ratio and more to politics and law: the terms and enforcement of indenture; the significance of vagrancy legislation; restrictions on emigration; and the use of taxation to compel wage labor. Some scholars always strongly emphasized coercion over input ratios in explaining

87. (U.K.) 3&4 Wm.IV c.73 (1833).

88. For an overview of writing on West Indian postslavery apprenticeship, see K. Smith, "Fragmented Freedom," and see other work cited below, on the British Caribbean, Africa, and Mauritius.

89. J. Ward, *British West Indian Slavery*.

90. R. Allen, *Slaves, Freedmen, and Indentured Labourers*. See also the comparison of enforcement rates in Table 1.3.

91. Engerman has always recognized the duality of coercion and consent in indentured labor, but the development of his work might be seen as a gradual concession that economic factors are strongly conditioned by others, and notably by the law: what starts as economic history increasingly sounds like a prospectus for sociolegal history. Klein and Engerman, "Transition from Slave to Free Labor"; Engerman, "Economic Adjustments," "Servants to Slaves to Servants," "Coerced and Free Labor," and "Economic Response"; Steinfeld and Engerman, "Labor—Free or Coerced?"

the transition from slavery to "freedom": the ability to control labor, and to control its access to land, was more important than the size of the respective factor inputs.[92] Local studies continue to produce evidence of the importance of penal law and its symbiotic connection with vagrancy and other criminal legislation in the West Indies, as in Africa and elsewhere in the empire.

Yet much recent work on indentured and other labor in the postslavery empire remains relatively incurious about the details of the law and its enforcement.[93] In part this may be a reaction to an earlier phase of research that emphasized the degree of exploitation under law, relying in large measure on official inquiries and the sources generated by political agitation against imperial indentured labor.[94] Recent work has been more inclined to attempt explanations that eschew "preoccupation with the most visible and sensational aspects," notably the use of penal sanctions, on the ground that it gives a highly distorted view of labor relations.[95] The emphasis is on wider social and economic contexts, including the movement later in the period of indentured labor to a more consensual regime of labor relations, and the immense influence of the international economy as export markets set limits to production, making labor costs critical, and generating vast flows of migrant labor from the poorer populations of the empire. It has been argued, too, that a plethora of penal law may be an indicator of its ineffectiveness, the unrealizable hopes of its authors.[96]

92. Bolland, "Systems of Domination"; Bolland, "Politics of Freedom."

93. Caribbean studies on postslavery apprenticeship, some of it comparative, include Green, *Slave Emancipation*; the scholarship cited in K. Smith, "Fragmented Freedom"; M. Turner, *Chattel Slaves*, and Turner in this volume; Altink, "Slavery by Another Name"; Boa, "Experiences of Women Estate Workers." On indentured immigrants, see the work summarized in Northrup, *Indentured Labor*; Laurence, *Question of Labour*; Lai, *Indentured Labor* (discussing penal sanctions, 127–35, and a summary of immigration statutes, 303–13); Saunders, *Indentured Labour*; Saunders, *Workers in Bondage*; Mohapatra in this volume; and work cited below. The general treatments vary greatly in the detail with which they consider penal sanctions; few examine the law itself at all closely. Relatively little work has been done on enforcement of low justice by magistrates on postslavery nonindentured populations: see Paton, "Penalties of Freedom," 289 (on convict labor after 1838 in Jamaica), and De Barros in this volume.

94. Tinker, *New System of Slavery*.

95. R. Allen, *Slaves, Freedmen, and Indentured Labourers*, 57–58 (see also below).

96. Ibid., for a recent example of such arguments. The relative lack of emphasis on law in the recent literature as a whole is reflected in the very useful summary by Northrup, *Indentured Labor*, in which a relatively small part of the book (mainly part of chapter 5 on "Indentures") deals with the issue of coercion under a number of heads, and reports some statistics of enforcement found in the literature. But the argument is framed (as it is in much of the literature) alternately as a moral assessment or a description of rational economic choices (e.g., 116, the regime in British Guiana was harsh, but without sanctions it could not have existed). The discussion of coercion and consent reflects the recent literature's preoccupation with opportunities opened to migrants to escape worse conditions, and its vagueness about the impact of

There is, however, good reason to examine penal sanctions closely for reasons other than sensationalism. The penal and other clauses of the employment statutes are not an irrelevant gloss on markets: on the contrary, they are crucial constituents of the labor market. Master and servant law was carefully designed to create labor markets that were less costly, more highly disciplined, less "free" than markets in which the master's bargain was not assisted by such terms. Even where indentured labor coexisted with a more open labor market, employers were well aware that the effect of a bounded sector under more coercive sanctions was to depress wages in the wider labor market as well.

Recently, with the belated recognition that penal sanctions and specific performance of labor contracts were part of even English law until 1875, some economic historians have abruptly abandoned the notion that "free labor" (defined by the absence of penal sanctions and specific performance) was the important distinction, turning instead to discussion of "free markets" in labor (defined by the absence of collusion among buyers and/or sellers).[97] Free labor may not be as widespread as we believed, it seems, but free markets are. The definition begins to seem vacuous: the hypostatized "free market" can be as much an incurious imposition on the evidence as the presumptive "free laborer" ever was. The mere fact of bargaining does not make for freedom:

---

criminal law (e.g., 129, "protest was impeded by penal codes") and the exact terms of contracts. A wider frame must consider in detail the role of law not only in creating low-wage migrant labor markets, but also in destroying the economic standing of the countries from which such laborers came (e.g., Parthasarathi, "Rethinking Wages," on the higher standing of living for Indian as compared with British industrial and agricultural workers in the eighteenth century, and the work summarized in Davis, *Late Victorian Holocausts*, 277-394, on the interaction of environment and government policy). A question for future historians may be whether the emphasis on the voluntary rather than coercive aspects of markets in much late twentieth-century historical scholarship can be explained by recent policy enthusiasms and economic developments, including the late twentieth-century boom in international trade and capital movement, insistence on removal of trade barriers, and transformation of millions of peasants into workers in international labor markets. The most recent comparable period was the half century before World War I—the last period of great international capital flows and trade, and the period in which indentured labor was at its height.

97. For example, Shlomowitz, "Transition." In this article the author (a Chicago-school economist who has written widely on the condition and recruitment of indentured labor) tends to conclude from some evidence of bargaining by labor (and complaints from employers) that a free market existed at the Cape and in the West Indies, whether labor was under penal sanctions or not. But no convincing evidence is cited on the question of whether collusion among employers in fact existed, nor is consideration given to other means (many of them legislated) to inhibit competition for labor, nor of the actual operation of the penal laws. For another view of the Cape evidence used, see the chapter by Banton in this volume; for a summary of Shlomowitz's similar arguments with respect to Pacific islanders in Queensland, see Munro, "Historiography."

slaves bargained, whenever conditions permitted, but it did not make them free. The crucial questions are about the limits on freedom, the constraints, disincentives, and boundaries. Master and servant legislation was a catalog of constraints and disincentives: the penal sanctions, of course, but also minimum terms, maximum wages, discharge certificates, obligations and offenses, and a host of other terms of the bargain and conditions of enforcement, all constitutive of the boundaries of the market within which bargaining could take place. The details are crucial, because in any time or place they combine with the relative demand for and supply of particular kinds of labor to determine who has what kinds of freedom in the employment relation, and how much. They describe the bounds of who could use the law, and for what ends.

Uses of the Law

The most obvious use of the master and servant acts was to regulate the labor market: in the words of the Statute of Artificers, "the hiring, keeping, departing, working, wages, or order of servants . . . and the penalties and forfeitures concerning the same." Master and servant regimes combined a residual attachment to the subordination of bound labor with an emergent conception of the wage worker as party to a personal, contractual relationship of limited duration. Freedom to choose one's employer did not imply the freedom to remain unemployed; if the master and servant acts did not themselves compel engagement and the whip of hunger did not suffice, then the head tax, land laws, or the law about vagrancy took up the burden. Everywhere the policy of master and servant reflected its medieval genesis in the plague years: it was predicated on labor shortage, and in particular on defeating the tendency of the market to bid up wages. In fully supplied markets like those of industrializing England, where workers were well habituated to the wage nexus, the increasing rates of prosecution are at first glance paradoxical. They are explained, on the one hand, by masters' attempts to defeat the market by tying skilled and experienced workers to long contracts and, on the other, by employers rallying to the defense of individual contract making against the incursions of trade unionism. In many overseas colonies, however, the problem was not merely one of using repressive law to hold wages below the level at which willing labor market participants would freely agree to work, but of creating a reliable pool of wage workers in the first place. A broad array of solutions married the penal sanctions of master and servant law to slave emancipation, sponsored immigration, labor obligations imposed on native "squatters," and taxation schemes designed to force subsistence producers into the wage nexus.[98]

In the colonies, these uses were most pronounced in wage-labor-intensive staples economies, particularly those organized around plantation agriculture or mining. Where the colonial staple rested on independent commodity production, these uses were far less evident. The explanatory significance of the production function is underlined in these studies by two kinds of comparisons. Contemporaneous colonies with similar statutes in place nevertheless showed markedly different patterns of use — as, for example, between West Africa[99] and Kenya[100] or southern Africa[101] in the late nineteenth and early twentieth centuries. The same staple commodity, extracted using similar technologies, could be associated with quite different patterns of recruitment and enforcement arising out of differences in local dependence on wage labor, as for example in the gold industries of British Columbia[102] and British Guiana.[103] In India, master and servant was prominent in tea plantations but much less important for the railways and textile manufacture.[104]

One way of holding workers to long contracts was to punish desertion; another was to penalize third parties who gave aid and comfort to runaways or enticed them away by offers of employment. "Harboring" and other crimping offenses were commonly proscribed in the statutes regulating maritime labor. Some of the general master and servant acts gave magistrates summary jurisdiction over such third-party offenses, relieving aggrieved employers of the trouble and expense of suing in tort. Other common mechanisms for tying workers to their original contracts and warning off employers who might otherwise try to poach them included requirements for discharge certificates or testimonials from former employers. Hiring a worker without a proper certificate, or fraudulently supplying one, was one of the few employer offenses punishable by imprisonment in several jurisdictions. The fact that enticing someone else's workers by offering better conditions was punished with greater severity than mistreating or starving one's own employees points up the underlying policy of the master and servant acts as a constraint on market freedom and wage competition.

Along with the regulation of worker mobility and labor market partici-

98. Among other examples in this volume, see the chapters by Mohapatra and Chanock.
99. Rathbone in this volume.
100. David Anderson in this volume.
101. Chanock in this volume.
102. Craven in this volume.
103. De Barros in this volume.
104. See the chapter by Michael Anderson in this volume.

pation, master and servant had an important role to play in enforcing work-place discipline. Besides the mobility-related offenses (absenteeism, desertion, quitting without notice, etc.), master and servant statutes typically supplied punishments for extremely broadly defined breaches of workplace discipline, in such terms as "misdemeanor," "miscarriage," "misconduct," "ill-behavior," "disobedience," "carelessly or improperly" performing work, or "neglect of duty," as well as such other more specific lapses as drunkenness, impertinence, or riding one's master's horse.[105] These provisions gave expansive discretionary powers to employers and justices and served both instrumental and symbolic ends. What was perhaps most pronounced and significant about these regimes was their readiness, whether by express statutory authority or in the informal common practice of magistrates, to enforce specific performance of the employment contract, an outcome allegedly abhorrent to the common law.

Another cluster of uses has less to do with regulating the labor market or workplace discipline than with upholding the sanctity of contract. Master and servant law was about holding people to their agreements. In this connection it had more than a little in common with imprisonment for debt. Both schemes punished the defaulter's body when property was wanting to satisfy his or her obligations. Lack of property transformed fines into incarceration, amounting in many places to systemic racial discrimination, and as such was regularly pointed to as its own reluctant justification. Moreover, indebtedness often reinforced the employment contract in upholding the obligation to work. Payments in advance, whether in cash or kind (e.g., passage money), were familiar means of creating this dual obligation in many settings. Merchant credit tied workers to employers in the Newfoundland fishery[106] and the Canadian fur trade;[107] money advances brought workers into the ambit of the penal contract in India.[108]

The connection between propertylessness and wage employment underscores the uses of master and servant law in preserving social order and relations of superordination and subordination. There was a nexus between propertylessness and criminality: those with no material stake in society were considered prone to disorder and so must be controlled. Criminalizing worker unruliness was consistent with a belief in the criminal inclinations of the propertyless. Master and servant law was also a way of keeping people in

---

105. The three specific offenses are all from (E. Africa Protectorate) n.4 of 1910.
106. Bannister in this volume.
107. Craven in this volume.
108. Michael Anderson and Mohapatra in this volume.

their place. The penal statutes made it clear that the contract of employment was an agreement between unequals. The social structure was displayed and reinforced in proceedings before the justices and reflected in specific master and servant regimes in pass laws and discharge certificates, curfews, licensing and registration, and such institutionalized forms of employer self-help as the power of private arrest. It answered European minorities' concerns about their security and the maintenance of cultural boundaries in dealing with native servants, and provided a social subsidy for conspicuous consumption to establish the prestige hierarchy among settlers and colonial administrators.[109]

Distinctions of class, race, age, and gender were coded into the legislation and reified in differential rates of prosecution, conviction, and punishment. Almost without exception statutes were gender-neutral in England, although the judges made a few important decisions that stigmatized servants who were unmarried mothers.[110] Colonial legislation sometimes provided especially for women servants, particularly in regard to the age of majority, marriage, child-bearing, and corporal punishment. Moreover women frequently had more complaints made against them because they were more often absent from work, due to pregnancy, child-rearing, and illness.[111] Women were less likely than men to be incarcerated for master and servant offenses in some colonies, and more likely in others, including some West Indian jurisdictions where flogging was banned for "apprentice" women after 1834: as a result, far more of them were sentenced to solitary confinement than were men. The incarceration of "apprentice" women in workhouses in Jamaica nonetheless led to flogging and other mistreatment and neglect.[112] Although women were a minority in long-distance indentured labor, British policy was to increase their numbers, and the proportion grew to about 30 percent in the case of Indian immigrants to British Guiana by the end of indenture, and 33 percent in Mauritius.[113] Female labor was even more important to some economies, particularly in the immediate postslavery period. Field "apprentices" in some islands of the West Indies were mostly women, and they suffered most of the penal sentences. Moreover, the freeing of children immediately at the beginning of "apprenticeship" gave planters and farmers in both the West Indies and the Cape Colony an intense interest in reclaiming their labor. Women in St. Vincent and other West Indian jurisdictions strongly resisted the indenturing

109. Mohapatra and Munn in this volume.
110. Hay in this volume.
111. For example, Lal, "Nonresistance," 207.
112. Boa, "Experiences of Women Estate Workers"; Altink, "Slavery by Another Name."
113. Northrup, *Indentured Labor*, 74–78. For the experience of women in Mauritius, see Carter, *Lakshiv's Legacy*.

of their children to estate labor; in the Cape, however, legislative tradition and social practice made it difficult to resist the long-maintained policy of compulsory apprenticeship without parental consent.[114]

Hand in hand with the uses of master and servant law in social *order* went a view of its use in social *change*. Especially during and after the amelioration and abolition of colonial slavery, settlers and administrators alike embraced an ideology of contract making as a civilizing influence. Penal contracts and restrictive practices were, in this view, a necessary transitional stage in the natives' journey out of savagery. The imperial government introduced "apprenticeship" in 1834 as the way station between slavery and full emancipation. Seventy years on, the same idea enjoyed a resurgence as explanation or exculpation for the introduction of penal contracts to recently acquired colonies in Africa and points east, long after breach of the contract of employment had been decriminalized at home.

The idea that workers of color were to be locked up or whipped for their own good was accompanied by the detailed institutionalization in dietary, housing, and sanitary regulations of a protective impulse that had long been an aspect of master and servant legislation. The longer the term of the contract and the more complete the authority of the employer, the more assiduously did the law seek to ensure that the worker's surrender was, if not entirely voluntary, at least informed. Many jurisdictions, although by no means all, coupled the penalties for workers' breach with expeditious procedures for the recovery of unpaid wages and gave justices the power to release servants from their bonds to unduly cruel masters. These features should not be dismissed: actions for wages, in particular, were extensively used by workers where they were available. But protective provisions were subject to Adam Smith's caveat: "Whenever the legislature attempts to regulate the differences between masters and their workmen, its counsellors are always the masters. When the regulation, therefore, is in favour of the workmen, it is always just and equitable; but it is sometimes otherwise when in favour of the masters."[115] The protective provisions underscored the inequality of the bargain and so the subordination of the worker.

Finally there are what may be called the contrarian uses of master and servant, in which the law became an arena of political and social struggle. This had two quite distinct manifestations. The first, encompassing conflict be-

114. Boa, "Experiences of Women Estate Workers"; Brereton, "Family Strategies"; Turner in this volume; and the subsequent section, "An Example: The Cape Colony." For women's role in the work force in Fiji, and their resistance, see Etherington, "Criminal Law"; J. Kelly, "Coolie."

115. A. Smith, *Wealth of Nations*, 1:157–58.

tween colonial legislatures and imperial authorities, was most pronounced
in the battle over postemancipation "apprenticeship." That there were not
more such moments is due at least in part to the ineptitude and negligence
of officials on both sides. The other manifestation was the challenge posed
by workers and, increasingly, their economic and political organizations. By
the end of the nineteenth century, this struggle had resulted in the formal repeal of the penal provisions in Britain and their practical abandonment, for
the most part, in the white dominions. Workers in some other regions of the
empire had yet to enter, let alone pass through, the penal contract regime.
In many places, master and servant law, with its vaguely worded offenses and
stinging punishments for breach of the contract of employment, would remain on the statute books until independence, and beyond.

An Example: The Cape Colony

Unlike the West Indies, with their dependence on imported African slaves
and Indian indentured immigrants, the colonies in southern Africa had substantial indigenous populations that were simultaneously dispossessed of land
by force and legal enactments and the source of labor to render profitable
the property now in the hands of the colonizer.[116] Early British rule in the
region built upon the preexisting foundation of colonial Dutch law to elaborate the distinctive combination of employment, vagrancy, tax, and land law
that shaped southern African employment relations in the first half of the
nineteenth century. These were then elaborated, as Martin Chanock shows in
this volume, in the law-obsessed regime of what became the Union of South
Africa in 1910.[117]

During the wars against frontier peoples carried on by the Dutch in the
eighteenth century, children of San (Bushmen) and other groups were sometimes captured by Boer commandos and compelled to work. Settlers were not
allowed by the regime to enslave the resident Khoikhoi, but the presence of
slavery colored all labor relations. The Dutch attempted to turn the indigenous Khoikhoi and others into farm laborers, using Netherlands models of
service. From 1721 the children of Khoikhoi women and male slaves could
be indentured to the age of twenty-five years, and eventually the law made
all Khoikhoi children subject to indenture. Dutch employment models were

---

116. In the later nineteenth century much indentured Indian labor was imported into Natal
and the Transvaal, which briefly saw the use of Chinese also, whose contracts were often three
times as long as those of Indians: Northrup, *Indentured Labor*, 161; N. Levy, *Transvaal*, 245.
See below.

117. And over many more areas of law: Chanock, *Making*.

distorted (apprenticeship to age twenty-five became in some cases indenture *for* twenty-five years) but complaints to magistrates (*landdrost*) perhaps afforded some protection. On the other hand, they were almost always themselves local farmers, sharing their neighbors' interest in ensuring cheap and plentiful labor.[118] During or shortly after a revolt of Khoikhoi servants in the eastern Cape in 1803, an ordinance requiring labor contracts to be signed in the presence of a magistrate also provided corporal punishment for servants in breach.[119]

The Dutch regime ended in 1806.[120] The British regime largely codified existing Dutch practice. In 1812 the British governor proclaimed the forced apprenticeship from ages eight to eighteen of all "Hottentot" children with parents in the service of a farmer or other inhabitant.[121] The justification — that the farmer had maintained the child in infancy—was one of the classic policy defenses of heritable slave status in law, but the instrument was an adaptation of English pauper apprenticeship.[122] If the farmer did not want the child, the *landdrost* could apprentice him or her to another master. As with English pauper apprentices, neither the parents' nor the child's approval was required: the indentures were signed and exchanged between the *landdrost* and the master.[123] This system had the added advantage to employers that parents who wanted to stay with their children were deterred from leaving the service of the farmer. Further legislation in 1817 and 1819 extended the apprenticeship system to orphans and children not in the care of their parents (terms easily abused) and to "Bosjesman" (Bushman) children. What was presented as protective legislation was in fact designed to provide a stable labor force for white farmers, and, in the process, to accelerate the process by which the Khoikhoi and San were separated from traditional means of subsistence and made into a settled, low-wage agricultural work force.[124] The unusually strong

118. Newton-King, *Masters and Servants*, 120-24, 137ff.; Boeyens, "Black Ivory," 188.

119. Plakkaat, Indiensneming van Hottentotte deur middle van huurkontrakte, Batavian Republic, 18 Apr./9-10 May [*sic*] 1803, in S. Naudé, *Kaapse Plakkaatboek* (Cape Town, 1951), 6:24. We owe this reference to Robert Ross.

120. The Dutch East India Company ceded control to Britain in 1795; Britain ceded control to the Batavian Republic in 1803, which lost the Cape to the British again in 1806 (confirmed in 1815).

121. The "Hottentots" were mainly Khoikhoi. One *landdrost* recommended apprenticeship to age twenty-four.

122. For another colonial variation on pauper apprenticeship, see Craven in this volume.

123. (Cape) Procl. 23 Apr. 1812. The *landdrost* was a permanent official with the powers of a chief police officer and commander of the local militia; like an English justice of the peace, he was in large measure responsible for local government. In 1827 they were replaced by resident magistrates on the British model. Elphick and Giliomee, *Shaping of South African Society*, 290-91, 497. On pauper apprenticeship in England, see the chapter by Hay in this volume.

124. Newton-King, *Masters and Servants*; Elphick and Giliomee, *Shaping of South African*

emphasis on child apprenticeship in the Cape (compared to the postemancipation West Indies, which had at least some legislative provisions in common) derived from its usefulness in also securing adult workers and from the long prior history of child and family labor in the region. The Cape "apprenticeship" statute of 1835 had even included a clause allowing married women to contract, in spite of coverture.[125] As many Boers left the British Cape for the interior, they carried the institution with them: indenturing children appears in the Transvaal as early as 1848 and was legally embodied in that Boer territory by an Apprentice Act of 1851, which regulated compulsory labor obligations for such persons to the age of twenty-five.[126] The purpose, as in the past, was the procurement of labor by a European farming community hungry for bodies to work the land it had seized in continuous settler incursion and warfare since the eighteenth century.

Separate enactments addressed the recruitment and retention of adult African labor by regulating master and servant relations, vagrancy, access to land, and a host of other questions.[127] Slavery in the Cape Colony had been intensely exploitative.[128] When it ended, the colony's comprehensive and rigorous "apprenticeship" statute (1835) significantly anticipated future developments. Runaways (those who were absent for more than six days) could be punished by hard labor for a month, up to thirty lashes, and an extension of their indentures.[129] The Cape master and servant acts of 1841 and 1856 were unusual in their details of offenses and punishments; the latter was a model for a great deal of other legislation in southern and eastern Africa in the later nineteenth and early twentieth centuries.[130]

Labor control in the region also relied on pass law and vagrancy legislation. In the Cape, the Dutch had acquiesced in settler's demands for pass laws as early as the 1780s, both to prevent desertion and to deter white employers from poaching their neighbors' servants at a period of great competition for labor.[131] Under British rule, proclamations in 1809 (the so-called Caledon Code) and 1812 introduced master and servant based partly on En-

---

Society, 40–41. The group names are contested; Khoisan has been proposed as an indicator of the probable merger of peoples, but questioned by other historians.

125. (Cape) n.1 of 1835; Scully, *Liberating the Family?*, chs. 3, 5.

126. Boeyens, "Black Ivory," 188.

127. White British settlers, brought under a scheme of indenture to the eastern Cape in 1819–20 that envisaged recreating an idealized "traditional" English social structure, quickly repudiated the status as one of "slavery": the racial division would be paramount in southern Africa. Crais, *White Supremacy*, ch. 5.

128. Worden, *Slavery in Dutch South Africa*; R. Ross, *Cape of Torments*.

129. (Cape) n.1 of 1835, pt. 5, ss.7, 10. R. Ross, "Rather Mental than Physical."

130. See below, and the chapters by Banton and Chanock.

131. Elphick and Malherbe, "Khoisan to 1828," 32–33.

glish models. The Khoikhoi now had the right to complain against masters; limits were set on the duration of contracts, which were to be in writing; farmers could not detain workers at the end of them. But the code also provided for whipping, loss of wages, and imprisonment for breach of contract by the worker; systematized the pass law system; and enacted heavier penalties for "vagrant" contraventions of it.[132] The avowed purpose was to force Khoi (who were in violent struggle with white colonists over the ownership of land and cattle) into labor contracts with white farmers; the legislation made it easy to treat individual Khoikhoi as criminals and vagrants. Protective clauses limiting the duration of contracts were ignored in practice, while the more coercive clauses were widely used, along with taxation and restricted access to land, to force Africans into wage labor on white farms.[133]

A complication (for farmers) was the enactment in 1828 of an ordinance "For improving the condition of Hottentots," apparently designed by the British authorities to free the Khoikhoi of the felt oppression of the earlier vagrancy legislation.[134] In contrast to Jamaica or Mauritius, where the Colonial Office was willing fairly early to approve much vagrancy legislation, the colonial secretary on the advice of the governor of the Cape disallowed the 1834 Vagrancy Bill on the grounds that it reimposed limits on the free movement guaranteed to the Khoikhoi in 1828. Moreover a minority of Khoikhoi who lived on missions enjoyed sufficient security to exercise considerable bargaining power. Denied vagrancy legislation of the West Indian kind, south African farmers first turned to master and servant legislation instead.[135] The 1841 statute (renewed in 1846) was made significantly harsher in 1856, in the aftermath of a widespread panic among whites who believed that their farm laborers were plotting to rise and massacre them.[136] The harshness of southern African labor law was probably due in large measure to the fact that it was often a product of warfare or shaped by white fears of catastrophic revolt.

132. (Cape) Procl. 1 Nov. 1809 and 23 Apr. 1812.

133. Elbourne, "Freedom at Issue," 114, 121–23; R. Ross, *Beyond the Pale*; Crais, *White Supremacy*, ch. 8; Newton-King, "Labour Market," 176–77.

134. (Cape) n.50 of 1828. However, (Cape) n.49 of 1828 facilitated tightly controlled flows of African labor from outside the colony, part of a long history of imported labor, with the effect of reducing local wages.

135. Worden, "Between Slavery and Freedom," 133; but see R. Ross, *Beyond the Pale*, 102ff., for evidence (including unpublished work by Worden) that (Cape) n.50 of 1828 was undercut by strong government measures to prevent Khoikhoi and ex-slaves from settling on land. See also Elbourne, "Freedom at Issue," 127ff.

136. On (Cape) Ord. 1 Mar. 1841 and (Cape) n.15 of 1856, see the chapters by Banton and Chanock in this volume, and also Elbourne, "Freedom at Issue," 143–44, and the opposed treatment in Shlomowitz, "Transition," 244–45. The background to the 1856 statute is discussed in R. Ross, *Status and Respectability*, 162–63.

San children were captured in the commando raids of the eighteenth century; the 1856 statute was enacted in the immediate aftermath of the 1850–53 war against the Xhosa, when many Khoikhoi rebelled.[137] By the later nineteenth century vagrancy legislation was enacted, and with pass legislation, stringent land and residency laws, and penal master and servant statutes, the legal tools of the new Union of South Africa were in place at its formation in 1910.

This brief survey of Cape legislation in the first half of the nineteenth century illustrates a central issue in studying imperial employment law (and one to which we return later): the way in which master and servant was knit into larger measures of control such as vagrancy or pass, taxation, and residence or settlement regulations, all of them usually administered in a similar way, by inferior magistrates in summary hearings. It also returns us to the larger comparative questions about the uses of this type of law across the whole extent of the empire and, in particular, to questions about how it was enforced.

Enforcement, Repression, and Resistance

The sheer mass of similar legislation, accompanied by other measures such as vagrancy, settlement, and pass laws, suggests that from medieval England to the wider reaches of the late nineteenth-century British Empire, the project of creating "free" labor, disciplining it to often extremely heavy physical work, and controlling its wage demands through criminal sanctions was a sustained project, deeply embedded in law and economy and culture. As many of the studies in this volume show, it could have huge impact, even where its defenders deplored the effectiveness of resistance to their efforts. It was also an integrated project, in which the master and servant provisions were but parts of a larger whole. For example, a Mauritius act of 1864 defined desertion (punishable under master and servant legislation) as vagrancy, bringing the servant simultaneously under that harsh body of law, which was otherwise used to compel servants out of their indentures to reengage.[138] Statistics of prosecutions also suggest that in some jurisdictions, notably southern Africa, master and servant law more narrowly understood (desertion, neglect of work, other breach of contract) was less heavily relied upon than pass offenses. But official statistics can be greatly misleading. Not only were the pass laws designed to compel workers to seek work and to stay until the completion of the contract, whatever the working conditions, but they were remarkably

---

137. We owe this observation to Elizabeth Elbourne.
138. (Mauritius) n.4 of 1864; R. Allen, *Slaves, Freedmen, and Indentured Labourers*, 65ff.

easy to enforce, even if the "offense" prompting arrest was suspected desertion. Overseers might accompany constables to the compounds to lay charges
of "neglecting their master's work," as in Kimberley in the 1880s. But as the
statistics for that jurisdiction also show, in the rapid shifts in annual figures,
it was a matter of bureaucratic convenience which offense was recorded: pass,
vagrancy, and breach of contract provisions were mutually reinforcing, often
proved with the same evidence (or lack of it), and equally designed to hold
"labor" in place or, if it was no longer wanted, to expel the men and women
and children who constituted it.[139]

Reliable comparative figures on enforcement in such different jurisdictions over so much time are extremely difficult to construct. They are even
more difficult to interpret. However, the chapters in this volume and some
other studies at least allow comparisons of orders of magnitude for the later
nineteenth century, and we also have some scattered indications of how enforcement of the law appeared to contemporaries in earlier periods. That the
penal sanctions of the law were put fully into force in many jurisdictions is
abundantly clear. In the later nineteenth century the imperial bureaucracy
gathered and published statistics for many colonies that give a sense of the
size of the policing operation involved. The largest immigrant concentrations of indentured Indian labor were in Mauritius and the British Caribbean,
where there were also repeatedly enacted, constantly amended, and highly detailed master and servant acts. The pattern of enforcement differed, although
all were plantation societies in which cheap labor was crucial to profitability.
Tables 1.3 and 1.4 compare enforcement statistics for Mauritius and British
Guiana to those for England and an industrial city in one of the "white" dominions, Canada.

These figures are open to a number of interpretations. The striking dis-
proportion in the rates of prosecution in England and Canada, on one hand,
and the plantation societies, on the other, suggests how different was the use
of master and servant in different settings. In England even those areas with
higher rates (such as Wolverhampton, an industrial area in a county that always had some of the highest rates of prosecutions) saw one-fiftieth the rate
of servant prosecutions as did the plantation societies. In England master and
servant prosecutions were increasingly resented in the nineteenth century for
their taint of criminality, but they were exemplary; the vast majority of disputes, although settled in "the shadow of the law," never got to court, let alone
punishment. The relatively high rates in Macclesfield may result from the fact

139. Worger, *City of Diamonds*, 125, 144, 138.

TABLE 1.3.
Servants Prosecuted Annually, Selected Places and Periods

Jurisdiction and Dates	N/Year	Indentured Population	As Percentage of Total Servant Population	Per 100,000 Workers	Per 100,000 Population[a]
Canada					
Toronto, 1847–77	22				44
England					
Macclesfield,					
Cheshire,					
1823–24	60		5	500?	333
Wolverhampton,					
Staffordshire,					
1860s	170				266[b]
Hanley,					
Staffordshire,					
1864–66					43
England and Wales					
1860s	9,700				48
1860s, males only	9,003				88
Mauritius, 1860s	14,197	71,000	20	19,996	4,569
British Guiana					
1880s	3,476	18,700	18.6	18,588	1,349
1900–1914	3,211	11,200	28.7	28,741	1,115

Sources: Toronto: chapter by Craven. Macclesfield: chapter by Hay; *British Census of 1821*, PP 1822 1:35-6; and Sylvester, *History of Cheshire*, 87–90. England and Wales, and Wolverhampton, 1860s: PP 1861 to 1870, *Return of Judicial Statistics for England and Wales*; Wrigley and Schofield, *Population History*, 588–95; *Victoria County History of Stafford* (1908), 1:326. British Guiana: Mandle, *Plantation Economy*, 19, table 2; and chapter by Mohapatra, Table 14.1. Mauritius: R. Allen, *Slaves, Freedmen, and Indentured Laborers*, 17, 66–67.

[a]The per 100,000 population rates for British Guiana and Mauritius are probably low, as prosecutions of nonindentured workers under other legislation may not be counted.

[b]Assuming that the parliamentary returns are for Wolverhampton township only, population approximately 64,000 in the 1860s.

that Thomas Allen, a popular arbiter of labor disputes, whose notes are the source, was frequently called upon by both masters and servants to resolve questions that might not have come before a magistrate elsewhere.[140]

The level of prosecution in the sugar colonies is of another order entirely.

140. See the chapter by Hay in this volume.

TABLE 1.4.
Outcomes of Master and Servant Cases, Selected Places and Periods

Jurisdiction and Dates	Prosecutions of Servants as % of Cases[a]	Masters' Success Rate (%)	Claims by Servants as % of Cases	Servants' Success Rate (%)
Toronto, Canada				
1847–77	38	55	61	65
Macclesfield, England				
1823–24	60	n/a	40	n/a
Hanley, England				
1864–66	63	83	37	80
Mauritius				
1860s	65	75	34	75
British Guiana				
1880s	100?	60	Nearly none?	n/a
1900–1914	99	54.3	< 1	n/a

[a] The total number of cases and the proportions of cases brought by masters and by servants after 1846 in England are affected to an unknown extent by the diversion of some wage cases to the county courts. See the chapter by Hay and Table 2.1.

In Mauritius, it appears that the immediate postemancipation regime was as harsh as slavery: indeed, the Colonial Office interrupted the early importation of Indian labor when the degree of exploitation came to its attention. Planter pressure produced the common imperial pattern in ex-slave colonies: a master and servant regime with highly detailed regulations that supposedly balanced penal sanctions with labor standards. There were more than 70,000 indentured workers in Mauritius by the 1860s, and each year 20 percent of them were prosecuted for desertion and other offenses; in turn, about 10 percent of the workers brought complaints, mostly for unpaid wages. The prosecutions of workers declined markedly after the 1860s, to about 7 percent annually, and the number of complaints against masters fell even lower. Why is less clear. Contemporaries credited the increasing refinement and stringency of employment, vagrancy, and other legislation, notably the consolidated master and servant act of 1867.[141] The facts that in the later nineteenth century employers made large deductions from wages for absenteeism and often refused to pay wages for 10 to 40 percent of days actually worked suggest that recourse

141. Carter, *Servants, Sirdars and Settlers*, 213, notes that prosecuting police received half the fines.

to the courts became more difficult for workers, and less necessary for employers.[142] Some recent work, in reaction to Tinker and others who emphasized legal disabilities and reports of exploitation in official inquiries, emphasizes instead a "maturing" labor relations system, with increasing numbers of nonindentured Indian workers, which may have made harsh enforcement unnecessary later in the century. Mauritian labor therefore was less likely, over the course of the century, to be subject to the specific (and highly penal) legislation governing "new immigrant" indentured labor. Even for those subject to it, the argument is made that the laws were largely nugatory, their frequent reenactment and high rates of absenteeism a testimony to their ineffectiveness.[143] Yet without detailed information about the use of other employment statutes, the stringent vagrancy laws, pervasive policing, and less formal controls, including official toleration by complaisant magistrates of employers who coerced their workers and withheld their wages, the case for a more "mature," less exploitative labor system remains unproven. All these means were used by Mauritian employers.[144]

What is clear is that in British Guiana and Trinidad, sugar plantation economies developing rapidly after the abolition of slavery, prosecution rates remained high throughout the later nineteenth and early twentieth centuries. As Mohapatra shows in this volume, between one-fifth and one-third of indentured workers were prosecuted annually, with the highest rates occurring after the turn of the twentieth century. Each year between 6 and 7 percent of all indentured workers were imprisoned, while proceedings against masters were virtually nonexistent. David Trotman has shown that in the heavily policed society of late nineteenth-century Trinidad, 18 percent of all offenses and 23 percent of convictions and committals were for breach of contract.[145]

142. R. Allen, *Slaves, Freedmen, and Indentured Labourers*; prosecution rates calculated here from his table 5. Compare the statistics of Carter, *Servants, Sirdars and Settlers*, 210–11, table 6.1.

143. R. Allen, *Slaves, Freedmen, and Indentured Labourers*, who argues against the view that a "new system of slavery" continued after midcentury by pointing to a growing "old immigrant" Indian population, free of indentures, successfully developing shopkeeping and other commercial activity, that by late in the century had bought significant amounts of land. Sugar estates were increasingly subdivided, and workers increasingly provided by Indian subcontractors. Shorter-term contracts became much more common not only because "new immigrants" under five-year indentures formed a smaller and smaller part of the work force, but because employers could thereby escape the labor standards of the statutes governing indentured labor. By the end of the century the number of contract laborers was less than half what it had been in the 1860s.

144. For evidence of these techniques of labor control into the 1870s, see Carter, *Servants, Sirdars and Settlers*, ch. 6.

145. Trotman, *Crime in Trinidad*, 188, 295.

The problem with relying on statistical series of master and servant convictions alone to describe enforcement is illustrated by the figures for Assam in India. There were half a million contract workers in the tea gardens by the early twentieth century, but the annual prosecution rate never reached 1 percent. As Mohapatra shows, however, the authorities tolerated a system of employer self-help based on frequent, usually unrecorded, arrests of workers without warrant, often accompanied by severe corporal punishment. This was a labor regime possibly as harsh to workers as that of the West Indies but relying on private enforcement of the labor contract, authorized by statute.[146]

These different patterns in plantation societies heavily dependent on Indian labor show that coercion cannot be measured directly by prosecution statistics, but that where rates were low, other forms of coercion to maintain the boundaries of the low-wage sector, including private corporal punishment, were strikingly in evidence. An equally revealing instance is Kenya, where prosecution rates indicate there was relatively little use of master and servant legislation and that its use diminished over time. But as David Anderson shows in this volume, flogging remained the norm, quietly countenanced by the local and imperial state until they were embarrassed by particularly brutal punishments resulting in deaths.[147]

Studies by other scholars have found evidence of the extensive use of highly repressive legislation in other colonies, where active prosecution was coupled with employer self-help. In British Honduras there was a customary practice of public whippings and imprisonment in the 1830s for breach of contract; there was no summary procedure for workers to recover wages. Regulations adopted by public meeting when "apprenticeship" ended in 1838 finally provided for wage recovery as well as more formal master and servant provisions, by which workers could be imprisoned as long as six months for breach of contract. Lengthy punishments, coupled with truck payment and advances, kept mahogany loggers in perpetual debt. Working conditions were thought by many commentators to be among the worst in recent imperial history. Imprisonment for breach of contract was reduced to three months in 1857, but other enactments provided for additional repressive measures, including the right of employer or agent to apprehend a laborer without warrant and remove him forcibly to his designated place of work. By the 1870s magistrates were dealing with hundreds of cases of absence, insolence, assaults, and neglect of work, virtually all resulting in conviction and sentences of three months' im-

---

146. Mohapatra in this volume. (Bengal) n.6 of 1865 ss.35ff. provided that the private arrest be followed by notification of the police and, in theory, confirmation by a magistrate; (India) n.1 of 1882 s.170 widened the power.

147. David Anderson, this volume.

prisonment with hard labor; there were a tiny number of cases brought by workers.[148]

Direct coercion by whipping or arrest, unsanctioned by any magistrate, was most common in Africa and Asia, particularly in the later nineteenth century. Earlier on, in the period of abolition and "apprenticeship," the pressure of public opinion in Britain, and the determination of a few crucial figures like James Stephen in the Colonial Office, meant that new labor ordinances were usually closely scrutinized, while the use of stipendiary magistrates and the requirements for inspection and reporting of abuses made it more difficult (although far from impossible) to use private force to keep cheap labor within a bounded labor market.[149] But the Honduras regulations and the complacency about Kenyan practice are only two of many accommodations to colonial employers made by the Colonial Office later in the century. As Banton's chapter shows, it approved longer and longer contractual terms, and adopted the justification, a matter of faith among employers, that the nonwhite worker was not yet civilized enough to be disciplined by love of contract alone.

The widespread acceptance in the nineteenth-century empire that "natives" and "coolies" were not entitled to the same protections as white labor sometimes influenced also the views and actions of the high courts. We have emphasized that master and servant law, enforced by magistrates, was largely ignored by most colonial courts. It is instructive to observe those occasions on which they took cognizance of it. One instance is Ceylon (now Sri Lanka), where the formal legal edifice of master and servant acknowledged what was really at the heart of plantation society and economy: the planter's informal yet virtually absolute control of his work force. Chief Justice Bonser, at the end of the nineteenth century, wrote:

> No doubt on many estates what I may term the patriarchal system prevails. The superintendant punishes the coolies himself for any disobedience or faults, and so long as the superintendant does not abuse his position, and the coolies acquiesce, that system is probably much preferable to one in which the interference of the Police Courts is being constantly evoked by the superintendant, and this court would certainly not be anxious to interfere. But it must be distinctly understood that such a system has no support from the law, and only rests *on the acquiescence of the coolies*.[150]

148. Bolland, "Systems of Domination."

149. British Honduras was something of an exception, as it only became a colony in 1862, although under British control from 1798: Bolland, "Systems of Domination," 601.

150. *Marden v. Muniandi* (1899), 1 CLR 33, quoted in Samaraweera, "Masters and Servants," 129.

In this and other judgments, the high court relied on a variety of ratio-
nales for tolerating what contemporary accounts show to have been a system
of brutal private exploitation that compared unfavorably with West Indian
slavery. In the early nineteenth century the magistrates who enforced master and servant laws in Ceylon did not punish the servants they convicted as
provided by the statutes but simply returned them to their estates and the
informal justice of their masters. And there, as a novelistic account noted, apparently accurately, "as long as the man is working for you, you have a right
to do what you like with him—that is, anything short of killing him."[151] The
practice became an embarrassment to some lawyers, and the Colonial Office
did not like it. It was outlawed in 1865: henceforth magistrates were to enforce
the punishments provided by statute, not by employers. But the magistrates,
most of whom were planters themselves, continued their former practice. The
authority they sustained was that of English, white employers over imported
Indian labor. The central reality of employer self-help in plantation settings
was notorious also in Africa, and the difficulty of controlling employers, or
the magistracy so often subordinated to them, was one of the strongest arguments for ending indentured labor.[152]

The common element in most enforcement regimes was *performance*—requiring the servant to work out the full term of his contract. This took a
variety of forms. Some master and servant statutes expressly provided for performance orders. By the Statute of Artificers, a servant who quit before his
term could be jailed until "bound to the party to whom the offence should
be made, to serve and continue with him for the wages that then shall be
limited and appointed." Several seventeenth-century American statutes included similar provisions,[153] or more generally required "unfaithful, negligent
or unprofitable" servants to "make satisfaction" to their masters.[154] An early
Jamaica statute requiring that masters care for their sick servants added the
proviso that if the servant's incapacity was caused by his own misconduct, his
term was to be extended to make up the time lost to sickness and the cost of
medical care.[155] Express provisions for performance orders were fairly com-

151. Samaraweera, "Masters and Servants," 128, quoting William Knighton, *Forest Life in Ceylon*, 134.

152. David Anderson in this volume; Tinker, *New System of Slavery*, esp. ch. 9.

153. For example, (Rhode Island) "Breach of Covenant" (1647); (Mass.) "Regulation of Seamen" (May 1693) contains an early example of the very common provision that an absenting
seaman may be imprisoned, "so he may be secured and forthcoming to proceed on the voyage."

154. For example, (Mass.) "Liberties of Servants" (1641); (Mass.) "Masters, Servants, Labourers" (May 1649); and (Virginia) 14 Car.II n.101 (1661), among others, required workers who
deserted one employer to work for another to perform the original contract and pay damages
to both masters.

155. (Jamaica) Act of 20 Oct 1664.

mon throughout the empire well into the twentieth century. Thus a South
Australian statute of 1935 gave justices the jurisdiction to "direct the fulfil-
ment of the contract," while by a Kenyan act of 1938 the contract could be
extended by the length of time the servant was absent from work, whether
he was away of his own volition or because he was serving a term of imprisonment.[156] Even where there was no statutory provision for specific performance, magistrates commonly enforced it by the threat of fines or jail.
Throughout the empire, workers charged with desertion or insubordination
were presented with the choice between returning to work today or after a
month's imprisonment at hard labor. Specific performance of the employment contract was at the heart of master and servant law.[157]

In many jurisdictions, though, the contract could be extended not only
to make up for lost time but as an additional punishment or disincentive to
misconduct. This took the form of statutory provisions for obliging servants
to work *multiples* of the lost time. Among the earliest examples is a Virginia
statute of 1642, providing "that all runaways that shall absent themselves from
their said masters service shall be liable to make satisfaction by service at
the end of their times by indenture (viz.) double the time of service so neglected, And in some cases more if the commissioners for the place appointed
shall find it requisite and convenient."[158] There was similar legislation in other
American colonies in the seventeenth century, and in Nova Scotia and for
Newfoundland in the eighteenth. Most were for double the time of absence,
but Connecticut provided for a *triple* extension.[159] Nor was the penalty restricted to absenteeism: a Virginia statute of 1659 complained about "stubborn and incorrigible servants" who were "resisting their masters and overseers." It provided that servants who laid "violent hands" on their employers
were to serve them two years after the term of their indenture.[160] The penalty
also appears in some early West Indian statutes. In Barbados, for example,
servants were to work a whole day for every two hours of absence by a statute
of 1661. A Jamaican statute of 1664 required five days' work for each day's absence; the same provision appeared in Pennsylvania in 1700.[161] Provisions for
extended terms recur in the West Indies in postemancipation statutes of the

156. (S. Australia) n.112 of 1878 as am. to 1935; (Kenya) n.2 of 1938.
157. In Fiji, at the turn of the twentieth century, about 40 percent of men's indentures were
extended to make up for lost time, and over 50 percent of women's: Lal, "Nonresistance," 211.
158. (Virginia) 8 Car.I n.22 (1642). See the chapter by Tomlins, who finds such provisions
used extensively in Virginia, less so in Massachusetts.
159. (Connecticut) "Master, Servants and Sojourners" (1672).
160. (Virginia) n.13 of 1659.
161. (Barbados) n.30 of 1661; (Jamaica) Act of 20 Oct. 1664; and (Pennsylvania) 12 Wm.III
c.49 (1700).

1830s, carefully phrased to soothe Colonial Office sensitivity to the reemergence of anything resembling slavery.[162] They first appear outside the Western Hemisphere in 1835, in the Cape Colony, where runaway "apprentices" could be punished by a month's imprisonment, thirty lashes, and additional service "after the expiration of their apprenticeship with their employers" at the justice's discretion. In an uncharacteristic moment of inattention, James Stephen reported the Cape statute to be unexceptional, calling it a "mere transcript" of an imperial order in council with a few accommodations to local conditions.[163] By 1838, 954 Cape "apprentices" had been sentenced to periods of additional service.[164] Natal statutes of 1870 and 1891 required indentured immigrants to work two days for every day of absence in aggravated cases, and a similar penalty applied to apprentices in British Guiana as late as 1893.[165] In the exceptionally punitive regulation of indentured immigrant labor in Mauritius, attempts were made to combine the extension of indentures with the much-despised "double cut," whereby Indian workers were docked two days' pay for every day of unauthorized absence.[166]

These comparisons of enforcement across the empire challenge Daphne Simon's early conclusion that master and servant law was not at the heart of the economy, even despite its use in the most heavily industrialized parts of England. She argued that its coercive penal aspects were used overwhelmingly by small, uncompetitive capital, seeking to retain work forces that would otherwise move, in times of higher wages, to larger competitors. This was her explanation for the very high rate of prosecutions in the Staffordshire small metal trades and potteries and the Sheffield cutlery sector.[167] The evidence for England suggests a considerably wider use of the law.[168] In many colonial settings the most punitive forms of the legislation were sought by

162. For example, (Nevis) n.112 (1834).

163. (Cape) n.1 of 1835 pt. 5, ss.7, 10; CO 323/51, ff. 327–30, Stephen to the earl of Aberdeen, secretary of state for the Colonial and War Departments, 16 Mar. 1835 (information from Dr. Mandy Banton).

164. Worden, "Between Slavery and Freedom," 125, 132; Worden, "Slave Apprenticeship."

165. (Natal) n.2 of 1870; (Natal) n.25 of 1891; (British Guiana) n.1 of 1854 as am. to 1893.

166. Mauritius introduced the "double cut" in its postemancipation statute, n.16 of 1835 s.20; workers whose absence exceeded three days could also be sentenced to imprisonment. (Mauritius) n.22 of 1847 applied the penalty to Indian indentured immigrants, who were to forfeit any claim to wages or rations during their absence and were in addition to pay a halfpenny out of every shilling of monthly wages for each day's absence. After 1862 the fine could be imposed directly by the employer, without recourse to a magistrate. The double-cut was abolished in 1909 after protests from India. Tinker, *New System of Slavery*, 188ff., shows that planters used these fines to keep workers perpetually in their debt. Tinker's chronology is unreliable, and he apparently did not consult the statutes but relied on official correspondence and inquiry reports.

167. Simon, "Master and Servant."

168. Hay in this volume.

very large mining and plantation concerns, and their successful use could depend upon a high level of concentration of ownership. In periods when many small employers were in a desperate competition for labor, and wage rates were rapidly rising as a result, employers called for and sometimes got from the state what they believed would be remedial legislation. In the Kimberley diamond field in West Griqualand (absorbed by Cape Colony in 1880), both pass and master and servant legislation were enacted in such conditions in 1872.[169] This legislation, backed by expanded police forces and streamlined magistrates' court procedures, resulted in high levels of prosecution and convictions.

These aspects of labor control became *more* rigorous and punitive in Kimberley as industrial concentration in the diamond mines increased, culminating in closed compounds and strip searching. In the early years, when very large numbers of black laborers were required, attempts to impose stringent master and servant legislation and similar measures like wage cutting did not succeed: workers responded by leaving the market, leading mine holders to attempt to retain them by ignoring or subverting the regulations. (In this period too the London-dominated colonial state was not prepared to enact specifically racist legislation.) Over the next two decades periodic depressions in the diamond market reduced labor demand and also increased the concentration of capital in the industry. Both processes, ultimately culminating in monopoly, permitted the effective imposition and enforcement of the most far-reaching legal controls over labor. The domination of large capital prevented competitive evasion of the law by other employers seeking to retain or attract labor, while the immense political resources of the diamond cartel defeated attempts to introduce workmen's compensation, or to mitigate the reach of master and servant and other punitive law for whites. The new omnipotence of local legislatures meant that the concerns voiced from London in earlier decades were no longer to be heard in South Africa.

The use of the law in other southern African jurisdictions suggests further contrasts with the British experience of master and servant.[170] Southern Rhodesian gold mines in the early twentieth century experienced mass desertions: "desertion *was*, in many cases, a form of combination—and in some cases an extremely effective form." Desertion rates among forced labor in the early 1900s approached 20 percent before reaching the mine, and exceeded 60 percent in the first two weeks of labor. This was an immediate, col-

169. (Griqualand W.) n.14 of 1872. The following account is based on Worger, *City of Diamonds*, 92, 114–19, 122–24, 131, 136–38, 217–18.

170. There is a large literature. For a study offering comparisons to both Worger and van Onselen, see N. Levy, *Transvaal*.

lective response once armed coercion was removed or became less vigilant. Desertions from unhealthy mines were common immediately after payday. In many cases workers deserted Southern Rhodesia to seek higher wages in the mines of the South African Rand. Pass laws were intermittently effective in controlling desertions, while new recruits were forced into the mine labor force by increased taxes. Ambitious state participation in recruitment through the Rhodesia Native Labour Bureau (RNLB) was matched by new employment legislation: nineteen statutes between 1900 and 1915, including the 1901 master and servant ordinance and a new act in 1912, modeled on South African legislation, which led to prosecutions of workers who "refused or neglected to do work," showed "gross carelessness in handling tools," were "impertinent," or who "wilfully destroyed compound huts and other property." These provisions were not much used by mine managers, who found it difficult and time-consuming to prosecute many men successfully. Instead, they relied on frequent unauthorized flogging and extralegal fines (although fines were also possible under the ordinance), part of the efficiently concentrated violence and control now made possible by the compound system imported from South Africa.[171]

In nineteenth-century mining districts in England, the law was also used against collective action, including strikes.[172] High rates of prosecutions in some districts (the counties of Staffordshire, Lancashire, and Yorkshire are instances) may reflect the proximity of lower-wage and higher-wage employers and employments. During economic upturns, workers sought to increase their returns by abandoning lower-paid work. In both England and Africa, employers sought to immobilize their workers. In England they used master and servant prosecutions; in Africa, violence and exactions without due process, albeit carried on in the shadow and spirit of oppressive legislation. In England, by the nineteenth century, trade-union lawyers were making life increasingly uncomfortable for employers and magistrates, increasingly discrediting the penal law.[173] In the labor compounds of twentieth-century southern and eastern Africa, legal recourse was not possible. Resistance could only take the other, covert, and extralegal forms that desperate indentured laborers everywhere had turned to when they could not turn to law.[174] Like the employment law of so many other jurisdictions throughout

---

171. (S. Rhodesia) n.16 of 1911; van Onselen, "Worker Consciousness," 9–13; van Onselen, *Chibaro*, 80, 94–95, 98–99, 106, 143. Chibaro ("slave") was the name given by RNLB workers to the contracts enforced by (S. Rhodesia) n.5 of 1901 and its amended versions.

172. Hay in this volume.

173. Frank, "Constitutional Law."

174. Van Onselen, *Chibaro*, 237ff.

the old and new British Empires, that of eastern and southern Africa was profoundly racist in intent and effect. An editorialist in Kimberley in the 1870s
demanded that the state support "class legislation, restrictive laws, and the
holding in check of the coloured races till by education they are fit to be our
equals." These were also the demands of white workers in racially divided
colonial societies. In this case, legislation in 1876 was disallowed by London.
But even when there was reluctance in the Colonial Office to sanction explicitly racist legislation, it might mean little in practice: in a racially divided
society it was well understood, by judges, administrators, and the public, that
only in the most exceptional circumstances were punitive master and servant provisions to be applied to whites. In India too, colonial administrators
viewed native workers as immature, justifying both the protective clauses for
emigrant labor and the penal sanctions in India itself.[175]

Master and Servant as Imperial Law[176]

The ubiquity of this body of law, over so many jurisdictions and over such a
long period of time, raises a number of questions about legal systems and their
evolution. Medieval and early modern legal systems were typically pluralis-
tic aggregations of local law, mostly governing private relationships, limited
by geography, corporate charters, specific trades, linguistic and ethnic communities, religious bodies, and local custom. The highly centralized, state-
dominated regimes of the modern civilian- and common-law systems are the
product of developments over half a millennium, from their origin in competing jurisdictions of church and state law in the twelfth century through the
development, in common-law countries, of modern appellate systems in the
nineteenth. In the more distant past, most people's entitlements and duties
were defined and enforced largely by microjurisdictions, often insulated from,
but at times subject to, local legal representatives of increasingly powerful
central states.[177] In England the central state's expression was Parliament and
the royal courts, as distinct from the borough and hundred and other local
courts. Of crucial significance in articulating the relationship between local
power and central authority was the office of the justice of the peace, created

175. Chanock in this volume and Chanock, *Making*; Worger, *City of Diamonds*, 118, 121, 135;
Michael Anderson in this volume.
176. The following discussion is a tentative and abbreviated version of some arguments that
will appear more fully developed in a second volume by Craven and Hay.
177. For an argument about medieval local citizenships, see Somers, "Rights, Relationality."
For illustrations of the fate of manorial custom and some other limited bodies of law, including
those of trades, see Hay and Rogers, *Eighteenth-Century English Society*, chs. 6, 7, and Arthurs,
Without the Law.

by a centralizing monarchy in the fourteenth century. His role was sometimes that of an agent of the central state, sometimes that of local feeling, depending on the century, the place, and the man.

Within and between the early modern legal systems of Europe, and across their spreading colonial possessions, the law of the fifteenth through seventeenth century was fluid, plural, and local.[178] This is said to be true also of the legal regimes of Islamic and Asian polities. These common characteristics gave important purchase to localized rights within larger legal regimes. They allowed merchants, travelers, and religious and ethnic minorities of all kinds to find protection and opportunity and common ground. Some of that diversity particularly characterized some early English possessions, notably India where eighteenth-century British policy was to preserve the existing complex structures of local and personal law, but also many others.[179]

By the nineteenth century Britain (like other European states) had largely subordinated local jurisdictions to the central courts, often by destroying or reshaping local bodies of customary law through legislation and the decisions of the royal judges. The imperial state also increasingly, in the eighteenth and nineteenth centuries, imposed a superordinate structure of British imperial law (especially criminal law) and English procedural elements both on the formerly heterogeneous systems of older possessions with plural law (such as India) and on new possessions either captured from other colonizers (Quebec, British Guiana, St. Lucia, South Africa) or appropriated from indigenous peoples.

This major change has been noticed by theorists of comparative law, who see in it a problematic issue for their rather relentlessly taxonomic field. What *is* a dominant legal system? What counts as a settled "family" of law when it incorporates not only a mixture of two or more of the world's major systems (e.g., civil, common, Islamic) but also the discovery or invention or reification of indigenous or customary law for the purposes of colonization?[180] The York Master and Servant Project provides a different frame for the question. In one way ours is a much more constricted view. The topic explored in this and a succeeding volume is not all of private law, or criminal law, or constitutional law, but only the contract of employment. The word "only" is (intentionally) provocative: with land law and vagrancy law, the contract of employment was the crucial legal instrument for making colonies profitable, for shattering and rebuilding the original elements of the colonial economy and society in a different image. It was the body of law arguably of the greatest significance to

178. Tomlins and Mann, *Many Legalities.*
179. Benton, *Law and Colonial Cultures.*
180. For example, Örücü, "Mixed and Mixing Systems."

the greatest number of all those subject to British rule, at home and throughout the empire. Yet it is curiously absent from most accounts of comparative
law.[181] We have already emphasized one reason for this anomaly. The law of
the individual employment contract, in England and Scotland and Ireland,
and throughout the British Empire, was administered by lay justices or other
inferior magistrates; these disputes were rarely considered in the high courts.
Yet it was also embodied in statute, a product of state, not of local and private legal ordering.[182] Neither magistrates nor statutes have been among the
main concerns of comparative lawyers. As statute, master and servant law was
found in the most diverse kinds of legal, social, and economic regimes, reflecting little of their other legal characteristics.

The explanation begins in the long history of master and servant law in England. From its fourteenth-century inception it was special law, deliberately
insulated from the high law of the judges in the central courts of the king. It
was law, more exactly legislation, for dealing with poor people, for recalcitrant serfs or laborers or artisans, and then for ex-slaves, "native" workers, and
indentured "coolies." During the entire period covered by this book it was
speedy, cheap, shorn of doctrinal formality and procedural complexity, administered by magistrates, usually lay justices. All those characteristics made
it uninteresting to lawyers, more rarely considered by judges than most other
parts of the law, and hence of almost no interest whatever to modern scholars of comparative law.[183] The same characteristics made it suitable for em-
bodiment in municipal regulation, colonial legislation, or received doctrine,
in colonies of civilian as well as common-law traditions, in unitary as well as
pluralist legal regimes.[184] It was immensely adaptable, and much adapted. In

181. But see Hooker, *Legal Pluralism*; Mommsen and de Moor, *European Expansion and Law*;
and Benton's chapters on imperial jurisdictions in *Law and Colonial Cultures*.

182. For the contrasts between high law (that of the royal trial and appellate courts, law reports, and treatise literature) and low law (that of the justices of the peace and other magistrates,
courts of request, manorial and other local courts, and policing), see Hay, "Time, Inequality,"
166–71, and Hay, "Judges and Magistrates." Karsten, *Between Law and Custom*, draws a different
distinction in defining "high" and "low" law.

183. Before the nineteenth century lawyers were most likely to deal with employment cases
when they raised the poor-law issue of settlement: service for a year was one of the grounds for
obtaining settlement in a parish, making that parish obliged for poor relief to the servant. Master and servant cases became numerous in the English and Scottish high courts in the nineteenth
century largely because the unions began testing the law by contesting magistrates' decisions;
a few politically committed lawyers were responsible for a very high proportion of cases by the
1840s and 1850s. Frank, "Constitutional Law"; Frank, "Warrington Cases." In India, the persistence of master and servant law into the twentieth century (and hence review in the courts)
contrasted with reforms in other areas of Indian law: see Michael Anderson in this volume.

184. For an instance of postslavery and immigrant indentured labor subject to such legislation in a civilian regime not within the British Empire, see Conrad, *Destruction of Brazilian*

more than 100 different jurisdictions, it found a place either as one of several nested subsystems within a well-developed body of plural law (as in India) or as the dominant part of low law (as in Mauritius). It fitted into common-law regimes for the same reason that it was adaptable to civilian regimes such as Quebec, St. Lucia, Ceylon, and South Africa. In this process diverse groups of colonies developed master and servant law with strong family connections, even when their "dominant" lawyerly legal regimes (civilian or common law, Islamic or Hindu, or customary) were quite different.

From an early period, the imposition of master and servant law marked a clear assertion of the colonial state's sovereignty over its laboring subjects. Recent accounts of colonial legal systems describe a fluid multijurisdictional law throughout much of the world of European empires up until a period of transition from the late eighteenth to the mid-nineteenth century. Hegemonic colonial state legal projects are then seen to subordinate the polycentric law of an earlier period in world and colonial history.[185] But master and servant law clearly shows a central state project much earlier than this. As we have remarked, in England itself it was a distinct project of the central and local state from early medieval times. It is true that there was a recurrence to particularistic legislation and very variable standards of local enforcement in some periods, of which the long eighteenth century (1660–1820 or so) was one; some local and peculiar jurisdictions retained their own employment law even in England, and terms of contracts might depend on local practices.[186] But the long story of the penal sanctions is the story of the statutes: state law, not local law; law analogous to criminal law, not to the private law that arises out of custom and community. In the British colonies of the seventeenth century, it was already entrenched.

From the mid-seventeenth century the imperial legislation is multitudinous, but equally centered on penal sanctions and speedy administration.[187] Private law in conquered colonies was usually respected and preserved (Mauritius, Quebec, India), a tenet of English common law given imperial emphasis by Chief Justice Lord Mansfield in *Campbell v. Hall* (1774) as England drew back from the initial purpose of wholly replacing French with English law in

---

Slavery, 22ff., 148ff., and Dean, *Rio Claro: A Brazilian Plantation System*, 96–97, 145, 156ff. Brazil copied some British criminal procedure in the early nineteenth century, but we have not compared the Brazilian master and servant laws. For the insulation of master and servant regulations from Quebec's civil code, see Craven in this volume.

185. Benton, *Law and Colonial Cultures*.

186. Hay, "Master and Servant in England," and in this volume.

187. Intense local conflict might result in delegation of legislation to municipal bodies: see Craven's chapter for the example of Quebec. Another instance of such pluralism is early law in Madras, India: Ahuja, "Origins."

Quebec.[188] But criminal law was much more likely to be remade by the imperial power and to show the effects of English law, imposed or absorbed in procedure and statute: imposed in its entirety in Quebec, absorbed in other colonies as procedure, codes of offenses, evidentiary rules, legislative sources, and judicial rulings.[189] The law of master and servant, like the criminal law to which it was related, was also the product of the colonizing power or its local representatives. But as an instance of inferior law, administered informally by magistrates and justices of the peace, it was also very distant from the ideologies and procedures of the high courts, where criminal law often boasted all the procedural safeguards of English doctrine, and where the distinctiveness of a colony's private law was often partially preserved.[190] Master and servant law was low law: a marvel of efficiency, coercion, and finality.

Finally, both in Britain and in Britain's imperial possessions, for most of this history, the penal law of master and servant was the product of deeply undemocratic polities. Britain itself had one of the most restrictive franchises in the Atlantic world and Western Europe until the last quarter of the nineteenth century; repeal of the penal sanctions became possible only then. In European settler jurisdictions where democratic franchises had a longer history, the penal clauses sometimes endured longer, perhaps because they were less enforced.[191] But in many of Britain's wide imperial possessions, the populations most subject to the law of master and servant were denied the vote throughout the whole period we have described. Comparative legal histories, imperial legal histories, only make sense when freedom to change law, freedom to use law, freedom to resist law are given as much emphasis as the freedom to enter markets.

188. Adam Shortt and A. G. Doughty, *Documents Relating to the Constitutional History of Canada, 1759–1791* (Ottawa, 1918), 1:522–31. The decision, on Grenada, had greatest implications for Quebec.

189. Hay, "Meanings." Some more coercive aspects of private law were also imposed, notably imprisonment for debt: see the chapter by Craven.

190. Chanock, *Making*, 119–20.

191. See the chapters by Craven and Quinlan in this volume.

TWO

England, 1562–1875

The Law and Its Uses

Douglas Hay

In March 1857 a potter named William Baker was imprisoned for a month in the Staffordshire house of correction for leaving his employers, whom he had contracted to serve for a year, but whom he left after four days after a dispute about pay. He served the month, but on his release from jail he refused to work for them. His employers had him rearrested, and he was recommitted for another month at hard labor. This time his case went to the high courts. His lawyers asked Queen's Bench to release him on a writ of habeas corpus, arguing, among other points, that the original contract had ended with conviction and imprisonment. The judges rejected the "ingenious subtleties" of this argument: "his duty to perform still exists."[1] Magistrates had been sending recalcitrant workers to prison for at least 500 years; there was ample statutory authority for it; and why should a worker be allowed to escape serving his master simply because he served time in prison for trying to avoid it in the first place? The judges of the Court of Queen's Bench continued to refuse to release workers who had been repeatedly convicted for breach of the same contract. They had precedent on their side: Lord Ellenborough, chief justice of that court, had ruled more than forty years before that there was nothing to prevent recommittal to prison of the worker, presumably as often as necessary. Otherwise the breach would amount to the right of the worker to dissolve the contract. Perhaps the worker was even obliged to labor for his master while in jail, if he commanded it.[2] After all (as Ellenborough said in another case, justifying dismissal of disobedient workers with loss of all wages), "the question really comes to this, whether the master or the servant is to have

---

1. *Ex parte William Baker* (1857), 26 Law J. Rep. M.C. (1857) 193; also a fuller version 155–68; also *Justice of the Peace* (1 Aug. 1857), 486–88.
2. *R v. Barton-upon-Irwell* (1814), 2 M&Sel 329, 105 ER 404.

the superior authority."[3] But Baker's lawyers did not give up: they went to Exchequer. There Chief Baron Pollock took a very different view. It was, of course, the case that an initial absence from work, or other misbehavior, was punishable by one to three months at hard labor: a wide range of statutes provided for it. Indeed, Parliament had learned the year before that 5,560 workmen and women had been summarily convicted and imprisoned in England, Wales, and Ireland in the two years 1854 and 1855 for breach of contract.[4] But, said Pollock, repeated convictions were another matter. It was "contrary to the general spirit of the English law . . . that a man should be punished thus over and over again, for what substantially is the same matter," and "the rights of labourers . . . are to be considered as well as the interests of the masters." The law provided for repeated imprisonment of apprentices, and that might well be necessary, but that "would not be suitable and proper in the case of a man grown up and of full age, possibly surrounded by a wife and children." Repeated imprisonment, he said, "is about as inconvenient and as improper an instrument to enforce a contract as can be well developed. I think that the treadmill is a very bad instrument to enforce the labours of workmen from week to week and from month to month, for the period of a year."[5] Indeed, he calculated, a man might spend almost fifteen months in prison for repeated breaches of a year's contract of employment. And, not surprisingly, he found some legal as well as policy reasons for releasing Baker, seconded by his fellow judges.

Pollock handed down his decision in the last decades of fines and imprisonment in English employment law: his judgment became ammunition for the unions in presentations to parliamentary committees in the 1860s, and for other critics of the law.[6] Imprisonment was only one, and the least common, form of remedy obtained by masters. Far more frequent was abatement (deduction) of wages for time absent, and dissolution of the contract with wages forfeited. Imprisonment was, however, the ultimate sanction, the harshest, and ultimately the most contentious. Moreover, the threat of imprisonment was used, as it had been for centuries, to enforce performance of the contract, and even when the threat was carried out, masters could, and did, have their penitent servants released back into their employment before the full sentence was served. Master and servant penal sanctions were designed, and

3. *Spain v. Arnott* (1817), 2 Stark 256, 171 ER 638.

4. *Abstract Return of Numbers of Persons Summarily Convicted . . . for Breach of Contract, 1854 and 1855,* Parliamentary Papers (hereafter PP) 1856 (441), 50:633. On the statutes, see below.

5. *Ex parte Baker* (1857), 26 LJR at 163.

6. *Report from the Select Committee on Master and Servant,* PP 1866 (449), 13:71, evidence of William Evans, 5 June 1866, questions 1374, 1397; Edgar, "Jurisdiction of Justices of the Peace," 687–90.

used, to secure performance of the employment contract, a remedy not available in any other part of contract law.

The legitimacy of both penal sanctions and of the lay magistracy which heard most master and servant cases was under concerted trade-union attack from the 1840s. Organized labor prevented an expansion of the penal regime by massive mobilization and publicity in 1844; continued pressure in the 1850s and 1860s weakened parliamentary support for the old regime.[7] Pollock's comments and those of some other high-court judges at midcentury also eroded the legitimacy of the penal laws, although the bench, as always, was not all agreed, and the case law oscillated to the end of the penal regime in 1875, under continued union pressure.[8] But trade unions were not a new invention. Well-organized trades were able to stage massive strikes from the early 1700s, and the history of effective collective militancy probably goes back much farther.[9] The threat of disorder they posed, and the claims to consideration they exacted from Parliament, did much to shape the law of master and servant. Yet before the 1840s they had not been able to prevent the enforcement, indeed expansion, of the penal law, sometimes by Parliament, sometimes by the judges.

We now know a great deal about the law and its uses in the third quarter of the nineteenth century, but that is the last 5 percent of its very long run. This chapter sets out an argument about the longer history. Imprisonment and whipping and fines,[10] rather than civil remedies, were deeply entrenched in English employment law, and so too was its administration by the magistrates.[11] The law also gave remedies to workers, a fact of great significance for the public perception of the law.

Neither central state law nor local practice were static. For centuries they

---

7. For the period after 1840 the pioneer work of Simon has recently been greatly extended: see below.

8. With respect to repeated conviction, Pollock and his brethren took a similar view in *Youle v. Mappin* (1861), 30 Law J. Rep. M.C. 234; their view of Baker was derided by Queen's Bench in *Unwin et al. v. Clarke* (1866), 35 Law J. Rep. M.C. 193.

9. Rule, *British Trade Unionism*; Rule, *Experience of Labour*; Rule, "Employment and Authority"; Dobson, *Masters and Journeymen*; Randall, *Before the Luddites*; Randall, "Industrial Moral Economy."

10. Fines, defined here as forfeitures of wages, or other payments, made to the state, an institution, an informer, or (when beyond compensation for loss) to the master, are rare for workers' offenses in England in earlier centuries: apart from (England) 5 Eliz. c.4 (1562) ss.12, 13 (described below), they occur in only nine statutes, all dealing with offenses by seamen or related to embezzlement, where some statutes gave double damages to masters for fraud or spoiled work. The term was sometimes used loosely to describe abatements or costs; fines were much used from 1867 until they were abolished, with other criminal penalties, in 1875 (see below).

11. In other publications I describe the statute and case law, and the causes of their evolution from 1700 to 1840, in more detail.

were the product of trade organization, social structure, legislation, and continual renegotiation. Master and servant law offered remedies to both parties, and it was embedded in highly specific local cultures of work and social relations, which preserved and legitimated it. Then in the first three decades of the nineteenth century both the doctrine in the hands of the judges and the nature of its enforcement by lay magistrates, including the use of imprisonment, became more inimical to labor, at a time of rapid industrialization and increasing trade-union organization. By midcentury the coercive aspects of the law had become the object of sharp public debate, not least because (for the first time) a number of solicitors and a few barristers, working for the unions, brought a large number of test cases before the high courts. When the unions finally succeeded in forcing the repeal of virtually all penal clauses in 1875, a type of contract originally based on the need to subordinate labor was restated as if it were a contract between fully equal parties. All these changes can be explained only when the statutes and case law are set in the context of actual enforcement: who complained, about what offenses, before which magistrates, and with what results.

The Law to the Eighteenth Century

By the seventeenth century the roots of master and servant law lay in the distant past, but it was still recognizably the same plant, and flourishing. In the fourteenth-century Ordinance of Labourers (1349) and Statute of Labourers (1350), and further statutes of 1361 and 1388, the central state embraced legal regulation of labor.[12] It sought to compel service by the idle, curb movement by agricultural servants and artisanal and manufacturing workers, suppress their wage demands by fixing legal rates and by making annual hiring the norm, and tie workers to their employers for the duration of their contracts and to their social status for the duration of their lives. Employers poaching labor were subjected to some of the same penalties as workers defying the law. The legislation, an express response to rapidly growing wages in the generation after the Black Death, put great powers in the hands of the men charged with local enforcement of the law. The emergence of the English gentry, their appointment as justices of the peace, and their role as local enforcers of state labor law were all intimately connected, caused by the reaction of central government to the demographic crisis of 1348–50, in which a third to half the population of England died.[13]

12. (England) 23 Edw.III cc.1–8 (1349); 25 Edw.III st.2 (1350); 34 Edw.III cc.9–11 (1361); 12 Ric.II cc.3–9 (1388).
13. R. Palmer, *Black Death*, esp. chs. 3 and 14–19, cites all the older literature in making this

The law of the fourteenth and fifteenth centuries already distinguished agricultural "servants" and "labourers," the two main groups of agrarian workers. The former were usually hired by the year, usually young, and usually unmarried and living in their masters' household from their teens. Laborers, on the other hand, were hired by the day, might be married, and worked for several employers. "Artificers" might be servants, or they might be masters, members of the huge range of craftsmen in the manufacturing trades, including the large textile industries and building trades of the Middle Ages. As masters they employed many laborers (especially in the building trades), and they also took apprentices and employed journeymen who had completed their apprenticeships but had not become masters themselves.

All these terms appear in statutes and records of the courts over the centuries.[14] Their importance for the law of master and servant from the sixteenth century to the nineteenth is that they appeared again in the key statute that shaped the law until the nineteenth century. The Elizabethan Statute of Artificers (1562),[15] sometimes called the Statute of Apprentices, recodified the "great number of acts and statutes concerning the retaining, departing, wages and orders of apprentices, servants and labourers, as well in husbandry as in divers other arts, mysteries and occupations."[16] Its forty-eight sections also mention workmen and artificers, and scores of specific trades. The reasons for a great recodification of labor law are debated, but it seems clear that both the central state and local authorities thought labor should be controlled closely, forced into service, and kept from bidding up wages. The aim was to control inflation, prevent trades leaving towns for the countryside, and forestall or repress widespread and dangerous riot and disorder caused by recurrent

---

argument and reviews the terms of the legislation. For enforcement of the labor statutes in one county, see Poos, *Rural Society*, chs. 9 and 10. It has been suggested that the legislation also was one of the influences on general contract law, in the rise of assumpsit and decline of covenant: Baker, *Introduction*, ch. 16.

14. Poos notes variant forms and a range of possible ambiguities, while accepting the basic structure described by Kussmaul, *Servants in Husbandry*, which draws sharp distinctions between servants and others in the seventeenth and eighteenth centuries. In contrast, Hassell Smith, "Labourers," has unusually detailed evidence that shows a wider range of types in the late sixteenth century, with variants such as older married servants, varying periods of employment, and specialized laborers, all of which agree with the evidence of a very complex range of employment patterns arising in master and servant cases in the eighteenth century also (below).

15. Although the statute was enacted in 1563, and is often so cited, in this book we follow the uniform conventions of dating statutes used in the *Chronological Table of the Statutes* (London: HMSO, many editions), which also sets out the variant numbering of some statutes enacted before 1714.

16. (England) 5 Eliz. c.4 (1562), preamble. Contemporaries used the terms "workman" and "labourer" to cover a great variety of employed persons: Hassell Smith, "Labourers," esp. 12.

harvest failure and depression.[17] Thus economic purposes were inextricably mixed with issues of governance, in particular of the young and disorderly: the statute intended to curb "the licentious manner of youth" and keep them "under government" until age twenty-four, thought to represent maturity.[18] Concern with subordination had been, and continued to be, central to the law of master and servant.

Therefore almost all the elements of earlier legislation were recapitulated and elaborated, with innovations and changes, in the Statute of Artificers: compulsory service, apprenticeship, penalties for leaving work, attempts to tie workers to particular status and employers, and official wage rates. Now wage rates were to be adjusted as necessary by the justices; seven-year apprenticeships (long common in many towns) were presented as the norm and required to exercise a trade; year-long hiring was made mandatory in a list of named trades; a quarter-year's notice was required on either side; those without work were to be forced to take service; mandatory testimonials served as passes to control labor movement; there were minimum hours and set times for meals according to season with penalties for infractions; compulsory work could be demanded in harvest.[19] Several clauses gave justices their core jurisdiction. One justice could imprison a youth refusing to be apprenticed; the single justice had powers of initial investigation and a bench the power to discharge mistreated apprentices or, for fault in the apprentice, to pass sentence of "due correction [whipping] and punishment." The sections dealing with adult workers were equally expansive. One or two justices could end agreements between masters and servants on complaint, and a bench of justices could fine employers in breach forty shillings. The servant who left the master, or failed to give notice, or refused to serve for official wages, or promised or covenanted to serve but then did not, could be imprisoned by two justices until she or he agreed to serve. Two justices could imprison for a year the worker who assaulted a master.[20]

The law envisioned employment relations for several different kinds of

17. Woodward, "Background," which also reviews the earlier interpretations of Fisher and Bindoff; Loades, *Mid-Tudor Crisis*, ch. 3; Sharp, *In Contempt of All Authority*, 53–54, 77, 158, 258.

18. Paul Griffiths, "Masterless Young People," 152; Woodward, *Men at Work*, 56, quoting a well-known commentary of c. 1573.

19. Work on the statute has overwhelmingly concentrated on the wage-fixing and the apprenticeship clauses; the jurisdiction to decide disputes between master and servant has been relatively ignored. On the interrelationships of these issues, see below.

20. Ss.35, 5, 6, 9, 21. The last two sections, and some others, specified two justices in the county commission, and in corporate towns the mayor and two aldermen or "two discreet burgesses if there be no aldermen." I refer to all of these as "magistrates" or "justices." The jurisdiction of two sitting together came to be called the "double justice."

workers. In England, age distinctions were critical for apprenticeship.[21] It took several very different forms, based on the Statute of Artificers and later acts. There was voluntary apprenticeship by the parents (or a charity) of children usually in the midteens, male or female, to a master for a term of years to learn a trade: the parties entered into indentures (articles of agreement) and the parents or charity usually paid a premium, ranging from a large sum for a wealthy and skilled trade to very little if anything for husbandry, domestic work, and the like. The master clothed, fed, trained, and maintained the apprentice, acted in loco parentis, and was entitled to any wages the apprentice might make.[22] In sharp contrast, parish (pauper) apprentices were poor and often very young, even seven or eight, compared with the usual fourteen years of age of voluntary apprentices. They were bound without their consent or that of their parents to masters in the poorer and unskilled trades to the age of twenty-four (later twenty-one); few obligations were specified on either side, but the master promised the parish that the pauper apprentice would not become a charge on the taxpayers, and many pauper children from large towns were sent away long distances to serve their indentures. Overseers of the poor, to whom the law in such cases gave powers to apprentice that were normally exercised by parents, brought such children before two justices to approve the indentures, and refusal to accept such an apprentice exposed the master selected by the overseers to a fine.[23] Magistrates (and special courts in London and some towns) had jurisdiction over disputes between apprentices of all kinds and their masters. The apprenticeship clauses of the Statute of Artificers were repealed in 1814, a crisis for skilled trades. Their enforcement had never been uniform or consistent, but (with restrictive customs of entry into trades) they were probably increasingly important to servants and in the eighteenth century, and increasingly opposed by large masters.[24]

Adult workers, in 1600 and still in 1700, fell within the jurisdiction of the magistrates by the terms of the Statute of Artificers, a few subsequent statutes, and some case law in the high courts. They might also, in London and some towns, still be subject to guild regulations.[25] The law continued to en-

21. In the British American colonies of the 1600s they were equally important for indentured labor contracts entered into in England: see the chapter by Tomlins in this volume.

22. Apprentices in artisanal trades earned wages (either working with the master, or working with his permission for another) from medieval times: Woodward, *Men at Work*, 60–61; J. Lane, *Apprenticeship*, 101–3.

23. J. Lane, *Apprenticeship*, ch. 4.

24. Brooks, "Apprenticeship"; J. Lane, *Apprenticeship*; Rule, *Experience of Labour*, ch. 4.

25. For examples in the building trades, sixteenth to eighteenth century, see Woodward, *Men at Work*, 28–35. M. Walker, "Extent of Guild Control," suggests that the survival of guild

visage three main kinds of servants: artificers; agricultural "servants in husbandry" hired by the year, often with specialized skills; and day laborers.[26] A series of statutes enacted after 1700 also provided rights, remedies, and penalties for silk weavers, tailors, colliers, glassworkers, and many other groups of workers, in response to petition, riot, or problems with the labor supply. By 1800 some twenty-six enactments (many still contingent on the 1562 statute), and by 1875 another twenty-seven, defined and redefined rights and duties and remedies for most if not all adult English workers and their masters. Because repeal of earlier acts was rare before the nineteenth century, the statute law was cumulative. Case law interpreted, expanded, and elaborated it in many particulars. The judges decided, for example, that the wage-fixing clauses of the Statute of Artificers, even as they were falling into desuetude in the early eighteenth century, gave jurisdiction to the magistrates to make summary orders for wages against masters; they also changed their minds about whether domestic servants fell within the law.[27]

Some general principles ran through the whole body of law. By the eighteenth century a contract, oral or written, for workers other than day laborers was presumed (following the statute) to last a year, particularly in husbandry, unless specific terms had been explicitly negotiated, or the periods or terms of payment or other details altered the case. Such a "general hiring" was presumed to continue unless three months' notice was given on either side. Agricultural workers were paid their wages (apart from subsistence) at the end of the term to ensure their work during harvests, and long arrears of wages were common in many trades.[28] The master until the early nineteenth century was assumed to have responsibility for the sick or injured worker, who could not be dismissed until the end of the year. In general, throughout the eighteenth century the judges appeared to require the consent of a magistrate for a lawful dismissal. However, an unmarried pregnant worker might be dismissed after 1777 on the master's own authority. After 1797 both the judges and Parliament were reluctant to recognize the right of domestic servants to apply

---

powers in incorporated towns was greatly eroded in the 1720s and 1730s. For London, see Gadd and Wallis, *Guilds*.

26. Kussmaul, *Servants in Husbandry*, argues that yearly service was an early modern role rapidly disappearing in the eighteenth century, except perhaps in the North; more recent research suggests that use of the annual hiring in farm service was expanding in some areas in the late eighteenth and early nineteenth centuries in areas of high demand for labor; see the work cited in Gritt, "The 'Survival' of Service." For nineteenth-century printed contracts of farm servants, see Miller, "Master and Man."

27. On these and other issues in the case law mentioned in this and the following paragraph, see below.

28. For example, Rule, *Experience of Labour*, 129-30.

to magistrates on grounds of mistreatment or unpaid wages, as disruptive to household authority. This had the effect, later in the period, of limiting the reach of some of the penal sanctions also.

However, most workers, including servants in husbandry, journeymen and apprentices in many trades, and also day laborers, were punishable by imprisonment for breach of contract. Offenses included absence, refusing to begin on an agreed contract, working for another, disregarding orders, and insubordination. The sentence was one month by the 1562 statute, but up to three months for each offense by a number of eighteenth- and nineteenth-century acts. In contrast, until 1844 employers were never threatened with imprisonment for breach.[29] The legislation, like most of the case law, was gender-neutral.[30] Particular statutes for specific trades, in which outworkers received work to be done and then returned it to the employer when complete, also penalized work that was retained too long: the prime purpose was to discourage embezzlement, but the acts could be used for general labor discipline. The penalties included not only imprisonment but also (in many trades) abatement of wages, whipping, dismissal, or sometimes several of these penalties. Whether dismissal entailed the loss of wages for the entire contract changed over this period, and with magistrates' practice and their knowledge of the law. Their jurisdiction, under the case law and the statutes, to order masters to pay wages owing was an extremely important recourse for working people. The only alternative until 1846 (when larger sums could be sued for in the new county courts) was an action in the high courts. It was an unthinkably expensive and risky course for most; in contrast, magistrate's orders for wages were cheap to pursue, and very numerous.[31]

Although many employment contracts, express or implied, of the early modern period lasted a year, we know that many others did not. In spite of

29. Jail as an immediate punishment for breach by the master (rather than imprisonment for nonpayment of a fine, or contempt of an order) did not become possible until 1844, when masters of ships could be imprisoned for refusal to pay seamen's wages by (U.K.) 7&8 Vict. c.112; in 1848 it became possible to commit a master in default of distress by (U.K.) 11&12 Vict. c.43s.22. Mistreatment of apprentices became punishable by imprisonment by (U.K.) 14&15 Vict. c.11 (1851). Penal sanctions were largely removed by (U.K.) 30&31 Vict. c.141 (1867); while they could now also affect masters, they were almost never jailed: Steinmetz, "De-juridification," 277.

30. The only exceptions were (England) 5 Eliz. c.4 (1562), s.24 re the age (twelve to forty) at which women could be forced to serve; the poor-law statute (England) 43 Eliz. c.2 (1601) binding boy apprentices to twenty-four, girls to twenty-one or marriage; and (U.K.) 38&39 Vict. c.90 (1875), exempting convicted children, young persons, or women covered by the factory acts from any forfeiture of wages beyond actual damage to the employer. On the case law with respect to unmarried mothers, see below.

31. See Table 2.1. It is possible that some cases were pursued in courts of request, small-debt courts established in some towns by statute; for the use of county courts after 1846, see below.

the Statute of Artificers and fifteenth- and sixteenth-century municipal regulations, journeymen were often hired by the month or the week, and many apparently left their masters before the end of a year.[32] Agreements could be varied by explicit terms, most safely expressed in writing. Such written contracts became more common in England in the early nineteenth century, particularly in factory settings, and as the forms of master and servant were being transmuted into those of the modern contract of employment.[33] However, a number of specialized types of contracts took written form much earlier. One was the collier's bond, a form of annual contract (usually for eleven months and fifteen days) with specific terms and penalties that was well established in the Durham coalfield by the early eighteenth century and may have had much deeper roots.[34] Miners had some highly distinctive forms of contract from medieval times, differing in different parts of the country.[35] Annual bonds were also used in the pottery industry in the nineteenth century, to the advantage of masters. Finally, an entirely separate body of statute law governed seamen, who were required to sign "articles" with the masters of vessels, under terms largely dictated by the law rather than by voluntary agreement.[36] In general, workers who made written agreements with their masters for a period longer than the presumptive annual hiring, or with other specific terms, often did so by a covenant which took the form of an indenture. These "covenant servants" could sue or be sued in covenant as well as proceeded against before a magistrate. Such agreements, often for many years, were commonly entered into with highly skilled workers whom masters were anxious to retain.

This in outline was the law; with some significant differences many of its terms could also be found in Ireland (under different statutes) and Scotland (a partly civil law regime).[37] This complex, ancient, much-used and well-known body of statute and case law was entwined with another range of social prac-

32. Woodward, *Men at Work*, 65–66.

33. See below.

34. Levine and Wrightson, *Making of an Industrial Society*, 184, 360ff., 394ff., who argue that it was not found on Tyneside before 1703, but note some scattered evidence of annual bonds for seventeenth-century Lancashire colliers and other northern workers. See also Frank in this volume.

35. The most notorious exception by the later eighteenth century to the usual forms of contract was the Scottish collier's bound "serfdom" under a series of early modern statutes. Whatley, "Scottish 'Collier Serfs'"; Campbell, *Lanarkshire Miners*, ch. 1.

36. For example, (G.B.) 2 Geo.II c.36 (1728), made perpetual by (G.B.) 2 Geo.III c.31 (1762). In general, see Dixon, "Seamen and the Law."

37. The Irish Parliament enacted a number of master and servant statutes, with some significant differences from the English corpus; the Scots law, both statute and common, was distinctive until the 1830s. Both regimes will be dealt with in future publications.

tices—the "custom of the trade," or "custom of the country"—that generated further law as well as social expectations.[38] Within trades, or branches of trades determined by geography, or for a wider range of occupations in such a district, the shared understandings on which contracts of employment were created, sustained, and dissolved were often distinctive. When sufficiently common and notorious and well established to convince the high-court judges that a custom existed in the legal sense, the courts recognized these social practices as enforceable terms of the contract. Thus the right to strong beer during harvest, or the month's notice common in London, might be recognized as part of the local law. Of course, in the absence of high-court litigation, some customs might still have local legal force even if they never came to the attention of the royal judges.

The detail of master and servant law in England thus varied by historical period, trade, and geography. Equally variable was the way in which its terms were enforced in circumstances of breach.

Enforcement by the Magistracy before the Eighteenth Century

The details of enforcement are still not well understood for some earlier periods. The complexity of guild and town regulation, and the coexisting powers of justices, created much local variation in the sixteenth and seventeenth centuries.[39] The best-explored records are those of county quarter sessions and some borough courts. In the seventeenth century some master and servant cases, and others arising under 5 Eliz. c.4, came before benches of magistrates at quarter sessions. There were many prosecutions on indictment and information for infringements of the sections of the Statute of Artificers requiring a seven-year apprenticeship, but these were proceedings between competitors in trade, or by organized trades trying to keep out interlopers, rather than proceedings between masters and servants.[40] However, the sessions of many counties and boroughs also record scattered cases of servants and apprentices bringing masters before the court on wage claims or for brutal mistreatment, and masters accusing servants and apprentices of sauciness, threats, and repeated running away.[41] The number at quarter sessions is very small, prob-

38. The word "country" was often used with the local connotation of "county" in early modern England; the usage probably also was intended to distinguish such terms from the custom of towns, many of which had distinctive customary law.

39. Woodward, *Men at Work*, 66 and n. 73; it does not appear, however, that Woodward used magistrates' notebooks or house of correction registers. See also M. Walker, "Extent of Guild Control"; Gadd and Wallis, *Guilds*.

40. For example, Sharpe, *Crime*, 42–43.

41. Ibid., 121.

ably because the magistrates heard only rather unusual cases there.[42] In the seventeenth-century Staffordshire quarter sessions records there are equally few master and servant cases noted: some had been forwarded to sessions because the local justice of the peace had not turned up to hear the case.[43] At the end of the century there are still occasional orders for both wage payment and committals of recalcitrant servants in the quarter sessions records of many counties, but they are rare.[44]

Constables' records reveal other details. The constables, usually householders required to take the office in a parish for a year, were under the direct supervision of the magistrates. In some counties, in the early and middle decades of the seventeenth century, the justices or high constables ordered the constables to bring servants to sessions once or twice a year to have their contracts extended or ended with the testimonial required by the Statute of Artificers.[45] It appears that some constables were required also to prepare lists of masters and servants and to report on the wages being given; in such places they also submitted returns of apprentices. They also suppressed alehouses, on the ground that they led servants to neglect the business of their masters.[46] The constables and justices were probably most active under the early Stuarts, in the early years of James I, and especially the 1630s. The *Book of Orders* of January 1631 particularly sought strict enforcement of the law administered by justices out of sessions, including forced apprenticing of pauper children (upheld by an opinion of the chief justice of Common Pleas in

42. In Warwickshire there are scattered instances: a miller demanding wages from a gentleman in 1633 (both sides represented by counsel); another miller, the servant of a gentleman, presented for leaving service without license in 1638. In the years 1650–57 the Warwickshire sessions dealt with only five wage cases (some of them also discharges) concerning ordinary hired servants. L. E. Stephens, S. C. Ratcliffe, and H. C. Johnson, eds., *Warwick County Records* (Warwick, 1935–46), 1:166; 3:125, 137–38, 138–39, 140–41, 241. There were similar numbers of cases after 1660, usually it appears when a justice had bound a master to answer a wage dispute at quarter sessions under s.6 of the Statute of Artificers. Ibid., 6:205, 212, 217.

43. Stafford Record Society, *Collections for a History of Staffordshire* (Stafford, 1940), 85–86, 138. Sessions referred the last case to a justice of the peace to have a hearing and make an order; in the second the servant may have appealed to sessions because he was not confident of winning his case before a neighboring justice.

44. For example, William Le Hardy and G. L. Reckitt, eds., *Buckinghamshire Sessions Records* (Aylesbury, 1933–) (hereafter *Buckinghamshire*), 2:131, 222–23, 234. Other quarter sessions records are surveyed in Kelsall, *Wage Regulation*, 127ff. He realized that most cases were being tried by individual justices, citing the notebooks of Devereux Edgar, described below.

45. George Fox, the Quaker leader, reported attending such a sessions in 1648, exhorting the many servants present to do their duty, and the justices to give them sufficient wages: Lipson, *Economic History*, 3:261.

46. Kent, *English Village Constable*, 17, 27–28, 187 n. 1, 189, 193, 218, 293. (Engl.) 5 Eliz. c.4 (1562) ss.10, 11, 22, and 48 conferred on constables new powers and continued some found in earlier statutes for the control of labor.

1633, and apparently resulting in great mistreatment by many unwilling masters) and the obligations of servants and of masters.[47] Petty sessions, in which magistrates began to sit regularly as "double justices" to exercise the jurisdiction conferred on two rather than one justice by many statutes, emerge clearly in this period. We find masters being fined "for retaining a servant without entering the name thereof in any Petty Session." These years are also important because the 1633 "resolutions" of Chief Justice Heath—interpretations of some aspects of master and servant, including forced apprenticeship and dismissals—were treated as law until the restoration of the monarchy in 1660.[48] In this period too, there is one of the recurrent attempts to multiply and reform the institutions to punish and reform the idle poor: the Elizabethan bridewell or house of correction.[49] Later in the century, however, organized supervision of all hirings, consistent regulation of wages, and enforcement of the testimonial clause of the Statute of Artificers had all become much less common; in the 1670s testimonials (discharge certificates) were said to be rarely required.[50] As central state supervision receded, particularly after 1660, master and servant cases rarely appeared in the records of the courts. They had always been heard mainly before one or two justices out of sessions.

When we turn to the work of the single or double justice, the evidence is more varied, although scattered and very incomplete. We have two main sources for the whole period: printed handbooks for the instruction of justices, and surviving personal notebooks and petty sessions records of summary jurisdiction. Table 2.1 summarizes the decisions of a number of selected justices, and petty sessions, over several centuries.

Justices' notebooks in Stuart England show great variation in the work of magistrates dealing with disputes between servants and masters; the sources are summarized in the first part of Table 2.1. Bostock Fuller of Tandridge (Surrey) noted only five master and servant cases between 1608 and 1620: several complaints against masters were agreed, but he sent a maidservant to the house of correction "for striking her dame and threatening her after and for departing from her service"; a third party accused of retaining a runaway servant he sent to quarter sessions. Between 1667 and 1680 Sir Thomas Sclater, near Cambridge, heard perhaps 300 employment cases in the town and sur-

47. Forster, "North Riding Justices," 120ff.; Barnes, *Somerset*, ch. 7. Much of Kent's evidence also comes from the 1630s.

48. Barnes, *Somerset*, 188–89; *Warwick County Records*, 6:3; Barnes, *Somerset Assize Orders*, nos. 186–88, reprints them. See below.

49. Innes, "Prisons for the Poor."

50. Edward Chamberlayne, *Angliae notitia* (6th ed., 1672), 383. On the later use of testimonials, see below.

TABLE 2.1.
Master and Servant Cases Heard by Selected Justices of the Peace, Borough Justices, Petty Sessions, and London Chamberlain's Court, England, 1608–1871

Source[a]	By Masters	% by Masters	Masters' Success Rate (%)[b]	By Servants	% by Servants	Servants' Success Rate (%)[b]	Master and Servant Cases as % of All	% Accused to House of Correction[c]	% Convicted to House of Correction[c]
Fuller JP 1608–20 Surrey	2[d]	25	100	3	75	67	—	100	100
Sclater JP 1667–83 Cambridge	12[d]	50	—	12	50	25	9	8	—
Bromley JP 1687–1709 Warwickshire	4	50	—	4	50	—	—	—	—
Hill JP 1693–1705 Buckinghamshire	10	36	—	18	64	—	5	0[e]	0
Edgar JP 1700–1716 Suffolk	149	55	—	121	45	—	10	10	—
Hunt JP 1744–49 Wiltshire	5	29	—	12	71	—	3	0	—

Tew JP 1750–64 County Durham	177	47	96	203	53	80	27	12	33
Ward JP 1766–68 Northamptonshire	29	44	—	37	56	—	25	4[f]	—
Wyatt JP 1767–76 Surrey	4	27	—	11	73	—	7	50	—
Clifton JP 1772–1812 Nottinghamshire	8	42	—	11	58	—	9	—	—
London Apprentices 1787	183	71	—	53	22	—	100	35	—
Aylesbury PS 1800–1807 Buckinghamshire	6	60	100	4	40	75	20	33	50
Yate JP 1801–3 Herefordshire, Gloucestershire, Worcestershire	20 (4)	59	100	14	41	20	20	25	25
Whitbread JP 1810–14 Bedfordshire	23	35	70	43	65	65	6[g]	17	25

TABLE 2.1.
Continued

Source[a]	By Masters	% by Masters	Masters' Success Rate (%)[b]	By Servants	% by Servants	Servants' Success Rate (%)[b]	Master and Servant Cases as % of All	% Accused to House of Correction[c]	% Convicted to House of Correction[c]
Turner JP 1811–27 Suffolk	19	100	—	0	0[h]	—	24	—	—
Allen BJ 1823–24 Cheshire	60	60	94 (59)	40	40	92 (53)	10	13	—
London apprentices 1823–59[i]	100	—	—	—	—	—	100	30	—
Jee JP 1842–50 Warwickshire	1	25	—	3	75	—	10	0	0
Hanley PCt 1864–66 Staffordshire	24	63	83	14	37	80	1[j]	8	10
Sleaford PS 1866 Lincolnshire	62 (est.)[k]	87	100	9 (est.)	13	25	16	(23)	(23)

Berkeley PS 1866–71 Gloucestershire	28	93	89	2	7	100	9	14 (25)	17 (29)

SOURCES: Bostock Fuller: *Notebook of a Surrey Justice*, ed. Granville Leveson-Gower, Surrey Archaeological Collections 9 (1888): 161–232. Sir Thomas Sclater: Bodleian Library, Oxford, MS Rawlinson D1135, D1136, and D1137 (sample years 1667/8, 1671/2, 1675/6, 1679/80); Jacqueline Karn, "Sir Thomas Sclater, Compounder of the Peace: A Study of Law Enforcement in Restoration Cambridgeshire" (unpublished manuscript, Oxford University, n.d.), using slightly different categories, finds 6 wage cases in country parishes, and 14 masters' cases, 10 in the country and 4 in town. Sir William Bromley: Warks. R.O., CR 103 (part of the notebook is published in *Warwick County Records*, vol. 9, 1964). Sir Roger Hill: Bucks. R.O., D/W 97/8/8 (extracts also in *Records of Buckinghamshire* [1961–65] 17: 182–88). Devereux Edgar: Suffolk R.O., qS 347-96 and HA 247/5/4. William Hunt: *The Justicing Notebook of William Hunt, 1744–1749*, ed. Elizabeth Crittall (Wiltshire Record Society) (Devizes, 1982). Edmund Tew: *The Justicing Notebook (1750–64) of Edmund Tew, Rector of Boldon*, ed. Gwenda Morgan and Peter Rushton (Woodbridge [England]: Boydell Press for the Surtees Society, 2000). Sir Thomas Ward: Warks. R.O., CR 162/688 (1766–68 only). Richard Wyatt: *Deposition Book of Richard Wyatt, JP, 1767–76*, ed. Elizabeth Silverthorne (Surrey Record Society: Castle Arch, Surrey, 1798). Sir Gervase Clifton: Nottinghamshire Archives, M8050–51, notebook 1772–1812. London Chamberlain's Court for apprentices: Corporation of London R.O., CF10/1 (1787 only). Aylesbury hundreds petty sessions: Bucks. R.O., PS/AY/M/1, 2. The Reverend Henry Gorges Dobyns Yate: Hereford and Worcester R.O., BB88/1. Samuel Whitbread: *Samuel Whitbread's Notebooks, 1810–11, 1813–14*, ed. Alan F. Cirket (Bedfordshire Historical Record Society, 1971). George Turner: Suffolk R.O., HD 258/1. Thomas Allen: Cheshire R.O., D 4655. London Apprentices, 1823–59: Corporation of London R.O., CF11/1. Richard Jee of Hartshill: Warks. R.O., CR 261. Hanley Police Court: Staffs. R.O., D 26/1/1. Sleaford Petty Sessions: Lincolnshire Archives O., LAO PSJ 10/1. Berkeley Petty Sessions: Gloucs. R.O., PS/BE/M1.

a JP = justice of the peace; PS = petty sessions; BJ = borough justice; PCt = police court.

b Includes settled by agreement; those in parentheses are known to be imposed without agreement. Most sources do not clearly distinguish the basis of the outcome.

c Those in parentheses include imprisonments in default of fine.

d One is a third party.

e He notes committals for other offenses, but none for breach of contract.

f Underestimate, based on one mittimus; outcomes of most cases not recorded.

g Likely underestimate, because of multiple entries for other offenses. See Hay, "Patronage, Paternalism and Welfare," 39–40.

h The source is "information and complaint" forms, subsequently bound; wage orders may not have been preserved.

i Annual average.

j See text.

k Proportions, and success rates, estimated from January to July only.

rounding country parishes: a four-year sample shows half by servants, half by
masters. Annual hirings, day laboring, and taskwork (threshing, driving hogs,
claying a house and barn, sewing, cooking, harvesting) all gave rise to wage
claims.[51] The masters prosecuted runaways, a harborer, and servants who refused to continue in service or enter on service having made a contract. The
occupations were half agricultural, half in trades.[52] Sir William Bromley of
Baginton (Warks), MP and speaker from 1710 to 1713, was too important a
man to do much day-to-day business as a justice. Between 1687 and 1709 he
heard only eight employment cases, mostly the usual complaints but also that
of one servant who was discharged after confessing that she had committed
perjury for her master at an assize trial. Bromley granted warrants in all cases
but did not record outcomes. Sir Roger Hill of Denham (Bucks) heard eighteen complaints by servants and ten by masters for wage claims, unjust dismissal, and disobedience or absconding, a small proportion of his activity as
a justice between 1689 and 1705.[53]

Devereux Edgar, an active justice of the peace in parishes just northwest of
Ipswich (Suffolk) heard several hundred matters a year between 1700 and 1716,
and 10 percent (270 cases) concerned employment contracts.[54] Most involved
farm servants; a few complainants were rural tradesmen such as blacksmiths
or bricklayers, or gentlemen. A little over half the cases were complaints by
masters, usually against servants who had deserted (89 cases) or misbehaved
(25). Servants usually complained about unpaid wages (117 cases, almost all
successful); some also came before Edgar about mistreatment (9), or to ratify
a mutually agreed parting (8). In more than 10 percent of complaints by masters, Edgar sent the servant to the house of correction (17 cases).

Table 2.1 shows that on average these justices heard cases from servants 57
percent of the time.[55] It seems to have been 5 to 10 percent of their business;
the proportion of prosecuted servants who ended up in a house of correction
was also in that range. The differences in activity among Fuller, Sclater, Bromley, Hill, and Edgar reflect the fact that the amount and type of local business a "single justice" dealt with depended on his social status (greater gentry
usually doing less work than minor gentry), his age, and his zeal, religious or
administrative, and the nature of the local economy.[56] Justices also tended to

51. He sent one case, for wages in arrears amounting to more than eleven pounds, to quarter
sessions.
52. I am grateful to Jacqueline Karn for sharing with me her research for four sample years
of the notebooks: see note to Table 2.1.
53. Again, when process is mentioned, it is always a warrant.
54. See also Hay, "Master and Servant in England," 233.
55. Counting total numbers gives 47 percent by servants.
56. For example, the extensive archive of Sir Nathaniel Bacon of Stiffkey suggests that he

specialize: some pursued poachers, some did more master and servant business. Many justices probably kept no records at all, or in more fugitive form than a notebook. For these reasons it is helpful, particularly before the eighteenth century, to look at the handbooks published to guide the conscientious justice.

They appeared in numerous editions in the seventeenth century, and some contained advice about practice, as well as the usual bare-bones recital of statute law and doctrine. William Lambard's *Eirenarcha* appeared first in 1581 and was repeatedly reissued with changes until 1619; editions of Michael Dalton's *Country Justice* run from 1618 to 1742. William Shepherd's *The Whole Office of the Country Justice of Peace* (and similar titles) was widely available in editions from 1649 to 1663, supplemented by several editions of his *The Justice of Peace His Clarks Cabinet* (1654, 1660). Before Richard Burn's *Justice of the Peace and Parish Officer* came to dominate the genre (thirty editions between 1755 and 1869), there were some less able compilations, and lawbooks for "everyman" that nonetheless sometimes provide evidence of practice.[57]

The doctrine as they presented it revolved largely around interpretations of the Statute of Artificers, and typically authors recited the main provisions of 5 Eliz. c.4. Most also cited (England) 7 Jac.I c.4 (1609) as authority for one justice sending an "idle or disorderly" apprentice or servant to the house of correction, probably the basis of many convictions of servants who were imprisoned in the seventeenth century.[58] The Statute of Artificers was given a wide construction. It covered servants in husbandry and handicrafts but not servingmen; "and yet where the words of the statute be, servant generally, there it seemeth to extend to all."[59] But the interpretation of contracts in master and servant disputes turned also (as did the important poor-law issue of settlement) on whether the trade came within the terms of the annual "general hiring." Thus Dalton adds in 1655 that although earlier interpretation suggested husbandry was not within the requirement of a year's hiring, such was now held to be the case.[60] Covenant servants were punishable for departing,

---

was involved only in more important magisterial business, usually with local or national political significance: Hassell Smith, *County and Court*; Hassell Smith, *Papers of Nathaniel Bacon*.

57. Among them the works of John Bond, William Nelson, Giles Jacob.

58. Dalton (1618) 60; (1619) 69; (1622) 69; (1655) 87. See Shoemaker, *Prosecution and Punishment*, 37–39, 54–55; J. Innes, "Statute Law," 34–35. Similarly vague language in (Engl.) 2&3 Anne c.6 (1703) s.16 encouraged the forcible enlistment of "all lewd and disorderly men servants" into the navy, a provision already made for vagrants by (Engl.) 11 Wm.III c.18 (1698).

59. Dalton (1618) 62; (1677) 125–26, on exclusion of pippin-mongers, plowing or digging "for in those trades strength is more required than skill," and questioning an upholsterer, a reference to a decision of Coke (*Tollin*). All these are issues of the right to claim a right to exclude others from the trade for lack of apprenticeship and/or wage fixing.

60. Dalton (1655) 89. Settlement cases (to establish in which parish a pauper could receive

even in occupations that could not be set to compulsory service by the Statute of Artificers.[61] Wage fixing is very briefly mentioned in 1618; by 1655 Dalton reproduces the text of the Statute of Artificers, s.15, and adds also two scriptural quotations, "Thou shalt not oppress an hired servant, that is needy and poor, but thou shalt give him his hire speedily, for therewith he sustaineth his life. Deut. 14:14,15. And the hire of the Labourer is kept back, cryeth and entreth into the ears of the Lord. Ja. 5:4." The doctrine that Scripture was part of the common law was reinforced during the interregnum; Dalton clearly believed that it bolstered the authority of justices to order wage payments.[62]

How far could a master discipline or dismiss a servant? Dalton in 1618 thought "that the master may strike his servant with his hand, fist, small staffe, or stick, for correction: and though he do draw bloud thereby, yet it seemeth no breach of peace" provided "hee doth it not outragiously." However, he could not beat or force a runaway back into service but had to make complaint to the justices or sue in covenant (if a covenant servant, presumably).[63] By 1677, however, the master could take him up, and "retain and keep him whether he will, or no," and a constable could take the servant back to his master.[64]

An important point is that the handbooks agree that the master could not discharge the servant during the term without the latter's agreement, or (under the statute) for cause "to be allowed by one Justice of peace at least." Dalton pointed out that before 5 Eliz. a master might have done so. A servant who was denied wages or meat or drink, or who was beaten, or who was licensed by the master to leave, had cause, but again "by the stat. of 5 Eliz to be allowed of by the Just. of peace, before the servant may lawfully or safely depart."[65] The 1655 edition notes the obligation of executors for wages and of masters to keep sick servants and not abate their wages. One question (reconsidered by the judges in the eighteenth century) was that of the pregnant servant. In Chief Justice Heath's opinion of 1633, reprinted by Dalton, undeclared pregnancy at the time of hiring, or conception during service,

poor relief, one ground for which was service for a year) provide the principal evidence of the doctrine of master and servant in the high courts for much of the period.

61. Dalton (1618) 62; (1655) 93.

62. For other instances of scriptural quotation in legal argument in this period, see Hay, "Laws of God," 6off., and Banner, "Christianity."

63. Dalton (1618) 150, citing (Engl.) 33 Hen.VIII c.12 (1541); 38 Hen.VI c.25 (1459).

64. Dalton (1677) 128. Such self-help by masters was common in the empire: see the chapters by Prabhu Mohapatra and David Anderson in this volume.

65. Dalton (1618) 64, 65; Shepherd (1656) 149, 152. By the 1655 edition, however, joint consent by the parties was said not to be within the statute, and no approval needed from a justice. Dalton (1655) 94; Shepherd (1656) 149, item 7, 9, where the point is said to be "thought by some," citing Dalton.

was a valid cause for discharge, but the master could not do so under his own authority—the servant had to be "lawfully discharged" by a justice.[66] On wage recovery, Dalton noted in his earliest edition that although the servant had "his wages for the time he served," he apparently had no action to recover them, "but must crave the help of the Justice of peace herein." And he is clear that a servant departing before time, or refusing to work, lost all wages.[67] On the other hand, a servant dismissed without cause got all his wages, presumably for the entire period of the hiring.[68] During the commonwealth some sources suggest that the authority of a single justice was less certainly grounded, but later in the century such anxieties apparently largely disappeared, as central government greatly reduced the degree to which it tried to direct the local enforcement of law.[69] By the eighteenth century, Parliament was enacting a large amount of legislation giving the justices jurisdiction.

Over the whole period magistrates not only enforced employment contracts but also set wage maxima (and sometimes minima) under the Statute of Artificers and later legislation, supervised the administration of the poor law, and identified and punished rogues and vagabonds under the law of vagrancy. All these activities were closely concerned with the regulation of labor; they existed in continuum with the law of master and servant. In many ways master and servant law in early modern England reflected the concerns of the central state, and its local representatives the magistracy, as much or more than those of employers or workers. What were those concerns? Briefly, social and political stability. In the seventeenth century, massive popular risings (1607), civil war and republican revolution (1642–60), and a parliamentary coup against the monarch (1688) were national instances of instability rising above a host of local riots, often associated with trades plunged into depression by cyclical changes, or whole working populations impoverished by the spectacular increases in the cost of living caused by periodic harvest failure. Although eighteenth-century political stability was much more assured, local disorder, still often associated with trades and harvests, was frequent.[70] The law of master and servant was close to the heart of these concerns.

Punishment for breach of contract was less visible than the public exhibitions of cruelty that dominated the criminal law, but such cases were more

66. For example, Dalton (1677) 173, title "Poor"; also Shepherd (1656) 149.

67. Dalton (1618) 64, citing 10 Ed.IV c.49 and yearbook cases. In the 1655 edition he cites Sir Robert Brooke's *Abridgement*, 40, title "Apportionment" 16. On this doctrine of the "entire" contract, see below.

68. Shepherd (1656) 147, no authority cited.

69. I shall describe this in other work.

70. Hay and Rogers, *Eighteenth-Century English Society*.

common and gave the authorities a range of remedies. In deciding disputes magistrates in early modern England were expected to pay as much attention to the maintenance of social and political and economic stability as to the demands of the parties before them. The penal clauses and wage-recovery elements of the law were still deeply embedded in poor-law policy, the control of vagrancy, and the setting of wages. All underwent significant change between the seventeenth and the nineteenth centuries, changes that helped shape the law of employment. For example, before the Statute of Artificers the policy of wage setting had been to establish maxima; under the statute provision was made both for setting maximum rates but also for adjusting rates upward to match prices levels when necessary. The frequency and significance of such rates has long been a disputed issue.[71] The most recent examination of the surviving evidence up to 1725 shows a slow rising trend, gradually flattening, of magisterial activity from about 1610 to 1700, when the number of references to the practice stabilizes until about 1720. In general the justices seem to have been active in making assessments, at least in the earlier part of the period, in cities and market towns, and in counties where textile production was prominent. The importance of the industry, the large number of workers involved, and the potential for social disorder and interruption of production during sharp swings in the export trade made both local and central governments particularly sensitive to the sector. General wage setting in towns (where undermining of apprenticeship and the control of poor relief were effective tools for employers) seems to have declined after 1670, and a narrower scope of occupations appears in the ratings; the system embodied in the 1562 statute retained some vitality, however, in the counties, specifically with respect to agricultural occupations, for a longer period of time, undoubtedly reflecting the interests of country gentleman justices of the peace.[72] Later legislation was enforced as, or explicitly provided for, the setting of *minimum* wages in the all-important textile trades.[73]

The interpretation of the legislation in the early eighteenth century, when labor was in a better bargaining position due to the stagnation of population growth since the late seventeenth century, was to set maximum wage rates. Moreover, Parliament showed a continuing, perhaps increased, inter-

---

71. Minchinton, *Wage Regulation*, reprints the work of Tawney (1914) and Kelsall (1938, 1942); a recent account is M. Roberts, "Wages and Wage-Earners," on which the following paragraphs are largely based.

72. M. Roberts, "Wages and Wage-Earners," 40, 113, 114-16, 335-36, 408 graph 4.

73. (England) 39 Eliz. c.12 (1597); 1 Jac.I c.6 (1603). M. Roberts, "Wages and Wage-Earners," 27-37. After midcentury inflation ceased to be a problem for workers, and some legislation provided maximums, such as a statute for building workers after the great fire of London: (England) 19 Car.II c.3 (1667).

est in the policing of wage rates at this time. Thus the 1720 Tailors Act provided actual rates rather than a mechanism for setting them.[74] Wage setting under the Statute of Artificers continued in many parts of the country until the middle decades of the eighteenth century, although paternalists recognized the practice was dying out. One lamented in 1755 that he had seen only one example, twenty years before: "Numberless disputes about hiring and wages that now daily occur, would be prevented, if this law was observed and properly published."[75] The evidence, then, suggests that wage setting continued to be important to the justices in many parts of the country until at least the middle of the eighteenth century, and sometimes later, at least in the sense of setting a nominal ideal wage, which they hoped would create consensus among employers and perhaps at all levels of the trade. The public policy aimed at was wage stability, in the name of social stability, including stability of labor supply. Thus in 1725 the Lancashire justices commented that "the more northern part thereof ought not to demand so much, but be content with what the custom of the country hath usually been." In some industries, a legitimated and legal wage was felt to be necessary, to bring the prestige of Parliament to a settlement of major strike activity and thus to curtail riot and other breaches of order, at least at the time of enactment, and, it was hoped, for the future.[76]

After midcentury the pressure for legislation, now conceived again as the regulation of minimum wage rates, came from labor and from some paternalist justices; the position of employers was that there should be no such regulation at all. This conflict is registered in the well-known inconsistency of Parliament over wage setting in several important industries in the mid- to later eighteenth century. It continued to enact wage-setting clauses in other statutes in response to conflicts in particular trades, often accompanied by riot and sabotage: the central concern for public order (and the long-held suspicion of many paternalists that the new theories of political economy were nonsense) are important continuities with the world in which the Statute of

74. (G.B.) 7 Geo.I st.1 c.13 (1720). It may have been enacted in part also because the judges apparently ruled that justices could not order wage payments for tailors under the Statute of Artificers. I have not located the case, but it is referred to in a 1704 case (*R. v. London*, 6 Mod. 204; 2 Salk 442; 3 Salk 261; 87 ER 958; 91 ER 814). In 1668 the judges had observed that tailors were "within the statute" (*R v. Jo. Seellers*, 1 Lev 243; 83 ER 389). On the other hand, it seems likely that in the period (see below) in which King's Bench was divided on the issue, doubts expressed by some judges about other trades were again extended to tailors.

75. *The Laws Relating to Masters and Servants: With Brief Notes and Explanations . . .* (London, 1755), 7 n. The argument that wage setting declined in part because of legal obstacles (Kelsall, "Wage Regulation," 193, citing Holdsworth, *History*, 11:467, and Lipson, *Economic History*, 3:263–64) is incorrect; I discuss this in other work.

76. Kelsall, "Wage Regulation," 168–69; M. Roberts, "Wages and Wage-Earners," 229ff.

Artificers was drafted.[77] Over these centuries, disputes over unpaid wages and absconding servants thus had a much wider significance than simply the interest of the parties. Servants leaving for other masters were usually going to higher wages, wages that were therefore more likely to be prima facie illegal, in contravention of the rates set by the justices. But forcing the servant to return to the original master made more sense than prosecuting the parties for giving and taking unlawful wages under the statute, as less disruptive of social relations.

Subordination also remained at the core of employment relations. Pamphlet attacks on servants in the early eighteenth century and parliamentary recommendations to force idle young people into employment contracts probably reflect both high demand for labor due to low population growth and the role of subordinate servants in a perceived crisis in social order.[78] Evidence that this was the case is the Tailors Act of 1720: it was the last statute that enacted the very old policy of compulsory recruitment to labor for idle workers in the trade.[79] It was also the first of a series of important statutes enacted between 1720 and 1823. The resulting body of law, as interpreted by the judges of the high courts, was considerably harsher toward workers than that of a century before.

Parliament and the Judges to 1823

Throughout the seventeenth century magistrates relied on the Statute of Artificers and the vagrancy statute of 1609 in punishing insubordinate or runaway workers. Between 1720 and 1792, ten acts of Parliament imposed or increased imprisonment for leaving work and/or for misbehavior.[80] Two of the four earliest, in the 1720s, marked an important departure in penal sanctions: two and three months in the house of correction, rather than the traditional maximum of one month derived from one of the clauses in the Statute of Artificers.[81] Moreover, almost all the eighteenth-century master and servant

77. See below. On late eighteenth-century attitudes to Adam Smith's arguments, see Hay, "The State and the Market."

78. A. Moreton [Daniel Defoe], *Every Body's Business Is No Body's Business* (1725), and Defoe, *The Great Law of Subordination* (1723); Sir Thomas Parkyns, *A Method Proposed for the Hiring and Recording of Servants* (1721); Great Britain, Parliament, House of Commons, *Journals*, 20:256–57, 11 Feb. 1723/4. See Tomlins, "Subordination," and M. Roberts, "Wages and Wage-Earners," 42ff. For a somewhat different explanation from Tomlins's, see below, pp. 87–88.

79. (G.B.) 7 Geo.I st.1 c.13 (1720), s.6.

80. (G.B.) 9 Geo.I c.27 (1722); 12 Geo.I c.34 (1725); 13 Geo.I c.23 (1726); 2 Geo.II c.36 (1728); 13 Geo.II c.8 (1739); 20 Geo.II c.19 (1746); 22 Geo.II c.27 (1748); 6 Geo.III c.25 (1766); 17 Geo.III c.56 (1777); 32 Geo.III c.57 (1792).

81. (G.B.) 7 Geo.I st.1 c.13 (1720, tailors); 12 Geo.I c.34 (1725, woolen trade).

statutes introduced significant new language: all but one[82] specified that the imprisonment was to be with "hard labour"; and two, an important act of 1747 and another of 1792, introduced with Proclamation Society backing, added that the prisoner, once in the house of correction at hard labor, was there "to be corrected"—that is, whipped.[83]

Some of these statutes may have enacted what had earlier been done informally or served to reinstate penalties that had suffered judicial and legislative erosion.[84] Nevertheless most of the new acts were actively promoted by groups of manufacturers, mineowners, and other employers.[85] Often their efforts were met by petitions, campaigns for public support, and riot by workers in the trade, urging the legislature to recognize customary practices and claims. Parliament, still dominated by country gentlemen and professional politicians, sought to restore industrial peace and forestall dangerous public disorder through concession and mediation, in a manner not that different from Tudor and Stuart governments and parliaments.[86] The result was often a balancing of the claims of capital and labor, although the cumulative effect of longer sentences was to advantage employers over workers; Parliament reacted to disorder not only with concessions but with an escalation of penalties.

Thus the 1720 Tailors Act was Parliament's response to the masters' complaint that 7,000 London journeymen had combined to raise wages and reduce hours. Parliament responded with penalties for combination and for breach of contract, and even (as we have seen) for compulsory recruitment of idle labor. But it also provided for wage fixing and wage recovery, and the (relative) industrial peace that followed was extended in 1768 with an extension of the terms of the act to five miles around the city; the tailors continued to be one of the most militant and effective unions throughout the eighteenth century.[87] In many similar statutes, clauses giving jurisdiction

---

82. (G.B.) 6 Geo.III c.25 (1766).

83. (G.B.) 20 Geo.II c.19 (1746); 32 Geo.III c.57 (1792). The society was named after, and intended to implement the reforms, of a proclamation by George III against vice and immorality in 1787. The proclamation itself was the product of moral entrepreneurship.

84. Thus the application of the vagrancy statute commonly used in the seventeenth and early eighteenth centuries to discipline servants, (England) 7 Jac.I c.4, was affected by a narrower definition of "idle and disorderly" in (G.B.) 17 Geo.II c.5 (1743): Richard Burn, *Justice of the Peace* (7th ed., 1762), 3:415.

85. A detailed account will appear in other work.

86. Hay and Rogers, *Eighteenth-Century English Society*, chs. 6–8.

87. (G.B.) 7 Geo.I st.1 c.13 (1720); 8 Geo.III c.17 (1767). See Dobson, *Masters and Journeymen*, 60ff. (emphasizing masters' advantages), and Moher, "From Suppression to Containment," 78ff. (noting the balance sought by Parliament). Moher incorrectly gives 1766 as the date of the second statute.

to the magistrates over master and servant offenses were followed by specific provisions in the workers' interest (e.g., limiting the numbers of apprentices to be taken by masters, or expediting wage recovery) and others favor-
ing masters (such as new powers to counter combinations or embezzlement).
Thus a 1777 statute promoted by well-organized employers in the putting-out
trades was primarily concerned with embezzlement of materials but also increased the penalties for neglect of work or working for another master from
a maximum of one month to a maximum of three and a minimum of one. Another, enacted in the same year, gave the worsted manufacturers a unique private inspectorate, under the supervision of the magistrates, which was mainly
used for the prosecution of embezzlement but also for disciplining workers in
breach of contract.[88] Particular statutes concerned workers in woolen manufacture; others affected mariners, tailors, shoemakers, leatherworkers, lace
makers. The statutes of widest application were the 1777 statute already mentioned (17 Geo.III c.56), and three others. The first of these was (G.B.) 20
Geo.II c.19 (1746), enacted in 1747, under which a justice could punish "misdemeanour, miscarriage, or ill behaviour" by the servant or apprentice with
up to one month's imprisonment at hard labor "with correction," or abatement of wages or discharge. "Abating" of servants' wages does not appear in
any earlier statute, but the denial of some wages as a punishment became one
of the most common forms of punishment for workers in breach.[89] Under the
1747 statute the justice could also order masters to pay wages owing up to five
or ten pounds (depending on occupation) and release the worker from the
contract on proof of mistreatment by the employer.[90]

88. Felters, hatters, and workers in woolen, linen, fustian, cotton, iron, leather, fur, hemp,
flax, mohair, silk by (G.B.) 17 Geo.III c.56 (1777); worsted by (G.B.) 17 Geo.III c.11 (1777).

89. It was probably also done by magistrates before the act. There are suggestive references
to related issues in a number of sources. A case before the lord mayor in 1703 for wages that were
deemed "extravagant" resulted in a decision that "fifteen shillings be abated thereout" (Corporation of London Record Office, Mansion House Justice Room Charge Book [1699–1705],
fol. 189v). A 1744 source cites Dalton to the effect that "A servant ought not to be discharged
by reason of sickness, or any other disability by the Act of God; nor may his Wages be abated
for those Causes." Giles Jacob, Compleat Parish Officer (1744), 166, citing Dalt.129. The Statute
of Artificers s.9 provided that deserters were to be committed to ward until they were bound
to serve and continue "for the wages that then shall be limited and appointed, according to the
tenor and form of this statute"; although this appears a clear reference to official rates of wages,
it may have come to be interpreted as a reference to abatement. A reference forbidding officers' abating of soldiers' wages, except for clothing, appeared in the Soldiers Act (England), 18
Hen.VI c.18 (1439) s.2. On the related issue of the "entire contract," see below. Abatement was
not novel in 1867 (as suggested in Steinmetz, "De-juridification," 277).

90. Occupations named were servants in husbandry hired for one year or longer, artificers,
handicraftsmen, miners, colliers, keelmen, pitmen, glassmen, potters, and other laborers em-

A 1766 statute, (G.B.) 6 Geo.III c.25, allowed one justice to commit to the house of correction for a minimum of one and a maximum of three months any servants who absented themselves from their service before the term of the contract or were guilty of any other misdemeanor. Apprentices could be forced to make up time lost by absence, or suffer three months' imprisonment.[91] In its origins this statute too reflected the tumultuous industrial relations of the eighteenth century. During the massive colliers' strike on Tyneside in 1765, a correspondent of the earl of Northumberland explained why the 1747 statute had not been used:

> [T]his is very well, where two or three or a dozen men desert their service, and has been many times properly executed with good Effect, but where there is a general Combination of all the Pitmen to the Number of 4,000, how can this measure take Effect? in the first place it is difficult to be executed as to seizing the men, and even if they should not make a formidable Resistance which scarce can be presumed, a few only can be taken, for upon the Face of the thing it is obvious that the whole persons guilty can not be secured, so the punishment of probably twenty or forty by a month's confinement in a House of Correction, does not carry with it the least Appearance of Terror so as to induce the remaining Part of so large a Number to submit, and these men that should be so confined would be treated as Martyrs for the good Cause, and be supported and caressed, and at the end of the time brought home in Triumph, so no good effect would arise.

The strike was provoked by the (well-founded) suspicion that the employers intended to enforce testimonials of completed past service (discharge certificates) of the kind required in some of the Scots collieries, and in England in the sixteenth century by the Statute of Artificers. The Scots colliers were serfs, and the English miners believed that a discharge certificate enforcing the annual bonds under which they worked would be virtual serfdom for them also.[92] The men were successful; the masters denied that they planned to require testimonials. But this was but one battle in ongoing industrial warfare.

---

ployed for any certain time or in any other manner. Extended to laborers in husbandry for less than a year by (G.B.) 31 Geo.II c.11 (1758). On orders for wages under this statute, see below.

91. Applying to an artificer, calico printer, handicraftsman, miner, collier, keelman, pitman, glassman, potter, laborer, or other person.

92. J. B. Ridley to the Earl of Northumberland, quoted in Hammond and Hammond, *Skilled Labourer*, 14, and Levine and Wrightson, *Making of an Industrial Society*, 398ff.; see also Campbell, *The Lanarkshire Miners*, ch. 1; (England) 5 Eliz. c.4 (1562) s.10 (departed servant without testimonial to be whipped and used as a vagabond).

Matthew Ridley MP, one of the largest coal masters in the district, was one
of the main movers of the statute passed in 1766, which (like that of 1747) explicitly included "miners, colliers, keelmen, pitmen" and six other categories
of workers who entered contracts for set terms. The statute tripled the period
of imprisonment for breach of contract to three months at hard labor.[93]

George White, clerk to the Commons Committee on Artisans and Machinery, reviewing the existing state of the law in 1823, termed the 1766 statute
"the most cruel, unjust, and oppressive statute in the code." He pointed out
that if a worker left employment because of a dispute, one justice could decide
it constituted misbehavior: men had been jailed or instantly dismissed for "a
few angry words, singing, appearing dirty, smoking tobacco, not finishing his
work to please his master, or not doing enough—in short, every thing that the
master chuses to style misbehaviour."[94] In spite of White's hopes for an amelioration of employment law, (G.B.) 4 Geo.IV c.34 (1823), covering apprentices and the same workers as the 1766 statute, did not repeal it or the other
eighteenth-century statutes. It expanded workers' remedies against agents,
and permitted claims for up to ten pounds in wages without right of appeal,
but it also confirmed all the justices' powers.[95] It has been suggested that most
prosecutions after 1823 took place under this act (which reiterated the penalties of three months' imprisonment, abatement of wages, and discharge), but
we know that well into the nineteenth century the 1747 and 1766 acts were
sometimes cited in the courts as the basis of conviction.[96]

There was therefore often confusion or vagueness about the exact state of
the law. Some statutes overlapped, some were deficient in that they did not
cover particular trades or particular circumstances. The result, as White observed, was a body of law only imperfectly known by workers (and justices
of the peace). "The ignorance which pervades the working classes, as to what
laws they are bound by, is deplorable indeed; and, in fact, what little they do
know, they continually ask one another, 'Well, but are you sure it is not repealed?'"[97] The safe answer was, probably not. As late as the 1850s and 1860s

93. (G.B.) 6 Geo.III c.25 (1766).

94. George White, *A Digest of All the Laws Respecting Masters and Work People* (London,
1824), 94–95. An earlier edition, different in important respects, with Gravener Henson as joint
author, is *A Few Remarks on the State of the Laws, at Present in Existence for Regulating Masters
and Work-People* (1823).

95. Appeals to quarter sessions against orders for wages had been allowed under the statutes
of 1747 and 1766.

96. Simon, "Master and Servant," 165, 167, citing *Report from the Select Committee on Master
and Servant*, PP 1865 (370) 8:7, questions 5, 10, 11; *Report*, PP 1866 (449) 13:11, 25, questions
11, 12, 273. Simon tends to exaggerate the importance of the 1823 statute. On its passage, see
Steinfeld, *Coercion*, 96–100.

97. White, *Digest*, 44. Employers and magistrates were also confused. See *R v. Hoseason*

the judges were divided about whether the 1823 statute had in some way effected a constructive repeal of the 1766 statute; most doubted it.[98]

An extensive body of case law grew up around the statutory regime, rooted ultimately in interpretations of the Statute of Artificers, even after most clauses of the statute were repealed by 1814. A large number of reported cases, well over 100 important ones in the eighteenth century alone, glossed the main statutes and sometimes provoked new attempts at legislation. Among other issues (including what trades were covered, whether it was necessary to be working for only one master, and the standing of contractors for specific jobs) two instances may be given. One was the jurisdiction for wage recovery by servants; another was whether domestic servants were in fact subject to the law of master and servant. They illustrate the kind of interplay that took place between Parliament and the courts.[99]

Orders for wages were originally derived from the Statute of Artificers. A generously wide interpretation of the wage provisions in the Statute of Artificers (and, by inference, the penal sanctions) was given by the judges between 1699 and 1720, after a number of failures to enact wage-recovery legislation. An order for wages would be enforced on the presumption that it was for husbandry, unless it explicitly mentioned another occupation; hence, the usual course was simply to use the word "servant," and the judges hinted strongly that this was what magistrates should do to avoid trouble.[100] Early in the century they held that justices could also order wages for "labourers," and that the word was not restricted to laborers in husbandry: "courts of law," they said, "are indulgent in remedies for wages." The court extended the remedy to covenant servants, and "statute servants" whose trades were mentioned in the act. A coachman got his wages in 1713, on the ground that the order did not mention his occupation (although his petition did). And as another judge pointed out in a 1714 case, although the Statute of Artificers appeared to give no authority to the justices to deal with wages of gentlemen's servants, "they do it everyday."[101] Around 1720 chief justices Parker and Pratt reversed this

---

(1811), 14 East 605 at 607, discussed below, and also the ironmaster testifying to the defeat of a combination ("I am not prepared to say on what Act of Parliament he was committed"), quoted in Orth, "English Combination Laws." It might have been the 1801 Combination Act; however, it could equally well have been either the 1747 or 1766 master and servant acts.

98. See the cases cited in notes 1 and 8.

99. I shall discuss the case law in more detail in other publications. For a recent overview and interpretation over the long term, see Deakin, "The Contract of Employment"; for questions litigated in the early nineteenth century, see Steinfeld, *Coercion*; for the origins of that litigation, see Frank, "Warrington Cases," and Frank, "Constitutional Law."

100. *R v. Gregory* (1699?), 2 Salk. 484, 91 ER 417; *R v. London* (1704), 6 Mod. 204, 2 Salk 442, 3 Salk 261, 87 ER 958, 91 ER 814.

101. *R v. Gouche* (1701), 2 Lord Raym. 820, 2 Salk 441, 92 ER 48, 91 ER 383; *R v. Cecil* (1710),

line of cases,[102] but Parliament stepped in: to a 1702 statute[103] that already provided for wage orders for woolen, linen, cotton, fustian, and iron workers, more statutes were added by 1747.[104] The plethora of trades covered and the use of more generally inclusive language gave back to the justices the jurisdiction over wages. Some of the judges seem also to have relaxed the interpretation of the wage clauses of the Statute of Artificers again, implying that justices could order wages for the few groups still not covered by legislation, notably domestic servants.[105]

Domestic servants in London, early in the century, had been presumed to be subject to penal sanctions, either under the Statute of Artificers or the vagrancy statute (England) 7 Jac.I c.4 (1609) already noted, or perhaps on a rather general sense of what was required. As Miss Western told her brother, after being insulted by one of his servants, "she had known servants very severely punished for affronting their masters; and then named a certain justice of the peace in London who, she said, would commit a servant to Bridewell at any time when a master or mistress desired it."[106] Blackstone at midcentury appeared to sanction the doctrine that domestic servants could not leave employment, or be dismissed, without a quarter's warning on either side, except upon showing reasonable cause to a magistrate in the same manner as other servants under the Statute of Artificers.[107] One of the most expansive rulings as to what other servants were covered was that of Chief Justice Mansfield in King's Bench, who ruled in 1777, supported by his brothers, that all those working for a set time or by the piece were in fact servants: "He is a servant by the nature of his work, and here he is a servant each day he worked

---

2 Lord Raym. 1305, 92 ER 355; *R. v. Wotton* (1713), Sess Cas 12, 93 ER 11; *R v. Dalloe* (1714), Sess Cas 17, 93 ER 16.

102. *R v. Helling* (1717), 1 Str 8, 93 ER 350; *R v. Clegg* (1722), 1 Str 475, 93 ER 643. This is probably the context for Defoe's 1724 anecdote of magisterial impotence in a weaver's case of neglect of work: Tomlins, "Subordination," 56–61.

103. (England) 1 Anne st.2 c.22 (1702).

104. The most important were (G.B.) 7 Geo.I st.1 c.13 (1720, tailors); 13 Geo.I c.23 (1726, woolens); 20 Geo.II c.19 (1746), "artificers, handicraftsmen, miners, colliers, keelmen, pitmen, glassmen, potters, labourers for a certain time, or in any other manner."

105. *Shergold v. Holloway* (1735), 2 Sess Cas 100, 93 ER 156, per Lord Hardwicke. Shoemaker, *Prosecution and Punishment*, 90–99, suggests that the uncertainty of justices' powers to order wages except in husbandry under 5 Eliz c.4 inhibited justices in London, such as William Norris of Hackney; a dearth of cases in notebooks of justices of the peace may reflect instead the London custom of a month's warning on either side. *Justice in Eighteenth-Century Hackney: The Justicing Notebook of Henry Norris and the Hackney Petty Sessions Book*, ed. Ruth Paley (London Record Society, 1991).

106. Henry Fielding, *The History of Tom Jones, a Foundling* (1749), book 7, ch. 9.

107. William Blackstone, *Commentaries on the Laws of England* (London, 1793 ed.), 4:425–26; presumably he meant outside London. On dismissal, see below.

for his master."[108] By the 1780s Burn concluded that the statute of 1562 included all those "employed in trades, as procure their sustenance by bodily labour."[109]

But in 1796 Lord Kenyon reaffirmed (apparently reluctantly, although he liked to overrule Mansfield) the stricter interpretation of the early eighteenth century, effectively taking from domestic servants (and any other occupations not explicitly mentioned in the Statute of Artificers or subsequent legislation) the summary wage remedies, and equally depriving their masters of recourse to the magistrates.[110] Thus, by 1797, a master dealing with a recalcitrant coachman had to convince the court that the servant also performed odd services on his hobby farm.[111] This decision apparently added country interest to what was already felt, by some, to be a need for legislation to cover London domestic servants. Repeated attempts to enact such legislation were unsuccessful.[112] A few years after Kenyon's decision, it was argued that a statute was badly needed to "rouse the indolent" among servants and "reform the vicious." It could only be done by "coercion and fear."[113] The author deplored negligence, drunkenness, quarreling, swearing, embezzlement, insolence, insubordination, and fraud and suggested that dangerous numbers of servants were combining in revolutionary Jacobin clubs. "Low attornies" helped servants take their masters to law, complaining of mistreatment or un-

108. *Hart v. Aldridge* (1774), 1 Cowp 55, Lofft 493, 98 ER 964.

109. Richard Burn, *Justice of the Peace* (14th ed., 1783), 4:158–59. The practice of Lord Chief Justice Mansfield (1756–88) in two employment cases is discussed in Steedman, "Lord Mansfield's Women."

110. *R v. Inhabitants of Hulcott* (1796), 6 Term 583, 101 ER 716, cited in Blackstone, *Commentaries* (1793 ed.), 1:426 n. 3. Christian, the editor, comments that until this case magistrates had exercised jurisdiction over domestic servants, and that it would be "very useful to the public" if they could do so again. The date of this edition of Blackstone is misleading; the work was issued in parts. Bird argued in his popular work that the Statute of Artificers "related more particularly to artificers and servants of husbandry, but it is imagined that it may be well construed to give justices a general jurisdiction over servants of every description, and such jurisdiction is in fact exercised by them." James Barry Bird, *The Laws Respecting Masters and Servants* (1795; 3rd ed., 1801; 5th ed., 1806), 2; 3–4 (3rd); and 52 (5th).

111. Public Record Office (London), KB 1/29 pt.1, Mich 37 Geo.III no.1, affidavits in application for a rule nisi against Edward Read esq. for wrongful committal of Thomas Brown for conspiracy.

112. In 1795, reflecting on the London custom of only a month's notice, Patrick Colquhoun thought the "errors and improprieties, as well as crimes" caused by the "ill-regulated passions" of domestics would be curbed "if examples could occasionally be made, by inflicting slight punishments upon them; in the same manner as upon other servants for breaches of moral contracts." *Police of the Metropolis* (London, 1796), 438; see other suggestions in 1725, 1784, 1796 for legislation, cited in Hecht, *Domestic Servant Class*, 88–89; and Hill, *Servants*, 101.

113. [Anon.], *Reflections on the relative situations of master and servant, historically and politically considered; the irregularities of servants; the employment of foreigners; and the general inconveniences resulting from the want of proper regulations* (London: Aspin, printer; sold by W. Miller, 1800).

paid wages; the magistrates were intimidated by the lawyers, and juries were likely to sympathize with the servants. These last allegations sound like fantasy, but may reflect the fact that some servants in London probably had access to the courts, even King's Bench, by using "low attornies" on contingent fees.[114] The author's recommendation was for an act that would provide mild but criminal penalties, under a summary process: in short, the extension of master and servant legislation. He advocated it in its full extent, moreover, in that he thought the wage clauses should also be copied. He cited the Statute of Artificers and 20 Geo.II c.19 (1746) as possible models.

In fact, a bill had been introduced by an MP for Nottingham, and the author of *Reflections* was undoubtedly seeking to ensure its success. "A Bill for the Better Settling of Disputes between Masters and Mistresses of Families and their Menial or Domestic Servants" was given first reading 5 March 1801.[115] It provided simply for the summary determination before magistrates of all issues to do with wages, notice, liveries, leaving service, and improper dismissal, with the proviso that the master or mistress might be represented by an agent. The sanction for breach in the servant was a month in the house of correction, abatement of wages, or discharge. A master or mistress who mistreated a servant or refused necessities might also find the servant discharged. There was an appeal to quarter sessions, but no certiorari. The bill was modeled closely on the 1746 and 1766 statutes for other workers. It was never enacted.

The fear was that such legislation would give domestic servants too much power, because they would have the right, like workers in other trades, to go to the justices for wage orders and to complain of mistreatment. Lord Sydney, the home secretary, believed in 1787 that "the Lords would never suffer such a power to be given as might subject them to be summoned by a servant."[116] For masters, the oversupplied domestic labor market of early nineteenth-century England made dismissal without a character usually a strong enough sanction in domestic service, and gentlemen and peers did not want their domestics taking them before magistrates. Cases against domestic servants continued

114. This very interesting practice in the work of King's Bench as an original jurisdiction in London and Middlesex is being investigated by Dr. Ruth Paley.

115. Ordered for second reading 22 April, amended in committee, and again given first reading 20 May. The report recommending the bill is in PP 1801 (62) 3:135, *Select Committee on State of Laws between Masters and Servants*; amendments in Sheila Lambert, ed., *House of Commons Sessional Papers of the Eighteenth Century* (150 vols., New York, 1977), 127:936 and 937.

116. Derbyshire Record Office, D239M/0 134, Thomas Coltman to Sir William Fitzherbert, London, 17 Feb. 1787. See also *Reflections*, 25, and John Huntingford, *Laws of masters and servants considered; with observations on a bill intended to be offered to parliament to prevent the forging and counterfeiting of certificates of servants characters; to which is added, an account of a society formed for the encouragement of good servants* (London, 1790).

to come before the courts in the nineteenth century as from time to time masters sought unsuccessfully to use other legislation.[117]

The justices of the peace must often have puzzled over the (often cursory) discussions of the case law in their handbooks. But the eighteenth-century innovations in master and servant law were arguably greatest in the realm of legislation, and statutes were undoubtedly the surest guide for magisterial practice. It is probably misleading to assume that the lay magistrates of the eighteenth century were always aware of the doctrine in the high courts, or greatly constrained by it. Historians have noted the lack of recourse to exact authority by magistrates in the early eighteenth century (a declension from the early seventeenth), and in London petty larcenies, which in theory should have gone to jury trial, were punished summarily with sentences to Bridewell. Magistrates acted in quite informal ways under the pressure of huge numbers of cases.[118] The supervisory authority of King's Bench over master and servant convictions, or indeed many other kinds of cases, seems hardly to have mattered in many parts of the country. In the county of Stafford, where hundreds of justices decided thousands of cases summarily, of various kinds, between 1740 and 1820, only a tiny number were questioned in King's Bench. Not a single one in the eighteenth century concerned master and servant.[119] Justices were still remarkably free to decide for themselves the contours of master and servant law.

Enforcement in the Eighteenth and Nineteenth Centuries

At the beginning of the eighteenth century there were still occasional committals of servants by quarter sessions, but they were rare. Punishment of masters by the sessions was even rarer.[120] Virtually all imprisonment and most other remedies of masters and servants and apprentices were firmly in the hands of the single and double justice. In some places, much enforcement

117. For example, *Kitchen v. Shaw* (1837), 6 A&E 729: 6 Geo.III c.25 does not apply to domestic servants.

118. Beattie, *Policing and Punishment in London*, 24–26; King, *Crime*, ch. 4.

119. Hay, "Dread of the Crown Office." For a rare instance of a habeas corpus for an imprisoned servant noted in a Surrey magistrate's notebook, see below (Richard Wyatt). The eighteenth-century decisions by Mansfield and Kenyon, discussed above and also in Steedman, "Lord Mansfield's Women," cannot be assumed to have had much effect on magisterial practice, without more research. The impact of high-court decisions appears to be much greater in the early nineteenth century, in part because of fuller newspaper reporting, and other changes: see below.

120. For example, *Buckinghamshire*, 3:101 (a case of 1707). The only master punished in a sample of 2,800 Staffordshire cases at sessions and assizes was for contempt of an order: Staffs. Record Office, Q/SR Translation 1795, Thomas Hulse (fined one shilling and one week in jail).

was in specialized borough or city courts, such as the chamberlain's court in London, which dealt with apprentices.[121] The London lord mayor's court had equivalents in municipal governments across England, where lay mayors and aldermen had substantially the same powers as lay justices did in the county commissions of the peace. There were no professional stipendiary magistrates anywhere until their appointment in London in 1792; they were appointed for some of the large urban areas in the middle decades of the nineteenth century. Many of the sources for understanding enforcement are similar to those for the centuries before 1700: justices' notebooks, and the printed sources of law, but now also manuscript notes of judges, parliamentary inquiries, and far better statistics of accusation, conviction, and incarceration.

In some jurisdictions, most prominently the City of London, company or guild regulation of trades still gave certain courts a customary or chartered jurisdiction over apprenticeship.[122] From medieval times, apprenticeship disputes in the City commonly came before the chamberlain, and the jurisdiction was still active in the eighteenth and nineteenth centuries. Apprenticeship and adult employment disputes could also be brought before the lord mayor's court; these tended to be more serious cases, at least in some periods, and cases could be remitted from the chamberlain's to the lord mayor's court.[123]

The early eighteenth-century practice, at least in London, was to give runaway, absent, recalcitrant, or rude workers a short sharp shock in Bridewell, as London's principal house of correction was called. Almost three-quarters of committals were for less than two weeks; about half included whipping and hard labor.[124] The chastened servant or apprentice was then released to her or his master; new misbehavior meant a return to Bridewell. In Middlesex and Westminster, essentially London outside the City, 7 percent of all commit-

121. J. Lane, *Apprenticeship*, chs. 10, 11, gives many illustrations of master-apprentice conflict over three centuries, but does not use notebooks of justices of the peace or similar sources, citing only scattered evidence from quarter sessions, settlement examinations, and the ordinary criminal courts. Most legal proceedings by apprentices, and by masters, thus escape notice. Hill, *Servants*, is similarly vague about adjudication. Rushton, "Matter in Variance," attributes the decline of apprenticeship cases at quarter sessions from about 1750 in the Northeast to "proletarianization of the young"; it was probably due rather to the enactment of 20 Geo.II c.19 (1746), which gave two justices wide authority in apprenticeship cases.

122. The wider powers of guilds exercised in earlier times (e.g., Woodward, *Men at Work*, and the work cited there) were in eclipse, in part because of decisions that they were in restraint of trade: see, for example, *Harrison v. Godman* (1756), 1 Burr 12. For a local study, see Neale, *Bath*, 63–69; for an overview, M. Walker, "Extent of Guild Control."

123. Masters, *Chamberlain*, 13, 28, 55, 93–97.

124. Shoemaker, *Prosecution and Punishment*, 174–75, 188–89. My survey of early eighteenth-century provincial houses of correction shows (so far) very few committals, but the sources are extremely patchy.

tals in 1663–64, 1690–93, and 1721, were for master and servant offenses. In 1721 they amounted to 56 out of a sample total of 711 committals (8 percent) for a wide variety of petty offenses.[125] It is clear from the court books of the summary hearings held before the lord mayor in the City that throughout the seventeenth and eighteenth centuries he heard each year (among hundreds of other cases of felony, assault, and public order) a regular trickle of employment cases involving both apprentices and adult workers: dismissed apprentices, unpaid or disputed wages, mistreatment, refusing to obey a master's commands, desertion from service. Some disputes were settled, some accusations were dismissed, orders were made for wages, servants were committed to Bridewell and whipped (and sometimes discharged early at the request of the master).[126]

At the beginning of the nineteenth century we can distinguish the relative importance of the lord mayor's and the chamberlain's courts. In 1809, the first surviving year of continuous records for the City of London Bridewell, the lord mayor or aldermen committed fourteen men and boys, but the chamberlain's court committed thirty-five apprentices, the oldest twenty-four, but most of them in their teens.[127] It seems likely that the boys tried by the lord mayor were often apprentices also, brought before the lord mayor as an matter of convenience or for more serious offenses.[128] Thus a total of forty-nine committals, all but a dozen of them apprentices, were for employment offenses. They amounted to about 9 percent of all the prisoners sent to Bridewell that year, very similar to the proportion a century earlier.[129] The offenses for which apprentices were tried and imprisoned were insolence and abusive language, desertion, disobedience, neglect of duty, defrauding the master, repeated absence without leave, and striking the master.

Of course, not all were sent to Bridewell.[130] In 1787, for example, the cham-

125. Ibid., 89 (table 2).

126. Examples are: Corporation of London Record Office, Waiting Book, vol. 3 (1664–68), fols. 140, 140v, 145v, 147, 148v, 151v, 152; Justice Room Charge Book, 1699–1705, fols. 177, 180v, 181v, 189v, 190, 191v, 192; GJR/M 3 (Apr.–May 1762), 27, 29 Apr., 3 May 1762; MJR/M 1 (Nov.–Dec. 1784), 15, 16, and 18 Nov. 1784; MJR/M 27 (Dec. 1786–Feb. 1787), 27 Dec. 1786, 8, 29 Jan. 1787.

127. Guildhall Library (London), Manuscripts Division, Ms. 33138, vol. 1, Prisoners Committal Book, 1809–16. The series is continuous to vol. 9, which ends in 1916.

128. For example, case 281, a fifteen-year-old named Drury, was sentenced by the lord mayor to one month for neglect of duty but discharged early by the chamberlain. However, only the lord mayor tried adults: of the fourteen cases cited, ten were adult seamen (deserting ship), two were boys (neglect of duty, absence, and pilfering), one a man of twenty-three (leaving work unfinished), the last a man of fifty-three ("quitting his duty").

129. Most convictions in the lord mayor's or other courts were for the usual range of criminal offenses, and prostitution and vagrancy. On the seventeenth-century figures, see below.

130. Corporation of London Record Office, CF10/1-18, Apprenticeship Complaint Books,

berlain's specialized jurisdiction dealt with a total of 236 disputes between masters and apprentices: 183 brought by masters, 53 by apprentices.[131] The latter complained of such injuries as a master locking up shoes, failing to give instruction or clothes or bedding, and (frequently) abusive beatings. In most such cases the chamberlain admonished both parties; a proportion were dismissed as frivolous; no masters were punished. Masters complained of the usual absenteeism or rudeness or saucy language or idleness; also venereal disease, revealing the master's secrets, and hunting bullocks, among other misdemeanors. Often the apprentice was reprimanded, but in 35 percent of cases the apprentice went to Bridewell, usually for a short term: five for three days, forty-three for ten days. But there were also thirteen sentences of a month, and three sentences of two months. They might be released early as a result of a master's leniency and the concurrence of the court.[132] From 1823 to 1859 the number of boys complained against was about 100 a year except for the late 1830s and early 1840s when the numbers averaged about 150; over the whole period the percentage imprisoned averaged 30 percent, again with a peak in the late 1830s and early 1840s, when it was over 40 percent. The net effect was that many more apprentices (over 50 a year) were committed to Bridewell between 1834 and 1842 than earlier or later in the nineteenth century; but in only one of those years were more committed than had been in 1787. As late as 1858 the City chamberlain warmly recommended that his jurisdiction be copied elsewhere: it benefited all parties, he believed, and in particular provided both remedies against mistreatment and wholesome discipline for apprentices. Its great virtues were that the court sat daily, cost a shilling to invoke, emphasized conciliation, and was not a criminal court; nor were any ordinary criminals (at that date) confined to Bridewell with the imprisoned boys. The numbers rapidly declined after 1859: in 1862 there were thirteen prison sentences and in 1872, twelve.[133]

1787–1917 (discontinuous). Earlier records were destroyed by fire in 1786: Masters, *Chamberlain*, 93, 95.

131. CF10/1. See Table 2.1.

132. Masters, *Chamberlain*, 96–97. Such cases recur throughout the Bridewell Prisoner's Committal Books also: for example, for 1809, ten of the cases noted above for that year are early dismissals, including that of one Pickman, sentenced by the chamberlain to one month, but discharged five days early "by the master's request to the chamberlain." Guildhall Ms. 33138 vol. 1, case 538 for 1809.

133. As noted, the Apprenticeship Complaint Books cover 1788 to 1917, with gaps. There is also a summary of sentences in the Apprenticeship Committment Book, CF11/1, covering the period 1817 to 1916, compiled by a contemporary: the summary appears on a sheet inside the front cover, and on two sheets in Misc. MSS 368.8, covering complaints and commitments for 1823 to 1859. One estimate for 1858 was that nearly three thousand apprentices were within the

Outside London the house of correction registers in several counties record the numbers of both apprentices and adults imprisoned for breach of contract. In Gloucestershire and Staffordshire about a quarter of the inmates imprisoned for employment offenses were apprentices. Some were quite young: in the Littledean (Gloucester) house of correction between 1792 and 1828, seven of the ninety-seven apprentices were between eight and ten years old, and fully three-quarters were under fifteen. A fifth were girls, including six eleven-year-olds, and again almost three-quarters of all the female apprentices in prison were under the age of fifteen.

The house of correction registers also give us some insight into the numbers, identities, and sentences of the adult workers convicted of the most serious master and servant offenses, and their punishment.[134] The prison sentences in early eighteenth-century London (60 percent of them for less than two weeks) contrast sharply with the evidence a century later, from several counties: in Staffordshire less than 7 percent of sentences of workers were this short. The increase in statutory penalties during the eighteenth century was reflected in early nineteenth-century average and modal sentences of about a month, ranging from a week to three months depending on the offense. It was possible to pass such sentences because of the greatly increased capacity of county prisons and houses of correction (which earlier were often decayed and tiny lockups) in the period 1790 to 1850. In Gloucestershire, the new houses of correction were most used by employers nearby, whose expenses in sending and retrieving imprisoned servants were low. But the building of new prisons clearly affected rates of imprisonment and was designed to do so. The planners of Bedford's new prison, opened in 1820, listed their targets: poachers came first, followed by "servants in husbandry and other labourers for misbehaviour in their employment."[135] An analysis of over 5,000 inmates recorded for Gloucestershire and Staffordshire houses of correction in the three decades after 1790 shows that 26 percent in the first county, 39 percent in the second, were men, women, and children imprisoned for breach of contract. (In Staffordshire, poor-law and bastardy cases was the only larger category, 48 percent.) Higher proportions, and higher absolute totals, are concentrated after about 1800. This pattern continued to the middle of the

---

chamberlain's jurisdiction: Masters, *Chamberlain*, 95; B. Scott, "Custom of Apprenticeship," 183–87.

134. See Hay, "Master and Servant in England," 241–63, for sources, statistical data, and an interpretation of secular and regional change of imprisonment of servants in houses of correction in Littledean (Gloucestershire), 1792–1828; Northleach (Gloucestershire), 1791–1816; and Stafford, 1793–1814, on which this paragraph is based.

135. Bedfordshire Record Office, Q/S rolls 1820/69.

century and beyond: in Staffordshire usually sixty to eighty apprentices and servants were imprisoned annually for breach of contract.[136] They ranged in age from children of eight to men in their seventies, with a concentration of men and women in their late teens and early twenties. But nearly a third were over twenty-five, and a fifth over thirty. They worked at every skill level, in many trades: pottery (20 percent of prisoners) and the various metal trades (13 percent) were the dominant industries of the county, but mining (9 percent), the cotton and leather industries (each with 6 percent), and hatting (3 percent) were also important; a very wide variety of other artisanal and industrial occupations accounted for 16 percent of the cases. Finally, the bare categories of "servant" and "labourer," undoubtedly many of them agricultural workers, comprised 28 percent of those imprisoned for master and servant offenses. Women were a minority overall, but a majority of those imprisoned in some occupations. In Staffordshire, 15 percent of those in the house of correction were women; most were about twenty years of age and were either cotton workers or described simply as "servants," the two groups in which the majority of those punished were women.[137]

At the beginning of the eighteenth century many servants in London Bridewell apparently were whipped. There is very little evidence of such sentences in the county houses of correction 100 years later, except for a few runaway apprentices.[138] Yet it was sometimes used in exemplary cases for adults, usually under the statute of 1746, which called for "correction": in one reported case from rural Norfolk in 1811, the comments of the jailer suggest that whipping with a cat was far from unknown in such cases.[139] The persistence of whipping in the statute law and in practice in England is notable. From scattered evidence it appears that whipping was probably used quite widely into the early eighteenth century, and thereafter when magistrates particularly wanted to make examples. Whipping was also used on vagrants and petty thieves and soldiers. Whipping had always been demeaning, a deliberately hu-

136. In Gloucestershire totals were about the same at the beginning and middle of the nineteenth century: Hay, "Master and Servant in England," 259. In Essex houses of correction in 1753–54 and 1788–93, servants and apprentices sentenced for breach of contract comprised 8.1 percent and 6.6 percent of the inmates. King, "Summary Courts," table 4.

137. Proportions of women by occupation: cotton, 62 percent; metal trades, 7 percent; potteries, 6 percent; husbandry, 3 percent; "servant," 69 percent; miscellaneous, 24 percent. No women were prosecuted in day labor, hatting, leather, or mining.

138. Hay, "Master and Servant in England," 245.

139. (England) 20 Geo.II c.19 (1746); Craven and Hay, "The Criminalization of 'Free' Labour," 86–87, is in error on this point. The case is *R v. Hoseason* (1811), 14 East 605, discussed (with other evidence) in Hay, "Patronage, Paternalism, and Welfare," 40–44; Hay, "Master and Servant in England," 245–46, and below.

miliating punishment from medieval times. It was from the seventeenth century associated with slavery in the British West Indies. In those colonies and in England it branded the bodies of workers with a particularly emphatic mark of subordination.

The magistrates' notebooks show large numbers of cases in which the threat of imprisonment secured performance of the contract by the servant, who agreed at the hearing before the magistrate to go back to work. For many more the threat sufficed: employers routinely used it in arguments with their workers.[140] Even when the worker or apprentice went to prison, the employer might arrange for early release, perhaps after an exemplary few days or weeks.[141] This was particularly likely when the charge was refusal to work, absence from service, neglecting work, or being an idle and disorderly apprentice. More than 20 percent of Stafford prisoners convicted of these offenses were released before they had served half their sentences. Deserters, however, were least likely to be released early. Men were slightly more likely than women to be released early.

The justices' notebooks to the early nineteenth century, from both rural and industrial areas, show the same variations in activity seen in earlier centuries.[142] Those in Table 2.1 fall into several types.[143] Some justices in rural farming areas heard relatively few cases, either in absolute terms or as a proportion (less than 10 percent) of their case loads. These men, William Hunt in Wiltshire, Richard Wyatt in Surrey, and the famous philanthropist and MP Samuel Whitbread in Bedfordshire, all heard twice as many complaints from servants as from masters. It seems likely that they were known to be sympathetic to servants' complaints, and Whitbread, whose decisions we know, gave judgment in about the same proportion to masters and to servants. His notebooks show a willingness to investigate cases in depth, on one occasion seeking expert opinion on whether a field of turnips had been properly hoed.

140. For example, an incident in 1778 recounted in the *Autobiographical Memoir of Joseph Jewell, 1763–1846*, ed. A. W. Slater (*Camden Miscellany*, vol. 22) (London, 1964), 133.

141. The judges note an instance without comment in the reported case *R v. Barton-upon-Irwell* (1814), cited in note 2, above. See also Steinfeld, *Coercion*, 53–57; Frank, "Constitutional Law."

142. On Edgar, see above. The notebooks of Edgar, Wyatt, Hunt, Ward, and Allen are described more fully in Hay, "Master and Servant in England," 232–39, and those of Allen and Whitbread in Hay, "Patronage, Paternalism, and Welfare." On Hunt, Wyatt, Norris, and William and Ralph Brockman (both of Kent), see also Oberwittler, "Crime and Authority," 10, who calculates that 10 percent of their business was master and servant but gives no details.

143. Several rural Kent justices had relatively little business, hearing two to nine cases a year, amounting to 2 to 30 percent of their workload: on Gabriel Walters, and William and Ralph Brockman, see Landau, *Justices*, 177–78, 195. William Norris of Hackney similarly had few cases in the 1730s, for reasons discussed above.

Other rural justices, the Reverend Henry Gorges Dobyns Yate in Hereford and George Turner in Suffolk, also had small case loads but a quarter of them were employment cases. Also in contrast to the first group, both heard more complaints by masters, and Yate, whose decisions we know, was five times as likely to find for a master as for a servant.[144] If the first group of justices were paternalists, regarded by servants as fair-minded, Yate and Turner seem likely to have been avoided by servants because they were not.

In the same period (1750 to 1823) justices in areas where rural industry was important, or in towns with large manufacturing populations, were occupied with master and servant cases more than 10 percent of the time, sometimes much more. Some of these men clearly had the confidence of both parties. The Reverend Edmund Tew in Boldon, near Sunderland (Durham), heard many cases from mariners, boatbuilders and other maritime trades, and masters and workers in salt making and blacksmithing, as well as farmers and farm laborers. Masters complained about as often as servants, and were slightly more successful. Sir Thomas Ward of Northamptonshire dealt with many workers in the textile trades (like Tew, he had about twenty-five cases a year). Servants were charged with leaving work unfinished, neglecting work, refusing work, misbehavior, and embezzlement, but he also heard more cases against masters brought by servants, who paid about a day's wages in fees for process. Masters got warrants in 70 percent of cases, servants in only 5 percent (when mistreatment was alleged), as was common in such cases. Finally, Thomas Allen, a borough justice of Macclesfield (Cheshire), heard about 100 employment cases a year, almost all in the dominant silk-weaving industry of the town. He claimed to be accepted by the community as an impartial arbiter, and, again, servants brought almost as many cases as masters. Almost half were "settled," and where he had to make a decision, servants and masters were equally likely to be successful.

The heavier case loads of justices in industrial areas are suggested also by other evidence. In the nineteenth century, records of magistrates administering the law in industrial areas frequently show high levels of activity. Petty sessions records from an industrial area of Gloucestershire in the 1820s show the justices active in textile cases, both master and servant and embezzlement, a role also reflected in the heavy use by masters of incarceration in the houses of correction at Horseley, Littledean, and Northleach.[145] In the early nine-

144. Most masters were farmers, others were brickmakers, a timber merchant, mealman, cordwainer, mason, and several gentlemen; Yate frequently granted a warrant "with permission to settle privately."

145. Gloucestershire Record Office, PS/SD/M1/1, Stroud (7 Nov. 1822 to Mar. 1825); on the houses of correction, see above.

teenth century the Reverend Edward Powys in the Staffordshire potteries committed 179 workers to the Stafford house of correction for breach of contract over a period of fifteen years (two-thirds of all his committals), suggesting a total master and servant case load (including penalties other than imprisonment, and also wage orders) of perhaps 2,000 over that period of time, about 130 a year.[146]

All the justices in both agrarian and industrial areas in this period, with the exception of Hunt in Wiltshire, sent a significant proportion of workers to the house of correction (Table 2.1): they were likely to be laborers who contracted to harvest and then absconded or failed to turn up, repeated runaways, or servants who had been openly disrespectful or disobedient (if self-respecting in their own eyes). Cases of independent contractors for particular jobs also still appear in the justices' records, claiming payment, or brought before the justice for not completing work. One striking aspect of some justices' work is a high proportion of young women: in the case of George Turner, 40 percent of accused servants were women or girls.

That pattern can be found also in rural records forty years later. In Berkeley (Gloucestershire) the petty sessions register shows the justices punishing agricultural servants, and again young women constitute 43 percent of those accused, most of them farm servants such as dairymaids (Table 2.1). For being absent from work, they received seven to ten days in the house of correction, with costs deducted from their wages; a repeat offender, Sarah Hale, who was accused not only of being absent but also of being abusive, profane, and disobedient, was sentenced the second time to three weeks in prison. A girl who refused to milk a cow was fined and paid costs totaling ten shillings, over a month's wages; another who stayed out all night lost two weeks' wages.[147] Male servants were also punished harshly: the proportion of servants sentenced to prison is higher than in any other sessions register or justice's notebook examined for this study. Moreover, only two servants brought cases before the Berkeley justices in a five-year period.[148] A similar pattern is found in Sleaford (Lincolnshire) in 1866, again a rural area, where masters brought the great majority of cases and were always successful. A third of the accused servants were women, as were three of the four seeking wages. Only

---

146. Based on his committals to the Stafford house of correction, 1801–14, and an estimate of the proportion of committals to all master and servant cases of 10 percent, probably a conservative estimate.

147. Cases of Sarah Hale, Hannah Cox, Sarah Pinkett, E. Trayhrme. Fines were probably abatements of wages.

148. See below on the changing ratio of masters' and servants' applications to justices in the nineteenth century.

one wage case succeeded; three were dismissed, and in two cases the servants lost their jobs.[149]

This domination of justices' hearings by masters in the second half of the nineteenth century appears also in the industrial town of Hanley (Stafford-shire). We know too that the justices on the bench there were almost all pot-tery manufacturers. The two who heard most cases were Joseph Clementson and Samuel Keeling. On one occasion, Clementson stepped down from the bench to prosecute a cupmaker who had worked for him for fourteen years, securing a fine of ten shillings and costs for three days' absence.[150] The Hanley magistrate's court records relatively few cases, but press reports suggest that many cases were being handled elsewhere, perhaps by individual justices. In Hanley skilled workers accused of disrupting industrial processes, with seri-ous consequences, were likely to be prosecuted.[151]

The very scattered soundings in individual justices' notebooks and petty sessions registers over the eighteenth and nineteenth centuries summarized in Table 2.1 suggest that justices in industrial areas had heavier case loads, probably representing the greater density of population (and thus contracts of employment) in areas of rural industry that by the later period had often become urban manufacturing districts. But it is clear from analysis of the post-1858 statistics, as well as Table 2.1, that many breach-of-contract cases were also brought before rural justices. In fact, they formed a similar propor-tion of summary convictions (between 4 and 10 percent) between 1858 to 1875 in rural as in industrial counties, and the soundings from before 1858 show many justices as busy with employment law in agricultural as in industrial

149. Lincolnshire Record Office, PSJ 10/1.

150. On Clementson, Keeling, and Brownfield, see J. Jenkins, *Victoria County History of Stafford*, 8:137, 149, 164, 166–68. In 1866 William Evans, the editor of the *Potteries Examiner*, testified to a parliamentary committee that apart from one stipendiary magistrate (Davis) who moved about to the six petty sessional courts of the townships of Stoke on Trent, including Hanley, all the other magistrates were in the trade. PP 1866 (449) 13:71, questions 1387–94 (5 June 1866). He did not appear to think that the justices often sat without the stipendiary present, but the Hanley petty sessions book suggests that there they usually did.

151. The Hanley court heard 38 cases in twenty-one months in 1864 to 1866, a case every few weeks on average, and only a small percentage of the total (mainly drunk and disorderly charges, some bawdy house and factory act prosecutions): Staffs. Record Office, D26/1/1. Hanley in 1861 had a population of 31,953: J. Jenkins, *Victoria County History of Stafford*, 8:145. The pottery district stipendiary magistrates acting in 1871–72 (SRO D1142/1 [1871–72]) heard only 4 em-ployment cases out of about 450 hearings. Steinberg, "Capitalist Development," a recent de-tailed account, suggests the record is incomplete; more prosecutions were reported in the press in Hanley, for a total of almost 33 prosecutions per year between 1864 and 1875, about 18 of them potters; clearly other magistrates were hearing cases, a fact also suggested by the annual parliamentary returns. As a comparison, between 1792 and 1814, in the whole county, probably about 80 potters were prosecuted yearly.

districts.[152] The motives of prosecutors often differed between areas. Master and servant law was very useful in keeping skilled workers to their jobs and ensuring discipline in demanding industrial processes. But it was also very attractive to employers in rural parishes faced with surly dairymaids who were in fact also domestic servants, and in London and many towns it gave masters the power to discipline apprentices when they could not do so themselves.

In industry and mining, master and servant penal law shaped not only the individual employment contract; it was critical also in collective bargaining, and always had been so. Most accounts of master and servant quote George White on the usefulness of the laws in breaking strikes. Because in many trades the work was never fully completed, the result of a strike was a prosecution for leaving work unfinished. It was easier for the master to prosecute on the grounds of being absent from service, general "misconduct," and other such master and servant offenses than to secure convictions under the far more notorious combination acts. Obviously the tactic was limited by the size of the strike. But massive solidarity was (as always) the exception. The use of the master and servant acts to break smaller strikes was undoubtedly common. Such cases typically surface in the court or prison records in the form of several convictions by the same magistrate on the same or succeeding days, and usually of men with the same occupation. By this measure, between 10 and 20 percent of workers committed to the house of correction at the beginning of the nineteenth century in Staffordshire were there as a result of a collective dispute. The combination acts were much less important to unions than the master and servant laws.[153]

Variations in enforcement, and the use of master and servant law against strikers, will be illuminated by further detailed work in local archival and printed sources.[154] Three important general changes, however, appear to have taken place after about 1800 and before the central state began collecting annual statistics of master and servant cases in 1858. These changes greatly altered the social significance of master and servant prosecutions. One was the growth in the use of written contracts and perhaps testimonials on completion of work; a second was the increasingly criminal context of master and servant proceedings as summary jurisdiction expanded; the third was the hardening attitude of the high courts in the face of labor unrest.

---

152. For a preliminary analysis of the statistics of enforcement after 1858, see Hay, "Master and Servant in England," 260–62 (figures 5, 6, 7, 8).

153. Ibid., 250–55.

154. On its use against strikers in the nineteenth century, see Frank, "Constitutional Law."

Written Contracts and Testimonials

Written contracts for "covenant servants" were not uncommon in early centuries; we have also seen that the colliers' bond was an important form. The
bond used in the northeast coalfield (and later in the potteries, apparently
from the 1830s) became a more elaborate instrument in the course of the
eighteenth century, with clauses negotiated by masters and men, and usually
entered into in late autumn. It bound the worker for a little less than a year,
prescribed set fines for offenses and wage rates for piecework, but did not
guarantee full-time work. Yet these skilled workers were prevented from seeking other work when times were slack: "[I]f any of them elope to other work
[they] are imprisoned," it was reported in 1731 from Wearside, and the masters ensured that they had legislative backing to prosecute for breach of contract.[155] Masters colluded to ensure that wage rates were comparable so that
they were not in the position of competing for labor, hence raising wages. The
bond was usually collectively negotiated, but because it included employer-
administered fines for poor work or absence or lack of output, and was inescapable proof of a contract, it was a powerful instrument for employer self-
help as well as prosecutions before the justices.

In other industries too, written contracts enhanced the disciplinary power
of masters. Thus the standard form contract devised by the lawyers of Messrs.
Cooper and Co.'s Cotton Mill in Ashbourne, Derbyshire, in 1796, provided
that the (female) worker should work for thirteen hours daily at weekly wages
of four shillings for a six-day week "only and to be at her own liberty at all
other times." This appeared to give her more liberty: in theory, the common law made her answerable every hour of the day and night.[156] But the
contract continued that if she were absent from service the company could
abate her wages or discharge her.[157] Apparently Cooper & Co. continued to
take workers before the local magistrates for other remedies such as imprisonment, but the justices began to object, "that the Master has taken the Law
into his own hands by specifically reserving a right of abateing wages pro-
portionately for such absence."[158] Counsel advised that the power reserved by

155. Levine and Wrightson, *Making of an Industrial Society*, 409. Legislation dealing with
breach of contract by colliers included (G.B.) 20 Geo.II c.19 (1746); 6 Geo.III c.25 (1766);
(U.K.) 4 Geo.IV c.34 (1823).

156. The motive may have been to deny settlement under the poor law or to remove the
contract from the terms of the general hiring, which imposed obligations on both parties.

157. "Case" for the opinion of J. Balguy, 4 Apr. 1796, Staffs. Record Office, Q/SR Translation 1796/136. Balguy was counsel in many leading employment cases: cf. Cald. 12, etc.

158. "Case" for the opinion of J. Balguy, 4 Apr. 1796. They also raised a second objection:
that servants who were minors were incapable, without parental agreement, of entering into

the master was concurrent with that exercised by the justices, and so did not prevent them from hearing the case, "when the master waives all authority and applies to the Magistrate." If the magistrates accepted this reasoning, the employer now had the advantages of both penal enforcement and dismissal at will under the contract. The increasing use of written contracts (and it was undoubtedly widespread) marks a significant transition in practice.[159]

As new technologies developed, the employers of the first industrial revolution sought to bind their skilled workers for long terms. In 1790 the manager of a Lancashire foundry wrote his aristocratic employer, "In a few days I expect to have all our best people bound down for three years; this has required vast manoeuvring."[160] In the glass industry, five-, six-, or seven-year contracts became the norm for skilled men.[161] Boulton and Watt, the steam engine manufacturers, used contracts of three to five years, with a clause providing that unjustified absences would be made up at the end of the contract by two days' labor for each day absent.[162] Wedgwood, the great potteries manufacturer, signed almost all his men to formal written contracts, longer for the more highly skilled. In an acid works in Prestonpans, Scotland, men were bound under indentures for twenty-one years.[163] From the evidence of the miner's bond, the pottery, and other growth industries including cotton spinning, written contracts increasingly superseded the assumptions of yearly (or lesser) service that had been doctrine and magisterial practice in medieval and early modern law. They became common in new industrial manufacturing concerns with large work forces.

George White claimed in 1823 that master and servant law had become even more unfair with the spread of written agreements. He argued that the combination of traditional penal sanctions, the new practice of written contracts, and the greed of wage-cutting employers had produced a particularly exploitative use of 6 Geo.III c.25. Illiterate workmen signed contracts drawn up by attorneys, only to discover later that they did not embody what had been verbally agreed. According to White, when the worker threatened to

---

any other contract than one of apprenticeship. Balguy advised that if the minor gave notice, "the Magistrate cannot enforce the performance of it against him," but that if she deserted, the penal laws applied.

159. But there was a simultaneous evolution of the law in cases where contracts were verbal, and the terms supplied by the courts. I deal with this elsewhere.

160. Birch, *Economic History*, 90.

161. *R. v. Inhabitants of Whitechapel* (1738), Sess Cas 120, 93 ER 161, for a five-year contract; for the nineteenth-century case law that arose around long contracts, see Deakin, "Contract of Employment" (glassworkers cited at note 75).

162. Roll, *An Early Experiment*, 64–65.

163. Sir John Sinclair, *The Statistical Account of Scotland* (Edinburgh, 1796), 17:68.

quit, his master declared, "I'll tell you what, Jack, . . . if you don't go to work this instant, I'll take you before a justice, and send you to the house of correction. You shall dance upon the tread-mill." Jack is arrested, the attorney attends, the contract is produced and read out by the justice's clerk, and explained by the magistrate: "I have it here in black and white, that you agreed to work for so much per week, and you must go to work, or go to the house of correction." White added, "Many such dupes have submitted to the house of correction sooner than work."[164] By the 1850s there is much evidence of employer prosecutions relying on such agreements, including the effect of works rules incorporated in the contract. This probably also eroded the willingness of magistrates and judges to consider customary practice as part of the contract.[165]

Testimonials (discharge certificates) were mandated by the Statute of Artificers, ceased to be required universally by the seventeenth century, and were feared by workers in the eighteenth century as a step toward servitude.[166] Employers never gave up hoping they could be made universal, for they promised a very high degree of control over recalcitrant servants, particularly as yearly hirings approached their end. The editor of the Northampton newspaper reported in 1790 that "respectable farmers" in another county, following the example of tradesmen, now required testimonials to deal with a "useful, yet rude," set of people: "servants in the husbandry line, call the last, *the saucy Quarter*, and are in common more insolent and careless in this than any other."[167] Requirements of testimonials in fact were enforced in some neighborhoods, and some trades, well into the nineteenth century. In the 1860s in the south Yorkshire collieries, employers required "clearance papers" from the last employer, stating either that the miner's services were no longer required, or that he had "legally left": in the latter case, he had a much better chance of being hired. They were particularly useful against strikers.[168]

164. White, *Digest*, 95–97. White referred to such contracts for terms as long as fourteen years, and he proposed legislation that would force registration (and hence examination) of long contracts, among its other provisions. The bill was not enacted; instead Parliament passed the 1823 master and servant act.

165. Steinmetz, "De-juridification," 273–74, 279–80, 289.

166. Beier, *Masterless Men*, 147, 154; and my comments above.

167. *Northampton Mercury*, 28 Aug. 1790; I owe this reference to J. M. Neeson. See also Christopher Tancred, *A Scheme for an Act of Parliament for the Better Regulating Servants* (1st ed., 1724), 19; Anon. ("P.S."), *A Help to Magistrates* (4th ed., 1708), 127.

168. *Report from the Select Committee on Master and Servant*, PP 1866 (449) 13:51–52, questions 928–40 (1 June 1866).

Magisterial Justice and the Growing Taint of Criminalization

In the first half of the nineteenth century the magistracy itself was changing rapidly in composition, notably in industrial areas. The law of master and servant, administered overwhelmingly by justices without the direct supervision of either judges or juries, depended for its legitimacy on the standing and indifference, in the good sense, of the justices of the peace and borough justices and stipendiaries (paid professional magistrates) who administered it. Country justices in early centuries and stipendiaries in the nineteenth were both removed by social class or profession from too close an identification with most of the masters who brought or defended master and servant cases before them. Yet much evidence shows that by the 1820s or so in industrial areas, magistrates in all inferior courts were increasingly drawn not from the country gentry but from middle-class professionals, clerics, and also from the trades that brought most cases before the courts. In so-called ancient boroughs (chartered before 1835), tradesmen and manufacturers had always sat on the bench; they did so too in the low courts of the new municipal corporations that replaced the old boroughs, and were established in many new urban areas by the 1835 Municipal Corporations Act. But such men were increasingly to be found in some county commissions of the peace by the 1830s and 1840s. As colleagues, competitors, and friends of masters who brought prosecutions against workers, they were the object of union enmity and workers' distrust.[169] The evidence of oppressive and one-sided interpretation of the law mounted throughout the first half of the nineteenth century. As it did so, the legitimacy of master and servant law in the eyes of labor was greatly weakened. The decline of the role of the country gentleman as a justice of the peace, particularly in manufacturing districts, probably also eroded the traditional personal authority of the justice, which had often enabled him to persuade servants to return to work, and masters to pay wages owing, without having to make committals or orders for payment of wages. In the early nineteenth century, as magistrates were increasingly likely to be employers in the same trade, resolutions that a country gentlemen might have imposed in a spirit of paternalism (or a gentlemanly dislike of men "in trade") were less and less likely.

It seems likely that wage claims became easier to pursue with the creation of the county courts in 1846. They had jurisdiction in civil claims to twenty pounds (raised to fifty pounds in 1850). Cases, particularly those involving

---

169. The latest account is Frank, "Warrington Cases," and Frank, "Constitutional Law."

setoffs, which could not be settled before magistrates, appear immediately.[170] In 1859 one observer suggested that as a consequence the right to bring summary wage hearings before justices was not of much importance to workers, and magistrates sometimes suggested that cases brought to them should be taken to the county courts.[171] Not all wage claims before justices disappeared (see Table 2.1), but they undoubtedly became less common. However, a consequence was that justices' hearings became increasingly the venue for masters, and less frequently a place where workers found justice in the form of wage orders. This change, together with others, made master and servant increasingly seem to be part of the regular criminal law.

Employment law had been penal for centuries, but it became increasingly criminal in character, a slow development that accelerated in the nineteenth century. The legislation of the eighteenth century created longer sentences, but the great increase in the capacity of local prisons and houses of correction in the first decades of the nineteenth century, together with the institution of rigorous disciplinary regimes, greatly increased the bite of such a custodial sentence. Hard labor, which was prescribed by many of the eighteenth-century statutes, was made very hard indeed by the installation of treadmills and the crank in local and county prisons. Bitter complaints about both were made in the parliamentary inquiries into master and servant law in the 1860s.[172] Other developments greatly increased the sense of workers that master and servant law had become *criminal* law. One was the deployment of the new police forces formed in the early nineteenth century, and their constantly increasing strength. The unions had opposed their creation, fearful (often with reason) that they would be used against strikers. But the police were also immensely useful to employers in making arrests under master and servant statutes; sometimes constables were sent by determined employers in pursuit of absconders to very distant parts of the country.[173] The taint of criminality now ran throughout master and servant proceedings from the initiation of

170. For example, Warks. Record Office, CR 2641/7 County Court of Warwickshire, Nuneaton, Minute Book, 28 Apr. 1847 to 20 July 1848, pp. 76, 131, 342, 407, 410, A11, A27, A59. Magistrates making wage orders under the 1823 statute were limited to ten-pound awards.

171. Edgar, "Jurisdiction of Justices of the Peace," 687–91; Staffs. Record Office, D26/1/1, Hanley magistrates' court. Steinmetz, "De-juridification," 296–303, suggests that the county courts probably were being used as often as magistrates in the 1870s. Evans, the editor of the *Potteries Examiner*, told the Select Committee in 1866 that he was not sure that pottery workers would prefer the county courts: *Report from the Select Committee on Master and Servant*, PP 1866 (449) 13:71, question 1399 (5 June 1866).

172. On the crank in Scotland, for example, see *Report from the Select Committee*, PP 1865 (370), questions 257–61.

173. For an instance, see Frank, "Warrington Cases."

process. Servants were usually brought before the court on arrest warrants, in police custody; masters were almost invariably summoned. Petty sessions registers from the 1840s show many cases of a worker (including dairymaids as young as fifteen) brought up from the cells, referred to as "the prisoner" as in serious criminal trials, and tried and sentenced in what after 1847 became a largely criminal court.[174]

It was now usually called the "police court." A momentous transformation of petty sessions, in existence under one form or another for centuries, began with legislation in 1847 and developed rapidly under further acts in the 1850s and 1860s and later. Each statute expanded the summary jurisdiction of the magistracy by bringing more and more larcenies and other criminal offenses into the magistrates' courts for determination, away from the quarter sessions and assizes where they had formerly been tried by jury. The "police court" was new, feared, and hated by those workers who now found themselves before its bench. The regular reporting of its proceedings in the press, which was never the case in the eighteenth and rare in the early nineteenth century, made the stigma public and permanent. The processing of workers as criminals apparently like other criminals, by police and magistracy, raised interesting tensions within the coalescing mid-Victorian ideology of the "respectable" working man. Baron Pollock's comments in 1857, painting a picture of a worker torn from the domestic hearth—"a man grown up and of full age, possibly surrounded by a wife and children"—expresses that unease.[175]

But how "criminal" was the law of master and servant in fact, in earlier periods or in the last years of the penal sanctions? However difficult it is to compile the statistics, the proportion of English workers sentenced to penal sanctions was never large, compared with the number of employment contracts.[176] But prosecutions were exemplary, intended to serve as a warning, to set limits, to deter. In this respect master and servant was like all criminal law.[177] It is useful, therefore, to make a comparison of the numbers punished by the "ordinary" criminal law, notably for theft, with the numbers imprisoned under master and servant, or punished by abatement of wages or the

174. For example, Berkeley (Gloucs.) Petty Sessions 1866–71, Gloucs. Record Office, PS/BE M1/1.

175. Note 1.

176. See the comparison with colonial master and servant prosecutions, discussed in the Introduction.

177. And also like the law of debt, which similarly relied on imprisonment. Master and servant was in part understood, like debt, as a surety for performance among a class without property to answer. Paul Craven and I explore this dimension of master and servant in forthcoming work.

threat of prison. In four sample years at the beginning of the nineteenth century, the number of workers imprisoned in the Staffordshire house of correction was 176. Based on the ratio of prison sentences to other sentences on conviction in such cases, from a variety of sources, we can estimate that there were more than 1,000 convictions of servants for breach of contract. In the same four years, the total number of theft convictions in the county was 169. In other words, there were six times as many workers punished for master and servant offenses as there were thieves punished by the "ordinary" criminal law. The total number of workers imprisoned exceeded the total number of convicted thieves (punished in a variety of ways) in these years.[178]

Later in the century, we have the national statistics for both master and servant and ordinary criminal offenses in the last quarter-century of penal sanctions. They reveal that between 1858 and 1875, the ratio of master and servant prosecutions amounted to between 12 and 32 percent (depending on the year) of the number of all theft prosecutions (both summary and tried by jury) throughout the country. This does not mean that master and servant prosecutions declined in numbers compared with totals in the early nineteenth century; rather, the enormous expansion of summary convictions for theft had changed the denominator of the ratio. In fact, the greatest number of master and servant prosecutions occurred between 1871 and 1875. In part this was due to the nature of the trade cycle (it was a period of labor demand, high wages, and increased use of master and servant prosecutions), but it also coincides with a great increase in the use of fines, enacted in 1867 as a substitute for most imprisonment in breach-of-contract cases. The number of fined workers greatly exceeded the decline in the number of those imprisoned. (The conviction rate for women greatly increased also.) In the last four years of penal sanctions (1872–75) for breach of contract, the ratio of master and servant prosecutions to all theft prosecutions varied between 25 and 32 percent. In the courts that heard both summary property and master and servant cases, the national ratio of accused workers to accused thieves varied between 31 and 41 percent in those four years. In counties where the law was heavily used, such as Staffordshire, it was much higher, even in the late 1850s, when general rates were lower.[179] In the mining district of that county, the ratio of

178. The years are twelve months from each of 1795–96, 1801–2, 1806–7, and 1811–12. Total theft convictions are those recorded at county assizes and quarter sessions; in this period only a tiny number of thefts were triable summarily, and these can be ignored. The sources for assizes and quarter sessions are all Q/S (quarter sessions) series in the Staffordshire Record Office and all Staffordshire assize records in the ASSI series for the western circuit in the Public Record Office.

179. For the national rates, see Hay, "Master and Servant in England," 260.

accused workers to accused thieves appearing before the magistrates was 89 percent.[180]

It might be argued that such high ratios removed some of the stigma, but workers continued until 1867 to feel the force of the carceral state. We have seen (Table 2.1) that justices and petty sessions before 1858, when the statistics begin, showed wide variation in the proportion of accused and convicted servants they sent to prison. The fullest sources tended to have rates of 5 to 17 percent of accused servants ending up in prison (although the rate for London apprentices was 35 percent). Of those servants actually convicted, 25 to 33 percent were incarcerated.[181] Comparing the national statistics for the whole country between 1858 and 1867 (when imprisonment largely ended), the proportion of accused workers ending up in prison varied between 14 and 16 percent; of those actually convicted of breach of contract, 22 to 30 percent were incarcerated.[182] It appears, then, that the more penal regime of master and servant that was created by the expansion of prisons, policing, and hard labor in the early nineteenth century continued almost until the very end.[183]

The Judges and an Increasingly Oppressive Legal Regime

In England in the nineteenth century, the law of master and servant itself apparently became more inequitable in its doctrine than it had been in the previous century. The high-court judges heard more cases about labor contracts, and they did so in a period, from 1800 to 1850, when "freedom of contract," notably a will theory of contract, was reaching its apogee and permeating the courts' reasoning in many areas of law. Its consequences for the common law of master and servant were many.[184] In the early decades of the nineteenth century the court of King's Bench was particularly active in changing master and servant law. An understanding of how much was changed can be seen

180. SRO Q/SB, Chief Constable's Return of Summary Convictions, 1858 and 1859.

181. Edgar, Tew, London 1787 apprentices, Yate, Whitbread, Allen.

182. Between 1867 (when most imprisonment ended) and 1875 (when fines also ended), imprisonment rates of accused workers varied between 3.6 and 7.5 percent nationally, and of convicted workers, between 5.7 and 12.4 percent.

183. It is possible that imprisonment for nonpayment of fines may actually have increased the proportion of convicted persons who went to prison: see Table 2.1 (Sleaford 1866, Berkeley 1866–71). It is not clear in the national statistical tables for 1858 to 1875, or in the instructions given for completing the returns, how such imprisonment was recorded.

184. I shall discuss other aspects of the case law in more detail in other publications. For a recent overview and interpretation over the long term, see Deakin, "The Contract of Employment"; for questions litigated in the nineteenth century, see Steinfeld, *Coercion*; for the origins of that litigation, see Frank, "Warrington Cases," and Frank, "Constitutional Law."

from a comparison with the doctrines of the eighteenth-century judges. An illustration is the doctrine of dismissal.

The eighteenth century had seen some expansion of the rights of masters. Reversing old doctrine, Lord Mansfield (chief justice, 1756–88) decided in 1777 that a master could dismiss an unmarried pregnant servant without application to a magistrate: to keep the unwed mother in the house "would be *contra bonos mores*, and in a family where there are young persons both scandalous and dangerous."[185] This was, however, seen as an exception. The general authority for magistrates was s.5 of the Statute of Artificers, reprinted in a great many justices' manuals:

> [N]o person which shall retain any servant, shall put away his or her said servant . . . unless it be for some reasonable and sufficient cause or matter *TO be allowed before two justices of peace, or one at the least* . . . or the mayor or other chief officer . . . to whom any of the parties grieved shall complain . . . which said justices . . . shall have and take upon them . . . the hearing and ordering of the matter.[186]

In the 1770s an expert in the field noted that the question of dismissal had not been before the courts much in the recent past, except for a case in 1753 and another in 1773. In the former, the court held that a discharge was illegal because it was not made by a justice.[187] Lord Mansfield tended to continue to deny the right of a master to dismiss on his own authority. In a 1773 case he declared (in a typically sweeping general dictum), "No person can be judge

185. *R v. Inhabitants of Brampton* (1777), Cald. 11. The social significance of the pregnant servant is discussed in Hill, *Servants*, ch. 3. See above for Chief Justice Heath's 1633 requirement for dismissal of the pregnant servant only by a justice, reprinted in Dalton until 1747; for the genesis of *Brampton*, see Steedman, "Lord Mansfield's Women." The argument of counsel for the crown was that 5 Eliz. c.4 applied to maidservants, "and therefore at least the intervention of a magistrate is necessary: without it, the contract could not legally be dissolved; nor is there any authority to support the contrary doctrine. . . . a master has not any such authority by law vested in himself" (12). The reporter of the case supports this argument in his notes but concludes that whether the jurisdiction of the justices extended beyond servants in husbandry, and whether masters on their own authority could dismiss on reasonable cause, "though there are authorities to show that he cannot, seems . . . from this case, not to be fully and absolutely settled" (14 note c). He admitted, however, that general practice, especially in large towns, was for masters to exercise such a power. He noted also that lawyers were raising a notable quibble: over the word TO emphasized in the quotation (below at note 186) from the Statute of Artificers: some cited the passage as "OR be allowed . . ."

186. (England) 5 Eliz. c.4 (1562) s.5 (emphases added). As well as justices' manuals, the clause was reprinted without comment in such works as *The Gentleman's Assistant, Tradesman's Lawyer, and Country-man's Friend* (3rd ed., London, 1720), 428; Giles Jacob, *The Compleat Parish-Officer* (London, 1744), 166; etc.

187. *R. v. Tardebigg* (1753), Sayer 100 and Burr. Settl. Cas. 322. See also the note in Cald. 13, note a.

in his own cause; and this first principle could not be meant to be overturned by any law or usage whatsoever."[188] He disregarded evidence that it was, in fact, the general custom in London.[189]

His 1777 decision against the pregnant servant arose from his hatred of sexual impropriety: he insisted on using the word "criminal" to describe the acts of both parents of a bastard child,[190] and he considered the master certainly had the authority to dismiss where a crime had been committed.[191] But in general, where an occupation was found to be within the statutes giving jurisdiction to magistrates, he stated that a lawful discharge could only be made by a justice.[192]

Mansfield's successor, Lord Kenyon (chief justice, 1788–1802), significantly strengthened the doctrine that approval of a magistrate was mandatory. He would not allow even Mansfield's exception of crime: "Where indeed the servant commits a crime, the master may apply to a justice to have him discharged; but if no such application be made, the relation of master and servant subsists."[193] Kenyon was a traditionalist in many ways, and also a popular

188. *Temple v. Prescott* (1773), cited Cald. 14.

189. The fact that the unwed mother in *Brampton* was a domestic servant also raised some questions in the minds of lawyers, because cases earlier in the century had suggested that only servants in husbandry fell under the Statute of Artificers, the source of the power of justices in such cases. In *R. v. Welford* Cald. 57 the following year (involving an unwed father) it was made clear that the servant was in husbandry "to take it out of the case of the *King* versus *Brampton*," probably in case *Brampton* could be explained by the fact that justices did not have jurisdiction over domestic servants; the case was not finally determined.

190. In *Brampton* he repeatedly denounced the behavior as "criminal," although counsel pointed out that it should not be so categorized. See also *R. v. Inhabitants of Westmeon* (1781), Cald. 129 at 134; *R. v. Inhabitants of North Cray*, 4 Dougl. 243 at 244.

191. Cald. 17.

192. There is a possible technical explanation for this doctrine. All these cases concerned settlement: whether a pauper was owed relief by one or another parish as his or her "parish of settlement." A settlement could be gained by a valid hiring for a year; hence a valid discharge for cause before the completion of the year's employment destroyed the claim to settlement and poor relief (throwing the obligation back on a previous parish of settlement). The cases I have cited were all litigated by the parishes concerned, not by masters and servants. And in evaluating what was a valid from an invalid discharge, often made years before, the high court had a strong incentive to look for the best evidence. "Fraud infects everything in these cases," Lord Hardwicke once said, and therefore a determination made by a justice, after a hearing, was among the best kinds of evidence. It was therefore convenient for the judges to insist that a valid dismissal for cause could not be established by the act of the master alone but only by the magisterial oversight prescribed by 5 Eliz. c.4. Whether that is the case, the argument that the judges were also enunciating an ideal of social ordering, an ideal that also possessed the legislature, can also be sustained, as Kenyon's stance suggests. Reported appeal cases of wage claims by servants on grounds of lack of a proper discharge before a magistrate would be very helpful. I have not found such cases for this period. Certiorari was not allowed under the 1746 act, but the cost of high-court litigation in the eighteenth century may be sufficient explanation.

193. *R. v. Inhabitants of Sutton* (1794), 5 TR 659. See also *R. v. Hulcott* (1796), 6 TR 583 at 587.

chief justice, enjoying a reputation as a paternalist and protector of the poor. His decisions in a wide range of cases fit the picture of a judge actively seeking to make the law a social censor and arbiter between the claims of different classes of men.[194] He was exacting about committals by magistrates, freeing men committed loosely as vagrants or under master and servant statutes.[195] In other labor cases, prosecutions for conspiracy to break the combination laws, he was indulgent toward the defense.[196] By the end of Kenyon's career as chief justice (he died in 1802), a popular treatise on employment law noted that "Neither for rudeness, or other misbehaviour of servants, can the master discharge him before the end of his term; nor can the servant leave his master on account of ill treatment by the master or mistress; but in these and like cases, application must be made to a justice for a discharge as directed by the statute of Elizabeth."[197] At the end of the century, then, the traditional authority and role of the justice of the peace was emphasized. It was reiterated in all the justices' manuals. Whether it was expected to obtain in practice, everywhere, at all times, is doubtful; the manuals also reproduced much obsolete law, including other clauses of the Statute of Artificers.[198] But it was an assertion of a legal and social ideal, stamped with judicial authority at the highest level.

Under Kenyon's successor, Lord Ellenborough, chief justice from 1802 to 1818, a very different temper appeared in King's Bench. The traditional doctrine of dismissal was utterly repudiated in 1817, after a series of cases that transformed master and servant law in other ways also.

The coverage of the penal statutes was widened: in *Lowther v. Earl Radnor and another* (1806), the application of the 1746 statute was held to embrace laborers of every class, including those who would later be deemed to be outside master and servant law because they were independent contractors.[199] A few years later, in 1810, the 1766 statute was before the court in the case

194. See Hay, "The State and the Market," and my account of Kenyon, in Harrison, *Oxford Dictionary of National Biography*.

195. *R v. Rhodes* (1791), 4 TR 220, requiring proper conviction (not just committal) on the vagrant act (G.B.) 17 Geo.II c.5 (1743); *R v. T. Cooper* (1796), 6 TR 509, in which the court held that warrant of commitment under (G.B.) 6 Geo.III c.25 (1766) merely says charged, not convicted; prisoner discharged from custody.

196. Dobson, *Masters and Journeymen*, ch. 9.

197. J. B. Bird, *The Laws Respecting Masters and Servants*, 3rd ed. (1801), 3. The passage does not appear in the 1st ed. (1795).

198. Although in none of those cases does a late eighteenth-century treatise suggest they are in force, as Bird does re s.5.

199. *Lowther v. Earl Radnor and another* (1806), 8 East 113, 103 ER 287. For later expansion in the categories of workers over whom magistrates were given jurisdiction, see Steinfeld, *Coercion*, 125–53; for earlier instances, see the discussion above of domestic servants.

of a thirty-six-year-old coal miner from Tipton, Staffordshire, one Joseph Thompson. He had been sentenced to two months in the house of correction in 1810 for absenting himself from work.[200] His lawyers, undoubtedly working for the union, sought to obtain mandamus to force the justices at quarter sessions to entertain an appeal. The issue was important: the 1766 statute provided for an appeal to quarter sessions "except [on] an order of commitment," and in his case the conviction, on which he might have appealed, was included in the order. If this was general practice (and it appears from other evidence that it was), it precluded any appeals from committals to the house of correction under the statute, although minor issues of service or pay (and wage orders against masters) could be appealed. Lord Ellenborough declared the statutory basis for an appeal was absent, "and it does not become us to scan the wisdom of the provision which the Legislature have enacted."

The following year, in *R v. Hoseason* (1811) King's Bench refused to allow criminal proceedings against a Norfolk justice of the peace who had convicted his own servant for disobedience, sentenced him in a summary hearing to imprisonment and whipping, and then insisted on the full bloody punishment being carried out. When he appeared in King's Bench he enjoyed the support of other prominent Norfolk magistrates. Lord Ellenborough regretted that Hoseason had acted as judge in his own cause, but decided any other justice would have done the same. The case was decided in the opening months of Luddism, and it seems likely that the decision was intended to reinforce country magistrates' authority at a time of social crisis.[201]

Arguably the most important of these cases was decided in 1817. The notion of the "entire contract," by which a servant not completing a contract was held to have forfeited wages for the entire period of employment, while noted in sixteenth- and seventeenth-century sources, was not enunciated in employment cases in the eighteenth century.[202] It is doubtful that magistrates in earlier centuries actually enforced it fully, and some eighteenth-century high-court language appeared to contradict the doctrine. Its strong reaffirmation in *Spain v. Arnott* (1817) by Lord Ellenborough affected many ser-

200. *R v. Justices of Staffordshire* (1810), 12 East 572, 104 ER 223. The master of the house characterized his behavior there as "orderly": he had served his entire time before the case was heard.

201. *R v. Hoseason* (1811), 14 East 605, discussed in Hay, "Patronage, Paternalism, and Welfare," 40–44, and Hay, "Master and Servant in England," 245–46.

202. See above at note 67 on the earlier sources. On the doctrine (the timing of adoption or expansion, and in particular its application by magistrates, is still unclear), see Atiyah, *Rise*, 415 (who gives its origin as *Spain v. Arnott*); Tomlins, *Law, Labor and Ideology*, 273–78; Steinfeld, *Coercion*, 291–97. Even in the 1850s, however, only some judges in county courts were applying the entire contract rule always: Steinmetz, "De-juridification," 306–7.

vants adversely in the nineteenth century, including the hapless waggoner
who brought it, after losing his position by insisting on having his dinner. The
case was also a powerful endorsement of the authority of the master over the
servant at all times, and also apparent confirmation of the master's authority
to dismiss the disobedient servant without judicial intervention: "After a refusal on the part of the servant to perform his work, the master is not bound
to keep him on as a burthensome and useless servant to the end of the year. . . .
the question really comes to this, whether the master or the servant is to have
the superior authority."[203] The case, very briefly reported and innocent of
precedent, became the leading authority for the servant's subordination, and
for the entire contract doctrine in employment cases. Ellenborough's insistence that a master had the right to dismiss on his own authority simply repudiated the long line of cases calling for adjudication by a justice, most recently endorsed by Kenyon.

The significance of Ellenborough's decisions was great, because the pro-
nouncement of the high courts (notably King's Bench) had a cumulative and
ultimately very great impact on magisterial practice. There is an irony here.
As long as the law was not tested in the high court, earlier doctrines and
local practices, many of them originating before about 1750, when the state
made no apologies for interfering on behalf of both capital and labor, probably guided most magistrates. These included regular adjudication of quantum meruit, frequent application by servants to magistrates for redress, and
a degree of paternalism that reflected the custom of the trade, the custom
of the country, or the custom of the magistracy. Once the high court began
to declare some of these interpretations of the law invalid, and to publicize
such doctrines as the complete loss of wages for incomplete work, or the paramount authority of the master in even small matters of discipline, the magistracy had to take notice. Ironically, it was forced to do so in part because
from about the 1820s, and very often by the 1840s, as we have seen, reform-
ers, trade-union lawyers, and finally Parliament increasingly insisted upon the
magistracy following the letter of the law as pronounced by the judges. This
subordination to high-court direction undoubtedly benefited some workers
in the 1840s who in an earlier period would have had no remedy against magisterial discretion amounting to caprice and oppression. But it also meant that
in cases where common-law doctrine had become highly unfavorable to labor,
more working people felt its impact more directly.

The triumph of free market ideology in the high courts in the early nineteenth century also seems to have increased the importance of master and

203. 2 Stark 256, 171 ER 638.

servant at this time. A will theory of contract was wedded to the penal sanctions of master and servant, in a market that was increasingly oversupplied with unskilled labor. There was a complex interaction of law and enforcement. A great deal of punitive legislation, the expansion of the prison system, and changes in the composition of the magistracy all made the penal sanctions more severe. In the same years the use of written contracts, the legalization of disputes that often had been resolved in the past by somewhat disinterested country gentlemen, and the decisions of Lord Ellenborough and other judges simultaneously weakened the protections from arbitrary dismissal or wage abatements that master and servant legislation had to some extent provided earlier in the eighteenth century.

Historians of emancipation have noticed the way in which the creation of harsher imprisonment, including the introduction of the treadmill, created employment regimes that were arguably worse than the last decades of slavery itself.[204] What has been less noticed by historians of English labor law is that the Colonial Office supervision of the postslavery regimes included the advice that local laws could be less harsh than those controlling laborers in England, where the law was allegedly moderated by its mild administration.[205] British workers, who by the 1830s compared their lot with that of West Indian slaves, and found themselves on treadmills like those in the colonies, were not so sure.[206]

The Last Years

It may be that master and servant law was most oppressive in the 1830s, when slavery was being replaced by harsh regimes of "apprenticed labour" elsewhere in the empire.[207] The 1840s stand out as a period when the English unions successfully contested master and servant law in both political and legal arenas. The 1844 attempt to extend the existing penal law to new groups of workers failed.[208] Throughout that decade a few able and politically committed solicitors, notably W. P. Roberts, actively defended union members in magistrates' courts with considerable success.[209] Roberts's tactic of feeing

204. Paton, "Penalties of Freedom"; Worden, "Between Slavery and Freedom," 128; Turner in this volume.

205. Green, "Emancipation to Indenture," 100.

206. Cunliffe, *Chattel Slavery and Wage Slavery.*

207. The only continuous statistics dealing with this period of which I am aware are those for committals of apprentices to the London Bridewell, where much higher rates are found between 1834 and 1842 (above).

208. Frank in this volume.

209. Frank, "Warrington Cases," and Frank, "Constitutional Law." The expanding bar, and

counsel to argue cases in Queen's Bench on writs of habeas corpus and certiorari had the effect of making master and servant law suddenly far more complex, and magistrates much more uncertain about their powers. His success with the judges incidentally made his clients, including many Chartists, unexpectedly enthusiastic supporters of the high-court judges. Then legislation in 1848 made it much more difficult to bring such appeals, and the high courts in the 1850s showed themselves much less willing to question the application of the more penal parts of the law on the grounds that contracts were void or committals technically deficient.[210] The continuing conflict in the courts, and the case law it generated as the modern contract of employment emerged, is now known in much more detail than before.[211]

By 1857, when the potter William Baker was spared repeated imprisonment by Baron Pollock, the law of master and servant had been under sustained attack by the unions for several decades. From 1858 its place in the criminal and labor law of England was registered in the annual judicial statistics; plotted, the sinuous line of convictions is fairly closely correlated with the business cycle, increasing in times of labor scarcity.[212] The largest number of convictions was recorded in the last years of the law. Master and servant acts remained important until concerted trade union protest and a widening working-class franchise made abolition possible. Until then it served masters everywhere. It disciplined low-wage rural workers and sustained class relations on the land. It held skilled industrial workers to their contracts when demand for their labor was rising, crippled strikes, and supported employer authority in all its dimensions.[213] The final move to civil contract appears in the statistics. With the 1867 Master and Servant Act, fines replace almost all imprisonment; after the 1875 Employers and Workmen Act, employment offenses disappear from the criminal returns. In the same year Parliament legitimized trade unions.[214] Half a millennium of penal employment law ended in England, but in much of the Empire it flourished.

---

the role of a generation of radical lawyers, needs further investigation in other decades. On the demography of the English bar, see Duman, *English and Colonial Bars*.

210. Frank, "Warrington Cases," and Frank, "Constitutional Law."

211. Simon, "Master and Servant"; Steinmetz, "De-juridification"; Deakin, "Contract of Employment"; Steinfeld, *Coercion*. American work that discusses English doctrine includes Orren, *Belated Feudalism*; Steinfeld, *Invention*; and Tomlins, *Law, Labor, and Ideology*.

212. For a preliminary analysis of some of these later statistics, see Hay, "Master and Servant in England." Steinfeld, *Coercion*, notes the correlation of prosecutions with the business cycle. A study with similar conclusions, based on press reports rather than official statistics, is Woods, "The Operation of the Master and Servants Act."

213. Steinberg, "Capitalist Development."

214. (U.K.) 30&31 Vict. c.141 (1867), (U.K.) 38&39 Vict. c.90 (1875). Steinmetz, "De-juridification," describes the administration of the law in England from the 1850s, and after 1875.

THREE

Early British America, 1585–1830

Freedom Bound

Christopher Tomlins

In 1614, when England's colonization of the American mainland was still in its infancy, the Elizabethan adventurer John Smith wrote passionately of the many "commodities, pleasures, and conditions" that America offered all those willing to pledge "labour and diligence." Smith's contemplation of widespread opportunity owed much to his excited anticipation of the new world's unprecedented natural abundance. Of equal importance, however, were his hopes for a world of unprecedented freedom from others' coercion. "Here are no hard landlords to racke us with high rents, or extorted fines . . . no tedious pleas in law to consume us. . . . So freely hath God and his Maiesty bestowed those blessings on them that will attempt to obtain them, as here every man may be master and owner of his own labour and land; or the greatest part in a small time."[1]

To many historians of labor in early British America, Smith's anticipation of the migrating everyman quickly made his own master will seem naive, if not downright misleading. Historians identify indentured servitude, not freedom, as the foundational reality of working life awaiting the European settler in the mainland colonies. And, although it is recognized that work in early America took a profusion of forms—wage work, independent production, and household production as well as servitude and slavery—it has been argued that nonetheless *all* performers of labor were alike in one transcendent essential, being subject to criminalized discipline, and hence all legally unfree.[2]

1. Arber and Bradley, *Smith*, 1:195–96, 197. See also S. Innes, "Smith's Vision," 3.
2. On servitude as the normal state of migrant labor, see Abbott Smith, *Colonists in Bondage*, 4, 3; McCusker and Menard, *British America*, 242, 238ff. On legal unfreedom as the "default"

Such views require qualification. Migrant indentured servitude was a crucial component in mainland British America's original work regimes and a majority of European migrants to mainland America throughout the seventeenth and eighteenth centuries did arrive as indentured servants. But high rates of natural increase in the white creole (native-born) population, on the one hand, and increasing rates of importation and natural increase of enslaved Africans, on the other, left indentured migrant labor of diminishing significance in the total working population well before the end of the seventeenth century. Given, in addition, that in most areas of settlement "most of the labor available . . . was family labor," one must question whether bound labor per se should be accorded the distinctive influence in mainland America's legal culture(s) of work.[3]

The notion that the legal culture of work was primarily a culture of generic unfreedom must also be reexamined. Alongside the statutory regimes defining indentured servitude and later slavery, one encounters law that recognized other, voluntary, work relations. Work's legal culture was not uniform and unfree, but highly differentiated.

This chapter offers the beginnings of a reconsideration of law and work in early America. By no means all the threads begun here are tied. Neither slave nor household relations, for example, receive here the degree of attention appropriate to their parts in a differentiated legal culture of work. The primary goal is one of ground clearing, to demonstrate the existence of historical questions that cannot satisfactorily be answered by allusion either to the ubiquity of servitude or to the reception of generic regimes of "master and servant" law from a colonizing metropolis.

I proceed by way of an examination of selected colonial statutory regimes, then of selected county court proceedings, each drawn from one of the

---

status of all labor, see Steinfeld, *Invention*, 3–5; Grubb, "Bound Labour," 29; Orren, *Belated Feudalism*, 4.

3. Rough estimates of the incidence of indentured servitude in total population have placed it below 10 percent by the later seventeenth century. See Abbott Smith, *Colonists in Bondage*, 336; Grubb, "Immigrant Servitude," 796. My own detailed estimates can be found in "Reconsidering Indentured Servitude." Summarizing, that article suggests that some 54 percent of all European migrants to the mainland (including convicts) were committed to an initial period of servitude, that the proportion of servants in total migration was substantially higher in the seventeenth century (60–65 percent) than the eighteenth (40 percent), and that the incidence of indentured servants in total colonial population did not exceed 10 percent at any point after 1675 and declined throughout the eighteenth century. See also Jones, *Colonial Wealth*, 3:1787, table 4.21 (servants 2.3 percent of the population by 1770s). These results contest Robert Steinfeld's contention that it was not until the last quarter of the eighteenth century that the incidence of indentured servitude had declined to "no more than a small fraction of the total labour force in any colony." Steinfeld, *Invention*, 11.

three principal regions of early settlement: the Chesapeake (Virginia, York County), New England (the Massachusetts Bay colony, Essex County), and the Delaware Valley (Pennsylvania, Chester County). This examination reveals not a generic legal regime enforcing a basic division between people who worked and people for whom they worked, but a variety of legal forms exhibiting a range of outcomes. Local statutes were the single most important determinant of those outcomes: as one might expect courts in each case were guided by the particular colony's legislation. But where statutes did not apply, courts constructed rules. They did so not by following on what historians have taken to be concurrent English law, but rather by paying attention to the nuances of local status and work practice.

The Chesapeake: Virginia and York County

Virginia's earliest history was shaped by three factors: environment, experience, and the designs of its Elizabethan promoters. The Chesapeake environment was hostile. Disease, dearth, and volatile relations with the region's indigenous inhabitants were constants throughout the half century following the first, temporary, settlement of the English at Roanoke in 1585. Itself the first transoceanic expression of Tudor-Stuart expansionism, Roanoke had parallels in the armed manors that Tudor adventurers had already established in Ireland. Autonomous "authoritarian settlements . . . centrally planned and highly structured colonies on classical and military lines," these were plantations designed for a migrant tenantry of soldier-farmers. Like their Chesapeake successors they were attempts to realize an idealized conception of social organization impossible in diverse, swarming England—a disciplined hierarchy organized in precise functional ranks of leaders and led.[4]

Reality was messier. The Irish plantations were far from models of disciplined settlement. Nor were the English migrants who returned to reestablish their Virginia outpost in 1607 experienced *coloni* soldier-farmers, but were predominantly gentry "cocooned" in status and unprepared for work. When promoters scoured for labor to keep the settlement viable during Jamestown's first decade, they found themselves forced to draw upon those very elements in England whose lack of social discipline they most feared and despised: vagrant children from the streets of London, convicts and rebels, wandering adolescent farm servants.[5]

It was the expansion of tobacco cultivation and the growing local demand

---

4. Canny, "Permissive Frontier," 17–44, at 18.
5. Morgan, *American Slavery*, 84ff.

for labor imports in the years after 1617 that truly set the stage for early Virginia's legal culture of work. An ad hoc contrivance that emerged piecemeal during the thirty years following the establishment of the Virginia Assembly in 1619, that legal culture was a local creation that responded to local contexts by drawing selectively on elements of English law.

The first step taken by the Assembly simply required the recording of indentures of servants departing England and made provision for their enforcement in Virginia. Without written agreements, planters had no legal means to retain immigrants in servitude longer than the one year customary in England — insufficient recompense for the cost of transporting settlers and maintaining them while in service.[6] The statute marked imported servants as a distinct segment of the population, but detailed attention was not paid to their legal status until the 1630s, when their numbers began to mount. In its first decade the Assembly was less concerned with defining the condition of indentured labor than controlling the costs of hired labor, selecting from among the many provisions of the Statute of Artificers[7] those which empowered magistrates to assess wages and which forbade laborers and artificers to leave work unfinished "unlesse it be for not payinge of his wages."[8]

By the early 1640s these hired labor statutes appear no longer in force, for they were not included in either the 1642 or 1652 Assembly restatements of Virginia law. Simultaneously the Assembly's attention turned to indentured servitude, establishing it as a distinct condition of explicit subordination.[9] Any action that implied an infringement of the immediate master's jurisdiction — absconding, clandestine marriage, fornication — became liable to severe punishment.[10] Servants had few legislated rights, the Assembly merely allowing them to take grievances before justices.[11] It also enacted the first statutory terms for servants migrating without indentures (four years if over twenty; five years if over twelve, seven if under).[12]

6. Billings, "Servants and Slaves," 48. Economic historians have provided considerable evidence for the "efficiency" of markets in indentured labor, by which is meant the rational adjustment of contract length to costs of passage and maintenance, and variations in human capital. See, generally, Galenson, *White Servitude*; Grubb, "Indentured Immigrants." Unfortunately little of this work covers the first half of the seventeenth century.

7. (England) 5 Eliz. c.4 (1562).

8. (Virginia) 7 Car.I n.30 (1631).

9. Court records from the 1630s and early 1640s indicate that hired workers and some artisans were ordered to perform agreed terms of service, or agreed tasks, but such orders peter out after the early 1640s: Tomlins, *Law, Labor, and Ideology*, 250 nn. 85 and 86.

10. (Virginia) 18 Car.I n.20 (1642); (Virginia) 18 Car.I n.21 (1642); (Virginia) 18 Car.I n.22 (1642).

11. (Virginia) 18 Car.I n.22 (1642).

12. (Virginia) 18 Car.I n.26 (1642).

Virginia's existing servant statutes were reaffirmed in the third general revision of colony statutes undertaken in March 1651/2, just as the colony was entering upon its heaviest period of migration. Evidence from the colony's fourth general revision of statutes (1662) shows that the subject was given further detailed attention during the 1650s. By 1662 the original measures dealing with wage fixing and the performance of contracts by laborers and artisans had long since disappeared. Provision for specific performance of labor contracts by free persons was confined to migrants. In the case of indentured servants, all the familiar restrictions remained in place, although the physical disfigurement (branding and hair cropping) of persistent runaways was discontinued. The default terms of servants imported without indenture continued to vary, those above sixteen now required to serve five years, those below until age twenty-four. For the first time, however, servants had gained specific protections in an enactment that ordered "compotent dyett, clothing and lodging," required "moderation" in correction of servants, and once more emphasized court oversight.[13] In 1677 masters were foreclosed from renegotiating indentures with their servants outside the presence of a justice.

The 1662 "restatement" of colony servant law remained in place until the passage, in 1705, of An Act concerning Servants and Slaves.[14] The previous thirty years had seen a momentous transition in the sources of Virginia's noncreole labor supply, beginning in the years after Bacon's Rebellion (1676), from youthful British servants to enslaved Africans. The 1705 act was a hybrid statute, drawing on the piecemeal measures of the previous forty years, passed to accommodate a bound labor force of increasingly bifurcated character. Beginning from the position that "servant" meant "imported servant," the statute defined slaves as a distinct category of imported servants, namely all those who were not Christians at their time of entry into Virginia.[15] As first provided in 1662, children born in Virginia were to be "bond or free, according to the condition of their mothers."[16] Powers and duties common

13. (Virginia) Acts 98, 100–105 (March 1661/2), in Hening, *Statutes at Large*, II, 113–19 (hereafter *SL*). Between 1660 and 1720 self-identified "servants" entered 115 petitions before the York County Court seeking redress in one or other aspect of their relationship with their masters. Of these 80 (70 percent) were successful and 15 (13 percent) were unsuccessful. In the remaining 20 cases (17 percent) the outcome was either ambiguous or went unrecorded. If the no-result cases are excluded, we can record a success rate of 85 percent. See York County Transcripts, Deeds Orders and Wills, III–XVI (hereafter DOW). In Maryland (1652–1797), servants have been identified as successful in 86.5 percent of the petitions they presented to the county courts (163 recorded decisions, 1652–1797) and 74.6 percent of those presented to provincial courts (59 recorded decisions, 1658–85). See Daniels, "Liberty to Complaine."

14. (Virginia) 4 Anne n.49 (1705).

15. This definition was first established in (Virginia) n.1 of 1682. See Guild, *Black Laws*, 46.

16. (Virginia) n.12 (Dec. 1662), in *SL*, II, 170; Brown, *Good Wives*, 135–36.

to all relations of servitude were specified, but particular discriminations in treatment and in the obtaining of redress were confirmed: thus, masters were forbidden to "whip a christian white servant naked"[17] but could brutalize a slave without fear of retribution. Servants, but not slaves, could complain to a justice of a master's neglect of duty, or mistreatment, or nonpayment of wages. Servants were also held entitled to maintenance if sick during their term of service, to freedom dues at the end of it, and to the protection of the courts in renegotiating indentures.

The creation of distinct legal categories (European or African, Christian or non-Christian) managed the substantial shift under way in the composition of *imported* bound labor. They implied that native-born whites formed yet a third, wholly free, civic category. In the statute this remained somewhat ambiguous, in that some provisions stretched beyond clearly "imported" persons to encompass persons "become servants of their own accord here, or bound by any court or church-wardens."[18] Amendments in 1726 shed further light. By this time the transformation of the bound labor force to one based on racial slavery was complete: the amendments altered the law dealing with runaways in a fashion that implied runaways would almost invariably be black. Clauses punishing refusals to work and misrepresentations of ability on the part of tradesmen and workmen "on wages" were confined in scope entirely to migrants. Thus the 1726 statute strengthened the association of whiteness and freedom, while allowing importation as a partial (and temporary) exception.[19] The Assembly confirmed the approach twice more (1748, 1753), revising the provisions of the 1705 code applying to white labor in ways that made it unmistakably a code of labor imported under indenture.[20]

The course of Virginia's statutory servant law shows that the legal character of indentured servitude emerged piecemeal as the practice itself became a reliable means for facilitating large-scale transoceanic transfers of

17. (Virginia) 4 Anne n.49 (1705). This prohibition had long since entered case law. See Complaint of Mary Adney against Jno Wright "for barbarous usage to her" (24 April 1683), York County, DOW, VI, 493–94.

18. (Virginia) 4 Anne n.49 (1705). "Servants of their own accord" ensured coverage of creole apprentices, who do not appear as a distinct legal category in Virginia until "apprenticeship" was incorporated in the revision of the statute, (Virginia) 22 Geo.II n.14 (Oct. 1748). Persons bound by courts and church wardens means paupers and criminals. The penalty provisions applied to servants for terms defined by "indenture, custom, or former order of court." Custom here means "custom of the country," the court-denominated term of service for migrants (overwhelmingly adolescents) entering Virginia without means to pay their passage or previously negotiated indentures.

19. (Virginia) 12 Geo.I c.4 (1726). In his *Office and Authority of a Justice of Peace* (Williamsburg, 1736), at 281–87, Webb reproduces the law of servant as well as slave runaways, but all his form examples assume the subject will be a Negro.

20. (Virginia) 22 Geo.II n.14 (Oct. 1748); (Virginia) 27 Geo.II n.7 (Nov. 1753).

youthful migratory labor and policing their activities once arrived. Virginia's "bastard-manorialism" provided the initial cultural context in which servitude's legal form developed, and its associated characteristics—authoritarian idealizations of hierarchical social relations, the dispersal of population on isolated plantations—continued to hinder the development of a public sphere, producing master-servant relationships initially cut off from anything other than perfunctory oversight. As Virginia's institutional complexity increased, servitude took on a more closely observed and regulated character. But its early form—hierarchical, youthful, and extended—remained a constant.

Ostensibly similar to English farm service in its enlistment of youthful workers in agricultural production, legally Virginia servitude owed less to farm service than to the explicit bindings of parish servitude (orphan or pauper apprenticeship) and to the law of vagrancy and its obsession with control of the mobile, the deviant, and the unruly young.[21] But if indentured servitude's development as a legal category distanced it from English farm service, it also distanced it from creole work relations. In Virginia, legal subordination to the authority of a master became a condition identified not only with youth, but also with persons imported from elsewhere, rather than with anyone who undertook "work" at large. More obvious in the case of slavery's bestowal of conditions of comparative elevation upon the unenslaved, one can nevertheless see well before the end of the seventeenth century complementary civic distinctions—youth or adult, migrant or creole, bound or free—wrought into the legal culture of work as a consequence of the presence of indentured servitude.

Slavery, nevertheless, finally enabled Virginians to achieve a stable relationship between work and civic status. In the wake of Bacon's Rebellion, planter elites had been torn between the need to secure and the need to appease their unruly white indentured labor force. The turn to a largely enslaved plantation labor force enabled them to pursue security and white appeasement simultaneously. "White men received political recognition as providers, masters and potential patriarchs." The enslaved were defined as incapable of enjoying any such status. "By the early eighteenth century, Virginia's political system had achieved a stability built on the division of white and black labourers . . . and an incipient Anglo-Virginian identity that rested precari-

---

21. See Ben-Amos, *Adolescence*, 59–60. In fact, the closest parallel to indentured servitude in early modern English law can be found in the husbandry apprenticeship clauses of (England) 5 Eliz. c.4 (1562) sections 18, 28. Generally, the statute law of indentured servitude in Virginia reflected a felt need to control dangerous adolescent youth—hence the impact of the failure of control represented by Bacon's Rebellion in 1676, and the resulting search for a replacement bound labor force and for civic accommodation with the existing one. Brown, *Good Wives*, 145–86. For England, see Griffiths, *Youth and Authority*.

ously upon the fragile bonds uniting white men."[22] In Virginia, the legal culture of work bestowed real civic capacity on everyman by becoming a legal culture of race.

YORK COUNTY, Virginia, occupies roughly half the lower peninsula between the James and York Rivers, an area of rich soils first entered by settlers in the 1620s and 1630s. Some 510 persons lived in the area when the county was created in 1634. At the end of the century the population was close to 2,000. Land distribution among freeholders was relatively even, but the population contained significant numbers of nonlandowners. Among tithables (all white males and all slaves above the age of sixteen), free heads of households outnumbered bound laborers until the late 1670s. At about the same time, slaves began to outnumber indentured servants.[23]

Records of York County's courts exist for most of the period from the county's founding, although before 1658 they are fragmentary and discontinuous. Work was a frequent subject. Proceedings arising from unfree relations were common, but others dealt with relations between free persons.[24]

Among disputes arising from unfree relations, historians have generally concentrated on those illustrating courts' coercive functions—the punishment of flight or other indiscipline. Indeed, these are constants of York's records. Take the case of William Keaton, bound by indenture in February 1641 to serve W. Hockaday five years, who "absenting himselfe [from] his sd master uppon pretence of being free . . . did runn away from his sd [master] June last to his great hinderance and damage." Keaton was ordered to serve "til the 28 Feb next accord. to indenture," and for his absence and also his "peremtory answeare [to] the Ct in refuseing the performance of [the order] herein" he was to receive thirty lashes "on his bare shoulders." Hockaday made no claim of time lost and thus received no "double the tyme of service soe neglected" as provided three years earlier for punishment of runaways. Double time "according to Act" was granted Thomas Curtis, however, whose servant Benjamin Hallyard "hath divers tymes runn away . . . to the number of 30 days." Hallyard was also sentenced to be whipped.[25]

Some early York entries suggest that in the 1640s the enforcement of service in Virginia did extend beyond migrant indentures to shorter-term local

22. Brown, *Good Wives*, 186.
23. See, generally, K. Kelly, "York County."
24. See, generally, DOW, I–XIX (1633–1746/7, with gaps); Judgments & Orders, I (1746/7–1765, with gaps); Order Books, I (1765–68); Judgments & Orders, II (1768–74); Order Books, II (1774–83); all located at Department of Historical Research, Colonial Williamsburg Foundation, Williamsburg, Va.
25. 25 Feb. 1645/6, in DOW, II, 101a; 25 Sept. 1646, in DOW, II, 169.

covenants. Take, for example, Edmund Smith who "hath divers Saturdayes absented himselfe from the servis of Mr John Chew being his covenant servant. It is therefore ord with the consent of the sd Smith that he shall serve the sd Chew twenty [day]es longer than by covenant hee is bound in consideration of his neglect." Here time was added to compensate for absence. Yet the proceeding stands apart from those involving multiyear indentures in two respects. First, the court made no mention of the statutory double-time provisions. Second, it required Smith's consent to the addition of time, which implies that other forms of compensation might also have been acceptable. John Duncombe's indenture of 30 July 1646, for example, had bound him to serve Nicholas Brooke one year or compensate him in tobacco "to the value thereof." When he did not perform, the court ordered with the consent of both parties that Duncombe arrange payment "of one thousand lbs tob on 20th Nov next in full consideration."[26] In enforcing covenants of service and assessing penalties—or compensation—for their neglect, the York court was already in the 1640s allowing that service could take different legal forms.

During the second half of the century the parameters of difference become easier to observe in the proceedings, which make clearer qualitative distinctions between indentured migrants and creole hirelings. In May 1674 Henry Jenkins sought recovery of a debt of 400 pounds tobacco and cask owed by one Richard Crane as wages for a year's service. Crane alleged that Jenkins had absented himself "a great part of his time." Had he been an imported indentured servant, Crane could have claimed double time for Jenkins's absences.[27] Had the court been governed by contemporary English law, Crane could have had Jenkins imprisoned. Certainly he could have expected abatement of the wages. Instead the court merely discounted the debt in proportion to Jenkins's absences and ordered payment for the time he had actually spent in Crane's employ. "Ord that he be paid but 200 lbs tobo. & ca. & costs als exec."[28] Similarly, Michaell Robbarts successfully recovered payment of a debt of corn and tobacco owed him by Mr. David Condon for service as an overseer, notwithstanding testimony of frequent absence offered by Condon and others.[29] When, in February 1690/1, one David Jenkins sued Captain James Archer under similar circumstances, and "itt evydently appearing in ct by the oathes of severall evydences that Jenkins did voluntarily leave his cropp before compleated, contrary to the condicons & w/out any occas-

26. 20 Oct. 1646, in DOW, II, 185; 24 Jan. 1647/8, in DOW, II, 322.

27. In imposing double-time penalties for absconding, the court would ritually cite the prior obligation to serve by indenture, custom, or court order. (See note 18.)

28. 25 May 1674, in DOW, V, 68. See also 6 May 1686, in DOW, VII, 163–64, 177–78.

29. 26 Jan. 1684/5, in DOW, VII, 6, 15–16.

sions of sd Archer," the suit was dismissed. There is no indication that any-one thought Jenkins could be restrained from departing, however, or that he could be punished for it.[30] Nor, when George Glascock refused to complete a term as laborer for William Cheseley, did Cheseley do anything more than "aske the sd Glascock what he would allow him and he would finish the crop and discharge the sd Glascock of any further trouble." The parties agreed on damages of 100 pounds of tobacco, which Glascock neglected to pay. This brought them to court, but in a civil action for recovery of the debt, not a criminal complaint against an absconding servant. Moreover, when Chese-ley failed to pursue the matter, the outcome was a nonsuit of 50 pounds of tobacco to Glascock.[31]

Such proceedings confirm clear distinctions in the way legal authority was made available to discipline the performance of work. These laborers and overseers were subject to a different legal regime than migrant servants im-ported under indenture, one that invoked no criminal sanctions to punish departures but instead placed disputes in a civil realm of compensatory ad-justments, one that did not treat contracts for services as entire but instead apportioned wages owed according to actual time worked.[32]

Further evidence comes from proceedings arising from statutory prohi-bitions on fornication and bastardy. By the statute of March 1661/2, anyone convicted of fornication, whatever their status, was liable to pay a fine of 500 pounds of tobacco. A servant woman convicted of bastardy, however, was in addition to serve "two yeares after her time by indenture is expired" or pay her master 2,000 pounds of tobacco.[33] Pregnancy, childbirth, and maternal care all represented intrusions upon a master's command of a servant's covenanted time, compensated by additional time.

In certain bastardy cases, however, persons described as servants, but who were not indentured, were not required to serve compensatory time. When another paid their fine on their behalf, the court might specify service to re-pay the debt, as indeed it might specify service for any debtor without mone-tary resources. But the defendant had to consent, and the service was not in itself a penalty. Thus, Elizabeth Mullins, "servant woman to Mrs Elish. Vaulx" and summonsed for bastardy, was fined 500 pounds of tobacco for for-

30. 24 Feb. 1690/1, in DOW, IX, 1. On freedom to depart, see also the deposition of Henry Shittle, 24 Mar. 1684/5, at DOW, VII, 59.

31. 24 Apr. 1685, DOW, VII, 69.

32. For a contrary view, see Steinfeld, *Invention*, 47-48, where it is argued that "ordinary agreements to enter service" differed little in their legal effects from the indentures that bound migrants. Steinfeld's analysis, however, relies on interpretation of statutes, not on research in local case law.

33. (Virginia) 14 Car.II n.100 (1661).

nication "and is willing to serve her sd Mrs Vaulx halfe a [year] Mrs Vaulx by her note to the Ct obligeing herselfe to pay" the fine. Vaulx testified that Mullins's child "was borne in her servitude," though Mullins was "free before I had her to Court."[34] Again, in May 1709 Rachel Wood, "English servant woman" to Mongo Ingles, was ordered to serve "one whole year after her time by indenture custom or former order is expired" for bastardy, but the order was later rescinded, for "on consideracon of the law in that case . . . [the Court] are of oppinion that (the sd Woods time by indenture being expired) there is no service due to her master." Wood's obligation was subsequently reinstated, once Ingles showed that her indenture had not expired, but this outcome only reinforces the lesson that local law treated indentured servitude as a distinct category of working relationship.[35]

Consider finally the evidence of disputes arising from the performance or nonperformance of promises to undertake work. In 1632, the Virginia Assembly adopted a provision of the Statute of Artificers by requiring artificers or laborers retained "in greate" to perform "uppon penaltie of one mounthes imprisonment" and a statutory penalty payable to the party aggrieved, in addition to damages and costs.[36] There is no indication that the Assembly statute remained in effect beyond the early 1640s, but York records in the 1660s and 1670s do furnish isolated examples of orders to perform contracts.[37] None of these proceedings specified what sanction backed the order, and none invoked any criminal penalty, but none allowed an alternative to performance except where mentioned in the original agreement.

Well before the end of the century, however, performance had ceased to be the sole course of action offered. In 1686, in a suit brought by Mr. Thomas Ballard Jr., Jeremiah Wing was ordered to "finish the glaseing work he was to doe & finish some considerable time hence," or pay damages of forty shillings and costs. More interesting than this was a case from August 1679. Thomas Sloper had been retained by Robert Spring to work "for halfes" with a servant of Spring's in sawing boards. Spring petitioned that "sd Sloper never came to worke . . . accord. to agreemt." Spring did not try to compel performance, claiming damages in mitigation. Witnesses confirmed both the bargain and Sloper's neglect. Once before a jury, however, the plaintiff's case was rejected and costs awarded the defendant.[38]

34. 24 Jan. 1680/1, DOW, VI, 279, 288.
35. 24 May 1708, DOW, XIII, 137; 24 May 1709, DOW, XIII, 216; 24 Jan. 1709/10, DOW, XIII, 263.
36. 8 Car.I n.28 (1632).
37. 12 Nov. 1666, DOW, IV, 111 (enforcement of a penalty clause); 10 Jan. 1670/1, DOW, IV, 306 (order to undertake work specified).
38. 6 May 1686, DOW, VII, 163; 24 Aug. 1679, DOW, VI, 114, 116.

The law of artisan work was revisited in the early eighteenth century in a tangle of damage and debt suits brought by Robert Hyde, housewright, against James Morris, a carpenter, in a dispute over unfinished carpentry work. The damage suits all alleged Morris's breaches of agreement and failures to perform. The debt action invoked "the statute of Queen Eliz made in the fifth year of her reigne entitled an act containing divers orders for artificers"—that is, the Statute of Artificers—to have Morris fined five pounds for the nonperformance and departure. Hyde alleged he had retained Morris "in order to finish the sd Hyde's inside work of his house so far as he the sd Hyde would have it done & to be payd therefore so much as it should be worth," that Morris had neglected Hyde's work, and that the work remained unfinished sixteen months later. Morris did not deny that the work was unfinished but brought in accounts for thirty-five days of carpentry work at five shillings per day. That is, Morris claimed a credit for the work he had performed in setoff against damages for the overall neglect. Hyde protested vehemently, stating that the contract was entire. He had "never agreed w/the sd Morris to work by the day." But the court allowed the setoff. As a result Hyde's suits netted him a grand total of nine shillings and sixpence. Hyde continued the punitive debt action, but in October 1705 the court threw it out.[39]

Like other cases involving accusations against artisans, overseers, and wage laborers departing or neglecting work, the Hyde-Morris affair underscores the absence of resort to criminal proceedings in cases involving unindentured labor. In situations where one might expect to encounter criminal sanctions—where, indeed, statutory criminal sanctions were express in English law—one finds none. Indeed, Hyde's is the only attempt to invoke the Statute of Artificers in 150 years of York County court records. His failure underscores the statute's irrelevance, even in the highly abbreviated form in which it had been adopted in 1632, and confirms that even that version did not survive the revisions of early Virginia law undertaken before midcentury.

Second, the outcome in these and earlier suits suggests the unpopularity in Virginia by the last quarter of the seventeenth century, if not before, of construing retainers of wage and artisan labor strictly as "entire" contracts. Morris, after all, was credited for work he had actually done, even though the thirty-five days were spread over sixteen months, were not accounted save as a lump sum, and had left the task he had undertaken unfinished. Where contracts were apparently held indivisible (almost always in relation to disputes over the completion of artisan work in the building or repair of houses)

39. (England) 5 Eliz. c.4 (1562). See, variously, 2 Mar. 1704/5, DOW, XII, 295 (continued through XII, 348); 24 Mar. 1704/5, DOW, XII, 322 (continued through XII, 448).

recovery was routinely allowed off the contract on a quantum meruit basis, with the net value of what had actually been accomplished determined by referees.[40] The only instances in the York records in which artisan labor is subjected to compulsion involve statutes that penalized indentured migrants for failing to exhibit craft skills they had claimed.[41]

Taken together, the Virginia statutes and York County records suggest that what developed in Virginia was not a generic legal culture of labor unfreedom but a stratified legal culture that accommodated distinct regimes of work and status, significantly more oppressive than those to be found in England for some, significantly less oppressive for others. By occupying the legal-cultural space of unfreedom, migrant servitude established a context— a base line, in effect, constituted by explicit legal obligations and procedures applicable to both parties—for the relatively greater autonomy of creole artisan and hireling labor. In this way, indentured servitude performed a role in early Virginia's legal culture not dissimilar from that which Edmund Morgan has famously attributed to slavery in the region's later colonial years. By furnishing an "other"—both materially and ideologically—it assisted forms of freedom to evolve.

New England: Massachusetts and Essex County

Labor, Stephen Innes argues, enjoyed substantially greater mobility in the economic culture of New England than in contemporary old England. Material conditions—the abundance of land relative to deployable workers—explain the opportunity for mobility, but local legalities were decisive in securing it. One response to scarcity, after all, is to restrict a resource's circulation. Indeed, early in the history of settlement in Massachusetts (as in Virginia), colonywide wage regulation was proclaimed on two occasions by the Massachusetts Court of Assistants. But the proclamations were as quickly rescinded. As to other English regulatory legislation, Massachusetts settlers simply did not receive it.[42]

The absence of carryovers from English law indicates that no metropolitan-standard legal culture of work was imported into Massachusetts. In good part, this was an outcome shaped in the early development of the

40. See, for example, the dispute between John Alford and Mr. Thomas Shelston over carpentry work done by Alford. 24 Jan. 1667, DOW, IV, 163 (continued through IV, 185).

41. See, for example, 17 May 1742, DOW, XIX, 99.

42. *Records of the Court of Assistants of the Colony of the Massachusetts Bay, 1630–1692* (Boston, 1904), 2:3, 36. S. Innes, *Creating the Commonwealth*, 175–80. See also Tomlins, *Law, Labor, and Ideology*, 241–49.

colony's legal culture. The Massachusetts Charter described a basis for civil authority in the commonwealth that rested substantially on the discretionary rule of leaders confined only by the ambit of activity "not repugnant to the laws and statutes" of England. In England local legal cultures actively refracted the sweep of metropolitan legalities, but in New England matters went further still, toward the founding of local legalities on "a popularly based determination to uphold rule by fundamental law." The relationship between people and law throughout the first generation of settlement is best represented in language that appears in the *Lawes and Libertyes* of 1648, as the product of a struggle over the "Countenance of Authoritie." The phrase signifies acceptance of the legitimacy of governmental rule over the lives, liberties, and properties of inhabitants, but simultaneously conveys two fundamental principles: that rule should have a definite basis or expression rather than be discretionary and mysterious; and, hence, that it should be knowable. This "Countenance of Authoritie" and the civic freedoms that embodied it constituted the colony's public sphere.[43]

Insofar as the *Lawes and Libertyes* defined the colony's legal culture of work, they sketched a set of relationships in which authority's countenance was as much protective as coercive. The earlier, and briefer, *Body of Liberties* had drafted liberties of servants that were exclusively concerned with the servant's welfare.[44] The *Lawes and Libertyes* codified these provisions verbatim, adding to them several more restrictive orders adopted piecemeal by the Court of Assistants and the General Court.[45] As a code of conduct for those in service, the *Lawes and Libertyes* recalled aspects of English law but with little of its detail and virtually none of its provisions subjecting hired labor to legal discipline. Only covenanted servants—those explicitly bound by written indenture or other form of explicit contract to furnish services on demand for a prescribed term—were clearly subject to restraint.

That statutory work disciplines should be thus circumscribed is not particularly surprising, given the local urge to hedge the operations of "authoritie." But the explanation lies also in the demography of the early New England

43. S. Innes, *Creating the Commonwealth*, 201, 204–15; Coquillette, "Radical Lawmakers," 179–211. On locality and legality in England, see Somers, "Relationality."

44. *Colonial Laws of Massachusetts. Reprinted from the Edition of 1672. With . . . the Body of Liberties of 1641*, edited by William H. Whitmore, Record Commissioner (Boston, 1890) (hereafter *Colonial Laws of Massachusetts*), Tit. "Liberties of Servants" (clause 85–88), protecting well-conducted servants from the "Tiranny and crueltie" of masters.

45. These prohibited servants from dealing in commodities without permission (1630), required "workemen" (paid by the day) to work a full day "alloweing convenient tyme for foode & rest" (1633), provided for the return of runaway servants (1635), allowed towns to assess wages (1636), allowed payment of wages in corn (1641), and enabled town constables to call upon artificers and handicraftsmen not otherwise employed to work in the harvest for wages (1646).

work force. The migrating population for whom the *Body* and the *Lawes* were prescribed was one of families, in which the capacity to labor was represented by the head of household and household dependents (wives and children), and unattached adolescent servants, laboring in return for passage and subsistence. Under these circumstances, disciplinable service took on a pronounced identification with two overlapping categories: "outsiders" and youth. The three kinds of people who could lawfully be subjected to the loss of liberty that servitude entailed were all in one form or another outsiders to the local community—"lawfull captives, taken in just warrs," that is, Indians; strangers who "willingly sell themselves, or are solde to us," that is, imported indentured servants and/or slaves; and finally persons "who shall be judged thereto by Authoritie," that is, persons temporarily cast out—convicted of criminal offenses, or delivered by court execution to serve creditors.[46] As to youth, as a practical matter at first, migrant indentured service effectively added up to youthful service. Then, when migration fell away after 1640, drying up the supply of imported servants, it left creole youth virtually the only source of deployable labor easily available to local inhabitants. Because youth was outside the community of household heads (and because youth is always everywhere considered simultaneously socially vulnerable and socially dangerous, and hence proper for restraint), justifications of its subjection to "authoritie" were relatively easy to come by, as they were not for adult males. Throughout the remainder of the colonial period, the propensity of statutes to identify disciplinable service almost exclusively with youth is one of the most prevalent characteristics of the legal culture of work in Massachusetts.[47]

ESSEX COUNTY, Massachusetts, abuts Massachusetts Bay, north of Boston. English settlement began in the late 1620s and during the 1630s settlers founded townships along the coast from Lynn in the south to Newbury in the north. By 1700 settlement had spread west across a rough rectangle of territory approaching 800 square miles in extent. Faithful to its geography, in which it was a microcosm of the region, this was a county whose people were largely dependent either on farming or on the sea for their livelihoods.[48] Landed or maritime, Essex County livelihoods were intensively laborious. They were also intensively social, requiring the concerted effort of several rather than the isolated labor of a single individual. As such, they could become intensively legal.

Essex County court records are substantially complete for the period from

46. *Colonial Laws of Massachusetts*, 4.
47. Tomlins, *Law, Labor, and Ideology*, 244–47.
48. Vickers, *Farmers and Fishermen*.

the courts' creation in March 1635/6 through the late seventeenth century.[49] The eighteenth-century record is less complete but still informative. As in Virginia, the records describe a legal culture of work that is overtly stratified. In Essex's case this was largely by age. Unlike Virginia, immigration quickly ceased to be a significant source of labor. Hence the distinction between creole and migrant had less salience. As in Virginia, hired labor was significantly freer from restraint than in contemporary England, but distinctive practices developing out of maritime wage work add a layer of legal relations wholly absent from the Virginia record. Finally, the Essex and York records appear to grow more distinctive over time. From the beginning the social relations of work that developed in the two regions were different, but with sufficient initial similarities to suggest that settlers enjoyed at least some points of common reference. By the end of the seventeenth century, however, the different characters of the regional populations, and of the local economies and local law they had produced, had resulted in very different legal cultures of work.

Certain of the work relations illustrated in the Essex record clearly belong in a category of unfree labor. Indentured servants, though demographically insignificant after the first decade, nevertheless furnished business for the court. Mostly this took the form of masters of servants seeking court-ordered punishments of servants for insubordination and court-ordered compensation for time lost to illegal departures from service. Whipping was the response to most servant offenses, whether absconding, insubordination, or drunkenness. Few early proceedings mention any addition of compensatory time — William Poole, servant to Colonel John Endicot (a justice of the peace) was the first runaway to be required to make up time lost.[50] Massachusetts never adopted statutory time-on penalties for runaways but left matters to the courts. The occasional court orders providing for compensatory service have as a result a discretionary quality quite distinct from the statute-guided routines of the Chesapeake.[51]

Essex court records confirm the close association of service and youth that we find everywhere in early America. William Dodge's runaway was a

49. Published as *Records and Files of the Quarterly Courts of Essex County, Massachusetts* (hereafter *RFQE*), vols. I–VIII, 1636–83 (Salem, 1911–21; repr. 1988), vol. IX, 1683–86 (Salem, 1975). See also Works Progress Administration, unpublished typed transcripts of the quarterly courts (hereafter WPAT) (Peabody-Essex Museum, Salem).

50. See *RFQE*, I, 3 (Sept. 1636), 4 (Dec. 1636), 5 (June 1637), 8 (June 1638), 9 (Sept. 1638).

51. The first statutory mention of compensatory service came in (Mass.) *Province Laws* c. 23 (1694–95), giving the court discretion to add up to one year's service in the specific case of "sons and servants" who deserted the service of parents or masters to enter on board any ship or vessel. A wider grant of discretion in (Mass.) *Province Laws* c.17 (1758–59) permitted courts "to order satisfaction to be made" by runaways "by service or otherwise, as to them shall seem meet."

"boy." Richard Gell, before the court for stealing in 1640, was "an apprentice boy." Benjamin Hammon, who slandered his master in December 1640, was "yong" and "rash."[52] As the record becomes more detailed, evidence increases of how strong the relationship was in early America between the legitimacy of restraint in service, indentures or other written authority, and youth. In the Essex record, however, the relationship again has a discretionary quality that underlines both the exceptional nature of migrant servitude and the ambiguities imparted to the legalities of "restraint" in servitude by the region's greater reliance on long continuities in family labor. Locally, "youth" meant roughly from age ten, when minors were considered able to earn their keep, until twenty-one, when males attained legal majority. Migrant servants tended to act as if attaining majority conveyed an immediate right to depart. But legal majority in Essex did not necessarily signify independence. The ambiguities could breed controversy, particularly because Massachusetts had no "custom-of-country" legislation defining "default" terms of service in the absence of indentures.

Consider Richard Coy, who had arrived in New England in 1638, aged about thirteen, with two elder siblings and several other juveniles. Coy became servant to William Hubbard but left him in 1645, claiming he was to serve only seven years. Hubbard, it was alleged, had told Coy, "hee shod not akept him agaynst his will Butt if you will stay with me still i will giue you wagges as to other men." But in court Hubbard claimed Coy was to have served ten years, not seven, or until age twenty-four, not twenty-one, and Coy was ordered to return to him (although he left again, permanently, well before the ten years were up). In renewed litigation Hubbard based his claim not on an indenture but on an amortization of his costs, which "cannot here be lesse worth than £15 or £16," adding "for a boy of 13 yeares of age to be layd out here for 10 yeares service cannot . . . seem injurious to ye servant or much advantageous to ye Master all wch considered it seemeth to mee the plaintiffe hath no cause to complaine." The court agreed. Similarities abound in the case of William Downing and Phillip Welch, arrested to court in 1661 for refusing to serve their master Samual Symonds. Both were "Irish youthes" who had been "stollen . . . out of theyr beds" in 1654 and sold into servitude. Now being "aboue 21 years of age" both refused to serve longer, "7 yeares seruice being so much as ye practise of old England, & thought meet in this place." Symonds claimed that both were to serve nine years (i.e., until approximately age twenty-four). He had no indenture but produced a covenant of sale to

52. *RFQE*, I, 4 (Dec. 1636), 18 (June 1640), 23 (Dec. 1640), and see also 25 (Mar. 1641), 27 (June 1641).

that effect. He also sought damages for time and work lost to their refusal to serve. A jury held in a special verdict that if the covenant of sale were legal the terms should stand, and this outcome was confirmed by the court. But it allowed Symonds no compensation, the servants' refusal and departure creating no additional grounds for recovery.[53]

Daniel Vickers has recently underlined the early New England farm economy's dependence upon the labor of children.[54] This was no English-style service-in-husbandry, nor was it plantation-style indentured servitude—New England farms generated neither the demand for continuous labor imports common to the plantation regions nor the revenues to pay for them. Instead, close-knit patriarchal households retained their own male children in generational subordination over an extended period of household dependency from late infancy through adulthood and beyond. Where the labor of offspring was insufficient the household might add an imported servant, but servants were supplemental, and their "careers" followed the dominant household-familial pattern, coming into households young and remaining over extended periods of time, rather than forming a distinct culture of work.[55]

If migrant servitude was an exceptional form for supplementary labor to take in Essex, slavery was even more so. Adult creole servitude was not unknown but as elsewhere it was confined to the discharge of debts and as a means of restitution for crime. Apprenticeship was a more common means of mobilizing youthful labor, and by the eighteenth century had become both the principal subject of Massachusetts' labor statutes, and a synonym for servant.[56] Apprenticeship was not confined to trade education, but was the means households used when they wished to convey a child's or youth's labor to others for an extended period.[57]

"Bound" labor, in Essex, thus meant the labor of children, debtors, and convicts. But children, debtors, and convicts were not the sum of the Essex

53. *RFQE*, I, 381–82 (Mar. 1655); II, 294–97, 310–11 (June 1661). See also WPAT, vols. III, VI. See also *William Deane v. Mr Jonathan Wade*, "for prosecuting him after the manner of a runaway, the plaintiff being free," *RFQE*, II, 62–63 (Mar. 1658), WPAT, vol. IV.

54. Vickers, *Farmers and Fishermen*, 52–60, 64–76, 82.

55. James Coleman, for example, joined William Cogswell's household approximately at age nine, and had remained there "15 yeares prentice and covenaunted servant." *RFQE*, VI, 68 (Sept. 1675). In his dispute with Symonds, Welch at one point offered to remain "if his master would give him as good a portion as any of his children." *RFQE*, II, 297 (June 1661). For a classic illustration of Massachusetts's pattern of partible inheritance, retention of children, and supplemental, life-cyclical service, see the evidence in litigation over the will of John Cogswell, *RFQE*, II, 307–8 (Sept. 1653); VI, 68 (Sept. 1675), 151–60 (June 1676); WPAT, vol. XXIII.

56. Tomlins, *Law, Labor, and Ideology*, 244–46.

57. In August 1644, for example, Ezekiell Wathen, a boy of about eight and a half years, was committed to Thomas Abre as an apprentice until he was twenty years old, "if his master live so long" with no further ado. *RFQE*, II, 72.

labor force. Farmers seeking additional assistance also had resort to adult hireling labor, though more often to each other. The latter could amount to no more than a mutual helping-out. Or it could comprise paid task work, such as the hiring of an artisan to undertake construction or repair of a house or a boat. Both forms of relation generated disputes, but these show little evidence of any resort to criminal law to underwrite employment commitments.

Hireling relations gave rise to several different kinds of dispute. Occasionally employers complained about excessive rates of pay. Only four such complaints were filed during the first forty years of court sessions in Essex, however, and only the first resulted in any material penalty.[58] Complaints against employers for nonpayment of wages were more frequent, arising in both agricultural and maritime employment, and better than half of the seventeenth century suits prosecuted by hirelings to recover wages were successful. Wage recovery suits continued to appear in the eighteenth-century record, characterized by a noticeable rising incidence of resort to quantum meruit claims, usually presented in tandem with a count of indebitatus assumpsit. Formerly plaintiffs had simply alleged a debt on the basis that the task or term agreed was complete but the sum agreed was unpaid. Whereas debt implied recovery after completion, however, quantum meruit implied valuation of what had actually been done. Unsurprisingly, in this light, eighteenth-century wage suits also give increasing prominence to *rates* of pay agreed between the parties, rather than actual lump obligations accumulated.[59]

Most interesting among the complaints arising from hireling relations, however, were breach of contract, nonperformance, or departure complaints. As in Virginia, punitive strictures on hirelings were rare from early on. In 1655, for example, when Richard Jacob established that Mordecai Larkum (a married adult) had neglected his service, Larkum was neither imprisoned nor compelled to perform, but instead ordered to pay damages of twenty-five shillings (ten to fourteen days' wages) in lieu.[60] In September 1659, John Godfrey was found liable in damages to Francis Urselton "for not pforming of a somers work, which he promised to doe . . . for the wch he receiued pt of his pay in hand" but in November Urselton was nonsuited when, in a parallel action "of debt of fiue pounds & for fiue months service" he attempted to have Godfrey penalized five pounds for his departure and ordered to perform the outstanding service. The debt action can only be explained as an attempt to invoke the English Statute of Artificers' penalties on laborers

58. See *RFQE*, I, 3 (June 1636), 49 (Dec. 1642); II, 152 (Mar. 1659); V, 37 (May 1672); also WPAT, vol. XVIII.

59. See, for example, *Follet v. Morrill*, Ipswich Common Pleas, New Entries (hereafter NE) no. 92 (Mar. 1756); *Lufkin v. Ellery*, Ipswich Common Pleas, NE no. 55 (Mar. 1757).

60. *RFQE*, I, 404, 416 (Sept. 1655).

leaving work unfinished, and the nonsuit indicates the statute was considered inapplicable—indeed no other attempt to invoke it can be identified in the Essex court records during the entire colonial period.[61] In March 1670 Thomas Knowlton sued William Knowlton for breach of a covenant to be his journeyman, for which William had received an advance of fifty shillings, but the court merely required that he return the advance and pay five shillings damages for the breach.[62] From the other side of the hiring relation, when Thomas Rumerye sued John Norman for wages for sawing timbers, Norman defended himself by showing that he had paid in full, excepting only an amount withheld "Bee Cause Rumery . . . Left his work." The defendant had not pursued the plaintiff for his premature departure, nor withheld all his wages, but had simply refused to pay in full for incomplete performance. The court found the defendant had no cause to answer.[63]

Damages, too, were the order of the day in actions brought against artisans for failure to complete work. In June 1661 Georg Emory recovered five pounds from John Norman Sr. "for not finishing a house according to agreement." The court did not order completion but provided for further damages to become due in two months if the house remained incomplete.[64] In 1662, in settling Zarubbabell Endecott's action against John Norton "for nonperformance of covenant in building a house" for which he had already been paid, the verdict for the plaintiff was purely for damages, with performance simply left up to the defendant as an alternative means of compliance.[65]

Essex County's fishing and maritime economy adds further dimensions to the legal culture of work on display in the court record. Seeming to have much in common in distinction from landed agricultural labor, the respective legal cultures of fishing and maritime work were actually less similar than one might assume.

The Massachusetts fishery began using a work force recruited in the west of England on seasonal retainers, but developed into a locally based fishery in which independent "companies" of fishermen (crews of men and boys) contracted with local merchants for advances of supplies, secured by a promise of exclusive rights to purchase the catch on their return. The merchant-

61. *RFQE*, II, 175 (Sept. 1659), 185 (Nov. 1659); WPAT, vol. V.

62. *RFQE*, II, 223 (Mar. 1670); WPAT, vol. XV.

63. *RFQE*, VIII, 108–9 (June 1681); WPAT, vol. XXV. See also *Clements v. Merrill* (Mar. 1682).

64. *RFQE*, II, 282–83 (June 1661); WPAT, vol. VI. In a countersuit (at 283) Norman sought to recover payment for the work that *had* been completed, but a verdict was given for the defendant, the evidence tending to show he had indeed been paid.

65. *RFQE*, II, 388–89 (June 1662); WPAT, vol. VII. See also *Fisk v. Waler*, *RFQE*, I, 26 (June 1641).

fisher relationship was one of clientage, built on credit rather than wage-based employment. Members of a company were a partnership rather than a crew under a master's authority. Neither relationship depended structurally on legitimated compulsion, although of course neither promised substantive equality. Clearly, clientage could become oppressive if creditors chose—as they commonly did—to use debt to enmesh clients in obligation. Usually, their goal was to guarantee that the indebted supplier always return to the merchant-creditor, thus assuring the latter of a continuing supply of fish. Where, however, the merchant himself became active as an owner and operator of boats, debt often became a direct means of obtaining crews and controlling their labors. Dr. Richard Knott, who operated a fleet of shallops, appears to have been particularly adept at preying on indebted itinerant seamen, first assuming their debts and then converting that control into an obligation of the seaman to labor for him. William Jarmin had come to Marblehead in the mid-1670s "and meeting with bad voyages Run himselfe into Mr. Brown his debt." Jarmin allowed Knott to assume his debt, but Knott then demanded payment, obtaining execution of him as a debt servant for three years in lieu.

Job Tookey's relations with Knott two years later tell a similar tale. Another itinerant seaman, he became insolvent through injury. Knott offered to assume his debts in exchange for Tookey's agreement to go on a seven-month fishing voyage, at forty shillings per month and outfit. Tookey worked a month preparing the voyage but then reneged on the agreement, claiming the vessel in question was short-manned and that he himself was ill with gout. Tookey also claimed that Knott had agreed to pay him for his month and to allow him to seek a voyage with another boat, but instead Knott had obtained a warrant ordering Tookey attached to answer in damages "for denying and disobeying the said Knotts commands." Tookey spent ten weeks in gaol awaiting the county court's June 1682 session. Once before the court, the action was withdrawn.

Knott's maneuvers illustrate the merchant-proprietor's power in the fisheries. They do not, however, indicate that this power derived from the legitimated authority of a master. Indeed, neither case confirms Knott's magisterial power over a "servant." Knott lost the first action and withdrew the second. What both illustrate, rather, is the formidable persuasive power inherent in debtor-creditor relations and in the coercive procedural sanctions (incarceration pending hearing was the inevitable fate of anyone with no assets to attach sufficient to cover the size of the suit) that applied in such cases.[66]

66. See, generally, Vickers, *Farmers and Fishermen*, 85–203. On William Jarmin, see *RFQE*, VII, 333–36 (Mar. 1680); on Job Tookey, see VIII, 330–38 (June 1682); WPAT, vol. XXXVII.

Two other cases arising from shipboard relations in the fishery in the early 1680s indicate, however, that issues of hierarchical authority were beginning to impinge directly on the fishery in ways that suggest a transformation in its conduct. By the 1680s, the introduction of ketches and schooners was changing the collaborative, shallop-based fishery in structure and scale. Voyages were lengthening; crews becoming larger; work for the merchant for a proportion of the catch, or wholly on wages, was replacing the sharing of earnings; ship masters were being appointed to oversee, coordinate, and command an increasingly complex process.[67] Violent arguments between ketch masters and crew resulted. In June 1682, for example, complaint was made against William Russell for his "abusive carriages" toward Thomas Jeggles, master of the ketch *Prosperous*. Russell had first argued with and sworn at Jeggles, then absented himself, and then had returned to attack Jeggles and other members of the crew with a knife. He was sentenced "to be severely whipped." The following year another ketch master, Peter Hinderson, complained against two members of his crew, Robert Bray and Richard Bale, for their abusive carriage and willful disobedience in refusing to do their duty in hauling up the anchor and otherwise obstructing the departure of the vessel from harbor, and assaulting him. At issue in both cases—implicitly in the first, explicitly in the second—was the ketch master's authority to command. The growing scale and complexity of fishery operations, these incidents suggest, was putting pressure on the legal culture of "men in partnership."[68]

As changes in capitalization undermined collaborative work relations, the fishery threatened to become more like the Atlantic maritime industry, whose legal culture of work routinely pitted masters against men in fights over wages and discipline and prescribed rules that reinforced norms of shipboard authority.[69] Examining its application in Essex in occasional seventeenth-century and more frequent eighteenth-century cases, one detects some local variations tending to moderate commanders' authority. Ironically, Dr. Richard Knott features again as an early illustration, this time on the receiving end. In 1677 Knott was jailed in Lisbon for departing the *John & Ann* (on which he had sailed as surgeon). The consul offered to secure him, in the normal fashion, "tell the ship was redey to sayle" but the captain eventually decided "to Clere himm, and pay him his waeges; which I did rather than to be troubled with him." Back in Essex, the resourceful Knott then brought

67. Knott was in the forefront of this process, adding a ketch in 1681 to his fleet of shallops. His dispute with Job Tookey began when Tookey refused to remain on Knott's new ketch, preferring the relatively greater freedom of the small-boat shallop fishery.

68. *RFQE*, VIII, 348 (Nov. 1683); IX, 145 (Nov. 1683); WPAT, vol. XL.

69. See, generally, Rediker, *Devil*.

suit against the captain for abusing him, and won. Also successful that year was Thomas Hewson, a local man who had joined the *John Bonadventure* at Gravesend for a voyage to Massachusetts Bay, thence to the Iberian Peninsula and a return to London for discharge. At Marblehead he "uniustly left and absented ye shipp," which departed without him. Notwithstanding the terms of the voyage, Hewson sued for wages owed at the time his departure. The court granted his suit, in effect applying a quantum meruit rule to an entire agreement.[70]

The crew of the *James* six years later was less fortunate. Having agreed a voyage from Gravesend to the Isle de May, thence to New England, and thence to the West Indies, "[receiving] ye full propotion of our wages in Every [port of call] according to ye Customs of ye Country for aible semen 25s a month onely too months pay keept in ye Mrs hands as an obligation to performe . . . & those persons yt doth nott performe ye voye shall loose there too months pay & suffer ye Law," eight (of eleven) crew members left ship in Salem. Although they maintained "that theire agrement was to be clear from the ship Losing 2 months wages," they were ordered to return to their duties, any refusing to be escorted on board by the constable.[71]

The indulgence shown Thomas Hewson compared with that shown the crew members of the *James*, whose terms of voyage were sufficiently ambiguous to allow the interpretation they had offered to be taken seriously, may have reflected preference accorded a single local man returning home, as against a group of absconding strangers. Too, the members of the *James*'s crew were defendants trying to avoid a criminal penalty for desertion, whereas Hewson was a plaintiff mounting a civil action for wages owed. Hence the different outcomes may have reflected nothing more than the difference between a case in which local legal practice amenable to the apportionment of wages took precedence over transatlantic maritime law disciplining seamen, and one in which the opposite prevailed. At the same time, the return to duty enforced upon the crew of the *James* suggests that the more integrated Massachusetts maritime economy became with that of the Atlantic as a whole, the less distinctive its legal culture of maritime work would become. In the fishery in contrast, and to some extent in the coasting trade, generic maritime rules remained of limited influence, whereas local practice continued to be influential.[72]

70. *RFQE*, VI, 328–30, 331 (Sept. 1677); WPAT, vol. XXVII.

71. *RFQE*, IX, 59 (June 1683); WPAT, vol. XXXIX.

72. For examples of continuity in wage payment and contracting in the fishery and coasting trades, see *Lufkin v. Ellery*, Ipswich Common Pleas (Mar. 1757), NE no. 55; *Emerson v. Foster*, Ipswich Common Pleas (Mar. 1768), NE no. 33; *Noyes v. Boardman*, Ipswich Common Pleas

The legal culture of work, landed and maritime, on display in the Essex court records was in important respects quite different from that of the early Chesapeake. Statutory legal discipline structuring hierarchical work relations was substantially less in evidence, courts were left with greater discretion, and the household was a more active locale of authority. In both regions, however, the existence of unfree—legally subordinated—working populations permitted the development of exceptional degrees of legal freedom in work relations for white male and, to a lesser extent, female adults.[73] In New England the subordinated populations were essentially life-cyclical; that is, they were defined by age. Their legal subordination was thus temporary. In the Chesapeake, the fact of a practice of temporary legal subordination in the form of juvenile servitude paved the way for the more permanent and extreme subordination of race enslavement, with its concomitant effect of more fully underwriting the freedoms of whites.

The Delaware Valley: Pennsylvania and Chester County

Pennsylvania, in William Penn's words, was founded as a "colony of heaven," a society of Christian harmony. Penn's idealism is not in doubt, but it came with a social and political context attached. Granted the "true and absolute Proprietarie" of the colony by Charles II, Penn thought "subordination and dependency" inevitable in human society. Along with his desire for a New World order of "love and brotherly kindness" came a certain nostalgia for an organic English past and ambition for restorative "balancing" of society's different orders.[74] Unsurprisingly, these sentiments found their way into Pennsylvania's sociolegal design. Abhorring indiscriminate settlement, for example, Penn instead planned to create "agricultural villages" of up to twenty families, each village set in a 5,000-acre tract, recalling the nucleated, manor-centered settlement pattern of downland England.[75]

Basic contradictions existed between the legal and political culture implicit in the proprietor's conception of the colony's organization and those more characteristic of the areas from which most of its early settlers actually came. Penn's nucleated agricultural villages were displaced by "sprawling

---

(Mar. 1768), NE no. 75; *Gage v. Vickre*, Ipswich Common Pleas (Apr. 1790), NE no. 117. In 1792, however, a federal fisheries act expressly applied maritime employment law to the crews of fishery vessels of twenty tons or more: c.6 (2nd Congress, 1st session) s.4. Vessels of this size had long been commonplace in the Massachusetts fishery.

73. On the relativities of adult gender inequality in seventeenth- and eighteenth-century New England, see Ulrich, *Good Wives*.

74. Fischer, *Albion's Seed*, 461.

75. Lemon, *Poor Man's Country*, 42–70.

townships" of dispersed farmsteads, the typical settlement pattern of the English pastoral uplands. Disputes over proprietorial control of settlement patterns, squatter "invasions" of the proprietor's manors, the collection of quit rents, and the very legal character of possession all fed the political conflict that characterized early Pennsylvania.

Like other aspects of early Pennsylvania society, the legal culture of work that Delaware Valley migrants created reflected the influence of the largely rural society centered on dispersed family households with which they had been familiar in England. As such it varied from the model implicit in proprietorial plans.

Servitude was present in the region before Penn's charter was granted, in the scattered fortified outposts of the Swedes and Dutch, and brought northward from Maryland by migrating tobacco planters. Penn's relations with the preexisting settler population were generally accommodating, and this no doubt extended to their labor practices. His earliest agreements with his co-investors also endorsed the transportation of indentured labor. The "Certain Conditions or Concessions" agreed in 1681 contemplated a head-right system of land grants that would reward the first purchasers of Pennsylvania land for mass importations of servants, along Chesapeake plantation lines; the *Laws Agreed Upon in England* (1682) sketched the beginnings of a regulatory system to control the process of servant importation. Under these auspices, approximately one-third of the flurry of arrivals recorded between 1682 and 1686 were indentured servants.[76]

At its first two meetings in 1682 and 1683, the provincial Assembly adopted a detailed set of disciplinary measures expanding upon the regulatory role hinted at in the *Laws Agreed Upon in England*. These measures declared punishment of servant insubordination to be the business of the courts, established a servant registry and pass system, prohibited the sale of servants out of the province or assignment of servants without court oversight, rendered property in servants immune from attachment, penalized harboring or trading with servants, and prescribed five days' additional service for each day an absconding servant was absent, together with costs of pursuit. The Assembly also established statutory terms of service and freedom dues for servants imported without indenture. Codified in 1700, these measures remained the core of Pennsylvania's statute law of servitude throughout the eighteenth century.[77]

76. Cushing, *Printed Laws*, 191; George et al., *Charter*, 99–103; Nash, *Quakers*, 54; Herrick, *White Servitude*, 35.

77. Herrick, *White Servitude*, 31, appendix 289–91; George et al., *Charter*, 113, 119, 151–53, 166; "An Act for the better Regulation of Servants in this Province and Territories" (1700), in

Notwithstanding the overtones of the proprietor's original plans, servitude in Pennsylvania was in important respects a very different institution from that created in the early Chesapeake. Pennsylvania law from the beginning placed great emphasis on oversight of the master-servant relationship. Provision for court supervision of punishments and assignments, for example, helped realize Penn's adage that masters be careful to "mix kindness with authority." Kindness, of course, was in the eye of the beholder: requiring runaways to serve five additional days for each day of absence was one of the more severe responses to absconding anywhere on the mainland. It gave considerable edge to Penn's further advice, this aimed at the servant's ears, that "if thou wilt be a *good* servant, thou must be *true*."[78] As important, however, is the nature of the population thought appropriate for regulation. None of the measures enforcing service ever touched wage workers or artisans. Hirelings were "privileged to withdraw from their service if they so wished, though this might mean the forfeiture, wholly or in part, of the wages earned." Wages were not regulated and were generally recorded at levels that compared extremely favorably with English experience.[79]

Nor did the character of servant migration into Pennsylvania follow the pattern that had prevailed in the Chesapeake. In the earliest years the influx was not dissimilar: a movement of young unattached males. This flow, however, never reproduced the levels that had been apparent in the Chesapeake and dwindled virtually to nothing by the end of the century. Some of the abatement resulted from interruptions in overall migration occasioned by European warfare, but the region's economy—not concentrated agricultural settlements or plantations but dispersed farm households producing a wide variety of crops and home manufactures—did not stimulate the levels of demand for labor that had characterized the tobacco-planting, land-engrossing staple economy of the Chesapeake. In the Delaware Valley, servant labor was supplementary to the immediate nuclear family and demand dictated by its needs. Most of the area's deployable servants were children and adolescents: offspring of the first settlers' English neighbors, bound in England and

---

Laws of the Province of Pennsilvania (Philadelphia, 1714), ch. 49. According to Herrick, the 5:1 penalty for absconding was Penn's own proposal.

78. Quoted in Illick, *Colonial Pennsylvania*, 114.

79. Herrick, *White Servitude*, 3. See also Benson, *Kalm's Travels*, 204; Schweitzer, *Custom and Contract*, 54; Offutt, *Law and Society*, 4. For examples of early proceedings involving artisans, see *Neeld v. Madox*, "An action of the Case for Breach of Articles," Chester County Court, *Docket and Proceedings* I, 135 (Mar. 1689/90), and the transcribed *Records of the Courts of Chester County, Pennsylvania* (Chester County Archives, Westchester, Pa.), 190–92. A defendant artisan might be liable in damages for failure to undertake or complete an agreed task, but could not be forced to do the work.

brought along as part of the migrating family group; and children of local Delaware Valley neighbors bound out as domestic servants and farm apprentices.[80]

Some farmers turned to slaves during the early eighteenth century to fill the gap caused by the interruption of European migration but never on a scale remotely comparable to the Chesapeake colonies.[81] And when migration resumed in the 1720s, Pennsylvania's rural servant labor force quickly again became predominantly a mixture of creole children and migrants, the latter ranging from unattached youth, through the offspring of incoming migrant families (predominantly German and Irish), to entire family groups of children and adults. Other sources of bound labor—transported convicts—simply helped confirm that, for European settlers, servitude was a status increasingly explicitly demarcated (as elsewhere) by age and origin, a condition for children and outsiders. Public records of bindings show little incidence of servitude among creole adults.[82]

The incidence of servitude of any kind in rural Pennsylvania remained low. No more than 20 to 25 percent of Chester County estates included any bound labor (servants or slaves), and those seldom had more than one. Sharon Salinger argues that "the broad economic orientation" of the farm economy made "reliance on unfree labour unnecessary."[83] Clearly Pennsylvanians had no scruples about using unfree European labor. Unfree labor, however, was supplementary to total demand for labor rather than the basis of the provincial economy's culture of work.

CHESTER COUNTY, Pennsylvania, lies on the Western bank of the Delaware River, more or less due west of the city of Philadelphia. Founded in 1682/3, the county stretched in a rough wedge some thirty miles to its northern and western borders, 600,000 acres largely of dispersed family farms engaged in a mixed grain and livestock husbandry. To the southeast, across the river, was West Jersey and the Delaware Bay. To the southwest was Cecil County, Maryland's northern edge.[84]

Regular influxes of transatlantic migrants, and the contiguity of the Delaware and Chesapeake Bays and the waterways that fed them, encouraged con-

80. Nash, *Urban Crucible,* 15. B. Levy, *Quakers,* 138.
81. Schweitzer, *Custom and Contract,* 45–47; Illick, *Colonial Pennsylvania,* 115.
82. On eighteenth-century Delaware Valley migration and servitude, see, generally, Grubb, "Immigration and Servitude." On convicts, see Ekirch, *Bound for America.* On creole adult bindings, see Grubb, "Servant Auction Records," 157.
83. Schweitzer, *Custom and Contract,* 46–47; Salinger, *Indentured Servants,* 70–71; Tomlins, "Reconsidering Indentured Servitude," 15–20.
84. Lemon, *Poor Man's Country,* 98–183.

stant population dispersal and mobility throughout the Delaware Valley region. Many migrants entering through Philadelphia stayed in Pennsylvania,
but others headed north toward New York and the Hudson Valley, or south
to the Chesapeake, or west into Appalachia and beyond. Indenture records
show that servants landing in Philadelphia moved into the city's craft shops
and the surrounding farming regions, but also south to the Chesapeake, or to
the Jerseys and New York. Runaways were pursued into Pennsylvania from
the Chesapeake; runaways from Pennsylvania headed in all directions. Geography, then, gave Delaware Valley labor more opportunity for movement
than perhaps any other locale of settlement. Indeed, prosecutions of absconding apprentices and servants were sometimes joined in the Delaware Valley
courts by prosecutions of absconding *masters*, abandoning failing businesses
and their dependent apprentices and fleeing south or west to begin anew.[85]

James T. Lemon has observed that Pennsylvania's "relatively open society"
meant that people in motion encountered few hindrances.[86] Although accurate, we should note that Pennsylvania's "relatively open society" existed as
such on the basis of quite sharply defined distinctions between freedom and
restraint. We have seen that mobility rendered Penn's original ambitions
for orderly settlement under manorial supervision unworkable: the dispersed
farm household became the locus of social order, not the nucleated village.
Nevertheless, the impulse to control movement remained. Pennsylvania's pass
law required all persons traveling beyond their counties of residence to carry
official certification of their place of residence, on pain of apprehension and
return, or incarceration as a presumptive runaway.

In practice, control of mobility focused on bound servants, and the county
courts were instrumental in its implementation. During the period 1715-75,
restraint of runaways accounted for 80 percent of all proceedings against servants initiated by masters in the Chester County Court. Virtually all were
found in favor of the master. The severity of the penalty—five additional
days service for each day absent—made runaway time a valuable resource, and
masters recorded absences diligently, often presenting them for balancing at
the end of a term of service, rather like book debt. At the same time absconding appears quite exceptional: the average number of proceedings was but
three per annum. It has been estimated that 95 percent of all servants under

85. See, for example, Chester County General and Quarter Sessions (hereafter CCGQ),
Feb. 1728/9 (petition of Joseph Wade); Nov. 1742 (petition of William Grimer), Chester
County Archives. Philadelphia Mayor's Court, July 1763 (petition of Ephraim Hyatt); Phila-
delphia County General and Quarter Sessions, Mar. 1774 (petition of John Davis), Philadelphia
City Archives.
86. Lemon, *Poor Man's Country*, 71-97, esp. 96, 97.

TABLE 3.1.
Master-Servant Disputes in Chester County, Pennsylvania,
Court Proceedings, 1715–1774

	Master Plaintiff			Servant Plaintiff			
	Runaway	Bastardy	Other	Freedom Dues	Release	Treatment	Other
1715–24	19	3	4	1	1	4	—
1725–34	38	—	6	11	3	1	4
1735–44	34	6	3	14	5	2	4
1745–54	44	12	9	20	10	6	4
1755–64	20	3	—	6	6	4	2
1765–74	36	3	—	18	7	7	1

indenture quietly completed their terms without incident. Penalties may have discouraged absconding but on the Chester evidence the principal predictor of the incidence of runaway proceedings (as in the related matter of detentions under the pass laws) was change in the overall flow of migration into the area.[87]

Servants also petitioned the courts, though less frequently than masters and with more ambiguous results.[88] Servants petitioned primarily for enforcement of their right to freedom dues. But they also petitioned for enforcement of masters' other contractual obligations: to provide promised instruction, or to furnish appropriate food, clothing, and accommodation. Less often they sought dissolution of indentures allegedly obtained deceptively or unfairly, or simply asked courts for relief from intolerable situations.[89]

Servant petitioners have often been thought vulnerable to intimidation to

87. Table 3.1; see also Grubb, "Bound Labour," 31; Brophy, "Indentured Servitude," 108, 104.

88. Masters were plaintiffs in 63 percent of master-servant disputes presented to Chester Co. General and Quarter Sessions, 1715–74; servants (including parents of minors), 37 percent. These proportions coincide exactly with those found by Brophy, "Indentured Servitude," for the subperiod 1745–51. Masters' vastly superior win-loss ratio was almost entirely accounted for by runaway cases, which appear in the record as administrative determinations based mechanically on indentures proven and accounts presented. Excluding runaway cases, masters lost one case in every ten filed, and their actual win:loss ratio in cases with determinable outcomes was 7:1. Servants lost roughly one case in every twelve filed, but at 4.5:1 their actual win:loss ratio was still substantially lower than that of masters because more than 50 percent of servants' cases filed had no determinable outcome. The latter suggests frequent resort to informal accommodation: it is unlikely that the court was simply ignoring servant petitions because over the years the share of servant-initiated cases in total master-servant filings increased steadily, from fewer than 19 percent in 1715–24 to more than 45 percent by 1765–74.

89. CCGQ, May 1747 (Bartholomew McGregor); CCGQ (at a Court of Private Sessions), Dec. 1724 (Henry Hawkins).

withdraw or at least compromise their suits. Fragments in the record suggest, however, that servants could be quite forthright in asserting their claims, or at least that the legal discourse of intermediaries could function as an equalizer. Thus Margaret Moffett informed James Gill "to take notice that I intend to apply to the next Court of General Quarter Sessions . . . in order to be relieved from the indenture of servitude which you have wrongfully obtained from me at which time and place you may attend if you think fit and shew cause if any you have why I should not be discharged from your service." Moses Line desired that Robert Smith take notice "that I intend to . . . compel you to comply with the terms of a certain indenture of servitude entered into between us." Nor do the petitions themselves reveal any especial hesitancy in their authors' invocation of legal intervention, written by and large in plain language that straightforwardly catalogs grievance. Rather, where servants were publicly obsequious, it was toward the court, not the master. George Brandon, seeking dues and a formal release after seven years' service to Edward Richards approached the court "most Humbly," praying that "your Honours will be so good as to see that Justice is Dun me," continuing "for I have no other Fathers in this Strange Land but your honours too whome [to look] for Reliefe." But respectful language did not divert Brandon from pursuit of his rights, and when Richards's promise to pay "in 2 or 3 weeks time" proved unreliable, Brandon returned for an order to compel performance. The same blend of supplication and consciousness of right was on display three years later when John Jacob Nies came to seek payment of his freedom dues. Though "a Foreignerr," Nies was still "one of his majesties Subjects." Though humble in his desire for "the Clemency of the English nation," he pointedly reminded the "Honourable Bench" that "by the Laws of this Province" it was "the sole Gaurdian [*sic*] of the Oppressed and Seeing them Righted." The court issued the order he sought.[90]

Servants thus did not yield the juridical space of the county court to their masters. They invoked the court's statutory authority to supervise master-servant relationships in an attempt to blunt the asymmetries of power inherent in their situation. That the court may have chosen to mediate settlements in the majority of disputes meant that petitioners could be vulnerable if justices were capricious in composing settlements. But servant petitioners were not unwilling to press complaints even against members of the bench when they felt slighted.[91] Nor should one assume that masters were confident of the court's favor. In 1751, after losing a dispute over possession of a minor

90. CCGQ, Nov. 1731 (Margaret Moffett); Feb. 1775 (Moses Line); Feb. 1747/8 (George Brandon); Feb. 1751 (John Jacob Nies).
91. CCGQ, Aug. 1766 (Daniel Blare).

servant, David John complained bitterly to the quarterly court that "if your nobel honors letts any of your m[e]mbers serve us so we may expect to keep not a sarvant amongst us."[92]

The policing of disputes between masters and indentured servants, therefore, was no more crudely one-sided in Pennsylvania than elsewhere. It was clear, nevertheless, that the courts pursued their role within the compass of a general understanding that, both socially and legally, the relationship of master and indentured servant was legitimately one of authority and subordination. The master's authority was to be overseen, but its lawful exercise protected. Emblematic of this was the courts' almost mechanical processing of runaways, which nicely exemplified the key characteristic of servitude— namely, the legality of restraint.

As elsewhere, however, indenture was the condition of legitimate restraint. This is made abundantly clear in local proceedings. In May 1732, for example, Jonathan Strange sought redress against one Humphrey Reynolds, who had neglected his promise to "faithfully and truly serve him the sd Jonathan" three months in consideration of two pounds, one shilling, and eightpence advanced by the plaintiff. But Strange's action was a civil suit seeking damages for Reynolds's failure to perform, not an invocation of the criminal penalties so routinely applied to indentured runaways. And unlike the summary disposal of those runaways, Strange's suit (like most civil suits in Chester, and elsewhere) simply languished on the docket (in this case for three years) before being composed, privately, by the parties themselves.[93]

"Servants," in short, were a distinctive legal subset of the Delaware Valley's working population, distinguished by an indenture and rendered subject to a unique legal regime. The tenor of that distinctiveness emerges in Joanna Long's 1763 petition for relief from the ill-treatment accorded her by her master, Richard Hall, of Springfield. About four months before, Long told the court, she had gone to work for Hall "as a hireling" and had "tarried with him a considerable time on wages." With "fair speeches and specious promises," Hall and his wife prevailed upon Long to bind herself to them for a term of two years. Her situation then changed abruptly. "Ever since your petitioner signed the said Indenture, she hath been very ill used by them," and the previous week had been "beat and abused . . . in a barbarous manner," causing her to abscond. Long's complaint was referred to two justices for a

92. CCGQ, Nov. 1751.
93. Chester County Common Pleas (hereafter CCCP), May 1732, Chester County Archives. Strange's complaint described Reynolds as a "yeoman." See also CCCP, Feb. 1740/1 (Thomas Bissett agt William Morrison); CCQS, Feb. 1740/1 (Petition of John Cartwright); CCCP, May 1726 (Foster agt Stringer); CCGQ, Feb. 1729/30 (Petition of Samuel Chance).

hearing and settled, though the settlement was not recorded. But clearly by binding herself she had brought about a drastic change in her social and legal circumstances. In the same way, it was the *absence* of an indenture that allowed Martha Liggett to depart the service of James Caldwell without penalty, "it not being satisfactorily made out to this Court that the said Martha Liggett is legally bound." It was also what made Brigett Cochran, who "hired with" John Walters of Concord township in October 1773 but departed after two weeks and was later accused of stealing from him, a "singlewoman" in court proceedings, unlike her alleged accomplice, James Hannell, who was his indentured "servant." And it was what saved Mary Broom, brought into court for "disobedience to the orders" of her master Daniel Humphreys, from punishment, she having nothing to answer for, "it not appearing that she was Bound by Indenture."[94]

Whether workers on wages remained liable to the less exacting but still serious sanction of loss of earnings in the event they broke agreements to serve (as observers alleged)[95] cannot easily be determined from the Chester court record. Civil suits seeking payment for work invariably alleged prior performance but supplied few details. The form of wage work transactions suggests the predominance of casual daywork: work debts were either paid immediately at the conclusion of a task or cumulated over time to be presented in periodic mutual accountings in the normal fashion of book debt.[96] Such a pattern is unlikely to generate disputes over the "entirety" of a contract. Moreover, the amounts of payment in dispute were generally small enough to be settled by a hearing before an individual justice rather than in the county court, and records at individual justice level are very sparse indeed prior to the late eighteenth century.

Nevertheless, cases that have been traced suggest one should *not* assume that wage laborers in breach of employment contracts faced loss of unpaid earnings in colonial Pennsylvania. In July 1767, for example, Eneas Foulk appeared before Richard Riley, justice of the peace of the Chichester township, to seek payment for work undertaken on behalf of Isaac Pyle. Pyle replied that Foulk had not been paid because he "had not compleated his work according to Bargain." Nevertheless, Riley's decision was for payment for what had been completed, "that the value of the work done & due to the plantiff is

94. CCGQ, Feb. 1763 (Petition of Joanna Long); Nov. 1768 (Petition of William Buffington, on behalf of his niece Martha Liggett); Feb. 1774 (Examinations of Brigett Cochran, James Hannell); Aug. 1774 (Discharge of Mary Broom).

95. Benson, *Kalm's Travels*, 204.

96. The Diary of Benjamin Hawley of East Bradford township, Chester County, 1769–82 (transcribed by the Bishop's Mill Historical Institute), Chester County Historical Society, Westchester, Pa.

but 15/- and no more."[97] Part payment was also judged appropriate some years later by Isaac Hicks, a Bucks County justice of the peace, in William Force's suit against James Moon seeking payment "for four months service of the six he hired for." Moon contended that "as the Plff did not stay out the time agreable to contract he owes nothing particularly as he suffered by his going away," but Hicks gave the plaintiff judgment "for the Bal[ance]." Balancing worked both ways. In May 1797, again before Hicks, John Butler demanded payment for thirty days' work, which he had been hired to perform by John Bulgar. Bulgar contended "that he hired the Plff to assist him in gitting his Indian Corn & Buckwheat for which he agreed to pay him 3/9 and that the gitting lasted but 12 days." He acknowledged that Butler had remained with him for the remainder of the period alleged, but employed only on "trifling matters." Hicks allowed the plaintiff judgment, but at a rate reduced by one-third, two shillings, threepence per day, for the final eighteen days.[98]

In the Delaware Valley as elsewhere, then, the indenture established a crucial line of legal status in the culture of work, a line of demarcation between enforceable and unenforceable obligation. The indenture signified when and when not the assertion of capacity to control or restrain another was legally allowable, what labor was not "free" and what was. There, as elsewhere, it existed in an environment crosscut by numerous other and intersecting lines of social demarcation — of age and gender, of race — to which the culture of work was also closely related. Occasionally, lines became crossed. In Chester County as in Essex, juvenile migrants could be found arguing that their service obligations ended once they reached majority. In February 1741/2, Joseph Helm, previously bound to Thomas Treese for a term of six years, absented himself from Treese's service, claiming that he had reached the age of twenty-one and that the remainder of his term was void. Instead of treating Helm as a runaway the court decided he should work at his trade on wages "either with his Master or if the sd Apprentice shall chuse it with some other person by his said Master's Appointment" until "the Cause receives a full Determination."

---

97. Richard Riley, "A Record of all My Proceedings Relating to the Office of a Justice of the Peace," 2 vols. (June 1765–Feb. 1776), Historical Society of Pennsylvania, Philadelphia, Pa.

98. Isaac Hicks, Docket, 1794–1831, 2 vols. (Hist. Soc. Penn.), 26 Jan. 1795, 1 May 1797. John Graves, Justice of the Peace, West Chester Township, Civil Dockets A–Q (1795–1832), Chester County Historical Society, also recorded a number of proportional settlements of disputes over wages or work payments due: 17 Oct. 1805 (*John Bell v. Jesse Mattock*); 5 Sept. 1815 (*John Webber v. Abner Few*); 4 May 1818 (*Joseph Mattock v. Samuel Stark*); 23 Apr. 1821 (parties not recorded); 14 May 1825 (*Daniel Massey v. Daniel Hastead*); 17 July 1828 (*Paul McCloskey v. John Felty*). These proceedings help clarify an important question that has been a matter of contention among historians, namely precisely when entire contract rules came to be adopted in service contract disputes. For a valuable summary of what is at issue, see Steinfeld, *Coercion*, 291–92.

The matter did not continue, apparently accommodated between Helm and Treese, but in 1737 the court had treated the attainment of majority as sufficient to end a term of indentured service, and it did so again some years later, notwithstanding the existence of an indenture for a longer period.[99]

More often, however, lines of demarcation complemented each other in practice. Collectively, they sustained in the Delaware Valley a substantively differentiated culture of work that, as elsewhere, was more plural than singular, that shared no generic legal regime of authority and subordination lending people at work a common identity as "servants" and their employers common advantages as "masters," but that rather ascribed different legal identities according to the different kinds of people—youth or adult, migrant or creole —involved. As elsewhere, too, that culture of work was itself a hierarchy, one in which the legal freedoms of adult white creole males stood out against, and were buttressed by, enforceable obligations of service visited more weightily upon others. We have observed the same hierarchy in the Chesapeake and in Massachusetts, so to encounter it in the Delaware Valley is no surprise. As in Essex County, however, the subordinations encountered in Chester were essentially temporary and life-cyclical. Not until African enslavement had established race as the cardinal measure of servility does one find a segment of the early American population designated as a permanent underclass of workers. It is in racial slavery, in America, that one finally encounters "master and servant" not as a temporary and essentially contained legal hierarchy but as an expansive polarity of freedom and its absence.

Postscript

"None but negers are sarvants."[100] For working white Americans, this, in the early nineteenth century, was the transcendent principle of the legal culture of work that had emerged from the colonial period. Once due allowance is made for the slower-than-imagined atrophy of early America's statutory categories of temporary youthful and migrant servants, it was also an accurate claim. But during the first half of the century, the claim became increasingly hollow. The ambit of master and servant grew until it absorbed the employment contract as a whole, underwriting "an employer's right and capacity, simply as an employer contracting for the performance of services, to exert the magisterial power of management, discipline and control over others."[101]

---

99. CCGQ, Feb. 1741/2; Aug. 1737 (Mathias Lambert); Aug. 1770 (Robert Potts). But see also Nov. 1775 (George Reab).

100. Quoted in Janson, *Stranger*, 88.

101. Tomlins, *Law, Labor, and Ideology*, 230–31.

To be sure, the importation of master and servant doctrine into nine-teenth-century employment law was an importation of a general concep-tual structure and language of legitimate authority in work relations, not of specific criminal disciplines. "Free labor" was not a meaningless designa-tion. But the importation was nevertheless deeply significant, for what dis-tinguished the nineteenth-century version from what had gone before was its all-encompassing quality, finding disciplinary authority in the contract of employment itself, rather than in the particular sociolegal status—youthful, indentured, and so forth—characteristic of the worker. "We understand by the relation of master and servant nothing more or less than that of the *em-ployer* and the *employed*."[102] This had its consequences. Wage labor through-out the eastern states, for example, found itself challenged by legal strictures that tightened the looser economic disciplines of the previous century.[103] In the antebellum South, the status of "free labor" remained qualitatively dis-tinct from slavery, but white workers found the claims to legal privilege and civic status they had built on their difference from slaves increasingly vul-nerable. Indeed, what crept into their discourse was intimations of a willing-ness to work *as hard as* slaves in order to keep racial privilege within their grasp.[104]

Ironically, given the intervening American Revolution, English influence was felt strongly in this nineteenth-century revision of master and servant in America. This was not a matter of specific statutory example; indeed, as the thesis writer Timothy Walker put it, "what a contrast is here presented to the laws of England, which leave hardly anything to the discretion of the employer and the employed."[105] Rather it was a matter of the influence of au-thoritative English common-law reports and treatises, the product of com-mon-law judging, and reconceived common-law doctrine, all of which en-couraged American legal culture in a rejection of earlier delimited, parochial, and regionalized approaches to master and servant in favor of more expan-sive, universalized conceptions. During the colonial era, we have argued here, America's colonial legal cultures had severally felt the original influence of English law but had simultaneously refracted it through regional cultures of settlement that, in combination with distinctive local environments, had pro-duced differentiated legal cultures of work. But the impulses of the nineteenth century lent themselves to nothing so much as an overpowering indifference

---

102. T. Walker, *American Law*, 243.

103. Steinfeld, *Coercion*, 29–38, 290–314; Tomlins, *Law, Labor, and Ideology*, 273–78.

104. Tomlins, "Nat Turner's Shadow," 511–12, 516–17.

105. T. Walker, *American Law*, 250. For the best available comparative study of English and American labor contract law during the nineteenth century, see Steinfeld, *Coercion*.

to that earlier history. The new nation sought a new legal culture not of discrete differences but of transcendent universals.

Time was, Horace Gray Wood acknowledged in his 1877 *Treatise on the Law of Master and Servant*, that "servant" might have been a term of discrete application and legal consequence, that "others, as clerks, farm hands, etc. were denominated laborers or workmen, and were in many respects subject to different rules." But investigating that history would "serve no practical end." It was enough "to know how the relation *now* exists" in America. And how did it exist? The answer was succinct. "All who are in the employ of another, in whatever capacity," were now servants.[106] A decade after the Civil War's erasure of southern difference, all working people—at least conceptually—were at last in the same legal boat.

106. Wood, *Master and Servant*, 2–4.

FOUR

Law and Labor in
Eighteenth-Century Newfoundland

Jerry Bannister

The case of eighteenth-century Newfoundland presents historians of the law of master and servant with three questions. First, how did the adjudication of master and servant relations evolve in the absence of a colonial assembly? Although the island's fishery had operated since the seventeenth century, and permanent settlement grew in the early eighteenth, Newfoundland did not have its own legislature until 1832. Second, how did the passage of a parliamentary statute affect the local administration of the law of master and servant? While King William's Act[1] (1698) confirmed the system of fishing admirals, no statute provided for the regulation of wages and contracts in the Newfoundland fishery until Palliser's Act[2] of 1775. Third, how did the practice of appointing naval officers as judges affect the civil administration of the law of master and servant? This chapter considers the relationship between statute law and local custom in a pre-industrial economy dependent upon the labor supplied by indentured servants.

In Newfoundland, where the management of disputes between masters and servants represented the single most important responsibility for local courts, magistrates relied primarily on a customary law of master and servant. An amalgam of transplanted English practices and local customs, this legal regime differed from the Anglo-American model in form but not in func-

For their comments on earlier versions of this article, I thank Allan Greer, Douglas Hay, Christopher Munn, Jim Phillips, Daniel Vickers, and Vince Walsh. The research received funding from the Institute of Social and Economic Research at Memorial University of Newfoundland, and the Social Sciences and Humanities Research Council of Canada.

1. (Engl.) 10 Wm.III c.14 (1698).
2. (G.B.) 15 Geo.III c.31 (1775).

tion. The island's courts reinforced masters' authority through the effective criminalization of breach of contract. Both naval surrogates and civil magistrates decreed punishments for servants who were insubordinate, neglected their duties, or refused to work. Supported by merchants and governors, the courts applied paternalistic discretion to discipline unruly servants: the protection of servants against breach of contract was seen as a contingent privilege, not an absolute right. Those who challenged their masters' authority were subject to public whipping and the forfeiture of all their wages. Naval governors placed additional restrictions on Irish Catholics and fishing servants who stayed in Newfoundland after the expiration of their contracts. The regulation of labor operated essentially the same before and after Palliser's Act, which simply codified customary laws already in force. Servants pursued their own interests and frequently went to court to seek redress for breach of contract and severe beatings, and to secure liens to protect their wages. However, evidence from a case study of an outport district indicates that these efforts met with mixed success. At the end of the eighteenth century, when the heyday of wage labor in the fishery had passed, the threat of being whipped for insolence and neglect of duty still hung over servants.

Master-Servant Relations in a Fishing Society

The Atlantic cod fishery dominated the development of Newfoundland. By the mid-eighteenth century, the migratory fishery had evolved into a hybrid of resident and English-based operations: a significant number of servants and a growing class of planters had begun to settle permanently on the island for the first time. Some year-round settlement had always existed to serve the fishery's needs but was becoming increasingly permanent. The population of settlers on the island reached 3,000 in 1720; it doubled in thirty years and nearly doubled again by 1780, to more than 10,000. It is difficult to speak of immigration in any traditional sense of the term. Migration and settlement consisted of three different modes: seasonal (those who resided only during the summer fishery and returned to England or Ireland each autumn); temporary (planters who stayed for a few seasons and servants contracted to serve two summers and a winter); and permanent (traders and planters with fixed capital, and servants who stayed after serving out their time). By 1715 the growing presence of permanent settlers was creating sustained pressure for some type of local government beyond the system of fishing admirals. The threshold of settlement needed to support basic governmental institutions was crossed well before the first appointment of a governor and justices of the peace in 1729. The cod fishery did not become a predominantly Newfoundland-based economy until after the Napoleonic Wars.[3]

The island's social structure differed considerably from that of Georgian England or colonial America. Newfoundland divided socially into three distinct groups: merchants, planters, and servants. No discernible middle class or community of established farmers existed in the eighteenth century. The family did not begin to become the dominant social unit until the late eighteenth century. Prior to 1800 capital relied predominantly on the wage labor supplied by servants contracted out from English and Irish ports, many of whom had no ties or experience with the fishery. Dominated by young, single men, the migratory fishery had limited demands for women's labor. For most of the eighteenth century, women made up less than a third of the total population. At the top of this society, a caste of British merchants dominated the fishery. Based primarily in Devonshire and Dorset, they controlled the flow of capital and sold the extensive supplies needed each spring, such as food provisions, fishing gear, clothing, and alcohol. Newfoundland had a carrying trade operated by sack ships, as well as persistent interlopers from New England, but the West Country merchants commanded the bulk of the fishery's capital. They met each August to determine the price to be paid for cured salt codfish, which they further influenced through the fish culler employed to grade the quality of its cure. After their accounts were settled at the end of the fishing season, most merchants returned to England, where some of them, such as the Lesters of Poole, were prominent members of the gentry.

Planters were middlemen who drew on the merchants' capital and contracted wage labor, although merchants also hired servants directly. Typically, planters owned inshore fishing vessels manned by servants hired for set wages. They were divided between those who settled in Newfoundland and others, known as by-boat keepers, who came over each summer; but both performed essentially the same economic roles as merchant client and fishing master. By the mid-eighteenth century, their ventures had become largely dependent on the merchant credit: each spring a planter borrowed from a merchant, usually via a local agent, the necessary supplies for the summer fishery; in return he was bound to sell all of his catch only to that merchant's firm. Because mer-

---

3. Unless otherwise noted, the summary of Newfoundland society in this and the following paragraphs is based on the major secondary sources: Head, *Newfoundland*, 82–100; Handcock, *Origins*, 91–120; Mannion, *Peopling of Newfoundland*, 1–17; Lahey, "Catholicism and Colonial Policy," 49–53; Mannion, "Maritime Trade," 208–33; Matthews, *Lectures*, chs. 14–15; Ryan, "Fishery to Colony," 138–56; Cadigan, *Merchant-Settler Relations*, chs. 2–4; O'Flaherty, *Old Newfoundland*, chs. 4–6.

chants influenced both the cost of provisions and the price paid for codfish, planters often found themselves in debt when their accounts were settled in the autumn. Forced to obtain further credit to procure sufficient winter supplies or a passage back to the British Isles, some of them fell into a cycle of debt and dependence in which fish and provisions formed the sole currency. In order to protect their interests, planters searched wherever possible for ways to cut labor costs.

Servants supplied virtually all of the labor in the fishery. Throughout the eighteenth century, the terms "fisherman" and "servant" were used interchangeably, as officials assumed that all workers served under the direction of a master.[4] Craftsmen were regularly hired for monthly wages, but no class of artisans emerged until the nineteenth century. Workers in Newfoundland were commonly engaged each spring in ports such as Poole and Waterford—many were also contracted out locally as needs arose—to serve in the Newfoundland fishery for two summers and a winter for annual wages ranging from ten to thirty pounds. Known popularly as a "shipping paper," the covenant stipulated the servants' duties and the terms of service.[5] Wage labor suffused the means of production; servants resisted attempts to impose a system of shares. Despite their reliance on wages, workers in Newfoundland fit the standard model of early modern servants: with few exceptions, they depended on their masters for accommodation, transportation, food, and most other basic provisions.[6] Although some of these obligations became codified in statutory law, others remained unwritten customs. Each spring, for example, servants were expected to sign on the doctor's books of a local surgeon, chosen by the master, and pay a fee at the end of the fishing season, usually between five and ten shillings. Working conditions were exacting: during the height of the fishing season, between late June and mid-August, servants could work as much as eighteen to twenty hours a day to take advantage of the run of fish. They were typically organized into crews of six: four men fished in small vessels under the direction of a boat's master; the other two worked ashore preparing the fish under the supervision of skilled splitters and salters. Living conditions were at times brutal, most foodstuffs

4. On the use of the term "servant" in local nomenclature, see Story, *Dictionary*, 461.

5. A standard shipping paper reads: "Then I Thomas Leaman agreed and shipped myself with Mr. William Collens for this Winter, and the next Summer ensuing, and I am to do the best of my endeavour for the good of the voyage; and in consideration of my due performance, I am to have for my wages the sum of £26 sterling; and, after allowing my Country charges, to have the balance of my account in good bills of exchange. To be clear the 20th of September 1788." Sheila Lambert, ed., *House of Commons Sessional Papers*, vol. 90, *Newfoundland, 1792–93* (Wilmington, Del.: Scholarly Resources, 1975), 427.

6. On the standard definition of servitude in this period, see Steinfeld, *Invention*, ch. 2.

had to be imported, and there were sporadic reports of near starvation in re-mote outports. When servants settled up with their masters in the autumn, the stakes were high for both parties.

The treatment of servants must also be considered in the context of religion. While the established planters and merchants were largely English, most servants came from southern Ireland. Put simply, the island had a propertied class dominated by one religious faction and a labor force supplied by another. Irish servants were a relatively cohesive group with a distinct identity and, for many, a separate language; translators were routinely needed in court. Census records usually separated Irish servants from the rest of the population. Governors portrayed the Irish as a united community, despite the divisions between factions from Munster and Leinster. They reputedly had strong Jacobite sentiments and were repeatedly accused of being disloyal to the British crown. In 1750, for example, Governor Drake had warned that the Irish were "notoriously disaffected to the Government, all of them refusing to take the Oaths of Allegiance when tended to them."[7] Attitudes of governors ranged from tolerance to outright bigotry, but local authorities did not actively pursue religious persecution until 1755, when Governor Dorrill outlawed the celebration of Mass. These regulations went further than the English Penal Laws: penalties for attending Mass included arrest, fines, and house burnings; Dorrill also outlawed the hoisting of Irish flags.[8] These draconian measures, which coincided with the expulsions of the Acadians from Nova Scotia, reflected fears of an Irish rebellion and alliance with the French. When St. John's was captured in 1762, large numbers of Irish servants allegedly sided with the French, and one writer claimed that, "during the time the French were in possession of the Island, the merchants and inhabitants suffered more cruelties from the Irish Roman Catholics, than they did from the declared enemy."[9]

Concerns over sedition underlaid the desire to control masterless men. That most of these men were Irish Roman Catholics was lost on no one in the eighteenth century. One of the consistent tenets in imperial policy was the aim to prevent surplus labor from accumulating after the summer fishery had ended. Merchants, planters, and their legitimate servants were never prohibited from settling on the island. But servants who lived in Newfoundland without a written contract to serve under a master were referred to as "diet-

7. Provincial Archives of Newfoundland and Labrador (hereafter PANL), Colonial Office Papers, series 194 (hereafter CO 194), vol. 12, p. 186, report of Governor Drake, 24 Dec. 1750.

8. PANL, Colonial Secretary's Letterbook (hereafter GN 2/1/A), 2:202, 216, 251-62, 264, 277.

9. G. Williams, *Newfoundland*, 9-10.

ers," a designation that linked idleness with a propensity for crime and social unrest.[10] In 1764 Governor Palliser promulgated a penal code designed to
control the mobility of laborers. "For better preserving the peace, preventing robberies, tumultuous assemblies, and other disorders of wicked and idle
people remaining in the country during the winter," Palliser ordered:

> That no Papist servant man or woman shall remain in any place where
>   they did not fish or serve during the summer preceding.
> That not more than two Papist men shall dwell in one house during
>   the winter, except such as have Protestant masters.
> That no Papist shall keep a publick house or vend liquor by retail.
> That no person keep dyeters [dieters] during the winter.
> That all idle disorderly useless men and women be punished
>   according to law and sent out of the country.[11]

This proclamation, which magistrates were to read at quarter sessions each
year, was renewed by Governor John Byron in 1770 and Governor Robert
Duff in 1775.[12]

The relations of production and exchange contained inherent tensions.
A fundamental cleavage separated servants from those who contracted their
labor. The point of economic exchange—where masters had to settle accounts
and to pay outstanding wages—was a forum in which competing interests
regularly collided. From the servants' standpoint, securing their wages represented the most important goal. They also brought complaints to acquire
more favorable working conditions, which involved petitions for breach of
contract alleging, inter alia, that their masters had acted improperly, broken customary arrangements, or had beaten them severely. Servants utilized a
range of extralegal measures to promote their interests: from refusal to work
or intimidation of their master, to desertion or assault, and to the seizure of
goods to secure their wages. From the masters' viewpoint, the chief objective
was to limit costs generally and servants' wages in particular. Masters routinely brought suits against servants for breach of contract on the grounds
that the specific duties outlined in the shipping paper were either completed
improperly or left undone. Masters often accused servants of neglect of duty
or insolence in order to justify withholding all or part of their wages. In some
cases they seized the season's catch as it lay ready for transport, sold it to another merchant agent, and thereby avoided having to split the proceeds to

10. On the term "dieter," see Story, *Dictionary*, 140.
11. PANL, GN 2/1/A, 3:272.
12. PANL, GN 2/1/A, 4:285, 6:101–2.

pay for their servants' wages. Masters commonly relied on the more effective paternalistic practice of using alcohol and other provisions to control labor costs. By advancing servants their wages during the fishing season, usually through the sale of rum, masters could ensure that their servants had little or no claims for wages left when accounts were settled. With a preponderance of young unattached men, laboring under harsh conditions with few local ties to kin, the island had the prime ingredients of a violent society.

The Development of Naval Government

The history of written law in eighteenth-century Newfoundland begins with the 1699 Act to Encourage Trade to Newfoundland.[13] Known popularly as King William's Act, it codified the customary regulations established in the Western Charters first granted to English merchants in 1634. It confirmed the tradition that the master of the first English ship to arrive in a Newfoundland harbor after 25 March was by right the admiral of that outport for the upcoming fishing season. The second and third masters then became the vice- and rear-admirals, respectively. Admirals had the choice of the best fishing rooms—tracts of the waterfront used for wharves, flakes, and stages—and were empowered to settle disputes over the possession of the remaining premises. Like the earlier charters, the act contained regulations for the conduct of the fishery, such as prohibitions against damaging stages, stealing fish nets, or selling alcohol on Sunday. It also reaffirmed the existing method for dealing with serious criminal offenses: suspected felons had to be brought to England for their trial. The fishing admirals, in order to preserve the peace and good government in their harbor, were enjoined to ensure that all of the act's regulations were enforced, and to keep a written journal for each fishing season. To augment this rather limited legal regime, King William's Act offered one significant reform: the naval commanders of the warships sent to patrol Newfoundland each summer could act as appeal judges to the fishing admirals' decisions. The implications of this provision extended much further than the Board of Trade had originally envisaged, as the Royal Navy became the dominant judicial and political force in eighteenth-century Newfoundland.[14]

King William's Act reflected imperial policy toward Newfoundland. The British government viewed the island not as a permanent colony but rather

13. (Engl.) 10 Wm.III c.14 (1698).

14. Unless otherwise noted, the summary of the legal system in this and the following paragraphs is based on Bannister, *Custom of the Country*. For a synopsis of the history of naval government, see also Bannister, "Naval State."

a seasonal fishing station to be used solely for the benefit of the West of England fishery. Although never a productive source for sailors, Newfoundland was seen as a nursery for seamen, and the Admiralty played a dominant role in its administration. The right to settle and to hold property was in theory subordinate to the needs of the fishery, although in practice property rights were often recognized and enforced. Settlement continued to expand throughout the eighteenth century, often supported by the West Country merchants and traders, although its legal status remained uncertain, as governors made sporadic and ineffectual efforts to restrict property use to the fishery. While some year-round habitation was inevitable and indeed necessary for the operation of the migratory fishery, the full trappings of colonial government were not. Conventional wisdom held that the island's limited development did not merit the institutions normally allocated to settled colonies. In his treatise on the British empire, John Oldmixon pronounced that in Newfoundland, "there is no need of much Law, for the inhabitants have not much land and no money."[15] British officials took a pragmatic view toward Newfoundland, remaining skeptical about granting the island its own legislature right up to the eve of representative government in 1832. But this does not mean that Newfoundland was somehow anomalous. The administration of most colonies in the first British Empire was largely ad hoc, leaving local communities with a relatively limited amount of official supervision and regulation. London was invariably wary of initiating policies that would place added burdens on the treasury. Between 1689 and 1763 Parliament passed relatively few acts relating directly to the management of individual colonies. In the wake of the consolidation of the navigation system in 1696, the English government focused on defending specific domestic industries against foreign and colonial rivals. By protecting the West Country interest in the cod fishery, King William's Act formed part of a broader policy of using statutory law to promote English commerce.[16]

The growth of permanent settlement and local propertied interests placed increasing pressure on the English government to appoint civil magistrates to govern during the winter. As early as 1701 the government was receiving reports that "quarrels and differences happen here after the fishing season is over, and in the rigor of the Winter masters beat servants, servants their master."[17] Although the tens of thousands who worked each year in the migratory

15. John Oldmixon, *The British Empire in America* (London: J. Nickolson & B. Tooke, 1708), 1:18–19.

16. See Madden and Fieldhouse, "Imperial Policy and Legislation," 2–5; Steele, "Governance," 105–26, 300–323.

17. PANL, CO 194/2, p. 132, report of George Larkin, 1701.

fishery still dwarfed the year-round population, the growing presence of resident dealers and traders precipitated legal reforms. Pushed to establish some type of a judiciary, in 1729 the British government appointed the naval commodore as governor, with the power to appoint justices of the peace and to hold quarter sessions. The fishing admirals reacted strongly against this usurpation of their power, however, arguing that the commissions of the peace, issued by writ of the Privy Council, contravened the superior power granted them by parliamentary statute. The attorney general ruled that the commissions bestowed by the governor did not contradict King William's Act because the magistrates' authority extended only to breaches of the peace and other criminal matters.

Although the fishing admirals sharply contested the authority of the governor and magistrates in the early 1730s, by 1750 they were no longer an independent force. In the second half of the eighteenth century the fishing admirals came firmly under the control of the island's naval government. In 1749 Governor Rodney launched an ambitious series of reforms: within two years the island had a local court of oyer and terminer (an annual assize court that tried felonies at St. John's); a highly organized system of customary "surrogate courts" (convened in the outports by naval officers); and a central court in St. John's (presided over by the governor). By the mid-1760s Newfoundland was divided into nine districts, administered by civil magistrates, and five maritime zones, governed by naval surrogates. It had many of the standard English institutions used to administer justice—for example, constables, coroners, a sheriff, and a grand jury—and magistrates took recognizances, held petty sessions, and organized quarter sessions on a regular basis. Naval government comprised an entrenched customary regime based on two levels of authority: the seasonal administration of the Royal Navy, which had up to ten warships patrolling the coast from midsummer to early autumn; and the year-round sessions held by civil magistrates. With the backing of the naval governor in St. John's, the island's justices of the peace heard a variety of criminal and civil disputes summarily and in petty sessions; belatedly, Palliser's Act conferred upon the court of sessions statutory authority to administer the law of master and servant.[18] The office of the justice of the peace, which was filled largely with surgeons, operated as closely to the English model as local conditions permitted. The naval surrogates presided over the autumn quarter sessions in each district, usually with the justices of the peace, and reported back to the governor in St. John's. Warships were also dispatched at magistrates' request to convene a "special court" to deal with local crises.

18. (G.B.) 15 Geo.III c.31 (1775) ss.17–18.

In the wake of problems with the surrogate courts in the late 1780s, Parliament passed new legislation for Newfoundland in 1791. The Judicature Act[19] provided for a temporary court of civil jurisdiction and a chief judge to preside over the judiciary. It was limited to one year, during which John Reeves, the first chief justice, was appointed to assess the need for further reforms. In addition to its cognizance in all civil causes, the court of civil jurisdiction was empowered to hear wage disputes during the governor's summer residence, after which authority reverted to the court of sessions. In his 1791 report to the secretary of state, Reeves recommended the establishment of some form of legislative authority in Newfoundland, but he abandoned this initiative the following year. In 1792 a second Judicature Act[20] created a supreme court with both civil and criminal jurisdiction. It codified the system of surrogate courts that had long operated customarily and empowered the governor to institute such courts throughout the island's districts. The supreme court and surrogate courts had a monopoly on civil pleas, save maritime causes (to be heard in the vice admiralty court), and wage disputes, which could be heard in the court of sessions or before two justices of the peace. Again the act was for one year only and had to be renewed annually until 1809 (49 Geo.III c.27). Naval officers began to withdraw from their customary position as sole surrogate judges — after 1791 civilians began to sit on the surrogate bench — but the governor and his junior officers still dominated local government. Naval rule prevailed until a reform movement in Newfoundland pressured the British government to pass the 1824 Judicature Act (5 Geo.IV c.67), which abolished the surrogate courts and established a new system of civilian circuit courts.

The Newfoundland Law of Master and Servant

Named after Hugh Palliser, governor from 1764 to 1768, the 1775 act contained a significant range of provisions regulating master-servant relations.[21] It was designed to uphold the imperial policy that Newfoundland should remain a fishing station and not a settled colony. Masters were prohibited from bringing servants to Newfoundland without the governor's permission (s.12). All servants were to have written contracts, which, if a dispute arose, the master was obliged to produce in court (ss.13, 15). During the period of service, masters were forbidden from advancing servants more than half their wages, forty shillings of which was to be withheld to pay for the servants' passage

19. (G.B.) 31 Geo.III c.29 (1791).
20. (G.B.) 32 Geo.III c.46 (1792).
21. (G.B.) 15 Geo.III c.31 (1775). On Palliser's administration, see Whitely, "Governor Hugh Palliser," 141-63; J. Crowley, "Empire versus Truck," 311-36; Janzen, "Showing the Flag," 3-14.

home at the expiration of the contract (ss.13, 14). All of the fish and oil produced by the masters' fishing operations were liable first for the payment of servants' wages (s.16). On the other hand, any servant who willingly absented himself without permission, or neglected or refused to work according to the terms of the contract, was to be fined two days' pay for each day of absence or neglect of duty. Those who absented themselves without leave for five days were deemed to be deserters and thereby forfeited all of their wages to their master. Surrogates and justices of the peace were empowered to issue arrest warrants for deserters and, on the oath of at least one creditable witness, to confine them in prison until the next sitting of the surrogate court or court of sessions. Convicted deserters were liable to be publicly whipped as vagrants and shipped back to their country of origin (s.17). Finally, the district court of sessions and the St. John's vice-admiralty court were empowered to hear and determine any wage dispute or offense committed by masters or servants against the act's provisions (s.18).

Historians have tended to focus on the wages and lien system in Palliser's Act, but the salient aspect of the law of master and servant was the effective criminalization of breach of contract. Justices presided over the enforcement of a penal regime that employed whippings to punish actions that threatened the master's authority. Sean Cadigan has argued that in spite of the provisions in Palliser's Act for whipping servants for breach of contract, "local courts chose to ignore them."[22] The problem with this argument lies in the broader assumption that magistrates were somehow reluctant to discipline servants in the eighteenth century. Cadigan concludes that the pressures engendered by the judicial resistance to enforce servant discipline eventually undermined the system of wage labor and contributed to the rise of the family fishery in the nineteenth century. Servants won an overwhelming proportion of their suits to recover wages, thus placing their masters, who were typically planters, in an increasingly untenable financial position. With indentured labor becoming increasingly unattractive, fishermen turned to their family and kin to supply the bulk of the labor needed for fishing operations.[23] Newfoundland was practically unique, therefore, in that the potential for judicial repression of indentured labor was never realized. Cadigan's work forms part of a broader reaction in Newfoundland historiography against what is seen as the myth of mercantile oppression. In other words, the scale is now tipped in favor of stressing servants' rights over labor discipline.[24]

Palliser's Act constituted neither a new nor a unique law of master and ser-

22. Cadigan, *Merchant-Settler Relations*, 84.
23. Ibid., ch. 5.
24. See Janzen, "Newfoundland and the International Fishery," 280–324.

vant. Its basic provisions were copied from regulations formally promulgated since at least 1753, when Governor Hugh Bonfoy issued rules for the settling of debts and wages. Bonfoy ordered debts to be adjusted "according to ancient custom": in cases where a planter could not "discharge his just debts and servant's wages," the creditors were to "secure (to be by them paid) the wages due to the servants employed in the fishery, [so] that the voyages may be continued to the end of the season, and a just division of the debtor's effects be made to each creditor."[25] In 1793 a committee of the House of Commons inquired into the enforcement of this custom and traced its origins back to 1749.[26] During his tenure as governor Palliser enforced the customary law of master and servant. In September 1764 he reiterated Bonfoy's proclamation on servant's wages, including the proviso "according to ancient custom."[27] In practice, such customs were a mixture of the laws, regulations, and traditions that had been adopted over time to ensure the smooth operation of the fishery. These provisions were recurrently altered and augmented according to the perceived needs of those in power. While some aspects doubtless were "ancient," in the sense of originating before formal government in Newfoundland, others were recent measures. To deal with the problems associated with settling debts at the end of the fishing season, Palliser issued a notice "to the merchants and traders," which stated, "I desire you will meet and consult together and suggest to me the means you think best for answering these ends."[28] At the same time he published another proclamation, this one directed to the "boatkeepers, inhabitants, and others concerned in the fishery," which provides a fascinating glimpse into the process of law making:

> And whereas I have it under consideration to make one general order rule or regulation for a certain and speedy method by which merchants may recover their debts, in order to enable me at the same time to provide a security for the boatmen and fishermen against all sorts of impositions and oppressions from the merchants, I desire you will meet and consult together and let me know what has been the ancient practice before these illegal methods became so common what are the several hardships the fishermen feel and suggest to me the method you think best to answer these ends.[29]

25. PANL, GN 2/1/A, 2:63–64.
26. See *Third Report from the House of Commons Committee*, f. 192, in Lambert, *House of Commons Sessional Papers*, 430.
27. PANL, GN 2/1/A, 3:275.
28. PANL, GN 2/1/A, 3:242–43.
29. PANL, GN 2/1/A, 3:243.

By working to identify and enforce legitimate local customs, Palliser was adhering to English common law.[30]

The District Courts: A Case Study of Trinity, 1760–1790

The district of Trinity encompassed the outports from Cape Bonavista down to Bay de Verde. District court sessions were held at Trinity harbor, which was the center of the cod fishery on the island's northeast coast.[31] From 1760 to 1790 the courts dealt with 300 writs, orders, and various actions; 149 suits and trials were entered into the minute book. By examining the fifteen years before and after 1775, the relative local impact of Palliser's Act can be ascertained. The most salient trend was the decline in the proportion of master and servant disputes before the courts: from 67 percent of the total case load in 1760–75, to 16 percent in 1775–90. This was not a by-product of an overall decline, since 45 percent of the total cases were heard after Palliser's Act. When broken down into five-year periods, this drop in master and servant suits can be clearly traced. The vast majority of master and servant disputes (more than 83 percent) were heard *before* the passage of Palliser's Act and, therefore, judged on the basis of the customary law of master and servant. The frequency of master-servant disputes brought before the district courts waned as the fishery's reliance on wage labor started to decline. During the heyday of the migratory fishery, the government was particularly concerned over the flow of laborers into Newfoundland. It is therefore not surprising that 60 percent of the total master-servant cases in Trinity occurred in the 1760s, when Irishmen from Leinster and Munster flocked to Newfoundland in search of work (see Table 4.1).[32]

These data suggest that eighteenth-century Newfoundland did not significantly diverge from the trend in the Anglo-American law of master and servant to criminalize breach of contract.[33] Servants were much more likely than masters to bring a case to court; they initiated more than three-quarters of the total cases. Of the suits brought before 1775, 38 percent were for wages and 30 percent for breach of contract, of which one in three involved complaints of severe beatings at the hands of their masters. In terms of verdicts, however, servants never won more than half of the total suits, with whippings

---

30. See C. Allen, *Law in the Making*, ch. 2; R. Walker and Walker, *English Legal System*, ch. 1.
31. See Handcock, *Trinity*.
32. Head, *Newfoundland*, ch. 7.
33. See Hay and Craven, "Master and Servant in England and the Empire"; Craven and Hay, "Criminalization."

TABLE 4.1.
Actions before Trinity District Court, Newfoundland, 1760–1790 (% of actions)

	Merchant-Planter	Master-Servant	Criminal Trials	Other	Number of Actions
1761–65	—	—	100	—	5
1766–70	12	79	—	10	52
1771–75	18	50	11	21	28
1776–80	—	29	14	57	7
1781–85	32	16	19	32	37
1786–90	35	15	5	45	20

SOURCE: PANL GN 5/4/B/1, boxes 1, 2.

ordered in more than 10 percent of the total cases (see Table 4.2). These data confirm the prevalence of servant discipline: in a quarter of the verdicts in the masters' favor, the court ordered servants to be publicly whipped.

The bulk of the master and servant disputes was heard from 1666 to 1770, when the naval surrogate in Trinity was Lieutenant John Cartwright, commander of HMS *Guernsey*. A vigorous administrator, Cartwright maintained excellent relations with the English fish merchants. During these years, Benjamin Lester, who was the most prominent merchant in the region, never lost a major suit.[34] In 1766 Lester brought an action against Edward Cole for refusing to ship himself and another servant for deserting his service. Lester's offer of three pounds was considered charity in a season that witnessed a glutted labor market. Both defendants were seen as part of a dangerous group of idle Irishmen. Lieutenant Cartwright ruled: "In order therefore to suppress such wick'd practices and intolerable idleness it is hereby ordered as an example to others that the said Cole and Mahany shall at the common whipping post receive on their bare backs two dozen lashes each with a cat of nine tails."[35] This decision enforced a paternalistic law of master and servant. In effect, surplus laborers had to accept any contractual terms offered to them under threat of corporal punishment and deportation as vagrants.

Contextualizing Labor Disputes and Court Actions

To assess the impact of punishments at the local level, the various types of social regulation need to be weighed together. For example, four court ac-

34. On Benjamin Lester, see D. F. Beamish, "Benjamin Lester," *Dictionary of Canadian Biography*, 4:491–92.
35. *Lester v. Cole & Mahany*, 1 Nov. 1766, Trinity District (PANL, GN 5/4/B/1).

TABLE 4.2.
Verdicts in Master and Servant Cases, Trinity, Newfoundland, 1761–1790

	Verdict for Servant	Verdict for Master[a]	Arbitrated or Dismissed
1761–65	—	—	—
1766–70	16	22 (5)[a]	3
1771–75	7	5 (1)[a]	2
1776–80	1	1	—
1781–85	2	4 (2)[a]	—
1786–90	1	1	1
Total	27	33	6

SOURCE: PANL GN 5/4/B/1, boxes 1, 2.
[a] Servant whipped.

tions brought in the space of a year in Trinity displayed the multiple faces of paternalistic authority. First, in May 1755, John Stanweth, a ship's carpenter, complained that John Goold, a fishing servant, had struck him in the face. In response, Thomas Warden, the local justice of the peace, ordered Goold to receive a dozen lashes at the whipping post.[36] At the next sitting of the court, Benjamin Lester alleged that John Walden, one of his servants, had been drunk and ill-behaved. According to the memorandum: "The next day John Walden down upon his knees in publick company and acknowledge[d] what he had said to be false and asked Mr. Lester's pardon and it was forgiven him upon condition not to be guilty of the like for the future."[37] This act of contrition symbolized the potent mix of retribution and mercy, of personal relations and public authority, which suffused the administration of law. The third example occurred in November 1755, when the servants' contracts were being settled. John Brock brought an information against one of his servants for refusing to go to sea. The magistrates issued a warrant for the man to return to work and, if he did not, authorized Brock to seize his servant's chest, clothes, as well as any other property, and "turn him out of doors and not allow him any victuals."[38] Such a threat loomed particularly large as winter approached and the servant would have been hard pressed not to relent. Lastly, in February 1756, Warden recorded that John Johnson was put into the stocks for being drunk and abusive toward his master.[39] As calculated ex-

36. *Stanweth v. Goold*, 30 May 1755, Trinity District (PANL, GN 5/4/B/1, box 1).
37. *Lester v. Walden*, 18 June 1755, Trinity District (PANL, GN 5/4/B/1, box 1).
38. *Brock v. Sargent*, 12 Nov. 1755, Trinity District (PANL, GN 5/4/B/1, box 1).
39. See the minutes for 15 Feb. 1756, Trinity District (PANL, GN 5/4/B/1, box 1).

amples in a small community, such incidents were sufficient to establish an effective penal code in the minds of those laboring in the local fishery.

Many of the suits brought before the courts each autumn were the climax of a running battle that can be discerned only through an extended case study. In 1773, for example, Walter Welch presented a petition to the surrogate court in Ferryland detailing how he had been beaten and unfairly dismissed by his master, William Saunders.[40] Contracted to work as a splitter, Welch had arrived in Ferryland the previous May. After returning from his first fishing voyage, he was ordered to work with the shore crew washing fish. Welsh had apparently signed his shipping paper in Ireland; whether he had worked previously in Ferryland is uncertain, but he probably had some experience, since splitters required a relatively high degree of skill. To be forced to wash fish with the shore crew would have been an insult to any splitter and was likely used as a form of "working up," that is, using demeaning tasks as a type of punishment.[41] Saunders admonished him for doing a poor job and struck him two or three times, upon which Welch complained to Robert Carter, the local justice of the peace. Summoned to explain the beating, Saunders told Carter that the next time he thought Welch deserved it, he would beat him even worse. Welch asked to be released from his contract, but Saunders refused, claiming that Welch was a good splitter whom he could not do without. Welch then allegedly skulked away and hid himself. Saunders remonstrated to Carter, who ordered a fine of three shillings for each day Welch neglected his duty.

Some time later another altercation occurred when Welch returned the key to the provisions chest. Saunders apparently thought too much had been taken and ordered Welch to go to sea again. The next morning he commanded Welch to cut wood and afterward refused to allow him to bring his clothes to the washerwoman. Ordered back to work, Welch refused on the grounds that it was a Sunday. His master then pushed him into his house and struck him twice on the nose; he ran outdoors but was struck on his side and collapsed, bleeding over the dirty linen he was still carrying; seeing this, Saunders kicked it into the dirt. The next morning Welch again went to Carter. Saunders informed Carter that Welch had refused to work and was "otherwise very saucy for which reason he struck him." He said he was now willing to release his servant from his indenture, but Welch maintained he would serve his whole time and then have his wages.

40. Unless otherwise noted, the material in this and the following paragraphs is based on *Welch v. Saunders*, 11 Sept. 1773, Ferryland District (Provincial Resource Library of Newfoundland and Labrador, St. John's [hereafter PRL], 340.9/N45, VT, Rare Books).

41. On the practice of "working up," see R. Morris, *Government and Labor in Early America*, 265.

But Carter would have none of this and gave Welch his clearance. He asked for the shipping paper, which Welch refused to give up, and Carter replied that if he did not deliver it within twenty-four hours, he would be flogged. At the surrogate court—where Captain James Howell Jones presided alongside Carter—Welch was found to be "a very troublesome and litigious person and has several times neglected his duty." The court sentenced him to receive corporal punishment and to be paid only for the time he had done his duty. For the assault Saunders was fined three pounds. While a cursory reading of this decree might suggest a simple case of punishment for insolence and a fine for assault, the dispute between Welch and Saunders had encompassed specific grievances over an entire fishing season. Through the use of violence, the law (rules for neglect of duty), control of work conditions, and then violence again, Saunders reacted to perceived instances of substandard performance, desertion, improper use of provisions, and refusal to work. In response, Welch sought redress through the law (by appealing to Justice Carter), objected to unfair work conditions, complained again to Carter, and then petitioned the surrogate court. Carter discharged his office according to the customs of the country, by which he tried to arbitrate the dispute, then fined Welch for desertion, and finally used the threat of flogging. None of these proceedings would have been recorded if Welch had not petitioned the visiting naval surrogate. Unfortunately for Welch and countless other servants, in such cases the surrogate courts consistently upheld the authority of the local justice of the peace.

Paternalism Reconsidered

A strict paternalism guided the regulation of labor disputes. Servants enjoyed conditional privileges, not inalienable rights: what paternalism granted it could also take away. Whether a merchant or planter acceded to a servant's request or periodically acted altruistically is not the point: what matters, at bottom, is that such decisions were almost exclusively within the master's discretion. Magistrates were not unusually cruel—local courts routinely responded favorably to petitions for wages and redress for breach of contract—but these choices were the prerogative of the naval governor, his junior officers, and the justices of the peace.[42] Such discretion can be plainly seen in Governor Byron's response to a servant's petition against his master for nonpayment of wages in 1770. The servant admitted that he had been unable to

---

42. For a critique of the traditional model of paternalism, see Hay, "Patronage, Paternalism, and Welfare," 27–45.

perform his duties due to illness, but he insisted that he had become sick through no fault of his own after being shipped to work in the fishery. Byron ordered Robert Carter, a justice at Ferryland, to look into the matter. He reminded Carter that masters not only had an obligation to take care of their servants but also were legally obligated to pay wages to those who had signed a contract. Nonetheless, Byron added an important caveat: "where circumstances shall be made appear against servants, who shall abuse an *indulgence* of this sort, by feigned sickness or sickness brought on by drunkenness the masters may deduct two days for one of every day neglected of their duty."[43] Allowing such indulgences meant neither that magistrates were recognizing a legal right nor that servants necessarily felt beholden because of such treatment.

As a group of Irish servants discovered in 1790, benevolence and discipline were flip sides of the same coin. Suspected of having stolen some salt codfish from a merchant's flake, twelve men were examined by the local justice of the peace. Three of them confessed and were convicted of larceny, but the merchant recommended one man, who was his servant, for mercy because he was "an old man hitherto bearing an exceeding good character."[44] While the court sentenced all three to be deported to Ireland, it gave one of them an additional sentence: "Decreed that Thomas Quinn be punished with twenty four lashes on his bare back, as follows, viz. eight at the point beach, eight at the north side room, and eight at the court house, and to walk from place [to place] with a fish hung round his neck." There is no evidence to suggest that Quinn was any more guilty of the crime than his two accomplices. The determining factor behind the decision to whip him instead of the others was simply the prerogative of the bench, which followed the lead of the complainant. From the servants' perspective, the capriciousness of paternalism meant that they had little influence over their fate when they entered the courtroom as defendants. If they were granted mercy, it was due to the whim of magistrates and masters who together selected those worthy of special consideration.

As Greg Dening and others have pointed out, the incidence of judicial violence cannot simply be counted but must be measured in terms of social im-

43. PANL, GN 2/1/A, 4:263-64 (emphasis added).

44. *Hill v. Quinn, Dullahanty, and Lundrigan*, 14 Oct. 1790, Ferryland District (PRL, 340.9/ N45, VT, Rare Books). The minutes stipulate that Patrick Lundrigan was a servant of the merchant whose fish had been stolen, and the other two men—Roger Dullahanty and Thomas Quinn—may also have been working under the complainant's direction. The men testified that they had been drunk the night of the theft and could not remember what they had done. The original information had been taken by Henry Sweetland, a local justice of the peace, who issued a search warrant and then examined the suspects. The hearing and sentencing took place two weeks later, at a formal sitting of Sweetland and two other justices of the peace.

pact. The bare numbers of public whippings mattered less than the context in which they occurred.[45] Magistrates at times explicitly cited the threat of corporal punishment in order to discipline servants. In Ferryland in 1785, for example, James Kane brought an information against three of his servants for refusing to work. The court ruled that the men were guilty of disobeying their masters' orders; they were each fined two days wages and ordered to return peaceably to their duty. If any future complaint should be made, the servants were to be summarily whipped.[46] Legal power could be wielded as much by sheer intimidation as by individual acts of judicial violence, and the specter of punishment and brutality penetrated deeply into the *mentalité* of maritime life. Evidence of labor discipline in Newfoundland conflicts with the model advanced by Marcus Rediker. Where Rediker sees what amounts to naked class conflict between workers (violent popular resistance) and capital (violent legal repression), I would argue that magistrates were far more circumspect in their use of corporal punishment. What made whipping so effective was not its indiscriminate application but rather its deliberate calibration in response to varying local conditions.[47]

Even in cases that did not involve lengthy disputes or appeals, magistrates faced complex suits that forced them to wade into the tense relationships that regularly developed between servants and masters. In August 1786, for example, John Clinch, a justice of the peace in Trinity, heard a complaint that clearly exposed the cracks in a captain's authority over his crew. John Andrews, master of the brig *William*, brought an information alleging that Thomas Taylor, a mariner under his command, had assaulted him and had been insubordinate while the vessel was readying to sail from St. John's harbor. According to Andrews, after the crew had raised and catted the anchor, Taylor used an improper method to clinch the stopper (the rope securing the anchor to the cathead) and, insisting his way was best, refused to follow Andrews's orders. A heated argument ensued over the correct way to fasten the stopper—Taylor reputedly derided Andrews's seamanship as lubberly—and the confrontation turned violent.[48]

Because the circumstances surrounding the use of violence bore directly on the question of culpability, the court investigated the details of the affray. The information recounted how the fight broke out:

45. Dening, *Mr. Bligh's Bad Language*, 113–15. See also Thompson, "Folklore, Anthropology, and Social History," 255.

46. *Kane v. Colbert et al.*, 30 Aug. 1785, Ferryland District (PRL, 340.9/N45, VT, Rare Books).

47. Rediker, *Devil*, ch. 5. See also Linebaugh and Rediker, *Many-Headed Hydra*, ch. 5.

48. Unless otherwise noted, the material in this section is based on *Andrews v. Taylor*, 23 Aug. 1786, Trinity District (PANL, GN 5/4/B/1, box 2).

[T]he said Andrews then Damned him for a Jowling rascal—the said
Taylor returned the compliment in the same words, the said Andrews
not expecting such an answer, supposed it a mistake, and desired a repe-
tition of his answer, which the Taylor immediately gave, viz. What do I
say—I say you are a damned rascal at [the] same time looking the said
Andrews full in the face, such behaviour exasperated the said Andrews
so far as to strike him, which the said Taylor likewise immediately returned—from whence a scuffle ensued, sometimes one down sometimes the other, at length the said Taylor getting his knees on the said
Andrew's breast, and taking him by the stock said, now you bugger
I'll choke you—after a short time the said Andrews disengaged himself
from the said Taylor, with his shirt and waistcoat torn in pieces and full
of blood—During the scuffle the mate and men stood by mute.

Andrews's testimony placed him on a firm legal footing, since maritime law
permitted masters to flog disobedient seamen. Masters were not permitted
to beat seamen cruelly, that is, to injure a man or cause severe bleeding, and
they could not legally flog ill crewmen or deny food or water as a form of
punishment. But they could expect assistance from the crew, who were legally
obliged to constrain any disobedient seaman. In cases where a servant's insolence was proved in court, magistrates could sentence the offender to be
whipped, fined, or imprisoned (or a combination thereof), as well as dismissed
from the ship.[49] The court first had to determine whether the initial beating
was justified and whether Andrews had used excessive force. If it ruled that
Taylor had assaulted Andrews and disobeyed lawful orders, the court had a
wide range of penal options at its disposal.

The court heard testimony from the entire crew. For his part Taylor denied striking Andrews or using abusive language, adding that he had obeyed
the order to cat the anchor. Next the five other mariners serving aboard the
William testified. The men all stated that they had not seen Taylor actually
strike the captain, but they gave varying accounts of the incident. Two of
them testified that they had tried to separate Taylor and Andrews during the
scuffle, while two others affirmed that a great deal of blood had spilt about the
deck. Another seaman claimed that not only had Taylor made no resistance
to the first beating, but Andrews had taken off his coat and renewed his attack
a second time, grabbing Taylor by the shoulders and tearing his shirt. The
final witness was the mate, who testified only that he saw an altercation during
which the captain struck Taylor. Since none of the witnesses stated that they

49. R. Morris, *Government and Labor in Early America*, 262–73.

had seen Taylor strike Andrews, the prosecution focused on the defendant's alleged insubordination, particularly his use of impertinent language.

This case provides important insights into how local courts viewed the problem of labor discipline. Although the jury's verdict found both parties at fault, the crewman was punished much more severely than the master. Thomas Taylor was fined three pounds plus the jailer's fees, while John Andrews had to pay all of the court costs. To buttress the master's blighted standing, the court ordered Taylor to ask Andrews for his pardon, and he was to be discharged from the brig's crew. In a revealing statement, the jurors ruled that "in consequence of the said John Andrews renewing the attack the second time, they cannot award any corporal punishment to be inflicted on the said Thomas Taylor." By phrasing the judgment in the negative, the court acknowledged that Taylor would have been whipped had Andrews not persisted in beating his crewman. The judgment illustrates how local courts could function at three interrelated levels: the rule of law (apportioning fines based on the relative culpability of the two parties, and ordering the discharge of a disobedient seaman according to maritime law); judicial discretion (issuing the additional requirement that the seaman personally apologize to the ship's master); and mercy (publicly pronouncing that the accused would not be whipped, despite the fact that he had been disobedient). Power was not simply exercised by meting out punishments to the full extent of the law but rather flowed through parallel forms that mutually reinforced both the legal and social order of class relations. In short, Taylor was never whipped but was punished nonetheless.

Conclusion

Law in eighteenth-century Newfoundland evolved according to the needs of those in power. Authority was exercised in an inherently paternalistic manner; servants were, in effect, at the mercy of those who sat on the bench. This does not mean that servants were correspondingly docile—they pursued their interests as best they could and periodically rebelled—but the decision of whether to convict a servant or order a whipping was the prerogative of the bench. Newfoundland does not fit the basic interpretive dichotomy of state law (statute) versus folk law (unwritten law).[50] The island's courts relied ex-

---

50. A recent collection of essays treats unwritten law and folk law as largely one and the same thing, employing a series of dichotomies—for example, oral versus written, flexible versus fixed—to construct an inclusive definition of folk law. Renteln and Dundes, "What Is Folk Law?," 2–4.

tensively on unwritten law: custom and common law formed the foundation of governance. For most of the eighteenth century, statute law was of secondary importance; Palliser's Act was a reactive measure that codified customs already in force at the local level. Without the constraints of the panoply of English institutions, the naval government was divested of many obligations and processes of accountability, leaving governors relatively free to respond to local problems using whatever resources they deemed necessary. The fact that many aspects of this legal regime were informal did not make them ineffective. In the absence of a local legislature, the British government tailored the law of master and servant to suit available legal resources and the demands of propertied interests. When Parliament passed new legislation in 1791–92, it made the minimal changes required for a functional judiciary and entrenched legally the system of surrogate courts that had long operated customarily.

The development of the law of master and servant bears on the larger issue of locating Newfoundland's place in the British Empire. As David Hancock has argued, the first Atlantic empire was characterized by decentralized opportunism. English colonies developed under a system different from that imposed in other empires: it was fundamentally agricultural in nature, organized around settlement by Europeans, and governed by representative institutions staffed by civilian authorities.[51] After the American Revolution, the British Empire became increasingly divided between its remaining colonies in North America and others, mostly in Asia, where militaristic oligarchies governed non-European societies.[52] Yet the case of Newfoundland belies the assertion that the empire can be simply divided schematically into colonies with representative government and civil courts (where settlers of British origin formed the controlling majority), and those with autocracy (where colonial elites ruled over predominantly non-European peoples).[53] Newfoundland was populated overwhelmingly by servants from England and Ireland, but its authoritarian system of naval government persisted well into the nineteenth century. As late as 1818, fishermen were liable to be whipped for relatively minor offenses, and naval officers continued to administer law until 1824. As in other staple economies, laborers toiling in the cod fishery were kept in their place by an autocratic regime which did not shrink from using violence and intimidation.

51. Hancock, "A World of Business to Do," 3–5, 34.
52. Bayly, *Imperial Meridian*, esp. ch. 4.
53. Marshall, "Britain without America," 590.

FIVE

Canada, 1670–1935

Symbolic and Instrumental Enforcement in Loyalist North America

Paul Craven

Master and servant in Canada has a paradoxical history. There was a great deal of penal legislation. In contrast to the neighboring United States, fines and imprisonment remained available well into the nineteenth and, in some provinces, twentieth centuries. Indeed, new legislation to punish workers for disobedience and desertion was enacted after 1875, the year of final repeal in Britain, and even after the Canadian Parliament's own Breaches of Contract Act two years later. But compared with Britain and the other white dominions, let alone other parts of the empire, in most parts of Canada enforcement was sporadic, convictions relatively few, and punishments rarely harsh. It is easy enough to construct an explanation for inconsiderable enforcement out of the structure of the economy and the characteristics of the labor force, but these cannot at the same time account for the variety and persistence of penal legislation. The answer seems to lie as much in the symbolic as the instrumental uses of employment law in this part of the empire.

The British colonies and territories that became Canadian provinces in the second half of the nineteenth century included military, crown, legislative, and company regimes, and both common-law and civilian jurisdictions.[1] Ex-

1. Nova Scotia (Acadia, [hereafter N.S.]) was first ceded to England by France in 1714, but British settlement and civil administration began only in 1749. Prince Edward Island [P.E.I.] and New Brunswick [N.B.] were carved out of old N.S. in 1769 and 1784 respectively. Quebec [Que.] (Lower Canada [L.C.], 1791–1840; Canada East, 1840–67) came under British rule in 1759–60, while the settlement of what is now the province of Ontario [Ont.] (Upper Canada [U.C.], 1791–1840; Canada West, 1840–67) did not begin in earnest until the arrival of the Loyalists after the American Revolution. Although U.C. and L.C. were joined in legislative union as the Province of Canada (Can. [Prov.]) from 1840, most of the legislation of that period discussed here applied to just one or the other of its predecessor colonies. All these colonies con-

cept Rupert's Land, granted to the Hudson's Bay Company (HBC) in 1670, these regions came under British rule a good two centuries later than the American colonies discussed by Tomlins in this volume. The local master and servant statutes of the various Canadian colonies were distinctly different not only from any English act but from one another's as well, a function of different reception dates, external influences, and local conditions. Nova Scotia and Quebec adopted local legislation so early in their British colonial histories that for practical purposes they could hardly be said to have received the English statutes.[2] The Nova Scotia legislation, which depended heavily on seventeenth-century Virginia statutes embellished with some Irish borrowings, influenced subsequent enactments in New Brunswick and Prince Edward Island. Some of the earliest Quebec legislation was also based on seventeenth-century American colonial statutes.[3] English master and servant acts to 1759 were supposed by treatise writers of the 1830s to have been received in Ontario, but they were considered not to be in force by 1847, when the first local legislation was enacted.[4] The law governing HBC employment relations in Rupert's Land as late as 1870 was notionally that of England in 1670. The new provinces in the prairie west based their master and servant acts on Canadian precedents, while British Columbia received early nineteenth-century British statutes before adopting a version of Ontario's reformed master and servant act in 1897.

In all these jurisdictions, the law defined employment relations in contractual terms, summarily enforceable by justices of the peace. The range of available sanctions varied considerably. In the Virginia-influenced Atlantic colonies, absentees and deserters were required to "make satisfaction by service"

---

federated to form the Dominion of Canada (Can. [Dom.]) in 1867 or shortly thereafter. The northern territories draining into Hudson Bay (Rupert's Land) and the region west of the Great Lakes were under the control of the Hudson's Bay Company (HBC) until the mid-nineteenth century, although that control was fiercely contested by its Montreal-based rival, the North West Company, before the two merged in 1821. The Canadian province of Manitoba [Man.] was created out of the old Red River Colony (Assiniboia) in 1870. The North-West Territories [N.-W.T.] in the western interior became the provinces of Saskatchewan [Sask.] and Alberta [Alta.] in 1905. The Pacific coast colonies of Vancouver Island and British Columbia [B.C.] were created in 1849 and 1858 respectively, united under the latter name in 1866, and joined Confederation in 1871. For Newfoundland, which joined the Canadian confederation in 1949, see the chapter by Bannister in this volume.

2. Writing in the 1830s, Beamish Murdoch considered that (N.S.) 5 Geo.III c.7 (1765) and (N.S.) 28 Geo.III c.6 (1787) amounted to a complete code, so that none of the English master and servant statutes was in force there: Murdoch, *Epitome*, 2:5.

3. For example, (Que.) 5 Geo.III, Ordinance of 31 May 1765 (desertion by seaman), was based on (Mass.) Prov. Laws (May 1693).

4. Craven, "Law of Master and Servant"; Webber, "Labour and the Law."

by working twice the time they were absent or more. Although it remained a common remedy in statutes regulating apprentices and merchant seamen, performance did not appear in the general master and servant statutes passed elsewhere after 1800; instead, convicted workers were subject to fines and imprisonment. Nevertheless, specific performance remained a common object of magistrates' practice in worker misconduct cases throughout the nineteenth century and into the twentieth.

For much of the period considered here, master and servant statutes in the Atlantic region and Quebec did not provide remedies for wages complaints. In some of these places, justices of the peace had an expanded civil jurisdiction, so small wage claims could be determined relatively expeditiously.[5] In others, unpaid workers faced the prospect of protracted and expensive civil litigation. Until 1834 in Quebec, wage claims had to be taken to the Court of King's Bench, whose inferior term had jurisdiction over all claims up to ten pounds sterling. Thereafter, they could be tried summarily in one of the small-claims courts.[6] Before an 1841 reform permitted them to recover wages up to twenty pounds before two justices, merchant seamen in Nova Scotia had to proceed in Vice-Admiralty.[7] Beginning with Ontario's 1847 statute, summary wage recovery was commonly provided for by the master and servant acts themselves.[8] That the legislation provided a quick and cheap remedy for breaches of contract by either party may have made it seem fairer.[9] Nevertheless, the Ontario act (and others that followed it) clearly distinguished prosecutions of workers, who might be arrested on warrants and punished by fine or imprisonment, from claims against employers, which proceeded by summons and ended in damages. Where wage recovery was available under master and servant acts, it was used heavily, although a successful action did not guarantee payment.

Neither the legislatures nor the courts exempted domestic or menial servants from coverage by the Canadian colonies' general master and servant

5. N.B. justices could determine small civil complaints either alone or with a three-man jury, while in N.S. debts of less than twenty shillings could be determined by a single justice of the peace. (P.E.I.) 2 Wm.IV c.26 (1833) was the first in the region to provide for summary wage recovery, in this case before two commissioners of debt for amounts up to five pounds.

6. Hogg and Shulman, "Wage Disputes"; Hogg, "Legal Rights," 4, 35. For small-claims courts, see Fyson, *Court Structure*. Statutes providing for summary wage recovery included (L.C.) 6 Wm.IV c.28 (1836), (Can. [Prov.]) 12 Vict. c.55 (1849), and (Que.) 59 Vict. c.48 (1895).

7. (N.S.) 4 Vict. c.50 (1841). Earlier legislation had been disallowed: A. Stone, "Admiralty," 406. In N.B., sailors could recover wages of up to twenty pounds before a single justice of the peace: (N.B.) 6 Wm.IV c.44 (1836).

8. These included (Can. [Prov.]) 10&11 Vict. c.23 (1847), (Can. [Prov.]) 12 Vict. c.55 (1849), (N.-W.T.) Ord. n.5 (1879), (B.C.) 60 Vict. c.26 (1897).

9. Craven, "Law of Master and Servant," 188–89.

statutes, which were rarely limited to specific occupations.[10] The chief exception was the merchant seaman,[11] whose written engagements (articles) were closely supervised, and who could be imprisoned at the employer's expense for misconduct in port, "that he may be secured and forthcoming to proceed on the voyage he has so agreed for."[12]

Throughout Canada, justices of the peace and other local officials could bind out orphans or destitute children as apprentices or servants. Similar provisions were often included among the powers of corporate officers in acts incorporating workhouses and orphanages. Under Nova Scotia's and New Brunswick's variants of the Elizabethan poor law, this extended to the involuntary binding of the adult poor as well, sometimes through the institution of "pauper auctions" whereby the services of the indigent were sold to the lowest bidder.[13] Combined with vagrancy provisions for whipping or jailing the idle and dissolute, these poor-law regimes effectively criminalized unemployment for all but the unremittingly feeble.[14] In Ontario, which rejected English poor law early in its history,[15] the pauper apprentice provisions were used to regularize guardianship or fostering arrangements but do not seem to have played a significant part in labor recruitment or discipline.

Despite royal instructions advising the governor of Nova Scotia, Britain's first permanent settlement in Canada, to avoid discouraging the slave trade, furnish a twice-yearly account of "what number of Negroes our said Colony is supplied with," and ensure that "each Planter do keep a proper Number of White Servants, and that they appear in arms at all times as they shall be required,"[16] these northern colonies were not destined to become lands of plantation agriculture worked by black or panis (native) slaves or brown coolies under the watchful eyes of white men with guns. Native people figured prominently in the fur trade, although more as producers for exchange than

10. In some of these colonies, apprentices were subject to different legislation than ordinary servants.

11. Some similar occupations were also covered by special legislation, notably *voyageurs* in the fur trade and workers on fishing vessels.

12. (Que.) 5 Geo.III, Ord. 31 May 1765. The same language appears in N.B. and P.E.I. statutes.

13. The low bid would be paid out of the local poor rate to subsidize the pauper's maintenance. See Aiton, "Paupers"; P.L.I.S., *Manners, Morals and Mayhem*.

14. (N.S.) 28 Geo.III c.6 (1787), s.6, provided for binding out anyone convicted of a clergyable offense and "all discorderly [*sic*] and beggarly persons who shall be found strolling in this Province," for seven-year terms.

15. Smandych, "Poor Law"; for the influence of English poor-law reform on Ontario in the 1830s, Baehre, "Paupers."

16. Provincial Archives of Nova Scotia (hereafter PANS) RG 1 v.350(a), instructions to Cornwallis, 29 Apr. 1749.

as subordinate employees. Some temporary local exceptions aside, they did not form a substantial part of the wage labor force except in British Columbia. Neither did these colonial economies depend to an appreciable extent on African slavery, although slaveholding persisted into the early nineteenth century.[17] Successive waves of blacks arrived from the thirteen colonies and the United States as slaves or servants of white settlers, as former slaves freed by military proclamation during the revolutionary war and the war of 1812–14,[18] and as runaways seeking their freedom on the "underground railroad" in the two decades before the American civil war. In pockets of settlement they supplied a pool of cheap disposable labor whose presence conditioned local employment practices and race relations. Chinese, Japanese, and East Indian contract workers fulfilled a similar although more extensive role in British Columbia later in the century, particularly in railway construction, coal mining, and the fishery.

These were overwhelmingly white settler colonies, peopled largely by smallholders and other producers seeking to establish a degree of economic independence by accumulating capital toward family-based commodity production. For some this meant the exercise of a trade, but for most it meant direct participation in resource extraction—in the fur trade, the fishery, lumbering, and farming (and often a combination of these). During the settlement phase of the colonial economies, less a span of years than a moving shadow, money was scarce, goods were dear, and labor was frequently set off against store credit. Long-term contracts were rare. People took casual, occasional, or seasonal work to clear a debt or complete a purchase; their long-term attachment was not to paid employment but to clearing or improving the family farm and acquiring property to settle their children.[19] Labor market development was quite uneven, constrained by a double scarcity, of workers and of the capacity to pay them, although there was no shortage of potential work. Distinctions emerged and hardened between city trades and country crafts. Skilled workers in garrison towns, administrative centers, and major

---

17. Ontario abolished slavery by legislation; elsewhere in British North America it was extinguished by judicial action (or inaction). See in general Winks, *Blacks*; for N.S.: Pachai, *Beneath the Clouds*; Hartlen, "Bound"; J. Walker, *Black Loyalists*; A. Robertson, "Bondage"; A. Robertson, "Tenant Farmers"; Cahill, "Slavery"; Clairmont and Magill, *N.S. Blacks*; for P.E.I.: Holman, "Jupiter Wise"; Hornby, *Black Islanders*; for N.B.: Bell, "Slavery"; Raymond, "Negro"; Spray, *Blacks*; Jack, "Loyalists"; for Que.: Trudel, *L'esclavage*; and for Ont.: Fleming, "Negro Slaves"; Brode, "Simcoe."

18. As late as 1832, the N.B. legislature debated "the great and unnecessary burden of the black refugees" on local poor rates: *Saint John Courier*, 25 Feb. 1832.

19. Bittermann, "Farm Households"; T. Crowley, "Rural Labour"; McCalla, *Planting*; Radforth, "Shantymen"; Webber, "Labour and the Law"; Wynn, *Timber Colony*.

ports were organizing for standardized shop rules and wage scales while their country contemporaries were still taking payment in green fish and store credit.

By the middle of the nineteenth century significant industrial enclaves had emerged in Montreal, Hamilton, and Toronto.[20] In the next quarter century, and particularly in southern Ontario, the factory system took root in many smaller centers as well.[21] Urban trade unionism's confrontation with the industrialists' assault on established work practices, recruitment, and workplace discipline was accompanied by a contest about the reach of law. Employers had little success attacking strikes as criminal combinations,[22] but rather more in using the master and servant legislation to hold workers to their contracts. An opportunistic alliance between the governing party and Toronto's trade-union "junta"[23] resulted in Dominion legislation purportedly decriminalizing trade unions (1872) and breaches of employment contracts (1877). The former was largely window dressing because in removing a phantom liability it also created new strike-related crimes;[24] the latter was far narrower in scope and effect than its expansive preamble suggested.[25]

In what follows, I track the local origins and enforcement of master and servant legislation regionally, from east to west. This geographic organization is necessarily asynchronous, but it is consistent with the fact that while western regions sometimes borrowed from eastern predecessors, the reverse rarely happened. It recognizes the regional distinctiveness of employment law, which survived Confederation in 1867 and was reinforced by the 1877 Dominion legislation.

Atlantic Canada

The early legal history of Atlantic Canadian labor is embedded in race relations. For three decades after the arrival of the Loyalist refugees from the American Revolution, the status and security of black workers were constantly before the courts. At Shelburne, Nova Scotia, a center of Black Loyalist settlement, the issue presented itself in numerous guises: blacks claiming to have been unlawfully detained as slaves;[26] whites charging others with em-

20. For late nineteenth-century urban social conditions, see Copp, *Montreal*; Piva, *Toronto*; Kealey, *Canada Investigates Industrialism*.
21. Gilmour, *Spatial Evolution*; Heron, "Factory Workers."
22. Craven, "Workers' Conspiracies."
23. Kealey, *Toronto Workers*, ch. 8.
24. Craven, "Workers' Conspiracies."
25. Craven, "Modern Spirit."
26. PANS MG4 v.141, Township Book (Shelburne Gen. Sess.) (hereafter TB) (*Molly, a*

ploying blacks whom the applicants claimed as their slaves;[27] protests by free blacks who feared being removed from the province by their employers and sold into West Indian slavery.[28] There were other manifestations of the marginal status of black workers, particularly where their numbers threatened white wages. Disbanded soldiers rioted in 1784 to drive the blacks from town. Frequent prosecutions of blacks for petty thefts, often from their employers, were followed by judicial beatings and in some cases banishment from the county.[29] Black children were routinely taken from their parents and bound out to whites;[30] indentures were routinely sold and assigned to other masters.[31] Black workers, whether slaves or notionally free, had little effective recourse against the violence of some white employers.[32]

Nova Scotia's first master and servant act (1765) applied to servants bound by indenture or hired for six months or more,[33] while the similar New Brunswick act of 1786 applied only to indentured servants and apprentices.[34] Cover-

"negro wench" v. *Gray*, 12 Apr. 1786); PANS RG 60, box 1 (Shelburne General Sessions case files, 1783–96) (hereafter SGS1) file 6 (Andrews, 23 Aug. 1785); SGS1 file 49 (*Postell v. Gray*, 5 July 1791).

27. PANS Mfm 13,375 Shelburne General & Special Sessions (hereafter SGSS) (*McLeod v. Cocken*, 17 May 1786); TB (*White v. Licet*, 12 Apr. 1786); SGS1 file 2 (*Gernon v. James*, 23 Jan. 1785); SGS1 file 31 (*Lion v. Summers*, 26 Oct. 1787).

28. PANS RG 34 series M Shelburne (Dixon, 29 July 1791); RG 34 series P Shelburne County file 8 (*Connor v. Harris*, 1 Nov. 1791), and file 14 (two blacks carried to Guadeloupe by a French privateer, 13 May 1804).

29. SGSS ("Joe, a Black Man," on complaint of Sommerville, 15 Sept. 1785); SGSS (Westley, 5 Jan. 1791); RG 60, box 2 (Shelburne Gen. Sess. case files, 1796–1820) (hereafter SGS2) file 87 (Mathews, 6 Aug. 1810); SGS2 file 108 (Thomas, Oct. 1819); SGS2 file 109 (Brown, 1819).

30. SGS1 file 58 (*Robertson v. Williams*, 4 Apr. 1795); SGSS (*Van Lyle v. Clarke*, 3 Jan. 1787/8). In 1786 the Shelburne justices resolved, "That the Act respecting the Poor, be particularly attended to, . . . particularly that part of it respecting the binding out the Children of the Poor, more especially the Blacks, that they may be brought up usefull, and not burthens to the Community."

31. SGSS (*Van Lile v. Clerk*, 3 Sept. 1788); SGSS (*Wise v. Greenwood and Fraser*, 5 Aug. 1789). Assignment of indentures was not limited to black servants. (N.S.) 28 Geo.III c.6 (1787) permitted masters to sell and assign the unexpired terms of indentures and required the purchaser to give security not to carry the worker out of the province.

32. Indictments and trials of the Andrews family for the murder of Jude, their black servant: PANS RG 42 Magistrates Court, Shelburne County Courts of Oyer & Terminer (1801, v. 1, file 4); SGS1 file 27 (*Davis v. Gray*, 5 Nov. 1786). In contrast, a black servant (or slave) convicted of assaulting his master was sentenced to an immediate public whipping, to two months confinement at hard labor with additional whippings, and to remain in jail until his court fees were paid: TB (*R. v. Isaac*, a Negro, 6 Apr. 1784).

33. (N.S.) 5 Geo.III c.7 (1765) s.1. Murdoch, *Epitome*, 2:3, maintained that it referred "chiefly to such menial servants as are bound by indenture, and to servants hired for six months, or a longer term, as agricultural or fishery servants, by written contract, and does not appear to embrace common servants, or apprentices to trades and professions."

34. (N.B.) 26 Geo.III c.37 (1786).

age was extended to monthly hirings in 1787 in Nova Scotia and 1795 in Prince Edward Island.[35] These acts enforced employment contracts by specific performance or damages; imprisonment was incidental.[36] Jail time as the routine punishment for workers' breach first appeared in Atlantic Canada in a New Brunswick statute of 1826.[37] Yet both before and after the 1765 act was passed, magistrates at Halifax, the Nova Scotia capital, assumed the power to imprison deserting workers. While the details are sketchy, the 1771 case of an indentured servant jailed for refusing to return to his master's service,[38] and another in 1792 of imprisonment for resisting a twenty-month extension of the term of indentures to make up for an absence, suggest that jail was being imposed for refusing to obey the court's performance order.[39] In 1815, however, new bridewell legislation empowered the Halifax justices to imprison, among other classes of disreputable persons, "runaways, stubborn servants, apprentices and children."[40] Of the fifty-eight people jailed for employment-related offenses between August 1834 and May 1841, at least thirty-nine were seamen, most of them committed on the authority of the merchant shipping legislation, and fifteen were "runaway" or "refractory" apprentices, committed on "common law" or "Police Act" authority. Of the four remaining, two were listed as "deserting from" (without more), one as "absconding from his father's service," and the last as "absconding from his master."[41]

Outside Halifax, the justices required misbehaving servants to perform

35. (N.S.) 28 Geo.III. c.6 (1787); (P.E.I.) 35 Geo.III c.4 (1795).

36. By (N.S.) 28 Geo.III. c.6 (1787) misbehaving workers could be punished by abatement of wages. By (P.E.I.) 35 Geo.III c.4 (1795) servants who left their employers at the expiry of their term without prior notice risked forfeiting all wages or, if there were no wages due, a month's imprisonment.

37. (N.B.) 7 Geo.IV c.5 (1826); (N.B.) 7 Geo.IV c.12 (1826) provided imprisonment for desertion by seamen, and (P.E.I.) 5 Geo.IV c.12 (1824) by fishery workers. The latter provision was copied from Palliser's Act, (G.B.) 15 Geo.III c.31 (1775), the imperial legislation governing the Newfoundland fishery. (P.E.I.) 2 Wm.IV c.26 (1833) routinized abatement and imprisonment as punishments for workers' breaches, and introduced expedited wage recovery and fines for withholding wages.

38. In October 1751 two indentured servants were in jail for desertion, as was another in June 1771: PANS RG 34 series J (Halifax County Prisoners in County Gaol, 1751–1849). In 1752 the magistrates complained that the only punishment for "disorderly servants who . . . absent themselves without leave from their service" was to jail them at their masters' expense: PANS RG 1 v.210, Minutes of the Governor's Council (Transcripts), 22 Dec. 1752; a workhouse was provided in 1754.

39. PANS RG 34 series 312 P1 Halifax County Minutes of Proceedings (*Bethell v. Munro*, 5 Dec. 1792). Performance orders could be severe. In 1769 the Halifax quarter sessions extended an apprentice's term by a full year because his father had kept him from his work for four days: PANS RG 60 Halifax County Gen. Sess., v. 1 (*Turner v. McKinnon*, 18 Sept. 1769).

40. (N.S.) 55 Geo.III c.9 (1815).

41. PANS RG 34 series J Halifax Police Return of Commitments.

their contracts, but they did not jail them.[42] Prosecutions under the master and servant acts were scarce in the rural Maritimes, and uncommon even in the cities. Most of the employment law business of the Halifax and Saint John police magistrates involved seamen. Nevertheless, about 10 percent of the work-related cases heard in mid-nineteenth-century Halifax arose under the master and servant (as opposed to the seamen's) acts, almost all of them apprenticeship cases.[43] Throughout the Maritimes, and indeed in all the Canadian colonies, justices were profoundly reluctant to release apprentices from their indentures, even where mistreatment was clearly proved.[44] The belief that a master should be permitted to recoup his investment in the apprentice's upkeep and education persisted well into the early twentieth century.[45]

Between 1846 and 1858, the Halifax police court heard about 500 employment-related cases.[46] Eighty-five percent involved merchant seamen, reflecting Halifax's status as a busy international seaport and the particular importance of police, magistrates, and prisons in the shoreside regulation of seafaring labor. Three-quarters of the employment-related cases arose out of complaints by shipowners and captains that sailors had left their vessels or were refusing to proceed to sea.[47] In about one-sixth of these the court released the men, usually because of technical defects in their articles. In five of every six cases, however, sailors who left their ships or refused to go to

---

42. For example, PANS RG 34 series P King's County, box 3 (*Burbridge v. Whealon*, 26 May 1772); additional papers are in PANS MG 1 Chipman Collection (hereafter Chip.), v. 182, no. 76; Inferior Court of Common Pleas, Hants County, box 1, judgment book of George Deschamps, 31 May 1773; SGSS (*Bull v. Shorta and Slator*, 23 May 1787). Murdoch, *Epitome*, 2:5, observes that the 1787 master and servant act "gives the sessions of each county power to make regulations to punish ill doing servants, and to apprehend and restore runaway servants; but no fine or penalty is pointed out, to give a force and sanction to this general power."

43. After 1851 an apprentice or minor servant who deserted his employment or misconducted himself might be ordered to return to his master, or imprisoned for up to twenty days, "unless sooner discharged by his master." (N.S.) *Rev. Stat.*, Part II, Title XXXIII, c.125 (1851).

44. Chip. v. 186, nos. 48–50 (*Pulk v. Chase*, 19 Apr. 1805); PANS RG 34 series P Cumberland County, Amherst General Sessions Proceedings (*Bulmer v. Berry and Wife*, 26 Oct. 1790).

45. The master's common-law right to use corporal punishment was limited to "moderate" correction of apprentices and minor servants, to whom he was in loco parentis.

46. Here I summarize the master and servant business of this court for a broken run of seventy-five months from Jan. 1846 to Jan. 1859, representing slightly less than half the total period, and including 243 employment-related cases. These volumes (in PANS RG 42 Series D [hereafter HPC], vols. D1–D9) are entitled "Police Court Minutes" except D7, which is "Stipendiary Magistrates Court Minutes." For the history of the court, see Girard, "Rise and Fall," and Marquis, "State or Community?"

47. Fingard, *Jack in Port*, explains the pattern of desertion by three main factors: the economic impetus for sailors from British ports to desert in North America where higher wages were available; sailors' resistance to cargo handling and other port duties; and their desire for freedom and recreation after weeks or months at sea.

sea were convicted. Half were imprisoned; half were ordered to return to work, usually with an express threat of jail for noncompliance.[48] Holding unruly sailors in custody at the masters' expense until their ships were ready to receive them was the characteristic pattern in Canadian ports as elsewhere. Sailors who offered to resume their duties,[49] or whose masters consented to take them back,[50] were usually permitted to return to their ships. Roughly three-fifths of those imprisoned were committed "until the vessel is ready for sea and the aid of the Police given to put them on board."[51] Those who deserted absolutely or refused to go on the voyage were more likely to receive fixed sentences, usually of thirty days and occasionally at hard labor.[52] In part this was because some deserters were not sentenced until their ships had already left port. Sailors also came before the court for employment-related misconduct other than absenteeism, such as being drunk and disorderly on board, or assaulting a ship's officer. The assaults were treated as ordinary criminal offenses prosecuted in the name of the crown; they did not result in the cancellation of articles or discharge from employment. The court heard approximately as many work-related assault complaints from sailors as from their officers.

Perhaps the most surprising aspect of the Halifax police court's master and servant business, especially when compared with its urban contemporaries in Montreal and Toronto, is the virtual absence of workers other than seamen and indentured apprentices. In the seventy-five months surveyed here, only one ordinary servant came before the magistrates for absenteeism. Elizabeth Johnson was "brought down on complaint of her Master with absenting herself from his house without his leave and having been found in a House of Ill fame." She was sentenced to thirty days in the bridewell "as a vagrant" — suggesting that the penalty was for being a "found-in," rather than for leaving her work.[53] The Halifax police court records examined here bridge a watershed in Nova Scotia's master and servant legislation. Until 1851, except for merchant shipping, it kept largely to the old remedies of "satisfaction by service" and

48. HPC D7, 21 June 1855 (*Walton v. Moore and Brown*), 23 June 1855 (*Crowhurst v. McLachlan and 6 others*), 22 Apr. 1856 (*Pyke v. Brown*).

49. HPC D8, 7 Sept. 1855 (*Condon v. Broomfield and 8 others*); HPC D5, 14 Oct. 1853 (*Allen v. Harrington*).

50. HPC D6, 11 Sept. 1854 (*Oliver v. Common*); HPC D4, 2 Apr. 1852 (*William M. v. Coony*).

51. HPC D6, 19 July 1854 (*James v. Jones and 2 others*): in this case one of the defendants was discharged, "being a minor and having signed the articles as such."

52. The test of desertion in the 1836 legislation was whether the absentee had taken his clothes or kit with him. For example, HPC D5, 1 June 1853 (Eliott).

53. HPC D4, 6 Nov. 1851.

annulment of the contract.[54] Imprisonment, which had always been important in the regulation of shipping labor, was introduced for apprentices and minor servants in Nova Scotia's 1851 statute revision. What is most revealing about the 1851 legislation, though, is that thenceforth it was the province's only general master and servant act.[55] In Nova Scotia, from 1851 on, master and servant legislation applied only to apprenticeship indentures, employment contracts of other minors, pauper indentures—and merchant seamen.

In New Brunswick, a staunchly Loyalist colony, imprisonment had been available for indentured workers' breach of contract since 1826. Otherwise, its master and servant legislation essentially paralleled that of Nova Scotia.[56] There are no police court minutes for Saint John in the period, but the New Brunswick seaport's jail records suggest a pattern of employment law enforcement similar to Halifax.[57] Between 1852 and 1864, about 228 prisoners spent time in the cells for employment-related offenses.[58] Almost all were sailors, half of them charged with deserting ship and the rest with a range of offenses from disobedience to mutiny. Six prisoners were absenting apprentices[59] and one was in jail for "harbouring" deserting seamen.[60]

Atlantic Canadian master and servant legislation reflected the region's eighteenth-century origins in its reliance on performance remedies and its emphasis on the enforcement of long-term and long-distance bargains. In this, the region resembled its close geographic and commercial neighbor, New England. For most land-based workers and their employers, including those in agriculture and in the region's important timber and shipbuilding industries, the whip of hunger was a more important enforcer of employment bargains than the justice of the peace.

54. The eighteenth-century acts were repealed by (N.S.) *Rev. Stat.*, Title XLI, c.170 (1851).

55. (N.S.) *Rev. Stat.* Part 2, Title XXXIII, c.125 (1851), while entitled *Of Masters, Apprentices, and Servants*, applied only to minors. It survived unchanged through the subsequent statute revisions of 1859, 1864, and 1873.

56. (N.B.) *Rev. Stat.* Part 2, Title XXXIV, c.134 (1854).

57. For a critique of the Saint John magistrates from the point of view of a shipowner, see *N.B. Courier*, 20 Mar. and 8 May 1847.

58. Where someone is held for examination, then on remand, and then to serve a sentence, I have counted the three (or more) separate entries as one occurrence. The number of individuals is somewhat smaller than 228, however, due to recidivism. Provincial Archives of New Brunswick, Saint John County Jail Records, RS 383.

59. These were apprentices to land-based trades; the count of sailors includes a few ship's apprentices.

60. It is hard to determine whether seamen or debtors made up the greater part of the Saint John jail population. The Charlotte County jail at Saint Andrews held 105 prisoners in 1835, including 57 debtors, 21 "seamen deserting or refusing to do their duty," and 3 seamen imprisoned for mutiny.

Quebec

In the St. Lawrence valley heartland of New France, settlement had stag-
nated until the 1660s, when the French crown took direct control of what
had been a company colony and imported a labor force of indentured workers
and soldiers.[61] As in other colonies where labor was scarce and opportunities many, employers and governors sought to provide against desertion and
indiscipline. Ordinances of October and December 1663 and March 1667 required indentured *engagés* to serve their assigned master for three years and
established penalties for servants' desertion and drunkenness, as well as for
the third parties who harbored or debauched them.[62] In addition to heavy
fines payable to the master,[63] which must have been transmuted into extended
terms of servitude,[64] corporal and shaming punishments upheld the labor
obligation.[65] Workers might be imprisoned pending trial, but not as a punishment upon conviction.[66] Deserting servants were often expressly ordered
back to work.[67]

By the turn of the eighteenth century, indentured immigration was a
thing of the past. New France had developed into a society of peasant smallholders, largely self-sufficient, who paid their seigneurial dues and store debts
in wheat, credited labor, or seasonal wages earned in timbering or the fur
trade. There was little demand for agricultural labor in the countryside, where
the unpropertied were more likely to farm on shares than to work for wages.
Even in the towns, construction and portside laboring supported only a small
wage-earning population. Artisan shops were mostly small, employing perhaps one or two apprentices on three-year indentures and a journeyman or

61. Dechêne, *Habitants and Merchants*; Greer, *Peasant, Lord, and Merchant*; Greer, *People of New France*.

62. *Jugements et déliberations du conseil souverain de la Nouvelle-France* (Québec, 1885 *et seq.*) (hereafter *JDCS*), 1:29, 75, 382.

63. *JDCS*, 1:153.

64. There was no imprisonment for ordinary debts in New France; in the early, labor-starved, years of the colony debtors were sometimes condemned to work off the amounts they owed: *JDCS*, 1:166, 167; 2:218.

65. Pierre Pichet, a domestic, was fined ten livres for drunkenness and four livres for each day he missed work: *JDCS*, 1:77; another domestic was fined and put in the pillory for two hours wearing a sign identifying him as a "serviteur engagé qui a delaissé le service de son maistre"; others were warned that they would be pilloried for a first offense and branded and beaten for a second: *JDCS*, 1:744–45, and see *JDCS*, 1:747–48 and 777; another was condemned to beg his master's family's forgiveness for his "rebellion": *JDCS*, 3:70. A Quebec City police regulation in 1676 fixed the pillory as punishment for a first offense of desertion and corporal punishment and branding for a second: *JDCS*, 2:63.

66. *JDCS*, 1:104, 310.

67. *JDCS*, 3:451.

two.[68] Most employment contracts were made in writing, even those for casual day labor, although the latter were not usually notarized. They could be enforced in the civil courts or at arbitration.[69]

The fur trade began in informal exchanges between colonists and local Indians, but as it reached further into the interior it acquired a regular work force of its own. In the seventeenth century one or two entrepreneurs might secure working capital from a sponsoring merchant with which to purchase trade goods and supplies and hire a crew of canoemen for a trading journey into the interior. By the eighteenth century, the French trade had penetrated to the center of the continent, requiring much greater organization and capital. Specialist merchants contracted workers on a seasonal basis to make the round trip between Montreal and the *pays d'en haut* and hired others on three-year indentures to man the trading posts in the interior. Both groups of workers were recruited in the less fertile rural parishes around Montreal. They, or their families, typically had property to answer for their defaults, and it appears that breaches of fur trade employment contracts led to awards of damages in the civil courts.

Following the cession of Quebec in 1763, British merchants replaced many of the French ones at Montreal, but the organization of the fur trade, including enforcement of the employment contract, did not at first change. During the short military regime that preceded the establishment of full civil government, several canoemen charged Edward Chinn, an English merchant resident in Montreal, with failing to pay their wages for a fur-trading trip to Michilimackinac. Chinn had earlier, without success, sought the convictions of the leaders of the party for stealing furs from the packs. Now he relied on the evidence of French-Canadian merchants that it was customary when furs went missing that "the whole crew of the canoe, besides paying for the goods, forfeit their wages." Characterizing the dispute as "an affair of commerce, that may be attended with the utmost bad consequences, to alter the established rules," the court found Chinn entitled "in equity and usage" to withhold the men's wages until he received satisfaction for his losses. In approving this decision, General Burton promised to publicize "the established rules, between merchants and their hired canoemen, employed in the traffic, to and from the upper countries."[70]

However, as the pressures of competition and increasing overhead costs pushed the Montreal fur trade ever closer to monopoly, merchant employers

68. Moogk, "Indentures"; Hardy and Ruddel, *Apprentis*.

69. Houses were built for a price fixed in advance, and wages for casual labor were typically calculated by the task rather than by time: Moogk, *Building*, 60, 81–82, 93, 111–12.

70. Public Record Office, WO 71/49/255–60 (General Court Martial, Montreal, Dec. 1763).

called on the government to help make their servants "strictly conform to their agreements."[71] When this assistance came, it abandoned the "established rules" and "equity and usage" and replaced them with English-style master and servant legislation. Boatmen who contracted in writing for voyages to the interior were liable to a month's imprisonment if they deserted their employment before setting out, and three months' imprisonment and loss of all wages if they deserted during the voyage.[72] The law was further refined by a 1790 enactment, which was to remain on the statute book for a century. Duly contracted voyageurs who refused to commence the voyage were to be imprisoned for fifteen days; those who deserted in the back country were liable to jail terms of one to three months.[73]

Even before turning its attention to the fur trade, the Quebec executive had addressed employment discipline in the merchant marine. An ordinance of 1765 provided that articled seamen who refused to do their duty were to be imprisoned until called for by the shipmaster, so as to be "secured and forthcoming to proceed on the voyage."[74] The penalties became more stringent over time. An act of 1807 prescribed jail sentences of twenty days for unauthorized absences of six hours or more, thirty days if the seaman took his clothes and kit (thereby indicating an intention not to return), and forty days for a second offense. In every case the offender was to be delivered back to his ship once the sentence was served. Shipmasters could obtain the release and delivery of convicted sailors on request, and were required to pay the men one shilling and sixpence per day to maintain themselves while in jail.[75] Quebec also adopted special employment legislation for the fishery. An 1836 enactment, applying only to the Gaspé, provided a five-pound fine for desertion, with a month's imprisonment on default of payment.[76] Subsequent legislation, in force in both Quebec and Ontario, was still more severe. By 1857 the justices could sentence deserting fishermen to a month's imprisonment; in 1869 the maximum sentence became three months.[77]

By the Quebec Act (1774) and Constitutional Act (1791), the province was to have English criminal and French-Canadian private law, to be administered in English courts—a formula that was to result in "legislative paralysis

71. Cited in Podruchny, "Unfair Masters," 51 n. 27.
72. (Que.) 28 Geo.III c.3 (1788).
73. (L.C.) 36 Geo.III c.10 (1796).
74. (Que.) 5 Geo.III, Ordinance of 31 May 1765.
75. (L.C.) 47 Geo.III c.9 (1807).
76. (L.C.) 6 Wm.IV c.57 (1836); (Can. [Prov.]). 4&5 Vict. c.36 (1841) increased the fine to ten pounds.
77. (Can. [Prov.]) 20 Vict. c.21 (1857); (Que.) 32 Vict. c.37 (1869).

and judicial chaos" as French-Canadian and British elites jostled for control of the colony.[78] Employment law was stranded in the no-man's-land between the two:[79] both systems viewed it as contractual, but in the English master and servant tradition breach was punishable in much the same manner as petty crimes. Despite the guarantee of French civil law, British merchants managed to insist that imprisonment for debt, which had been introduced after the Conquest, remain available.[80] It was only consistent that penal master and servant law should apply to enforce work discipline. It was no less consistent that wage recovery should be left to the civil courts. In 1802 the chronically deadlocked Assembly suspended its efforts to enact master and servant legislation and delegated the framing of employment regulations to the justices of the peace in the three judicial districts. This expedient survived for more than a century and had a profound, anomalous, and lasting effect on employment regulation in the province.

The 1802 legislation directed the justices in quarter sessions of each of the three judicial districts to make regulations "to restrain, rule and govern" apprentices,[81] domestics, hired servants and journeymen, and for the conduct of masters and mistresses, subject to the approval of the district court of King's Bench; penalties were not to exceed ten pounds or two months' imprisonment.[82] Justices in the Quebec district were at first uncertain of their power to enforce penal regulations,[83] while in the district of Trois Rivières it is possible that no regulations were made before 1856.[84] The following account focuses on the Montreal justices, who adopted master and servant regulations in 1802,[85] 1810,[86] 1817,[87] and 1821.[88] Municipal government passed from quar-

78. Kolish, "Legal Metropolis."

79. Quebec City justices complained in 1802 that they were "souvent très embarasseés pour remédier aux plaintes portées devant eux . . . faute d'une loi précise et claire qui puisse les guider": Hardy and Ruddel, *Apprentis*, 89; Larose, "Contrats," 69; Hogg, "Legal Rights," 30–31.

80. Kennedy, McClure, and Lanctot, *Laws of Quebec*, 29; Brunet, *Les Canadiens*, 228; Kolish, "Debt."

81. For an extended discussion and econometric analysis of apprenticeship indentures and their enforcement at Montreal in this period, see Hamilton, "Apprenticeship."

82. (L.C.) 42 Geo.III c.11 (1802); continued by (L.C.) 43 Geo.III c.4 (1803), (L.C.) 47 Geo.III c.4 (1807), (L.C.) 51 Geo.III c.13 (1811), and (L.C.) 55 Geo.III c.4 (1815).

83. Fyson, "Criminal Justice," 57.

84. Larose, "Contrats," 71.

85. Archives Nationales du Québec à Montréal (hereafter ANQM), TL32 S1 SS11, Montreal Quarter Sessions Register, 19 July 1802.

86. *Montreal Gazette*, 17 Sept. 1810.

87. *Montreal Herald*, 21 June 1817.

88. Ibid., 14 Mar. 1821; *Compilation of the Bye-Laws and Police Regulations in Force in the City of Montreal* (Montreal: James Starke, 1842), pt. I, pp. 117–20.

ter sessions to an elected council in 1833, but the old regulations remained in effect until 1865, when they were succeeded by a new penal bylaw which was still in force in 1931.[89]

The earliest version emphasized reciprocity, limiting the servant's duty of obedience to commands within the scope of their agreements, and providing for specific performance by the servant only where the master or mistress had fulfilled his or her part of the bargain. Neglect of duty was punishable only if repeated. A misbehaving worker, jailed for up to two months, could be released upon expressing "a penitent desire to return to his or her duty and service." Later versions of the regulations abandoned these more generous provisos. After 1821, servants could no longer complain to the magistrates of mistreatment by their masters; their only recourse became expensive and protracted civil litigation. The regulations also become more punitive. The ostensibly mandatory penalty for most kinds of worker indiscipline became imprisonment and a fine.[90] Nevertheless, Montreal's justices in the 1830s frequently ordered misbehaving workers back to their employment without additional punishment. Later in the century the words received a stricter construction: "This by-law imposes imprisonment in each case besides a fine, and the judge has no other alternative but to follow."[91] In most respects, the 1802 bylaw and its successors were reasonably comprehensive master and servant enactments. The justices in their weekly and special sessions were to hear and determine complaints arising between employers and their apprentices and employees, including the usual categories of work attendance and discipline, mistreatment by the employer (until 1821), notice of termination, and third-party interference in the employment contract. There was, however, no provision for summary disposition of wages complaints.[92]

Surviving records of the Montreal weekly and special sessions[93] for 1829, 1832–35, and 1838–43 show the justices actively enforcing not only the municipal regulations but also the special legislation for voyageurs and merchant seamen. Three-quarters of the employment-related cases involved desertion, and three quarters of those accused were convicted.[94] Half of those convicted

---

89. *Bylaws of the City of Montreal* (Montreal: 1931), c.XX, n.9 (passed 10 May 1865).

90. In 1865 this was extended to breaches of the notice provision, which had formerly been punishable by fine alone.

91. H. A. Germain, *Report of Penal and Civil Prosecutions and Complaints* (Montreal, 1887) (hereafter Germain).

92. After 1836 the justices could decide claims for sailors' wages under (L.C.) 6 Wm.IV c.28 (1836).

93. ANQM, TL32 S1. For another view of these and related cases, see Pilarczyk, "Servants' Rights" and "Masters' Rights."

94. The conviction rate varied from 59 percent (domestic servants) to 88 percent (appren-

were ordered to return to work, with or without a fine.[95] About 40 percent were sentenced directly to jail, although most of the others were threatened with imprisonment if they did not return to work or pay a fine.[96] Seamen and voyageurs were the most likely to be committed directly to prison, for terms ranging between two days and two months; apprentices were the most likely to be offered the choice between returning to work directly or after a spell in jail—usually one or two months. Costs were almost always awarded against the convicted deserter, and in some cases could be substantial. Thus Mary Ann McDonough, who quit her job as wet nurse when her employer demanded that she make beds and sweep rooms as well, was fined fifteen shillings for desertion plus costs of one pound, three shillings, and eleven pence. Her wage had been six dollars—approximately one pound, ten shillings—a month.[97]

The majority of desertion cases turned upon proof of a contract of employment for a fixed term,[98] either in writing (often by a notary) or in the presence of at least one witness.[99] A few cases were dismissed when the court found that the defendant lacked the capacity to contract.[100] When there was a contract and capable parties, the most common defense was the employer's failure to live up to the terms of the bargain. The court dismissed desertion complaints when the servant's wages had not been paid on time;[101] when an apprentice milliner took a husband with her father's consent, despite a clause in the indenture prohibiting marriage;[102] and, in one notorious case, when two sailors succeeded in persuading the court that they were not deserters but only left their ship to inform the justices that their captain had abused

tices); other groups, including seamen, journeyman tradesmen, and voyageurs, came within two or three points of the mean.

95. These figures do not include those ordered to return to work after serving a jail sentence (most commonly seamen). Only two of eight convicted voyageurs were ordered back to work, probably because their parties had already left without them. Apprentices were the most likely to be ordered back (86 percent), and domestic servants among the least (31 percent).

96. Fifty-four deserters (43 percent of the 126) were sent directly to jail; 31 (25 percent) were ordered to return to work or go to jail; 12 (10 percent) were fined with jail time in default of payment. In the remaining 2 cases deserters were sentenced to pay a fine and to go to jail.

97. *Lindsay v. McDonough* (Special Sessions [hereafter SS], 27 May 1842).

98. Thus *Coursol v. Roy* (SS, 13 May 1842).

99. Thus *Cleighton v. Cosgrove* (SS, 18 June 1841) was dismissed for failure to prove a contract despite the fact that the defendant, a domestic servant, had continued in the plaintiff's service for nearly two years before leaving in midmonth, and despite evidence from two witnesses that she had told them she was employed by the month.

100. For example, *Choquette v. Lafrance* (SS, 31 May 1834) and *Fullum v. Desormier* (SS, 3 June 1842).

101. *Davis v. Verdon* (SS, 21 July 1841).

102. *Brown v. Williams* (Weekly Sessions [hereafter WS], 19 Nov. 1833).

them and threatened them with a pistol.[103] The court held that the captain had not treated them "as a well conducted master of a vessel in the British Empire should," and let them go. This case was unusual because the defense of ill-treatment, although frequently relied upon by deserting sailors and apprentices, was nearly always unsuccessful.[104] Apprentices who were physically assaulted, verbally harassed, deprived of sufficient food, or exposed to contagious disease were expected to find their remedy in the civil courts and not in self-help. The justices' theory of such cases echoed the eighteenth-century approach and anticipated the view expressed by the Court of Queen's Bench at Montreal a half century later: "It will readily be admitted than an apprentice should be held strictly to his bargain, else dishonest people might gain undue advantages by having their children taught the rudiments of a trade and then allowing them to desert their employment."[105]

The 1802 statute contemplated that master and servant regulations adopted in quarter sessions would apply to the whole judicial district, but by 1811 city justices could no longer impose their regulations on the rural parts of the district. An act of 1824 gave local justices power to enforce master and servant regulations in the country parishes, and in 1836 the legislature adopted substantive master and servant regulations applicable outside the three main towns.[106] These provincewide rules were at first modeled on the Montreal regulations then in force. By 1845 the two regimes had diverged to the extent that the maximum penalty in urban master and servant cases was ten pounds or two months' imprisonment, while in the country parts it was a fine of two pounds, ten shillings or an order to make up lost time,[107] with a jail sentence of fifteen days on default of either of these.[108]

These regulations and legislation survived the codification of Quebec's civil law in 1866. Despite the formal apparatus of Roman law underpinning the analysis of employment as lease of service in the Civil Code of Lower Canada, its authors did not interfere with the existing master and servant regime, which was at such odds with the civilian tradition. Instead, article

103. *Burn v. Harris and Flanders* (SS, 27 May 1841).

104. For example, *Martin v. McIntosh* (WS, 11 and 26 Jan. 1841).

105. *Baker and Lebeau* (1884), 7 *Legal News* 299, per Ramsay J.

106. (L.C.) 4 Geo.IV c.33 (1824); (L.C.) 6 Wm.IV c.27 (1836).

107. In 1875 a Superior Court judge held that it was "a monstrous case of oppression by a master, and of ignorance in a magistrate" to have convicted a former apprentice of desertion for failing, at the end of his term, to make up time lost to sickness: *Ex parte David and Collerette*, 19 *Lower Canada Jurist* 111.

108. (Can. [Prov.]) C.S.L.C., Class D, c.21 and Class K, c.25 (1845). The gap was narrowed in 1849, when country justices were authorized to impose a five-pound fine, a thirty-day jail sentence, or both: (Can. [Prov.]) 12 Vict. c.55 (1849).

1670 merely recited that "The rights and obligations arising from the lease or hire of personal service are subject to the rules common to contracts. They are also regulated in certain respects in the country parts by a special law, and in the towns and villages by by-laws of the respective municipal councils." The codification commissioners did not set out the details of these regulations because, as they put it, "they are more matters of police than of principle and in many instances in fact are departures from formal principles."[109] In the result the code articulated a splendid abstraction that simply did not apply in important respects to most workers in the province.[110]

Montreal's master and servant regulations also survived the Dominion Breaches of Contract Act, 1877, which purported to decriminalize breaches of the employment contract.[111] In 1881 Quebec passed a new masters and servants act by which misbehaving workers and apprentices, third parties interfering in employment contracts, and employers who mistreated their employees or discharged them without paying their wages all became liable to a twenty-dollar fine.[112] However, neither the old acts nor the new applied to Montreal or any other "incorporated cities, towns and villages which have passed or may hereafter pass by-laws regulating the relations of master and servant." This was not an insignificant exception. Montreal's Recorder's Court fined and imprisoned eighty-four "guilty servants" in 1886 alone.[113] Provincial legislation of 1894 made the twenty-dollar fine the standard penalty for master and servant infractions throughout the province, "any special law or all by-laws to the contrary notwithstanding."[114] Nevertheless, when Montreal's charter was revised and consolidated in 1899, council's power to "regulate the responsibilities and duties of masters and servants" and to enforce such bylaws with fines and imprisonment was confirmed.[115] For greater certainty, a further amendment in 1912 declared that the Recorder had jurisdiction to impose any fine or penalty set out in the city bylaws.[116]

The validity of Montreal's penal bylaw was not tested in the courts, and

109. In art.1671, the commissioners dealt in a similar fashion with the special legislation governing seamen and voyageurs.

110. Cairns, "Employment," 705.

111. The pre-Confederation Quebec statute notionally repealed by the federal act had already been replaced by another penal statute, which was expressly unaffected by the Breaches of Contract Act: Craven, "Modern Spirit."

112. (Que.) 44&45 Vict. c.15 (1881). A two-month jail term could be imposed in default of payment. The employment contract could be annulled for repeated offenses.

113. Germain.

114. (Que.) 57 Vict. c.40 (1894): offenders could be imprisoned up to thirty days in default of payment.

115. (Que.) 63 Vict. c.58 (1899).

116. (Que.) 2 Geo.V c.56 (1912).

employers continued to drag misbehaving workers before the Recorder in significant numbers until the First World War.[117] During the last quarter of the
nineteenth century, however, the scope of the regulations and their applicability to contemporary employment relations were regularly put in issue. Although in some respects the outcome nibbled slightly at the margins of the
Recorder's jurisdiction,[118] this was more than outweighed by a series of decisions extending his court's punitive grasp.

Several decisions wrestled with the question whether pieceworkers fell
within the scope of section 3 of the bylaw, which made it an offense for workers
to quit without proper notice "before the time agreed upon shall have been
expired." In the first of these cases to be decided, a lather, engaged at ninety
cents per 1,000 laths, was held to be an *engagé* (hired worker) punishable under
this provision as he had agreed by notarial contract to work for a year.[119] In
1890 the court upheld the application of the section to a journeyman shoemaker engaged for a year at so much per dozen pairs. In a close analysis of the
French and English texts of the bylaw, Judge Pagnuelo decided that although
journalier ordinarily meant day laborer, it had been rendered as "journeyman"
in the English text, so that the statute applied as well to *compagnons* (journeymen) as to *journaliers*.[120]

The Montreal bylaw was rather imaginatively adapted to the changing circumstances of an industrial city in a series of decisions about workplace rules.
The underlying difficulty was that section 1 of the bylaw cast a broad net over
all sorts of indiscipline by all sorts of workers, while the notice requirement in
section 2 applied only to workers engaged "for a fixed period, by the month,
or longer space of time, or by the piece or job."[121] Many factory workers were
employed for indefinite terms and were paid by the week or the month. The
bylaw seemed to offer their employers no recourse if they quit without notice
on payday. In *Angers* (1872), a wages case, the Montreal Circuit Court upheld
a factory rule that workers who quit midweek without notice would forfeit
any wages due:[122] "Les grands manufacturiers, qui font gagner le pain à tant

117. Montreal Recorder's Court minutebooks have not survived. Annual statistical summaries of bylaw offenses in the municipal records show a fluctuating stream of "apprentices,
servants or journeymen guilty of deserting or absence without leave, ill-behaviour, idleness,
refusing to obey, malicious damage to their master's property, etc."

118. Thus in 1884, a Superior Court judge held that a *commis* (a clerk or salesman) was not
a *serviteur* within the meaning of the bylaw and so was not subject to arrest and punishment for
leaving his employment without permission: *Martin v. DeMontigny et al.*, 1 Mtl L.R. 260.

119. *Dinelle v. Gauthier et al.*, 3 Mtl L.R. 134.

120. *Ex parte Joseph Gagnier*, 7 Mtl L.R. 18.

121. In *Dakley v. Normon* (1886), 9 *Legal News* 213, Recorder de Montigny held that s.2 of the
bylaw did not apply to someone who was employed by the week.

122. *Martineau v. Angers et al.*, *Fontaine v. Angers et al.*, 4 *Rev. Leg.* 74; in *Augé v. The Do-*

de pauvres gens doivent trouver protection devant les tribunaux . . . sans cette protection les travaux entrepris se trouveraient sans cesse arrêtés, selon le gré des employés et au grand dommage des contractants." In 1882, Recorder de Montigny took *Angers* for authority to fine and imprison a weaver who worked by the fortnight and had quit at the end of a pay period without giving the fifteen days' notice required by a company rule. The Recorder based the conviction on section 1 of the bylaw, thereby avoiding the requirement of a fixed term of a month or more in section 2. The same principle was applied in the small-claims courts to uphold company rules providing for deductions from wages for lateness or absenteeism.[123]

Benjamin Antoine Testard de Montigny's late nineteenth-century Recorder's Court enforced the master and servant bylaw with mechanical rigidity, grounded in the unwavering conviction that employers' hard-bought rights must be protected from the depredations of the contemptible beings they had to employ:[124]

> Some female servants have undertaken to become a nightmare to those who cannot dispense with their services. Laziness and love of luxury combined have rendered them more and more exacting and insolent, and those defects in them are only equalled by the unscrupulous manner in which they break their engagements and cause trouble to their masters. Many apprentices and journeymen mechanics are equally guilty in this respect.

De Montigny's appointment as Recorder in 1880 coincided with a steep increase in the number of desertion prosecutions, and he presided over its peak. If there was a touch of irony in the fact that an ultramontanist Quebec lawyer and former papal zouave was the sternest upholder of this vestige of English employment law, the irony was redoubled in his successor, Robert Stanley Weir, an Ontario-born lawyer and former schoolteacher, who had little use for the penal bylaw.[125] In two decisions issued on the same day in 1905, Weir significantly narrowed the scope of the master and servant bylaw, effectively subsuming it to the stated policy of the 1877 Dominion statute that breaches of contract "are in general civil wrongs only, and not criminal in their na-

minion Wadding Company (1888), 11 *Legal News* 138, the Circuit Court held that illness excused failure to provide the notice required by company rules.

123. *Boyer v. Slater* (1889), 13 *Legal News* 274; *D'Elle Sigouin v. Montreal Woollen Mills Co.* (1890), 14 *Legal News* 2.

124. Germain. Germain was the Recorder's Court clerk.

125. Weir's coappointee, Alexandre Eudore Poirier, a former criminal lawyer, *Hansard* translator, journalist, and political candidate, resigned in 1907.

ture."[126] In the first, he held that the offense of "enticing any apprentice or servant" to abandon his employment, in section 4 of the bylaw, was to be construed as applying only to apprentices and *domestic* servants, and not to other kinds of employees: "the by-law is peculiar in that it makes a penal offense of what is ordinarily subject matter of damages."[127] In the second case, he found that the bylaw did not apply to workers on indefinite hirings (in this case, a blacksmith on weekly wages) but only to those who contracted for a fixed term. Strict construction was necessary, not only because the bylaw was penal but also to counter the "erroneous impression . . . that desertion of service is punishable as an offence without regard to the terms of the contract."[128]

Ontario

Although founded in the late eighteenth century, Ontario (Upper Canada, Canada West) did not legislate for employment relations before the mid-nineteenth century.[129] During the first half century of settlement, the English statutes (to 1792) were notionally in force, but a series of high-court decisions so limited their application that in 1847 the legislature could declare there to be no act in force to regulate the relations of master and servant. Despite contemporary treatise writers' assurances that penal sanctions were available, what little evidence has survived about the uses of the English statutes in early Ontario is largely negative. It consists of justices' records that do not mention master and servant cases, and jail records that do not enumerate misbehaving servants or apprentices among those committed. In fact, there may be more reported cases in the high court raising doubts about the reception of the English statutes than there are surviving records of master and servant cases before the justices.[130]

126. The pendulum began to swing away from de Montigny's law as early as 1901, when Poirier held that a cigar maker, paid by the piece and not employed for a definite term, was entitled to quit upon either finishing the cigars or returning the unused tobacco—he was not punishable under the bylaw, nor could third parties be punished for inducing him to leave his employment: *Youngheart vs. Chaw et al.* (1901), 7 *Rev. Jur.* 274. This prosecution seems to have been occasioned by a strike.

127. *Sommer v. Waldman* (1905), 12 *Rev. Jur.* 94.

128. *Lamothe v. Bissonette* (1905), 12 *Rev. Jur.* 195.

129. (U.K.) 9 Geo.IV c.51 (1828) empowered local justices to determine disputes between the Canada Company (which sold land in southwestern Ontario) and its indentured servants but does not appear to have been enforced.

130. Craven, "Law of Master and Servant"; Webber, "Labour and the Law." Exceptions include a few convictions by justices that were appealed to quarter sessions, as for example the decision of R. P. Boucher, justice of the peace, in *Keys v. White* (Northumberland & Durham), 14 July 1845. While there is scant evidence that misbehaving servants were jailed in Ontario be-

In 1847 the local legislature adopted its first master and servant act. Drafted to help employers in the Ottawa Valley timber industry enforce contracts in a volatile labor market,[131] it was amended in the Assembly to broaden its application and give workers summary actions for wages and mistreatment.[132] If the result was not entirely one-sided, neither was it perfectly balanced: where masters could be summoned, servants could be arrested; where employers could be fined for mistreatment, workers could be imprisoned for misconduct. This act was followed in 1851 by another providing in broadly similar terms for apprentices.[133]

Jail records and justices' returns of convictions show that there was a relatively steady although unspectacular flow of desertion and wage cases[134] in rural and small-town Ontario from 1847 to 1877 (when most of the penal provisions were repealed). Of approximately 13,000 summary convictions returned from ten rural counties, slightly more than 1,000 involved master and servant complaints, mostly wage recovery and desertion.[135] Master and servant accounted for about one of every eleven cases heard by the justices out of sessions. Although the overall rate (one in eleven summary cases) is reminiscent of some English counties in the same period,[136] three-quarters of the

---

fore 1847, runaway apprentices sometimes were. Newspaper advertisements about absconding apprentices sometimes offered a reward to "anyone securing him in one of His Majesty's jails in this province," for example, *Kingston Chronicle*, 13 June 1823. A few absconding apprentices appear in the pre-1847 jail registers, but whether they were serving sentences or merely awaiting collection by their masters is hard to tell. Thus Toronto alderman Gurnett committed Dennis Clock, an absconding apprentice, to jail on 21 June 1840 and ordered his release the following day. By contrast, John Doyle, a fifteen-year-old runaway, was sentenced to two months' hard labor in November 1841 "in default of finding security," and seventeen-year-old Robert Stevenson was sentenced to three months' hard labor in March 1843 "for deserting his apprenticeship." Several of the high-court cases limiting the effect of the English statutes arose out of disputes between masters and apprentices. Nevertheless, the legislature did not adopt an apprenticeship statute until 1851.

131. For Ontario forest workers in this period, see Radforth, "Shantymen."

132. (Can. [Prov.]) 10&11 Vict. c.23 (1847).

133. (Can. [Prov.]) 14&15 Vict. c.11 (1851).

134. There is some evidence of suits for wages in the lowest civil courts before 1847. Thus the *Brockville Gazette* (21 May 1830) reported a district court suit for wages by a worker in a blacksmith's shop. I am grateful to Howard Baker for this reference.

135. Quarterly returns of convictions were collected from clerk of the peace records, newspaper reports, and quarter sessions minutes for ten counties (Essex, Huron and Bruce, Kent, Lincoln, Northumberland and Durham, Oxford, Perth, Simcoe, Victoria, and Waterloo) and master and servant convictions (but not overall rates of returns) from two additional counties (Carleton, and Prescott and Russell). These data are extremely sparse and there is little overlap between surviving returns of convictions and surviving jail records for most places throughout most of the period. The following discussion is based on 1,185 master and servant or apprentice returns by justices in these twelve largely rural counties between 1847 and 1880.

136. See Hay in this volume. While the rural Ontario rates are low in comparison to other

cases heard by Ontario justices were wage claims. Only 20 percent involved desertions,[137] while complaints of disobedience and ill-treatment made up the remaining 5 percent.[138]

Workers charged with desertion were nearly always convicted (89 percent of known outcomes),[139] but they were rarely imprisoned (16 percent of those convicted). Only six deserters (3 percent) were sentenced to jail directly;[140] twenty-nine others were committed for failing to pay a fine.[141] Servants committed or awaiting trial for employment offenses accounted for barely 1 of every 265 prisoners in the province's jails. They never amounted to as much as 1 percent of the total jail population in any county in any of the years examined, and they averaged less than four-tenths of 1 percent.

The most common penalty for desertion (87 percent of those convicted) was a fine, in amounts ranging from a few pennies to $20 or more.[142] Half the fines were for $2 or less; few exceeded $10. (Laborers' day wages averaged between $1.00 and $1.25 in the period.) Ten percent of the convicted deserters were simply ordered to return to work.

At least 90 percent of wage claims succeeded, at least to the extent that employers settled accounts or were ordered to pay.[143] However, although more than a third of the workers convicted of desertion were required to pay their fines "forthwith," fewer than 8 percent of employers were ordered to pay up immediately. In two-thirds of the wage cases, the justices fixed a future date for payment, usually twenty-one days after the decision. In many cases the wages were still outstanding when the justice returned the conviction sometime after the notional due date, and several returns indicated that the em-

---

parts of the empire, they are higher than Karsten, *Between Law and Custom*, suggests in his discussion of the "informal" law of employment (e.g., pp. 335–36).

137. Related complaints such as "absconding apprentice," "leaving work," and "refusing to commence work" are counted among the desertion cases.

138. There was considerable variation across the province, although this may be an artifact of the sparseness of the record. The ratio of claims against masters to complaints against servants was 28:1 in Kent, 7:1 in Huron and Bruce, and 1:3 in Lincoln.

139. Outcomes are known for 237 of the 242 desertion prosecutions. Nine were dismissed or withdrawn, and 18 were "settled," often with the defendant paying the costs.

140. Four of the six jail sentences were imposed by the same justice of the peace, Simcoe County's Alexander Gaviller.

141. In imposing fines, justices often specified jail terms in the alternative, or in default of payment; where they did not, imprisonment could follow upon failure of distress.

142. This includes some sentences of fine and imprisonment that are also counted as imprisonment (above). One absconding apprentice was fined fifty dollars; he gave notice of appeal to quarter sessions but abandoned it when he returned to work: *Treble v. Kenrick* (Huron & Bruce), 28 Aug. 1869.

143. Outcomes are known for 97 percent of the 899 wage claims; 8 percent of these were dismissed or withdrawn.

TABLE 5.1.
Master and Servant in Urban Ontario, to 1877

	Years	Cases	Wages (%)	Desert/ Disobey (%)
Toronto	1847–77	1,787[a]	61	38
London	1856–77	199	63	37
Hamilton	1859–61, 1863–66	208	81	17
Belleville	1874–77	76	87	13
Galt	1866–77	48	52	48

SOURCES: Toronto: Police Register of Criminals and Warrant Register, Toronto City Archives and Police Museum; police court reports in *Toronto Globe* and *Leader*. London: Police court reports in *London Advertiser* and *Free Press*. Hamilton: Police Court Register, Hamilton Police Museum. Belleville: Hastings Co. Police Court Minute Book, Archives of Ontario RG 22. Galt: Police Court Records, Archives of Ontario RG 22.

[a] Includes 8 complaints of mistreatment and 5 cases of third-party interference.

ployer had left the jurisdiction. In consequence, the actual wage recovery rate was probably much lower than the 90 percent success rate.

The returns are too sparsely distributed across the counties and the period for reliable comparative or longitudinal analysis of the frequency and disposition of rural master and servant cases. A rough approximation of patterns in the incidence of these cases can be gleaned by examining annual variations in the ratio of wages to desertion and disobedience cases. The desertion ratio peaks in 1854 and 1872, years of considerable labor unrest and trade-union activity in the province. Claims for unpaid wages are disproportionately high in the recessions of the late 1850s and mid-1860s.

While the ratio of wage claims to prosecutions for desertion and disobedience averaged 3:1 in the rural counties, in urban Ontario (see Table 5.1) it ranged from 4:1 (Hamilton) to less than 2:1 (Toronto, London).[144] Leaving settled cases aside, over the whole period Toronto workers were successful in two-thirds of their decided wage claims and were acquitted in slightly less than half of the decided employer complaints. Workers' success in wage

144. Urban police courts have left a more thorough record than county justices. The best run of evidence about summary proceedings in Ontario master and servant cases is the Toronto Police Register of Criminals (so-called), the police court "blotter" of the province's largest city. For the history of the court, see Craven, "Law and Authority." While volumes for 1858–60 and 1865–73 are missing, other sources of information—the statistical report that was compiled in some years, local newspapers, and surviving warrant registers—can be used to fill out the record. Less extensive city police court data exist for Hamilton ("blotters," 1859–61 and 1863–66) and London (newspaper reports). Comparable records have survived for some smaller towns; the Galt cases are discussed in Craven, "Law of Master and Servant," 200–205.

claims rose from the early 1850s through the depression at the end of the decade, then declined through the succeeding expansion, leveling off in the mid-1860s. The long-term linear trend was for workers' success in wage claims to fall off gradually from about 70 percent of decided cases early in the period to about 60 percent near the end. Workers' success in desertion and disobedience cases climbed to the early 1850s, fluctuated until about 1864, and climbed again until it reached a plateau at about 60 percent after 1869. The long-term linear trend for these cases was a fairly steep increase from a worker success rate of approximately 25 percent early in the period to better than 50 percent by 1876. Toronto workers were less successful in wage claims than their rural counterparts but more successful in defending against prosecutions.

A second aspect of disposition is the rate of settlement and withdrawal. We have no way of knowing what proportion of potential cases might have been resolved before reaching the courthouse. Recorded settlements and withdrawals reflect events inside the courtroom, including mediation and persuasion by the magistrate or clerk. While there was significant fluctuation in rates of settlement in Toronto, rates for wage and desertion complaints tracked one another quite closely. Nonpayment and discipline cases were often two sides of the same coin. Employers refused to pay workers whose conduct they deprecated; workers walked off the job when employers treated them unfairly. The trend was for settlement rates to decline over the period. Nearly 30 percent of the discipline cases were withdrawn or settled in the early part of the period, compared with fewer than 10 percent by the end. (This may help explain the steep increase in worker success rates, reflecting an increased employer propensity to press prosecutions to a legal conclusion.) The downward slope in settlement rates for wage cases was less steep (from about 18 percent to about 12 percent).

In Toronto, almost 24 percent of convicted workers were ordered to return to work, often with a reprimand, but without fine or imprisonment;[145] 60 percent were fined, about half with the alternative of a jail term. In the whole period only forty-seven workers, fewer than 16 percent of all those convicted, were sentenced to jail without the alternative of a fine. More than half the jail sentences were imposed between 1870 and 1875.[146]

The Toronto jail register for 1870–73 includes fifty-five committals of forty-seven individual workers under the master and servant and apprentice

145. This includes 4 percent who were mulcted for costs and discharged, usually on the understanding that they were to return to work.

146. (Can. [Prov.]) 14&15 Vict. c.11 (1851) limited the options for apprentices and minor servants. This complicates the analysis, particularly since the record often leaves it uncertain whether a minor was involved.

legislation. This is the greatest number of such committals for any four-year period. A close examination of these cases gives a revealing glimpse of the uses of the law in a period of heightened industrial conflict, and on the eve of the trade unions' repeal campaign.[147] Committals included workers detained under warrants to await their trials, usually for one or two days, as well as those serving sentences. While the greatest number of committals (twenty-two) occurred in 1872, more workers were actually serving sentences for employment-related offenses in 1870. The experience of even a few hours' detention in Toronto's Don Jail would have disposed many to accept the magistrate's offer of a return to work. Four of the workers who were sentenced to jail in this period were indentured apprentices. One, who had taken two days off to see the Barnum show, did not improve his prospects by his flippancy in court; another had run away to Buffalo and, on his return, taken a job with another employer; a third had broken an earlier promise to return to work. Two others were minors, one apprehended at the station on his way to California, the other caught up in a dispute between his employer and his family. The rest of the jail sentences, as well as a number of committals for trial, involved collective resistance and industrial action.

Employers used the master and servant acts increasingly in the early 1870s to respond to collective action by their workers. Sometimes this took the form of group prosecutions, when employers brought up two or more workers together on misconduct charges: there were several of these in the mid-1850s, and then very few until another flurry in 1869–72. While they typically involved several workers at once, group prosecutions could also be serial. In 1871, for example, when the owners of the Gurney foundry were fending off the molders' union, they prosecuted a series of desertions. After dealing out fines and warnings in the earlier cases, the magistrate finally imposed a jail term, presumably in the interest of greater deterrence. Employers also used the acts to break strikes, whether by imprisoning the leaders or, as in the 1872 typographers strike, to keep strikebreakers at work.

Of the twenty-five total committals in 1870 and 1871, nineteen were accounted for by a single employer, the Beard Brothers stove factory. The company had been one of the city's premier molding shops before its founder, sometime Toronto mayor Joshua George Beard, retired in 1864, leaving the business in the hands of his three sons, who sold the old foundry to build a larger one. Between October 1865 and September 1871, they launched no fewer than thirty-three separate prosecutions against fifty-five defendants for

147. The Toronto Trades Assembly first lobbied the provincial government to repeal the master and servant act in March 1874: Kealey, *Toronto Workers*, 149, and see Craven, "Modern Spirit."

offenses under the master and servants and apprentices acts, and for conspiracy, making them by far the greatest consumers of the police magistrate's labor regulation services.[148] The Beards are a classic illustration of Daphne Simon's characterization of the master and servant acts as the weapon of the marginal manufacturer.[149] Their new factory was undercapitalized in comparison to its competitors. It relied disproportionately on inexperienced workers: 40 of their 100 employees were "boys," many of them articled to the firm or its principals. It quickly gained a reputation as a "scab shop," obliged — to quote the scarcely unbiased organ of the molders' union — "to take the offscourings of creation, all the drunken scallawags and botch workmen that found their way to Toronto." Nine Beard employees were sentenced to jail terms in 1870, and six the following year.

The Beards accounted for four of the twenty-seven committals before trial in 1870–73; thirteen others were individuals arrested for unrelated breaches of the employment statutes.[150] The rest were group prosecutions. Four printers were held for trial during the 1872 strike: one was subsequently sentenced to twenty days in jail, and another, who was given the alternative of a fifteen-dollar fine or thirty days, joined him there. A group of six deckhands spent some hours in jail before their court appearance, where they were fined for refusing to obey their mate's orders to take on wood after they had finished unloading cargo. John Webster, a master coach builder, charged two coach smiths with desertion: one was sentenced to two days in jail, and the other to a month at hard labor. Lastly, in 1873, founder Thomas McGaw had two brass finishers (described as "boys" in the police register) arrested for desertion: at trial, magistrate MacNabb discharged them with a caution.

When employers made master and servant prosecutions part of their arsenal against the unions, they politicized the law and invited a challenge from the local labor movement. The Ontario-based Canadian Labour Union and the Toronto Trades Assembly had been pressing for the repeal of the province's master and servant act since 1874. Their opportunity came in February 1877, when the Ontario government took the position that it was without jurisdiction to repeal an act that criminalized breach of contract. Criminal law fell within the exclusive purview of the Dominion government. Armed with the precedent of the British Employers and Workmen Act, 1875, the unionists appealed to the federal minister of justice, Edward Blake, who realized that with one stroke he could resolve a constitutional anomaly and pre-

148. The Beard conspiracy prosecution is discussed in Craven, "Workers' Conspiracies."
149. Simon, "Master and Servant."
150. Only one woman spent any time in jail awaiting trial for a master and servant offense in these four years, and she was charged with theft as well as desertion.

empt labor movement criticism of his government over the prime minister's heavy-handed intervention in a recent railway strike.[151] Despite the promise of its title, "to repeal certain laws making breaches of contracts of service criminal," Blake's bill merely clarified the constitutional boundary between the Dominion's exclusive jurisdiction over the criminal law and the provinces' exclusive jurisdiction over property and civil rights. "Wilful and malicious" breaches of the employment contract were made punishable under the general criminal law. Ordinary cases of desertion and disobedience could now be punished as offenses (but not as crimes) under provincial legislation. Punishments for provincial offenses could include fines and imprisonment.

The real effect of the 1877 statute, then, was not to do away with fines and imprisonment for breaches of the employment contract but rather to permit the provinces to implement or repeal penal sanctions when and if they chose to do so. The Ontario legislature responded immediately by abolishing imprisonment for master and servant offenses, although it was retained for apprentices. In Quebec, municipal bylaws providing for mandatory imprisonment were still being enforced after the turn of the twentieth century. The 1833 Prince Edward Island enactment, whose penal provision was specifically repealed by the Breaches of Contract Act, was a dead letter long before 1877; nevertheless it was thought still to be in effect in 1906[152] and was not officially repealed until 1951.[153] Dominion statutes providing imprisonment for breach of articles by merchant seamen remained in force well into the twentieth century, as did several provincial acts stipulating jail terms for uncooperative child workers and others imposing imprisonment for nonpayment of fines.

The West

In 1670 the Hudson's Bay Company was granted a trading monopoly over the entire Hudson Bay drainage basin (Rupert's Land). Commercial rivalry with other fur traders based in the St. Lawrence–Great Lakes system led the HBC to expand its operations and, in 1821, to merge with the Montreal-based North West Company, effectively adding nearly all of what is now western and northern Canada to the company's trading empire. This vast region was not a colony of settlement, although it incorporated the small community at Red River (Assiniboia), granted by the HBC to Lord Selkirk in 1811. The

151. Craven, "Modern Spirit."

152. Canada, *Labour Gazette*, July 1906, 57.

153. (P.E.I.) 2 Wm.IV c. 26 (1833) was not reprinted in post-Confederation consolidations, but is listed in the schedule of statutes repealed by (P.E.I.) Revised Statutes, c.2 (1951).

royal charter of 1670 authorized the HBC's governor and council to make and enforce laws and ordinances: while the extent of its jurisdiction over native people, Red River settlers, interlopers, and others not necessarily "belonging" to the company was contested terrain, the HBC had undisputed legal authority over its own employees.[154]

The HBC recruited actively in the Orkneys and elsewhere in Scotland and northern Europe where the men "did not know too much and had been accustomed to obedience,"[155] for artisans and laborers to staff its trading posts and transport network. Its employment pool expanded with the 1821 merger to include *Canadiens* as well as Red River Métis. For its posts and supply system west of the Rocky Mountains and along the Pacific coast, the company hired Kanakas, natives of Hawaii. Hiring was by multiyear contract at fixed rates of wages.[156] Recruitment for service in remote parts was not without risk to the company, as new hires sometimes pocketed their advances and failed to show up for transport. The voyageur legislation specifically targeted this offense in Quebec. In the 1850s the HBC tried and failed to prosecute defaulting Orcadian recruits under the British master and servant act of 1823.[157] While the fur trade depended on the labor of aboriginal producers of furs, food, and other natural products, as well as on the domestic labor of native concubines (or their slaves),[158] the HBC did not count them among its employees. It employed Indians for wages as guides and in transport.[159] The wage nexus with aboriginal workers became increasingly important as the HBC diversified its trading activities and its reliance on local produce and when, in the nineteenth century, its focus of operations shifted to the Pacific coast.[160]

At the company's "factories" on the bay, and at inland posts, difficult work-

154. An imperial act, (U.K.) 43 Geo.III c.138 (1803), gave Canadian courts jurisdiction over offenses committed in the North-West; the HBC maintained that this did not extend to Rupert's Land. This conflict was addressed by the (U.K.) 1&2 Geo.IV c.66 (1821), which gave courts in Upper Canada jurisdiction to determine civil and criminal disputes arising throughout the North-West, subject to the HBC's charter rights. The territorial courts intended by the 1821 legislation were never established: (U.K.) 22&23 Vict. c.26 (1859) (Preamble). For most practical purposes, company justice prevailed: W. Ward, "Administration of Justice," 5.

155. Helmcken, *Reminiscences*, 88.

156. For example, the 1836 arrangements to indenture twenty Orcadians and twenty Canadians: Oliver, *North-West*, 738.

157. Burley, *Servants*, 105–7.

158. Van Kirk, *Tender Ties*; on native slavery, see Mackie, *Trading*, 293–95, 300–308.

159. For example, in 1843 the HBC assigned "2 voyaging Servants . . . assisted by 26 Indians to be engaged for that purpose" to work two boat trips to York Factory: Oliver, *North-West*, 859. In Manitoba in 1872 several Swampy Cree were imprisoned in default of fines for breach of their contracts as boatmen for the HBC: Harring, *White Man's Law*, 130. Makahonuk, "Wage-Labour"; Goldring, "Employment Relations."

160. Mackie, *Trading*.

ing conditions, harsh discipline, scarcity of food and other supplies, confined circumstances, makeshift accommodation, bitter weather, and the occasional threat of armed attack made fertile ground for worker discontent. Desertion was a dismal option.[161] Resistance took a number of forms, from drunkenness to work refusal to outright mutiny. Individual factors' responses to indiscipline ranged from feeble pleading to brutal chastisement. Formal sanctions included fines, stoppage of privileges, whippings, imprisonment, and transportation home to face "condign punishment" there.

It is a nice question whether HBC discipline policy was mere employer self-help or something more akin to colonial employment legislation. Was the company making law and administering justice, or just taking the law into its own hands?[162] Its legislative powers were circumscribed by the requirement that it hew "as near as possible" to the laws of England at 2 May 1670, the date of its charter.[163] The applicable English employment legislation for the whole period of company rule was therefore the Statute of Artificers.[164] Yet there was little in the great statute that could be directly enforced in Rupert's Land.[165] It is suggestive that while in the early eighteenth century the company required its factors to read the Piracy Act to post employees each month,[166] there was no required reading of the Statute of Artificers. An official circular published at Moose Factory in 1815 complained of servants' "disobedience, neglect of duty, Combinations, and desertion, to the great injury of the Company, the degradation of the Officers, and the subversion of all order and discipline," and warned that "all Crimes, Offences or misdemeanours, which are cognizable by the Laws of England will in future be punished according to the said Laws." The circular included a table of "leading offences" and "probable punishments."[167] Among the litany of charges pressed by the company against Nor'Wester Duncan Cameron in 1816 was "seducing His

161. For example, Thomas Anderson, laborer, fined five pounds "for deserting from the Arctic Discovery Expedition" in 1836: Oliver, *North-West*, 772.

162. Smandych and Lynden, "Administering Justice."

163. See, for example, Adam Thom's 1851 opinion as to whether Presbyterian ministers could solemnize marriages in Rupert's Land: Oliver, *North-West*, 383. (Can. [Dom.]) 49 Vict. c.25 (1886) fixed the reception date for Canadian law at 15 July 1870. For a discussion of what law was in force in the territories between 1870 (when control passed from the HBC to Canada) and 1886, see Ward, "Administration of Justice," appendix A.

164. (Engl.) 5 Eliz. c.4 (1562).

165. Nevertheless, in 1832 chief factors were authorized by council, "to engage strong, healthy half-breed lads not under fourteen years of age, as apprentices . . . on a term not less than seven years": Oliver, *North-West*, 686.

166. Muir, "Structures, Symbols," 42; the Piracy Act was (Engl.) 11 Wm.III c.7 (1698).

167. Oliver, *North-West*, 1285ff. Bindon, "HBC Law," 45, considers this the company's "first code of penal laws." The better view seems to be that it was a compilation and restatement of preexisting policy and practice: see Burley, *Servants*, 223 n. 92.

Majesty's subjects settled on Red River and the servants of the Earl of Selkirk to desert and defraud their masters."[168] This neatly encapsulated the dual role of Selkirk at Red River, and by extension the company in Rupert's Land, as both viceroy and employer.

The governor of Assiniboia issued a warrant for the arrest of three absconding HBC employees in 1823, and in 1837 his council petitioned the company for copies of Burns's *Justice* and a magistrates' manual.[169] Nevertheless, the council at Red River did not concern itself expressly with master and servant issues before 1857, when it adopted regulations for river transport, requiring masters and boatmen to make written contracts and prescribing imprisonment for up to thirty days for the servant's breach, as well as civil recovery of advances or unpaid wages.[170] The model seems to have been the Quebec voyageur legislation.

The Dominion of Canada acquired control of the North-West from the HBC in 1870.[171] The province of Manitoba, created in that year out of the old district of Assiniboia, adopted its first master and servant statute in 1871.[172] It was patterned on then current Quebec legislation (although "drunkenness" as an employment offense was peculiar to Manitoba).[173] The act provided fines and up to two months' imprisonment in default of payment for worker and third-party offenses. It included a compulsory notice provision, breach of which was to be treated as desertion. Workers who brought valid complaints against their employers could be released from their contracts and awarded a month's wages over and above the amount otherwise due to them. In the absence of a written contract, justices determining wage claims were bound to rely on the master's sworn statement about the conditions of employment. The compulsory notice provision was repealed in 1880, as was the master's oath.[174] Imprisonment in default of payment was dropped from the act in 1883, restored in 1891 when Manitoba's master and servant and apprentices and minors acts were combined, and finally abolished in 1913.[175]

Research to date suggests that the Manitoba master and servant legislation was used mostly for wage recovery, although its penalties for worker breach were not entirely neglected. The Winnipeg police court heard 10 employer

168. Oliver, *North-West*, 203.

169. Ibid., 246, 281.

170. Ibid., 427; a similar enactment was made in Apr. 1862 (ibid., 497).

171. Imperial Order-in-Council, 23 June 1870.

172. (Man.) 34 Vict. c.14 (1871).

173. Drunkenness had been an employment offense in New France. The Man. drunkenness provision was inherited by N.-W.T. and subsequently by Sask. and Alta.

174. (Man.) Consol. Stat. 1880 c.41.

175. (Man.) 46&47 Vict c.33 (1883); (Man.) Rev. Stat. 1891 c.96; (Man.) Rev. Stat. 1913 c.124. The apprentices and minors act was (Man.) 40 Vict. c.26 (1877).

complaints and 17 wage claims in 1873 and 1874, but a total of only 3 master and servant matters in the next five years.[176] The same court heard 134 wage claims and 4 complaints against employees in the eleven months beginning 1 October 1909.[177]

In 1873, to consolidate its contested sovereignty in the rest of the former HBC territories, the Dominion government established the North-West Mounted Police (NWMP). Its inspectors and superintendents were ex officio justices of the peace, so that the NWMP had principal responsibility not only for the apprehension of lawbreakers, but for summary justice as well.[178] The Manitoba master and servant act of 1871 was extended to the North-West Territories in 1873.[179] Between January 1879 and September 1889, the NWMP reported 315 master and servant prosecutions, 265 of them for unpaid wages.[180] In desertion cases, which accounted for most of the remainder, the police justices seem to have taken the same tack as Ontario magistrates before 1877, using the threat of penal sanctions to enforce specific performance of the employment bargain, so that several cases were "dismissed upon agreeing to return to work." In just two cases were convicted workers jailed without the option of a fine, although several more suffered imprisonment for inability or unwillingness to pay.[181]

One unusual feature of master and servant enforcement in the North-West was large-scale actions for wages. On several occasions the NWMP intervened to preserve the peace when large employers were unable to meet their payrolls. Two of these instances, involving 79 and 54 workers respectively, arose out of the bankruptcy of the Saskatchewan Coal Mining and Transportation Company, in which former NWMP superintendent J. M. Walsh was concerned.[182] Others occurred during construction of the Cana-

176. Provincial Archives of Manitoba (hereafter PAM) G 2762, Winnipeg Police Minute Book, 1873–79.

177. PAM G 4137, Winnipeg Police Record Books, vols. 17, 18.

178. (Can. [Dom.]) 37 Vict. c.22 (1874). HBC factors were also appointed as justices: W. Ward, "Administration of Justice," 35.

179. Oliver, *North-West*, 1005. (N.-W.T.) Ord. n.5 (1879), (N.-W.T.) Rev. Ord. c.36 (1888), and (N.-W.T.) c.3 (1904) continued the policy of fines for worker misconduct, with up to a month's imprisonment in default of payment.

180. These statistics, and the account which follows, are based on the police commissioner's annual reports in Canada, *Sessional Papers*, 1879–89 (hereafter NWMP).

181. For example, four agricultural laborers spent fourteen days in the Crane Lake police guardroom in 1888 in default of ten-dollar fines for deserting employment: NWMP 1888, 121. Thirteen cases imposing fines with a jail alternative have "imprisonment" or "served imprisonment" in the "Remarks" column.

182. I am grateful to Alan McCullough for information about this company and the CACCC discussed below. For Walsh, see R. C. Macleod, "James Morrow Walsh," *Dictionary of Canadian Biography*, 13:1071–72.

dian Pacific Railway (CPR). Fifteen CPR bridge builders who had been discharged without pay received judgments for wages at Calgary in June 1884.[183] In April 1885, when 1,200 trackmen in the Kootenay District struck for unpaid wages, NWMP Inspector Steele instructed the five policemen under his command "to use the very severest measures to prevent a cessation of the work of construction." One man was shot, the Riot Act was read, resisters were fined $100 each or six months' hard labor, and the strike collapsed the next day.[184]

Although the CPR sometimes prosecuted workers for desertion, the railway relied on the services of the NWMP most heavily during strikes.[185] Several much smaller employers made disproportionate use of the master and servant legislation, most prominently the Canadian Agricultural, Colonization and Coal Company (CACCC). This ranching concern was founded by an entrepreneurial English aristocrat, Sir John Lister-Kaye, who imported his cattle stock from the United States and his sheep and laborers from England.[186] About 110 men were recruited on one-year contracts with the promise of free passage, board and lodging, and a homestead once their term was up. They arrived in the North-West in late August 1888; over the next few months at least 10 of them were charged with breach of contract or deserting employment. One case was settled when Inspector Sanders persuaded the accused to drop a charge of assault against his foreman. Three others were dismissed.[187] Six men were convicted: they all served jail terms in default of paying ten-, twenty-, and thirty-dollar fines. Sir John wrote a formal letter of appreciation to police superintendent Antrobus, who closed his report of the matter by observing, "I have always endeavored, in the interests of the public, to assist any company starting in the Territories to the best of my ability, and have impressed upon my subaltern officers and non-commissioned officers and men the necessity of carrying out my wishes in this respect."[188] In October 1889, however, disappointed by a lack of government support for its latest colonization project, the CACCC dismissed most of its remaining English recruits.

In 1905, when the new provinces of Saskatchewan and Alberta were cre-

183. The "Remarks" column of the NWMP tabulation indicates that the CPR appealed these judgments, perhaps on the ground that payment had to await its paymaster's approval: *Manitoba Daily Free Press*, 9 June 1884.

184. NWMP 1885, 16–17.

185. There is an extended account of police intervention in the Dec. 1883 running trades strike at NWMP 1883, 10ff.

186. McGowan, *Grassland Settlers*, ch. 5.

187. *Manitoba Daily Free Press*, 3 Dec. 1888.

188. NWMP 1888, 121.

ated out of the old North-West Territories, they inherited the territorial master and servant ordinance of 1904, which imposed fines for worker misconduct and imprisonment in default of payment, as well as a summary action for unpaid wages. In both provinces, the thirty-dollar fine or one month in default for drunkenness, absenteeism, disobedience and dissipating the master's effects survived into the 1940s.[189]

In the unorganized territory west of the Rocky Mountains, the HBC had established its commercial dominance in competition with Russian and American traders and extended its trading network from Alaska to Mexico.[190] But the Oregon boundary settlement of 1846 and the California gold rush of 1848–49 made it clear that continued British sovereignty depended not on claims of first discovery and commercial exploitation but upon settlement and the establishment of civil authority. In 1849 the imperial government granted Vancouver Island to the HBC for agricultural colonization.[191] The company's land policy (and that of its satellite, the Puget's Sound Agricultural Company) was expressly Wakefieldian. Land prices were to be set high enough to introduce "a just proportion of labour and capital." The ideal settler would have small but independent means, with "enough to pay for his land, and passage out for himself and five labourers . . . under contracts for 5 or 7 years, as the Hudson's Bay Company hire their servants."[192]

There was to be a civil government, with a governor of the company's choosing. It preferred its chief factor at Fort Victoria, James Douglas, but settled instead for Richard Blanshard, an English barrister without ties to the company, who was willing to serve without salary.[193] Arriving in March 1850, Blanshard found the HBC embroiled in labor conflict. The company had recruited an extended family of Scottish miners on special indentures to build and work an underground coal mine at Fort Rupert on the northern tip of Vancouver Island.[194] Almost from the day of their arrival at Fort Rupert

189. (Sask.) Rev. Stat. c.149 (1909); (Sask.) Stat. 1918–19 c.61; (Sask.) Rev. Stat. c.205 (1920); (Sask.) Stat. 1923 c.63 (adding the offense of "abandoning employment"); (Sask.) Rev. Stat. c.247 (1930); (Sask.) Rev. Stat c.294 (1940); (Alta.) Stat. & Ord. Consol. & In Force, c.50 (1910); (Alta.) Stat. 1911–12 c.4; (Alta.) Stat. In Force c.50 (1915); (Alta.) Rev. Stat. 1922 c.180; (Alta.) Rev. Stat. 1942 c.136.

190. In 1838 the HBC was granted a twenty-one-year monopoly of the Indian trade west of the Rockies.

191. The grant was expedited by the retirement of James Stephen, who had opposed it as a "Proprietary Lordship" that could not be maintained "any longer than the inhabitants are too few and too feeble to shake it off." Quoted in Knaplund, "Stephen," 268–69.

192. HBC Governor Pelly to chief factor Douglas (1849) quoted in Lamb, "Blanshard," 18–19.

193. Ireland, "Blanshard"; Lamb, "Blanshard."

194. For secondary accounts, see Lamb, "Blanshard"; Ralston, "Miners"; Bowen, "Colliers"; Newsome, *Coal Coast*; and Burley, *Servants*.

in September 1849 the miners' expectations and experience clashed head on with those of the HBC managers and ordinary employees. When two miners refused to dig a drain as ordered, the post's acting manager charged them with breach of contract and fined them fifty pounds—a year's wages. The clan stopped all work. The company responded by confining the men in irons for several days, then placed them under house arrest. The strike spread to other groups at the fort, especially after the arrival of a ship bringing the first news of the California gold discoveries and a supply of rum.

In the meantime, an HBC ship had arrived at Fort Victoria with a group of intending settlers and other new employees: among the complement was J. S. Helmcken, a recent medical graduate who had contracted to serve the company as surgeon and clerk at Vancouver Island for five years. Governor Blanshard appointed Helmcken justice of the peace at Fort Rupert: "This is the only appointment I have yet made in the Colony, for as there are no independent settlers, all cases that can occur, requiring magisterial interference, are disputes, between the representatives of the Hudson's Bay Company and their servants."[195]

Helmcken's diary of his short tenure as magistrate reveals much about the relationship between company discipline and civil authority, albeit in extreme circumstances.[196] He had no legal knowledge, no law books,[197] and no authority: "The men who left off work were not brought before me, Mr. Blenkinsop being well aware that I could not do anything with them, not having any constables or other coercive force."[198] His efforts to interpret and apply the men's employment contracts were ineffectual, even when sanctioned by the governor himself. Denied a remedy and encouraged perhaps by Helmcken's construction of their agreements, several miners and others deserted the fort. The sorry affair culminated when three runaway sailors were found murdered, apparently by Indians. Helmcken resigned his commission as justice of the peace; not long afterward, Blanshard resigned the governorship to be succeeded by Douglas, as the company had wanted all along.

Two years later, when gold was discovered on the mainland, the colony of

195. Blanshard to Colonial Secretary, 10 July 1850, quoted in Lamb, "Blanshard," 11. Helmcken himself was less sanguine about the conflict of interest: *Reminiscences*, 309.

196. Helmcken's diary (hereafter Diary) for 27 June to 20 Aug. 1850 is in Provincial Archives of British Columbia (hereafter PABC) C/AA/403/R3 (Magistrate's Court Fort Rupert). Forty years later Helmcken published another version in the *Victoria Colonist* (1 Jan. 1890), reprinted as an appendix in *Reminiscences*, 297ff.

197. "Anyhow 'law' without power to compel obedience thereto is worse than useless." Helmcken, *Reminiscences*, 309. Nevertheless he had detailed written instructions from Blanshard: Lamb, "Blanshard," 11, 13.

198. Diary (transcript of letter to Fort Victoria, 16 July 1850). Helmcken's call for volunteers to act as special constables went unanswered.

British Columbia was created. Douglas became governor, while remaining in office at Vancouver Island, although he was now required to relinquish his position in the HBC.[199] Both colonies received mid-nineteenth-century English statutes—"having all the English laws, we had enough."[200] When the two were united as British Columbia in 1866, the common reception date was fixed at 19 November 1858.[201] This meant that until 1897, when British Columbia adopted its first local master and servant act on the reformed Ontario model, the British statute of 1823[202] was in force in the colony, and in the Canadian province that it became in 1871. While few records of British Columbia master and servant cases cite statutory authority, the 1823 British act was expressly relied upon in a handful of prosecutions launched by Fraser River salmon processors against Indian fishermen in 1877.[203] There were local enactments in 1870 and 1871 to prevent desertions from merchant ships and one in 1877 to regulate coal mines.[204] The local shipping acts addressed crimping and other third-party interference between seamen and their employers; direct enforcement of sailors' contracts depended on British legislation received by the colony before 1871, and Dominion legislation thereafter.

Master and servant proceedings in the records of the Victoria police court in its busy years of the Fraser River and Cariboo gold rushes resemble those of its Atlantic coast contemporaries, although on a smaller scale.[205] Most of the workers prosecuted were merchant seamen—thirty-three for desertion, fifty-seven for disobedience—who, upon conviction, were ordered to return to their ships or sent to jail for up to a month or until called for by their masters. There was just one case of someone not identified as a seaman "improperly absenting himself from his employer": he was ordered to pay costs or spend twenty-four hours in jail. One man was jailed for a month on the charge of "labourer: breach of contract."[206] But of 138 wage cases for which disposi-

199. Helmcken had by now become speaker of the Vancouver Island legislature, and son-in-law to Douglas. Another son-in-law succeeded Douglas as HBC chief factor in 1858.

200. Helmcken, *Reminiscences*, 336. Earlier imperial legislation giving Canadian courts jurisdiction in the region was repealed when the colonies were created: see, for example, (U.K.) 12&13 Vict. c.48 (1849).

201. Douglas had issued a reception proclamation for the old colony of British Columbia on that date.

202. (U.K.) 4 Geo.IV c.34 (1823); Hay in this volume.

203. D. Harris, *Fish*, 49–55. The only record of these prosecutions is the *New Westminster Mainland Guardian*, 18, 21 July, 11 Aug., 25 Sept. 1877. At least one of these decisions was to have been appealed, but no record or report has been found.

204. (B.C.) 33 Vict. n.14 (1870); (B.C.) 34 Vict. n.166 (1871); (B.C.) 40 Vict. c.15 (1877).

205. PABC GR-0848, Vancouver Island, Police & Prisons, vols.1–5 Charge books, 1858–71. There are no master and servant cases recorded after 1869 and very few after 1864.

206. There was one other breach-of-contract case recorded, but without any indication that it involved a contract of employment.

tions are known, only 8 were sailors' claims.[207] The success rate in wage cases was about 60 percent overall. Sailors won 75 percent of their wage cases; Indians lost most of theirs. Of 5 wage claims by Indians, 1 was settled and the rest dismissed (1 for nonappearance). This was perhaps unsurprising in view of the advice given by Victoria stipendiary magistrate A. G. Pemberton: "I never convict on Indian testimony unless it be corroborated by white evidence."[208]

During the gold rush years, local administration in the British Columbia interior was entrusted to officials called gold commissioners, who licensed and regulated mining claims while acting as justices of the peace and, in some cases, constables, sheriffs, and bailiffs as well. The gold commissioners' casebooks show them dealing with employment disputes, but in the context of civil litigation rather than enforcement of the (British) master and servant act. For example, wage claims before the Cariboo gold commissioners took the form of actions requiring defendants to show cause why they should not be ordered to pay the plaintiffs various sums for work and labor.[209] Similarly, when the men it had hired to construct a drain "backed out," the Bed Rock Drain Company did not prosecute them as deserting servants but sued them severally in damages for breach of contract.[210] There is no indication of reliance on the master and servant act in the surviving records of the gold commissioners' courts.[211]

In theory, the British act of 1823 remained in force in British Columbia until 1897, when the province adopted its first local master and servant act. But there is little or no evidence of its use to prosecute workers after the 1877 Fraser River fishery cases. Between November 1890 and November 1897 the Victoria police court records forty-five employment-related cases (some of

207. There are several actions for seamen's wages in the records of the court of vice-admiralty at Victoria in the 1860s: PABC C/AA/30.33/2. At the police court, 53 of 138 wage claims were dismissed, 17 of them for failure of the complainant to appear. In 84 cases the court ordered wage claims to be paid in full or in part; distress warrants issued in at least 6 of these.

208. Pemberton had been asked by the colonial secretary to answer a newly appointed magistrate's question about the admissibility of Indian evidence in cases of liquor selling. Pemberton might have meant his response to apply only in such cases. PABC GR-1372 F-15-2 A.C. Anderson re duties of JP, 12 July 1864.

209. PABC GR-584 v.18, Cariboo gold commissioners casebook, 16 Sept. 1866–12 Apr. 1869: e.g., *Cooney v. Curry*, 18 Sept. 1866; *Huskin v. Heron*, 25 Sept. 1866; *Chisholm v. Crane & Boyle*, 28 Sept. 1866; *Johnson v. Robinson*, 28 Sept. 1866; *Caine v. Donahue*, 15 Oct. 1866. For a similar case involving work on shares, see *Stewart v. Williscroft*, 22 Aug. 1867.

210. PABC GR-584 v.22, Richfield gold commissioners notebook, *Anderson v. Wight et al.*, 10 June 1864. *McKinney v. Jack*, 3 Oct. 1867, in the same notebook, appears to be an action for wrongful dismissal from employment; no disposition is recorded.

211. For accounts of popular intervention by miners' meetings in one case of wage default and another of wrongful dismissal during the Yukon gold rush, see T. Stone, "Mounties as Vigilantes," 123–25 and 131.

them involving more than one worker) but nearly all are merchant shipping cases.[212] All the employment-related cases (except one of embezzlement) in a sample of Vancouver police court proceedings between 1890 and 1910 involved merchant seamen.[213] The British act does not appear to have been used to intervene in strikes by coal miners or cannery workers, although other legal and extralegal repression figured prominently. Nor, with the sole exception of the 1877 prosecutions, does it seem to have played a direct part in the subordination of Indian, Chinese, and other nonwhite labor. The penal provisions of the 1823 British act seem to have become a dead letter in British Columbia after 1877, although it remained the basis for wage recovery in the police courts until 1897. The provincial enactment that succeeded it was modeled on the Ontario statute then in force and so made no provision for enforcing the employment contract against the worker.[214] It was essentially an act for the summary recovery of unpaid wages up to fifty dollars. During the legislative debate the attorney general explained, "that as the acts of England in force in 1859 [*sic*] only became law here insofar as they were applicable to this province, it was thought best to bring in this act."[215] This suggests that the British act, which had been repealed there in 1875, was considered inapplicable, a conclusion consistent with its apparent disuse.

The 1897 debate focused on a section of the bill that enabled enforcement of written employment contracts made outside the province for performance in British Columbia. Provisions of this sort were common throughout the empire and had the effect of subjecting extraterritorial contracts to local regulations and enforcement. But populist and labor politics in late nineteenth-century British Columbia were racist and nativist, and the provision in section 8 became the focus of opposition.[216] "It is not often that a member in charge of a bill is met by such an entire misconception of its purpose," noted the *Victoria Colonist*. "This provision was wholly in favour of the workmen, but the house struck it out under the mistaken notion that thereby they were preventing the hiring of foreign labourers."[217] The following year, an amendment was introduced to make employment contracts with nonresi-

212. PABC GR-0605, Provincial Court (Victoria), Police Court record books, v.1. The exceptions are a single wages claim and a case of alleged enslavement.

213. Vancouver City Archives, series 182, Vancouver Police Court calendars. The sample consisted of all the cases listed in one month per quarter in each of 1890, 1895, 1900, 1905, and 1910. There were just eighteen employment-related cases in these twenty months, several of them with multiple complainants or defendants.

214. (B.C.) 60 Vict. c.26 (1897); section references to (Can. [Prov.]) 22 Vict. c.75 (1859) appeared in the bill as published in the *Victoria Colonist*, 16 Feb. 1897.

215. *Victoria Colonist*, 19 Feb. 1897.

216. For labor politics in this period, see Robin, *Politics*, ch. 4, and Robin, *Spoils*, ch. 2.

217. *Victoria Colonist*, 20 Feb. 1897.

dents "void and of no effect" against workers who came to British Columbia to perform them. The government, having learned from the 1897 debate, sought to cut its losses; the premier objected that the bill was "unpatriotic and against the whole principle of confederation as it legislated against other parts of Canada and would be calculated to arouse sectional jealousies." His amendment to the amendment, restricting the bill's application to contracts made outside Canada, was hotly debated but eventually carried.[218] In 1899, however, the act was amended to invalidate all employment contracts made out of the province.[219] There was a renewed attempt in 1904 to restore the 1898 provision making other Canadian employment contracts enforceable in British Columbia.[220] One member argued that this would "destroy the usefulness of the present act, which he considered protective to the workingmen." Another surmised that "every employer of labour in the province would like to see every Chinese and Japanese out of this province, but what could they do? Labour conditions here were quite different from those in other parts of the Dominion." A third maintained that the "object of this amendment was to dump the off-scourings of the street corners of the east into this province."[221] In the face of such compelling pressure the bill was withdrawn.[222]

Conclusion

In England, and in many colonial settings, master and servant legislation played a substantial economic role in the recruitment and retention of scarce labor, in limiting or directing labor mobility, and in habituating labor to emergent capitalist relations of production. In Canada, however, despite a proliferation of master and servant statutes, many of them at least occasionally enforced, these acts did not play a central part in regulating the labor mar-

---

218. (B.C.) Bill No. 30, 1898; *Victoria Colonist*, 18, 24 Mar., 7 Apr. 1898. The bill exempted contracts for skilled labor that was unavailable in the province and for teachers and performers.

219. (B.C.) Bill No. 10, 1899; *Victoria Colonist*, 18 Jan., 1 Feb. 1899; BC Legislative Assembly *Journal*, 1 Feb. 1899; (B.C.) Stat. c.43 (1899). The act was also amended in this session to provide for the administration of medical benefits deducted from wages. This provision was the subject of further amendment motions in 1900 (Bill 55), 1901 (Bill 86), 1902 (Bill 24), 1907 (Bill 44), 1908 (Bill 16), 1909 (Bill 83), and 1924 (Bill 38). Another set of employment standards amendments dealt with the form of wage payment: 1905 (Bill 75), 1906 (Bill 29), 1914 (Bill 13), 1915 (Bill 69), 1916 (Bill 46). The 1906 version, which proposed a fifty-dollar fine for nonpayment of fortnightly wages, sparked an extended debate over "class legislation," the "penal clause," and the greater reliability of Chinese than white labor: *Victoria Colonist*, 2, 9 Mar. 1906.

220. (B.C.) Bill No. 56, 1904 provided for replacing the words "British Columbia" in the exclusionary section of the act with the word "Canada."

221. *Victoria Colonist*, 5 Feb. 1904.

222. Ibid., 11 Feb. 1904.

ket or disciplining workers, except perhaps in merchant shipping. Reconciling this apparent enthusiasm for legislation with its general irrelevance for economic life is a central problem in this chapter. The solution proposed here is that while master and servant enforcement could bear only marginally on labor market problems in the Canadian setting, it was nevertheless valued for its side effects. The occasional exemplary prosecution served as a useful reminder of superordination and subordination in a British society bordering the American republic. Unequal relations, whether of class or of race, found clear expression in an employment regime that could curtail liberty for insubordination. The rough policy of master and servant law could lend legitimacy to employer authority and, especially in the absence of other institutions to enforce the law's provisions, sanction employer self-help.

It is difficult to point to more than a small handful of instances in which the actual enforcement of Canadian master and servant acts made an arguable difference in the operation of a local or sectoral labor market. At the same time, it is possible to identify several recurring contexts in which master and servant law was used in a variety of ways, although generally to limited practical effect.

Enforcement of the master and servant acts played a small but tangible part in reinforcing distinctions of race and class (and gender, at least to the extent that magistrates in some parts were reluctant to jail women) and delineating the gulf between respectable and disreputable.[223] Differential treatment of black workers in eighteenth-century Nova Scotia or Indians in nineteenth-century British Columbia resulted not from the express policy of the employment legislation but rather from the magistrates' determination to put such people in their place.

Some English employers called on master and servant law to bolster their symbolic authority over British employees indentured for service in Canada, particularly in the context of colonization schemes—thus Captain William Owen, R.N., who brought thirty-eight servants under indenture to colonize Campobello Island in 1772 (only to find it occupied by squatters from New England). Having first erected a flagpole, a pair of stocks, and a whipping post, Owen called his flock together on a Sunday, "performed Divine Service and read the reciprocal duties of Masters and Servants."[224] Thus too, though a century later and 5,000 kilometers to the west, Sir John Lister-Kaye and his Canadian Agricultural, Colonization and Coal Company. In the absence of relatively autonomous civil authority, the Hudson's Bay Company cloaked its

223. Craven, "Law and Ideology."
224. Owen, *Narrative*, 130.

sometimes brutally arbitrary, and always determinedly self-interested, discipline of indentured workers in the mantle of British law. As late as 1924, James Aikins, Manitoba's Anglophile lieutenant governor,[225] charged one of his employees with deserting employment: "[T]he prosecution was brought for the purpose of warning farm labourers who have a tendency to quit their job at a time when they are most needed, that they cannot legally do so, after an agreement has been made to serve for a period of time."[226]

It would be a mistake, though, to imagine that such appeals to symbolic authority were typically successful; on the contrary, they seem often to have arisen out of the master's despair at the workers' intractability. Owen's servants abandoned his "plantation" at the first opportunity. The same John Muir who told his diary after witnessing a sailor's punishment, "them that's bound must obey, Servants must be subject to their masters,"[227] was soon to resist the HBC's interpretation of his own contract and become complicit in the work refusal and subsequent desertion of his crew of miners.

In the Canadian context, appeals to penal employment law were often counsels of despair. Colonel John Prince, whose career as Upper Canada militiaman and legislator included summary executions of Patriots in the rebellion of 1837–38 and successful sponsorship of a bill against poaching, supported Ontario's 1847 master and servant act because it was so hard to keep domestics to their agreements: "The only cure he saw for the evil he described was, to send any young lady he saw so acting for a month to jail."[228] This was a rearguard action against creeping democracy and the practical realization, as one Reform supporter put it in the same debate, that "there was no use in endeavouring to compel an unwilling servant to perform his contract."[229] The bill passed, but few if any of Prince's "fine young girls" were jailed in consequence. As late as the 1877 parliamentary debate on the breaches of contract bill, one or two members continued to insist that only the prospect of imprisonment would compel workers to keep to their engagements.[230] But this was a minority opinion, and the official view—in English Canada, at least—was that employment agreements should be treated no differently than any commercial contract. In de Montigny's Montreal, the ineluctable incarceration

225. Aikins was also president of the Canadian Bar Association: "[H]is notion of 'Law' was inseparable from conceptions of Britishness, Christianity, and 'civilisation'": Pue, "British Masculinities," 91.

226. *Winnipeg Free Press*, 18 Sept. 1924. The man was convicted in absentia and sentenced to pay five dollars and costs or suffer ten days' imprisonment.

227. Newsome, *Coal Coast*, 28.

228. Quoted in Craven, "Law of Master and Servant," 189.

229. Ibid.

230. Craven, "Modern Spirit," 155.

of "exacting and insolent" servants was a corollary of ultramontane conservatism, to be dismantled by his liberal Protestant successor.

Ideology could give way to practicality, of course. Toronto newspaper publisher George Brown, who had inveighed against the 1847 bill as brutal, tyrannical, and impractical—"compulsory service is worse than useless"[231] —expressed no qualms about using it in 1872 as he attempted to break the typographers' strike. But employer recourse to the master and servant acts to undermine union organizing and strikes was not especially effective in the Canadian context. It could not relieve against festering discontent, as the experience of the Beard foundry showed. It could backfire, becoming a rallying point for public criticism of employer heavy-handedness, as it did in 1872. The rhetoric of strikebreaking in Canada relied more successfully on appeals to public order and industrial peace than to the sanctity of individual employment contracts.

As for practicality versus ideology, Edward Blake, the sponsor of the Breaches of Contract bill (1877), acknowledged that it could not be made to apply to merchant shipping.[232] This was the single arena in which contracts of employment were regularly enforced by imprisonment. The pronounced interest of the mother country in regulating sailors' labor markets throughout the empire led to imperial disallowance of colonial Canadian legislation varying the rules about seafarers' employment.[233] As late as 1886, when the Dominion government was required to respond to complaints about Canadian shipboard discipline made by the secretary of the British and Foreign Sailors Society, it reassured the Colonial Office that Canada had "laws similar to those which prevail in the United Kingdom" and adequate facilities for enforcing them.[234] As a result, police courts in Saint John, Halifax, Vancouver, Victoria, and other seaports processed considerable volumes of sailors' desertion and disobedience cases, sending scores of seamen to prison each year, while rarely hearing a single complaint against other categories of workers under the local master and servant legislation. Special legislative treatment of sailors' labor discipline has persisted as a lasting residue of imperial labor regulation. In a recent review of labor standards compliance, the International Confederation of Free Trade Unions draws attention "to the provisions of the Canada Shipping Act under which imprisonment including forced la-

231. *Toronto Globe*, 14 July 1847.

232. Craven, "Modern Spirit," 156–57.

233. Apart from the N.S. sailors' wages acts (note 7) these included a N.B. seamen's act and P.E.I. legislation permitting sailors to be arrested for debt. For the corresponding Australian case, see Quinlan, "Balancing Trade."

234. PABC GR 0996–5–1024/87.

bour may be imposed for breaches of discipline, even when the safety of the ship was not endangered."[235]

Finally, something must be said about the lingering demise of master and servant law in Canada.[236] It is hard to measure this by the passage or even the enforcement of specific statutes. Some enactments were unenforceable from the outset: an early example is Nova Scotia's attempt to introduce Elizabethan-style wage fixing in 1777: "The Justices took it into consideration, and put it of[f] for further consideration," until the measure expired.[237] Other statutes became unenforceable as a matter of political practicality, although they lingered on the statute books. Nor can the decline readily be measured from a moment of reform. The best example to the contrary is Ontario in 1877, when penalties for worker breach were simply abolished, but even there the labor movement was not necessarily opposed to a penal law: in its official view the fundamental unfairness was not that workers could be jailed for breach of contract but that employers could not, and it readily conceded imprisonment for absconding apprentices. This theory of geese and ganders survived into the populist western farmers' movements of the 1920s and 1930s and even resulted in legislation. In Alberta the United Farmers government introduced a fine of up to $2,500 with three months' imprisonment in default of payment for coal mine operators who failed to post bond guaranteeing miners' wages.[238] In Manitoba, the Liberal-Progressive government made employers liable to six months' imprisonment in actions for wages by domestic servants.[239] The last act came in the final decade of the twentieth century, when Ontario's first social democratic government thought to put an end to linguistic inequality in a province that had abandoned imprisonment for breach of contract more than a century before: henceforth there were to be no masters and servants on the statute book, but only employers and employees.[240]

235. ICFTU, "Labour Standards."

236. A recent assessment of "the 20th century employment law regime in Canada" does not mention master and servant, as good an indication as any of its perceived demise: Fudge and Tucker, "Pluralism or Fragmentation?"

237. Perkins, *Diary* I, 8 July 1777. (N.S.) 17 Geo.III c.2 (1777) expired after one year and was not renewed.

238. (Alta.) Statutes c.46 (1928); an amendment reduced the minimum fine from $1,000 to $100 and added a penalty of $100 or thirty days' imprisonment in default for failing to make monthly returns of wages paid: (Alta.) Statutes c.43 (1934).

239. (Man.) Statutes c.26 (1934).

240. (Ont.) Employers and Employees Act, R.S.O. 1990, c. E.12.

SIX

Australia, 1788–1902

A Workingman's Paradise?

Michael Quinlan

You can send a man to prison, like a thief, if he has a row with a squatter after signing an agreement, but we can't send the squatter to prison if he's in fault. The Masters and Servants Act is all wrong and we'll alter it when we get a chance.[1]

Ned the shearer's speech, in William Lane's 1892 novel, *A Workingman's Paradise*, summarized sixty years of Australian pastoral workers' struggles. They culminated in 1891 when troopers clashed with armed unionists amid widespread arson of shearing sheds, and hundreds of strikers were jailed. Master and servant law was not a prominent issue in the dispute, but the subordination of workers through individual contract making ensconced by that law was. Lane wrote *A Workingman's Paradise* in the aftermath of defeat to help thirteen strike leaders jailed after a show trial in Rockhampton. The novel is a scathing account of the exploitation of working men and women. Its ironic title points up the paradox that Australia offered real opportunities to working people, along with denial, political repression, and exploitation.

Employment Regulation in the Australian Colonies: An Overview

European settlement in Australia began in 1788 with the establishment of a penal colony under military rule. As the free population grew, a civil court structure slowly emerged and the founding colony of New South Wales was granted a Legislative Council in 1825. Three years later it enacted the first master and servant statute in the Australian colonies.[2] Employment regula-

---

I would like to thank Barrie Dyster for many helpful comments on earlier drafts of this chapter.
    1. W. Lane, *Workingman's Paradise*, 196–97.
    2. (N.S.W.) 9 Geo.IV c.9 (1828).

tion in the convict colonies took two forms. Various categories of convict workers were subject to governor's orders or regulations backed by a disciplinary penal code. Free emigrant and pardoned convict workers were subject to a combination of governor's orders specifying wages, rations, and hours of work[3] as well as English master and servant law. While the adoption of colonial master and servant acts signaled the shift to a free labor market, the regulation of convict labor remained significant until 1840 in New South Wales and even later in Tasmania and Western Australia.[4] Given this overlap, and the impact of the convict experience on colonial master and servant laws, it is important to look at the regulation of convict labor, as well as the regulation of free labor before 1828.

Between 1788 and 1868 132,308 men and 24,960 women were transported to the Australian colonies from Britain and Ireland, most arriving before 1840. While transportation was promoted as a means of moral improvement and imparting regular work habits, for colonial authorities and employers the working of convicts soon came to be seen in the more pragmatic light of workplace discipline, output, and efficiency. Convicts dominated the New South Wales work force and were the main focus of labor regulation until 1828. Military rule imposed a prescriptive, interventionist approach in the early period. Governors, local officials, and even many private employers were naval or military officers, and troops were stationed to maintain order among convicts and suppress Aboriginal resistance. Convicts directly engaged on government work (like chain gangs building roads) were subject to regulated hours and ration levels with discipline backed up by harsh punishments. The governors had authority to issue general orders regulating convict workers' wages, hours, clothing and corporal punishment. The first governor of New South Wales (Phillip) set working hours at eleven and a half per day but soon introduced task work to deal with slow workers. In 1798 Governor Hunter, realizing that task work was expensive to administer and prone to exploitation by sawyers and others who wanted to establish a custom of not working in the afternoon, ordered a return to the system of fixed hours. In 1804 Governor Bligh reduced the hours of work, except during harvest. The regulation of convict wages and hours remained a contentious issue for later governors.[5]

Private and semifree forms of convict labor emerged from a very early period. Beginning in the 1790s, convicts who had served part of their sen-

3. A similar device applied in Western Australia: Battye Archive, State Library of Western Australia, Perth, WA CSO 2/85, Proclamation 25 Mar. 1830.

4. Tasmania ceased receiving transported convicts in 1852, whereas Western Australia received them from 1850 to 1868.

5. Coghlan, *Labour and Industry*, 48–66.

tences might be granted tickets of leave, a form of parole typically followed by a pardon. These almost-free workers were not bound to a government establishment or particular private employer and could hire themselves out. Other convicts, assigned to private employers in a wide variety of industries, could perform additional work for private reward after completing their specified hours or tasks. Tacit bargaining quickly emerged whereby employers (especially those using skilled workers or when labor was scarce) were obliged to provide wages or extra rations. By 1800 convict malingering and working on account caused the governor to formalize the assignment system, prescribing hours of work and fixing annual wages in addition to rations.[6] Even so, masters in both New South Wales and Tasmania found it necessary to pay premiums to avoid the time and expense of prosecuting servants for idleness or the risk of losing their service altogether.[7] In 1823 New South Wales governor Brisbane abolished prescribed wages for assigned servants in an unsuccessful attempt to eradicate this practice.

The categories just described were not static and the economic efficiency of convict labor—the subject of much recent debate[8]—appears to have declined over time due to a range of factors including changes in the economy and the strengthening free labor market. Tasmania[9] introduced a formal multitiered system of probation in 1839. A response to British government pressures to replace assignment and its heavy-handed abuses of convict servants with a system based on contemporary penal theories of discipline and moral reform, probation was a conspicuous failure. A report by future Victoria governor Charles La Trobe concluded that it would have been better to have modified the preexisting assignment system by introducing fixed wages and "judicious checks" on the treatment of convict servants.[10]

The regulation of convict workers must be seen as contested terrain. Even in the slave societies of the Americas, as Mary Turner has shown, the management of slave labor could entail forms of bargaining as employers and the state sought to encourage cooperation or discourage resistance.[11] Convicts were not slaves, of course: their unfreedom was temporary, and they retained access to the courts even to bring their overseers to account for mistreatment or nonpayment of wages.[12] But like slaves, even within the limits of their unfreedom Australian convict workers could and did take advantage of the scar-

6. Dyster, "New South Wales."
7. McKay, "Assignment," 30–31.
8. See, for example, Nicholas, *Convict Workers*, and Oxley, *Convict Maids*.
9. Officially named Van Diemen's Land until 1856.
10. Brand, *Convict Probation*.
11. M. Turner, *Chattel Slaves*.
12. Neal, *Rule of Law*, 138; Kercher, "Contract Law," 299–302.

city of labor and exploit their capacity for resistance and work refusal to win improved conditions from employers and the state. For the most part this activity was informal, tacit, or individualized, as collective revolts risked not just the lash but hanging.[13]

Some protest methods drew on customary practices in Britain, such as the burning of hay stacks and other acts of incendiarism or sabotage. Some convicts had "form," having been transported for machine breaking, taking part in protests sweeping the agricultural districts (including 600 rioters in 1831), or forming trade unions (in the case of the seven Tolpuddle martyrs). However, this group was small and not especially conspicuous in dissent or organization.[14] Resistance occurred among both assigned convicts and those retained by the government. Nor was it restricted to men.[15]

In the ambiguous legal context of a penal colony, justices of the peace were empowered to correct breaches of convict discipline summarily, dealing out the lash for a wide range of vaguely worded offenses such as insubordination and insolence. Abuses of power were especially common in country districts where magistrates were also major landholders and employers. Even after the passage of a summary jurisdiction act in 1832,[16] considerable scope remained under offenses such as "neglect of work" and "abusive usage to his overseer." Neal argues that, consistent with the need to establish order in a penal society, "the ratios of corporal punishment and surveillance (by police, the military, overseers and informers) were much higher than for England."[17] Nevertheless, as Maxwell-Stewart observes, punishment alone could not ensure acquiescence to the workload objectives of masters, but on the contrary might inflame resistance and a desire for revenge, including sabotage. Throughout the convict period authorities and private masters were forced to rely not on punishments alone but also on inducements such as "indulgences" (extra rations), remissions of sentences, and tickets of leave.[18]

Before the passage of local master and servant laws, the regulation of free labor within the penal colony posed a problem for the governors, especially when employers complained of workers bidding up wages at harvesttime. In

13. H. McQueen, "Convicts," 3–30; Atkinson, "Protest," 28–51; Nichol, "Malingering," 18–27; Maxwell-Stewart, "Bushrangers"; J. West, *Tasmania*, 245, 459–60, 665; Blair, "Revolt," 78–107.

14. J. West, *Tasmania*, 652, 661.

15. Reid, "Convict Women," 88–105.

16. (N.S.W.) 3 Wm.IV n.3 (1832).

17. Neal, *Rule of Law*, 133–37, 165.

18. Maxwell-Stewart, "Bushrangers," 84–86, 196–205, 230–31. The problematic character of labor control is also revealed in fluctuating official attitudes to task work: Brand, *Convict Probation*, 253; Hirst, *Convict Society*, 33–57.

1797 a New South Wales General Order fixed piece rates and time wages for free agricultural labor. Three years later, the governor ordered the same annual wage (ten pounds, plus board and lodging) for assigned convicts, an implicit acknowledgment of convicts' bargaining power.[19] However, despite the governors' powers of enforcement, wage fixing was largely ineffective. By 1800 many classes of labor were receiving more than twice the established rate. Despite Governor Bligh's Order of 1806 imposing a ten-day jail term and five-pound fine on masters who paid wages in excess of the specified rates, there is little evidence of prosecutions. Evasion was habitual.[20] By the 1820s wage fixing was effectively abandoned in New South Wales.

The magistracy, vested with broad regulatory powers by the early governors, relied on English master and servant legislation in deciding cases involving free workers—illegally as it was later held.[21] By the early 1800s free workers were pursuing claims for unpaid wages in the courts, which treated employment as a simple commercial contract.[22] In 1818 Governor Macquarie proclaimed English master and servant legislation to be in force in New South Wales. Despite Deputy Judge Advocate Wylde's doubts about the validity of the proclamation—concerns shared in London—magistrates continued to apply English law in New South Wales and Tasmania well into the 1820s.[23] Outside the colonial capitals, part-time magistrates, many of them military men or employers, did not draw clear distinctions between the employment rights of free workers and convicts, especially in the more remote country districts.[24]

The growing importance of free workers in the local labor market, together with uncertainty about the use of the English statutes and the boundaries between free and convict labor account for the introduction of local master and servant legislation, beginning with the New South Wales act of 1828. The shift to free labor came later in Tasmania, helping to explain why it took a further nine years to introduce a master and servant law there. Be-

19. Dyster, "New South Wales," 83–90.
20. Coghlan, *Labour and Industry*, 57–58.
21. Castles, *Australian Legal History*, 81, 298.
22. Kercher, "Contract Law," 299–306.
23. Castles, *Australian Legal History*, 388–89; Neal, *Rule of Law*, 110, 134.
24. Neal, *Rule of Law*, 117–18, 133–37, 161. The distinction was more consistently made in the colonial capitals. A survey of Hobart Bench Books for the 1820s and 1830s reveals a clear distinction between free and unfree servants both in recording the case and in the punishment inflicted, with magistrates indicating a knowledge of English law: Hobart Bench of Magistrates, Record of Cases Heard in Petty Sessions, 7 Aug. 1820 to 3 Apr. 1824, and Records of the Hobart Police Office, Sept. 1836 to Apr. 1837, Archives Office of Tasmania, Hobart (hereafter AOT) LC 247. Some employers criticized this distinction in treatment: for example, a letter from "Fair-play," *Tasmanian*, 31 Mar. 1837.

tween 1840 and the end of the century, colonial master and servant acts were the dominant form of employment regulation throughout Australia.[25] Some of these statutes provided for apprenticeship, which was otherwise dealt with in separate master and apprentice statutes. The early master and servant acts also made special provision for assisted immigrants brought to the colonies under indenture: their employment relations later became the subject of separate legislation in the 1850s.[26] From the 1870s colonial legislatures introduced specific wage recovery laws in response to the problem of insolvent companies and contractors failing to pay wages.

Nearly two-thirds of the statutes were enacted between 1828 and 1868. Legislative activity was influenced by loosening imperial controls, changing political structures (and rising working-class influence when the franchise was extended after 1850), experience with particular legislative devices, worker resistance, and cyclical shifts in economic conditions. For example, there were clusters of legislative activity in the early 1840s, the mid-1840s, and the early 1850s, all periods in which employers experienced particular difficulties securing or retaining workers.[27] Remoteness from European sources, volatile markets for the colonies' pastoral and mineral exports, and dependence on an equally volatile flow of British investment all contributed to periodic labor shortages. Perceived crises in labor control were magnified by the mercantile and pastoralist interests that dominated colonial legislatures for much of the nineteenth century.

While early laws responded to the growth of a free labor market within the colonies, their form and application was also shaped by the prescriptive and punitive regime of labor regulation that marked the convict period. The penal context, the military background of many early magistrates and officials, and stubborn adherence to metropolitan social norms in the face of colonial experience fostered expectations of worker deference among magistrates, land-

25. New South Wales enacted its first master and servant statute (9 Geo.IV n.9) in 1828, Tasmania (1 Vict. n.15) and South Australia (7 Wm.IV n.3) in 1837, and Western Australia (4 Vict. n.2) in 1840. Victoria, which separated from New South Wales in 1851, continued the New South Wales statute then in force—(Victoria) 16 Vict. n.2 (1852); (Victoria) 18 Vict. n.16 (1855)—before enacting its first master and servant act (27 Vict. n.198) in 1864. Similarly, Queensland, which separated from New South Wales in 1859, enacted its own act (25 Vict. n.11) in 1861. In most of these colonies there was a succession of master and servant statutes, each of which wholly replaced its predecessor. Master and servant legislation enacted after 1900 (South Australia, Tasmania) continued wage recovery machinery for workers who were not covered by arbitration awards or factory legislation.

26. (New South Wales) 16 Vict. n.42 (1852); (Tasmania) 18 Vict. n.2 (1854); (Victoria) 18 Vict. n.16 (1855).

27. This cyclical pattern is reinforced if lapsed bills are also considered: for one such New South Wales bill, see *Maitland Mercury*, 16 Sept. 1846.

holders, merchants, legislators, and other members of the emergent colonial elite. Although such expectations were bound to be disappointed, they nonetheless shaped early laws and were even carried over to neighboring free colonies through legislative imitation. Reliance on prescriptive legislation remained an enduring feature of labor regulation in Australia for reasons canvassed elsewhere.[28]

The first laws introduced by unrepresentative legislatures were short and simply worded statutes that granted sweeping powers to aggrieved employers and scant redress to servants. They incorporated significant departures from metropolitan legislation: for example, the New South Wales act of 1828[29] supplied up to six months' imprisonment for absenteeism or desertion, double the maximum penalty for those offenses under the corresponding English statute of 1823.[30] Unlike its English counterpart, the New South Wales act made no provision for wage recovery. In these and other respects it was a more one-sided law with more coercive provisions intended to restrain workers from exercising their economic advantage in the understocked colonial labor market. The English authorities recognized the comparative harshness of the New South Wales act, but accepted it on the basis that special circumstances obtained in the colony.[31] Approximately a decade later, though, when South Australia,[32] Tasmania,[33] and Western Australia[34] adopted similar enactments, conferring wide powers on employers, containing harsh penalties, and empowering a single justice to determine cases. However, the imperial authorities took a different view from that of 1828. The laws were disallowed by the Colonial Office for being too sweeping in scope, lopsided, and arbitrary.[35] The colonies responded by modifying their laws to reduce penalties and require that two justices adjudicate cases. However, other elements such as broad coverage provisions and powers to deal with a wide range of employee misbehavior were retained. Tasmania's attorney general fought a largely successful battle with British authorities by pointing out a trend away from balancing employer and servant offenses in the English legislation, which struck a responsive chord at a time of Chartist activism.[36]

28. Quinlan, "Pre-Arbitral Labour Law," 25–39.
29. (New South Wales) 9 Geo.IV n.9 (1828).
30. (U.K.) 4 Geo.IV c.34 (1823).
31. Davidson, "Tasmania," 42.
32. (S. Australia) 7 Wm.IV n.3 (1837).
33. (Tasmania) 1 Vict. n.15 (1837).
34. (W. Australia) 4 Vict. n.2 (1840).
35. Davidson, "Tasmania," 51–53; Cashen, "Masters and Servants," 32–43; F. Crowley, "Master and Servant," 94–115.
36. Davidson, "Tasmania," 53–54.

In 1840 the New South Wales act of 1828 was replaced.[37] While the push for a new law originated with employer concerns about labor shortages, the combined influence of British authorities and local working-class protests resulted in a less oppressive act with more moderate penalties. Five years later another perceived labor market crisis in New South Wales produced a new act, based more nearly on English legislation than its predecessors, but including as well a compulsory discharge certificate system and enhanced powers to jail offending servants.[38] An attempt to require discharge certificates in South Australia in 1847 failed in the face of strident working-class and other opposition.

Labor shortages associated with the gold rushes of the early 1850s led to renewed attempts to restrict labor mobility and better discipline workers. The penalty provisions of the 1854 Tasmanian act[39] were so stringent that the governor advised magistrates "that the law should be administered with great caution lest injustice be done in cases where a light punishment would suffice."[40] While harsh penalties had symbolic importance, the law's legitimacy would be undermined if they were invoked too often. By the mid-1850s, moreover, ebbing labor shortages and growing working-class opposition led to a new phase of moderation in master and servant legislation. Imprisonment (except for nonpayment of fines) was restricted in Tasmania in 1856,[41] New South Wales in 1857,[42] and Queensland in 1861.[43] These predated similar moves in Britain in 1867,[44] although three other colonies lagged behind, Western Australia achieving this in 1868,[45] South Australia in 1878,[46] and Victoria in 1891.[47] Unlike Britain however, the Australian colonies did not repeal or even retitle their master and servant laws in 1875, or for many years after.

The free colony of South Australia provides an interesting illustration. Aware of British reforms, the *South Australian Register* saw a paradox in less liberal colonial legislation. Criticizing a halfhearted attempt to remove the prison penalty from worker offenses in 1877, it pointed out:[48]

37. (New South Wales) 4 Vict. n.23 (1840).
38. (New South Wales) 9 Vict. n.27 (1845).
39. (Tasmania) 18 Vict. n.8 (1854).
40. AOT VDL CSO 24/258/10687, Colonial Secretary to Chief Police Magistrate, 10 Nov. 1854.
41. (Tasmania) 19 Vict. n.28 (1856).
42. (New South Wales) 20 Vict. n.28 (1857).
43. (Queensland) 25 Vict. n.11 (1861).
44. (U.K.) 30&31 Vict. c.141 (1867).
45. (W. Australia) 32 Vict. n.8 (1868).
46. (S. Australia) 41&42 Vict. n.112 (1878).
47. (Victoria) 55 Vict. n.1219 (1891).
48. 6 Dec. 1877.

It is strange that in spite of our democratic tendencies in these colonies the Imperial law on this question should be more liberal than our own and more in accordance with the altered relations subsisting between different classes of society. . . . The old relationship between employers and those in their employ has virtually ceased. The bond between them now is purely a commercial one. In the former meaning of the words they have practically ceased to be masters and servants. Hence both should have the same kind of remedy in the Civil and not the Criminal Courts.

Even this limited reform was dropped in the face of opposition, and in the absence of effective working-class mobilization.[49] The attorney general argued that fines were insufficient to address the enormous property damage that misconduct by drovers and other servants could inflict. Another member (Williams) argued that laws must reflect the local context where, unlike Britain, the population was thinly spread and laborers held the property and lives of employers in their hands. Stripped of its rhetoric, here we find an explanation of the "great anomaly . . . that while practically the working man is paramount the old penal clauses against him are retained."[50] Although Australian workers had more bargaining power than their English counterparts, harsher laws were nevertheless retained to redress this "imbalance" and maintain orderly production, especially in those remote areas which were a critical source of colonial exports and wealth generation.

In the turbulent mid-nineteenth-century economy, legislators came under increasing pressure to address the issue of wage recovery against insolvent employers. During the burst of railway construction in the 1850s and 1860s navvies in New South Wales, Queensland, and Victoria were involved in a series of disputes over nonpayment of wages, failure to supply rations, and the truck system. In July 1858 there was a strike and riot by navvies working on the Melbourne–Murray River line in Victoria, with a similar dispute by men on the Sandhurst line one year later. In 1863, when a contractor on the Windsor line in New South Wales simply abandoned his contract (leaving his men unpaid), the matter was referred to Parliament. In 1866 a far more serious dispute occurred among navvies working on the Ipswich-Toowoomba railway line in Queensland involving a strike, riot, and threatened march on the capital, Brisbane. While the abuses of the truck system did not lead to a

49. *South Australian Advertiser*, 15 Dec. 1877; *South Australian Register*, 15 Dec. 1877, 8 Nov. 1878.
50. *South Australian Register*, 8 July 1878.

significant legislative response,[51] the problem of wage recovery was a different matter. Legislation adopted in Victoria[52] and Queensland[53] in 1870 was followed in 1879 by less generous provisions in South Australia[54] and New South Wales.[55] Wage protection bills introduced into the legislatures of Queensland and South Australia in 1890 both lapsed in the industrial and economic crisis that descended on the colonies. The only exception was Western Australia, which experienced a mineral and construction boom in the 1890s after decades of sluggish growth, and enacted a contractor's wage law in 1898.[56]

The depression of the 1890s led to one belated legislative development. In 1870 the British Parliament had introduced a law restricting the capacity of creditors to attach the wages of indebted workmen.[57] Given higher general wage levels (especially for unskilled workers) in the colonies, local legislatures chose to ignore this development until the hard years after 1890. In 1893 South Australia enacted a law on workmen's liens.[58] Victoria adopted a stronger law in 1898,[59] followed by New South Wales in 1900.[60] These acts protected the first two pounds of the worker's weekly wage. However, a Tasmanian act of the same year placed the weekly wage before attachment at one pound, probably as a consequence of the colony's lower wage levels and more depressed economy.[61]

Before proceeding to a more detailed examination of the nature and application of master and servant law, it is necessary to identify three categories of workers for whom special regulatory controls applied, namely assisted European immigrants, non-European indentured workers, and Aboriginal workers.

Assisted Immigrants and Indentured Non-European Labor

The remoteness of the Australian colonies in comparison to other destinations for European immigrants (most notably North America) meant that

51. Some laws dealing with indentured non-European workers banned this practice, but (W. Australia) 63 Vict. n.15 (1899) was the only general prohibition of payment in kind before 1900.

52. (Victoria) 34 Vict. n.385 (1870).

53. (Queensland) 34 Vict. n.16 (1870).

54. (S. Australia) 41&42 Vict. n.112 (1878).

55. (New South Wales) 42 Vict. n.22 (1879).

56. (W. Australia) 62 Vict. n.35 (1898).

57. (U.K.) 33&34 Vict. c.30 (1870).

58. (S. Australia) n.575 of 1893.

59. (Victoria) 62 Vict. n.1573 (1898).

60. (New South Wales) n.6 of 1900.

61. (Tasmania) 64 Vict. n.10 (1900).

labor supply not only varied with wage levels and discipline but also required government intervention in its own right, especially during periods of acute labor shortage. An Aboriginal population decimated by European invasion (war, massacre, introduced diseases, and social dislocation) could not meet expanding labor requirements. At particular times and in specific areas Aboriginal workers figured significantly in certain occupations, most notably sheep herding, pearling, and domestic service. Although they were ostensibly subject to master and servant laws, there is little evidence of litigation involving aboriginal workers, who seem generally to have been treated in a far more patronizing, exploitative, and capricious way than Europeans.[62] Several colonies adopted protective legislation for natives engaged as pearlers or seamen,[63] but no corresponding action was taken on behalf of Aboriginal land-based workers.[64]

As convict transportation wound down colonial governments had to provide passage assistance to free emigrants or support for employer efforts to recruit offshore workers privately.[65] Employers tended to recruit indentured immigrants for longer terms and at lower wage rates than were customary within the colony. As a result, immigrant workers often became disenchanted soon after arrival, sought to dissolve their indentures, or simply absconded. Colonial master and servant acts were extended to enforce contracts made abroad for service in the colony. The New South Wales master and servant act of 1847 set the maximum term of such contracts at five years, far longer than most contracts made within the colony. South Australia initially set a one-year limit,[66] but in 1849 this was waived for contracts made in Britain or other Australian colonies after lobbying by the Patent Copper Company.

62. Though there are few references to Aboriginal workers it is clear that on occasion they stood up for their rights. While debating a proposed reform of master and servant law in 1847 one member of the Legislative Council of New South Wales referred to a case where an Aboriginal worker threatened to charge a constable with false imprisonment. *Maitland Mercury*, 19 June 1847.

63. (W. Australia) 37 Vict. n.11 (1873); (W. Australia) 39 Vict. n.13 (1875); (W. Australia) 50 Vict. n.25 (1886); (Queensland) 48 Vict. n.20 (1884).

64. For Aboriginal employment and its regulation, see Saunders, *Workers in Bondage*, 11–13; McGrath and Saunders, *Aboriginal Workers*; Mumewa and Fesl, "Unknown God."

65. Earlier the British government encouraged the indenturing of immigrants to New South Wales and Tasmania. A U.K. act of 1823 authorized the use of seven-year contracts, fixed punishments for employers "poaching" indentured workers, and empowered two justices to enforce the terms. Similar provisions were included in United Kingdom acts for the Australian Agricultural Company (1824) and the Van Diemen's Land Company (1825), as well as the Australian Courts Act of 1828. For a discussion of the former company's use of indentured labor, see J. Perkins, "Australian Agricultural Company." For the U.K. acts, see above, p. 13, n. 39.

66. F. Crowley, "Conditions," 33; (New South Wales) 11 Vict. n.9 (1847).

Three years later, after further employer representations, the restriction was removed altogether.[67]

Colonial governments and employers with investments in offshore recruitment also feared labor poaching by their neighbors. In November 1840 South Australia responded to attempts by settlers in New South Wales and Tasmania to crimp local workers by introducing a Labour Enticement Bill. Modeled on a New Zealand law, the bill required customs officials and shipmasters to check departing colonists.[68] The bill lapsed with the onset of recession. However, the measure received considerable attention in Western Australia, which subsequently amended its master and servant act to require that labor brought to the colony at public expense must remain there for two years.[69] Labor shortages induced by the gold rush resulted in feverish efforts to obtain and retain immigrants. In 1852 New South Wales enacted legislation[70] providing passage assistance for working men, women, and apprentices under indentures to remain in the colony for at least two years or with a particular employer for the term of a contract (to a maximum of seven years). The act, later copied by Victoria, regulated emigration agents who did the recruiting in Britain and elsewhere. Indentured immigrants were subject to the disciplinary provisions of master and servant laws. However, more severe penalties applied to absconding and to those hiring absconders (a fine of five shillings for each day of employment). Although New South Wales did away with some of these special disabilities later in the decade,[71] other colonies continued to experiment with more stringent provisions for immigrants as late as the 1870s and 1880s.[72]

In Tasmania, concerns about labor supply were intensified by the recent cessation of convict transportation and the colony's lack of gold or other attractions. Problems enforcing the contracts of indentured immigrants had been widely publicized in the Tasmanian press.[73] The Tasmanian act of 1854[74] borrowed heavily from the 1852 New South Wales act.[75] The original bill re-

67. State Library of South Australia, Adelaide (hereafter SA) CSO A(184) 97, J. S. Walters, Manager of Patent Copper Co. to Governor Sir Henry Young, 12 Jan. 1849. Walters complained, "[I]f one or two break their contract who are vital to operations we must still pay the others although their labour is now useless." See also Cashen, "Masters and Servants," 36.

68. *South Australian Register*, 28 Nov. 1840; *South Australian*, 15 Jan. 1841.

69. *Perth Gazette*, 6, 13 Mar. 1841; Crowley, "Master and Servant," 113.

70. (New South Wales) 16 Vict. n.42 (1852).

71. (New South Wales) 18 Vict. n.30 (1854); (New South Wales) 19 Vict. n.35 (1855).

72. (W. Australia) 40 Vict. n.10 (1876); (S. Australia) 41&42 Vict. n.112 (1878); (Queensland) 46 Vict. n.7 (1882).

73. For example, *Hobarton Guardian*, 22 June 1853.

74. (Tasmania) 18 Vict. n.2 (1854).

75. (New South Wales) 16 Vict. n.42 (1852). There is extensive archival evidence of this

quired a four-year stay in the colonies and penalties of up to six months' imprisonment for repeated absconding. Both these deviations from the New South Wales legislation, as well as the five-shilling fine for hiring absconders, were removed from the final act despite support for them by some leading employers. Critics of the more punitive provisions, including the colonial land and emigration commissioners, argued that excessive severity would disadvantage the colony and undermine efforts to get the clergy of Scotland and others to promote emigration. Even the employer-sympathetic *Launceston Examiner* declared that the colony's new master and servant legislation savored "too much of the slave market and the assignment system to be palatable."[76]

Such laws highlight the colonies' dependence on assisted European immigrants. During economic downturns, when even those arriving under indenture might find their services no longer wanted, such measures became redundant. Unemployed immigrants were housed in special depots. Those refusing even the most miserly wage or unattractive job offer risked being thrown out to fend for themselves. In 1850 the director of an Adelaide depot for unprotected females complained to the colonial secretary that eight needlewomen recently arrived on the *Tory* were insolent and unruly; two were expelled for refusing service at thirteen pounds per year (they demanded sixteen pounds). At the same time, he acknowledged that others seeking work as seamstresses would fail because supply already exceeded demand.[77]

Colonial governments were notably less keen to help employers secure immigrant workers from the Asia-Pacific region. From the 1830s rural employers especially made repeated attempts to recruit indentured workers from India and China.[78] Their efforts were opposed by the labor movement and others in the colonies, as well as by the Colonial Office which had designated Australia as a site for European settlement.[79] At first, employers relied on the foreign contract provisions in the master and servant acts. Later legislation was enacted, not to sponsor large-scale non-European immigration but to regulate recruitment and employment practices. While European immigrants were recruited on the presumption that they would remain as permanent residents, the laws regulating indentured non-Europeans prescribed that

---

legislative borrowing in AOT VDL CSO 24/242/99551, which includes the documents quoted in this paragraph.

76. 18 Apr. 1854.

77. SA CSO 1850/1994, Depot for Unprotected Females to Colonial Secretary, 2 Sept. 1850.

78. Between 1847 and 1853 3,500 Chinese were introduced into New South Wales: Darnell, "Regulation of Life."

79. Quinlan and Lever-Tracy, "Asian Workers," 159–82; Saunders, *Workers in Bondage*, 16.

they were temporary "guest workers" who would return home after completing their contracts. Indeed, after 1880 there were legislative moves to restrict the numbers of Asian, especially Chinese, residents already in Australia, many of whom had arrived during the gold rushes.

India presented particular problems. Regulations introduced there in 1839 prohibited the indenturing of Indians as overseas agricultural and pastoral workers, although at least one innovative partnership brought twenty-five Indians to the Moreton district (later part of Queensland) in May 1844 by labeling them as "domestics."[80] British authorities in India were concerned at the treatment of indentured workers, especially in light of complaints and publicized instances of abuse. Colonial authorities in Australia also had little real enthusiasm for Indian or other Asian labor. In 1854 a select committee recommended against legislation to encourage Asian recruitment, expressing doubts about whether Indian and Chinese laborers already in the colony fully understood their agreements, and questioning the physical suitability of a group of Eurasians from India.[81] Several colonies did enact laws dealing with Indian labor, although they were never of much significance. Queensland passed enabling legislation in 1862, but by the time official approval was received from India, the colony had discovered another source of non-European labor for its sugar plantations, namely the New Hebrides and other Pacific islands. Introduced under five-year indentures for an annual wage of six pounds (well below the prevailing rate in the colony), these workers were reputedly docile and obedient. The switch to islanders was reinforced by continuing Indian government reservations over exporting its nationals and increased intercolonial competition for indentured Indian (and, to a lesser extent, Chinese) labor following the imperial abolition of chattel slavery in 1834.

Pacific Islanders never proved as tractable as was hoped. They absconded in large numbers and engaged in collective dissent.[82] Nevertheless, their employment was successful enough to ensure that around 60,000 were introduced over the next thirty years. Despite early enthusiasm about their suitability for the work and climate, large numbers died. The Queensland government responded by requiring employers to provide medical care and contribute to the maintenance of hospitals, and by appointing inspectors to

80. Sanders, *Workers in Bondage*, 14–15.
81. *Report from the Select Committee on Asiatic Labour*, Legislative Council of NSW, *Votes and Proceedings*, 27 Nov. 1854.
82. Islanders were brought under the local master and servant act by (Queensland) 31 Vict. n.47 (1868), which imposed a twenty-pound fine for harboring runaways.

visit plantations and living quarters.[83] Nevertheless, in 1884 the registrar-general's returns indicated a death rate of 50 per 1,000 per annum, about five times the rate among Europeans in the colony. One member warned the Assembly that unless such matters were addressed, the imperial government would intervene to ban the traffic in Pacific Islanders.[84] Additional protective legislation was adopted in 1885, 1886, and 1892, and the employment of Pacific Islanders was restricted to particular regions so their behavior could be more effectively monitored.[85]

The Queensland sugar industry's use of Pacific Islanders was Australia's only large-scale experiment with indentured non-European labor. Attempts to grow cotton in Queensland during the 1860s failed, and the other colonies' primary industries did not lend themselves to the kinds of intensive cultivation that fostered demands for indentured plantation labor elsewhere in the empire. Those promoting the use of indentured non-European workers also had to deal with unenthusiastic imperial authorities and significant opposition from organized labor and others within the colonies who embraced an exclusionist and racist sentiment.[86] Even in Queensland such opposition ensured that Pacific Islander employment was restricted by legislation to a narrow band of tropical or subtropical agricultural work.[87] In the end, the proponents of indentured non-European labor were overwhelmed by a rising tide of chauvinistic and racist sentiment. Their defeat was sealed with federation (1901) and the adoption of an avowedly racist "White Australia" immigration policy that excluded non-Europeans for the next seventy years.

Coverage, Penalties, and Procedure

Unlike the English master and servant legislation, but in common with that of many other colonies, the Australian statutes applied generally to an overwhelming majority of workers, including (in some of the earliest laws) independent contractors as well as hired servants,[88] and often including ap-

---

83. (Queensland) 44 Vict. n.17 (1880).

84. Queensland Legislative Assembly *Debates*, 5 Feb. 1884 (248f).

85. (Queensland) 49 Vict. n.17 (1885); (Queensland) 50 Vict. n.6 (1886); (Queensland) 55 Vict. n.38 (1892).

86. J. Harris, "Pacific Island Labour," 40–48; Quinlan and Lever-Tracy, "Asian Workers," 166–68.

87. (Queensland) 44 Vict. n.17 (1880) s.7. In practice, there was some slippage.

88. (New South Wales) 4 Vict. n.23 (1840); (Tasmania) 4 Vict. n.12 (1840); and see the report of a petty sessions decision applying the act to itinerant carriers: *Melbourne Daily News*, 22 Jan. 1849.

prentices along with the rest.[89] Domestic servants, including women, were expressly included, a calculated response to their scarcity and "troublesome" character, as well as their propensity to abscond.[90] Nevertheless, the punishment of female offenders created a moral dilemma for authorities. Women were written out of the South Australian master and servant act in 1847 following public outrage at the jailing of a "respectable looking girl" in late 1846. They were written back in again in 1849 when a wing of Adelaide jail was set aside for the confinement of women.[91] New South Wales, Victoria, and (after 1856) Tasmania all prohibited the imprisonment of women convicted of master and servant offenses, but there was some confusion over whether they could be kept in jail pending trial.[92]

The statutes commonly described workers' offenses in broad and indefinite terms. Familiarity with the more extensive powers over convict behavior and aspirations for worker deference led employers to stretch such definitions even further, for example, by charging insolent free servants with "misconduct."[93] By the 1840s magistrates were generally construing the statutory usage more narrowly, although as late as 1878 one court refused to award costs to the successful complainant in a wage suit because he had been "unnecessarily insolent" in demanding his wages.[94]

Virtually all the colonial statutes identified offenses arising out of worker mobility and absconding. In an often understocked labor market, employers found it difficult to retain workers and were not above poaching labor from one another. Workers sought short contracts to enhance their bargaining power. They frequently left before completing their agreements if dissatisfied, or accepted cash advances and then failed to turn up. The colonial press

89. The inclusion of apprentices meant they tended to be treated as just another category of servant, subject to proposals for more stringent controls during periods of labor shortage. For instance, in December 1851 the Hobart police magistrate responded to complaints from shipbuilder John Watson about the absconding of an apprentice to the gold fields by proposing that magistrates be empowered to issue an arrest warrant prior to a hearing. The attorney general killed the proposal, arguing it would have little practical effect and "the proposed law would be one of unusual stringency and severity and for which I am not aware of any precedent." AOT VDL CSO 24/187/6810, Colonial Secretary to Chief Police Magistrate, 29 Dec. 1851, and Attorney General to Colonial Secretary, 3 Feb. 1852.

90. *Launceston Examiner*, 4 Mar. 1858; female servants were also accused of using ill-treatment claims against their masters to nullify their agreements: *Port Phillip Patriot*, 22 May 1847.

91. Cashen, "Masters and Servants," 35–36.

92. (New South Wales) 4 Vict. n.23 (1840), s.20; (Victoria) 16 Vict. n.6 (1852); (Tasmania) 19 Vict. n.28 (1856); (Victoria) 55 Vict. n.1219 (1891) excluded domestic servants from coverage altogether.

93. A. Merritt, "Masters and Servants," 84–88.

94. *South Australian Register*, 2 May 1878.

abounds with such complaints, which are also commonplace in official inquiries into immigration and policing. These views may have been simplistic and one-sided, but they influenced legislators. Absconding was treated as
a serious offense in every colonial act, and some provided especially severe
punishments for workers who failed to work out advances.[95] Minimum notice
requirements also restricted worker mobility: for example, Tasmania's 1854
master and servant act required one month's notice unless otherwise specified in the agreement. The colonial secretary advised Spring Bay magistrate
James Ratcliffe that this period of notice was to apply even when the term of
the agreement had expired or the period of engagement was only one week.[96]
Virtually every colonial act prohibited "harbouring" or "enticement," with
fines of up to fifty pounds for inducing workers to break their agreements, or
employing or sheltering absconders. These actions were subject to common-
law proceedings in England but were not covered by the master and servant
legislation there (except in merchant shipping). Though directed primarily
at employers, on occasion they were used against union officials and strike
organizers.

Perhaps the most interesting strategy to restrict worker mobility was an
experiment with compulsory discharge certificates, first introduced in New
South Wales (1845–57) and later adopted in Tasmania (1856–82) and Victoria
(1851–90).[97] Employers were to give servants a written discharge when they
completed their contracts and to require the production of a certificate at the
point of hiring. Employers and workers could be fined five pounds for failing
to supply or require a certificate, and there was a ten-pound fine for forgery.
Like discharge certificates and pass laws elsewhere in the empire, the system
targeted absconding. This was recognized by its opponents, who called it a
form of slavery.[98] It was readily abused. When employers refused to issue discharges, the only legal remedy available to the worker was prosecution. Masters were liable to a five-pound fine, but the magistrate might reduce this to
as little as a shilling if the master claimed the worker had been insubordinate
or neglectful. No similar discretion existed when authorities prosecuted mas-

95. (New South Wales) 4 Vict. n.23 (1840); (New South Wales) 9 Vict. n.27 (1845); (New
South Wales) 11 Vict. n.9 (1847); (S. Australia) n.9 of 1847; (S. Australia) 26&27 Vict. n.7
(1863); (Queensland) 25 Vict. n.11 (1861); (Victoria) 27 Vict. n.198 (1864); (Victoria) 54 Vict.
n.1087 (1890).

96. AOT VDL CSO 24/259/10755, 25 Nov. 1854.

97. In Victoria it applied only to rural servants after 1864. Queensland and Western Australia did not require the use of discharge certificates although their acts—(Queensland) 25 Vict.
n.11 (1861) and (W. Australia) 32 Vict. n.8 (1868)—provided for them. An attempt to introduce
the system into South Australia in 1847 failed.

98. *Port Phillip Patriot*, 2 June 1846.

ters for hiring servants without a discharge.[99] In the end, widespread evasion by both employers and workers, as much as political opposition, caused the system's demise.

Several of the colonial acts made servants liable for the loss, spoilage, or destruction of their master's property, especially livestock.[100] Individual shepherds and stockmen were often left in charge of large numbers of sheep and cattle at remote outstations. In the aggregate, these flocks and herds were critical capital investments: wool accounted for over half of Australia's annual export earnings throughout the nineteenth century. Losses were inevitable. Shepherds were responsible for flocks of more than 1,000 sheep for long periods on stations where fencing was rare and there was an ongoing danger from disease and predators (dingoes). From the employers' viewpoint, absconding could cause a double loss of labor and capital on pastoral leases. Thus when John McCormack absconded from a station near Blinman, South Australia, in April 1870 the manager, Paul Phillips, had to employ several men to collect his scattered flock and still lost between sixty and seventy sheep.[101] It is not surprising that pastoralists were exceptionally vigorous in prosecuting workers for loss of property.[102] Even so, the provision was pernicious. It failed to recognize that losses might not result from negligence or malice. The New South Wales act of 1845 left the penalty entirely to the discretion of the magistrates. The 1847 South Australian act limited damages to twenty pounds—an amount equal to a year's wages in many instances. The harshness is typified by a case in December 1847 where an old shepherd with one eye and a long record of diligent service was forced to work off some lost sheep.[103] Another shepherd was jailed for six weeks because his wages did not cover the loss.[104] Employers claimed losses to offset wage claims, as in the case of a Chinese shepherd, Hue Bow, who had served a five-year term on Hugh Gordon's Strathbogie station. The court ordered his wages forfeit to compensate Gordon for forty-four lost sheep, and fined Bow four pounds for absconding, even though his contract had expired.[105]

    99. Ibid., 27 Dec. 1845.
    100. (New South Wales) 9 Geo.IV n.9 (1828); (New South Wales) 4 Vict. n.23 (1840); (New South Wales) 9 Vict. n.27 (1845); (S. Australia) n.9 of 1847.
    101. *South Australian Register*, 15 Apr. 1870.
    102. A. Merritt, "Masters and Servants," 220.
    103. *Argus*, 3 Dec. 1847.
    104. *Port Phillip Patriot*, 24 Jan. 1846. In the 1840s the Port Phillip press alone reported dozens of cases where lost sheep were the subject of a prosecution or wage offset. For cases over other damages (such as lost cattle and spirits), see *Port Phillip Gazette*, 22 July 1846, and *Melbourne Daily News*, 8 Apr. 1851.
    105. A. Merritt, "Masters and Servants," 265–66.

Due Process and the Magistracy

No account of master and servant laws would be complete without consideration of the magistrates who administered the laws. In the period before representative government, the courts were an especially important site of struggle over the emergence of civil society out of a penal settlement.[106] Magistrates were critical to the maintenance of order, and enjoyed significant political influence. Both part-time justices of the peace and full-time stipendiaries (police magistrates) actively shaped master and servant law through correspondence with the colonial secretary or governor, evidence to government inquiries, and other means. On occasion their input was invited by colonial authorities, but their advice was forthcoming even when it was not sought. In 1830 a meeting of West Australian magistrates urged the governor to permit employers to withdraw "indulgences" (additional rations) from servants as a disciplinary measure and to enable magistrates to modify ration regulations in cases of emergency.[107] In 1841 South Australian magistrates successfully pressed for a more stringent master and servant law.[108] A typical instance of individual activity occurred in 1856 when W. Abbott, the magistrate for Kangaroo Point in Tasmania, wrote to the colonial secretary to oppose an amendment requiring master and servant cases to be heard by two justices: "I am well aware that in several instances arbitrary sentences of solitary and other confinement by individual justices has been imposed, but the master as well as the servant would be damnified if the amended law is passed requiring the adjudication of two justices."[109]

Although most early laws enabling a single part-time magistrate to try cases had been disallowed, Tasmania briefly reintroduced this measure in the labor market crisis of the early 1850s. The magistrates' proposals for more effective administration invariably advantaged employer attempts to discipline workers. Unlike Abbott, most made no attempt to give even the appearance of balance.

In country districts the part-time justices who administered the law were generally major landholders or professional men who associated with these and other employers. The mobile work force and more fluid social relations of recently settled colonies meant that the ties upon which a more entrenched society might rely did not bind.[110] Landholders' behavior so often belied their

---

106. Neal, *Rule of Law.*
107. Both measures were refused: F. Crowley, "Master and Servant," 97; WA CSO 2/85.
108. SA CSO 1841/433, Chairman, Bench of Magistrates to the Governor, 10 Aug. 1841.
109. AOT VDL CSO 1/2/40, Abbott to Colonial Secretary, 30 Jan. 1856.
110. Neal, *Rule of Law*, 3.

aspirations to the status of the English squire, that they became labeled as a squattocracy or bunyip aristocracy.[111] It was not unknown for landholding magistrates to try their own servants, despite attempts to ban the practice.[112] More commonly they played musical chairs with one magistrate temporarily stepping down from the bench while his colleagues tried his servant. Even conservative newspapers were outraged. In 1846 a Melbourne paper remarked:[113]

> It is not so long since, that we held up to public reprobation the proceedings of certain country magistrates, who openly and shamelessly, alternatively appeared on the bench and in the witness box, to prefer and adjudicate in complaints against their respective servants—a course of conduct, which in the mother country, would have caused the names of such men to be swept from the precept as unworthy of the confidence of the Crown.

Such abuses of process and the blatant partiality exhibited by magistrates were recurring themes of public debate. Criticisms of antiworker bias generally focused on the rural justices. The press sometimes accused urban justices of being too lenient on workers or misreading the law, but rarely criticized stipendiary magistrates.

Colonial legislators were aware that blatant bias on the bench undermined the moral authority of the legislation. The point was driven home by press criticism, worker protests, and evidence before official inquiries. Nevertheless, even late in the nineteenth century efforts to restrict magistrates' powers met strong resistance from justices and rural employers. In 1885 Sir Samuel Griffith, Liberal premier of Queensland, tried to prevent justices of the peace from determining cases under the Pacific Island Labourers Act, following reports that planters had stacked recent cases in Bundaberg and Mackay. Magistrates and planters from these districts vehemently denied the allegations, and conservative rural members used their majority in the Legislative Council to repeatedly reject the clause. Griffith countered by claiming that only police (stipendiary) magistrates were allowed to sit on the bench in Sydney and employers of coolie labor were not allowed to adjudicate cases under the Coolie Act [sic] in British Guiana.[114] Several opposition members asked why the mas-

111. For contrasting accounts of class relations in rural Australia, see Atkinson, *Camden*, and S. Roberts, *Squatting*.

112. Governor Macquarie banned the practice in 1813: Neal, *Rule of Law*, 13. For later measures, see (S. Australia) 41&42 Vict. n.112 (1878), s.23.

113. *Port Phillip Patriot*, 16 Dec. 1846; see also 19 Nov. 1847.

114. In an earlier debate on the bill the member for Warrego (Donaldson) noted that land-

ter and servant act was not placed on the same footing if the clause was necessary to protect island laborers.[115] The government dodged this point and eventually dropped the measure.

All this is not to say that magistrates unambiguously served the interests of capital.[116] The behavior of country justices differed from those in large towns. Evidence also indicates changes over time, especially after 1860. The cohort of magistrates who had disciplined convicts retired. Later laws gave justices less discretion, and the basis of magisterial selection shifted. Further, after 1860 they had access to detailed handbooks such as the *Australian Magistrate*, and the development of representative government placed them under more critical scrutiny. Changing patterns of enforcement and legal challenges mounted by servants also influenced the behavior of magistrates.

Patterns of Use and Resistance

Examining the evolving form of master and servant law and the equally evolving nature of the magistracy that administered it only provides a partial insight into its nature and impact. It is also necessary to consider overall evidence on patterns of usage and the nature and effectiveness of various forms of worker resistance, because application of the law was a contested terrain.

There are no comprehensive statistics on master and servant prosecutions, but the available evidence indicates that the acts were used extensively, especially prior to 1860. Merritt estimated that there were 115,000 cases in New South Wales between 1845 and 1880, more than half of them (58,410) in the fifteen years to 1860.[117] Fragmentary evidence on other colonies suggests a similar pattern with especially vigorous use in the 1830s and 1840s followed by a gradual decline after 1860 in both general incidence and the range of occupations involved.[118]

---

holders were excluded from sitting on poaching cases in Scotland: Queensland (Legislative Assembly) *Debates* (15, 20 Oct. 1885) 1091, 1141.

115. See statements by Legislative Council members T. L. Murray-Prior and F. T. Gregory in Queensland (Legislative Council) *Debates* (29 Oct. 1885) 207.

116. This issue is taken up by McQueen in "Social Control." Note, however, that his evidence is restricted to Toowoomba, the largest town in the region, in the period after 1860.

117. A. Merritt, "Masters and Servants," iv, 191. Due to a rural bias in her sample (more rural than town court bench books have survived), Merritt's estimates for later periods may understate the decline, especially in residual use of the laws in the twentieth century.

118. On occasion fragmentary statistics were reported to Parliament. For example, police returns in the colony of Victoria indicate that 1,253 workers (mainly laborers and servants) were placed in custody under the master and servant act between 1859 and 1870 while 118 absconding apprentices were arrested between 1846 and 1870. These returns exclude noncusto-

If Merritt's figures are extrapolated to the other colonies, they suggest that there were no fewer than 167,000 master and servant cases in Australia in the period 1828–60. The total European population of the colonies grew from less than 80,000 in 1828 to around 1 million in 1860. This suggests a very high incidence of litigation. By comparison, Simon reports an average of 10,000 cases per year for England and Wales between 1858 and 1875. Based on Merritt's estimate, the comparable figure for the Australian colonies with a population less than a tenth the size would be an average of about 7,000 cases per year. Even if Simon's figures are a gross underestimate, it seems inescapable that the incidence of litigation was far higher in Australia.[119]

Merritt showed that litigation was spread across a wide range of occupations but with a significant concentration among rural workers, followed by domestic servants, tradesmen, and transport workers. Over time, domestics and (especially) rural workers became increasingly prominent. Absconding was the major employee offense, accounting for almost 40 percent of cases between 1845 and 1860. About 39 percent of convicted workers were imprisoned in this period but the proportion jailed declined rapidly thereafter to 15 percent in 1861–80, 5 percent in 1881–1900, and 1 percent in 1901–30. Forfeiture of wages was initially the second most common penalty, imposed in 20 percent of worker convictions in 1845–60 and more than 26 percent in the remaining decades to 1900. Fines became the dominant penalty, rising from 15 percent of worker convictions in 1845–60 to 46 percent in 1861–80 and almost 60 percent in 1881–1900. The proportion of convicted workers returned to service declined from 15 percent in 1845–60 to 5 percent in 1881–1900. Other remedies, such as cautions, were uncommon, falling from 8 percent of worker convictions in 1845–60 to 5 percent in 1881–1900.

Disputes over wages were the major worker complaints. They grew to dominate the master and servant litigation, rising from about 29 percent of all cases tried in 1845–60 to nearly 70 percent in 1861–80 and 78 percent in 1881–1900.[120] This growth accounts for the decline of worker offenses as a proportion of total cases. Again, these findings (from New South Wales) are consistent with evidence from other colonies.[121]

---

dial litigation: *Legislative Assembly of Victoria, Votes and Proceedings, Papers—Criminal Statistics, 1871.*

119. Simon, "Master and Servant."

120. A. Merritt, "Masters and Servants," 208–39.

121. A survey of Victorian and Queensland cases (taken from bench books) by McQueen indicated that absconding was the leading charge against workers, while wage complaints made up the bulk of worker initiated claims. At the same time, McQueen's survey indicates some disparities in usage between rural and urban centers that are consistent with evidence I have

Master and servant laws may have been overt class legislation, but their application was never unproblematic. Legislative attempts to restrict labor mobility through discharge certificates were undermined by employer connivance. Few employers were charged with refusing to issue a certificate and even fewer for hiring a servant without a certificate. Moreover, workers never fully acquiesced in their legal subordination. The form and application of the laws were continuously under challenge. Even more vulnerable workers subject to additional regulatory controls, such as indentured European and non-European immigrants, often rebelled. They deserted in droves, engaged in go-slows, and even went on strike. For example, from the 1860s onward the colonial press reported dozens of strikes by non-European sugar plantation workers in Queensland. At most, prosecution only partly discouraged such activity. At T. P. Smith's Woodland plantation near Marburg (west of Brisbane) twenty-seven Pacific island laborers struck for rations in June 1890. Nine of the strikers were convicted of absconding, but the magistrate imposed a fine of only one shilling (or six hours' jail in default) and recommended they be given rations daily rather than weekly.[122]

Worker resistance to the legislation took a number of forms. Much resistance was individual but it was also calculated. One method was outright evasion of the terms and conditions of contracts. The colonial press lamented that shearers failed to appear, absconded, or threatened to leave at the commencement of the shearing season in order to secure higher wages. Most escaped prosecution.[123] Claims that higher wages were paid elsewhere could be used as a bargaining chip, with pubs and roving bands of seasonal workers assisting in the spread of information.[124] Workers often timed their claims for when they calculated employers would be most likely to prefer concessions to prosecution.[125] Female servants were accused of breaking agreements in the knowledge that their exemption from imprisonment made prosecution unlikely.[126] Even individual actions had broader effects when aggregated.

The large number of employer-initiated prosecutions, especially prior to 1860, cannot be seen as unequivocal evidence of the laws' effectiveness in subordinating workers. Commenting on the 1845 New South Wales act, one newspaper observed that filling the jails with offenders only served to high-

---

derived from surveying reports in the colonial press. R. McQueen, "Legislation," and "Social Control."

122. *Brisbane Courier*, 25 June 1890.
123. *Port Phillip Patriot*, 23 Oct. 1845; *Argus*, 16 Nov. 1847.
124. *Port Phillip Gazette*, 8 Apr. 1846.
125. *Port Phillip Patriot*, 23 Oct., 29 Dec. 1845; 23 Nov. 1846.
126. They also asserted a customary right to leave upon marriage: *Argus*, 1 Sept., 5 Dec. 1848.

light the tyrannical and oppressive nature of the legislation.[127] Convicted workers thumbed their noses at courts and employers. Sentenced to three months' imprisonment for being absent, John Williams told the bench, "I thank you gentlemen, kindly, I would rather step it out than work for such a nigger driver as Captain Hutton."[128]

Even rural employers learned that swift recourse to the courts could not fully address covert forms of resistance and revenge. Following in the footsteps of convicts, free workers engaged in go-slows, worked to rule, withdrew voluntary initiatives, and resorted to alcohol. Drawing on British traditions of protest, the burning of hay stacks and other forms of incendiarism let the aggrieved rural worker impose a costly and difficult to detect revenge on his employer.[129] Other forms of sabotage were practiced.[130] Some protesting workers were caught and prosecuted, but many undoubtedly got away with implied threats or escaped detection. Minimizing cooperation with the employer could be at least as costly as specific acts of sabotage or dissent.[131] Many employers recognized these problems and used prosecution sparingly or in an exemplary fashion in combination with threats, the late withdrawal of charges, or a plea for a small penalty or warning in return for a pledge of cooperation by the worker. Magistrates also played their part, warning domestic servants of the consequences their behavior would have on future job prospects. However, such threats were less influential than in Britain where servants were in plentiful supply.

Multiple appearances by both employers and workers indicate both the limited deterrent effect of the law and the determination of workers to pursue claims against masters for nonpayment or ill-treatment. Merritt's survey found that in the period 1845–60 multiple appearances by employees accounted for nearly 10 percent of all cases—a figure roughly sustained in later

127. *Port Phillip Patriot*, 11 Feb. 1846.

128. Ibid., 27 Nov. 1848.

129. Complaints about incendiarism appeared regularly in the press in the 1820s, 1830s, and 1840s: see *Hobart Town Courier*, 6 June 1834. Initially associated with convict workers, the practice was carried on by free workers. Workers also made physical threats against employers (see, e.g., *Argus*, 25 Aug. 1846), but there is little evidence of threatening letters like those used in Britain.

130. For example, two rural workers at Arno Vale adulterated the wheat they were thrashing: *South Australian Register*, 15 July 1843. Other methods included scabbing sheep: *Port Phillip Patriot*, 31 Oct. 1845.

131. Rural employers tried to encourage more cooperative attitudes among free and assigned workers by such devices as agricultural society prizes awarded to shepherds rearing the most lambs and to servants displaying exemplary conduct: see, for example, *Australian*, 11 June 1830. Other proposals to foster stable and sober habits among bush workers included religious instruction, friendly benefits, and rural saving schemes: *Port Phillip Gazette*, 2 Aug. 1847.

periods.[132] Multiple employer appearances constituted more than 15 percent of all employer-initiated cases. Few employers rivaled F. W. Bacon of Goodooga in western New South Wales, who racked up sixty-five appearances between 1890 and 1903. Repeated employer resort to the courts was not necessarily a measure of the law's effectiveness in subordinating workers. Indeed, litigious employers often found it difficult to hire workers. Some, like Major Newman, tried the patience of even sympathetic magistrates.[133] Multiple employer appearances resulted almost twice as often from complaints by workers as against them.[134]

Terms and conditions of employment and the meaning of the legislative provisions themselves were sites of contestation. Master and servant laws could not abolish conflicts of interest inherent in the employment relationship. As Merritt and Tomlins have both noted, employers looked to the law to articulate the subordination and deference that they believed their workers owed them; but workers used law to assert their rights as contractual equals.[135] Verbal contracts especially were minefields of conflicting interpretations and memory. Early laws were sometimes amended so as not to recognize, and magistrates became reluctant to enforce, such agreements. The continued use of verbal agreements provided some servants with a ready escape clause, although this could be a two-edged sword.[136] Legal technicalities were used to void contracts; the meaning of such phrases in written agreements as "to make himself generally useful" were challenged.[137] Technical objections were more likely to be recognized and considered by a stipendiary magistrate or justices based in larger towns. The flexible interpretations of country magistrates defeated many a clever or technically sound objection.

In 1846 the *Port Phillip Patriot* observed that there seemed to be an infinite potential for complication, no matter how straightforward the case initially appeared.[138] This was not an isolated complaint. Many cases involved a complex web of claims and counterclaims over wages, work behavior, required tasks, ill-treatment, and numerous other matters. Cross suits were also common—a tactic especially favored by employers defending themselves against

132. A. Merritt, "Masters and Servants," 386.
133. *Argus*, 29 Aug., 1 Sept., 24, 27 Oct. 1848.
134. A. Merritt, "Masters and Servants," 396, 407.
135. Ibid., 322–26; Tomlins, "Subordination," 56–90.
136. Magisterial discretion could prove critical: see, for example, *South Australian Register*, 6 Feb. 1864.
137. Workers refused tasks that they did not consider part of the occupation, as in a case of a hutkeeper prosecuted for refusing to move hurdles: *Argus*, 3 Dec. 1847.
138. 10 Dec. 1846.

wage claims. For example, in April 1862 Thomas Brennan, an apprentice, sued his Adelaide employer Humphrey Bickford for seven pounds, fifteen shillings unpaid wages while Bickford claimed two pounds in damages to a reaping machine. Both won.[139] Some employers charged workers with absenteeism when they left work to lodge a complaint with a magistrate.[140] Even where no cross suit was lodged, magistrates imposed reciprocity by offsetting wage claims or (less frequently) mitigating the penalty imposed on workers. In exceptional circumstances the claim was dismissed. When John Hall, an Adelaide ginger beer maker, prosecuted his servant Henry Rosser for unlawful absence in May 1859, police magistrate Beddome dismissed the case, telling Hall that since he had recently discharged three other servants at a moment's notice it was natural enough for Rosser, whom he had engaged by the week, to go away when he liked.[141]

The growth in prosecutions by workers that eventually swamped employer-initiated actions was not simply a reflex to a tandem growth in wage evasion by employers. There is no evidence that the incidence of evasion grew over time and good reasons for suspecting the opposite. What had changed was that after 1845 the master and servant acts made it easier for workers to initiate and succeed in such claims. Workers' readiness to use these limited forms of redress should not be seen as indicating any particular affection for the laws but merely that they represented the only accessible legal remedies.

Another tactical response by Australian workers was to make the period of engagement as short as possible. This allowed workers to leave an undesirable employer or renegotiate better conditions upon renewal—possibilities that undoubtedly influenced employer behavior. Average periods of engagement were shorter than those in Britain. During periods of acute labor scarcity workers strove to engage for periods as short as a week, whereas terms tended to lengthen when market conditions favored employers.[142]

Some workers, especially tradesmen like compositors, sought to evade the legislation altogether by claiming that as artisans, handicraftsmen, or independent contractors they fell outside its scope.[143] There is evidence of this in all colonies. In March 1863 George White, one of two compositors charged with absence from the *South Australian Advertiser and Chronicle* office in Adelaide, claimed he was not a servant but an ordinary contractor who had no

---

139. *South Australian Register*, 4 Feb. 1862.
140. *Port Phillip Patriot*, 2 June 1847.
141. *South Australian Register*, 15 May 1859.
142. AOT VDL CSO 24/259/10755.
143. For examples of such claims involving compositors, cabinetmakers, and butchers, see *Port Phillip Patriot*, 6 Feb. 1840; *Argus*, 3 Oct. 1848; *Melbourne Daily News*, 20 Feb. 1849.

specified hours and was paid simply for work completed.[144] His challenge failed, but within two months the government's difficulties in applying the law at its own printing office led it to amend the coverage provisions.[145] The new clause brought "all persons contracting for the performance of work at a certain price taken in task by the piece, or in gross" within the ambit of the master and servant act. By October 1864 the coverage provisions were again under challenge, with a case (*Mullen v. Dawson*) going to the Supreme Court to test the claim that artificers and handicraftsmen were not covered by the 1863 act.[146]

Some of these challenges combined individual and collective resistance. In 1845, for instance, several women domestic servants in Melbourne combined to reshape their employment conditions by leaving their employers, demanding wages at short notice, and seeking redress through the master and servant act when these demands were not met.[147] Throughout the 1840s and 1850s coal miners in the Hunter Valley of New South Wales repeatedly challenged the magistrates' jurisdiction on the basis that neither the 1845 nor the 1857 act made specific mention of "miners." After a union was organized in 1850, this resistance was formalized. In 1856 striking miners secured a wage increase but refused to sign an agreement that they believed would bring them under the act. In 1862 the Supreme Court ruled that miners were covered.[148] However, by this time collective modes of regulating employment, including experiments with third-party conciliation, had assumed considerable importance in the industry.

The impact of the master and servant acts on the development of colonial trade unions is a complex and dynamic story. Collective action by workers began in the late eighteenth century (including a combination of reapers to raise wages in 1795),[149] but the first formal unions did not emerge until the mid-1820s. During the nineteenth century well over 4,000 unions were formed in the Australian colonies. While most were small and short-lived, the movement grew and exerted an increasing influence on employment con-

---

144. *South Australian Advertiser*, 1 Apr. 1863; *South Australian Register*, 1 Apr. 1863.

145. The bill was introduced at the suggestion of W. C. Cox, the government printer.

146. In the result actions were postponed against other workers, including a saddler charged with desertion. Nevertheless, the magistrate responsible for hearing the original case refused to entertain the argument in connection with charges of absence against another defendant when it was raised by the same defense counsel: *South Australian Register*, 16, 18 Oct., 6 Dec. 1864.

147. The tactic failed when the bench refused to entertain their claims: *Port Phillip Patriot*, 15 May 1845.

148. J. Turner, "Newcastle Miners," 30; J. Turner, "Coalmining," 86–91; *R v. Merewether*, 1 SCR 260; *Ex Parte Sperring*, 11 NSWLR 407.

149. Connell and Irving, *Class Structure*, 57.

ditions. Building workers pioneered the eight-hour day in the 1850s and by the late 1880s it was a standard condition for many urban craft workers. By 1890 there were more than 200,000 union members and, in terms of density and industrial gains, the Australian union movement could claim to be one of the strongest in world. Organization was so strong that, contrary to the Webbs' analysis, some noncraft unions attempted unilateral regulation. With notable exceptions (such as tailoresses, boot machinists, shop assistants, and teachers), most women workers remained outside the orbit of unionism.

Organization gave workers an alternative method of pursuing wage concerns that weakened the individual employment contract enshrined in master and servant law. Merritt suggests increasing industrial agitation in the Western Division of New South Wales during the 1880s probably explains declining pastoralist use of master and servant laws at this time.[150] However, employers also used master and servant laws to combat collective organization. Striking workers were charged with absence, absconding, or breach of agreement. Often a few individuals, including union activists or officers, were selected for exemplary treatment. Alleged strike instigators were charged with inciting a breach of agreement. Prior to 1860 the courts were used against striking workers in a wide range of occupations, including miners and urban tradesmen. In 1840, for example, three Sydney shipwrights were prosecuted for refusing work and several compositors working for the *Sydney Monitor* were charged with neglect of work. In 1841 a Melbourne master tailor prosecuted two journeymen for neglect of work and hiring themselves out to others. In 1857 four striking compositors at the Melbourne *Argus* were charged with breach of contract. In 1853 nine striking miners from the Newtown colliery near Hobart were jailed for two months for breach of contract. In 1858 eight German immigrant stonemasons who refused to scab on a strike in Victoria received a three-month sentence for the same offense.[151]

After 1860 this device became increasingly confined to a narrowing band of employments, notably in the pastoral industry and agriculture. The shift almost certainly reflected the growing strength of trade unions and the ineffectiveness of the laws in stopping collective action. In December 1878, when an Adelaide builder named Joseph Stevenson charged ten carpenters with inciting others to leave work contrary to the 1878 master and servant act, police magistrate Beddome dismissed the case.[152] Four years later, when

150. A. Merritt, "Masters and Servants," 212.

151. *Monitor*, 3 Dec. 1840; *Port Phillip Herald*, 19 Nov. 1841; *Argus*, 2 Apr. 1857; *Colonial Times*, 11 June 1853; Coghlan, *Labour and Industry*, 2:737–38.

152. *South Australian Advertiser*, 16, 18 Dec. 1878.

twelve striking mason's laborers were charged with unlawful absence and each was mulcted two days pay plus costs by the Port Adelaide magistrates, building unions held a protest meeting that declared that artisans should not be subject to master and servant law.[153] That these charges were brought at all was exceptional in this period of worker mobilization.

In some industries employer attitudes were slow to change, however. Moreover, there was a general revival of prosecutions during the titanic nationwide industrial struggles of the 1890s, when employers sought to assert "freedom of contract"—the right not to recognize or deal with unions. Australian employers could still play the jail card. In Britain, the Employers and Workmen Act, 1875,[154] effectively repealed master and servant law, removing the prison penalty for ordinary breach of contract. The Australian colonies did not adopt similar legislation, and in some, like New South Wales, the prison option survived (albeit in a restricted form) into the twentieth century.[155]

The master and servant acts had always been critical weapons of rural employers, and pastoralists continued to use them against the spread of unionism. In October 1890 the Australian Pastoral Company sought to defeat the Queensland Shearers Union's (QSU) attempt to organize roustabouts and laborers at the Bullamon and Noondoo sheep stations by charging thirty-nine strikers with breach of agreement. Almost all were convicted by a bench of magistrates that included the local government sheep inspector.[156] In the same month George Taylor, a QSU organizer, was charged with inciting ten men to breach their agreements following a strike at Amby Downs station. Frederick Vaughan, police magistrate at the Mitchell court, decided to make an example of Taylor, who had prosecutions dating back at least to 1888, by imposing cumulative penalties amounting to a fine of £194 or twenty months in jail. The Queensland Supreme Court found Vaughan to have exceeded his powers and overturned the conviction.[157] When the first of a series of major strikes erupted less than six months later, such legal niceties evaporated. One magistrate who bucked the trend and sympathized with the strikers was rusticated to an isolated location. More typical was Supreme Court Judge Harding. Passing sentence on thirteen strike leaders at the infamous Rockhampton conspiracy trial of 1891, he stated, "The indictment contains twenty counts and you shall serve three years on each count." He then paused, giving the men the impression they were to serve sixty years. Only after the whispered

153. Ibid., 16, 17, 18 Aug. 1882; *Newcastle Herald*, 21 Aug. 1882.
154. (U.K.) 38&39 Vict. c.90 (1875).
155. Tighe and Russell, *Master and Servant*, 83–84.
156. *Brisbane Courier*, 16 Oct. 1890.
157. *Maryborough Chronicle*, 21 Oct. 1890; *Queensland Times*, 3 Nov. 1890.

intercession of the crown prosecutor did he add sourly, "the sentences to be concurrent."[158]

Employers' use of the master and servant acts in the strikes of the 1890s aroused sufficient rancor for colonial labor electoral leagues (precursors to the Australian Labor Party) to make their abolition a key part of their platforms. Yet political resistance to the legislation already had a long history. Protests from Sydney workers, including a petition with 3,300 signatures, had mitigated provisions of the New South Wales enactment in 1840.[159] In 1843 shepherds from a number of districts in Western Australia formed a club to fight recent changes to the master and servant act of that colony.[160] Protests by rural workers against the 1845 amendments to the New South Wales act, including the compulsory discharge certificate system, failed, but widespread agitation by laborers, miners, and other workers in Adelaide, Glen Osmond, and the Barossa defeated similar amendments in South Australia two years later.[161] Responding to the coercive measures used in the gold rush of the early 1850s, Tasmanian workers (including women) turned from their twenty-year struggle against convict transportation to urge a reformed master and servant law.[162] Their agitation led to the introduction of a new bill in 1855, but its passage was halted when Parliament was prorogued following a scandal in the Convict Department. A less ambitious law enacted in 1856 substituted fines for imprisonment in convictions for misconduct.[163] However, dissatisfaction with the retention of the discharge certificate system led to further protests.[164] The harsh treatment of indentured servants such as Eliza Maguire, detained on allegations later found to be baseless, and a couple named Aherne, jailed after attempting to leave Tasmania because they could not find work, were made causes célèbres by the press.[165] In December 1857 T. D. Chapman was

158. The strikers were convicted of criminal conspiracy under the Combinations Act, (U.K.) 6 Geo.IV c.129 (1825), repealed in Britain but not in Queensland; George Taylor was one of those sentenced to prison on the appositely named St. Helena Island in Moreton Bay: Stuart, *Shearers' Strike*, 26, 49.

159. *Monitor*, 29 Sept. 1840; L. Thomas, *Labour Movement*.

160. *Perth Gazette*, 21 Jan. 1843.

161. *Port Phillip Patriot*, 11, 19, 23 Dec. 1845; SA CSO A 1847/467, John Goodlee, Chairman of Mechanics and others of Hindmarsh, 19 Apr. 1847; CSO A 1847/475, John Goodlee, Chairman of meeting of Working Classes of Hindmarsh to Governor, 28 Apr. 1847; CSO A 1847/1563, Memorial of the Mechanics, Artisans and Labourers of Hindmarsh and Bowden; *South Australian Register*, 21, 28 Apr., 8 May, 7 July 1847; Cashen, "Masters and Servants," 32–43.

162. AOT VDL CSO 1/42/714, Committee of Operatives to Governor, 21 Apr. 1855; reply from W. Champ, Colonial Secretary, 4 May 1855; VDL CSO 1/59/1254; *Hobart Mercury*, 4 May 1855.

163. AOT VDL CSO, Attorney General to Colonial Secretary, 29 Feb. 1856.

164. Davidson, "Tasmania," 162–74; *Colonial Times*, 1 Feb. 1856.

165. *Colonial Times*, 1 July 1856; *Tasmanian Daily News*, 1, 24 July, 20, 22, 24, 28 Oct. 1856.

elected with working-class support on a pledge to change the law. However, faced with a counterattack from rural employers, Chapman did an about-face and withdrew his reform bill.[166]

In all these campaigns, very similar arguments were mounted against the acts: they were more oppressive than their British counterpart; they were an assault on the rights of British subjects; they lacked reciprocity in terms of offenses, procedures, and penalties; they were polluted by a "convict leaven" in their treatment of free labor; they discouraged emigration. Taken together with the significant expansion of the franchise in the 1850s and the ineffectiveness of some coercive measures, these campaigns clearly had an impact. By 1868 the worst features of many of the earlier acts had been dropped and the rate of legislative activity had slowed. Subsequent reforms, such as enhanced means for recovering unpaid wages, benefited workers. Political agitation also became more institutionalized. Charles Don, an ex-Chartist stonemason endorsed by the Political and Socialist Labour League, was elected to the Victoria parliament (1859–64) promising to destroy the master and servant act and replace it with a lien law for wage recovery. He failed but a wage law was enacted within a decade (1870). Repeal of the master and servant acts was a formal policy plank of the 1884 Intercolonial Trades' Union Congress, with the editor of the official record expressing surprise such one-sided legislation had survived so long. His surprise might have been even greater had he known the laws would still exist thirty-five years later when Labor had been elected to government in all six colonies (now states).[167] There is no complete explanation for this paradox apart from the growth of unions and the concomitant concentration of Labor's energies on the compulsory arbitration system, which covered more than 80 percent of workers by the late 1920s and so displaced the individual contract and the master and servant acts that regulated and enforced it.

Conclusion

Employment regulation in the Australian colonies depended heavily on statutory mechanisms. This reflected a carry-over of prescriptive regulation from the convict period as well as the prominent economic and social role assumed by the colonial state. Master and servant laws were initially shaped by the

166. *Tasmanian Daily News*, 8 Feb. 1858.

167. In 1922 the editor of the coal miners' journal expressed equal surprise at the failure to repeal the New South Wales act, and made ambiguous reference to its use against shearers and shed-hands engaged in a go-slow strike. If correct, this appears to have been one of the last times the law was imposed on collective action: *Common Cause*, 10 Mar. 1922.

interaction between local legislatures dominated by pastoral and commercial capital and British authorities, the convict experience, a fluid labor market, and the refusal of workers (many of them immigrants in search of a better life) to accept the dictates of their masters. The close association between the magistracy and employers, especially in rural districts, undermined the moral authority of the legislation in the eyes of workers. Just as convict workers contested the regulatory regime that sought to govern their conditions of employment, so various forms of resistance among free workers made the punitive character of early laws increasingly problematic. The master and servant acts were always a site of struggle, and by the 1840s they had contributed to organized political agitation by workers. In the second half of the nineteenth century, these developments, together with the rise of unionism, restricted the effective scope of master and servant laws to a narrow range of occupations, notably rural workers and female domestics. Following a brief reversal in the 1890s, the long demise of the master and servant regime was accelerated by the introduction of compulsory arbitration at state and federal levels at the turn of the century. The acts remained on the statute books of a number of states until the 1970s. Ironically, recent legislative attempts to decollectivize employment regulation and promote individual employment contracts in Australia are reminiscent of earlier master and servant laws. The overt usage of subordination has been replaced by the new economic rationalist mantra of "freedom" and "choice." Like their counterparts of a century ago, workers today are finding that changes in terminology do not alter the realities of individualized bargaining.

SEVEN

The Colonial Office, 1820–1955

Constantly the Subject of Small Struggles

M. K. Banton

It must be remembered in dealing with a question of this kind that there is a constant tendency in Legislatures composed of employers to frame Laws which (they flatter themselves) will relieve them from the necessity of humouring and improving the Laboring population, and enable them to treat that population as a mere means of production bound to employ itself for their benefit according to certain Laws fixed with reference to the employers profits. Instances therefore of severe Legislation against Laborers in our tropical Colonies . . . cannot be neglected as mere exceptional accidents, but must be treated as instances of a Law which, unless simply allowed to take its course, will constantly be the subject of small struggles between the Colonial Authorities and the Home Government.[1]

Sir Frederic Rogers's words, penned during an examination of a Gambian master and servant ordinance in 1858, would have struck a chord with many officials throughout the lifetime of the modern Colonial Office.[2] Such "small

1. Public Record Office, CO series (hereafter CO) 323/86, F. Rogers, report on the Gambia Ordinance for the better regulation of artisans, sailors, laborers, and other servants, 21 Sept. 1858; the legislation was amended in light of Rogers's report and enacted as (Gambia) Ordinance, 28 Feb. 1859.

2. "Colonial Office" is used here to describe both the Colonial Office proper (1854-1966) and its predecessor the War and Colonial Department (1801-54). Before 1696, colonial affairs had been managed by the Privy Council, working through a number of temporary committees and commissions. From 1696 to 1782 the Board of Trade and the secretaries of state in partnership assumed responsibility. With the temporary abolition of the Board of Trade in 1782, the Home Office took over for almost twenty years. This chapter covers the period from about 1820 to the mid-1950s. It is concerned with the crown colonies, protectorates, and mandated territories rather than the dominions, which accounts for the lack of coverage of the development of South African labor legislation after the late nineteenth century. (See in this regard the

struggles" commonly attended the discussion of new or amended colonial labor legislation. The much greater "struggles" between the Caribbean colonial authorities and the home government that marked the drafting of instruments to abolish slavery in 1834 and regulate the intermediate state of "apprenticeship" to 1838 are well known, as is the central role of Rogers's predecessor Sir James Stephen. In 1840 Stephen grumbled that "among all the duties which are to be discharged here, the most unwelcome has always been that of revising our Colonial Legislation. . . . Such a mass of uninteresting details it would be difficult to bring together from any other quarter."[3] However unattractive the task, it was one that he did not shirk. Despite contemporary and more recent scholarly criticisms of his inability to delegate, the slowness of his administrative procedures, and his poor relations with other officials, few have doubted that his comments on colonial statutes were consistently thorough, detailed, and acute. W. L. Burn, William A. Green, Thomas C. Holt, D. B. Swinfen, and others have described his detailed scrutiny of pre-1833 slave codes, and his role in drafting the emancipation legislation and formulating the scheme of apprenticeship, and have analyzed Colonial Office principles behind the policy statements of the period.[4] As Swinfen stressed in his study of the process of colonial law review, in overseeing the enactment of slave and labor legislation officials in London were "motivated first by concern for the unrepresented classes and secondly by concern for the whole colonial community."[5]

My purpose in this chapter is to explain some of the many ingredients that went into Colonial Office oversight of master and servant law, from the able and informed work of Stephen, through increasing complacency in the late nineteenth century, to the ultimate capitulation to international pressure from the International Labour Organisation (ILO) and public opinion at home, which finally led to an acceptance within the office that the abolition of penal sanctions should be pursued. It is impossible in one chapter to explain developments in every area of the empire, and I have concentrated here on a number of specific examples to illustrate how the office worked, what general ideas about the nature of "native" labor emerged and changed over time, and how specific pieces of legislation came to be adopted, or resisted, or

---

chapter by Chanock in this volume.) British relations with the Union of South Africa (established 1910) were the responsibility of the Dominions Division of the Colonial Office (set up 1907) which became a separate government department, the Dominions Office, in 1925.

3. Swinfen, *Imperial Control*, 3.

4. Burn, *Emancipation and Apprenticeship*; Green, *Slave Emancipation*; Holt, *Freedom*.

5. Swinfen, *Imperial Control*, 137.

ignored. My examples come primarily from West, Central, and East Africa and from the West Indies.

The British government's decision in the late 1830s to draw up a series of orders in council to regulate the law in some colonies, and to be used as model legislation in others, has led to a widespread belief that the imposition of legislation from London was the norm. In fact, although model legislation might be circulated when entirely new provisions were sought (e.g., the introduction of workmen's compensation schemes in the early 1930s), or when an international standard was required (as, e.g., in copyright), it was rarely considered advisable in subject areas such as the regulation of labor, where the diverse requirements of individual colonial economies were thought to make conformity inappropriate. Instead, statutes were drafted in the colonies and, according to constitutional niceties, either discussed with the Colonial Office (and other government departments as required) at draft stage or enacted locally and passed to London for formal approval.

The secretary of state for the colonies could and did disallow colonial statutes, notably in the West Indies in the 1830s, when the plantation colonies enacted statutes to restore their access to cheap subservient labor lost by the imperial emancipation of their slaves in 1833. Over the whole period, however, ministers and officials were generally reluctant to enforce the veto. The recommendation to disallow a Virgin Islands master and servant ordinance in 1927 was sufficiently unusual to initiate an anxious debate in the office about the correct procedure. It was not uncommon for colonial legislatures to enact temporary legislation and submit it to London some months after it had come into force. Successive secretaries of state signaled their willingness to accept less than favorable provisions in such circumstances, arguing that revision could occur when the act was renewed. An advantage of temporary legislation for the Colonial Office was that, in theory at least, it gave officials an opportunity to watch it in operation and to determine if it were appropriate. But they generally omitted to seek reports about its operation or ensure that earlier recommendations were followed. In the meantime, employers and local officials quickly became accustomed to the provisions and were subsequently inclined to argue that they were basically sound, if requiring some minor revision, thus making it more difficult for the office to achieve major amendment.

The operation of master and servant legislation already in force was, in fact, rarely of concern to the office. In general, statutes were discussed with London only when they were enacted or revised, in which case the impetus usually came from the colony. The role of the legal adviser was more often to examine locally drafted statutes than himself to play a central role in drafting. As Stephen stressed, this was a tedious task. It was made more complex by the frequent failure of colonial legal officers to provide any comparative table showing the derivation of each provision of a statute.

Sometimes the initiative came from the Colonial Office, as in the nineteenth century when new legislation was required to support emancipation schemes. Very occasionally provisions of statutes came to the attention of the office quite by chance, and in circumstances where some reform seemed desirable. Only from the 1920s and 1930s did the office seek to play a role in standardizing legislation. In general, it deferred to the superior local knowledge of "the man on the spot." Almost total reliance on the knowledge of governors continued even into the period when interchange of personnel between the Colonial Office and the colonial service became common. In 1939 the secretary of state, Malcolm MacDonald, wrote, "Today if H.M.G. is to continue to trust its distant representatives, as we do and shall, it must be on the basis, not of lack of contact, but of co-operation, common objectives, and awareness of each other's problems."[6] Those values help explain, perhaps, why penal sanctions continued to be found in British colonies well into the twentieth century, after they had been abolished in most other imperial systems.

JAMES STEPHEN was appointed part-time counsel to the Colonial Office in 1813, a post that was made permanent in 1825. He became an assistant undersecretary of state in 1834, and from 1837 to 1847 was permanent undersecretary. Throughout this long period he retained responsibility for reviewing thousands of colonial statutes. On his retirement this work went to Sir Frederic Rogers at the Colonial Land and Emigration Board, and two additional officials were appointed in the Colonial Office to take on the remainder of Stephen's duties. Rogers followed Stephen's career path, becoming permanent undersecretary from 1860 until 1871. He retained responsibility for reviewing legislation until January 1867, when Henry Thurston Holland was appointed legal adviser and assistant undersecretary of state. Holland resigned in 1874 and was replaced by W. R. Malcolm, who was not designated "legal adviser" but was responsible for inter alia "general legal business," as were his successors, Edward Wingfield (1878–97) and Hugh Bertram Cox (1897–1911). J. S. Risley was appointed legal assistant in March 1901 and became legal adviser in 1911 when Cox retired. He held the post until 1931. Risley's successors, H. G. Bushe, H. H. Duncan, and K. O. Roberts-Wray, also

---

6. *The Colonial Empire: Statement Relating to the Period 1/4/38 to 31/3/39 to Accompany Estimates for Colonial and Middle Eastern Services, 1939.* Cmd. 6023, 1938–39.

made the Colonial Office their main careers, joining the permanent establishment as legal assistants, or assistant advisers, with a few years' experience of private practice (although Duncan had qualified late and also had previous commercial experience). Bushe, after twenty-two years in the office, was appointed governor of Barbados in 1941, but it was unusual for an adviser to have prior colonial experience. One who did was Albert Ehrhardt, appointed temporary assistant legal adviser in 1920 after twenty-four years in administrative and legal posts in West and East Africa and the Western Pacific.

The inefficient processes of the mid-nineteenth-century Colonial Office, which placed responsibility for administrative detail as well as high policy in the hands of overworked senior officials, nonetheless resulted in a broad overview of legislative development. By the late nineteenth century, legal advisers increasingly confined their comments to the legal drafting; officials in the office's geographical departments, often quite junior, gradually assumed responsibility for examining the policy implications of suggested legislation. Usually without legal training, they struggled to make sense of lengthy and complex drafts. By the twentieth century they and their political masters complained, "I feel a little out of my depth in this mass of detail," or "I have not studied the whole of this draft Bill, which is a very elaborate piece of work." One official admitted that he and his colleagues were "constantly baffled." Another shelved an unwelcome burden by taking draft legislation home and "forgetting" it for nearly nine months. The degree of Colonial Office oversight and understanding of master and servant legislation thus changed greatly over the years. The records of the office also show that specific enactments might be closely examined or totally ignored, for reasons of policy, administrative convenience, the enthusiasm or apathy of an individual, or pure chance.[7]

Some points about the structure of the Colonial Office should be noted. Traditionally, its organization was on geographical lines. In the nineteenth century, only the Chief Clerk's Department (later the General Department) dealt with matters affecting the empire as a whole. The result was an almost complete lack of interchange of knowledge between officials responsible for different regions. They might meet in the corridors of the Downing Street offices, or at their clubs, but there was no official forum for a sharing of expertise. It was not until the ILO and the British Ministry of Labour were established at the end of the First World War that the Colonial Office placed

7. CO 96/513, Lord Harcourt minute, 21 Feb. 1911. CO 691/117/7, R. V. Vernon minute, 21 Mar. 1931. CO 866/29/1166, J. G. Hibbert minute, 1 Oct. 1936. CO 691/141/9, F. G. Lee minute, 9 Apr. 1936.

overall responsibility for labor supervision with the General Department (although the geographical departments still had sole responsibility for specific territorial matters). In the late 1930s the British Trade Union Congress coordinated demands for the establishment of a specialist Labour Department within the office. Officials vetoed this but, in 1939, agreed to the addition of a Social Services Department, to include labor matters.

The West Indies and Africa in the Early Nineteenth Century

Stephen and Rogers were responsible for the review of colonial laws throughout the period that included the abolition of slavery in the British West Indian colonies and the introduction and early development of labor legislation in British Africa. Stephen's humanitarian stance, criticized publicly by those contemporaries who detected a bias against the colonists, is revealed in much of his legal work. He himself commented upon "the most anxious, if not the first duty of a government, to consult for the permanent interests of Society, as opposed to the immediate interests of the most active and powerful of its members; and to watch over the welfare of the many, rather than the present advantage of the few; and to protect those whose only property is the power of labour against the rapacity of the rich."[8]

Analyzing the social and political implications of proposed legislation, rather than just the legal drafting, Stephen greatly extended the narrow duties of a legal adviser. He habitually involved himself in policy decisions even before his duties were officially extended to combine the two roles. Rogers followed this practice and was equally industrious and conscientious in his attention to legal detail. Swinfen notes his belief in the moral responsibility of government, commenting that his private letters show him "liberal, but distrustful of the 'populace.'"[9]

Despite Stephen's lengthy reports on new or amended slave codes from his earliest years at the office, there is no evidence that he had an equivalent concern for the regulation of free labor in the Caribbean in the preemancipation period, and, indeed, this subject seldom came to his attention. The older British West Indian colonies had regulated labor contracts in the late seventeenth century and during the eighteenth, but few statutes were revised in the first three decades of the nineteenth. In 1814 Stephen examined a Jamaican Act for the Better Adjusting and the More Easy Recovery of the Wages of Servants, and for the Better Regulation of Such Servants, which was to remain

8. Swinfen, *Imperial Control*, 29.
9. Ibid., 30.

in force until 1940, and commented merely that there was no legal objection. His reports on Grenadan labor statutes of 1826 and 1829 were also limited to the brief "no legal objection," or "no objection in point of law." Such legislation comprised comparatively minor revisions of a long-standing body of law closely related to contemporary English legislation. His review of the 1827 Bermudan Act for the Protection and Government of Masters and Apprentices produced the same comment. In sharp contrast, his report on another Bermudan statute of the same year, the Act to Ameliorate the Condition of Slaves and Free Persons of Colour, consumed forty-three pages.[10]

In the early decades of the nineteenth century, master and servant law in England was familiar, centuries-old in its essentials, and not yet a political issue.[11] It is unsurprising, therefore, that at a time when the primary humanitarian focus was on slavery, Stephen and his colleagues regarded the amendment of West Indian master and servant legislation as routine. Attitudes were rather different, however, toward legislation for a comparatively new and unfamiliar territory, and in 1817 Stephen secured the disallowance of legislation framed in Sierra Leone to regulate a growing community of Kru[12] workers. It had enacted a pass and policing system, requiring the registration of all workers and declaring the unregistered to be vagrants punishable by hard labor for six months. Employers, masters of vessels, and workers were all subject to penalties for evasion (including allowing workers to leave the colony without permission), but the most distinctive feature was the proposed creation of groups of forty to sixty workers under a constable, all of whom were to be collectively and individually responsible for the good conduct, and for making good losses, of any of the others. The whole group could be expelled from the colony after three instances of pilfering, larceny, fraud, or felony, unless the offenders were identified and convicted. Stephen, perhaps unaware that the original constitution of the settlement was based on such a system, objected that the statute imposed on one ethnic group a system of government that he described as an "imitation of the old English law of frankpledge," and to the harsh penalties provided, but recommended disallowance mainly because no case had been made in support of a local requirement for such stringent legislation. "It is easy to conceive a state of things in which justice

10. CO 323/40, Stephen to Bathurst, 29 Dec. 1815. CO 323/43, Stephen to Bathurst, 8 Dec. 1826; CO 323/47, Stephen to Murray, 11 May 1830; (Grenada) Act of 23 May 1826; (Grenada) Act of 30 Dec. 1829. CO 323/45, Stephen to Murray, 25 Oct. 1828. CO 323/45, Stephen to Huskisson, 22 Feb. 1828.

11. See the chapters by Hay and Frank in this volume.

12. The contemporary term was *kroomen*. It is debatable whether this group, seen primarily as an occupational class, consisted only of ethnic Kru.

and policy may alike require at least the temporary enactment of a law like the present, however widely it departs from European models of legislation, and even from our own habitual views of Equity. In the absence of any such explanation, I am however of the opinion, that this Act is highly objectionable, because apparently unjust."[13]

In 1820, Sir Charles MacCarthy, governor of Sierra Leone, submitted for approval an Act for the Better Regulation of Mechanics, Kroomen, Labourers, Grumettas and Other Servants.[14] The preamble to the act noted that specific regulations for the control of workers were considered necessary, and drew attention to doubts whether the jurisdiction of magistrates in England over "servants and hired labourers in husbandry" extended to the "various classes of mechanics and labourers" in Sierra Leone.[15] Although less unusual than the 1816 legislation, the new act combined current English master and servant clauses with some important innovations, one of which was in fact a return to medieval (and long disused) English law. Thus the act extended to the colony the summary powers in employment cases that were held in England by justices. It provided, as in England, for forfeiture of wages, fines, and imprisonment for the servant in breach, but also allowed servants to make summary claims for wages. Penalties for neglecting work and other misconduct, working for more than one master, embezzlement, seducing a servant away from his master, making a combination or conspiracy all had close parallels in English law. But there were also penalties for insolence, enforcement of a stipulated period of service where none was specified in a contract, and the requirement that contracts with children under fifteen, and with non-English-speakers, be made in the presence of a justice of the peace and recorded. Most striking was the clause providing a fine (and imprisonment in default) for anyone who refused to hire himself when requested to do so. This kind of provision, originally found in the fourteenth- and sixteenth-century English legislation, had not been enacted there since a 1720 statute dealing with London tailors, and was utterly disused.[16]

The clause excited great interest within the office, but the secretary of

13. CO 323/40, Stephen's report on Sierra Leone ordinances of 1816, 11 July 1817; n.13 ("for the better regulation of Kroomen . . .") was disallowed.

14. (Sierra Leone) 1 Geo.IV n.25 (1820). *Grumetta* has been defined as "free laborer" or "local day laborer." By 1858 the term was considered obsolete and removed from Sierra Leone legislation transferred to the Gambia.

15. CO 267/51, MacCarthy to Bathurst, 25 July 1820. In 1774 it was ruled that the laws of a conquered or ceded colony remained in force until altered by the conqueror, whereas in colonies by settlement it was held that English common and statute law arrived as part of the "luggage" of the settlers. (Reception issues of both kinds as they arose in Canada are discussed in the chapter by Craven in this volume.)

16. (G.B.) 7 Geo.1 st.1 c.13 (1720). See Hay in this volume.

state, Lord Bathurst, accepted the governor's claim that "Kroomen do not belong to the Colony but resort here for hire . . . if . . . [they] are not lawfully employed they are living by petty thieving."[17] The Privy Council (also reviewing the legislation) complained that no proper report accompanied the act, but it directly criticized only one minor provision. When deliberations concluded in London, the act, passed for a two-year period only, had been in force for over a year, and the governor was merely asked to reconsider certain clauses if the act were renewed. The Sierra Leone legislation was renewed in 1822 and 1825. Despite evidence that a settled labor force was emerging, the clause making it an offense to refuse work was retained. In 1825, the legislation was automatically extended to the Gambia when the government of Sierra Leone took over its administration. It was amended in the Gambia during the 1850s at the instigation of the Colonial Office, but the parent statute remained in force until 1905 when its reform was initiated locally. Neither colony was affected by the demand for a radical change in much colonial legislation that accompanied and followed the abolition of slavery in 1834 and then of post-slavery "apprenticeship" in 1838. The only African colony included in that general review was the Cape of Good Hope.[18]

The Origins and Consequences of Cape Legislation

Lord Glenelg, the secretary of state, asked governors in the West Indies in 1837 to review legal codes in anticipation of the termination of the apprenticeship schemes set up in 1834. He stressed that legislatures, in formulating labor laws, should take particular care to avoid any system placing "the proprietary body in an invidious and apparently unfriendly relation towards those who are to live by the earnings of manual labour."[19] Concerned to safeguard an inexperienced and, they believed, less mobile wage-labor force, Glenelg and Stephen were prepared, as W. A. Green has noted, "to curb the authority of the planters in the interest of freedmen's liberty"[20] and insisted that vagrancy and contract laws must be more lenient than those of England. When laws drawn up in West Indian assemblies were found to conflict with principles set by the Colonial Office, officials in London attempted to impose their own model legislation to regulate contracts of employment.[21]

17. CO 267/56, MacCarthy to Bathurst, 23 Sept. 1822.
18. (Sierra Leone) 3 Geo.IV n.28 (1822); (Sierra Leone) Act of 29 July 1825; (Gambia) Act of 29 July 1825; (Sierra Leone) n.17 of 1905.
19. CO 854/2, Glenelg circular dispatch, 6 Nov. 1837.
20. Green, *Slave Emancipation*, 164.
21. See the chapter by De Barros in this volume.

The essential features of the model were that contract periods should be limited to four weeks if made orally, or one year if written, and written contracts were to be attested by a stipendiary magistrate. Breaches of contract subject to criminal penalties should be limited to three: failure to perform stipulated work; negligent or improper performance of such work; and causing damage to the employer's property by negligence or improper conduct. Maximum penalties should be a fine of one month's wages, fourteen days' imprisonment, or dismissal. Claims for nonpayment of wages or compensation for ill-treatment, as in England, could be made before a magistrate for summary settlement. Forwarding the model to the Cape in December 1838, together with copies of correspondence with West Indian governments, Glenelg stressed that given the differing conditions of the Caribbean and southern Africa, it would be sufficient for measures to "harmonise with the principles laid down."[22]

Legislators in the Cape, as in the West Indies, regarded this approach as interference. Stephen found that the statute they enacted infringed the principles of the model in several major respects: longer contract periods, heavier penalties, and administration by resident district magistrates rather than especially appointed stipendiaries (a problem also with legislation regulating the Cape apprenticeship scheme, already criticized by Stephen in 1835).[23] The ordinance added several new criminal offenses: behaving to the master with violence or insolence; scandalous immorality; drunkenness; or other "gross misconduct." Stephen complained that the terms were too vague, that the immorality and misconduct of workers were not more proper objects of punishment than when anyone else was guilty of them, and that true emancipation would be limited by such provisions since "much of the essence of slavery consisted, and must always consist, in the power of summary punishment for offences either wholly indefinite or defined merely by vague and general words." Rejecting the common claim of employers that people were simply not willing to work, Stephen expressed his abhorrence of the underlying intention that coercion and punishment should be substituted for the "impulse of self-interest" and noted with disapproval that workers laying complaints against employers risked imprisonment for making a "vexatious" or unproven claim.[24]

Stephen's examination of the ordinance and its subsequent revision led to voluminous correspondence with the governor, Sir George Napier. In the end, Lord John Russell, the new secretary of state, accepted Napier's claim

22. CO 49/32, Glenelg to Napier, 31 Dec. 1838.
23. CO 323/51, James Stephen to the Earl of Aberdeen, 16 Mar. 1835.
24. CO 48/207, James Stephen to Vernon Smith, 10 Oct. 1840.

that only "an intimate acquaintance with the local circumstances" could enable anyone to judge the "propriety or necessity" of the proposals, and he allowed the ordinance for a temporary, experimental period. Throughout its history, the Colonial Office preferred the opinion of "the man on the spot," and Stephen's reluctance to rely uncritically on such knowledge was unusual. On this occasion he minuted, "Explanations on matters of this kind, which cannot be made intelligible to a remote and comparatively ignorant reader, will generally be found to involve some error or fallacy; for there is nothing obscure or abstruse in the nature of the subject itself." Russell endorsed Stephen's recommendation for reports on the administration of the law, but the office had no machinery for regular review, and a detailed report was not submitted until 1850, although the ordinance was extended by order in council in 1844, and made permanent by the same process in 1846. Requesting confirmation of the order in October 1845, the governor referred to an 1844 request for a report, but now stated merely that, in his opinion and that of his Executive Council, the ordinance "is well fitted to attain the object for which it was framed," and had never been complained against.[25]

Very important changes were made to the Cape legislation in 1856. The new constitution of 1853 removed the requirement that the governor submit draft legislation but gave the secretary of state continuing power to disallow any statute within two years. The Cape act of 1856,[26] however, was never examined in London, apparently because a junior clerk, on receipt of the package of acts passed in that session, noted on them "these are for the Library."[27] Thus an act that was considerably harsher than its predecessors and that was to form the basis of laws enacted in southern, central, and eastern Africa during the next seventy or more years, was never reviewed in London. Before examining the terms of the 1856 Cape Act, it is instructive to consider how Gambian legislation was treated at midcentury.

The Colonial Office put pressure on the Gambia during the 1850s to reform its master and servant ordinance, on the grounds that since that law was passed "the Colony must have had the benefit of increased experience and confidence in dealing with the labouring classes and of the altered views prevalent since the abolition of slavery."[28] Clearly, the humanitarian views of the 1830s continued to inform office decisions, and the disquiet felt in 1820 about the compulsory work clause in the Sierra Leone legislation (extended

25. CO 48/207, Napier dispatch, 30 Jan. 1840. CO 48/207, James Stephen to Vernon Smith, 10 Oct. 1840. CO 48/253, Maitland dispatch, 17 Oct. 1845.
26. (Cape) n.15 of 1856.
27. CO 48/375, note by Frederick Lacock, assistant junior clerk, 3 Sept. 1856.
28. CO 401/9, Stanley to O'Connor, 18 May 1858.

with other laws to the Gambia in 1825) became acute when it came to the office's attention quite fortuitously in 1858.

Two Gambian magistrates, T. F. Quin and W. H. Selby, complained to the secretary of state that the governor had unconstitutionally reversed a decision of the bench. The governor, Colonel L. S. O'Connor, reported that Selby had illegally convicted four Africans for "refusing to accept one shilling per day as labourers," fined them twenty shillings each, and immediately imprisoned them for one month with hard labor in default. The incident had come to the attention of the governor only because one of the imprisoned men was the son of a local leader, recently commended for rendering important military assistance, who had complained. O'Connor initially assumed that the men had refused to accept work, but found that they were willing to work at the usual rate, which they considered to be one shilling and sixpence, but not at the lower rate that the man requiring their services, Selby's fellow magistrate Thomas Quin, had attempted to fix. Selby complained:

> [S]ome time ago 8d Stg. per diem was the current rate, however some short time ago it rose to a shilling and is going on increasing beyond all reason. . . . if there be no limit placed to the demands of these people, and if the Custom of the place be overridden then I see no reason why they should [not] go on progressing to 10/- per day, and thus render it impossible for the Merchant to carry on his business.[29]

When O'Connor freed the prisoners, both magistrates resigned. The episode confirmed Stephen's opinion that lay magistrates were not appropriate adjudicators of employment disputes. The secretary of state, Lord Stanley, considered O'Connor's intervention not only justifiable but necessary. Further, the correspondence alerted him to legal provisions that, he suggested, required amendment:

> A law which enables a justice to punish in a summary way any attempt of the labourer to stand out for higher wages by treating it as a wilful refusal to work, is open to the grossest abuse in any case, except when the wages are fixed by the law itself. And when applied to labourers not resident in the Colony but coming in search of hire, it would seem to be of a very suicidal character, inasmuch as the report of such injustice must tend to deter them from offering their necessary services.[30]

---

29. CO 87/66, Selby's report of 14 Aug. 1857 enclosed with O'Connor's dispatch no. 16, 24 Mar. 1857.

30. CO 401/9, Stanley to O'Connor, 18 May 1858. Justices in England had been empowered by (Engl.) 5 Eliz. c.4 (1562) to fix rates at the quarter sessions, a power not abrogated until 1814,

Stanley asked O'Connor to repeal the provision making refusal to accept work a criminal offense; he stressed the "questionable soundness" of a clause "imposing a severe punishment for the very vague offence on the part of the labourer of idling away his time"; and he asked for a careful general review of the law. Sir Frederic Rogers examined proposed amendments from the Gambia but found no great improvement. The "refusal to work" provision, instead of being repealed, had been amended to approximate contemporary English vagrancy legislation. As Rogers pointed out, "It still makes it the duty of the Stipendiary Magistrate to punish any laborer who, not being satisfied with 'the current rate of wages' refuses to receive employment except at a higher rate. This does in effect deprive the Laborer of the legitimate advantage which he possesses in a thinly peopled country."[31]

The clause making it a criminal offense for a worker to "idle away his time" also remained. O'Connor justified its retention, arguing that evidence of neglect of work could be had by comparing the work of individuals. Rogers, in the words that preface this chapter, advised the new secretary of state, Sir Edward Bulwer Lytton, to insist on Stanley's amendments. Writing to O'Connor, Lytton spelled out the problem: "What is popularly called the 'current' rate of wages is generally fixed by that paid to the low average class of laborers. Are the willing and the skilled workmen,—and there must be such even among the population which this Ordinance concerns to be forced to accept the same terms as the ignorant and the lazy?" He concluded that "Under no circumstances could H. M.'s Government sanction any enactment to impress labour by seizing on a man and compelling him to hire himself at any rate of wages, current or not, merely because he happened to be unemployed."[32]

This amendment was made, but Lytton did not press further for removal of the clause penalizing idleness, merely asking that its operation be carefully watched for potential abuse. No attention was given to identical legislation in the neighboring territory of Sierra Leone.

One can only speculate about the way in which Rogers and Henry Labouchere, Stanley's predecessor, would have dealt with the Cape act of 1856 had they examined it. The Cape's representative government would have been more difficult to deal with than the Gambia, but the office had been force-

---

although in desuetude by the mid-eighteenth century (see the chapter by Hay in this volume). Technically it may be argued that this authority was available to Gambian magistrates, having been transferred to the settler colony of Sierra Leone, with the body of English statute law, and thence to the Gambia, and not repealed in either territory.

31. CO 323/86, F. Rogers's report, 21 Sept. 1858.
32. CO 401/11, Lytton to O'Connor, no. 22, 27 Oct. 1858.

ful in its approach to elected assemblies in the West Indies in the 1830s. The contents of the Cape act were so stringent that, had they been known, they would have provoked a vigorous response.

The 1856 Cape Act to Amend the Laws Regulating the Relative Rights and Duties of Masters, Servants and Apprentices was a lengthy and comprehensive enactment.[33] In seventy-six sections, it gave limited recognition to workers' rights by introducing sick pay and requiring residential servants to be properly housed and fed, but established neither a standard nor an inspectorate and imposed no penalties on employers failing to comply. Penalties for a worker's breach of contract were increased, and the list of offenses lengthened to eight "minor" and six "major" offenses punishable by, respectively, imprisonment with or without hard labor of up to one month, or six weeks for a second conviction, and imprisonment up to two months for a first offense, or three for a second. "Minor" offenses included failure to commence an agreed contract, unauthorized absence from the workplace, negligent performance of work, drunkenness, abusive language, insubordination, and making a "brawl or disturbance." "Major" offenses included causing damage or loss to the employer's property; assault or attempted assault on the employer, his family, or fellow servants; and desertion. Workers convicted of a major offense, or a second conviction for a minor offense, could be sentenced to solitary confinement and/or a "spare" diet. No period of imprisonment canceled a contract. Should a worker refuse to recommence work after release from prison, he could be imprisoned for one month, and for subsequent one-month periods up to a maximum of six months, until he agreed to work. The period of imprisonment would be added to the term of the contract, as would any period of absence without leave. Where a worker was convicted of losing or damaging his employer's property, which included being unable to explain satisfactorily the death or straying of livestock, a magistrate might award compensation from future wages, effectively tying the worker to his employer.

Although Colonial Office officials did not examine this act and received no report on its drafting, they had, six years earlier, received, and apparently ignored, a report on the working of the 1841 statute that laid the foundations for new and harsher legislation.[34] This report, requested by the Cape Legis-

33. (Cape) n.15 of 1856.
34. *Cape of Good Hope: Master and Servant: Documents on the Working of the Order in Council of 21 Jul 1846* (Legislative Council, 1849). I am indebted to Robert Ross and Douglas Hay for bringing this report to my attention. A copy sent to the Colonial Office in Sept. 1850 was acknowledged without comment and is not filed with the covering dispatch.

lative Council in September 1848, presented responses to questions put to resident magistrates, justices of the peace, ministers of religion, field cornets, and residents of Cape Town and rural areas. As well as requesting some statistical data and factual information, the questionnaire asked such leading questions as "Do you think more severe punishments are desirable?" Most respondents considered existing law insufficient, including some who also claimed to have no knowledge of the statute. They suggested that punishments should include hard labor, spare diet, corporal punishment, use of stocks, prolongation of contracts, fines, employment on public works, and compulsion to serve without wages. Some stressed that dissolution of a contract harmed only the master and that imprisonment with full rations was not only considered by servants to be no punishment at all but also had the effect of depriving the master of labor. Asked if there was any misconduct not reached by the 1841 statute, they mentioned neglect of property and livestock, desertion after accepting wages in advance, "wilful damages" done to the master, distributing alcohol to other servants, and inciting fellow workers to strike. Asked if they favored the enactment of vagrancy legislation, most replied in the affirmative. Although a few stressed the necessity of protecting workers against ill-usage, and one resident magistrate reported that complaints were usually settled amicably, another believed that "an extreme sense of philanthropy" had created the problems that were now so difficult to control or overcome. He believed that "slavery, bondage, vassalage, apprenticeship—all a state of compulsory labour, call it by what name you may,—appears to be essentially necessary to a favourable advancement of all young countries, when progressing from a state of infancy to maturity."[35] The strength of feeling against the efficacy of the 1841 statute is particularly striking in view of the governor's statement of 1845 that its provisions "have never been complained against."

The influence of the Cape legislation of 1856 was far-reaching. A 1908 report from the East Africa Protectorate noted that children employed to herd livestock, and regulated by provisions based on those of the Cape act, were expected to keep watch by night and day and were held responsible for the loss of animals.[36] In 1912 three domestic servants were convicted under the Northern Rhodesian master and servant ordinance for "creating a disturbance" by dancing and playing music on their afternoon off.[37] A study of Tanganyikan

35. Ibid., George Marsh, resident magistrate, Mossel Bay, 12 Oct. 1848.

36. (Kenya) n.8 of 1906, provisions copied from (Transvaal) n.13 of 1880, but originally from (Cape) n.15 of 1856.

37. Hansen, *Distant Companions*; (N. Rhodesia) n.18 of 1912 extended the operation of (Barotseland–N.W. Rhodesia) n.37 of 1908.

sisal estates in the middle years of the twentieth century found that "damage to property" provisions were commonly used against workers who "allowed" wild pigs or monkeys to eat the tender young leaves of sisal plants.[38] In the mid-1970s, D. G. Clarke, an economist, found that well over 50 percent of Rhodesian African workers were still controlled by legislation barely changed from the Cape model introduced into Southern Rhodesia in 1899 and 1901, and noted:

> So pervasive are the provisions, so stringent are their restraints on the employee and so heavily balanced in favour of the employer, that one can only surmise that the original architects of the legislation anticipated either the need to control considerable labour unrest, or sought to give legal ratification to an unequal bargain of employment struck between contractees whose political, social and economic status was inherently unequal.[39]

As British influence extended in southern Africa, the inequitable provisions of the legislation were extended into new jurisdictions. The 1856 Cape act was used as a model for statutes enacted in the Transvaal in 1880, and in Natal in 1894, and the provisions were then at last examined in London.[40] Edward Wingfield, appointed assistant undersecretary of state with responsibility for legal matters and for the West Indian colonies in 1878, examined the Transvaal ordinance. He recognized that provisions for the punishment of workers were very harsh, "but less so than those of the Cape Act which imposes imprisonment without the option of fine."[41] Lord Kimberley, then secretary of state for less than eight months, agreed that it was "a very severe law" but felt that, as similar legislation had long existed at the Cape, it was probably necessary.[42] They noted with approval that an employer could be fined for withholding wages, retaining a worker's property, or failing to supply articles stipulated in a contract. Harsher provisions would have raised questions, but it was assumed that the 1856 Cape act had been properly examined and approved, and the slightly more liberal provisions were seen as an improvement. Although Wingfield and Kimberley had no knowledge of the genesis of the Cape act, they did not ask for relevant papers, nor did they request a report on its use or consider that conditions might have changed in twenty-four years

38. Tambila, "Sisal Labour Force"; (Tanganyika) n.32 of 1923, effective 1 Jan. 1924.
39. Clarke, *Domestic Workers*.
40. (Transvaal) n.13 of 1880; (Natal) n.40 of 1894.
41. CO 291/6, report of E. Wingfield, 14 Dec. 1880.
42. CO 291/6, Kimberley minute, 17 Dec. 1880.

even if they had been comparable in the two territories at any time. They were prepared to accept a precedent uncritically.

Similarly, in 1892, officials sanctioned a Natal bill based on Cape and Transvaal laws with a minimum of discussion. It was not enacted, but two years later, a new government in Natal reassessed the bill, and the legislature voted to restrict it to African workers, stating that European "artisans and mechanics" should not be brought under legal provisions which, "though suited to native servants, could not with equal fitness be applied to a class of handicraftsmen who in many cases are possessed of considerable property and are fairly well educated." No real discussion of the amendment took place within the office. Edward Fairfield, an assistant undersecretary, noted that despite the extension of responsible government to Natal, the office was "supposed to look after the Natives and see that they are not oppressed." He argued, however, that unless the act was followed by repeal of an earlier law based on the Cape act of 1841,[43] "it cannot properly be said that *Native* Servants are exceptionally treated, as Non Native Servants remain under a somewhat drastic law. *Servants* are under exceptional legislation, as compared with other classes." In theory, at least, the Cape act of 1856 was racially nonspecific. However, as a report of the 1925 Economic and Wage Commission was to stress, an attempt had been made to restrict the scope of the act to indigenous and other non-European workers by a statutory definition of "servant" that excluded, so far as possible, occupations ordinarily followed by white employees.[44]

Whereas, after 1834, Stephen and Rogers had habitually sought details of local conditions and of the principles underlying new or revised legislation, their successors increasingly showed a willingness to rely on precedents set by the existence of comparable legislation in a neighboring territory. Fairfield, in 1894, acknowledged his ignorance by forwarding drafts to R. P. Ebden in the office's General and Emigration Department with the request, "as you have had so much to do with the Masters & Servants Act in Natal would you look into this?" Ebden merely pointed out that he knew nothing at all about Natal master and servant law, having dealt only with the Indian immigration legislation. Natal had, by this time, a substantial body of legislation designed to control the migrants recruited to meet its considerable labor demands. The paperwork went to Wingfield, who still had overall responsibility for legal

43. (Cape) Ord. of 1 Mar. 1841.
44. CO 179/189, statement of Harry Enscombe, attorney general, 12 July 1894. (Natal) n.40 of 1894. CO 179/188, E. Fairfield minute, 23 May 1894. Quoted in van der Horst, *Native Labour*, 37. See Chanock in this volume.

review, but he made no comment. No suggestion was made to the southern African governors in 1880 or 1894 that reformed English law (greatly changed in 1875) might be an appropriate model.

An Alternative Model: The Gold Coast, 1877

Neither Wingfield nor Kimberley had been in post in 1875–77 when the Gold Coast enacted legislation that followed the English reforms rather closely. The practice of handling most business of the office within regional departments ensured that more junior officials were often unaware of developments in other parts of the empire. The 1877 Gold Coast legislation, An Act for Regulating the Relations between Employers and Employed under Contracts,[45] was closely connected with the recent emancipation of slaves in the colony. An 1875 report had called for a law that would introduce "the idea of a limited service voluntarily entered into, yet obligatory during its continuance, and having for its object the mutual benefit of both the contracting parties."[46] Colonial Office officials, worried that emancipation might have an adverse effect on the economy and subsequent development of the territory, encouraged such legislation, which they suggested might be based on the English master and servant act of 1867.[47] This statute, although not fully meeting the demands of those who had agitated for reform of the law, enabled justices to treat disputes as civil proceedings and to determine appropriate compensation to be paid by the defaulting party. It thus introduced a greater degree of equality between employer and employee. But magistrates were also empowered to inflict up to three months' imprisonment if the guilty party was unable to pay, or to refer the case to the quarter sessions to be dealt with under criminal law if it appeared to them "that the injury to the person or property of the complainant has been wilfully and maliciously inflicted so as to amount to a criminal act, and not to be remedied by pecuniary compensation." The 1867 act was a model for the Gold Coast draft, with additional clauses to recognize local needs.

The colony's senior legal officer stressed that "the parties contracting in this country must be regarded as being in very many instances, on one side at least, in a state of quasi pupilage, and requiring to some extent to be protected against imprudent bargains."[48] The intention behind the legislation

45. (Gold Coast) n.16 of 1877.
46. CO 96/115, report on the working of the Slave Emancipation Scheme, 6 Mar. 1875.
47. (U.K.) 30&31 Vict. c.141 (1867).
48. CO 96/115.

was essentially the same as that behind the 1838 model; it was hoped that the introduction and regulation of labor contracts would protect emancipated slaves from exploitation, while at the same time ensuring a continuing supply of labor. Now, however, Colonial Office officials stressed economic concerns, and some at least distrusted the humanitarian ideals that had underlaid the work of their predecessors.

Like the English act, but unlike the legislation of southern Africa, the 1877 ordinance did not list specific offenses but allowed either party to make a complaint about any matter perceived as a breach of contract. It sought to make breach of contract a civil rather than criminal process, but, again like the English act, allowed penal sanctions to be imposed in the case of "aggravated misconduct," or if a party directed to find security failed to do so. Although the governor described the ordinance as "somewhat difficult,"[49] his limited correspondence with the secretary of state and ready acceptance of advice indicate their basic agreement on the legislation. In this case the local government saw no need to be constrained by the demands of European colonial interests because it regarded the legislation as part of the emancipation scheme and primarily concerned with the regulation of relations between African employers and African employees, although, as Dumett and Johnson have noted, there were in the Gold Coast those who hoped that a master and servant law would induce ex-slaves and others to honor contracts for long-term employment with European firms.[50]

While the draft Gold Coast legislation was still under consideration, the English act of 1867 was superseded by the Employers and Workmen Act of 1875,[51] which made a completely civil process possible. The final version of the Gold Coast ordinance reflected this major change. Magistrates were required to consider dealing with breach of contract as a civil matter before resorting to the remaining penal provisions. It empowered the courts to adjust and set off claims, to direct fulfillment of the contract, or to rescind the contract. How widely such powers were used was not reported to London. Magistrates would undoubtedly have found it easier to use penal provisions, and European employers probably argued, as they did in England in the 1860s, and in east and central Africa almost a century later, that a civil procedure was unenforceable where workers were not "fixed to the spot." Some additional revision had been made to make the ordinance suitable for extension to Lagos, which was now, and until 1886, administered as part of the Gold Coast

---

49. CO 96/122, Freeling to secretary of state, 15 Nov. 1877.
50. Dumett and Johnson, "Suppression of Slavery."
51. (U.K.) 38&39 Vict. c.90 (1875).

colony. Approving the ordinance, the secretary of state recommended that it should be regarded as experimental and its operation carefully watched, but he did not request any future report.[52] The Gold Coast legislation was further amended in 1890 and 1891, before being consolidated in 1893 by an ordinance that increased maximum contract length from two years to three but reduced penalties for "aggravated misconduct."[53]

The 1877 legislation shows that a very different model from that of the Cape of 1856 existed in Africa, even if it was unusual. Colonial Office records name the author of the 1877 statute, and of the earlier emancipation scheme, as the acting chief magistrate David Chalmers. Chalmers was a member of the Scottish Faculty of Advocates forced to seek a secure source of income following the failure of a commercial enterprise in 1866. Duman quotes the Scottish lord advocate, seeking a colonial post for Chalmers, as writing, "But for that circumstance I do not think he would have been disposed to accept the situation."[54] Chalmers saw service in the Gambia (1867), Gold Coast (1869), and Sierra Leone (1872). He returned to the Gold Coast in 1874, becoming chief justice there in 1876. Two years later he transferred to British Guiana as chief justice, remaining there until his retirement in 1894. Whether he influenced the revision of master and servant law in British Guiana is not revealed in the reports submitted by the governor and the attorney general. Neither do Colonial Office records indicate exactly who was responsible for drafting the earlier West African legislation referred to previously, or that of southern Africa, a lack of detail that can serve to erase any clues as to the genesis of a statute.

The legislation of individual colonies might be the product of a strong official or judge but often of a mining or planters' association. It was possible in crown colonies such as Gambia, lacking an elected legislature, to resist pressures from employers in a way that was not possible in the Cape or the Transvaal or Natal.

Another instance is Nigeria. In 1899 Sir Frederick Lugard, the first high commissioner of Northern Nigeria after the Royal Niger Company's charter was surrendered to the crown, drafted a master and servant proclamation. Although his attorney general, A. Davidson, had been appointed in April 1899 on Lugard's instructions, he remained in the United Kingdom until the end of the year to study African and Indian legislation and the Berlin agreements. Lugard's primary concern was to control migration; he explained that the

52. CO 96/122, secretary of state to governor, 9 Feb. 1878.
53. (Gold Coast) n.9 of 1890; (Gold Coast) n.6 of 1891; (Gold Coast) n.8 of 1893.
54. Duman, *English and Colonial Bars*, 126.

Niger Company's demands for labor made it difficult and expensive to obtain necessary labor for government projects. He therefore wished to introduce a third type of contract for service intermediate between foreign and local service, which should apply to laborers engaged for service more than 80–100 miles from home, but within the protectorate. Colonial Office officials disapproved of Lugard's decision to draft legislation himself, but his initial version was not in fact used. The attorney general and the chief justice re-drafted the legislation after studying the Lagos Bill of 1901 (enacted as Lagos no. 3 of 1902), the Central African native regulations of 1898, the Uganda porters regulations of 1899, the Southern Nigerian Proclamation no. 3, and "even the recent South African Proclamation Transvaal no. 35 of 1901."[55] The final version essentially followed the Gold Coast ordinance of 1893, while retaining Lugard's "extra local contract" provision.[56] Northern Nigeria had no legislature; legislative authority, by proclamation, was vested in Lugard.

The Colonial Office itself was still responsible for some initiatives in the later nineteenth century, particularly when other powers were involved. While displaying excessive confidence in British governors to avoid exploitation of workers, the office remained alert to possible foreign abuses, asking West Indian governors in 1892 to make foreign contracts unlawful, unless approved by a magistrate, in view of labor problems associated with the construction of the Panama Canal, and advising west African governors, three years later, to retain similar provisions, noting "there may be cases, such as that of the Congo Free State, where the labourers are ill-treated and the contracts are broken."[57] Colonial Office officials did not often consider the adequacy of such regulations, or the difficulties of enforcing them. When a Royal Navy officer expressed concern about the "trafficking" of labor on the west African coast in 1872, an official with responsibilities for indentured labor throughout the empire admitted that the British government could not hope to control the movement of laborers seeking improved prospects amongst the multinational interests of the coast. In 1878, the acting British consul in Samoa noted that, although the Pacific Islanders Protection Act dealt fully with recruitment of laborers, it gave no power to enforce regulations for their proper treatment on the estates of British subjects.[58]

---

55. (Lagos) n.3 of 1902; (British Central Africa Protectorate) n.1 of 1898; (Uganda) Queen's Regulations, 1899; (S. Nigeria) n.3 of 1901; (Transvaal) n.35 of 1901.

56. (N. Nigeria) n.22 of 1902; (Gold Coast) n.8 of 1893; CO 446/23, Lugard, 24 June 1902.

57. CO 854/31, 23 Dec. 1892; CO 147/99, confidential dispatch, 15 Jan. 1895.

58. ADM 1/6242 n.471, R. H. Meade, 20 July 1872: CO 83/18, A. P. Maudsley, 14 May 1878.

East Africa in the Early Twentieth Century

In the 1830s and the 1870s, Colonial Office officials and ministers had recognized, to a greater or lesser extent, the special considerations to be borne in mind in framing legislation for the regulation of a newly emancipated work force. Where the introduction, or major revision, of master and servant law was not directly linked to the abolition of slavery, officials in London rarely showed interest in establishing the nature or availability of labor. When, in 1911, mine companies in the Gold Coast sought to "reproduce the labour conditions of the Rand," an official of the West African Department who also served on the Indian Immigration Committee, stressed "there is no surplus of population . . . ample land . . . and the people are turning with great success to the cultivation of cocoa on their own lands . . . I see no reason to make it any easier than it is at present for the Mining Companies to tie down the labourers to the very unpleasant work at the mines."[59] Such local knowledge was unusual. This statement about west Africa was made at the end of a twenty-year period in which the southern African colonies, merged after the Boer War, had enacted and enforced the most oppressive master and servant legislation since the Cape act of 1856. Much African labor law in the late nineteenth century was profoundly conditioned by the enormous, and enormously profitable, discoveries of diamonds at Kimberley in 1867, and gold in Witwatersrand in the late 1880s. Kimberley was in the colony of Griqualand West, absorbed into the Cape Colony in 1880; Witwatersrand became part of the Transvaal. The insatiable, constantly growing demand for mine labor in both colonies led to hut taxes, pass laws, and master and servant legislation, often drafted by the mining companies, designed to increase the supply of African labor while simultaneously cutting its cost to the lowest possible level. A sharply divided work force, differentiated by race, was created, and sustained, in large part by legislation that made breach of contract criminal and that was enforced by expanded police forces and magistrates' courts.

As we have seen, much of this legislation aroused little interest in the Colonial Office in the late nineteenth century, because it seemed no more harsh than the original Cape act of 1856. Demands for migrant labor ensured that stringent legal provisions spread to neighboring territories. Southern Rhodesia adopted the body of Cape law as it existed at 10 June 1891, including the Cape master and servant acts of 1856 to 1889.[60] In 1911 a Bechuanaland Protectorate proclamation extended the provisions of the Cape acts, already in force and effect within the protectorate, to all "natives engaged or contracted

59. CO 96/513, W. D. Ellis minute, 24 July 1911.
60. Palley, *Southern Rhodesia*, 144.

in the Bechuanaland Protectorate to work as labourers in mines." The same provision was made for Swaziland, following complaints that "natives enlisting for work in the mines are not servants within the meaning of the Master and Servant Law, and consequently that breaches of contract by them are not punishable."[61]

How the office dealt with newly acquired territories was somewhat different, as the example of the East Africa Protectorate (EAP) shows. In contrast to the knowledge of Gold Coast conditions they were to demonstrate in 1911, officials in 1906 were ignorant of a territory for which they had assumed responsibility from the Foreign Office only the previous year.[62] When they examined new legislation there, they apparently assumed that there was a surplus of labor available for European enterprise. One tentatively noted that the provisions were probably necessary "in order to obtain reasonable service from the natives who are unused to the benefits and obligations of continuous labour."[63] The permanent undersecretary underlined the word "benefits" and added the marginal comment "including imprisonment for offences which are in no sense criminal!" but did not suggest disallowance.[64] The major concern within the office was that the ordinance contained provisions not only from Gold Coast law, but also from that of the Transvaal, where the use of Chinese indentured labor brought in under statute[65] had recently been the subject of enormous political controversy in the United Kingdom. However, although officials were well aware of such major contemporary issues, they lacked the detailed knowledge of master and servant legislation to recognize that although the EAP ordinance included clauses of the Gold Coast legislation designed to encourage civil procedures, an additional provision gave magistrates wide discretion to impose criminal penalties. Although penalties were more lenient, the Transvaal list of major and minor offenses was reproduced. The crown advocate drew up a comparative table detailing the origins of the various provisions of the ordinance, but he consistently misnumbered those sections of the Gold Coast ordinance that had been used in the draft and thus failed to highlight the new clause allowing penal sanctions.

Colonial Office officials believed the crown advocate to be the draughtsman, but Clayton and Savage have identified the authors as a subcommittee of the Colonists' Association appointed in January 1905 to consider labor law

---

61. CO 119/858, correspondence and minutes. The Cape acts in force were n.15 of 1856, n.28 of 1874, n.7 of 1875, and n.30 of 1889.

62. Initially the responsibility of the Imperial British East Africa Company (from 1891), the territory had been administered by the Foreign Office from 1895.

63. CO 533/16, W. D. Ellis minute, 12 Oct. 1906; (E.A.P.) n.8 of 1906.

64. CO 533/16, Ommanney marginal note.

65. (Transvaal) n.17 of 1904.

"following a number of demands to make contracts more binding."[66] In 1911 Colonial Office opposition to proposed Gold Coast legislation was fueled primarily by the direct involvement of the mine companies, who used their U.K. agents to discuss requirements with officials. In contrast, the central role of East African settler groups in framing the 1906 EAP ordinance was not recognized. Despite concerns about the allowance of three-year contracts, three month's imprisonment for major offenses, payment in kind, and the list of offenses copied from the Transvaal, Colonial Office officials allowed the ordinance largely because they believed, incorrectly, that it had already been in force for six months.

Unusually, the office did demand a report of the working of the 1906 ordinance that, when submitted in 1908, revealed a far from satisfactory state of affairs. In his covering dispatch, the governor admitted that although the ordinance was "as much for the protection of the native as for the benefit of the white settler, between whom the Government in the person of the various District Officers stands in the position of an arbitrator," officials had used it "to punish the native."[67] Officials now understood their proper role, but the governor thought the main problem was the Africans' ignorance of the law: "[I]t has been found in practice that a labourer who has been ill-treated generally prefers to return to his home, rather than wait and take proceedings against his employer. . . . Nor is this to be wondered at; the natives are in a low state of civilization and raw, and have not learned their rights under the Law." He believed that they would gradually come to do so without any official action.

R. W. Hamilton, principal judge in the EAP, took more practical steps. Reviewing the cases reported in the monthly returns of magistrates, he identified the most important provision of the ordinance as that giving magistrates the "widest discretionary powers of adjusting disputes"[68] and, in an attempt to encourage the use of these powers, issued a circular to magistrates in February 1907 drawing attention to the following points, among others:[69]

a. Proceedings under this Ordinance are only quasicriminal. The party complained against need not necessarily be placed in the dock and can give evidence in his own behalf. . . .

b. All process issued under the Ordinance is free. . . .

66. Clayton and Savage, *Government and Labour*, 32.
67. CO 533/42, Sadler dispatch, 25 Mar. 1908.
68. CO 533/42, R. W. Hamilton memorandum on the working of the master and servant ordinance, 11 May 1907.
69. CO 533/42, R. W. Hamilton, High Court Circular to Magistrates, no. 1 of 1907, 16 Feb. 1907.

c. The Government in fact stands in the position . . . of an arbitrator giving his services free to settle labour disputes.

d. To effect this the Collector [i.e., the magistrate][70] is given very wide discretionary powers of adjusting disputes, and his efforts should be directed to this end and the real cause of dispute thoroughly enquired into, and in cases of desertion the deserter should be carefully examined to ascertain the actual reason of his desertion.

e. The power to inflict penalties should not be resorted to except in those cases in which other adjustment is impossible or which obviously call for punishment.

f. The Magistrate must where the agreement between employer and employed exceeds one month in all cases call for the duplicate written agreement or an attested copy.

In discussing point (d), Hamilton noted cases in which potentially valid reasons for absence from work had been ignored, and workers treated as if they had pleaded guilty. Hamilton continued to be disappointed by the way the law was used. He later reviewed a case where a laborer had admitted desertion, but, in defense, claimed ill-treatment. The magistrate had not inquired into the allegation, but recorded a plea of guilty. Hamilton noted:

> In this case the Magistrate appears not to have understood clearly the meaning of the word "guilty" in a plea. A plea of guilty is an admission of the truth of all the elements of the charge, and of the absence of a defence. It is in order that this may be clearly brought out that Magistrates are directed to record the plea of an accused person in his own words. In the present instance this direction has only been partially followed with the result that the Magistrate has recorded an impossibility, viz: — a plea of guilty together with a defence.[71]

Revised EAP legislation[72] was submitted to the Colonial Office in late 1909, and considered there to be a "great advance." A section on "care of servants," which placed certain obligations on employers, was felt to be an excellent addition. An official noted that it would be "most useful for bringing to the notice of people who do not cease from troubling about native labour," demonstrating the office's growing awareness of outside criticism. Although the revised legislation was an improvement in part, the 1906 ordinance had

---

70. The term "collector" derived from Indian usage where it denoted a local official with magisterial powers.

71. *R. v. Onyinjo wa Duk*, Crim. Rev. 37/1910 (Oct. 1910), 2 E.A.P. Law Reports 109.

72. (E.A.P.) n.4 of 1910.

set a very low standard, and other clauses of the revision still caused concern. The possibility of imposing imprisonment with hard labor for absence from work was not liked, and officials had hoped for a reduction in prison terms for certain other offenses. Above all, officials disliked the reduced fine for withholding wages. The ordinance, unlike its predecessor, applied to "Arab and Native" workers only, "native" being defined as "a native of Africa not being of European or Asiatic race or origin." As in Natal in 1894, it was argued that many provisions of the new ordinance were "entirely unsuitable to contracts under which Europeans or other Non-Natives" were engaged, and that such people and their employers were sufficiently protected by the English common and statute law, and also by Indian legislation applied to the protectorate.[73]

Officials in London viewed the amendment as a tidying-up of local legal provisions and did not consider its implications for the future status of African workers. For the statute was another step in an incremental process by which the office, in the later nineteenth and early twentieth centuries, accepted an image of the African laborer as "primitive" and recreated that image in law. The result was the incorporation of unequal treatment in law, often justified in paternalist terms, precisely the kind of result that Stephen had feared and fought early in the nineteenth century. In this case, although the EAP statute led to no immediate practical change, it may have increased acceptance of harsher treatment, which would have raised objections if applied to non-African workers. The government of India was particularly concerned and had pressed the secretary of state for the colonies to appoint, in 1909, a committee to examine the working conditions of Indian migrants in British colonies. The classification in law of African workers as a special group also allowed employers to claim that their workers could not and need not enjoy conditions developed for quite different peoples. The Colonial Office apparently assumed in 1909 that the 1906 ordinance also was intended only for the control of African workers, through the emphasis on "bodily labour" in the wording of the act.

In 1920 Lord Milner, then secretary of state, publicly praised the Kenya master and servant legislation,[74] stating "it would be difficult to find a more comprehensive set of regulations to secure the well-being of natives." However, wartime amendments made under emergency regulations without referral to the Colonial Office had not only increased penalties but had also made

73. CO 533/62, H. J. Risley minute, 30 Dec. 1909. CO 533/62, A. C. C. Parkinson minute, 3 Dec. 1909. CO 533/61, memorandum by R. M. Combe, crown advocate, 12 July 1909; (Natal) n.40 of 1894.

74. For Kenya, see David Anderson in this volume.

desertion a cognizable offense, that is, one for which the police might arrest without a warrant. In 1919 the Labour MP Ben Spoor had suggested that "we shall shortly need in this Empire of ours a new Wilberforce to combat the tendency towards what might be described by many people, not as ordinary working conditions, but as very real slavery." Milner's parliamentary under-secretary, L. S. Amery, denied that the development "to the uttermost" of the resources of the empire would lead to exploitation. "The prime object, of course, of that development must be the welfare of the inhabitants of those regions. Our first duty is to them, our object is not to exploit them, but to enable them materially, as well as in every other respect, to rise to a higher plane of living and civilisation."[75]

In Africa, by the mid-1920s, the office's increased reliance on precedents had allowed legislation in the mandated territory of Tanganyika identical to Kenya's. Terms of the mandate required Britain to "protect the natives from abuse and measures of fraud and force by the careful supervision of labour contracts and the recruiting of labour,"[76] but in the office Milner's praise of the Kenyan legislation informed decision making for Tanganyika. Although Kenya and Tanganyika were dealt with by different departments within the office, criticism of Kenyan practice was so public and vociferous by this time that the Tanganyika and Somaliland Department must have been aware of it. The bill, under discussion in 1922 and 1923 at a time when the postwar regeneration of the Tanganyikan economy was only beginning, was more lenient than the Kenyan law, but despite requirements of the mandate and the lack of formal employer representation in government, the enacted ordinance copied that of Kenya exactly, retaining features of the 1856 Cape act which had by now spread northward into the territories administered by the high commissioner for South Africa and the British South Africa Company.

The perceived need for master and servant legislation in Tanganyika emerged from different circumstances than those of Sierra Leone in the early nineteenth century, or Kenya at the beginning of the twentieth. Tanganyika, as a conquered and subsequently mandated territory, had not inherited English statute and common law, but the legislation of the previous German administration. A 1909 ordinance had regulated the legal status and recruitment of African laborers and subjected them to a labor commissioner's disciplinary jurisdiction. It established a maximum contract period of seven months, or

75. *Despatch to the Governor of the East Africa Protectorate Relating to Native Labour and Papers Connected Therewith*. Cmd. 873, 1920. Parl. Deb., Commons, vol. 118, col. 2197, 2182.

76. Tanganyika Govt. Notice no. 8, 1923, "British Mandate for East Africa." See M. K. Banton, "Colonial Office Supervision of the Introduction and Revision of Labour Legislation in British Africa" (Ph.D. diss., University of London, 1993), 67–106.

180 working days within nine months (the "ticket system"), and required the registration of recruits and the licensing of recruiters. In 1907 the German colonial secretary, Bernhard Dernburg, attempted to introduce legislation based on the EAP master and servant ordinance, but had been stopped by pressure from European employers appalled to learn that such a law would place them too under the jurisdiction of officials. The 1909 ordinance imposed certain standards on employers, punishable through court proceedings initiated by a labor commissioner.

In the early years of British administration, German labor law was augmented to a limited extent by proclamations of March 1916 and September 1919, and by "regulations for peace and good order" issued in February 1919. A 1920 ordinance confirmed that German laws in place in 1914 should remain in force except where inconsistent with English law.[77] It introduced passes for Africans traveling between districts and provided for the enforcement of labor contracts with naval, military, and civil authorities. It made breach of contract a cognizable offense punishable by imprisonment for up to three months, or a fine of 1,000 rupees or florins, or both imprisonment and fine.

A government notice of September 1920 imposed a six-month limit on contracts and provided that an official witness a reengagement contract. These limitations reflected concern that the labor demands of planters were incompatible with a predominantly subsistence economy. An attempt was also made to outlaw the ticket system and to regulate employment and wage payment by the calendar month. The ticket system was regarded by British officials in Tanganyika as a German innovation, and disliked largely for that reason, but it was basically a South African device used in Kenya since 1905–6 and welcomed by settlers as a more effective method of keeping laborers at work than a system of full-time employment with monthly pay.

The 1920 notice served as a working arrangement to regulate labor relations while there was a comparatively small demand for labor for private enterprise. However, requirements of the League of Nations, together with the disposal and regeneration of ex-enemy estates, led the Tanganyikan administration by 1922 to recognize the need for more comprehensive labor legislation.[78] At a late stage in discussions with the Colonial Office (which on this occasion had been fully involved throughout) the governor, Sir Horace Byatt, made a further, unsuccessful, attempt to outlaw the ticket system. He complained that workers engaged for 180 working days might take nine, twelve, or even eighteen months to complete the contract, which exacerbated

77. (Tanganyika) n.5 of 1920.
78. (Tanganyika) n.32 of 1923.

labor shortages. Moreover, he claimed, it was "both morally and materially harmful to the native, who contracts habits of indolence and indifference."[79] Byatt overlooked the advantages of the system for both sides. Although a far less favorable picture emerges from Kenya, John Iliffe has observed that in Tanganyika "It gave migrants without wives time to cook food. It allowed for illness, exhaustion, and sheer boredom. It approximated to the work patterns of peasant agriculture . . . [furthermore] the employer could minimise his supervision costs, lay off his men cheaply when work was short, and yet know that a worker who failed to complete his contract could . . . spend six months in gaol."[80]

Evidence that the system led to inefficiency was provided by a 1926 report that "men [were] found with cards that they had had for many months, even a year; nominally they were working for a certain employer, and could plead this if called upon for any duties by their headmen."[81] This did not mean, as Byatt feared, that the system inevitably bred idleness. Many workers held tickets from more than one employer, and some were known to complete two, or even three, daily tasks for different employers in the same day. Other workers did daily-paid casual work for their employers after completion of their contract tasks.

A more contentious proposal from Byatt was that employers be permitted to withhold wages for absences from work and to inflict a fine of half-a-day's pay for each day of absence. Officials in London were uncertain: the scheme was unusual, did not exist in either Kenya or Uganda, and might concentrate too much power with employers. Sir John Risley, the legal adviser, told his colleagues that a similar system, known as the "double cut," had existed in Mauritius from 1878 until 1908 when it was replaced by a "milder provision" that might be more appropriate now. Such extraregional comparisons were rare and usually unavailable to officials in the geographical departments, but Risley would have remembered the storm that accompanied amendment of the Mauritius legislation, which had been recommended as early as 1897. The Colonial Office dealt more forcefully with Byatt's subsequent arguments than was usually the case and concluded the debate with a speed that suggests concern that he might hurry through legislation without approval.

Revision of the ordinance in 1926 legalized and regulated the thirty-day ticket system to be used alongside other legal forms of contract.[82] Workers

79. CO 691/62, Byatt dispatch, 27 Mar. 1923.
80. Iliffe, *Tanganyika*, 159.
81. Orde Browne, *Labour in Tanganyika Territory*, para. 79.
82. (Tanganyika) n.11 of 1926.

might be required to work on three days in every six, and absence without permission or "reasonable" excuse for more than six days constituted a "minor" offense. To reduce the long periods for which tickets were sometimes held, no contract could bind a worker for longer than twice the number of working days stipulated. The 1926 amendment also added provisions that wages must be paid in cash and that the death or serious injury of a worker must be reported to the nearest administrative officer. The following year a brief amending ordinance was sanctioned by the Colonial Office with no recorded comment.[83] This altered the definition of "servant" by removing all Africans employed as clerks, on the permanent establishment of the African Civil Service, or as "railway servants." Such initiatives came from Sir Donald Cameron, governor from 1925 to 1931, who recognized that the common argument that penal sanctions were essential for the regulation of workers unaccustomed to wage labor implied that such measures would be removed when a stable labor force appeared. Cameron later reduced penalties for desertion and, unsuccessfully, instigated discussions with Kenya about possible coordinated reforms. Although the Colonial Office sanctioned new Tanganyikan legislation, it did nothing to encourage similar amendment elsewhere in Africa.

The Master and Native Servants Ordinance was only part of a body of law designed to control Tanganyikan African labor. Unlike Sierra Leone, which had incorporated the regulation of vagrants in its early labor legislation, Tanganyika passed a separate Destitute Persons Ordinance empowering magistrates to order vagrants to find work, to detain them, or to send them back to their villages.[84] Colonial Office officials commented on the detail but showed no interest in the policy, regarding the East Africa Vagrancy Ordinance of 1920 as a precedent.[85] A few years later legislative provisions were introduced for particular categories of workers, a common feature of earlier English legislation. These included both the Departmental Offences Ordinance of 1927, which allowed the fining of African civil servants for offenses against labor discipline but excluded criminal procedures, and the 1928 Ordinance to Provide for the Protection of the Diamond Industry, which imposed harsh penalties for diamond theft on mine workers and merchants' employees.[86] A 1930 penal code regulated societies and assemblies, including labor organizations, and banned certain trade-union publications.[87] The wider framework

83. (Tanganyika) n.9 of 1927.

84. (Tanganyika) n.1 of 1923.

85. (E.A.P.) n.9 of 1920. The East Africa Protectorate became the crown colony of Kenya in 1920.

86. (Tanganyika) n.8 of 1927; (Tanganyika) n.21 of 1928.

87. (Tanganyika) n.11 of 1930.

on which such legislation rested—the use of forced (or "communal" or "voluntary") unpaid labor, the manipulation of taxation to mobilize labor, and often dubious recruitment practices—has been vividly described by Shivji.[88]

In the 1920s vigorous attacks on Kenyan practice eclipsed criticism of labor policy in Tanganyika, but in 1928 a complaint to the Permanent Mandates Commission about forced labor in Tanganyika brought to the attention of the office Raymond Buell's report of "the problems which have arisen out of the impact of primitive peoples with an industrial civilisation."[89] Officials had little interest in the opinions of an outsider; E. G. Mächtig in the Tanganyika Department commented that he had not found time to read Buell's book, "but I have no regrets."[90] Colonial Office officials similarly brushed aside complaints from critics such as Lord Olivier, C. R. Buxton, E. D. Morel, and W. M. Ross.

West Indian Reform

In contrast to its position on east Africa, the office had already been engaged for some years in an attempt at reform in the West Indies, responding to political pressure from several directions. In October 1917 the St. Kitts Universal Benevolent Association (formerly the St. Kitts Trade and Labour Union but reconstituted following enactment of the Trade and Labour Unions Prohibition Ordinance of 1916) called for repeal of the local master and servant act that dated from 1849.[91] Its members stated, "We feel that the Act has outgrown its usefulness, and should not be tolerated on the Statue [*sic*] Books of a civilised community, more-over it tends to keep our people in a state of serfdom, that is detrimental to progress and British Policy."[92] While agreeing with the governor that it was not "a suitable moment for making any change in the law," Colonial Office officials noted that the Indian government had already insisted on the removal of imprisonment as a penalty from various laws dealing with labor offenses committed by Indian migrants and expressed their opinion that all West Indian master and servant laws were out of date. Indentured laborers from India and from other parts of the empire had been imported in great numbers from the middle of the nineteenth century, but the systems under which they were recruited and worked were now under sharp

88. Shivji, *Working Class*.
89. Buell, *Native Problem*.
90. CO 691/100/4, Mächtig minute, 17 Aug. 1928.
91. (St. Christopher) n.84 of 1849.
92. CO 152/356, letter from St. Kitts Universal Benevolent Association, forwarded to secretary of state by governor in Oct. 1917.

attack.[93] In 1919, expecting that widespread criticism of labor legislation in the British Caribbean would follow, the Colonial Office asked governors to amend legislation in two respects. First, imprisonment should not be allowed as a punishment for breach of contract except in default of a fine, and then it should not exceed one month, nor should the fine exceed forty shillings; second, it should be made obligatory to allow time for the payment of fines.[94]

The amendments were speedily introduced in St. Lucia, St. Vincent, Antigua, Dominica, St. Kitts, and Montserrat.[95] The government of Trinidad vetoed total implementation but retained sanctions only for breach of indenture by an apprentice,[96] and the governor of Barbados claimed that the issue did not apply since the only penalty provided was the loss of one month's wages. Jamaica undertook to amend its legislation but failed to do so. The governor of British Guiana stated that he did not feel called upon to make any alteration, except by limiting the punishment for breach of contract under the existing (1853) ordinance to a fine of twenty-four dollars. For reasons that could not later be identified, no approach was made to Bermuda.[97] No further action was taken in the Colonial Office until 1927 when a master and servant ordinance enacted for the Virgin Islands, which had not previously had such legislation, was disallowed, and Sir Gilbert Grindle, deputy permanent undersecretary, reopened the general question of the use of penal sanctions for breach of labor contracts in the West Indian colonies.

There was no consensus of opinion within the West Indian Department. Although some officials wanted to encourage governors to abolish all criminal proceedings for breach of contract by a worker, others argued the legislation was obsolete and not much used. Another believed there was not "a particle of evidence" to suggest that existing legislation caused hardship, or "that there is any local demand among the labouring classes for its repeal."[98] One of the assistant legal advisers claimed that "the actual provisions if administered reasonably cannot be regarded as oppressive."[99] E. R. Darnley, head of the department, admitted that "we must give up Bermuda as impervious to suggestions from us," but insisted on pressing for reform in British Guiana and Jamaica. Echoing Stephen's criticisms of the Cape drafts in 1841, he stated,

93. See Mohapatra in this volume.

94. CO 152/364, dispatch to West Indies governors, 26 Sept. 1919.

95. (St. Vincent) n.1 of 1920; (Antigua) n.3 of 1922; (Montserrat) n.17 of 1922; also (Grenada) n.24 of 1919.

96. (Trinidad & Tobago) n.38 of 1921.

97. Traditionally Bermuda had been dealt with by the North America departments rather than the West Indian.

98. CO 318/393/10, L. B. Freeston minute, 12 June 1928.

99. CO 318/393/10, S. M. Campbell minute quoting opinion of A. Ehrhardt, 12 June 1928.

"It may be well not to push reforming zeal too far, but there are certain serious drawbacks about leaving on the Statute Books legislation reeking with the taint of slavery, and providing for insolence, misdemeanour, miscarriage, ill-behaviour and other obsolete and undefinable offences."[100] He instigated a thorough examination of existing laws, and dispatches were sent to governors spelling out the reforms required. Replies were less than satisfactory, but even Darnley agreed that little more could be done at that stage. For the first time, however, he was able to ensure an ongoing (if temporary) review of the West Indian legislation. Papers were regularly recirculated within the department, and where a governor was known to be particularly reluctant to implement change, the matter was tactfully dropped but reopened when his successor was in post. Officials in London examined existing legislation with more care, rather than unquestioningly accepting reports from the colonies. In 1930, for example, they found that although the governor of Barbados had previously claimed that no penal sanctions existed in the island's master and servant laws, there were provisions under which domestic servants could be imprisoned, with or without hard labor, and without the option of a fine, for such misdemeanors as "wilful negligence or improper conduct causing injury to property" and "insolence, misbehaviour, or insubordination."[101] Although the first was included in the 1838 model, a fine had been a possible penalty. Now, as Darnley expressed it, "Mary Jane" could be imprisoned for breaking a teacup.

The statements of Colonial Office officials rarely demonstrate any detailed knowledge of the labor needs of the various territories. The distinction that appears from the records to have been uppermost in their minds in dealing with the Caribbean and with East Africa was that between the "experienced" and the "primitive" wage laborer. In the early years of the twentieth century they were also more confident in their dealings with the West Indian colonies, with which they had a long familiarity. For the governors and their staffs the reality lay in local labor demand and availability. In the new and expanding settler economies of East Africa some means had to be found of providing the necessary labor. As Lord Olivier noted, these colonies were not advertised "as countries in which the white man could take up his burden, but as profitable and delightful places of residence for young Englishmen with a little capital."[102] In stark contrast the Caribbean colonies were already experiencing unemployment, with consequent migrations, which was to rise to acute levels in the 1930s. Inducing people to work was no longer the priority. The

100. CO 318/393/10, E. R. Darnley minute, 27 June 1928.
101. (Barbados) c.56 of 1891.
102. Olivier, *White Capital and Coloured Labour*, 21.

Colonial Office seems rarely to have appreciated that colonial governments were themselves large-scale employers and thus often sympathetic to the difficulties experienced by other local employers. In a new territory, as Lugard mentioned in 1899, the demands of the public works departments, and others, were considerable.

Reform Frustrated: The Colonial Labour Committee

In 1929 the election in the United Kingdom of the second Labour government brought new influences and interests into the Colonial Office. Although Lord Passfield's concern for colonial workers was not what one might have expected from the coauthor of *The History of Trade Unionism*, his presence in the office gave a growing lobby within the Labour Party direct access to the policy makers. His parliamentary undersecretary, Dr. T. Drummond Shiels, provided the "reforming zeal" and pushed the policy formulated by Leonard Woolf's Advisory Committee on Imperial Questions, often making himself unpopular with the permanent officials in the process. In November 1929 James Maxton MP complained about the "shocking conditions of the native [*sic*] population in the British West Indies," citing legislation that constituted "a peculiar device for perpetuating the economic slavery of the people."[103] Officials were anxious to play down the charges, but Shiels demanded an enquiry into the working of the master and servant ordinances. Passfield could not risk being accused of taking a less active role in this matter than his Conservative predecessor, and he approved further efforts to repeal obsolete West Indian legislation and to substitute statutes based on a St. Vincent ordinance.[104] Days after commenting on the draft reply to Maxton, Shiels received amending legislation from North Borneo[105] that provided corporal punishment, in addition to a fine or imprisonment, for willful breach of contract likely to "cause riot or danger to life or property," and he called for a complete overhaul of colonial labor legislation. By this time the ILO had agreed, in the face of strong opposition from employers, that a labor system based on long-term contracts, enforced by penal sanctions, constituted a form of labor restraint that should be the subject of a special study. Shiels objected to the

103. CO 318/396/12, James Maxton MP to Passfield, 24 Nov. 1929.
104. Although in 1933 governors were advised that the St. Vincent statute (n.30 of 1839, as amended by n.1 of 1920) should not after all be regarded as a satisfactory model as it was "open to objection on the ground that in section 19(1) provision is made for a penal sanction in respect of neglect of work or improper performance of an agreement by a servant." CO 318/403/5, dispatches to certain West Indian governors, 12 May 1933.
105. (British North Borneo) n.2 of 1929.

North Borneo provisions, but in the face of official opinion that it would be unwise to confront the North Borneo Company directly, he agreed to proceed more generally with a circular dispatch, of 6 August 1930, calling for the elimination of penal sanctions throughout the empire, a full examination of labor conditions, and a commitment to conform to international labor conventions. R. V. Vernon, head of the General Department, drafted the dispatch and Shiels concurred, but there is no evidence that Passfield saw the file. Shiels wanted to draw up a statement of general principles "representing the ideals to be aimed at," which could then be considered by region, with modifications introduced to meet local conditions. At this stage the labor legislation of each colony should be reviewed. Shiels thought it imperative that a general review should be carried out centrally, rather than asking governors to examine local conditions against a statement of agreed principles. Perhaps hoping for a new James Stephen, he suggested that an additional member of staff, preferably a lawyer, should be appointed, but Passfield, acting on the advice of senior officials, refused to approach the Treasury for funding. Instead he agreed that an interdepartmental committee, chaired by Shiels, might establish "general lines of policy," with the mechanics of application left for later discussion.[106]

Shiels wanted the committee to review the "more advanced" territories of the West Indies and Malaya first, since they required modern labor legislation most urgently. Other committee members, however, preferred a consistent approach throughout the empire but also agreed that master and servant ordinances (particularly penal sanctions for breach of written and verbal contracts), factory legislation, minimum wage–fixing machinery, the application of international labor conventions, and similar issues should have priority. Imperial consistency was, in this context, quite meaningless, of course, given that since the establishment of the Dominions Office in 1925 the Colonial Office had no voice in developments in southern Africa, which continued, as they had since the 1856 Cape statute, to influence practice elsewhere in Africa. Shiels had asked, unsuccessfully, for Dominions Office representation on the committee. As well as labor legislation per se, the committee would consider related legislation: vagrancy law, registration, land tenure, and taxation. It would look first at master and servant laws, which some members felt "contain

106. CO 323/1071/13, T. D. Shiels minute, 9 Jan. 1930. CO 323/1071/13, G. Grindle minute, 10 Feb. 1930. CO 323/1117/5, minutes of meeting of 20 Apr. 1931. The committee included representatives of the Ministry of Labour and the Home Office, then responsible for factory legislation. Shiels failed to persuade Passfield and officials that it would be appropriate to invite the general secretary of the Trades Union Congress to attend. CO 323/1117/5, Passfield minute, 11 May 1931.

provisions which are relics of a stage of development almost approximating to Slavery."[107]

Not all officials were happy with this program. Some suggested waiting until replies to the August 1930 circular had been received and considered, arguing that conditions varied so widely that no general legislative standard could be formulated. They feared that imposing a general standard from London would produce local resentment and might prove impossible in colonies where the governor did not have complete control of the legislature. Although Shiels was fully aware of this problem and had previously called for wider colonial franchises, he was not prepared to accept such an excuse for inaction. His Colonial Labour Committee (CLC) would "recommend standards to which it is desirable that all Colonies should ultimately confirm, but also . . . indicate what departures from this standard may temporarily be permitted in dependencies, or groups of dependencies, in various stages of development."[108]

At its second meeting the committee examined provisions normally included in master and servant laws. The relative merits of written and verbal contracts were explored, and the positive results of a general abolition of penal sanctions discussed. The widely differing current practice in various parts of the empire was quickly revealed, and the committee decided that it was impossible to legislate uniformly for "(a) the more primitive peoples (e.g. those in Africa and the Western Pacific), and (b) the more civilised peoples (e.g. in Malaya and the West Indies)." The laws of Africa and the Western Pacific should be dealt with first. This decision reversed the original intention of starting with the West Indies, where some groundwork had been done. It may also be seen as a diversionary tactic designed by some officials to steer Shiels's enthusiasm into an area where discussion was least likely to lead to early action.

Members of the committee quickly realized the difficulty of proceeding without details of the extent to which criminal penalties were applied. Figures were provided by J. F. N. Green for Tanganyika, but he stressed that where statistics were collated from different sources, such as reports of prisons, police, and labor departments, their reliability was doubtful. Furthermore, the office had insufficient information to allow meaningful analysis. The importance of a systematic collection of statistics had, to a certain extent, been recognized within the office. In 1918 a committee appointed to review the content and use of annual "blue books" of statistics asked for the inclusion of information about labor, agriculture, and industry. In 1919 the Colonial

107. CO 323/1117/7, CLC Minutes (1), 22 May 1931.
108. Ibid.

Research Committee requested the collection of labor information, as did the Imperial Mineral Resources Bureau, the International Health Commission, and the organizers of the Imperial Forestry Conference. At its first session in 1920, the British Empire Statistical Conference set up a Labour Statistics Committee and recommended the collection and systematized use of statistics in advance of inevitable demands from the ILO. But the Colonial Office had had ready access to details of convictions under labor legislation only once before, when they were collected for Indian migrants in the colonies in 1911–13.

The committee members studied summaries of master and servant statutes, and agreed that breach of contract could be satisfactorily handled on a civil basis by the existing legal machinery. That is, complaints made by either party should continue to be dealt with summarily by a magistrate or appropriate administrative officer. They recommended that offenses should be divided between those to remain within a labor code and to be regarded as simple breach of contract, and those to be removed from labor legislation and dealt with under existing, or revised, criminal law.

Two senior officials, heads of the West Africa and East Africa departments, who had not attended committee meetings because of Shiels's proposed emphasis on the West Indies and Malaya, grew alarmed by reports of its deliberations. At its next meeting, they presented inflexible opposition to the removal of penal sanctions and expressed doubts that committee members had sufficient knowledge of local conditions or of "native mentality" to know whether the removal of sanctions "would be likely to lead to the demoralisation of the labour forces, with, e.g., a consequent increase in the number of desertions, and other such acts."[109] Green pointed out that in Tanganyika attractive conditions of service had been found to ensure "the least trouble with . . . workers." He continued:

> [T]he retention of penal sanctions removes the incentive to a bad employer to improve the conditions under which his labourers work. The object to be aimed at should be a state of affairs where the worker willingly engages himself and remains at work because he is satisfied with his wages and other conditions of service. Penal sanctions should not be used to compel natives to remain at work under bad conditions.[110]

Shiels restored a measure of agreement by stressing that the committee was presently concerned not with immediate reform but with the general question of whether the office should aim for the elimination of penal sanc-

109. CO 323/1117/7, CLC Minutes (5), 26 June 1931.
110. CO 323/1117/7.

tions and, if so, how best to bring this about. Provisional recommendations were subsequently discussed with west African officials, who stated that employers rarely used the legislation and most actions were brought by employees. Broad agreement had also been indicated by east African officials in the United Kingdom. C. M. Dobbs, a Kenyan senior commissioner, had, however, presented a purely personal view, which can be discounted as in any way indicative of the Kenya government's position: "Of course I only employed a few natives—house boys, garden boys etc., but I would certainly never try to use the law to compel any boy to continue to work for me if he wished to leave, nor would I feel inclined to punish him if he left me." He would be only too happy to see desertion made a civil matter, except in the case of desertion with an advance of pay, which "is tantamount to cheating."[111]

In contrast, a letter from P. E. Mitchell, then senior native commissioner in Tanganyika, was detailed and informed and reflected a position already familiar to some officials from discussions with the governor. Mitchell deplored the growing tendency in east Africa for the "agricultural vote," that is, the European settler community, to bring pressure on governments to be influenced by the increasing severity on laborers in South African legislation: "From an East African point of view therefore it is in my judgment important that there should be as little delay as possible in getting labour legislation free of these objectionable features, and of penal clauses for matters which are not in their nature criminal, and in making it clear that freedom from these things is a matter of principle."[112]

He believed that offenses that master and servant legislation classed together should be divided into three groups: criminal offenses such as those endangering the health or safety of others; actions causing loss, directly or indirectly, to individual employers or employees; and mere breaches of contract. The first, Mitchell suggested, should be incorporated into ordinary criminal law. The last would be properly dealt with by way of liquidated damages under the summary procedure described in the CLC draft recommendations. The second could probably be dealt with in the same way, but some limitation of liability would be necessary since courts might assess loss to employers at rates that would almost certainly lead to imprisonment of the worker. An officer with power to sue on the worker's behalf should be appointed as a further safeguard. Mitchell believed that damages were better than fines because they emulated customary law and would be more readily understood by Afri-

111. CO 888/1, CLC 23, "Draft provisional recommendations regarding penal sanctions for the enforcement of labour contracts in the more primitive territories," extract from letter from C. M. Dobbs.
112. CO 888/1, CLC 21, P. E. Mitchell memorandum, 9 July 1931.

cans. He further stressed the necessity of ensuring, by wide publicity in the vernacular languages, that workers understood the regulations under which they worked. He advised extreme caution in dealing with desertion, claiming that it was sometimes provoked by employers toward the end of a contract in order to "immobilise labour and prevent it from seeking the best market and also as an excuse for not paying repatriation expenses." Mitchell's detailed response introduced members of the CLC to a range of practical local issues of which they were usually unaware.

Shiels's initiative was short-lived, not surviving the change of government in August 1931, and although CLC recommendations for the abolition of penal sanctions in the "more primitive territories" were finalized and circulated to governors of African and Pacific colonies in January 1932, there was no pressure for implementation. Although west African governments quickly agreed that local legislation could be amended to meet most recommendations, replies from central and east Africa were delayed and negative. While expressing general agreement with the ideals of the report, all, with the exception of Tanganyika, claimed that it was impossible to implement recommendations in the foreseeable future.[113] The reasons were familiar. Uganda claimed that the worker's "moral education is still at that more elementary stage where it is of more immediate urgency to inculcate some idea of the sanctity of an engagement," and stressed the difficulty of tracing deserters and the impossibility of recovering damages from men "of no immediate ascertainable property except the clothes, if any, in which they stand." Nyasaland foresaw increased breach of contract, and the disorganization of labor conditions. Northern Rhodesia believed that if penal sanctions were abolished for employees they must also be abolished for employers, leading to increased instances of illegal punishment by employers. The governor of Kenya, having waited to see his colleagues' replies, agreed with their reservations and stressed "the defenceless position in which the native labourer would be left if penal sanctions were abolished," also referring to widespread illegal punishment. Even Tanganyika took a step back from the positive position expressed by Mitchell. It now merely proposed to "consider" the elimination of those penal sanctions which were rarely used, and to encourage magistrates to make more use of the civil procedures already available. No amendment of the legislation resulted.

In the early weeks of 1931, before the establishment of the CLC, the Colonial Office had been discussing draft Tanganyikan legislation submitted by Donald Cameron. Cameron was convinced that master and servant law

---

113. CO 323/1209/14, dispatches from governors, 1932.

should be made to apply less and less to literate employees: "It seems absurd that such a special piece of legislation designed in the first instance for a primitive stage of society should apply to skilled and highly paid artisans who should engage for service on the ordinary basis of civil contract." He proposed that new legislation should "restrict its scope to those classes which stand in need of protection or discipline." Vernon regarded his proposals as "a real advance on the lines which we desire to encourage," and praised Cameron's hard work and "judicious pressure in the right direction." He delayed approval, however, because he was anxious to discuss the possibility of removing certain penal clauses covering drunkenness, failure to obey orders, giving a false name or address, failure to report the death or loss of an animal, and desertion. Having no familiarity with east African master and servant law, he incorrectly assumed these were new. Green found that proposed Tanganyikan legislation was already more liberal than that of Kenya, Uganda, or Northern Rhodesia. It would be difficult, he believed, to press the Tanganyikan government to go further without insisting on the same standard in neighboring territories. "In fact," he emphasized, "the whole question turns on the extent to which we are prepared to deal with Kenya. Tanganyika white opinion will, I am sure, go as far or further than Kenya is pushed." Shiels asked for the draft to go to the CLC to familiarize members with progress in Tanganyika and Cameron's suggestions for further improvement. However, Cameron left Tanganyika in February 1931 to become governor of Nigeria, and there was no indication that his successor had any interest in pursuing the matter. Without the new governor's endorsement, officials would not put Cameron's draft to the CLC; neither did it become law.[114]

After the change of government in 1931, the CLC met infrequently and had entirely abandoned Shiels's program of work. Shiels had hoped that Green would take over as chairman, but Green declined. He stated only that a more senior official was required to ensure progress, but there was little possibility that he would have been appointed; he was known as an active Labour Party supporter who had attended meetings of the party's Advisory Committee on Imperial Questions. Shiels's successor, the Liberal MP Sir Robert Hamilton, who had shown such interest in the EAP master and servant law twenty years earlier, also refused to take over the chairmanship, citing pressure of other work.

114. CO 691/117/7, Cameron dispatch, 29 Jan. 1931. CO 691/117/7, R. V. Vernon minute, 21 Mar. 1931. CO 691/117/7, J. F. N. Green minute, 18 Apr. 1931.

Managing the "Primitive" Worker

From the late nineteenth century until the 1930s, the Colonial Office made no general attempt to reform colonial master and servant law, largely because of a persistent belief that most colonial workers, particularly African workers, were insufficiently advanced to be regulated by modern employment law. Stephen and Rogers had denied that a regular work force could be procured and retained only by coercion and force, believing that even those totally unfamiliar with wage labor could quickly become skilled and valuable employees fully entitled to demand wages and conditions appropriate to their essential role within the colonial economies. Stephen and his political masters had also argued that a "primitive" work force, that is, the newly emancipated slaves of the Caribbean, needed protection, in the form of more lenient vagrancy and contract laws than those regulating the "advanced" work force of England, during a period of unaccustomed working relations. Similarly, they should be given greater powers of redress against their employers. In reviewing legislation drafted in the colonies, Stephen quickly identified provisions benefiting the employer, noting in 1840, for example, that a clause of the Cape legislation requiring a worker to give one month's notice, even where the contract was for one month only, was "very likely to degenerate into a restraint from which ignorant people will never be able to rescue themselves."[115] Lord Stanley, as secretary of state in 1858, suggested that the stage of development of the colonial administration was also relevant.

In the 1870s, when the Gold Coast postemancipation legislation was discussed, the view that inexperienced workers required protection against possibly unscrupulous employers, and against "imprudent bargains," continued. Long contracts were outlawed, and provisions made for contracts to be explained to illiterate people.

By the 1890s, however, official concern for an inexperienced work force was less marked. While pointing out that the office was "supposed to look after the natives and see that they are not oppressed," Fairfield showed no enthusiasm for ensuring this. In the period of the new imperialism, the views of Stephen and Rogers were replaced by a general acceptance that until a colonial work force became accustomed to regular wage labor it could be regulated only by harsher provisions than were appropriate in a more "advanced" economy. This message came not only from officials and employers but also from missionary commentators: "[O]ne knows that the Native must learn to persist in tasks that pall and to be faithful to promises of which he has repented, or

115. CO 48/207, J. Stephen to Vernon Smith, 10 Oct. 1840.

he can never make much moral progress." Others claimed that penal sanctions were necessary to promote industrial education: "If the African is to advance towards collective bargaining and attain a position where he can sell his labour to the best advantage, he must learn the nature of a contract." Although colonial officials believed that a reliable African work force needed to be fostered through the labor contract system, they refused to translate statutes into African languages or otherwise ensure an understanding of their provisions. It was not until the Colonial Labour Advisory Committee considered legislation to control strikes and lockouts in essential services after the Second World War that the Colonial Office suggested that regulations should be posted in workplaces. Many colonial officials described penal sanctions as merely an expedient designed to meet the particular conditions existing in "primitive countries" but, with very few exceptions, they made no attempt to remove experienced and skilled workers from the provisions of master and servant law, or to make separate regulations for the control of workers entering into a second or subsequent contract with the same employer. Within the Colonial Office there was a stereotyped view of "the African worker." As Bushe admitted in 1935, "[W]hen I came to the Colonial Office . . . I obtained the conception of a standard native with a black skin and a definite mentality and outlook and custom which might be regarded as common to Africa."[116]

By the late 1930s, many Colonial Office officials had accepted the argument that the African worker was not sufficiently advanced for modern employment practices. The official line became "the elimination of penal sanctions from laws governing the relation of master and servant is an ideal to be kept constantly in mind with a view to action being taken as and when the social progress of the native renders it practicable." Lord Hailey took this same "evolutionary" view in *An African Survey*, and the first labor adviser to the secretary of state, G. St. J. Orde Browne, expressed his opinion that calls for the abolition of penal sanctions were obstructive and "calculated to impede the African's progress and keep him a permanent child." Although Colonial Office officials tended to accept that there was a clear distinction between the "developed" and the "primitive" worker, the views of colonial officials and employers in different geographical areas varied little. When, in 1936, the British Honduras attorney general claimed, "It is extremely doubtful whether the majority of workers of this Colony can be said to be sufficiently evolved to understand the binding nature of contracts," Vernon responded irritably, "I do not think the A.G. is 'sufficiently evolved' to appreciate the difference

116. Willoughby, *Race Problems*, 204. Bodleian Library of Commonwealth and African Studies at Rhodes House, Orde Browne Papers (hereafter OBP), box 2/1, f. 136, n.d. H. G. Bushe, address to the African Circle, 20 Feb. 1935.

between civil contract and criminal law." But identical statements from the governments of east Africa were uncritically accepted.[117]

Furthermore, throughout the interwar period, despite attempts to introduce some coordination of practice and the beginnings of a coherent imperial policy in subject areas such as agriculture, health, and education, policy making within the Colonial Office was still dominated by the geographical departments that worked largely in isolation and dealt with issues pertaining solely to their own territories on an ad hoc basis or according to departmental precedents. Lack of formal communication between the departments obscured inconsistencies in policy and practice. In 1927 an official in the West Indian Department pinpointed this problem when he recommended disallowing a Virgin Islands master and servant ordinance: "I can trace no discussion of the general attitude we should adopt to this kind of legislation, i.e. whether to regard it as on the whole good, subject to certain alterations or to regard it as on the whole bad, to be tolerated as a concession to local opinion and to be restricted as much as possible."[118]

Not only was there no "general attitude," but there was often no appropriate knowledge of local conditions. Officials reviewing master and servant legislation tended to view it in isolation without considering its relationship to vagrancy, registration, and other related laws, or the extent to which legislative detail might be changed by the issue of regulations that were not required to be referred to the office. For example, in 1925 regulations in Tanganyika extended maximum contract periods from six to twelve months, thus removing a safeguard, previously commended by the Colonial Office, that enabled wage employment and a subsistence economy to coexist.[119] Officials also tended to assume that all colonial workers were on contracts, whether written or verbal, and therefore subject to the master and servant laws, whereas many employers believed that the master and servant law might be circumvented by employing workers as day laborers. They showed no interest in the development of case law, and rarely recognized the continuing use of Indian legislation in east Africa, or Roman Dutch law in southern Africa. Furthermore, the office lacked a reliable institutional "memory" despite its efficient systems of record keeping, and officials failed to build on expertise developed by their predecessors. They also became increasingly hostile to suggestions from outsiders who could genuinely claim to be experts in the field, notably officials of

117. CO 323/1429/7, Vernon to Margaret Bryant, Royal Institute of International Affairs, 31 May 1937. OBP, box 2/1, "Notes on the proposed programme of work for the Committee of Experts on Native Labour," f. 137, n.d. CO 318/423/6, report of British Honduras attorney general, A. McKinstry, 8 Sept. 1936. CO 318/423/6, Vernon minute, 22 Dec. 1936.

118. CO 152/403/13, S. Caine minute, 29 June 1927.

119. Reg. N.44 (1925) under (Tanganyika) n.32 of 1923.

the International Labour Organisation and the British Ministry of Labour, as well as a range of interested organizations and individuals.

The ILO: Abolishing the "Relic of Slavery"

When the Colonial Labour Committee restricted its 1931 review to the "primitive" work forces of Africa and the western Pacific, it stalled the West Indian Department's initiative of the late 1920s. Darnley, who had pressed so hard for reform, deferred further action to avoid making decisions counter to the committee's recommendations. He left the department during 1931. As the CLC made no recommendations for the Caribbean, the West Indian Department subsequently assumed that outstanding matters should "proceed departmentally subject to legal advice where required,"[120] but when other matters took priority, the paperwork was passed to the General Department for action. Disagreements between the General and geographical departments ensued, as the former refused to examine legislation, or to refer it to the CLC, with consequent delays in the reform of legislation both in the West Indies and in Tanganyika.

In 1932 the West Indian Department suggested that the recommendations of the CLC on penal sanctions "may be taken as an exposition of Secretary of State's policy on this question."[121] J. J. Paskin, labor coordinator within the General Department and secretary of the CLC, disagreed: "I do not think this can be regarded as an accurate statement of the position, as the recommendations represent only the views of the Committee, and only in relation to the territories which were under consideration. . . . Even in relation to those territories the Secretary of State did no more than express himself as being 'in general sympathy' with the Committee's recommendations." The West Indian Department was free to circulate CLC recommendations, but he emphasized that they had been drawn up for Africa and the western Pacific and "have been found at any rate not altogether suitable even for those places."[122]

In October 1933 Paskin recommended delaying reform of Leeward Islands legislation in view of the governor's statement that introduction would be difficult "at the present time of strong political agitation and racial ill-feeling,"[123] and he asked for piecemeal considerations of penal sanctions to be deferred until the ILO's Committee of Experts on Native Labour finalized its report on the terms of labor contracts. The report was completed during 1935

---

120. CO 318/403/4, S. M. Campbell, 22 Oct. 1931.
121. CO 318/403/5, S. E. V. Luke, quoted by Paskin.
122. CO 318/403/5, Paskin minute, 6 Jan. 1933.
123. CO 318/412/14, Paskin minute, 13 Oct. 1933.

and circulated to governors; it recommended the immediate abolition of penal sanctions. Early the following year, however, when a Labour MP described the Antigua master and servant ordinance as "a hopelessly out-of-date law, only made use of by scoundrels,"[124] Vernon, who had been Shiels's ally, stressed that the covering dispatch "did not actually call for a reply and will very likely not receive one":

> The result of all this is that reasons (may I say "pretexts"?) have been found from time to time for postponing amending legislation of the need for which there can really be no sort of question. These provisions in West Indian laws treating breaches of contract as penal offences are of course an inheritance from the period immediately following the abolition of slavery. They are absolutely out of date now; cannot possibly be justified by the British Government at Geneva; and I think it is time to tell the West Indies to get rid of them once for all before the question of the terms of contracts of employment comes up for consideration before the International Labour Conference.[125]

Despite the withdrawal of real ministerial support after 1931, Malcolm MacDonald and W. G. A. Ormsby-Gore, secretaries of state in the late 1930s, recognized that it would be inexpedient for the British government to be seen to obstruct developments led by Geneva. A new generation of Colonial Office officials was more sympathetic to reform of the law, and more willing to cooperate with others working toward the same goals, although the ILO and the Ministry of Labour were still regarded with some suspicion. When J. G. Hibbert replaced Paskin in 1936, he took up his duties with enthusiasm, quickly identifying employers as the primary obstacle to progress, especially in east Africa, and attacking their "awful oafish attitude" with gusto.

In 1937 increased pressure from the ILO and from MPs worried about labor unrest in Trinidad forced the office to examine again the subject of contracts of employment enforced by penal sanctions, this time in respect of all the territories for which it was responsible. Only then did it discover the extent to which a law described by the ILO as a "relic of slavery" was retained. The ILO was anxious to abolish penal sanctions for all contracts of employment, both written and verbal, but within the Colonial Office it was becoming increasingly clear that although the British government was responsible for the application of international conventions to dependent territories, it was often unable to impose amendments to colonial legislation. The office, repre-

124. CO 318/423/6, extract of a report of meeting between Susan Lawrence MP and Sir Cosmo Parkinson, n.d.
125. CO 318/423/6, Vernon minute, 24 Apr. 1936.

sented on the British government delegation to International Labour Conferences, delayed action by securing agreement that an initial convention on written contracts only should exclude the abolition of penal sanctions, which would be dealt with separately at a later date.

The Penal Sanctions (Indigenous Workers) Convention (no. 65) was finally agreed in 1939. It required penal sanctions to be abolished "progressively and as soon as possible," and immediately in the case of juveniles, but for certain offenses only. These were refusal or failure to commence service stipulated in a contract, refusal or failure to perform service stipulated, absence without permission or valid reason, neglect of duty, lack of diligence, and desertion. Application of the convention would thus allow retention of criminal penalties for such offenses as drunkenness, abusive or insulting language, using an employer's property without permission, damage, loss or serious risk to employer's property, and failure to report the death or loss of an animal. Despite these limitations, many governors considered application of the convention impossible. After consulting them, Colonial Office officials forecast, by no means accurately, that it should be possible to guarantee abolition of penal sanctions "progressively and as soon as possible" in Kenya, Northern Rhodesia, Nyasaland, Somaliland, Tanganyika, Uganda, Zanzibar, Sierra Leone, Seychelles, British Honduras, Jamaica, Fiji, British Solomon Islands, Gilbert and Ellice Islands, and Tonga. All relevant sanctions had already been abolished in a further seventeen territories. The office failed to agree with local governments that early abolition would be possible in Gibraltar, Malta, Cyprus, the Falklands, the Bahamas, Bermuda, British Guiana, the three South Africa High Commission territories of Basutoland, Bechuanaland, and Swaziland, Palestine, Transjordan, and the New Hebrides.[126] Consultation revealed the existence of penal sanctions enforcing contracts of employment in colonies that had not previously been recognized as having such legislation. Subsequently, the "small struggles" anticipated by Rogers multiplied and became increasingly intractable as officials struggled, with very limited success, to meet international demands for the reform of employment law.

It had always been difficult for officials in the Colonial Office to keep abreast of labor developments throughout the empire. The coordinating role of the General Department had been only partially successful, and in 1939 a Social Services Department was established whose remit included labor.

126. In the case of Palestine, Trans-Jordan, and the New Hebrides it was believed that no penal sanctions existed, but there was uncertainty because of the continued application of Ottoman law in the first two territories, and the mix of two legal systems in the Anglo-French condominium of the New Hebrides.

However, five years earlier a specialist Economic Department had been set up, and this division of responsibility resulted in a situation where officials responsible for the regulation of labor worked in isolation from those dealing with economic development, who often had more practical knowledge of labor requirements.

The outbreak of war delayed ratification and application of the penal sanctions convention. Harold Macmillan, parliamentary undersecretary from February 1942, commented that "The Conventions cannot become effective until two Member States ratify. . . . What other country is likely to ratify in existing circumstances? In the present state of the world, the whole thing seems to me rather unreal. In any case are there any commitments in the Convention which might prove hampering in war conditions?"[127]

Similar protests came from the colonies, but senior officials, reminded by Hibbert that both the previous secretary of state, Lord Moyne, and the minister of labour, Ernest Bevin, had told Parliament that the convention would be ratified, agreed that "we have little or no option in the matter."[128] Bevin subsequently became personally and incisively involved and pressed both the Colonial Office and the Dominions Office to approach governors who opposed application of the convention. Great Britain ratified the convention in January 1943, but, as Macmillan had predicted, no other member state ratified in wartime. The convention came into effect in June 1948.

Despite delayed ratification, in the early years of the war Hibbert pressed for reform of master and servant law. He welcomed the early decisions of Kenya, Northern Rhodesia, and Zanzibar to remove penal sanctions for juveniles and, in the case of the latter two, some that applied to adults, and he persuaded his superiors to seek improvements in Uganda, Tanganyika, and Nyasaland. All responded positively, although Uganda's governor, while anxious to abolish "out-moded and objectionable provisions and limitations,"[129] found it impossible to secure more than minimal improvements. Like Hibbert, he blamed employers, describing their views as "an expression of ill-informed obscurantism," but he entrusted examination of draft legislation to a committee with strong employer representation and claimed that it was impossible to obtain the opinion of workers or to identify anyone prepared to represent their interests.[130]

The worker's opinion rarely features in Colonial Office records. The mention of specific individuals in the Gambia in 1857–58 is a rarity, and it is not

127. CO 859/52/4, Macmillan minute, 24 Feb. 1942.
128. CO 859/52/4, Parkinson minute, 26 Feb. 1942.
129. CO 859/52/7, Dundas dispatch, 12 Dec. 1941.
130. CO 859/52/8, Dundas dispatch, 6 Aug. 1942.

until organized labor made its voice heard in distant London, by petition as from St. Kitts in 1917 or, more commonly, through the widespread labor unrest of the 1930s, that it began to impinge on the work of the office. Reports about individuals that did come to the attention of the office usually concerned major abuse, such as an incident in 1924 when a Tanganyikan sisal planter killed a worker who had provoked him, he said, by being "stupid, disobedient and lazy."[131]

While Hibbert was attempting to implement the penal sanctions convention and, indeed, to secure a practical improvement on its minimum provisions, emergency wartime regulations were formulated that increased penalties for breach of contract for many colonial workers. It was difficult for the Colonial Office to monitor developments, partly because of communications problems but primarily because the powers of governors had been extended by the Emergency Powers (Colonial Defence) Order in Council of 1939. In May 1941 Hibbert complained:

> In this loathsome era of Government by Order in Council Colonial Governments are having the time of their lives, and are passing all sorts of regulations under the Emergency Defence Laws, which normally would form the subject of Ordinances and have to be referred to the Colonial Office, and upon which a grandmotherly Colonial Office might occasionally frown. At the present time, the first intimation we here receive that such regulations have been made is by seeing them in the Gazettes.[132]

Emergency legislation regulated workers in employment deemed essential to the war effort, allowed conscription of civilian workers, and outlawed strikes and lockouts in essential services. In May 1942, for example, Northern Rhodesia promulgated a regulation reintroducing criminal penalties for workers in essential industries, identified initially as mining and associated manufacturing and the railway, but soon extended to farming. Even Hibbert could not deny the importance of the territory's role in supplying essential raw materials: "This is very regrettable and we shall get agitated Parliamentary Questions. But, there is a war on, and the maintenance of copper production is vital to the war effort. It cannot be efficiently maintained if there is any substantial amount of misconduct or absenteeism."[133]

In 1943, Hibbert left the office on temporary secondment. No one shared

---

131. The planter was found guilty of "voluntarily causing grievous hurt" and sentenced to eighteen months' imprisonment, reduced to six months' on appeal. CO 691/70.

132. CO 859/52/7, Hibbert minute, 21 May 1941.

133. CO 795/123/6, Hibbert minute, 1 June 1942.

his enthusiasm for the revision of master and servant legislation, or his concern, and that of outside critics such as the Fabian Colonial Bureau, that wartime labor regulation might reverse the minimal progress achieved. Many officials and lay advisers predicted a gradual and largely automatic decline in the use of penal sanctions at the end of the war and a widespread acceptance of abolition, and it was not until the 1950s that the Colonial Office, again at the prompting of the ILO, reconsidered the subject systematically. With the complexity of the issue now more fully understood, in particular the extent to which penal sanctions existed within legislation outside the narrow definition of master and servant, officials recognized that they would be unable to ensure the application of any further convention to those colonies which persisted in retaining penal sanctions. In 1947 this problem had been admitted outside the office for the first time when the cabinet was informed that the constitutions of many colonies made it impossible for the British government to impose application of conventions without a special act of the imperial Parliament: "Though much can be done by persuasion, it would be contrary to our Colonial Policy to take any steps which would weaken the constitutional position of Colonial governments, for the purpose of securing the introduction of legislation for which the territories concerned are not ready."[134]

In 1951 the ILO found that although the 1939 convention had been ratified only by the United Kingdom and New Zealand, Britain was not a leader. No penal sanctions for the breaches of contract specified in the convention now existed in French, Dutch, Italian, New Zealand, or United States dependent territories, and Australia was making progress toward implementation by the enactment of new legislation for Papua–New Guinea. Conversely, such penal sanctions persisted in Kenya, Tanganyika, Zanzibar, and Northern Rhodesia, as well as in Southern Rhodesia and the High Commission Territories.

A second international convention on penal sanctions, adopted in 1955, required all penal sanctions to be abolished no later than one year after date of ratification. Despite the continuing stated policy of the Colonial Office that penal sanctions should be removed, this effectively ensured that neither the office nor the Ministry of Labour recommended British ratification. To abolish all penal sanctions within one year of ratification was recognized by even the most optimistic as totally impossible. Furthermore, the rapid movement toward decolonization made the whole subject increasingly academic. Unable to influence the final form of the convention, officials steadily advised against U.K. ratification.

Although the abolition of penal sanctions had been Colonial Office policy

134. CO 537/5223, draft joint Colonial Office and Ministry of Labour paper to Cabinet.

since 1931, lack of political will, pressure of work, limited resources, limited understanding of both local circumstances and legislative development, reluctance (and, increasingly, inability) to interfere with the policies of colonial governments, all inhibited change. Personal attitudes and assumptions about "the working man" in general and "the native labourer" in particular, confirmed by the opinions of their counterparts in the colonies, encouraged many officials to accept harsh legislative control. Conversely, sporadic attempts to veto new legislation or reform existing laws often sprang from a personal interest and initiative.

In the 1830s and early 1840s the subject would have been of major importance whatever the views of individual officials. In contrast, in the late 1920s and early 1930s, there would have been little progress in formulating a policy without the personal interest of officials such as E. R. Darnley in the West Indian Department and J. F. N. Green in the Tanganyika and Somaliland Department. Then the brief presence of Drummond Shiels enabled Darnley, Green, and R. V. Vernon in the General Department to sidestep the obstructive attitudes of more senior officials. With the removal of ministerial support after August 1931, it was difficult to press for an unpopular policy. Furthermore, Darnley moved to the Pacific and Mediterranean Department in 1931, and Green retired in 1932. At a more junior level, J. J. Paskin, the first secretary of the Colonial Labour Committee, had no enthusiasm for Shiels's proposed program of work and advised the incoming secretary of state that it should not proceed. As has been noted, he also refused to undertake subsequent examination of draft legislation, arguing that the geographical departments should resume this responsibility, and he effectively blocked further progress in some colonies, notably Tanganyika, where, in the prewar years, local governments were increasingly amenable to change. In contrast, his successor, J. G. Hibbert, demonstrated a real commitment to the implementation of an international standard.

Conclusion

Sir Frederic Rogers's perceptive statement of 1858 anticipated the "small struggles" of the next 100 years, but his belief that allowing the law to take its course would avoid acrimonious debates between the colonies and the home government was only partially correct. In effect, "allowing the law to take its course," most notably in southern Africa, merely postponed problems and made their resolution almost intractable when international pressure for reform, which Rogers could not have predicted, was directed toward the United Kingdom. He stressed that legislatures composed primarily of employers would always tend to enact legislation which would "relieve them from the necessity of humouring and improving the labouring population." Despite widespread opinion that the experience of working for European employers under a contract labor system would benefit indigenous workers materially, morally, and educationally, it was equally clear to J. F. N. Green in 1931 that the retention of penal sanctions removed any incentive for bad employers to improve the conditions under which their laborers worked. For Africa, there is evidence that although European employers habitually complained about lazy, inefficient, and unreliable workers, they often preferred "raw" recruits to more experienced workers who were aware of their own rights under the law, and anxious to seek improvements to their working conditions.

Both Sir James Stephen, in the 1830s and 1840s, and David Chalmers, in the 1870s, believed that inexperienced wage laborers, and specifically newly emancipated slaves, should be regulated less harshly than the experienced workers of Europe. Rogers and Lord Stanley, in 1858, agreed that workers in a thinly populated territory had every right to take advantage of labor shortages to drive wages up and demand better conditions. The views of employers were often in sharp contrast. In the Cape, in the 1840s and 1850s, they demanded ever harsher punishments for breach of contract, apparently choosing to believe that nothing else would ensure a reliable labor supply. In east Africa, in the early years of the twentieth century, European settlers not only wanted severe legislation but also expected government direction of labor to meet their needs. They argued that there could be no comparison between African workers, who were often migrant, impossible to trace if they deserted, and not fully dependent on their wages (having retained at least some access to a traditional subsistence economy), and the settled work forces of Europe and some of the older colonies. By securing separate legislative control of the indigenous population and other racial groups, legislators were able to perpetuate such distinctions. Officials in London in the late nineteenth and early twentieth centuries appear to have been confident that harsh and separate regulation was a temporary necessity. They did not predict the long-term influence of ever harsher legislation in southern Africa.

The Colonial Office rarely had direct experience of dealing with employers, although the London agents of large-scale employers sometimes met officials. It failed fully to appreciate the constant pressure on governments of the settler colonies to meet the needs of employers, or to recognize that colonial governments, as large-scale employers themselves, were often sympathetic to the difficulties described. With its formal channels of communication through the governors, it was comparatively unusual for the office to be

made aware of local detail unless officials sought it out, and it was always reluctant to listen to outside critics. The "man on the spot" so trusted in London, was, in fact, the man at government house. On occasion other colonial
civil servants were able to present their views, as in 1931 when the Tanganyika senior native commissioner was asked to comment on CLC recommendations: an opinion was wanted urgently, and he was on leave in the United
Kingdom, but the endorsement of the governor was subsequently required.

The office's reliance on precedent tended to create a degree of regional
conformity. This was welcomed by officials since it reduced the diversity that
was so difficult to deal with, but it did mean that very different territories were
sometimes lumped together, with the probable result, as in east Africa, that
the colony most resistant to any reform of its legislation would be allowed to
set the pace. Throughout the period a majority view that the empire could
not be treated "as though it were one homogenous unit"[135] militated against
the successful formulation of an overall policy on master and servant legislation and penal sanctions, or the drafting of model legislation. And lack of any
machinery either to follow up the administration of a statute that had caused
concern at the time of enactment, or to take advantage of earlier discussions
within the office, prevented the development of a corpus of expert knowledge
and opinion.

As early as 1817 Sierra Leone considered much of the corpus of English
law inappropriate. There the solution was to follow English law with amendments and additions to meet local circumstances, sometimes reverting to now
obsolete features. In the late nineteenth and early twentieth centuries, legislators in southern and eastern Africa failed completely to consider the use
of English law, preferring to copy other African statutes. Only once, for the
Gold Coast in the 1870s, did the office suggest that English employment law
might provide a suitable model—a suggestion made at that time no doubt
because reform of the English law was so much in the news. West African
master and servant law continued to develop on separate lines, the governments not having settler pressure to contend with, and being supported by
the office in their occasional disputes with the mine companies. Failure to
insist on, or even to recommend, the use in new colonies of modern labor
regulation led to the entirely new introduction in Tanganyika, as late as 1924,
of legal provisions similar to those repealed in the United Kingdom nearly
sixty years before, and which proved, as in many other parts of the British
Empire, impossible to reform fully in the years before decolonization in the
1950s and 1960s.

135. CO 859/52/4, Gater, Colonial Office, to Leggett, Ministry of Labour, 3 Sept. 1942.

EIGHT

The British Caribbean, 1823–1838

The Transition from Slave to Free Legal Status

Mary Turner

The transition from slave to wage labor was effected in the British Caribbean by restructuring colonial labor laws. The process was set in train in 1823
when the imperial government, under pressure from abolitionists inside and
outside parliament, and with the full support of the West India lobby, took
the unprecedented step of drawing up a legislative program to prepare the
slaves for free status. It marked the seriousness of its intention by promising the owners £20 million in compensation and over the next decade laws
were framed to prepare the slaves for the "civil rights and privileges"[1] of other
classes of His Majesty's subjects. In 1833 slave status was abolished but the imperial government defined a new form of tied labor, designated by the time-
honored term "apprenticeship," to secure ex-slave workers for the plantations.

Dismantling slavery was the imperial government's first direct intervention in British Caribbean labor laws. In the representative colonies founded
in the seventeenth century, elected assemblies drew up their own legislation
for confirmation by the crown.[2] In the crown colonies captured during the
Napoleonic Wars existing slave codes had been left intact, or modified by
local ordinances issued by the governor, again confirmed by the crown.[3]

Statute law was complemented over the decades by customary practices,
some of which acquired much of the force of law. Customs acknowledged by
both owners and slaves made the labor system more flexible, capable of adapt-
ing to the economic needs of developing colonial societies. Slave workers ac-

1. Public Record Office, CO 854/1 circular dispatch, 28 May 1823.
2. Jamaica, Barbados, Bahamas, St. Kitts, Nevis, Antigua, Montserrat, Dominica, St. Vincent, Grenada, Tobago, and the Virgin Islands.
3. Demerara, Essequibo, and Berbice (united to form British Guiana in 1831); Trinidad
(ceded 1802); and St. Lucia (finally ceded to Britain in 1814).

cumulated de facto certain rights, which were acknowledged in the slave codes only belatedly, if at all. These rights originated in some cases in workplace disputes when slaves made claims their owners found it convenient or necessary to concede, claims that subsequently gained society-wide recognition. Slave workers claimed the right to bury their own dead and to travel (despite pass laws) to market, to church, and to visit wives and families on neighboring plantations. As small producers with gardens and, on some islands, provision grounds, they traded their own produce at market, dealt in small coins, and acquired inheritance claims to family land on the provision grounds. Most important, however, was their right to contest their terms of work.

Slave workers used their labor power to contest and shape the terms on which it was exacted. Verbal protests, covert withdrawal of labor, outright absenteeism, sabotage, and, most important, collective withdrawal of labor—strike action—were used to shape informal contracts within the master-slave relation. Slaves contested excessive punishment, increased or excessive work loads and work hours, inadequate rations or lack of time to work their provision grounds, inadequate clothing, removal from one property to another, tyrannical overseers, and rollbacks of their customary terms of work. Slave owners and managers were actively involved in the bargaining that resulted. Slave workers, individually or collectively, carried their grievances over the heads of overseers to attorneys (estate stewards) and owners, or to neighboring planters and magistrates. Owners, faced with the threat of a strike, invited neighbors and magistrates to mediate. And where labor was in short supply, where sugar production was interrupted, where the resident slave workers' case against a temporarily employed overseer was strong, concessions were made and overseers sacked.[4]

These procedures, most readily observed on the agro-industrial sugar estates, were costly for the slaves to establish and maintain. Action always risked and often earned punishment for both leaders and their followers. But workers who "took flog" as part of everyday work as well as for infractions of work discipline also put their bodies on the line to force changes in the terms on which they worked.

Labor bargaining in this form, variously calibrated and sanctioned by custom, can be traced throughout the slave colonies of the Americas. The extent to which statutory law afforded the slaves any form of legal redress for their grievances, however, varied considerably. There was scant provision in the representative colonies. The 1816 Jamaican Slave Code, for example, gave slaves the right to appeal to the magistrates only "wanton" punishments, or

---

4. M. Turner, *Chattel Slaves*, intro. and ch. 1.

workplace punishments in excess of the legal maximum.[5] But in the crown colonies taken over from the Spanish and the Dutch, the system for legal redress was more advanced. A government official, the *fiscal* in the Dutch mainland colonies and *procurador fiscal* in Trinidad, included the administration of the slave laws in their duties. The system of legal redress was underpinned, however, as the records of the fiscals in Berbice make clear, by workplace bargaining. Under the Dutch system, the official was expected to provide a court of last appeal for the slaves. Owners and managers paid a fee of twelve guilders for every slave who appeared before the fiscal, which made collective protests particularly expensive; it put a premium on settling disputes at the workplace.[6]

Dismantling the slave labor laws throughout the British Caribbean impacted, consequently, not only on statute law but also on customary law and on labor bargaining practices. This chapter reviews the laws devised by the imperial government to dismantle the slave labor system and substitute forms of free labor between 1823 and 1838. This redefinition of the labor laws allows us to see with some precision the moment of articulation between one system of labor extraction and another: chattel into wage slavery. The process took place in two stages. In the first (1823 to 1833), laws devised and in part imposed by the imperial government modernized the slave system, replacing slave codes designed to make slave workers and their progeny servants in perpetuity. In the second (1833 to 1838), a new labor code was introduced in most islands and territories, "to promote the industry of the manumitted slave."[7] This review concretizes exactly what changes in the terms of work, in particular what worker bargaining rights, characterized the workers' upgraded status from chattel slave to legally free apprentice in 1834 and indicates the influence of the apprenticeship system on contract and wage workers. It allows us, in short, to reassess the emotive designation, "free labor."

Reforming the Slave Labor Laws, 1823–1833

To restructure the labor laws throughout the Caribbean the imperial government was at first prepared to impose new laws on the representative colonies. This was made clear to the colonial governors in confidential dispatches outlining the reforms. Strenuous West Indian opposition, however, and a tremor of slave revolt induced a return to traditional constitutional practice: encour-

5. (Jamaica) 57 Geo.III c.25 (1816) ss.25–27.
6. House of Commons, *Report of Commissioners of Civil and Criminal Justice in the West Indies and South America, Second Report, Second Series, Demerara, Essequibo, Berbice*, Parliamentary Papers (hereafter PP), 1828 (577) 13:90 (Appendix A).
7. (U.K.) 3&4 Wm.IV c.73 (1833).

aging the assemblies to consider their own best interests through influenc-
ing colonial agents in London, the parliamentary-based Committee of West
India Planters and Merchants, and the colonial governors. Such influences
had prompted most assemblies, under the critical onslaught of the antislavery
movement, to make occasional changes to their slave laws. And in the postwar period the increasingly vociferous free-trade lobby highlighted the West
Indians' need to retain the favor of the imperial government if they were to
keep their privileged position in the British sugar market. But colonial response to imperial government initiatives was often hostile and the resulting
laws ineffective, leaving the Colonial Office with no recourse but disallowance.

In the crown colonies, where the governor exercised both legislative and
executive power on behalf of the crown, laws were imposed either directly
by proclamation or adopted by appointed legislative councils. The imperial
government's blueprint for dismantling the slave system is consequently most
clearly and succinctly formulated in the orders-in-council drawn up by the
Colonial Office for application or adaptation by the crown colonies. The
orders-in-council of 10 March 1824 and 2 November 1831 defined the reforms
required in the first stage in the dismantling process.[8]

The 1824 order, promulgated for Trinidad where the crown had full legislative power, was meant as a model for the representative colonies. Its main
thrust was to cut back the owners' power over the slaves, and its first concern was to improve the means of implementing the slave laws. The office
of Trinidad's *procurador fiscal* became a full-time, salaried appointment for a
nonslaveholding official to act as protector and guardian of slaves. The protector supervised the trials of slaves accused of felonies—punishable by death
or transportation—in the capacity of prisoners' friend, and of persons accused of cruelty to, or murder of slaves, together with manumission and property rights cases. It was a limited brief that put the criminal courts under
Colonial Office supervision, via the protector's detailed six-month reports
(on which payment of his salary was contingent). While the new office clearly
articulated with preexisting structures, it also marked an expansion of local
and imperial government authority over the local magistracy. The protectors themselves were directly appointed by and responsive to the Colonial
Office.

---

8. House of Commons, *Papers in Explanation of the Measures Adopted for the Melioration of the
Conditions of the Slave Population in the West Indies and South America*, PP 1825 (008) 26:205, e.f
Trinidad, order in council, 10 Mar. 1824, 124–38; *Papers in Explanation of Measures Adopted for the
Melioration of the Condition of the Slave Population in the West Indies*, PP 1830–31 (230) 16.1:93–138,
order in council, 5 Nov. 1831.

More innovatively, the 1824 order illegalized the use of the whip to coerce labor in the field. The whip—a focus of slave grievances and of antislavery propaganda—symbolized the personal power owners exercised at the workplace and the archaic nature of the slave labor system.

Persons superintending the labor of slaves in the fields were now prohibited from carrying "a whip, cat, or other instrument of a like nature for the purpose of impelling or coercing any slave or slaves to perform any labour of any kind," or of carrying it as an emblem of authority. Overseers, bookkeepers, and drivers were sent into the field disarmed. No alternative method of inducing labor was proposed in the order; although the colonial secretary, Earl Bathurst, in a confidential dispatch to the West Indian governors, recommended the introduction of task work to be complemented by a wage premium for extra labor, a suggestion taken up formally ten years later.[9] In the meantime task work and payments in cash, kind, or time for work over and above the estate routine continued to figure in informal workplace contracts.

Illegalizing the whip to coerce labor was complemented by limitations on workplace floggings. The existing slave laws all regulated workplace punishments: the number of lashes to be administered in any one day (from one to thirty-nine); the interval to elapse between the offense and the lashing; the need for the worker to recover between punishments. But there was no secure means of implementing them.[10] The owners' and managers' right to punish at will had only been effectively challenged in a piecemeal way by the slave workers themselves: overseers who breached customary punishment norms or inflicted cruel punishments were most likely to provoke strike action. The 1824 regulations went far beyond anything the slaves might have bargained for. Women, who made up between 50 and 70 percent of sugar estate workers and were commonly regarded as more "troublesome" than men, were entirely exempted from flogging. They were to be put in the stocks or imprisoned instead. Removing half the slave work force from the lash was a substantial innovation aimed at promoting reproduction among a steadily declining work force. Flogging for male workers was limited to a maximum of twenty-five lashes.

To implement these laws the order introduced a form of self-policing by owners and managers, supervised by the protectors and their assistants and backed up by fines and criminal prosecutions. All punishments of women slaves and of men given more than three lashes were to be recorded within

9. Ragatz, *Planter Class*, 415.
10. Stephen, *Slavery Delineated*, 40.

two days in a plantation record book. The record was to specify the offense, the time, place, nature, and extent of the punishment, and the names of the persons who had authorized and witnessed it, the witness to consist of one free person or three slaves. The accuracy of the record was to be sworn on oath every quarter when a transcript was deposited with the local assistant protector (on pain of a £10 to £100 fine) and transmitted with the original affidavits within fourteen days after collection to the protector. Failure to do so meant a fine of £5 to £100 and any falsification of the record was a misdemeanor, punishable by a £50 to £500 fine, one to six months in prison, or both. Owners who imposed excessive punishments could be prosecuted by the protector for cruelty, and the slave so mistreated could testify on his or her own behalf if traces of the punishment remained. The court could convict the owner of misdemeanor and order the slave forfeit to the crown.

Limits on workplace punishments were complemented by limits on working hours. The six-day week (already customary outside sugar production) provided for an eighteen-hour break from sunset on Saturday to sunrise on Monday, domestics and slaves engaged in "necessary work" (e.g., tending stock) excepted. Owners who violated these limits could be fined £5 to £50. These laws diminished the slave owners' and managers' authority; in its place, the order sought to promote the slaves' ideological formation, in particular the notion that Christian duty meant obedience to God and their masters. Plans were under way to invest money and personnel to revive the Anglican Church in the West Indies, making it a partner with the colonial state. The order consequently not only guaranteed the slaves' right to public worship (often contested by British Caribbean planters)[11] but facilitated it by decreeing that Sunday markets must close by ten in the morning, in time for Divine Service. Unfortunately this limited the slaves' customary right to Sunday trading and impinged on their living standards and social life.

The new code also extended slaves' personal rights into new areas. Slaves who were certified by licensed ministers and duly registered with the protector as capable of understanding the meaning of an oath were allowed to give evidence in court. Other provisions regularized the slaves' customary property ownership rights, introduced savings banks, and conferred rights to marry, to be sold in family groups (in specific circumstances), and to purchase manumission. The appointment of the protector and the magistrates as his assistants improved the slaves' access to legal redress in labor disputes and the new laws extended the forms of redress available to them. In Berbice,

11. M. Turner, *Slaves and Missionaries*, 78–80, 132–44.

for example, the protector carried more than twice the fiscal's case load and made systematic records. In every case, however, direct negotiations between workers and managers preceded appeal to the protector.[12]

The new code proved contentious even in the crown colonies. In Trinidad, where the changes were imposed directly, the governor, who was sympathetic to the planters, chose the *procurador syndic* for the office and salary of protector despite his close connections with the slave owners. It is not surprising that in the period 1824–29 only two slaves were certified as capable of giving evidence on oath and very few owners were ever prosecuted for breaches of the order. On the other hand, the new manumission regulations allowed more than 400 slaves (of a slave population of some 20,000) to buy free status.[13] In the other crown colonies the Colonial Office prompted legislative councils into action by threatening an imperial order to impose the necessary changes. Demerara held out against reform until 1825. Even then it contested the manumission provision until a parliamentary Select Committee ruled against the colony in 1828.[14] New laws were not implemented until 1826 in Berbice and St. Lucia.[15]

In the representative colonies, where a circular dispatch outlining the new measures was laid before the assemblies, reform took even longer to achieve. Adequate versions of the new legislation were not adopted until 1826 in Dominica, 1829 in Tobago, and 1830 in St. Vincent. The most spectacular resistance was that of Jamaica, the largest single slave labor unit in the British Caribbean, which did not comply until 1831 despite eight model drafts sent by the Colonial Office, two disallowances, and the presence in the assembly of a significant faction advocating cooperation with imperial policy.[16]

Where the imperial reforms were implemented, they resulted in some improvements in slave workers' conditions of employment. In Berbice the maximum number of lashes inflicted on men for disobedience and insubordination fell from seventy-five in 1827 to twenty-five in 1830, by which time most of them were punished by the stocks or imprisonment. For women, the maximum punishment for disobedience was reduced from seventy-one hours in solitary confinement in 1829 to four hours in the public stocks in 1830—a diminution that also minimized work time lost. The removal of the whip from

12. M. Turner, "Flog," 45–50.
13. Brereton, *Trinidad*, 60–61, 69.
14. House of Commons, *Slaves in Demarar, Order in Council Respecting Manumission of Slaves in Demerara or Berbice*, PP 1829 (301) 49:2–7.
15. Public Record Office, CO 111/102, *Berbice Royal Gazette*, 30 Sept. 1826, f.166; Mathieson, *British Slavery*, 154–58.
16. Ragatz, *Planter Class*, 418–19; M. Turner, *Slaves and Missionaries*, 120.

the field also reduced the proportion of complaints about punishment for protesting work loads and tasks that reached the protector.[17]

However inadequately implemented, the laws marked an imperial policy decision that the opposition of resident planters did nothing to change. As Colonial Office experience of planter recalcitrance and slave worker conditions accumulated, its determination tended to harden. The Colonial Office staff included James Stephen (son of Stephen the abolitionist) as legal adviser and Henry Taylor as senior clerk, both committed to the dismantling policy. They strongly influenced decision making under two notably indecisive colonial secretaries (Sir George Murray and Lord Goderich). Public pressure for emancipation made a qualitative leap forward in 1830–31 during the agitation for parliamentary reform and the Anti-Slavery Society abandoned its campaign to improve slave conditions to demand immediate abolition. These new political circumstances were reflected in the radical content and decisive handling of the 2 November 1831 order-in-council, which was intended as a model for legislation in the representative colonies. It repealed all the slave legislation enacted since 1824 and replaced it with a single law incorporating the more progressive provisions enacted under pressure of previous orders.

Lord Goderich spelled out what had been only hinted at in 1824: the new provisions were a "measured and cautious, but . . . decided advance toward the ultimate extinction of slavery." He attributed the prospect of West Indian bankruptcy and the threat of a slave revolt to a system in which "the people are not dependent on their own voluntary industry for their support; in which labour is not prompted by legitimate motives and does not earn its natural reward." It was time the slave owners acknowledged that the colonies whose interest they purported to defend were peopled for the most part by slaves, and that West Indian property was the direct fruit of their labor. It was unreasonable to refuse the slaves legal protection and adequate subsistence. The dismantling of the slave labor system was inevitable: "[I]t would be a fatal illusion to suppose . . . the ultimate extinction of slavery, by cautious and gradual means, can be averted." To contest this process could only result in disaster.[18]

The 1831 order expanded the power of the crown to appoint assistant protectors. Experience showed that the local magistracy could not be raised to new levels of conscientiousness in applying the slave labor laws under the

17. The rate fell from one in every three or four cases to one in every nine or ten: *Reports from Protectors of Slaves*, List of Offences, 1 July–31 Dec. 1827, PP 1829 (335) 25:255; Abstract of Offences, 1 July–31 Dec. 1829, 1 Jan.–14 May 1830, PP 1830–31 (262) 15:1ff.

18. House of Commons, *Papers in Explanation of the Condition of the Slave Population*, circular dispatch, Goderich to the Governors of British Guiana, Trinidad, St. Lucia, Mauritius, and the Cape, 5 Nov. 1831, PP 1830–31 (230) 16.1:59–88. Slaves belonging to the crown had been liberated in August 1831.

protector's leadership. Slave owners themselves, they were concerned to pre-serve, not to modify, long-established modes of discipline. It also expanded the powers of the protectors and their new assistants to initiate criminal or civil proceedings on complaints made to them by slaves, and they were given extensive procedural authority to conduct enquiries (ss.15–21). They could enter plantations and workers' huts to investigate and take evidence; anyone who obstructed them faced fines of up to £500 and up to twelve months' im-prisonment (ss.11, 12, 107). The protector's limited legal guardianship of slaves in court was transformed into active prosecution of slave complaints.

The distinguishing feature of the 1831 order, however, was that it set out the mutual obligations of slaves and owners: how much work in exchange for how much food, clothing, and medical care. The six-day working week was to con-sist of nine-hour working days, exclusive of breaks; task work was legalized and shift schedules imposed on manufacturing within the same time frame. Pregnant slaves and those under fourteen or over sixty were not to work more than six hours a day, and not at all at night. Owners who exceeded these limits, more stringent than any in England at the time, could be fined.

To complement these regulations, the order also fixed slave worker rates for wages-in-kind, a new level of intervention robustly justified by Lord Goderich. "The fact is," he wrote, "that the food of the slaves constitutes the largest part of his wages; and it can scarcely be required that the employer should judge in his own cause without appeal of the amount of remunera-tion which he is to supply to his labourer." The policy reflected in part re-cent parliamentary investigations of truck payment in industry. It introduced a new term to the vocabulary of West Indian slavery, for where the former slave codes had spoken of "allowances," as if the food was a gift, or "provi-sion ground," as if the ground of itself produced sustenance, the new language of *wages* acknowledged a contractual understanding of the slave system as an exchange of food for work.

The order detailed rates for ration-fed slaves some 30 to 50 percent above slave code terms, standardized the very variable scale and location of slave provision grounds (to half an acre per adult no more than two miles from the slave village) and almost doubled the time allowed to work them, from twenty-six (allowed in the slave codes) to forty days. The slaves were also to have seeds and tools supplied, sole ownership of the crop, and could not be dispossessed of the land before harvest.

These terms were more generous than those of the former slave codes and improved on the terms of many informal workplace contracts as well. How-ever, where slaves had previously cultivated their plots without supervision, under the new law their work on the grounds was subject to the same rules as work on the estate (s.16). This affected some territories and some slaves within those territories more than others. In British Guiana, for example, many of the slaves were supplied from grounds cultivated not individually but as part of the estate routine. Some proprietors leased crown land for this purpose.[19] More significantly, slave cultivators lost owner-occupancy and inheritance rights. The order affirmed the landlord's proprietorship, opening the way to rents and landlessness (s.13). Sunday markets, already much curtailed, were totally prohibited, depriving estate workers of their former participation in the cash economy.

In addition to food or the means to grow it, the order set annual allowances of clothing, utensils, household furniture, and certain personal items. All these, and especially the new right to two pairs of shoes and a bed, were improvements over the former slave codes. Slave workers were also to have regular medical attendance, recorded in a journal with details of diet and medicine, and open to inspection by the protector (ss.104–6).

Workplace flogging was further limited to a maximum of fifteen lashes in any twenty-four-hour period and colonial governors were required to limit other forms of punishment by proclamation. The order did not define what constituted workplace offenses, but reports by the protectors reveal that they included indecent language, uncleanly habits, and quarreling. "Punishments without cause" were prohibited, as were those "more than adequate to the fault," unusual, or more severe than used in the common jail (ss.37, 39, 40).

The day-to-day implementation of these rules depended, as in 1824, on owners and managers who were to keep detailed accounts in a more plainly titled "Punishment Record Book" and submit them on oath to the protector (ss.45–53). Owners and managers who breached punishment regulations were to be prosecuted for cruelty and, if found guilty, forfeit the slave or slaves to the crown; for two or three convictions the court was authorized to sequestrate all slaves in the offender's charge and prohibit his employment as superintendent or manager of slaves throughout the colony in addition to punishing him for misdemeanor (s.41).

The slaves' personal rights as defined in 1824 were confirmed and expanded: all slaves got the right to give evidence in court and all nondomestics the right to attend daytime services, rights that narrowed the gap between slave and free status (s.88). Most significantly, however, the order affirmed and enhanced the slave workers' right to legal redress. "Each and every slave" was "at all times . . . authorised" to take his or her complaint to the near-

---

19. *Select Committee on Extinction of Slavery*, PP 1831–32 (721) 20:180, question 2249, Rev. J. Austen; *Account of Extent and Situation of Crown Lands*, PP 1828 (146) 23:801–5.

est protector. In colonies with pass laws this right overrode the need for a pass should the manager refuse one. Managers were prohibited from punishing slaves who laid complaints on pain of prosecution for misdemeanor. The slaves risked punishment all the same, however, since complaints judged to be malicious earned thirty-nine lashes, or up to three months' hard labor (ss.13, 14, 43). It is not clear whether the provision about "each and every slave" countenanced collective complaints to the protectors, but in any event it did not preclude the established practice of workplace bargaining.

The political circumstances that radicalized the 1831 law also prompted an effort to short-circuit colonial obstruction. In the crown colonies, governors were to proclaim the order in force within one month of receiving it. In the representative colonies, the assemblies were instructed to pass declaratory acts incorporating the order or face exclusion from the benefits of a West India Relief Bill, which the Colonial Office was drafting for Parliament. Reception throughout the West Indies was hostile: slave owners protested reform of the system.[20] But in December 1831 the Jamaican slaves, using mass strike action and armed revolt, protested the system itself. They erupted in rebellion to demand free status and wage work.[21] They rattled the cage of the slave system and fueled the abolitionists' cause. The Commons marked its sympathies in May 1832 by appointing a select committee to consider measures for the extinction of slavery in conformity with the 1823 resolutions. The Colonial Office, for its part, concluded that the government must either bow to the colonists or move to abolition, and so advised the cabinet immediately after the December 1832 election for the reformed House of Commons.[22] Under renewed pressure from abolitionists, who had increased support in the reformed Commons, the government committed itself to emancipation in March 1833.[23]

Defining Labor Laws for Free-Status Workers, 1833–1838

To this point efforts to restructure the labor laws had been directed to improving the slaves' terms of work and their statutory civil rights while reducing the power of the slave owners. The decision to abolish slavery dramatically reordered imperial government priorities: concern now focused

20. Ragatz, *Planter Class*, 441–42.
21. M. Turner, *Slaves and Missionaries*, ch. 6.
22. Murray, *West Indies*, 194.
23. (U.K.) 3&4 Wm.IV c.73 (1833), Act for the Abolition of Slavery throughout the British Colonies; for promoting the Industry of the manumitted Slaves; and for compensating the persons hitherto entitled to the Services of such Slaves.

on the ex-slave owners now transformed into employers. The Abolition Act compensated them financially for their loss of slave property and compensated them for the loss of slave labor by inventing a new form of tied labor termed apprenticeship: it provided new mechanisms to discipline labor but left largely undefined the apprentices' terms of work. The act was essentially an employers' charter.

The ex-slave-owners got the compensation of £20 million they were promised in 1823 and twenty-five of the act's fifty-four clauses detailed its distribution. Compensation was calculated on a formula that compounded the value of a colony's exports with its number of slave workers. It was geared to worker productivity and favored the more fertile crown colonies, notably British Guiana and Trinidad, at the expense of the long-cultivated representative colonies.[24] Ex-slaves (except children under six) were returned to their former owners as bound apprentices without indenture to supply forty-five hours of compulsory labor a week for the wages in kind they were paid as slaves. As first proposed apprenticeship bound field and factory hands for twelve years and other workers for six. Strong pressure in the Commons, however, where a motion to limit apprenticeship to one year (the traditional hire period under English master and servant law) was narrowly defeated, obliged the government to reduce duration to six and four years respectively. The employers had a guaranteed, low-paid work force. And to discipline it, the Abolition Act, following the pattern developed by the appointment of crown colony protectors, provided for a core of 100 special magistrates recruited in Britain and paid by the crown. They had sole authority to adjudicate between masters and apprentices.

Most crucially, however, the apprentices' terms and conditions of work and their employers' disciplinary powers, the focus for detailed regulation in the 1824 and 1831 orders-in-council, and even the terms on which the special magistrates worked were left to be defined in the representative colonies by the colonial assemblies. The Abolition Act specified only the forty-five-hour workweek and prohibited Sunday work and merely bundled the other heads on which laws were required into one comprehensive clause (s.16). Abolitionist leader Thomas Fowell Buxton calculated that no fewer than twenty-nine vital issues affecting the apprentices' terms of work were delegated to colonial assemblies dominated by employers.[25] The act, as the abolitionists appreciated, provided an opportunity to give statutory force to regulations that limited the power of employers in relation to labor discipline and terms of work.

24. Mathieson, *British Slavery*, 252.
25. Ibid., 244, quoting *Hansard (Great Britain, Parliament, Debates)*, 1833, 19:1185.

But the imperial government that had threatened to use parliamentary authority in 1824 and 1831 to impose detailed regulations on the slave owners was not prepared to do so. It chose rather to allow the planters to retain the legislative powers they had used to sabotage reform of the slave labor laws modified only by the proviso that payment of compensation depended on crown approval of colonial abolition laws.

The skeletal framework of the Abolition Act and the contentious debates in the Commons demonstrated the government's policy shift without revealing an imperial standard interpretation of apprenticeship terms. The novelty of the apprenticeship scheme, however, made it particularly important for the Colonial Office to provide detailed guidance for crown colony governors and colonial assemblies as it had done in 1824 and 1831.

This imperial standard interpretation was circulated in October 1833, in the form of a draft order-in-council for British Guiana intended to serve as a model for all crown colonies. It confirmed in detail the dramatic shift in policy occasioned by the manumission of the slaves. The order gave priority to strengthening the colonial state. "An effective police establishment," the new colonial secretary Lord Stanley wrote, "is of the very essence of the whole measure."[26] An armed, uniformed police force was required, distributed in settlements, each with a house of correction, in every judicial district to back up the special magistrates. And public prisons were to be built to replace private estate lockups (s.1). The special magistrates' powers were modeled on those of the protector. Like him, they had the right to visit estates, but were now required to do so fortnightly where there were more than ten apprentices (s.2).

Strengthening the colonial state was, of course, necessary to replace the slave owners' authority. But the terms of work proposed for the apprentices' employment marked significant rollbacks as well as advances on the terms proposed for slaves in 1831. The Abolition Act reduced the compulsory working week to forty-five hours with time deducted for cultivating the provision grounds while maintaining the level of wages in kind. This apparent improvement was countervailed, however, by taking children under twelve off the payroll. They became their parents' responsibility, providing a practical demonstration of the "work or want" principle and ensuring the masters their traditional children's gang. This clause put a price on free status and pun-

---

26. *Papers in Explanation of Measures . . . Abolition*, circular dispatch, 19 Oct. 1833, Stanley to Governors of . . . colonial possessions not possessing local legislatures, enclosing Draft of a proposed Order in Council for carrying into effect the Act for the Abolition of Slavery, PP 1833–35 (177) 50:13–26. Stanley's perspective was undoubtedly sharpened by his recent (1830–33) experience as chief secretary in Ireland during the tithe war conducted by recently emancipated Catholics.

ished workers who omitted to pay it: failure to support children was made an "offence against the state" and defaulting parents could be hired out or sent to the public works or to hard labor to provide the earnings required (s.7).

Classification by function eliminated categorization by age and capacity, so the thirty-six-hour week for pregnant women, children, and the elderly as slaves was increased for free-status workers. The working day and the working week were deregulated. Hours of labor were no longer confined to daylight (out of crop) and could be spread across a six-day working week, Sundays still excluded. In British Guiana, this resulted in many apprentices working six seven-and-one-half-hour days, thereby minimizing their free or cash-earning time.[27]

The 1833 draft order applied new standards to workplace discipline. It categorized the "principal dangers" at the workplace as indolence, neglect and improper performance of work, injury to the employer's property, insubordination, and disobedience. The vagueness of definitions such as "disobedience" and "insolence," used to justify punishments in the protectors' reports, had been strongly criticized by the Colonial Office in 1831; to whip males and put females in the stocks "upon such vague and loose charges" invited the abuse of the slave owners' authority.[28] Once the workers had free status, however, the boot was on the other foot; what had by all means and methods to be restrained was abuse of power not by employers, but by workers. So the use of "vague and loose charges" continued.

The punishment schedule had some new features. The Abolition Act prohibited the renewal or prolongation of apprenticeship, but the order proposed to make absentees work extra time. For every hour of absence the apprentice was to serve two additional hours, up to fifteen a week. The resulting sixty-hour week would be six hours more than the legal limit for slaves in 1831. Extra work was to be the punishment for a first offense of indolence, carelessness, or negligence, and was among the punishments for careless use of fire, injury to property or stock, and disobedience. Apprentices could be made to serve out their time up to seven years after apprenticeship ended (s.7).

Flogging remained on the schedule but now required an order of the magistrates. Absences of two or six days made male workers "vagabonds" or "runaways" to be punished by two weeks' hard labor with fifteen lashes in the former case and up to a month's hard labor with thirty lashes in the latter.

27. See below, p. 318.
28. *Papers in Explanation of the Condition of the Slave Population*, circular dispatch, Goderich to the Governors of British Guiana, Trinidad, St. Lucia, Mauritius, and the Cape, 5 Nov. 1831, PP 1830–31 (230) 16.1:59–88.

Seven days absence meant either three months in jail with hard labor, or thirty-nine lashes. A third conviction for careless work would earn up to two weeks' hard labor and twenty lashes. Insolence, insubordination, drunkenness, and fighting were to be met with a week in jail at hard labor, or fifteen lashes (ss.5, 7). These provisions allowed for more lashes than the 1824 order-in-council had legalized, reversing the modernization process it had set in train and degrading free-status workers with a punishment they associated with slave status.

The draft order added to these restraints by reviving the pass laws, found in the earliest slave codes, for any purpose other than going to market or church, customary modifications originally established under pressure from the slaves themselves. And to leave the colony, apprentices required a passport issued by the governor on the written consent of the employer (s.6). Restrictions on freedom of movement were accompanied by restrictions on freedom of settlement. *Marronage*, defined as prolonged habitual absence from the estates by laborers who neglected "the duties imposed on them by law" and lived independently in settlements, remained as under slavery a crime. The special magistrates were empowered to "dislodge" and destroy the settlements and punish the inhabitants with to six months' imprisonment at hard labor and thirty-nine lashes (s.7).

The imperial standard interpretation of the Abolition Act focused on enforcing labor discipline and punishment schedules. The one innovation that marked the ex-slaves' new legal status as free persons was that the application of the labor laws was to be adjudicated by special magistrates.

Even this improvement, however, came at a heavy price. Following the heads of legislation recommended in s.16 of the Abolition Act to punish "combined resistance" and "riot," the 1833 draft (in contrast to previous orders) essentially prohibited the informal bargaining procedures that had customarily preceded slave appeals to protectors for legal redress. Labor bargaining became illegal and the punishments slave workers had risked were now written into the punishment schedule. If three or more workers combined together and combined to dispute (for example) their work load, or if they actually defied their employers' commands by combined and open resistance, they could be charged with unlawful conspiracy and get six months' imprisonment at hard labor and thirty-nine lashes. And a protest by three or more apprentices that became "tumultuous" and failed to disperse after a ten-minute warning could result in twelve months' imprisonment with hard labor (ss.5, 7). These rules, aimed at both workplace and larger-scale inter-estate combinations, were backed up by the pass laws. No equivalent laws were proposed to curtail employer combinations. The draft order strongly influenced the legal framework of apprenticeship in the crown colonies and was adopted with few modifications in British Guiana.

The spirit in which these regulations were interpreted is well illustrated by employer reactions in that colony to the first flicker of collective protest against apprenticeship.[29] On 4 August 1834, just three days after the emancipation celebrations had passed off without incident, apprentices along the Essequibo coast questioned the new contract terms and declared they would not work more than half a day without wages. The local magistrates (only five of the twelve stipendiaries allotted to Guiana were in the colony at this time) panicked and called for martial law. The governor, Sir James Carmichael Smyth, a soldier by profession with a year's experience of the local ruling class, refused; but when the protests continued he went himself with a few constables, explained the forty-five-hour rule, and warned the apprentices that continued resistance would put them in court. But the protests continued. In the upshot, the supposed ringleaders were rounded up and tried, not by a stipendiary in the terms of the order, but at the Supreme Criminal Court in Georgetown under an indictment for riot and sedition. The leader, Damon, was sentenced to hang: four others were to be transported and thirty-two flogged. Smyth, who considered the floggings could only harden the victims' resistance, pardoned these prisoners but the crown law office in London effectively supported the colonists by upholding the Supreme Criminal Court judgment. Damon was hanged and the three surviving apprentices sentenced to transportation began their journey to New South Wales. James Stephen alone argued from first to last that their crime was riotous assembly and their punishment twelve months in jail and thirty-nine lashes. He eventually prevailed. The men were pardoned and returned to British Guiana— in time to serve out the balance of their term as bonded labor.[30]

In the representative colonies little attempt was made to influence the assemblies' abolition laws. Notionally the Colonial Office was armed with the deterrent of disallowance and the carrot of compensation money to promote acts that conformed to the draft order. But the government was working within a strict time frame; the draft order was sent out in October 1833, and the new legislation had to be approved and in place by 1 August 1834, Emancipation Day. No less importantly the new colonial secretary in charge during

29. The proposed 1833 order was incorporated with few modifications in (British Guiana) n.43 of 1834.

30. PP 1835 (278) 50:276–327, for the protest, and trial and pardon; Green, "Apprenticeship," 49–51.

the crucial few months in which the local acts were under review and compensation awarded, Lord Stanley, took a strictly pragmatic view. Apprenticeship was a temporary arrangement to secure law, order, and continued production until "all classes" gradually fell into relations appropriate to a state of freedom.[31] He was prepared to set aside James Stephen's scrupulous reviews that had informed decisions on colonial legislation to this point in order to get the system into operation.

The colonial assemblies fully exploited this latitude; as late as 1838 some assemblies had not determined the apprentices' hours of compulsory labor, regulated their wages, or reformed punishment schedules, leaving women in some cases exposed to flogging and the chain gang. Some colonies even reduced the powers and obstructed the operation of the special magistrates and Jamaica had stripped them of exclusive power to adjudicate master and apprentice cases.[32] In the upshot the inadequacies of the scheme and its maladministration became public knowledge in Britain, and in February 1838 the antislavery veteran Lord Brougham launched a parliamentary campaign to terminate apprenticeship. This finally obliged the government to use imperial authority to implement the system. The Act to Amend the Act for the Abolition of Slavery in the British Colonies[33] (April 1838) was to be proclaimed wherever the local assembly had not adopted apprenticeship on acceptable terms. But the West Indian assemblies already alerted to this danger by the parliamentary attack on apprenticeship chose to forfeit two further years of bonded service from field and factory workers rather than their constitutional powers. Between March and July 1838 the representative colonies terminated apprenticeship.[34]

Apprenticeship was a short-lived scheme, but the contract terms it set out for labor extraction from persons of free status had long-term consequences in the British Caribbean and throughout the empire. It set standards, first of all, for full-time wage workers in the Caribbean as the Antigua case illustrates.

Antigua was the only Caribbean plantation society to take up the option allowed by the Abolition Act and move directly from slave to full wage labor. The assembly rejected the apprenticeship scheme as uneconomic. The slaves,

31. Burn, *Emancipation and Apprenticeship*, 169, quoting Stanley circular dispatch, 17 Oct. 1833, Public Record Office, CO 137/189.

32. (U.K.) 1&2 Vict. c.19 (1838) expressly repealed these provisions of (Jamaica) 1 Vict. c.26 (1837).

33. (U.K.) 1&2 Vict. c.19 (1838).

34. Marshall, "Termination of Apprenticeship," 8–45; Mathieson, *British Slavery*, 300. Montserrat, which had rejected wage work by only one vote in 1834, decided in Jan. 1838.

80 percent of a population of 37,000, were fed on imported rations and apprenticeship meant meeting the same "wage" bill for a 25 percent reduction in labor time.[35] The employers followed the apprenticeship model, however, by attempting to make its full-time wage-earning population into an alternative form of tied labor. A six-clause law freed the slaves but secured their labor for their former owners by house occupancy—a version of the English tied cottage system.[36] Wage levels fixed by the employer, labor discipline, and good conduct standards were to be enforced by the threat of eviction. This contract was for one year, exposing the workers to the threat of future eviction and/or rent charges. To enforce this system the Assembly again modeled legislation on the 1833 draft order: it set up a new, paid police force and planned houses of correction in every parish and a treadmill in the town jail. Its administration was in the hands of local magistrates, employers holding a crown commission.[37]

The Assembly did not make labor bargaining illegal, but employers used the new contractual regime to break with the overtime rate their slave workers had bargained for during the 1833 sugar harvest. The slaves had won two shillings a day plus their rations: after emancipation employers combined to cut the rate to a standard one shilling a day for able-bodied and ninepence for less efficient workers. Disputes inevitably erupted on this issue and many others, prompting the great mass of male workers to leave women and children at home while they sought better terms elsewhere only to find the island economy afforded few alternatives to estate work. The great majority were obliged to return home by September.[38]

Determined to head off a new round of labor bargaining the Assembly passed a Special Contract Act, which attempted to bind wage workers to the estate where they lived on more stringent terms.[39] At the same time it extended legal control, as the apprenticeship scheme did, to all categories of labor, including skilled workers and supervisors, some of whom had never been slaves, but belonged to the free colored and black population (ss.12, 15).

35. Higman, *Slave Populations*, 77; Green, *Slave Emancipation*, 124–25; Hall, *Leewards*, 18, 20.

36. House of Commons, *Papers Relative to the Abolition of Slavery*, PP 1833–35 (278-II) 50:297, Appendix B, Colonial Laws, Antigua no. 18, Act for relieving the Slave Population from the Obligations imposed on them by an act for the Abolition of Slavery (4 June 1834).

37. Ibid., PP 1833–35 (278-II) 50:298–304, Appendix B, Colonial Laws, Antigua no. 19, Act for establishing a New System of Police (31 July 1834).

38. Mathieson, *British Slavery*, 246–47.

39. House of Commons, *Papers Relative to the Abolition of Slavery*, PP 1833–35 (278-II) 50: 305–6, Appendix B, Colonial Laws, Antigua no. 21, Act for regulating Special Contracts between labourers and their employers (29 Dec. 1834).

Its workplace punishment provisions even exceeded the limits of the 1833 draft order (s.9), and while nonpayment of wages could result in an employer being fined, the only remedy for actual ill-usage was release from the contract.

The Special Contract Act was swiftly disallowed. The Colonial Office critique, reflecting the renewal of James Stephen's influence under Colonial Secretary Lord Aberdeen, condemned it in principle as subverting the rights of free labor. It focused on clause 12, which revived "the essential principles of the ancient slave code" by requiring the tenantry on every estate to labor in the service of the landlord at a rate of wages to be fixed by himself. Such restraint "on the free exchange of a man's labour for the best wages . . . that labour can command" was unjust to individuals and against the best interest of society at large. "No better elements of social prosperity could be desired," wrote the colonial secretary, ". . . than the anxious wish . . . of the labourers . . . to better their condition and the eager competition of the employers . . . for their services."[40]

The Colonial Office also saw the Antigua law as setting a precedent for wage-work legislation throughout the British Caribbean. On this basis the punishment schedule and the magistrate's powers were subjected to detailed criticism. In the transition to freedom, the colonial secretary emphasized, the law must guard against "the silent growth of a new code, depressing below the common level of society, in respect of civil rights and penal liabilities, persons who have been so long accustomed to regard themselves, and to be regarded by others as in a state of social inferiority and domestic and personal degradation."

Under imperial pressure the Antigua assembly responded with An Act for the Better Adjusting and More Easy Recovery of the Wages of Servants in Husbandry . . . and for the Better Regulation of Such Servants[41] which it identified with "the Laws which regulate the Hirings of the Labouring Classes in the Mother Country." It made ordinary magistrates the arbiters of labor relations, with powers to resolve wage disputes; punish employment offenses with imprisonment, fines, or discharge; and witness special contracts. Antigua already had legislation making "riotous assemblies" of twelve or more persons who failed to disperse after an hour's warning punishable by the death penalty.[42] Collective labor bargaining, of course, often generated "tumult"; and Antiguan employers were awarding themselves the legal right, disputed

---

40. Ibid., PP 1833–35 (278-II) 50:34–38, Aberdeen to Governor Sir Evan J. Murray Mc-Gregor, 28 Feb. 1835.

41. (Antigua) n.403 (1835).

42. (Antigua) n.384 (1834).

in the case of the Guianese apprentices, to hang any wage-worker protesters like Damon.

No less significantly, the apprenticeship scheme adumbrated the terms on which immigrant contract workers were employed. The pursuit of new sources of labor, by Guianese planters in particular, began as soon as abolition was decided to preempt both wage increases and labor shortages in land-rich territories at full emancipation. The first Indian contract workers arrived in British Guiana in 1838 and became the largest single element in the British Caribbean contract labor force until 1917. By midcentury the scheme was well established and tailored to employer requirements—a standard five-year renewable contract; a nine-hour working day; a pass system to restrict workers to the plantation; fines and imprisonment for workplace offenses—and the workers' only legal vent for grievances was appeal to the magistrates.[43] The employers reinvented "apprenticeship" and made it renewable.

The transition from chattel slave to free status was an epoch-making event of immense political significance. The labor laws that effected this change in the British Caribbean demonstrate however that at the workplace the transition took the form of a variant on the wage levels and labor discipline methods that characterized the slave labor system. The workers rejoiced they could no longer be flogged or locked up by their employers but found that a shilling a day and no allowances left men hard pressed to feed their families.[44] In fact flogging was not abolished but regulated, and alternative physical punishments—the treadmill and imprisonment—were used, together with fines and evictions. Labor penalties enforced labor discipline in a legal system administered by magistrates and police. Workers bound by contract faced an adjusted range of coercive pressures that confronted them with a choice between work and more or less "disagreeable alternatives."[45] And they were sent into this new battlefield disarmed. The laws denied free-status workers the customary right they established as slaves to use their labor as a bargaining tool. Free status introduced the slaves to a differently calibrated but no less rigorous system.

43. For a detailed account, see Mohapatra in this volume.

44. John Sturge and Thomas Harvey, *The West Indies in 1837* (London: Hamilton Adams and Co., 1838), 29.

45. Steinfeld, *Coercion*, 25, 26.

NINE

Urban British Guiana, 1838–1924

Wharf Rats, Centipedes, and Pork Knockers

Juanita De Barros

Master and servant legislation in British Guiana attempted to secure dependable, hardworking laborers who obeyed orders and completed their contracts. In much of British Guiana the legislation focused on indentured, primarily East Indian, sugar estate laborers.[1] In the capital city of Georgetown, the targets were different—primarily dock workers and gold diggers—but the goal was not: reliable workers for key industries, able to cut cane or load sugar when the harvest demanded or to mine gold in the bush for months at a time. With the end of slavery, the colony's legislators perceived a need for new controls over labor. They created a heterogeneous system that tied imported and indigenous laborers by indentures or contracts to plantations, mining companies, and other employers, or bound them by the freedom to wait casually on the docks for work to arrive.

Georgetown had long been the main port for the colony's sugar industry, and this continued even as much else altered in the city. Its borders expanded to encompass neighboring plantations. Its population grew from 12,600 in 1830 to 53,176 in 1891 and 57,777 in 1911 as it attracted first former slaves and then former indentured laborers from the sugar estates.[2] Its racial composition changed in these years from the Caribbean slave colony pattern—black, white, and mixed—to a multiethnic complexion. Its old residents had to share space with East Indians, Portuguese, Chinese, and Africans, all imported as indentured sugar estate laborers to replace the African slaves freed in 1838.

The colony's economy altered as well. The expected crisis in the sugar

1. For indentured plantation labor in British Guiana, see the chapter by Mohapatra in this volume.

2. Higman, "Urban Slavery," 41; British Guiana, *Report on the Census Results, 1891* (Georgetown, 1891).

industry following slavery's end in 1838 did not materialize. But despite reduced production costs, achieved by amalgamating and mechanizing estates,
importing East Indian indentured immigrants, and developing new markets,[3]
a crisis hit in the mid-1880s. Competition from Latin America and new, inexpensive, European beet sugar forced prices down.[4] Gold was discovered
throughout the interior in the 1880s, and the industry flourished in the early
1890s. By 1893 gold was the second most important export,[5] but production
declined later in the decade and continued to fall after the turn of the century.[6]

Georgetown was a nexus for the colony's workers. Dock laborers, usually
hired by the day, loaded sugar and other exports and unloaded imported food
and luxuries. Gold diggers offered their labor, registering with the police
magistrates (and later at the Institute of Mines and Forests) and buying gear
with cash advances from their employers. The distinction between dockers
and gold diggers, however, was illusory. Laborers in postemancipation British
Guiana worked at a range of occupations, migrating between the interior, the
plantations, and the docks.[7] Gold diggers often worked in the sugar industry between September and December after their terms in the bush expired.
In the 1920s, sugar workers left the estates for higher-paying jobs, primarily
on the docks, while plantation employers looked for surplus dock workers to
labor in the "country districts."[8] Local elites recognized labor's mobility in

3. Lancaster, "Hinterland Settlement," 2.

4. Ibid., 3; Parliamentary Papers (hereafter PP) 1896 (C.7944-11) 57:168, *Annual Report* (hereafter *AR*) *1894-5*.

5. Lancaster, "Hinterland Settlement," 7; PP 1895 (C.7629-16) 69:308, *AR 1893-4*; PP 1893 (C.6857-51) 59:463, *AR 1892-3*; PP 1897 (C.8279-12) 59:101, *AR 1895-6*.

6. Official encouragement of quartz over placer mining contributed to the decline in gold production. Planter opposition to the loss of field labor resulted in regulations discouraging the industry's growth: Lancaster, "Hinterland Settlement," 14, 15, 17. See PP 1910 (Cd.4964-6) 64:483, *British Guiana Report* (hereafter *BGR*) *1908-9*; PP 1911 (Cd.5467-7) 51:359, *BGR 1909-10*; PP 1912-13 (Cd.6007-2) 57:599, *BGR 1910-11*; *Census*, 1911, xxix; PP 1914 (Cd.7050-21) 57:659, *BGR 1912-13*; PP 1914-16 (Cd.7622-24) 43:767, *BGR 1913-14*; PP 1916 (Cd.8172) 19:343, *BGR 1914-15*; PP 1916 (Cd.8172-36) 19:373, *BGR 1915*; PP 1917-18 (Cd.8434-24) 22:341, *BGR 1916*; PP 1918 (Cd.8973-25) 17:181, *BGR 1917*; PP 1919 (Cmd.1-37) 35:429, *BGR 1918*; PP 1921 (Cmd.1103-11) 24:187, *BGR 1919*.

7. *AR 1893-4*, 309; see also *Report of Labour Commissioner, Together with Minutes of Sittings, and Evidence of Witnesses* (Georgetown: C. K. Jardine, 1890).

8. Rodney, *Guyanese Working People*, 99, 101; *Evidence Given before the Commission of Enquiry on the Conditions of Employment of and Rates of Wages Paid to Stevedores, Wharfmen and Others* (hereafter Employment Evidence), no. 27, Minutes of the Combined Court (hereafter MCC) 1924, 68, National Archives of Guyana (hereafter NAG); *Report of the Commissioners Appointed to Enquire into the Causes and Results of the Increased Cost of the Necessaries of Life*, MCC Special Session 1920, 29; *Report of the Commissioners Appointed to Enquire into the Conditions of Employ-ment of and Rates of Wages Paid to Stevedores, Wharfmen and Labourers* (hereafter Employment

their representation of Georgetown's quasi-criminal urban underclass. Characterized as "centipedes" and "wharf rats," these individuals, many of whom migrated from the plantations, worked or stole in Georgetown, frequently leaving the city temporarily for the goldfields, where they became "pork knockers," the men who worked placer claims.[9]

Postslavery Labor Law: The Nineteenth Century

With the end of slavery came new methods to control labor. The short-lived apprenticeship system (1834 to 1838) compelled former slaves (now called apprentices) in British Guiana and elsewhere in Britain's Caribbean colonies to provide forty-five hours of free labor for their former owners each week.[10] After 1838, the colonial government introduced a variety of measures designed to encourage former slaves to continue working on the plantations and to restrict nonplantation options. These included high import duties that increased the cost of necessities and hence the emancipated population's need for cash wages, and high prices for crown lands. British Guiana's government also began importing labor from Africa, Portugal, China, and especially India. These foreign laborers were bound to the plantations for up to five years and subject to harsh penalties for violating their contracts.[11] Yet legislation also attempted to control the indigenous, largely Afro-Guianese population.

With the demise of the apprentice system, master and servant ordinances regulated British Guiana's newly free laborers. An act of 1836 regulated workers contracted to perform "any Agricultural, Manufacturing, Handicraft, or other . . . Labour or Service." It protected servants from their employers by punishing mistreatment or nonpayment of wages with fines, imprisonment if the fine went unpaid, orders for damages, or, in extreme cases, cancellation of the contract. Servants, however, were liable for harsher penalties. Neglecting their duties, disobeying lawful commands (or convincing others to do so), using "insulting or threatening Language" to the employer, combining, dam-

---

Report), no. 15, MCC, 1924, 21, NAG. Indeed, the practice was recognized in the 1931 census, which asked about "principal" and "subsidiary" occupations (see *Census*, 1931).

9. E.N.N., "Centipedism," 14. Local elites named members of Georgetown's quasi-criminal and semiemployed urban underclass "centipedes." The term may have connoted the fear with which local elites regarded the city's subaltern population, but it may also have been used by the members of this class to represent themselves as dangerous and difficult to capture.

10. For postslavery "apprenticeship" in the Caribbean, see the chapter by Turner in this volume.

11. See the chapter by Mohapatra in this volume, and Laurence, "Labour Contracts," 9–27.

aging property, or committing any other breach earned servants fines of two days' wages or imprisonment, with or without hard labor. Those imprisoned for absence were obliged to make up the lost time.[12]

The British government disapproved of the British Guiana ordinance. Lord Glenelg believed it continued the "existing Relations between the Employer and the apprenticed Labourer," that its seven-year contracts were too lengthy, and that the legislation should not apply to African apprentices.[13] The imperial order in council of 1 March 1837 amended this law. Africans from the continent or the adjoining islands could not enter into such a contract, and apprentices (former slaves) could not contract for longer than twelve months. The ordinance expired on 1 August 1838.[14]

Subsequent legislation passed in 1838, 1846, 1848, and 1853 (the last remaining in effect until 1942) regulated "servants in husbandry, . . . sailors and boatmen employed on board vessels and boats belonging to the colony, . . . menial servants, and . . . artificers, handicraftsmen and other labourers in the colony."[15] As in the earlier legislation, the servant was given some recourse against breach of contract by the employer.[16] The emphasis of these ordinances, however, was on punishing worker misbehavior. They provided fines of up to twenty-four dollars and jail terms of up to thirty days for servants who did not begin service according to contract, absented themselves, refused to finish their contracts, misrepresented their work, or lost or damaged employer property. The 1848 ordinance provided for "immediate imprisonment" until the fine was paid. Servants guilty of "wilful misconduct or ill-behaviour" were liable for fines of ten dollars or imprisonment for seven days under the ordinances of 1846 and 1848; those guilty of "misconduct or wilful omission, or neglect of duty" could be dismissed immediately. Under the 1853 ordinance, workers who suspended their work or induced others to do so would lose fifty dollars to their employer and the wages for the unfinished work.

These ordinances coexisted with an earlier one, the 1827 Porters' Act, which regulated "porters and others plying for hire in Georgetown."[17] This legislation had three aims. It required licenses for day laborers and porters who moved "lumber, goods, wares, or merchandize" around the city and

---

12. (British Guiana) n.74 of 1836.

13. PP 1837–38 (180, 232) 52:13–14, *Copies of All Orders in Council or Colonial Ordinances . . . and of Correspondence* (hereafter *O&C*), no. 2, Lord Glenelg to Governor Smyth, 31 Oct. 1836.

14. *O&C*, encl. in no. 4, Imperial Order in Council, 1 Mar. 1837.

15. (British Guiana) n.18 of 1838; n.30 of 1846; n.2 of 1848; n.2 of 1853.

16. Chase, *Trade Unionism*, 36.

17. (British Guiana) n.9 of 1827.

its environs—including the docks—and "day-labourers on board any ship or vessel in the river." These workers had to register with the local government, carry tickets with their names, and wear badges around their necks. Unlicensed porters were liable to fines of twenty guilders[18] or three days' imprisonment in default of immediate payment, and anyone forging a badge, lending one out, or using one not his own was liable to a month at hard labor on the treadmill. Laborers could be hired by the day, half day, three hours, one hour, or trip. Free laborers were required to work on demand. The ordinance stipulated that porters and laborers were to "attend the call of any person when required," that is, to perform any work, for any duration, when so ordered; failure to do so would result in a fifty-guilder fine or seven days' imprisonment in default of payment. Wages were fixed at two guilders for a day's work in Georgetown and a little more for a day's work on board a ship.

The Georgetown Town Council Ordinance of 1860 repealed the 1827 legislation but retained some of its essential elements.[19] The so-called porter's bylaw covered all casual dock workers,[20] requiring them to register with the town council and carry a badge while working. Porters were obliged to perform any work asked of them, subject to a fine of up to twenty-four dollars, although they could refuse work by providing a reasonable excuse. The same fine applied to overcharging their customers. The 1898 version of the bylaw continued many of these provisions, although with some reductions in fines. Fines were determined and imposed by the Georgetown police magistrates and defaulters were liable for prison terms ranging from seven days to two months, depending on the amount owed.[21] Both versions of the bylaw emphasized that these were casual task workers, working for periods ranging from an hour to a day, depending on the demands of the task. The 1898 bylaw expressly excluded porters engaged by the week or month in any shop or premises in Georgetown.[22]

Pressures for Change in the Twentieth Century

In June 1916, the British government asked British Guiana to abolish the penal sanctions for labor offenses in its 1891 Immigration Ordinance. The colonial government delayed its response, soliciting the opinions of the Im-

18. One guilder equaled thirty-two cents. Mohamed, "Community," 20 n. 23.
19. (British Guiana) n.1 of 1860.
20. GD 45, Clementi to Long, 31 Jan. 1917, NAG; encl. Inspector General of Police Colonel De Rinzy to the Government Secretary, 15 Jan. 1916.
21. (British Guiana) n.3 of 1868; n.15 of 1893.
22. Bylaw no. 10 in (British Guiana) n.25 of 1898.

migration Agent General and the Planter's Association. Governor Egerton anticipated the amendments, directing the colony's magistrates not to imprison indentured immigrants, except for repeat offenders with three or more convictions.[23] In 1919 Colonial Secretary Alfred Milner suggested reforming master and servant ordinances in the West Indies. Imprisonment for breach of contract should be abolished except on failure to pay a fine, and then should be limited to one month. Fines should be no more than forty shillings with "reasonable time" for payment. Some colonies—Trinidad, Grenada, St. Vincent, St. Lucia, Antigua, St. Kitts, and Montserrat—cooperated, but British Guiana did not, merely amending its 1853 master and servant ordinance to limit the penalty for breach of contract to a twenty-four-dollar fine.[24] In 1928 the colonial secretary described this fine as "unnecessarily large" and complained that such offenses as "wilful misconduct or ill-behaviour" were "ill-defined" and should be abolished or reworded.[25] At the root of these complaints were British concerns about the imprisonment rates of East Indian sugar estate laborers. Indian public opinion required such changes if the indenture system was to survive.[26]

Georgetown's dock workers resisted the colony's labor laws, especially the insecurity of employment. Demand for their labor was largely seasonal. During harvest, work was plentiful, but in the "slack" season many laborers worked only two days a week.[27] Those who were unable to obtain work spent the day on Water Street by the docks, where they were considered part of the city's unrespectable poor, or "centipedes." In 1924 a former mayor of Georgetown, J. Wood Davis, described the scene when ships arrived: "I have myself seen when steamers come in and men having to get at the gate and close it as there is a rush of hundreds of men to get in. As soon as a certain number has been admitted the gate is closed and the remainder walk away and loiter practically the whole day up and down the street."[28]

From at least 1827 until 1905, dock workers were employed almost invariably by the task. Following the 1905 Georgetown riot, precipitated by a dock workers' strike, the minimum period of employment was increased from one hour to a quarter of a day. In 1916 casual workers in Georgetown petitioned

---

23. Egerton to Law, 4 June 1916, GD, Confidential, NAG; encl. copy of confidential circular to all stipendiary magistrates, 27 May 1916, from Geo. Ball Greene, Acting Assistant Government Secretary.

24. Amery to Rodwell, 23 July 1928, GD, Confidential, NAG. Governor Collet believed a forty-shilling fine insufficient: Collet to Milner, 6 Jan. 1920, GD, Confidential, NAG.

25. Amery to Rodwell, 23 July 1928, GD, Confidential, NAG.

26. Harcourt to Egerton, 19 May 1915, GD, Confidential, NAG.

27. Employment Evidence, no. 27, MCC 1924, 23, 46, 47, NAG.

28. Employment Evidence, no. 27, MCC 1924, 64, NAG.

for higher wages and a reduced workday.[29] After a brief strike, they accepted the offer of the Georgetown Chamber of Commerce—a pay increase, a ten-hour workday (with an hour for breakfast), and a minimum pay period of half a day.[30] Proposed legislation to limit the length of the working day for casual laborers on the wharves and on the sugar estates met resistance from the authorities, however. Inspector General of Police Colonel de Rinzy argued that tampering with a system that reliably provided labor for the sugar industry would result in trouble, "a miniature riot or, at any rate, some disorganisation of traffic."[31] The government secretary responded much as de Rinzy had: "[Their hours] depended so much on the character of the work and the time when it offer[ed] itself (for instance in loading or unloading steamers) that it appear[ed] to the Government unnecessary to propose to limit the exercise of their earning capacity."[32]

By 1924 the proposal's original sponsor, Francis Dias, agreed: dock laborers' working hours were necessarily uncertain due to the nature of their work and the varying number of ships in port, "a condition of affairs which [was] . . . beyond the control of their employers" and beyond the reach of legislation.[33]

The success of planters, shippers, and mine operators in securing a reliable postemancipation labor supply was partly illusory. In 1905 and 1924 dock and sugar estate laborers struck (sparking rioting in Georgetown), joined in 1905 by gold diggers. In other years (1906, 1912, 1917, 1918, 1919, and 1920), dock workers repeatedly struck or petitioned for higher wages.[34] The rate of prosecution suggests resistance was common. Before turning to the evidence about enforcement, though, it is necessary to consider the political economy of labor relations and labor law in the colony.

The Logic of Labor Law and Labor Markets

What Edward Jenkins, William Des Voeux, and other observers of late nineteenth-century British Guiana characterized as the "mild despotism of sugar" configured the colony's labor regime. "Mild" may have been an understate-

29. GD 11, Clementi to Long, 10 Jan. 1917, NAG; GD 45, Clementi to Long, 31 Jan. 1917; encl. Colonel Clark, Inspector General of Police to the Government Secretary, 22 Jan. 1917.

30. GD 11, Clementi to Long, 10 Jan. 1917, NAG; GD 45, Clementi to Long, 31 Jan. 1917; encl. Colonel Clark, Inspector General of Police to the Government Secretary, 22 Jan. 1917; GD 32, Clementi to Long, 23 Jan. 1917, NAG.

31. GD 45, Clementi to Long, 31 Jan. 1917, NAG; encl. De Rinzy to the Government Secretary, 15 Jan. 1916.

32. 22 May 1916, Minutes of the Court of Policy (hereafter MCP), NAG.

33. Employment Report, 13, 14.

34. Chamber of Commerce of the City of Georgetown 2 1912; *Report of the Inspector General of Police* (hereafter *IGP*), 1918, 505.

ment, "despotism" was not. The demands of the sugar industry determined when laborers worked. The industry's labor needs fluctuated with international pressures and the seasons. When the cane was ready for harvest, it had to be cut, ground, and shipped, and more workers were needed in the fields and the factories and on the docks. During slavery, labor was always available to the sugar estates, a situation partly replicated after emancipation by the indenture system. Indenture, however, obliged estate owners to find paying work for all laborers whatever the season, a difficulty employers sought to avoid by hiring casual workers. Master and servant legislation permitted task work, and government and employer policies sustained it. Nonindentured (free) laborers worked and were paid only when needed by the estate managers and shipping firms.

Field work on the sugar estates was similar in several respects to dock work.[35] In both settings, free laborers mostly worked by the task and experienced dramatic seasonal fluctuations in employment. Though the proportion of free to indentured workers is uncertain, it appears that free Afro-Guianese workers made up a significant proportion of estate cane cutters.[36] Edward Jenkins, writing in 1871, estimated that roughly one-third of the work force on a large estate such as Leonora was Afro-Guianese.[37] Work on the sugar estates had always been seasonal; after the mid-1880s, as industry historian Alan Adamson has shown, the "sugar-making season" shortened, becoming increasingly restricted to October, November, and December.[38] Nonindentured estate laborers lived in villages, which allowed them to combine wage labor on the estates with subsistence agriculture, thereby supplementing seasonal work on the sugar estates and allowing employers to keep wages low. Free East Indian estate workers were allowed additional privileges to ensure their continued presence on the estates, including cultivating rice and raising cattle.[39] Adamson suggests that "the increase in the size of the nonindentured labor force made it easier for planters to manipulate it as a reserve and to depress wages whenever drought or a fall in the price of sugar gave them the opportunity to do so."[40]

35. Adamson, *Sugar*, 119; *Return Showing Particulars Relating to Immigration of Indian and Chinese Coolies into British Guiana since the Report of the Commission of Inquiry in 1871* (1892), 211.
36. Adamson, *Sugar*, 147.
37. Jenkins, *Coolie*, 52, 94.
38. Adamson, *Sugar*, 147.
39. *Report, Commission to Enquire into Treatment of Immigrants in British Guiana*, PP 1871 (393) 20:483, 584. *Report to the Government of India on the Conditions of Four British Colonies and Surinam* (hereafter McNeill's Report), "British Guiana: Administration of Justice," PP 1914–16 (Cd 7744) 47:589.
40. Adamson, *Sugar*, 139.

Master and servant legislation encouraged casual employment on the docks and plantations; after the turn of the century it was amended to better support the gold and timber industries' labor requirements. In the latter part of the nineteenth century, there had been complaints that the 1853 act was insufficiently stringent.[41] T. J. Wakefield, who was "connected" with the gold industry, testified before the 1890 Labour Commission that the laws governing employers and servants were "insufficient." He pointed out that though he might register thirty men, only twenty would appear at the digging. To ensure the appearance of the others, he had to pay for arrest warrants and spend several hours at the Magistrate's Court. He recommended one of two changes to the legislation: the thirty-day jail term should involve hard labor, or employers should be refunded any advances.[42] In 1891, Georgetown's police magistrate reported that the 1853 ordinance was "quite unsuited to the present state of the labour market, and should be amended as soon as possible."[43]

The ordinance was amended in 1909 to address these concerns.[44] While it slightly improved protection for employees by introducing fines for non-payment of wages, it greatly increased the penalties for worker misconduct. Laborers who did not begin work as stipulated in their contracts, absented themselves, or failed to complete the work were liable to fines between forty-eight and ninety-eight dollars or to imprisonment, with or without hard labor, for a maximum of six months. Convicted laborers had to repay any advances to the employer or go to jail for up to six months. The ordinance provided for suspended sentences to allow the laborer to begin or complete the contract, where the employer agreed. Cooperative workers could have their sentences withdrawn, but the uncooperative could be compelled to finish their sentences. Laborers who did not complete their contracts could be barred from employment on "any mining claim or tract of land." In 1929 the Colonial Office recommended a reduction in these penalties, which "appear[ed] to exceed by far those necessary to ensure the due performance of contracts by labourers."[45]

The 1909 ordinance also limited deductions for advances or goods for the laborer's personal use, which could not total more than a third of the monthly wage or $15 a month. Employers had long used advances as a way of main-

41. In 1890 the *Berbice Gazette* argued that the colony's resources could not be exploited adequately unless "capitalists . . . [had] reliable labourers": *Demerara Daily Chronicle* (hereafter *DC*), 27 June 1890.

42. *Report of Labour Commissioner*, 15, 16.

43. *Report of the Police Magistrate for Georgetown for the Year 1891* (hereafter *PMG*), 542.

44. (British Guiana) n.26 of 1909.

45. Amery to Rodwell, 23 July 1928, GD, Confidential, NAG.

taining their hold over laborers in the interior.[46] It was not foolproof. In 1890 Samuel Goring, who had contracted to work as a gold digger in the Potaro district for four months, took the $2.50 advance but did not return to the steamer. Instead, according to witnesses, he got drunk at the Ice House rum shop and then contracted with another company. He was arrested at the police magistrate's office as he was registering with his new employer. Justice Abbott was outraged at Goring's "deliberate" actions and imposed a severe penalty: $15 or six weeks in jail.[47] James Henry was fined $15 or six weeks for refusing to carry out his gold digging contract. He claimed that he had been unable to cash the order his employer had given him for his $5.48 advance. Calling this defense "nothing at all," Abbott approved the employer's attempt—the first he had come across—to use an order for the advance: "Such a system would no doubt reduce the number of cases that were brought every day into court; and furthermore employers would be protecting themselves from dishonest labourers, who did nothing else but go about receiving advances with no intention of carrying out their contracts—and squandering the money in drink."[48] The editors of the *Chronicle* agreed, complaining that it was "becoming more and more common for dishonest fellows to register in Georgetown, take the advance, and proceed to Bartica by one steamer, and return to Georgetown by the next steamer."[49]

According to the nineteenth-century Guianese historian James Rodway, "great difficulty was experienced from labourers engaging themselves, taking cash advances, and then refusing to go with their party or running away."[50] He believed the Institute of Mines and Forests prevented this practice. Laborers had to register with the institute, which had a head office in Georgetown and branches in the districts.[51] It prosecuted laborers when they did not complete their contracts and, according to Rodway, "protect[ed] them in their legal claims on their employers."[52] The institute prosecuted laborers for

46. It was not common practice to provide advances to noninterior laborers. One of the few exceptions was the $2.24 advanced to William Johnson for materials to repair a couch. When he did not fulfill the contract, he was fined $12 or twenty-one days in jail: *DC,* 30 Sept. 1891. For a discussion of employers' use of advances and truck payment in postemancipation Belize in combination with labor legislation, see Bolland, "Systems of Domination," 607, 608.

47. *DC,* 29 June 1890.

48. *DC,* 9 Dec. 1890.

49. *DC,* 2 Aug. 1890.

50. Rodway, *Stark's Guide-Book,* 85.

51. Leechman, *Handbook,* 209. By (British Guiana) n.10 of 1914, (British Guiana) n.26 of 1909 was amended to permit employers to extend contracts without requiring a new certificate of registration, and providing for trials of offenses in the district in which they were committed (rather than where the contract was made or registered).

52. Rodway, *Stark's Guide-Book,* 85; for a less favorable view, see *Creole,* 11 Aug. 1906, 5.

breach of contract, 17 in 1890, and 256 over several months in 1891, 1892, and 1893.[53]

Once they had the men on site, gold operators were reluctant to let even sick workers leave the diggings. In 1891 Tyrrel Henry and nineteen others left their work on a placer, alleging unreasonable rules. When Henry and the others arrived, they found four ill men being taken to the boat. One who had asked to seek medical attention in town a week earlier died while being moved. Henry and the others refused to work unless they were promised they could leave if they became ill. The judge dismissed the men's concerns, saying that they must have realized when they registered that "they had to rough it to a certain extent." There was medicine at the placer and "medical comforts." Employers wanted to stop men "with trifling complaints rushing off to town when they might be treated on the placer." Justice Kirke fined Henry and each of his co-workers ten dollars or one month in jail.[54] At least one contemporary was not so sanguine about the standards of health care. In June 1890 W. Baily wrote to the *Chronicle*, noting that eight persons in Georgetown "who recently returned from the diggings" had died within the past two weeks from "illnesses contracted there and [for] which there was no medical attendance procurable to alleviate." Some of the larger companies supplied the laborers on the placers with medicine, but generally no one knew how "to administer or compound them."[55]

Evidence of Enforcement

Systematic evidence about the enforcement of master and servant legislation in British Guiana's nonplantation sector is sparse and scattered. In the 1890s the Georgetown police magistrate issued yearly self-contained reports detailing the numbers of those charged and convicted for several broad categories of offenses, including those against the master and servant acts. Before 1890 and after 1903 there are only aggregate statistics for the entire colony. The paucity of sources makes temporal comparisons impossible.

Georgetown newspaper reports in the early 1890s suggest that the master and servant legislation was mostly enforced against laborers who worked in the bush. (Dockworkers and other casual labor in the city were regulated by the municipal bylaws.) The growth of the gold industry in the 1880s and early 1890s, peaking in 1893–94, attracted many workers to the interior, and they

53. *DC*, Jan. to Dec. 1890; Jan., Apr., Sept. 1891; Jan., May, Sept. 1892; Jan., May, Sept. 1893.
54. *DC*, 17 Sept. 1891.
55. *DC*, 27 June 1890.

TABLE 9.1.
Occupations of Defendants, Master and Servant Offenses,
Georgetown, British Guiana

	1890	1891	1892	1893
Gold mining	123	63	116	50
Timber	22	34	8	9
Dock laborers	1	—	—	2
Seamen	24	15	16	4
Other	23	20	8	15
Other (interior)	13	6	12	25
Not stated	36	17	39	41

SOURCE: *DC*, Jan. through Dec. 1890; Jan., Apr., and Sept. 1891; Jan., May, and Sept. 1892; Jan., May, and Sept. 1893.
NOTE: Cases were withdrawn for want of prosecution by the party complaining or for want of evidence.

dominated master and servant prosecutions (Table 9.1).[56] Plantation managers testifying before the 1890 labor commission complained about their inability to compete with the gold industry for estate workers, particularly cane cutters.[57] Indeed, so great was the attraction that the inspector general of police anticipated "considerable difficulty in the future" in recruiting men for the police force due to the "great demand for labour at the Gold Fields."[58] Most of those prosecuted who were not listed as gold miners worked in other industries in the interior, as timber workers and coal burners. The newspaper record is supported by other contemporary accounts. In 1891 Georgetown's police magistrate observed that a "large number" of those charged under master and servant legislation worked at the "Gold Diggings and Wood cutting grants." Most of the contracts were made in Georgetown, so most of the laborers arrested elsewhere were brought to the city for trial.[59] The police magistrate attributed the increase in prosecutions in 1892 to the "very large development" of the gold industry. Twelve or more cases were investigated daily in his court and as many in the petty-debts court where laborers sued their employers for wages.[60]

56. The 1891 census indicates 3,222 gold diggers, though another account estimates 7,000 laborers working in the colony's gold fields in 1891, and others suggest 22,298 registered in 1891–92, up from 15,622 in 1890–91 and 7,224 in 1889–90: *Census*, 1891, vii; *AR 1891*; Lancaster, "Hinterland Settlement," 8, 11.
57. *Report of Labour Commissioner*; see, for example, the testimony of W. H. R. Greig, 30.
58. *IGP*, 1891–92, 302.
59. *PMG*, 542.
60. *PMG*, 478.

TABLE 9.2.
Master and Servant Offenses in Georgetown, British Guiana

	1890	1891	1892	1893
Embezzlement	3	3	1	—
Absence	84	76	143	70
Fail to enter service	11	—	—	13
Fail to fulfill contract	98	66	44	18
Insubordination: disobedient	14	9	10	4
Insubordination: disorderly	2	4	2	—
Neglect of duty	4	—	—	1
Breach of contract	32	8	9	54
Wrong certificate	—	1	—	1
Employer prosecuted for failure to provide promised articles	—	—	1	2

SOURCE: *DC*, Jan. through Dec. 1890; Jan., Apr., and Sept. 1891; Jan., May, and Sept. 1892; Jan., May, and Sept. 1893.
NOTE: The completeness of the newspaper accounts is uncertain. The terms used to describe offenses are those of the newspaper.

Workers in the gold and timber industries were overwhelmingly male and Afro-Guianese.[61] There were no women among those prosecuted for master and servant offenses in these industries, and only a small handful of East Indians.[62] In the sugar industry, on the other hand, the situation was quite different. Walter Rodney notes that most individuals charged under the master and servant acts between 1881 and 1905 were indentured immigrants working in the sugar industry.[63]

Absence and desertion were the most common master and servant offenses prosecuted in Georgetown in the early 1890s (Table 9.2). Some defendants attempted to justify leaving by citing inadequate provisions and other mistreatment, but these excuses were rarely successful.[64] Few employers were charged under the master and servant acts, although there may have been numerous actions for unpaid wages in the petty-debts court. Walter E. Roth observed that under the 1853 master and servant ordinance, in "case of a breach of contract, the servant [was] liable to fine or imprisonment" but the master could "only be sued in the Civil Court." This represented an "apparent inequality of punishment meted out to master and servant." Indeed, the worker "prac-

61. *AR 1893–4*, 310.
62. *DC*, Jan. to Dec. 1890; Jan., Apr., and Sept. 1891; Jan., May, and Sept. 1892; Jan., May, and Sept. 1893.
63. Rodney, *Guyanese Working People*, 234.
64. See, for example, the cases of Pieters et al., *DC*, 23 Jan. 1891, and Jones, *DC*, 17 Sept. 1891.

TABLE 9.3.
Outcomes of Master and Servant Prosecutions, Georgetown, British Guiana

	Charged	Convicted	Dismissed	Withdrawn
1891	767	495	113	159
1892	1,054	694	190	170
1894–95	533	339	14	180
1895–96	529	291	45	193
1897–98	588	365	49	174
1898–99	604	311	60	233
1899–1900	449	257	22	170
1900–1901	413	254	22	137
1901–2	267	133	13	121
1902–3	612	379	22	211

SOURCE: *PMG*, 1891, 1892, 1894–1903.
NOTE: In May 1902, the court at Providence was added to the Georgetown Judicial District. Overall, 1902–3 saw an increase of 436 criminal cases over the previous year. Summary convictions for master and servant offenses increased by 246. In 1903–4 there were 842 fewer criminal (including master and servant) cases in Georgetown than in the previous year. This was not a real decrease but "merely a transfer to other County tables": *IGP*, 1903–4, 555.

tically los[t] his wages—for, as a rule, the employer [would] not pay unless forced."[65]

Although many charges were prosecuted and sentences imposed, some were negotiated. Many master and servant complaints were withdrawn (Table 9.3).[66] Newspaper accounts in the early 1890s indicate that this typically happened when the laborer was willing to complete his contract or able to return his advance. Although Georgetown police magistrates rarely sent offenders directly to prison[67] and seldom imposed the maximum fine allowed under master and servant legislation, they frequently imposed the maximum jail term in default of paying the fines (Table 9.4).

The magistrates generally fined violators of the 1898 town council ordinance one or two dollars, although the maximum penalties for various offenses ranged between ten and twenty-four dollars. The town constables' reports do not single out employment-related offenses from other breaches of the 1898 bylaw, but in one month for which more details are available forty-eight convictions, mostly of unlicensed porters, resulted in total fines of only

65. Walter E. Roth, *Report of the Pomeroon District, for the Year 1911–1912* (Georgetown: The Argosy, 1912), 5; (British Guiana) n.2 of 1853.
66. See *PMG* for the years 1891, 1892, 1894–1903.
67. The exception was seamen, many of whom were jailed for refusing to obey orders.

TABLE 9.4.
Master and Servant Penalties, Georgetown, British Guiana

	Fine	Jail	Jail (in lieu)	Bound Over	Reprimand
1891	70	—	425	—	—
1892	131	—	563	—	—
1893–94	32	—	322	2	—
1895–96	37	2	252	—	—
1897–98	55	—	309	1	—
1898–99	43	2	260	6	—
1899–1900	41	—	215	1	—
1900–1901	22	—	228	1	3
1901–2	17	—	115	—	1
1902–3	72	44	260	1	2

SOURCE: *PMG*, 1891, 1892, 1894–1903.

forty-five dollars.[68] Given the low daily wages paid to most laborers, the reduced fines may have been irrelevant. Gold diggers earned between thirty-six and seventy-two cents a day plus rations, and casual wharf laborers about the same: forty-eight to sixty-four cents for a ten-and-a-half-hour day, though much less for broken days.[69] As Table 9.4 shows, most of those convicted of master and servant offenses in Georgetown ended up in jail for nonpayment of fines. The same pattern pervaded the whole colony. Thus in six months of 1900, 105 persons convicted under the master and servant ordinances were fined a total of $1,167.48. Only 8 paid their fines.[70]

68. Minutes of the Town Council and Lists of Business for 1897, 1899, 1900, 1902, 1904–6, 1909, 1914–16, 1918. The detailed report is for Feb. 1905; (British Guiana) n.25 of 1898.

69. Rodway, *Stark's Guide-Book*, 83; Leechman, *Handbook*, 209; No. 18, Hodgson to Lyttelton, Cd. 2822, 285; No. 25 of 1898, Schedule 7, NAG. The dock workers' day rate increased slowly until by 1922 it ranged between 84¢ and $1.80 a day: GD 11, Clementi to Long, 10 Jan. 1917, NAG; GD 45, Clementi to Long, 31 Jan. 1917, NAG; encl. Clark to the Government Secretary, 22 Jan. 1917; GD 32, Clementi to Long, 23 Jan. 1917, Employment Report, 3.

70. 16 Oct. 1900, MCP, NAG. The fines paid amounted to $65.48.

TEN

South Africa, 1841–1924

Race, Contract, and Coercion

Martin Chanock

This chapter will outline a number of themes in relation to the regime of master and servant law in South Africa in the period between the abolition of slavery, which was followed by the first legislation in 1841, and the 1920s, when industrial conciliation legislation was introduced. In that period, the laws of master and servant were only part of a larger ecology of legal and political mechanisms of labor control, and they are difficult to consider separately from that context. Other chapters in this volume analyze master and servant laws in a postslavery environment, or the coercion of labor in "tropical" colonies with peasant societies, or in settler colonies that gradually developed away from master and servant regimes. In South Africa all three models were present and interrelated.

Master and servant law in South Africa began as an attempt to tie rural labor after the abolition of slavery. By the early twentieth century, it had become, together with the pass system for African workers and the policy of influx control for urban areas, part of an ecology of coercive laws designed to limit the numbers of permanent African residents in towns and cities. The right to urban residence was linked to the labor contract. The labor contract was also adapted to the efforts to abolish sharecropping, to recruit labor from a family-oriented peasantry, and to tie labor tenants to farms in a phase of rising African urbanization. Competition between farmers and mines for control of labor, the large labor recruitment schemes for the mines, the institutionalization of migrant labor, and the confinement of workers in labor compounds all lay behind labor policies and the use of law.

In addition, master and servant law operated in the political context of a racially divided work force where the politics of labor law was dominated by the conflict between the industrial and political strength of white trade unions, determined to create and entrench a legally privileged position for white workers through highly effective strikes, and the powerful capitalist interests of the Rand. In this context, master and servant laws were part of a racially bifurcated industrial law in which they were eventually set alongside the system of industrial conciliation, which came to regulate the conditions of white labor contracts. Because I have set the discussion in this highly politicized context that rested on racial rule, my focus is not so much on the content of the laws or the conventional contextualizing of how the laws "worked" in practice. I have instead focused on how the laws were talked about, and what roles the representations of categories such as labor and contract served. The major discourses surrounding labor law were not legal and rule focused, emanating from lawyers or judges, but bureaucratic, political, value-oriented, and instrumental.

The white industrial labor force exercised considerable (and growing) electoral power. In addition, three periods of violent confrontation with white trade unions (in 1907, 1913, and 1922) forced the state to reconstruct the system of labor law affecting white workers. This was reinforced by a process in which the judges limited the application of the common and statutory law of master and servant to exclude industrial occupations. In the place of master and servant laws the models of industrial conciliation that were adapted for white workers were drawn from other white dominions, particularly Canada and Australia. The labor regime for black workers, however, was based on confinement in the mining compound; migrant labor extracted from rural areas by taxation; the seizure of land; prison; the extensive use of prison labor in public works and agriculture; whipping (judicially imposed and otherwise); strict control of movement and residence; rural labor extracted as "rent" from men, women, and children; and the denial of a legal capacity to organize and withhold labor. Yet despite their huge differences, for both legal regimes the idiom of contract was crucial.[1]

Passes

The pass marked the division between different types of labor in South Africa. The industrial conciliation regime, introduced in 1923, did not apply to

1. This bifurcation is, of course, too simple. There were other labor regimes making up the ecology within which the poles of "free" labor, and that governed by master and servant law, were situated. The regime of indentured Indian labor on the cane fields in Natal, the compounded imported labor from China in the Rand mines (for a brief period), the black mine labor recruited from outside of South Africa, and the labor tenancies in the rural areas of South Africa were all distinctive systems of unfree labor. In the latter case (see below) the links with master and servant law were eventually made.

"pass bearing natives." In addition, the pass became the key document for the registration of a labor contract under which the bearer became subject to the master and servant law, and by means of which desertion was identifiable and punishable.

Before the formation of the Union of South Africa in 1910, different legal regimes governed the movement of Africans in the different colonies. Unifying these laws was not a simple matter. In the Cape, an 1828 ordinance[2] and the abolition of slavery in 1834 proclaimed the notional equality of all before the law. Passes were not required for ordinary movement within the colony. But the eastward expansion, the desire to control the influx of "foreign natives" from the densely populated Xhosa country, and alarm about cattle theft led to the requirement of passes for Africans entering the colony from beyond its borders, and for those moving stock.[3] The Vagrancy Act, passed in 1879, also had far-reaching implications for freedom of movement and increased the "practice" of Africans carrying passes from their employer, or the owner of the land on which they lived.[4]

It was on the diamond fields of Griqualand West that the legal linkage between the pass and the labor contract was first made. Contracts of service had to be registered, and those without evidence of contract and registration were subject to arrest.[5] In the Cape Colony, the links between the right to be present, the right to move about, and employment did not apply. In Natal before 1901 passes were required for travel into and out of the colony and for moving stock. In 1901 a system of identification passes linked to registered employment contracts was introduced, with the intent to control desertion from employment. Every employed African had to carry a pass indicating the terms and length of the contract and produce it when required.[6] This was extended to farm residents by a 1904 act that required registration of terms of service.[7] In the Orange Free State, chapter 133 of the Law Book made all persons of color moving about the country without a pass liable to arrest as vagrants, and they could be bound in employment by magistrates.

In the Transvaal, however, the most detailed and comprehensive system of control had been developed. General regulations required all Africans traveling in the Transvaal to carry passes. In addition, there were laws relating to proclaimed labor districts. On entering such a district, an African "requires

2. (Cape) n.50 of 1828.
3. (Cape) n.22 of 1867.
4. (Cape) n.23 of 1879.
5. Worger, *City of Diamonds*; (Griqualand W.) n.14 of 1872.
6. (Natal) n.49 of 1901.
7. (Natal) n.3 of 1904.

in addition to his travelling pass an 'identification labour passport.' This pass-port must contain a complete record of the individual, and must contain the history of his movements until his return home."[8] A worker had six days to obtain the pass, on which all details of contracts of service had to be regis-tered. In 1909 this system was applied to urban areas in the Transvaal.

By examining the foundations laid in the Transvaal, a clear picture emerges of the fundamentals of the pass laws, and an idea of what was acceptable to the new British-run state, which was to be the legal and administrative model for the Union, as it faced the task of postwar reconstruction. As British gov-ernment established itself in the Transvaal in 1901 before the end of the Boer War, the Colonial Office in London came under pressure in Parliament about the harshness of the former republic's laws in relation to Africans and other persons of color, including Indians. Under particular attack were sections 150 and 151 of the Gold Law of 1898, which required passes, stipulated ten lashes for default and twenty-five lashes for other breaches of the labor law, and im-posed criminal sanctions for breach of labor contract, or "misbehaving in ser-vice." Only after considerable agitation and pressure from Whitehall did the new British administration in the Transvaal agree to abandon lashing, but it adhered to the essence (and the wording) of much of the existing law.[9]

The legal regime in the Transvaal was developed to suit the gold mines, large-scale recruiters of migrant labor. Milner, the British high commissioner, laid great emphasis on the claim that the new measures ensured that Afri-cans entered labor contracts voluntarily, by controlling recruiting agents and by government oversight of contracts before the issuing of labor passes. This was a crucial claim because once an African had "voluntarily" entered a con-tract, it was binding. Milner identified laborers and competing employers as the perpetrators of contract breaches, and both were subjected to punishment in the new regime. Under the old system, Milner wrote, "the frequency of desertion was one of the greatest evils. . . . in the great majority of cases the desertion was not so much due to any desire on the part of the native to escape his engagements, as to the temptations held out to him by unprincipled Euro-peans to do so." This "nefarious traffic" was to be stopped not just by encour-aging employers to cooperate with each other, but by subjecting employers to criminal penalties for engaging an African worker whom they knew was bound by a contract of service to another.[10] A person leaving service before the end of the contract was liable to a ten-pound fine or three months' im-

---

8. *Select Committee 1914* (*SC1914*). For form of citation, see Chanock, *Making.*

9. For Colonial Office involvement in South African labor regulation, see also Banton in this volume.

10. *General Pass Regulations*, s.12; Worsfold, *Milner*, 34.

prisonment and, after serving the sentence, would have to return to complete the term of the contract.[11] Milner concluded by defining the role of government in relation to labor. It was not the government's concern or intention, he wrote, to "procure labourers . . . by compulsion, and arbitrarily to reduce the rate of wages." But, he said, if employers "by combination among themselves . . . can prevent wages from being forced up to a preposterous pitch," it would be beneficial.[12]

> But in any case it is no business of the Government's to interfere in the matter, nor have the mine owners suggested that it should be. What they do ask is that the Government should do what it can to prevent the natives, whom they have obtained at great cost, and whose interests are safeguarded by the law in so many ways, from breaking away from their contracts in a mere access of childish levity or being tempted away by unprincipled labour thieves.

In 1901 the Native Passes Proclamation[13] divided the colony into labor districts, each with an inspector of natives. No person could employ an African without a pass, which was to be retained by the employer (s.7). Africans entering a "labor district" in search of work had six days to find work and could be imprisoned for a month with hard labor if they remained longer without work.[14]

In explaining Milner's reconstruction of the defeated republics, Worsfold accurately placed the pass law at the center of black-white relations. The pass, he wrote, "is the basis upon which rests the entire fabric of the legal relations between the native and the European." Natives could not leave their village without a pass, and it served as "a record of good or bad conduct" and as a certificate of identity. It had to be produced for policemen, Native Affairs Department officials, and employers:

> The control of the employer is now substituted for that of the chief. The native cannot leave the quarters assigned to him for a single night without the written permission of his employer. He must return to his quarters before sundown every day. To enable him to return to his "kraal" (village) or to seek fresh employment, he must have a proper discharge from his first employer, which includes a record of his behaviour, good, bad or indifferent.

11. *General Pass Regulations*, s.13.
12. Milner/Chamberlain, 6/12/01, 28.
13. (Transvaal) n.37 of 1901.
14. *Labour District Regulations*, s.4.

Worsfold concluded that the pass system "Rightly administered . . . is a means of putting into effect an industrial partnership between the white and the black races."[15]

The pass laws were taken for granted in the analysis of the "labour problem" set out by the Transvaal Labour Commission of 1903 and by the Lagden Commission two years later. The Transvaal Commission found that demand for African labor greatly exceeded supply, and that the needs of the mining industry in particular could not be satisfied from local resources. This led to the importation of Chinese labor for the mines. The Lagden Commission considered the broader question of why the African population was not mobilizing to meet labor demands.[16] "The British South African aboriginal Native has not fully met the labour requirements of the country," it wrote. Labor had to be imported from India, China, and other parts of Africa. "The economic disadvantage of this position is obvious."[17] But, in their analysis, "Any recommendation as to higher wages is quite out of place . . . any departure from the principle that the rate of wages must be a matter of free contract between employer and employee is unsound, nor is any relief from present difficulties to be found in such a measure."[18] Instead, "administrative measures" were desirable. Employers, analysts, and governments frequently argued that Africans were not subject to the disciplines of the market, and therefore other disciplinary mechanisms were needed. The Lagden report rejected direct or indirect compulsion, but there was a fine line to be drawn: it "would not only be legitimate but wise and just to keep in view all legislative and administrative measures" to create a "condition of things which at least will not perpetuate or aggravate the existing labour difficulty. It cannot but be an advantage to the Natives to be induced without compulsion to become more industrious."[19]

The commission sought to reduce "idleness" (i.e., not being in white employment). In the rural areas people were forced onto the labor market by the control of unregulated squatting on private land and the charging of rents for occupation of crown land. In towns the pass laws, in the form of the labor

---

15. Worsfold, *Milner*, 34.

16. *Report of the South African Native Affairs Commission*, 1903–5 (hereafter Cd 2399), 54.

17. Cd 2399, 57.

18. The details of the "contractual" relationships were rarely considered because "contract" served more as a political idiom than a legal agreement. As Diamond wrote of the Native Recruiting Corporation "contract," the mine at which the contracting workers were to work was not named, and the actual wages to be paid were not stipulated. When this was raised before the Native Grievances inquiry, Chief Magistrate Buckle, who conducted the inquiry, concluded that the need for specifying the wages in a contract was "overestimated." Diamond, "Native Grievances," 225.

19. Cd 2399, 58.

pass, were vital. The commission recommended "enforcement of laws against vagrancy in municipal areas and Native labour locations, whereby idle persons should be expelled."[20] The scale of the administrative and legal enterprise to which this strategy committed South African governments became enormous, involving the resources of a new and administratively weak state in a bizarre system to control the movement of the great bulk of its population.

As the 1920 Select Committee on the Pass Laws noted, there was long-standing opposition to the pass laws. In June 1918, following the European strikes, African municipal workers went on strike in Johannesburg. The effort was described as

> abortive . . . and the result was attributed to the existence of the pass laws and the system of registration of contracts under which they were unable lawfully to leave work at a days notice. The avowed object of the (African National) Congress from that time has been to abolish passes and contracts with a view to giving natives freedom of action to paralyse the industrial world by strikes. By this means it was hoped to secure the objects they had in view, which were not to be limited to the abolition of passes.[21]

Discussions of labor spilled over instantly, easily, and naturally, into the realm of the foundations of the racial political order.

The Urban Areas Act of 1923 contained provision for the registration of "every contract of service entered into by a male native" in proclaimed areas, and for compulsory reporting of the termination of contracts (s.12(1)a).[22] It reaffirmed the requirement that African males, on entering an urban area, report and obtain a pass allowing them to stay and seek work. This permission could be refused "whenever there is a surplus of native labour available

---

20. Cd 2399, 59.

21. In relation to the right to strike, the masters and servants and pass laws placed African workers in an entirely different position from whites. As African workers had to enter into monthly or six-monthly contracts of service they were not free to strike without legal punishment for breach of contract. White workers were perceived to be different. The Johannesburg magistrate wrote in 1918 that there could be no law against striking "except on the absurd basis that the workman should be practically a serf." In any case, as he pointed out, trade unionists outside and inside South Africa had realized that they "must contract only on an hourly basis, so that all the men affected may be free to end their contracts immediately and simultaneously without fear of legal consequences." *Reports of the Department of Justice*, 1919 (hereafter *UG36-1919*), 108. The Native Labour Regulation Act of 1911, sec. 14, also contained specific penal sanctions which made a legal withholding of labor impossible. Being absent from a place of work, neglecting to perform duties, and refusing to obey lawful commands were offenses under the act.

22. (S. Africa) n.21 of 1923.

within the proclaimed area" (s.12(1)c). Urban local authorities were required to render statistical returns on the numbers of work seekers, the numbers employed, and the likely demand for labor (s.16). If such returns showed a population "in excess of the reasonable labour requirements of that area," a local authority could compile a list of persons already in the area for compulsory removal (s.16). In the Transvaal and Natal, after the passing of the Native Service Contract Act of 1932, a person could be refused permission to remain if he did not possess a pass showing that he had been "released from the obligation of rendering service" to the owner of the land on which he was domiciled (s.12(1)c(ii)). A female could not legally be admitted to urban areas without the multiple permissions of the local authority, the native commissioner or magistrate in her district of origin, and her guardian (s.12(1)d). A person whose job ended had between seven and fourteen days to find another, or leave the urban area (though this did not apply to those born and permanently residing in urban areas).

The agenda to control movement and residence produced increasing numbers of pass law convictions. By the end of the 1920s, there were about 39,000 convictions in the Transvaal each year, by far the highest category of criminal convictions (39,000 out of 42,000 convictions unionwide).[23] The cost to the state, the Native Economic Commission noted, was "heavy" but "necessary."[24] The laws prevented "absconding from farms and other forms of employment . . . in general it prevents crime . . . [it was] a means of stopping wholesale entry into towns." The Economic Commission posed two questions: How far could the European social order allow free intermixture of Africans; and, "in the cases of farms, is the Native too irresponsible, too untied to his employment by his living requirements, to be allowed complete freedom of movement without economic disorganisation of agriculture resulting from it?"[25]

The Economic Commission considered a more comprehensive system of control. An African should carry a pass if moving beyond his or her residence. It should be an offense to employ someone without a pass, and new employees should be registered within seven days. They proposed a Central Bureau, "*in order that there may be a record of movement of Natives throughout the Union,*" to administer all this: "By these means we consider that a record of all Natives moving about the country would be built up at the Central Bureau and in the event of a Native not being at his home or recorded at the

23. Roughly calculated the standard fine for a pass offense was three or four months' income.
24. *Native Economic Commission, 1930–32* (hereafter *UG22-1932*), 722.
25. *UG22-1932*, 725.

local registration office . . . an enquiry at the Central Bureau should establish his whereabouts." All contracts of service over three months should be registered. Together with the bureau this would "go far to check desertion," by making it possible to trace offenders.[26]

Under Proclamation no. 50 of 1934, no African without a pass could be employed, and the employer was required to demand the pass and retain it in his possession until the end of the period of service, when it would be returned with the date of discharge. Anyone seeking a pass had to certify under pain of criminal penalty that he was not "under an unexpired contract of service," and no pass could be issued if he was. A small category of persons were exempted from the pass laws but had to carry and produce a document certifying exemption.[27]

Master and Servant Law: Content and Interpretation

Important master and servant legislation was introduced in the Cape of Good Hope in 1841 to provide a framework for labor discipline in the postslavery, postindenture era. The Cape legislation, "which studiously avoided all reference to colour," was accepted in London as a "comprehensive safeguard of the equality of treatment of all races."[28] It was however to develop into one of the cornerstones of the racially differentiated labor regime. Cape legislation of 1856 became a model for laws passed in the other colonies.[29] The different provincial laws were not unified and remained in force throughout the period under discussion, though refined and extended by a battery of Union legislation affecting labor. While this body of law originated in a postslavery rural economy with a racially subordinated population, it remained the legal base on which a massive industrial mobilization of labor occurred.

The basic thrust of the laws was to make breach of a contract of service criminally punishable. The term "servant" was defined as "any person employed for hire, wages, or other remuneration, or to perform any handicraft or other bodily labour in agriculture or manufacture, or in domestic service . . . or other occupation of a like nature." Failure to start work, desertion, negligence, insolence, refusal to obey commands, and the withholding

26. *UG22-1932*, 735–37.
27. (S. Africa) n.50 of 1934.
28. Mandelbrote, *Constitutional Development*, 374.
29. This legislation, and its astonishingly influential history, is examined by Banton in this volume; see also the editors' Introduction. It placed the relationship between master and servant firmly and explicitly within a contractual framework. See section 1, which states that matters arising out of any of the mutual relations between master and servant will be determined according to the law "applicable to bi-lateral contracts in general."

of wages became criminal offenses.[30] The definition of servant varied (some enactments included industrial workers as well as agricultural and domestic workers), and so did the type and length of contract covered by the law (written or unwritten, daily, monthly, or annual). Even without any reference to race, the laws could be adapted to apply to some workers in a racially segregated labor market and not to others. By 1926 the Economic and Wages Commission found that the definition of a servant, which was common to all the statutes, "was *evidently* designed to exclude occupations ordinarily followed by white employees and to restrict the Acts, as far as possible, to natives and coloured."[31] But this had not been so evident to the courts, which interpreted the statutes according to the then prevailing rules of statutory interpretation. The supreme courts narrowed the definition of servant to confine the operation of the acts. Innes ruled in *Clay v. Rex* (1903), T.S. 482, that a railway navvy (one of the few manual laboring jobs in which many of the workers were white), an occupation not mentioned in the act because there were no railways in South Africa when it was passed, did not come under the law. This was an important step toward exempting white workers. As it "attached criminal consequences to the breach of what is essentially a civil contract," he said, "the Masters and Servants Law must . . . be very strictly construed."[32] Although master and servant statutes were based on English models, Judge Wessels used an old Roman-Dutch law to distinguish between servants attached to the house and other workmen who hired out services:

The house servant belonged to a lower category. . . . It was the policy of the law of Holland to control domestic servants as much as possible because they were inmates or attached to the house of the master or mistress. We therefore find numerous *Keuren* or *ordinantien* all over the Netherlands of the same nature as our Master and Servant Acts. They make provision for penalties and punishments in case a domestic servant deserts his service or is not obedient to orders or fails to conduct himself decently.[33]

30. Hahlo and Kahn, *South Africa*, 774.
31. *Report of Economic and Wage Commission* (hereafter *UG14-1926*), 39 (emphasis added).
32. The criminal penalties involved in treating white workers as servants under the law extended not only to the "servant." Had such workers remained covered, trade-union activity would have been impossible. Strike action would have involved incitement to desert.
33. The Roman-Dutch law was based on the Roman law distinction between the letting and hiring of personal services, and the letting of services to do a particular task. The latter applied to highly skilled work, the former to more menial occupations. It was a fundamental distinction between different types of contractual regimes for labor and was easily adapted to a racial division. Someone who let personal services essentially contracted into a status of subordina-

The process of narrowing the definition of a servant must be understood in the context of increasing complexity in the manufacturing work force and the fact that the legislation was color-blind. Many jobs filled predominantly by white workers, such as printers, salesmen, and foremen, were excluded from the definition by this process of interpretation.[34] The 1926 commission remarked that not only had the act been construed in such a way as to keep out persons regarded as unsuited to its penalties but also that "proceedings are infrequently taken where white employees are concerned."[35] The Cape and Transvaal laws also made distinctions between the penalties applicable to those working in agriculture and those in other areas of bodily labor. Only the former could be sentenced to hard labor, spare diet, or solitary confinement.[36] Only agricultural employees could commit the crime of desertion, which was leaving employment with intent not to return. Negligence with the master's property, or its loss by breach of duty, were offenses. Rural workers were additionally liable for failing to report the loss of stock at the earliest opportunity and failing to preserve for inspection parts of animals alleged to have died. Loss of one animal out of several hundred was sufficient to sustain a conviction.[37] Once a period of imprisonment was imposed, its length was added to the contract period, and it was an offense not to return to the service of a master after serving a sentence. A maximum of six periods of consecutive one-month sentences could be imposed.[38]

The acts carefully protected the distinct status of masters and servants. Disobeying a lawful command of the employer was a criminal offense, as was the use of abusive language to an employer, employer's wife, or any other person placed in authority.[39] Prosecution for offenses was at public charge, but if the complaint was found to have been brought without reasonable or probable cause, the complainant was liable for costs.[40]

It would be wrong to see the courts' definition of "servant" as concerned only with the exclusion of white workers from the ambit of the master and servant laws. The narrow definition of servant had important implications for

---

tion: Jordaan, "Employment Relations." Wessels's lower-court judgment is quoted in *Spencer v. Gostelow* (1920), AD 617.

34. Gardiner and Lansdown, *Criminal Law,* 1414–15.

35. But they were sometimes. As late as 1923, 883 whites were prosecuted under the acts (as well as 18,369 nonwhites). These numbers, said the commissioners, "do not appear to be inordinate." *UG14-1926,* 39.

36. Gardiner and Lansdown, *Criminal Law,* 1418.

37. Ibid., 1412, 1422, 1424.

38. Ibid.

39. Ibid., 1420.

40. Ibid., 1428.

black rural workers as well. To be a servant, the work had to fit the definitions in the act, but there also had to be a contract of service for continuous employment over a defined period. The courts ruled that persons who did piecework did not come under the acts, nor did those who were employed by the day, or who might or might not come to work on any particular day.[41] For a criminal conviction a contract had to have come into force and still be in force. All of these cases concerned rural work practices: itinerant sheep shearers, tenants with undefined duties, and tenants who had never before been called on to work were not covered. Farmer employers were also restricted by rulings that held that contracts could not be for longer than the statutory period, which meant that those workers (of whom there were large numbers) who were working off loans were not servants under the acts.

While the master and servant law purported to describe and control legal forms of hiring and firing, employment practices and customs in the countryside did not fit easily into its provisions. As the Worcester magistrate wrote of the Western Cape in 1912:

> Magistrates were greatly exercised when administering the Masters and Servants Acts owing to the loose contracts entered into, which were generally of such a nature that they could only be described as invalid when compared with the construction of a legal contract under the said Acts as laid down by the Superior Courts. The universal agreement was a hiring by the day which has been held did not bring the servant under the provisions of the law. Custom seemed to be the principle which both masters and servants acted upon and they had periodical settlements (*afrekeningen*). Engagements were entered into for ploughing and harvesting, but no definite dates were mentioned for the commencement or finishing thereof. . . . Most frequently contracts for further service were made regardless of the provision in law that servants must enter into service within one month from the date of making the oral contract which was the local mode of contracting farm labourers.[42]

The picture is one of established and negotiated local practices that did not fit easily with a legalized administration. Customary practices could not be enforced through the courts: before the state could exercise its power, it had to shape and to regulate rural practices and to adapt the inherited standard forms of the master and servant law. The Wolmaranstad magistrate wrote in 1912 that the 1880 Transvaal law should be repealed and replaced by a new one

41. Ibid., 1413.
42. *Reports of the Department of Justice*, 1913 (hereafter *UG44-1913*), 49–50.

requiring registration of farm labor contracts on the urban model and heavier penalties for desertion: "The present law was unsatisfactory as farmers often had no proper contracts with their servants, only a sort of tacit understanding which had been running for years and was in conflict with sections 8, 9 and 10 of the Law."[43]

Nonetheless, the importance of the master and servant law to the authority of white farmer employers over labor was highlighted by the magistrate in the district of Ficksburg (on the border between the Free State and Basutoland) in 1912. He wrote, in relation to those Africans who lived on white owned farms, that

> The squatting agreements with farmers were purely civil contracts which did not fall within the Masters and Servants Act. The native was nominally the white man's servant but actually his own master and enjoyed all the lazy liberties of life which obtained in Basutoland. . . . the fact that the farmer was bound by the laws of the land enabled the native to treat him with an easy contempt. . . . the whole system was . . . demoralising to the entire labour supply.[44]

Indeed, squatting created particular problems for meshing rural practices with the master and servant law. Many living on white farms had complex arrangements with the farmer, which might include wages, or the provision of stock and food, or the right to keep stock and to have land plowed, or plowing on the half with the owner. It was a complex matter to sort out complaints arising from these circumstances under the master and servant laws. As the Winburg magistrate wrote, many Africans plowed on shares and agreed that they and their families "will perform such work for the farmer as they may be called on to do. As such 'agreements' when in dispute cannot be taken to a Law Court, and as they do not bring either party within the terms of the Masters and Servants Act, they lead to endless trouble and tend to complicate the labour question."[45]

There was strong pressure to bring all farm workers under master and servant law, and one way was to outlaw farming on shares. A member of Parliament, P. J. Theron, put it simply: "It would drive the Kaffir into the position which most people would like to see him in, and instead of having loose men in our employment, we should have men who were fixed in our service . . . you can get twice as much labour out of him."[46]

43. *UG44-1913*, 120.
44. *UG44-1913*, 208–9.
45. *Reports of the Department of Justice*, 1911 (hereafter *UG14-1911*), 277.
46. *Select Committee 9-1913 (SC9-13)*, 583.

These powers of control perceived in master and servant law could also, ironically, work against the interest of some poor whites. It made it far harder for those whites who did seek to work for white farmers. A Transvaal magistrate noted that "the greatest obstacle to the employment of white unskilled labour is not so much the cheapness or efficiency of native labour, but the greater power of control which the employer exercises over the latter. In the case of the native, the pass regulations and Masters and Servants laws give the employer the necessary control of his labourers which is lacking in the case of the white man."[47]

"The cry as to the scarcity of native unskilled labour was very nearly universal."[48] The most frequent complaints from white farmers involved the competition from mines for black labor. Master and servant law was one means of restraining the labor market. Indeed, as a labor market developed in rural areas, master and servant convictions increased. Improved job opportunities for black workers — for example, those reported from two Cape districts in 1914, where higher wages were paid to railway workers — led to desertion prosecutions by farmers. And, where there was a shortage of labor, workers "had no compunction about absenting themselves from their work in the middle of a job and so causing their employers much inconvenience and material damage."[49]

Another major complaint of farmers with the workings of an unfettered labor market was that, where labor was scarce, employers had to pay wages in advance to secure workers, many of whom deserted before completing their terms of service. In the face of established and negotiated practices, this was a problem that master and servant law alone could not control. One Natal magistrate reported in 1915 that the many cases before the courts did not reflect the true number of desertions because masters condoned the offense to avoid the trouble and time involved in going to court. This was due

> entirely to the pernicious custom which has arisen throughout the Division of making cash advances against labour. To such an extent has this custom grown that it is almost impossible to obtain the services of a Native unless a substantial advance in cash is made. In very many cases once an advance is received great difficulty is experienced in getting the servant to fulfil his obligations and many instances have occurred where

47. In the light of the discussion of the interpretation of the laws by the judges in the Supreme Courts above, the magistrate's assumption that the laws would not apply to white farm laborers was not necessarily correct in law but indicates what were the ruling assumptions about the law at the level at which it was administered. *UG39-1919*, 107.

48. *UG44-1913*, 80.

49. *UG28-1915*, 28.

a native has obtained such an advance from no less than four Europeans for the same period.[50]

The problems of indebted laborers did not occupy the magistrates or farmers, but attracted the notice of F. W. Lucas in his dissenting addendum to the report of the Native Economic Commission. He found that in Natal in particular most rural laborers were heavily indebted to employers. He quoted the Heilbron magistrate:

> Some natives owe accounts . . . which at their average wage of 10s per month they can never repay. The result is that the native is nothing less than a slave to the . . . employer until the debt is repaid. There are many of these cases. The result is Natives . . . desert from service and risk years of imprisonment so long as they can get away from the place they are at. . . . Persons who for some reason or other cannot keep servants gladly lend them £2 or £3 to hire them knowing that on the wages paid the Native has no hope of ever refunding the money.[51]

He wrote, "[M]any employers contend that the servant to whom a loan has been made is subject to the Masters and Servants law in respect of that loan until it has been repaid."[52] This law was "a cause of very great dissatisfaction among the Natives. Some Natives describe the law as one for legalising slavery." The Standerton magistrate affirmed that "many Natives consider the Act, as worked, reduces them to a state bordering on serfdom owing to the creation of conditions which have the effect of tying them down for years to one farm and one master whether they like it or not."

The employment relationship was the frontline of the assertion of white authority over blacks: the economic, political, and legal were inextricably combined. Any dissent by an employee was "defiance"; it contained an immanent political and racial challenge. The role of master and servant law in the rule of law in the countryside was central. The Newcastle magistrate believed one-quarter of the police force could be dispensed with if the act were not enforced. "Several Magistrates," wrote Lucas, "stated that their popularity among Europeans in their areas was in proportion to the severity with which they punished Native servants under the Act."[53] In the Free State in 1917, one in six criminal cases was a master and servant case.[54] In 1918 the figure was

50. *UG28-1915*, 156.
51. *UG22-1932*, 148, 155.
52. *UG22-1932*, 270.
53. *UG22-1932*, 273, 275.
54. *UG36-1918*, 66.

closer to one in four. In Natal in that year in the whole province one in five cases was a master and servant case, and in the Umvoti district nearly nine out of ten were.[55]

Master and servant cases were heard at the lowest rung of the curial ladder in the courts of the rural justices of the peace and, where higher sentences were possible (for example, in repeat offenses) by magistrates. In 1918 the jurisdiction of the justices of the peace, much of whose work was master and servant cases, was considerably increased "for the convenience of the rural population."[56] These employers' courts were also granted powers to impose sentences of whipping.[57]

The most important political and legal controversies regarding master and servant law in the rural areas, however, concerned squatters and their families. Most Africans living on white farms did so in return for ninety days of labor per year, often spread over the year as two days a week. The tenant in return received land to plow and graze, and rations on days worked. The heads of families did not always work and, according to the Native Economic Commission, did so "only exceptionally" when they had grown-up children. The principal source of labor to the farmers was the sons of the kraal head, while women were available for housework. The resulting flight of young men from the farms to the towns produced considerable friction between farmers and tenants.[58] In 1921 the Transvaal Provincial Division in *Maynard v. Chasana* ruled that the squatting agreement by which a right of residence on white farms was granted in return for ninety days' labor a year, and under which large numbers of Africans in the Transvaal lived, was not a contract under the Masters and Servants Act. Although the outcome of this particular case favored the farmer, the decision had broad implications in rural areas. The position taken under republican law, and subsequently enforced by the British, had been that a squatting agreement was a contract for the purposes of master and servant law, and that all members of a squatter family were parties to the contract entered into by the family head. An outcry among rural employers followed the decision. A parliamentary select committee urgently recommended that "the status quo which was disturbed by certain decisions of the Supreme Court in the matter of the relationship between the squatter

---

55. *UG36-1919*, 76. Even so Helen Bradford comments that "violence made up the fabric of Umvoti rural society. . . . Most Umvoti farmers regarded the Law and the Police as totally inadequate to their purpose of controlling and exploiting their workers." Bradford, "Industrial and Commercial Workers' Union," 293.

56. *UG36-1919*, 1.

57. (S. Africa) n.2 of 1918.

58. *UG22-1932*, 359.

and the owner should be legalised and restored so that the said relationship between the parties may again be considered to be governed by the Masters and Servants Act."[59]

But the kinds of arrangements that governed squatting were not easily rendered into contractual form. In practice, the farmer claimed labor when needed. The statutory riposte produced in Parliament to bring these arrangements under master and servant law, in the words of A. W. Roberts in evidence to the select committee, did "not enforce a definite contract, but rather allow[ed] a roaming, roving contract, or a lien on the services of the man, his wife and children." It made no mention of definite statements as to the nature of the work, the duration, or the pay. His objection that the proposal envisaged a number of "powers" for the farmer, rather than a labor contract, was the same as that for which the courts had rejected the arrangements. Roberts argued instead that rural labor contracts should have specific terms, and that breach should be dealt with as a civil matter. The response of the chairman to the latter was brief and withering. "What value would the contract have," he asked, "if you let the man go?"[60] It was common for younger men to work on the farm for three months in a year—which was usually not taken consecutively by the farmer, but over a period of, say, six months—and to leave for the rest of the year to find work elsewhere. What was the status of workers outside of the ninety-day service period? If the whole arrangement was not a contract under the master and servant law, then these men were not the servants of the farmer and would not be liable for criminal penalties if they failed to return.

Civil penalties did not appeal to the farmers' representatives. Senator Munnik explained that civil action was a "terrible business. . . . The native will be egged on to all sorts of things. If the native knows that the farmer has no control over him except by civil action it will mean that we will be landed in trouble." The squatters, he complained, had the "whip hand."[61] As Heaton Nicholls put it, "The difficulty is . . . you cannot arrest them or do anything to them. They can simply walk away and laugh at you."

How were Africans to be kept on the farm now that the towns beckoned? The old Transvaal republican law had made it illegal for people to leave a farm without the farmer's consent. The Land Act[62] had been an attempt to restore the position in relation to squatters to what it had been before British colonial

59. *Select Committee 12-1925* (hereafter *SC12-1925*), 1.
60. *SC12-1925*, 4.
61. *SC12-1925*, 75–76.
62. (S. Africa) n.27 of 1913.

reforms. But currently, as Senator Munnik complained, native commissioners would issue a trek pass to those who wanted to work in the towns. When they returned, sometimes after two or three years, the farmers would claim the whole period of back service under master and servant law, with the threat of criminal penalty. Since the ruling that such returning squatters were not servants, the commissioners would not support this claim.[63] Many Africans did not know the law, and it is difficult to gauge what effect the courts' decisions had on them. Officials and farmers were not likely to inform squatters of their rights. The evidence of Herbst, the secretary for native affairs, is revealing. Squatters would be surprised, he said, that they did not come under master and servant laws as they "have no knowledge of the law" and were "not concerned with what laws are made as long as they are happy where they are."[64] He was equivocal about the effects of Maynard's case, and his general view of law displayed administrative impatience with judicial intervention. Did the ruling intend that the acts no longer applied to squatters? In his opinion, "the law is in force today . . . but because of certain judgements . . . the provisions cannot be applied in the Transvaal."[65] There was no law in the Free State binding young persons over the age of sixteen, "but fortunately they do not know it."[66] Would a new law overcome the farmers' problem? "I think you will always find the judges will drive a wedge in it if they possibly can."[67]

African witnesses before the committee spoke of a different world. Contract was not a meaningful concept. Chief Cornelius Mapoche testified that squatters agreed to the arrangements "because they cannot do anything else," and there was nowhere else for them to go. The farmers insisted on engaging the whole family and "the father has no option but must agree." The children objected and ran away to the towns, leaving the old people helpless and liable to eviction. Farmers tried to keep people by seizing their cattle. As for the magistrates, "When there is any dispute between a black man and a white man the latter is usually favoured."[68] R. V. Selope Thema affirmed the absence of any real element of contractual agreement. In answer to the suggestion that the law did not force family heads to enter into labor contracts, but simply gave them a right to, he said that farmers forced family heads to contract the

63. *SC12-1925*, 70.

64. As Selope Thema said to the committee, people did not normally know what the law was until someone told them, and it was usually the farmer who did: *SC12-1925*, 38–39.

65. *SC12-1925*, 33. The law was in force, he explained, but it was only now that the judgment had been given "that the law was not of force" (*SC12-1925*, 39).

66. *SC12-1925*, 47.

67. *SC12-1925*, 36.

68. *SC12-1925*, 92–96.

labor of their children: "For the simple reason that they have no place to go in the reserves because they are so crowded . . . the head of the family accepts any conditions that the farmer will offer him."

Reinforcing the contractual power of the father would "not give parents the control over their children, it gives the farmer the control over the children of the native people." Contract was essentially illusory. "Today the people are forced by conditions to say I will enslave myself."[69] The farmers, Selope Thema said, should not endeavor to tie African labor but should pay enough to attract them.[70] He told the committee that the proposed contract would result in "driving the future generation of natives away from the farms. They will look upon the farming industry as one that will bring about enslavement."[71] The rulers sought coercive law to hold African labor; the ruled expected that the law would be systematically evaded. Much anger was expressed in Selope Thema's evidence. The effect of the application of the masters and servants law in the countryside was that "the magistrate gets the child and he is made a criminal, as every law does among our people."

The Native Economic Commission echoed the evidence of many witnesses that "the time has come for legislation to be passed to make the completion of a written contract between farmer and tenant obligatory. . . . An official form of contract allowing latitude for variations in the detail of remuneration to the labourer should be available, farmers' organisations being consulted in its drafting." Contracts should be executed before an official or the magistrate advised. This move to extend the administration of legalized relations in the countryside had an economic rationale enunciated by the commission. A nominal cash wage should be stipulated, and then deductions for use of land made. This would enable the farmer to have an idea of the cost of labor and would assist tenants "to a purely economic outlook in cattle."[72]

The relief given by Maynard's case was short lived. Legislation was introduced to give farmers the right to enforce the labor service provisions of squatters' agreements by making the masters and servants acts applicable to them. But the question of the father's power to contract was held over. In 1931 the proposed Native Service Contract Bill (ultimately enacted in 1934) returned to this question. It gave powers (notwithstanding any other law) to a father to enter into contracts binding his children up to age eighteen. A breach of contract by any one was to be held to be a breach of contract by all,

69. *SC12-1925*, 121.
70. *SC12-1925*, 101.
71. *SC12-1925*, 109.
72. *SC12-1925*, 396–400.

thus rendering them liable to ejectment. This power, said J. S. Marwick, "is going to be very effective in maintaining discipline amongst servants."[73]

The Political Ecology of Labor Law

Labor issues were central to the formation of the South African state. The decades following the South African War saw the construction of a divided regime. The Milner administration in the Transvaal put the resources of the state behind the mobilization of labor for the Rand mines. The oppressive recruitment of black labor, and the tightening of the pass laws, prefigured the potential unionwide application of the Transvaal system by the Native Labour Regulation Act, which was passed in 1911.[74] Unable to coerce enough African labor, the British government of the Transvaal, at great political risk, imported Chinese labor for the mines. This fueled the rise of the Labour Party in the Transvaal. The Labour Party and the White Union movement deployed an international socialist rhetoric in their developing struggle to protect white workers against "unfree" Asian competition and African encroachment. The struggle between capital and labor took place in the peculiar local context of immense concentrations of capital in the Rand mines, a racially divided labor force, and, after 1910, the politics of the imperial successor state dominated by the issues of Afrikaner loyalty, resurgent white nationalism and rebellion, "native policy," and anxiety about the poor white problem. Several strikes accompanied by widespread violence followed. One was broken by the intervention of imperial troops, and the last, in 1922, by the South African Defence Force.

It is difficult to draw a "legal" boundary around labor, the labor contract, the legal regulation of conditions of work, union membership, organization and the right to strike, and wage regulation, for in all of these legal discourse interweaves with political, placing at issue the nature of the society, state, and politics. Their South African context includes a legally imposed industrial color bar that preserved the upper levels of employment for part of the racial ruling class. Another part of the context was the broader unfolding consideration of legal regulation of the economy as a whole, in particular the development of market-oriented ideologies both in opposition to, and together with, regulatory ones. In this highly regulated and racially stratified society, the labor contract was pivotal in the development of legal thought. To what extent was it a "free" contract, between a free worker and an employer, amounting

73. *Select Committee 7-1931 (SC7-31)*, 18.
74. (S. Africa) n.15 of 1911.

to a mutually agreed bargain as to wages? What was the role of the state in
the regulation of wages, and in the control of breaches of contract, such as
strikes and desertions? And in what senses, and how far, could the livelihood
and well-being of white workers, and, therefore, of whites as a whole, be left
to a labor market where they competed with workers of other races? It is clear
that a political determination to entrench white power and a purely market-
and contract-based model of employment law could not have lived together.
In the decades after the formation of the union, the state undertook the difficult task of developing, at the same time, both a market approach to law and
economy with which to defend the system against the threatening predations
of "socialist" white labor, and a nonmarket justification for a racially bifurcated labor force. The regulatory ideology of the state and the market ideology of common law (and many of the state's economic advisers) provided the
poles of the discursive field within which the construction of the labor market color bar made possible the continued dominance of market ideology in
other sectors.

While labor law regulates the employment relationship, it also serves as a
tool of economic regulation. In South Africa it was pivotal in the preservation
of a white capitalist state. In addition to the racial division, and the emerging
competition for employment between white and black, the state was particularly dependent on the concentration of mining capital. The politics of labor
law were immediately governed by the existence of a white Labour Party,
and the White Union movement strong enough to mount a series of mining strikes accompanied by widespread civil disorder and rebellion, and by
the language of revolution. White politicians were haunted by fears that out-
breaks of this kind threatened the entire structure of white rule in the country.[75] Thus both controlling and, to an extent, satisfying the white labor constituency was the prime political necessity that drove the development of
industrial relations law. The Industrial Conciliation Act of 1923 reflected this
dual agenda. But this response was complicated by the particularities of white
politics in the period in which the urbanization of whites was strengthening
the Afrikaner composition of the white working class. This, together with the
pressures of the poor white problem, drove the Nationalist Party to join the
Labour Party in embracing strategies of racial regulation of urban labor. In
1924 this alliance was elected to government and proceeded further to entrench the position of white workers. These were the circumstances in which
the rhetorical and conceptual tools of law were deployed.

75. Sensitivity to the effect of white strikes on black workers was widespread. The chief
native commissioner, Taberer, told the Economic Commission in 1914 that Africans "have had
a very excellent example of how easy it is to defy law and order." *UG12-1914*, 37.

The core of the labor struggle, which culminated in the bloody strike of 1922 behind the slogan, "workers of the world unite and fight for a white South Africa," was the bitter conflict between white labor and the Rand mines. In essence, the mine owners preferred to use low-paid black labor, legally tied by the masters and servants laws and the Native Labour Regulation Act. They argued that the end of the color bar, and the consequent reduction in the cost of labor, was essential to the future profitability of their industry. White labor believed mine owners intended to exploit black labor more intensively at the expense of whites, and that eventually this would drive them out of employment in the country's largest industry.[76]

The different intellectual capital employed in the legal debates emerged from the legal evolution of nineteenth-century Britain. The U.K. Employers and Workmen Act of 1875[77] had been the watershed between a legal regime in which the labor relation was governed by master and servant law, and one that recognized "free" labor. But whereas in Britain the "legal imagery" of master and servant was "increasingly subordinated to the idea of contract,"[78] in South Africa the concept of contract was to strengthen and enhance the relation of master and servant. Before the triumph of the idea of contract in the nineteenth century, Holdsworth wrote, it was not considered that wages were settled by individual bargain (or prices), "or that the contract between employer and workman could be regarded as precisely similar to any other contract."[79] Contract involves the idea of free choice and therefore gives a new rationale for the acceptance of obligation. In South Africa, as the law developed, the emphasis of the master and servant regime in governing black workers was on their "choice" in accepting the terms of their employment. The new "master symbol" of contract was deployed to strengthen the master and servant regime. But in relation to white workers the development of contract in relation to employment was different. The existence of the white Labour Party and the trade-union movement underpinned the emergence of a dual regime. For white workers the coercive subordination of the whole person of the servant gave way to the idea of the contractual bargain for the sale of labor alone as a commodity, which, in the newly developing common law approach, was the product of a voluntary exchange between the parties. But

76. White employers, workers, politicians, and economists espoused the view that black labor was in an inherently stronger position than white because it did not depend solely on the sale of its labor to survive, but could "stay" on the land. For this reason, the added controls of the masters and servants laws and the restrictions on bargaining power for black workers were considered "fair."

77. (U.K.) 38&39 Vict. c.90 (1875).

78. Creighton et al., *Labour Law*, 19.

79. Ibid., 20.

in their case the contractual regime was to be diluted by the development of the statutory intervention that regulated the transaction.[80]

The new industrial conciliation legislation imposed on the trade unions after the end of the strike regulated white labor only. By 1923 the exclusion of Africans from the mechanism of industrial dispute settlement was taken for granted. It had been the subject of debate in the Transvaal Legislative Assembly in 1909. Some Labour members objected that the exclusion made Africans more attractive to hire because of their legally subordinate position. But Smuts stated the central rationale, that it was unthinkable that a legislative means of regulating strikes should apply to African workers because it was unthinkable that black workers should take part in legitimate concerted labor actions like strikes. The exclusion of black workers from the definition of employee effectively prevented trade unions from organizing black workers.

A year after the election of the Nationalist-Labour Pact Government in 1924, a major commission reviewed the labor and wage policies affecting all South African workers in the light of the new government's "civilised labour" policy. The political and intellectual context revolved at one level around the clash between voluntary contracting and individual bargaining, and a state-directed regime of wage determination. While the commission's report caused great controversy by supporting the concept of a free market in employment, it accepted extensive market interference for African workers. The commissioners noted that, despite a shortage of African labor, "the ordinary result," a rise in wages, had not taken place. The Native Recruiting Corporation advised that because African workers could satisfy their needs by intermittent periods of service, an increase in wages would merely mean that they would work for shorter periods and the amount of labor would be reduced. African workers were also subject to legal restrictions that affected their bargaining power and kept wages down. The masters and servants acts and the Native Labour Regulation Act provided for penal prosecution for breach of contract; permitted or required long contracts of service, usually six or nine months; and were built upon licensed recruiting and the compound system.[81]

The commissioners were on the whole satisfied that this was a reasonable regime. "[W]itnesses of great authority" told them that the penal clauses were a "necessary means of punishing breaches of contract by the native, who

80. There was little trace in the South African discussions with their repeated emphasis on the contractual obligations of employees of what Higgins said was "the truth of the doctrine of modern economists, of all schools I think, that freedom of contract is a misnomer as applied to the contract between an employer and an ordinary employee": Higgins, "New Province for Law and Order," 25.

81. UG14-1926, 37–38.

generally has no assets which it is practicable to seize by civil action; that it imposes no greater hardship upon the native than the corresponding civil action imposes on a white man, and that in any event it affects only those who break their contracts." Long contracts were needed to "secure economic working" from Africans who were not dependent on wages, and compounds were "inevitable" if large numbers of Africans were to be employed in centers of white population.[82]

The majority of the commissioners approved the application of master and servant law to "natives and the more ignorant class of coloured labourer." While criminal penalties were imposed for many acts that "otherwise would be visited merely by dismissal" (such as disobedience, breach of duty, and absence), the servants received a simple remedy against the withholding of wages and were in a better position than common-law servants if ill.[83] The commissioners remarked that "some differential treatment is inevitable where dealing with labour that is mainly illiterate and of inferior race." The statutes protected as well as penalized, and gave remedies to laborers who had "no possible chance of asserting their rights through civil procedures." While they might appear harsh, "As with all Acts affecting natives, a great deal depends upon the fairness and common sense of those who have to administer them." Finally, with a certain chilling realism, they claimed that "One point in favour of the Statutes is that they tend to reduce the number of assaults upon Native servants. The Master is given an alternative remedy for gross breaches of duty and frequently takes advantage of it."[84]

The minority report expressed concern about the spreading effects that a legal regime, meant primarily for blacks, might have upon whites: "These special provisions have the social result of dulling the public conscience against interference with the freedom of the individual not only for natives but for whites as well, so that a feeling tends to be established that the manual worker—whatever his colour—belongs to a different species of animal."[85] This was deleterious to white labor in that it made African workers more attractive to employers. Most farmers who gave evidence averred that they

82. *UG14-1926*, 38. The confining regulations under the Native Labour Regulation Act were, the commissioners thought, only the quid pro quo for the benefits that were given to African workers under the act, such as written contracts, the power of the director of native labour to cancel contracts, and the regulations regarding advance payments and remittances to relatives: *UG14-1926*, 39.

83. Penalties were light, in their view: two pounds or a month's labor for a first offense, "which is no greater penalty than that often imposed for breach of a municipal regulation." *UG14-1926*, 40. They did not consider the sum in relation to monthly earnings.

84. *UG14-1926*, 40.

85. *UG14-1926*, 328–29.

never used the acts because they were a waste of time, and also mentioned
the larger problem of getting a bad name and having disaffected employees. Nevertheless, they all urged that the system be continued because of its
"moral effect" on their employees.

While the majority of the commissioners found that the regime of master
and servant and other labor laws was harsh and discriminatory, they nonetheless accepted that it should continue. The minority, reflecting the views
of white labor, differed on both points. It concluded both that the laws gave
advantages to black workers, and that they should be swept away. Their analysis is important because it highlights the "common sense" that dismissed the
market approach to labor law and wage regulation, and which underpinned
the policies that followed. South African industry, they began, depended on
low-paid African labor. But there had never been enough, and industry had
imported Indians, Chinese, and Africans from Mozambique. The migrant
labor system and low pay had produced impoverished reserves, and detribal-
ized men who, not receiving the necessities of life, were "driven to extreme
measures such as crime or revolution."[86] White Labour politicians and activists had long been more sensitive than other whites to the potentially porous
boundary between legislative oppression of black labor and the status and
freedom of white workers. The greater powers that employers had over Africans made them preferable as employees. The opportunities for white labor
were undermined, in this view, as long as black labor was preferable to employers.

What was the alternative legal regime? While in theory it was the
common-law individual contract, it was admitted that the development of
trade unions had made this effectively obsolete. Most employer organizations,
as well as most unions, told the commission that the ideal means of settling
wages was voluntary collective bargaining. The majority report accepted with
approval the framework provided by the Industrial Conciliation Act. For this
purpose, it noted, effective trade unions must exist, so long as they had an exclusively industrial purpose and did not subordinate wage bargaining to an
outside political interest. The "motive force" behind the Industrial Conciliation Act had been the failure of the law to deal with the issues of the 1922
strike. The act subjected unions to tight controls in return for accepting their
role in the wage-bargaining process. Registered unions had to be representative and hold ballots before strike action. And while collective bargaining
might be voluntary, the agreed outcome could be made compulsory. Pro-

86. *UG14-1926*, 323–25.

vision was made for the establishment of industrial councils. Industry-wide agreements reached and registered with such councils had legal effect, and all in the industry had to comply. None of these processes applied to African workers. The commissioners observed that "So far as the natives are concerned the only method of settling wage rates appears to be that employers determine what they will pay."[87]

Conclusion

There is a broader context into which labor policies, labor law, and the law of master and servant in South Africa can be set. Following the abolition of slavery in the Cape in 1834, alternative ways of mobilizing and controlling labor became part of both the imperial and the various local agenda. These were constrained by international opinion, particularly opinion in Britain, and especially in the twentieth century by developing international standards. Forced labor was no longer legally justifiable, and the goals had to be achieved by invoking different legal concepts and mechanisms. While the use of tribute labor based on the supposed powers of African chiefs was looked on with increasing suspicion and ultimately renounced, indentured labor and laws based on criminal sanctions supporting the contract of employment between master and servant were acceptable as ways of dealing with workers who had no political voice. The key was the manipulation of the concept of contract. Contractual choice was presented as the opposite of slavery and the mark of freedom. It was also the justification for the coercion at the core of the masters and servants law.

In English law the contract of employment was transformed by industrialism, the rise of representative democracy, and trade unions. The 1875 act accorded a more equal status to both sides of the employment contract and abandoned penal sanctions for breach. In the colonial world this transition did not take place in the same way. While in England after 1875 both skilled and unskilled labor was governed by the same legal regime, in South Africa the division was deliberately widened along racial lines by both judges and legislatures. The transition that had taken place in English law affected the white working force only, whereas the labor contracts of black workers both in new industries and in rural areas continued to be conceptualized and governed according to pre-industrial models. The legal regime for white South African workers was also much affected by those developed in other white do-

87. *UG14-1926*, 50.

minions, such as Canada and Australia, reflecting the rise of trade unions and bitter conflicts over the right to strike, to organize, and to collective labor contracts. Black South Africans were excluded from this struggle.

In the United Kingdom and its white imperial offshoots, freedom of contract was the employers' tool in the struggle against trade unions and the struggle for better wages and working conditions. Contractual ideology was the basis of defense against the mobilization of labor to collective action. In South Africa, the idiom of contract played a different but crucial role in the bifurcated labor regime. In relation to Africans, the labor contract served to conceal the reality of legally enforced coercion. When "contract" was spoken to blacks, it affirmed a notional voluntary adherence to the institutionalized systems of coercion, of which each individual contract was a part. In relation to whites it was not simply an employers' defense but a positive reaffirmation of white labor's freedom in the midst of a system based on coercion. The irony in South Africa was that in the end white workers, who had full capacity to make political judgments, were controlled by statute, by awards and conciliation agreements that limited the application of contract to their working conditions, while blacks remained governed by the ideology of contract, denied on the one hand the capacity to make choices in the political realm, yet deemed to have the capacity to have chosen repression in their workplaces.

ELEVEN

Hong Kong, 1841–1870

All the Servants in Prison
and Nobody to Take Care of the House

Christopher Munn

The term "Servant" shall mean every Chinese regularly employed
in or about the Dwelling House, Office or Business Premises of any
Company, Corporation, or Person not being Chinese, in any of the
following capacities:

House Boy, Cook, Cook's Mate, Amah, Coolie, Watchman, Gar-
dener, Coachman, Horse Boy, and Boatman.[1]

When the British acquired Hong Kong in 1841, it was an isolated island community of a few thousand people. By 1870 it had grown into a large international trading city with a population of more than 124,000. Between the
small European colonial elite and the rapidly growing Chinese community
that dominated the economic life of the colony there were few ties: "[T]he
separation of the native population from the European," wrote governor Sir
John Bowring in 1858, was "nearly absolute." Linguistic, cultural, and social
barriers inhibited contact. The sojourning, unsettled nature of the Chinese
population aroused considerable anxieties among the Europeans about crime
and disorder. The absence of indigenous elites and the continued allegiance
of Chinese inhabitants to the emperor of China during a period of intermittent hostilities between Britain and China made rebellion and subversion a
constant fear, and encouraged the colonial authorities to deploy force and surveillance in their attempts to govern the island. The European elite did not
even exert much of a hold on the colony's labor, which was controlled largely

I am grateful to Martha Kanya-Forstner, Jerry Bannister, and Stephen Rockel for their comments on earlier drafts.
   1. (Hong Kong) n.7 of 1866: the Victoria Registration Ordinance.

by Chinese employers. "A few Chinese," admitted Bowring, "speak a strange 'jargon' by which they are enabled to convey their ideas to foreigners," but hardly a single European spoke any Chinese: "[T]he influence of the European settler upon the native mind may be said to be nil."[2]

Bridging part of the gulf between European settlers and the Chinese masses, and forming the largest group of speakers of this "strange 'jargon,'" or pidgin English, were the Chinese domestic servants. Europeans depended on them for their most basic daily needs and for insulation from the strange and difficult world that lay outside the home. Servants performed these functions very much on their own terms. They were quick to assert their interests and resist impositions. They inherited many of the attitudes and restrictive practices of the precolonial Canton system, when Europeans rather than Chinese had been the subordinate class. They formed a link in the tight monopolistic chain by which Chinese suppliers "squeezed" European households. Their intimate access to the private world of their employers and the ease with which they could abscond presented tempting opportunities for theft. And their close family connections with the mainland made them susceptible to intimidation and manipulation by the Chinese authorities during times of political tension. Alternately disowned by the Chinese authorities, branded as traitors, or ordered to take part in sanctions against the British colony, Chinese servants in Hong Kong occupied an uneasy position in the troubled relations between Chinese and British governments. The anxieties to which these problems gave rise encouraged the colonial government to single out Chinese domestic servants as a special category for legislation that went beyond the master and servant laws imported into the colony along with English law. This chapter examines that legislation and the relationship between European employers and their Chinese domestic servants during Hong Kong's formative years as a British colony.

This chapter is divided into four sections. The first describes the politics of master-servant relations in early Hong Kong and its background in the old Canton system of European trade with China. The second section explores how Chinese servants in Hong Kong were successful in asserting their interests against employers: it argues that in many households an understanding was reached in which servants were able to impose certain financial exactions and restrictive practices on their employers in return for providing the services on which Europeans depended. The third discusses the range of sanctions Europeans had at their disposal when this understanding broke down

2. Bowring to Lytton, 18 Sept. 1858, Public Record Office, CO series (hereafter CO), CO 129/69, 247.

through misconduct, crime, and political conflicts and argues that these sanctions were increasingly seen by Europeans as ineffective. The fourth section examines the additional schemes introduced by the colonial government to combat crime and control the colony's laboring population and the specific provisions intended to give European employers greater protection from, and control over, their Chinese servants: it argues that the criminalization of labor relations already present in English master-servant law imported into Hong Kong was taken a stage further in an attempt to assuage the fears of a tiny European community surrounded by a large and unassimilated Chinese population.

The sources for this study are problematic and incomplete. The statistics that survive on employment relations are sparse and of dubious value. Reports on cases in the lower courts—where most labor disputes were settled—are patchy in their coverage. The many anecdotal accounts of Chinese servants in European diaries, memoirs, and newspapers are often little more than the traditional grievances of employers everywhere, dressed in suitably exotic clothes: doubtless, they underrepresent abuse by employers, and, in their eagerness to generalize, stereotype, and orientalize, they form part of the problem. Statements by the servants themselves—except through the distorting medium of their employers—are entirely absent: the "hidden transcript" of what servants were saying about their masters behind their backs has not survived.[3]

The Political Economy of Master and Servant in Hong Kong

The British founded Hong Kong in the early 1840s on the principles of free trade and the free movement of labor. The large surplus population in China provided Hong Kong and many other parts of the world with a seemingly endless supply of cheap labor throughout the nineteenth century. "If," reported governor Sir Hercules Robinson in 1861, "we could offer the starving myriads of the opposite continent unlimited employment which would yield the settler even two meals a day of rice and fish with twopence a day for tobacco and luxuries, with common shelter and commonest clothing, I believe we might congregate a million souls under our rule within two years."[4] The abundance of cheap and skilled Chinese labor in and around the colony made it unnecessary for the merchants and professionals who dominated colonial society to seek labor from elsewhere: both the climate and government policy

3. See J. Scott, *Domination*.
4. Robinson to Newcastle, 5 June 1861, CO 129/81, 177–78.

were against the formation of a European proletariat of any great size.[5] "In this little colony," declared the *Hongkong Register* in 1855, "the Chinese are our butchers, bakers, tailors, shoemakers, carpenters, servants—in fact without them this would not be a colony."[6] While rightly pointing out the complete dependence of the small colonial elite on the Chinese community for its daily needs, the *Register* is misleading in suggesting that the Chinese in Hong Kong existed only to serve the needs of Europeans. Direct European control over the Chinese labor that streamed into Hong Kong in its early decades was extremely limited. In the official census for that year, out of a total Chinese population of 70,651, only 3,325 came under the heading "Chinese in employ of Europeans."[7] This category included the compradors, clerks, interpreters, overseers, and watchmen who worked for European firms and the colonial government. A large proportion, however, and perhaps the majority, consisted of domestic servants. The mere 571 merchants, civil servants, professionals, and petty tradesmen who made up the permanent European and American population of Hong Kong in that year would also have made frequent use of the thousands of casual laborers who sojourned in the colony.[8] The figures suggest, however, that, in contrast to their cousins in settler or plantation colonies, Europeans directly controlled only a very small part of the colony's labor force. By the end of 1855, Hong Kong's population had doubled in the space of four years with the influx of refugees from the widespread disorder in southern China: the Chinese in Hong Kong ran their own economy, which centered generally on trade. In early 1856, another newspaper, the *Friend of China*, conceded the importance of the Chinese community to the colony's wealth and well-being and pointed out that "we can no longer consider the Chinese here as only to be used as servants, compradors, and purveyors and tradesmen for the European inhabitants."[9]

5. Unemployed "European mechanics" from Australia and elsewhere were for a brief time a problem in the very early years of the colony. Although unable to compete in the labor market, English and Irish soldiers and sailors on shore leave added a considerable quasi-proletarian element to the colony's European population. *Friend of China* (hereafter *FC*), 13 Feb. 1844, 246; *Canton Press* (hereafter *CP*), 17 Feb. 1844; Emily Kerr to Mary Sword, 3 May 1845, quoted in Hoe, *Private Life*.

6. *Hongkong Register* (hereafter *HR*), 25 Sept. 1855, 154.

7. Population returns for 1855, *Hongkong Government Gazette* (hereafter *Gazette*), 12 Apr. 1856.

8. To this small, permanent community should be added a European garrison of around 500 and a temporary European population (composed largely of seamen) of about 300. The permanent European community rose to more than 2,000 in the mid-1860s, but it was still "surrounded by a dense Chinese fluctuating population in the proportion now of at least 60 Chinese to one European." MacDonnell to Carnarvon, 23 Nov. 1866, CO 129/116, 108. For a fuller survey of the population of early British Hong Kong, see Munn, *Anglo-China*, ch. 2.

9. *FC*, 13 Feb. 1856, 51.

It is doubtful if the Chinese in Hong Kong had ever only been there to serve the tiny European population. The founding of the colony in 1841 had attracted thousands of laborers to construct roads and buildings mainly for European use, but from the beginning the colony was a center of Chinese enterprise, some of it traditionally connected with the island (such as stone quarrying and fishing) but most of more recent invention, such as the flourishing trade in populating and supplying the expanding Chinese emigrant communities in places such as California and Australia. Europeans certainly found a useful role for Hong Kong in their activities along the China coast, as a shipping and banking center, as the headquarters of many merchant houses, and as a depot for opium and other commodities. Their activities were also closely linked to those of many Chinese merchants and middlemen. But their share of the direct control of labor in Hong Kong was small: it was also declining during a period in which a rapidly expanding population and frequent hostilities between Britain and China prompted calls from colonists for greater political control of the Chinese population. These controls were directed against crime and political opposition and included restrictions on labor generally and on Chinese employees of Europeans in particular. They were a clumsy and repressive response to real problems, at the root of which perhaps lay "the difficulty of dealing with a large Chinese population by means of a police who cannot speak their language."[10] But they also reflected the growing insecurity of a tiny European community, believing itself to be facing a deluge of crime.

At the heart of this insecurity lay the relations between Europeans and their Chinese servants. The oppressive, unhealthy climate and the cultural gulf that separated them from most of the colony's population made Europeans especially dependent on their Chinese domestic servants. In the early years of the colony especially, when men considerably outnumbered women in both the European and Chinese populations, male European householders directing male Chinese servants tended to be the norm, a considerable variation from the largely female realm of bourgeois domestic life.[11] Domestic servants had privileged access to the private lives of Europeans and enjoyed opportunities for cheating and stealing, which, in the opinion of many of

10. Julian Pauncefote, attorney general, commenting on (Hong Kong) n.7 of 1866, 27 Aug. 1866, CO 129/114, 523.

11. See Davidoff and Hall, *Family Fortunes*. The ratio of female to male Chinese employees of Europeans was about 1:13 in the late 1840s and early 1850s, 1:20 in the mid-1850s, and 1:8 in the mid-1860s (these figures include nondomestic employees). From the mid-1850s, female servants were increasingly employed as amahs (ladies' maids or nurses) in European households, and numerous Chinese women made a living as "protected women" or mistresses of Europeans: see C. T. Smith, "Protected Women."

their employers, they fully exploited. They were often the only Chinese with whom Europeans in Hong Kong came into extended contact, and it was from their domestics that many of them formed their usually negative stereotypes of "the Chinese character." Indeed, by the late 1850s, the Chinese domestic was already a well-defined type. "Atan," brother of "Attai," the stereotypical "China girl,"

> is bred up from his infancy for service among Europeans, and is surrounded from his dawning days with boys and coolies and compradors, who are constantly vaunting and displaying their wrongful gains, and are always laughing at the "cute" manner in which they individually have "done" their masters [and] often force the will-be "boy" to look on plunder as "proper pidgin" and on the successful plunderer as a kind of hero to be forthwith imitated.[12]

"Atan" had a long pedigree, rooted in "oriental monopoly" and "mandarin oppression," and predating the British acquisition of Hong Kong by many decades. Since 1760 European trade with China had been confined, under strict regulation, to the southern city of Canton. Among the restrictions had been a formal limit to the number of Chinese servants a foreign trading factory might employ as compradors (or manager-intermediaries), linguists, domestics, and porters. The provincial government usually relaxed the limit but also periodically used the restrictions as a tool in its disputes with the East India Company, which until 1833 monopolized Britain's trade with China. Chinese officials also frequently abused the Chinese servants themselves, whose allegiance they believed to have been tainted by their connections with Europeans. The right to employ servants without restriction ranked high in the requests of British embassies and petitions to the Chinese government, but the problem worsened in the 1830s, with the growing number of opium merchants in Canton and the deregulation of the British side of the trade with China.[13] It formed part of a large catalog of vexatious official measures, which British merchants claimed made their life in Canton intolerable. Government proclamations reminding the Cohong (the Chinese merchants who monopolized and managed European trade) that foreigners were not permitted to ride in sedan chairs or bring their wives to Canton seemed to be "promulgated with the evident design to hold up foreigners to the eyes of Chinese as an inferior and abject class which must tend to bring them into contempt with the lower

---

12. *China Mail* (hereafter *CM*), 11 Aug. 1859, 126.
13. For the many incidents and disputes involving Chinese servants, see Morse, *East India Company*.

orders of society."[14] Annual proclamations formally banning the employment of servants by Europeans charged British merchants with crimes too "shameful and atrocious" for the East India Company to place on record and warned the Cohong against buying young boys or procuring prostitutes for them.[15] Such allegations, and the generally low esteem in which foreigners in Canton were held, taught servants to despise their European masters. These servants, reported the *Canton Press* in 1838, belonged "to the very lowest class in the empire. They consider it a degrading service, and not one of them ever speaks to his employers but in a contemptuous or patronizing style. In order to gain the means of freeing themselves from this unpalatable thraldom, they pilfer and cheat as much as possible, and hold rather extravagant notions respecting the extent of their perquisites."[16]

Difficulties with servants plagued the besieged European community during the events that preceded the Opium War. When, in early 1839, the foreign residents of Canton were held hostage for the handing over of contraband opium, one of their greatest deprivations was having to do their own carrying, cooking, and housework.[17] Following their release from captivity in May and their exodus to the Portuguese settlement of Macao, the order from the Chinese government that Chinese compradors and servants should leave their British employers was the last insult that drove them to seek their final refuge in Hong Kong harbor.[18] While it would be rash to suggest that Hong Kong was founded because of a shortage of servants, Europeans in the new colony made ample use of the freedom they now possessed to employ Chinese servants in whatever quantities they wished. For their part, the Chinese servants, who came predominantly from counties close to Macao and Canton, brought with them to Hong Kong many of the attitudes and practices that had prevailed at Canton.

The Servant's Interest

Visitors to Hong Kong frequently commented on the large numbers of servants employed in colonial households, on the effete way in which Europeans

14. Protest by the English community to the East India Company, Oct. 1830, quoted in ibid., 4:236.

15. Ibid., 4:236; Morse, *International Relations*, 1:160.

16. *CP*, 14 July 1838.

17. *Chinese Repository*, 7 (Apr. 1839), 628.

18. The Public Notice to British subjects on behalf of the British Plenipotentiary of 21 Aug. 1839 cites the withdrawal of servants and the stopping of supplies as the main reasons for the planned departure to Hong Kong. *Chinese Repository*, 8 (Aug. 1839), 222.

traveled everywhere in sedan chairs borne by coolies, and on how the merchant community strove to "transact the everyday business of life with the least trouble."[19] It was generally accepted that a middle-class European household in Hong Kong needed several times as many domestic servants as it might need at home and would supplement this number, as the occasion demanded, from the large pool of labor available among the street coolies, who could be summoned at the click of a finger.[20] Vast numbers of servants stood in attendance at dinner parties, and when, on a moonlit evening in 1866, the judge John Whyte gave a picnic for 80 guests on the slopes of Victoria Peak, he employed 300 chair bearers to carry them and their improvised kitchen.[21]

Apart from the obvious facts that many Europeans had a great deal of disposable wealth and servants were cheap and in plentiful supply, three explanations might be put forward for this. First, in a small, wealthy, and deeply snobbish European community, many of whom were of lowly origins with high social ambitions, entertainment and display helped establish status and promote political influence. Governor Robinson complained in the early 1860s that it was impossible for a governor "to vie with the pomp and display of private individuals" in a community "where wealth is honour" and one that was "remarkable for the wealth of its members, for their boundless hospitality and costly display."[22] Lower down the social scale, the correspondent "Sub" described to the *China Mail* in 1862 how the need to return the lavish hospitalities offered to him by friends and acquaintances spoiled his plans to lead a simple life in Hong Kong. "The place was bad enough," he admitted, "without making it worse by lopping off the pleasures of society."[23]

The second explanation was Hong Kong's reputation of having one of the unhealthiest climates of any British colony. "A man is but half a man at Hong Kong," wrote one of the colony's early detractors: its humid heat sapped the energy of Europeans and afflicted them with diseases ranging from the fatal and inexplicable "Hong Kong fever" to the almost universal prickly heat and boils.[24] The use of servants reduced exertion, kept employers cool, and provided some of the few compensations to be found in such a trying climate. "So much of this imagined luxury," wrote the former civil servant Alfred

19. See, for example, Ellis, *Hong Kong*, 282; article on Hong Kong from the *Alta* of California, 1859, in CO 129/84, 219.
20. Weatherhead, "Hong Kong," 15, 24.
21. Diary of Matilda Sharp, 1866, in J. Smith and Savidge, *Matilda*, 62.
22. Robinson to Newcastle, 17 Sept. 1862, CO 129/90, 283–84.
23. *CM*, 25 Sept. 1862, 154.
24. Martin, *China*, 98. Hong Kong fever was believed to be endemic to Hong Kong. It devastated the European and Indian troops in Hong Kong in the colony's early years but was less prevalent among the civilian population.

Weatherhead in his materials for a lecture on Hong Kong, "is mere matter of necessity—and by no means implies enjoyment—or even comfort."

> We must lead a moderately bon-vivant sort of life, and with every appliance of comfort and luxury, with rare and choice wines, with ices and punkahs, with carriages and traps, with houses furnished in every style of elegance, with servants who understand our wants, and attend to them. . . . Luxury, kept on all sides within the limits of excess, is the secret of health in the East. There are few favorable specimens of an opposite system to be found.[25]

A third reason supplied by Weatherhead was the clear demarcation of responsibilities that Chinese servants maintained among themselves, so that the multiple duties necessary in even a small household could not usually be performed by a small staff: "No Chinaman with any proper self-respect would cook your dinner and open the door too—your house coolie would consider himself an injured individual, and grossly imposed upon, if you requested him to take a chit (note) for you next door."[26] A well-off merchant would employ a hierarchy of cooks, assistant cooks, amahs, and gardeners, as well as door, stable, punkah, house, and chair coolies, all under the charge of a comprador or major domo, "a long-tailed, sleek Chinaman, who is his general agent, keeps his money, pays his bills, does all his marketing, hires his servants, and stands security for their honesty, and of course cheats him unmercifully."[27] Some compradors exercised an almost dictatorial control over the household. "All the British residents were obliged to keep a compradore," recorded one fleeting visitor to the colony, "that is a man to whom they paid a certain amount of money and he kept house accordingly. You could not even suggest anything to him or ask questions."[28] Less affluent households would probably do without the comprador and the stables and would employ a much smaller hierarchy of servants. Few, however, could do without the services of a "boy," whom Weatherhead describes as "by no means necessarily a youth, but ofttimes a full grown, able bodied fellow. His pigeon is to run errands—convey chits—attend on you at dinners and parties, make all bargains and give orders to tradespeople, and act generally as your interpreter and representative."[29] Like other European employers, Weatherhead complained that Chinese ser-

25. Weatherhead, "Hong Kong," 33.
26. Ibid., 15.
27. Cooke, *China*, 57.
28. Venables, "Rebellion." I am indebted to Judi McBride-Wilson of Wellington, New Zealand, for this source.
29. Weatherhead, "Hong Kong," 16.

vants had "no notion of overworking themselves," and were "unquestionably very slovenly and dirty—will insist upon wiping the dinner plates with the washing towels, frying your dinner with lamp oil, will sweep round but never under sofas and bedstead etc., and it takes a long time and immense patience and perseverance to instil into them the faintest notions of European cleanliness and order."[30]

Doubtless these were the grumbles of English men and women throughout the empire, but a considerable amount of anecdotal evidence suggests that domestic servants were often very successful in asserting their interests against those of their employers. Indeed, the many ways in which servants guarded their privileges and resisted impositions caused some Europeans to believe that it was they who were being exploited or even persecuted by their servants. Restrictive practices were one obvious method, but servants also used a variety of other ploys to gain at the expense of their masters and mistresses. The greatest hold over Europeans was an economic one. In a swollen labor market that worked consistently in favor of employers, servants cost little enough, but it was still necessary for Europeans to pay their servants up to three or four times what Chinese employers paid theirs. Part of this price reflected the linguistic skills, cultural compromises, and political risks required of a servant to a European household, as well as the fact that employment did not always include board. A certain percentage of a servant's income would also go as security and commission to the comprador who arranged the employment and guaranteed the honesty of the servant.[31] But the differential is considerable enough to suggest both that domestic servants did well out of their European employers and that compradors, as brokers, maintained something of a monopoly on the supply of servants.

Compradors, or the cooks, boys, or other servants in charge of buying provisions, also did well on the "squeeze" system they operated in collaboration with those who ran the markets. "Our compradors," wrote Sir John Bowring, the fourth governor,

> invariably pocket large profits on domestic expenditure. They come to an understanding with the market people who also thoroughly understand one another, advancing prices wherever they are able and resisting their reduction with too successful pertinacity. We are in the hands of

30. Ibid., 15, 20.
31. The annual Colonial Blue Books for Hong Kong (CO 133) consistently record the monthly wages of the lowest class of servant during this period at £15 per annum, or about $5.50 per month. From 1864, the equivalent servants in Chinese households are priced at £3 15s per annum (about $1.40 per month) with board and lodging, rising to £4 10s in 1866.

Chinese servants and few persons (not being Chinese) are to be found in the colony capable of making a bargain with the sellers of commodities.[32]

The climate, the ignorance of the language, and the fact that most Europeans were "too much occupied, or too indifferent, to check the items of their household expenditure," helped to perpetuate this system.[33] Firm resistance from the market people helped ensure that it was maintained. The safest plan, observed an American reporter, was "to make all purchases through a 'comprador,' who cheats you some, but not nearly as much as if you deal with the Chinese direct."[34]

Governor Bowring, the editor of Bentham's works and an ardent free-trader, blamed such evils on the reckless spending and monopolistic mischiefs of the earlier East India Company, whose "table allowances were made on the most liberal scale, and enormous prices were paid for all the articles of consumption."[35] In their manner also, Chinese servants seemed to carry over to Hong Kong some of the attitudes of the old Canton system. The "fawning, cringing servile deportment" that characterized the Malay or Bengali servant seemed to be absent in the "quiet proud Chinaman." "None of your smirks, grins, and salaams for Fokey. He comes before 'se-tow' with an easy self assured air, holds his chin well up and his hands down, takes your orders with dignified gravity and quickly withdraws the moment they are comprehended."[36] Culturally, servants made few compromises. They cooked and served food in the English or Anglo-Indian style, but their dress and manners remained Chinese. Missionaries, who made few converts in Hong Kong, considered them a "somewhat inaccessible class of people."[37] They maintained their families on the mainland rather than bring them to Hong Kong. Even the "English patois," or pidgin, in which they spoke with their employers was the bare, functional minimum, and required as great an effort from employers as it did from the servants: it also added interpretation to the many important roles servants performed.[38] Servants protected themselves still further by "the prodigious lies" they invented "on every occasion as a matter of course: if taxed therewith they only laughed, evidently amused at

32. Bowring to Lytton, 29 Mar. 1859, CO 129/73, 308.

33. *FC*, 23 Nov. 1844, 584.

34. Article on Hong Kong from the *Alta* of California, 1859, in CO 129/84, 219.

35. Bowring to Lytton, 29 Mar. 1859, CO 129/73, 308.

36. Weatherhead, "Hong Kong," 20.

37. Benjamin Hobson to Arthur Tidman, 18 Sept. 1847, London Missionary Society Archives, South China and Ultra Ganges, box 4, School of Oriental and African Studies, London.

38. Weatherhead, "Hong Kong," 9.

our guileless simplicity." Matilda Sharp, a bullion broker's wife who kept a journal, records a dinner conversation with her friend, a "Mr Coe," who was

> anxious for my sympathy respecting his boy, whose family is in trouble with so frightful a mortality that he is constantly wanting to go and bury some relative. . . . This is the most common excuse with Chinese servants—they never honestly ask you for a holiday, but think they must always give some reason that will appeal to your feelings and make it impossible for you to say no. Mr Coe's boy's mother has so often had a fatal termination to her many illnesses that Mr Coe has told him today that if ever his mother dies again he will give him a good thrashing.[39]

Compulsively dishonest, impassive to the reprimands of their employers, servants were also capable of aggressively asserting their interests. Cold refusal was the simplest method: "'That no boy pigeon, that coolie pigeon,' is the form of your servant's remonstrance if you ask him to fill your bath or take a letter."[40] More calculated ploys were also used. Matilda Sharp's servants waited until the eve of her sister's wedding in 1865, when the household was busy with preparations, before deciding to go on strike to demand higher wages.[41] On the evening of 9 July 1848 three cooks employed by the soldiers of the Royal Artillery put a powerful emetic into the evening stew in protest at a decision made a fortnight earlier to serve supper at a later, more inconvenient time.[42] Food obtained by employers outside the market-squeeze system often remained uncooked. Weatherhead's servants put forward religious reasons for refusing to prepare a turtle he had acquired through his own channels.[43] When Henry Winiberg, the owner of the Winiberg Hotel, bought pigs and turkeys direct from the captain of a ship, the "Chinese servants resented it by throwing the pigs down a well in the yard used to supply the hotel with water."[44]

With the exception, perhaps, of the incident at the Royal Artillery's soldiers' mess, these were amusing enough little vignettes, all contributing to the quirky, childlike caricature that Europeans created out of their domestic servants and to the real-life chinoiserie that characterizes many reports from the colony. The queues and outlandish clothes, the quaint religious customs, the

39. Quoted in J. Smith and Savidge, *Matilda*, 58.
40. Cooke, *China*, 59.
41. J. Smith and Savidge, *Matilda*, 52.
42. The incident caused a brief panic in the colony and the cooks were later tried and acquitted on a charge of administering poison with intent to kill. *HR*, 11 July, 24 Oct. 1848, 111, 171; *FC*, 12 July 1848, 228; *CM*, 13 July 1848, 110.
43. Weatherhead, "Hong Kong," 20–21.
44. Venables, "Rebellion."

use of Canton pidgin English—"this grotesque caricature of the language of the nursery"—reinforced the comic impression and supplied Europeans with rich material for dinner-party conversations or their attempts at more ambitious insights into the Chinese character. Indeed, Weatherhead's lecture on life in Hong Kong would have been pretty thin without the pages he devotes to the antics of his domestics; he also depends on them for larger generalizations about the Chinese language or the conduct of Chinese defendants in the criminal courts.[45] Employers often made the most of the willow-pattern world in which they found themselves and deliberately orientalized and feminized their servants: the livery for the Sharp household, for example, consisted of "black satin shoes with soles one inch thick, blue hose tied at the knee, breeches very large of black or blue stuff, tied ditto, and a blue kind of smock. Pigtail ornamented with silk at the end and . . . head crowned by a black silk cap with a red tassel."[46] A few Europeans avoided having to deal with Chinese servants, by employing European, Indian, or Malay servants, who were "more docile and plastic than Chinese."[47] But many found their Chinese servants reliable enough. Alfred Weatherhead considered his servants to be generally loyal and honest: although he found their opium smoking disagreeable, and objected to the "swarm of so-called relations" that colonized his ground floor and outhouses, he and his wife seem to have achieved a modus vivendi with them.[48] Matilda Sharp developed some affection for hers:

> Now that I have got to know them and got to know their ways, I really like them on the whole very much. They cheat you fearfully of course, in every conceivable way, but then you know it, and they know that you know it, and so both parties reconcile themselves to what is inevitable. Yet though such cheats in some ways, in others they are scrupulously honest. You may leave things lying about in your room in perfect safety.[49]

The Master's Sanctions

Not all Europeans would have agreed with this last opinion. Where squeezing, lying, restrictive practices, and other nuisances might be tolerable and even amusing, direct assaults on an employer's private property were defi-

45. Cooke, *China*, 60; Weatherhead, "Hong Kong," 9–10.

46. Quoted in J. Smith and Savidge, *Matilda*, 25.

47. Junior, *Canton Chinese*, 256. The British Hotel advertised in 1843 that it possessed "European servants always in attendance." *FC*, 15 June 1843, 54.

48. Weatherhead, "Hong Kong," 19.

49. Quoted in J. Smith and Savidge, *Matilda*, 58.

nitely not so. When valuables went missing, servants were nearly always the first suspects, either as principals or accessories to the crime. If a servant also went missing at the same time as the valuables, it would be taken for granted that the two events were connected. A terse advertisement in the *Friend of China* in June 1845 by the merchant and government auctioneer Charles Markwick perhaps reveals as much about master-servant relations as any of the more cheerful descriptions by Sharp or Weatherhead. The advertisement offers a reward of $100 for information leading to the apprehension of his servants, who had absconded en masse with money, a watch, various boxes, cloth, and pistols. It describes the servants as follows:

> Assigh, —Mr Markwick's servant, about 23 years of age and about 5 ft 6 in high. Dull and Sulky countenance, speaks English indifferently.
>
> Assam, —Cooly, about 5 ft 8 in high and about 20 of age very active in his movements.
>
> Ahone, —Cooly, about 5 ft 7 in high, 25 years of age Dark complexion, slow and dull, speaks English.
>
> Ahoon, —Boy, about 13 years of age, slightly made, brother to the cooly Assam.[50]

In December 1849 newspapers reported a rash of thefts by servants, many with the aid of false or skeleton keys. A few of the many brief reports of such incidents from around this time illustrate the problem:

> On Saturday the drawing-room of Lieut-Col. Simmonds, Ceylon Rifles, was entered during the absence of the family at tiffin, evidently with the connivance of the servants, and a gold watch, gold guard chain, and other articles of jewellery stolen.[51]

> On Monday morning, a servant of Mr Drake's the Schoolmaster absconded with about two hundred dollars, chiefly in bank notes. Information was sent to the Chinese authorities of Cowloong, who traced the thief inland for several miles, but have not yet succeeded in taking him.[52]

> Absconded from the service of Mr Burgoyne, Wellington Street, a Chinese servant, stealing $30, (which he had been intrusted to receive by his master), and a musical box—playing 6 airs.[53]

50. *FC*, 7 June 1845, 809.
51. *HR*, 9 Oct. 1849, 162.
52. *CM*, 13 Dec. 1849, 198.
53. *HR*, 8 Jan. 1850, 6.

Absconded on the 11th instant, from the employ of Sergeant-Major Spence, Royal Artillery, a coolie named "Ah-mun," stealing a gold watch with gold dial, steel hands, No. 55, a silver guard chain, and a gold key attached.[54]

The items taken were standard: money, watches (which appear to have been greatly in demand in southern China), and mechanical objects. The temptations are understandable enough: $200 amounted to more than three years' wages for an average servant, who would probably have family and other obligations on the mainland; a gold watch, which might fetch around $30 or $40, was readily disposed of through one of the many pawnbrokers or fences who thrived in Hong Kong and Canton. The culprits could easily disappear into the mainland: despite the energies of the Kowloon authorities across the harbor in pursuing Drake's ex-servant, it was neither the custom nor a treaty requirement for the Chinese government to return suspected offenders to Hong Kong.

Very occasionally, attempts might be made to apprehend suspected servants before they made good their escape. A pursuit that took place in the crowded harbor of Hong Kong illustrates the tragic consequences that often resulted from a combination of misunderstanding and heavy-handed European reaction. At around sunset on 27 October 1846, Robert Duncan, a Scottish merchant, found that $200 was missing from his desk and that his cook had absconded. Believing that he might find the cook on a vessel in the harbor, he commandeered a boat and a policeman and, having checked several junks, approached a small passenger boat leaving the harbor on its way to the mainland. The passenger boat had been in a slight collision with a junk on its way out of the harbor, and boatmen from the injured junk were already in pursuit of it, firing muskets as warnings. Duncan's boat joined the chase. The eighteen men on board the passenger boat panicked and jumped overboard: five drowned; the remaining thirteen were captured by the police and sentenced by the magistrate to flogging and brief prison sentences for either being rogues and vagabonds or possessing arms with felonious intent. The Supreme Court set aside the verdict, but it also quashed the verdict by a coroner's jury of manslaughter against Duncan and the others involved in the chase. Duncan's cook was not among those on the passenger boat.[55]

Few actual cases of larceny by Chinese servants appear to have made it to

54. *HR*, 15 Jan. 1850, 10.
55. *Chief Magistrate's Report*, 29 Oct. 1846, CO 129/27, 338–48; *CM*, 29 Oct., 5, 26 Nov. 1846, 151, 153–54, 166–67; *FC*, 4, 7, 18, 21, 25 Nov. 1846, 1388, 1392, 1404, 1408, 1412; *HR*, 24 Nov. 1846, 191.

the courts. Europeans were well aware of the difficulties of tracing absconding servants, and their insecurity was heightened by a sense that such crimes came in waves, occasionally involved violence, and were sometimes combined with secret society activities or larger political conflicts. The newspapers, which took on the role of protectors of the European public, may have exaggerated the idea of crime waves by servants in the attention they gave to the problem and in their urging of vigilance. For example, a single theft by a houseboy in October 1862 was sufficient to recharge the *China Mail*'s campaign for the registration of servants.[56] Rare but well-publicized instances of violence by servants also fueled fears that Europeans were physically at risk even within their own homes. On 3 October 1845, a few months after the abscondment of Markwick's servants, the blacksmith Henry Clarke returned home after an evening drinking champagne at the Odd Fellows Arms to find his wife dead from wounds to the head. His two workmen, his cook boy, and the people who lived in a mat shed near his house had all absconded; Clarke's weapons and about thirty-five dollars were missing.[57] The newspapers noted that Clarke did not even know the names of his servants and linked the case to a new and alarming trend of violence against Europeans: a few months earlier there had been "reasons to suspect that an attempt had been made to poison a Gentleman and his wife, by putting some vegetable poison in their soup," and little more than a week after the murder of Mrs. Clarke, Chinese robbers had slit the throat of a European overseer working on the roads.[58] Foreigners, remarked the *Friend of China*, "have not that security over servants in Hongkong which they have in Canton, where detection and punishment would certainly follow a murder, or attempted murder."[59] Mrs. Clarke's murderers were not discovered, but where action could be taken it was swift. In early 1858, Look Ahsong, a coolie employed by Mr. Glatz, a watchmaker, was tried and hanged within a week of murdering Glatz's fifteen-year-old European apprentice.[60]

Nor were Europeans in Hong Kong safe from the kind of political manipulation of servants that the Chinese government had used against them in Canton. It was a constant theme among colonists that the Chinese authorities were trying to strangle the colony's livelihood through economic sanctions. Hong Kong's dependency on the mainland for supplies and labor provided the Chinese government with opportunities to deploy the tactics it had used in Canton on a larger and more threatening scale. Governor Bowring believed

56. *CM*, 9 Oct. 1862, 163.
57. *CM*, 9 Oct. 1845, 133.
58. *FC*, 8, 15 Oct. 1845, 948, 957.
59. *FC*, 8 Oct. 1845.
60. *FC*, 27, 30 Jan. 1858, 30, 31.

that "The power possessed by the Mandarins to prevent supplies reaching our markets, to drive away our population, to rob us of our servants, to disturb our revenues, to interrupt our trade, by that machinery of control and clanship which is one of the mightiest instruments of authority in China, and which can be called into action covertly in times of peace, as it is openly in times of war is a subject of the gravest character."[61]

In July 1841, during a truce in hostilities around Canton, the Chinese authorities prohibited laborers, artisans, and supplies from going to Hong Kong, and a brief strike took place among workers already on the island.[62] This attempt to smother the colony in its infancy does not appear to have had much success. When, however, formal hostilities erupted again in late 1856, the authorities in the nearby county of Xiangshan ordered all Chinese residents in Hong Kong to return to their native places, warning them that they and their parents would be severely dealt with as traitors if they remained in the colony: 5,000 Chinese were estimated to have left Hong Kong that year in response to the threat.[63] A further 20,000—more than a quarter of the Chinese population, including "the most respectable part of our population" and "almost all our servants"—deserted Hong Kong in July 1858 in response to similar threats, "thereby occasioning the greatest personal inconvenience to every individual of the community, and completely paralyzing all the ordinary operations of intercourse and daily life."[64]

At such times, servants of Europeans came under severe pressure. All were suspect: the Chinese authorities, reported the journalist George Cooke in 1857, "have a spy in every 'boy' who stands behind your chair, and in every coolie who pulls your punkah"; houses, he added, were "so arranged that all those long-tailed domestics who waited at dinner are, or can be, shut off from that part of the house in which the Europeans sleep."[65] Some servants were reported to have warned their employers in January 1857 of an unsuccessful attempt by agents of the Chinese government to poison the entire European community by adding arsenic to the bread baked by the only bakery still open to Europeans.[66] Others took advantage of the conflict. Just over two months

61. Bowring to Lytton, 22 Aug. 1858, CO 129/69, 108.

62. *CP*, 3 July 1841; *Canton Register*, 6 July 1841.

63. Proclamation by the Acting Prefect of Xiangshan, 25 Dec. 1856, CO 129/62, 295–98; population returns, *Gazette*, 28 Mar. 1857, 5.

64. Bowring to Lytton, 5 Aug. 1858, CO 129/94, 192. Memorial from Merchants and Inhabitants of Hong Kong, Executive Council minutes, 30 July 1858, CO 131/4, 215.

65. Cooke, *China*, 11, 80. For a partial substantiation of Cooke's assumption about spies, see the memorial by Ye Mingchen, Jan. 1858, *Chouban yiwu shimo* (Peking, 1930), 17/36.

66. William Tarrant to Bowring, 8 Aug. 1857, CO 129/64, 112. The poison attempt failed because too much arsenic was put in the bread, causing those who ate it to vomit.

after the poisoning attempt, Markwick the auctioneer had further bad luck with his servants when his door coolie, Ho Apo, strangled him in his bed and made off with his valuables. Bowring took special measures. Connecting the case with Chinese government plots "against English life and property here," and recognizing "the vital importance to this community under existing circumstances that the murder of an English master by a Chinese domestic servant should not go unpunished," he authorized a naval expedition to Ho's native village, about forty miles to the east of Hong Kong and in Chinese territory. The expedition captured two of the elders of the village and held them hostage in the debtors' jail at Hong Kong until Ho was delivered up ("the system universally employed by Chinese Authorities," Bowring explained). Within a week they were exchanged for Ho, who was convicted of murder and hanged. The Colonial Office had doubts about Bowring's methods, which were illegal both in English and in international law, but concluded that they were excusable in the interests of self-preservation.[67]

The murder of Charles Markwick, and the measures taken to secure his murderer, represent one extreme in the relations between Europeans in Hong Kong and their Chinese servants. The daily practice of disciplining servants was a more mundane affair, but it also included a similar mixture of criminal justice and coercion. The diary of one Hong Kong resident reveals the use that could be made of such resources. John Wright, a young English clerk in the Post Office between 1849 and 1853, kept a daily record of his life in Hong Kong. A bachelor, he shared a house with a group of male friends and reluctantly took charge of the messing arrangements. Less well placed than Matilda Sharp and lacking the comfortable retrospect of Alfred Weatherhead, Wright is frank about the difficult relations with his servants: they disobey or willfully misunderstand instructions, keep the house in a filthy condition, pilfer cutlery and food, and quarrel among themselves. There was, Wright concluded one day, after having given them a general scolding, "never a day's peace with them."[68] On 10 July 1850 Wright discovered that his boy had been stealing money and had broken his watch. Wright gave him to understand "that if he did not in two days return the two dollars he had stolen I would send him to the police and get him flogged."[69] At about 11:30 on the night of 15 September 1851 a member of Wright's household returned home to find the gate wide open and the door coolie absent without leave. Wright de-

67. Bowring to Labouchere, 23 Apr. 1857, CO 129/63, 17–24.
68. Diary of John Wright, PRO, Hong Kong, 25 Nov. 1851: I am grateful to Jocelyn Scrymgeour of Dunedin, New Zealand, for permission to quote from this diary.
69. This threat was sufficient to ensure the return of the two dollars. Wright Diary, 10, 11 July 1850.

termined to prosecute the coolie for neglect of duty, and the following morning took him before the magistrate. His diary entry for Tuesday 16 September reads as follows:

> 9 am at the Police Station to give the Coolie a charge — 2.30 pm made complaint before the Magistrate. Coolie fined five dollars — in default seven days imprisonment. He has gone to jail not being able to pay the fine. I was very sorry indeed to be forced to imprison him, but he justly deserved it, he exposed our property and had been warned on several previous occasions. Chinese servants are far too impudent and if all Europeans would similarly punish them, it would, I think soon bring them to their proper bearings, besides being a great benefit to society.[70]

Far from bringing the servants to their proper bearings, this incident appears only to have aggravated relations between Wright and his servants. A few months later, Wright woke up early one morning to discover that the watch he had hung at the head of his bed ("the only thing valuable I possessed") was missing, and that the cook, coolie, and boy were all "on the alert."

> As soon as it was at all light I went to the Police Office, stated the case and brought the policeman back with me, who took the cook, coolie boy and cook's father to the station house and returned to search their traps, but unfortunately without any luck. . . . At the Magistrate's Office at 10 o'clock. All up and arraigned before him. Remanded for forty-eight hours. They won't confess the beggars. . . . Our place is quite a chaos now and I feel as dull in it as possible. All the servants in prison and nobody to take care of the house. In a fix we are — considerable I guess.[71]

Wright arranged for a Post Office coolie to watch the house for a day or two, quickly engaged a new boy and cook, and returned to the case at the magistracy two days later, where the ex-servants were remanded for another week: "I am afraid there is not much hope for my watch." The following day he attempted to obtain his watch from Tam Achoy, a Chinese contractor "celebrated for getting back stolen watches . . . deeply skilled in cunning and a great blackguard," but Tam was unable to help him because the matter was already in police hands. Ten days later the case again came before the magistrate, and the old servants were obliged to find securities for their release, a common recourse in unproven cases. The cook and the boy found securities the following day, a Sunday, and returned to the house to collect their possessions:

70. Ibid., 15, 16 Sept. 1851.
71. Ibid., 2 Feb. 1852.

"[B]efore they did so," records Wright, shortly before going to church, "I had the pleasure of giving them a good thrashing, not to do them any serious harm, but just a lashing with a cane that made them servile again."[72]

Wright used the courts for three purposes: to threaten a servant suspected of pilfering, to discipline a negligent door coolie, and to prosecute his whole household staff for the theft of a watch. In the case of the watch he was as unsuccessful as most employers seem to have been; in prosecuting his door coolie, he spent the best part of a day on the case, lost the services of a servant for a week, gained no compensation for his troubles, and failed to improve discipline among his servants. It was a platitude among the colonists of nineteenth-century Hong Kong—and an important determinant of criminal justice policy—that Chinese convicts found prison far more comfortable than they did life outside.[73] No statistics for master and servant prosecutions survive for the 1850s to confirm Wright's complaint that not enough Europeans used the courts to punish their servants, but figures for the 1860s reveal a moderate but declining rate of prosecution.[74]

English law relating to masters and servants was applied in Hong Kong. Various local enactments empowered magistrates to impose fines on servants who left their employment without reasonable warning, went absent without leave, willfully disobeyed orders, used abusive or insulting behavior toward an employer, or damaged an employer's property.[75] Few prosecutions under these provisions made their way into the newspapers, but a handful of cases from the years 1846–47, when reporting from the Magistrate's Court was particularly thorough, give some indication of the kind of grievances taken to court. On 18 December 1846 an unnamed servant of Michael Gabriel, owner of the British Hotel, was fined five dollars (about a month's wages) and ordered to forfeit his wages for "neglect of duty and leaving the house without permission."[76] In February 1847 Chung-Ashun, a servant of a Captain Boate, was fined three dollars (or, in default, a week's imprisonment) for a similar

72. Ibid., 4, 5, 12, 15 Feb. 1852. Tam Achoy, probably the most prominent Chinese in the colony at this time, was recognized by the colonial authorities as a community representative.

73. See, for example, *CM*, 4 Oct. 1855, 158; 11 Aug. 1859, 126.

74. Seventy-six servants were brought before the magistrates for misconduct in 1864, 102 in 1865, 121 in 1866, 63 in 1867, 34 in 1868, 49 in 1869, and 27 in 1870. Between 5,000 and 7,000 Chinese were in the employ of Europeans during this decade, not all of them domestic servants. These prosecution figures suggest a rise in misconduct cases, peaking at about the time of the 1866 Registration Ordinance, when greater controls were imposed on servants, and declining considerably after the ordinance came into effect in 1867. Court returns, *Gazette*, 15 Apr. 1865, 31 Mar. 1866, 30 Mar. 1867, 29 Feb. 1868, 27 Feb. 1869, 19 Feb. 1870, 18 Feb. 1871.

75. (Hong Kong) n.5 of 1844; (Hong Kong) n.14 of 1845.

76. *CM*, 31 Dec. 1846, 187.

offense.[77] In the same month, Too-ahing, a servant of the trading company Mackay & Co., was imprisoned for a week for refusing to work because his employer declined to advance him a month's wages.[78] A tragic example, reminiscent of the Duncan case, occurred in September 1846. A Chinese baker, "a useful servant," in the employ of the bakery of MacMurray and Co. quit his job without giving the requisite one month's notice. His employers took him to the magistrate, who fined him two dollars and ordered him to finish the month. He disobeyed this order and was again taken before the Magistrate, who awarded him twenty lashes:

> As he still absented himself, Mr Woods [a partner in the firm] meeting him on the Queen's Road attempted with the assistance of two Constables to apprehend him. To elude them he entered the water, and was drowned either in an attempt to swim off to a boat, or by unexpectedly getting beyond his depth. Those in the boats made no attempt to assist him. The jury after adjourning to Friday forenoon, returned a verdict of Accidental Death.[79]

Newspaper reporting of cases before the summary courts declined in the 1850s, and although no statistics survive to clarify the matter, it might be fair to conclude that the prosecutions by Wright were something of a rarity.[80] With very few exceptions, the cases described above involve employees of commercial establishments rather than purely domestic servants. Europeans probably relied more on self-help in the form of violence, dismissal, or the stoppage of wages. An anonymous Chinese placard posted in Hong Kong in the early 1840s complained of cases in which Europeans in Hong Kong whose property had been stolen forced their employees to make good the loss, and cases in which employees had been beaten and abused.[81] The extracts from Sharp's and Wright's diaries quoted here also suggest that "thrashing" was an accepted practice. Violence was a common feature of colonial life: flogging was a staple punishment in the criminal justice system; heavy drinking and exasperation over cultural and linguistic barriers encouraged brutality in daily contacts between Europeans and Chinese. Respect for Europeans,

77. *CM*, 11 Feb. 1847, 211.

78. *CM*, 11 Feb. 1847, 3.

79. *CM*, 10 Sept. 1846, 122; *HR*, 8 Sept. 1846; *FC*, 5 Sept. 1846, 1324. The newspapers differ somewhat in their versions of the case.

80. A few prosecutions of non-Chinese servants for misconduct were reported in the early 1840s, and a somewhat complicated prosecution of a Chinese domestic servant is recorded in November 1844. *HR*, 17 Dec. 1844, 212; *FC*, 18 Dec. 1844, 612.

81. Anonymous placard posted in Hong Kong, Public Record Office, FO 663/47, reprinted in Sasaki, *Ahen Senso*, 313.

wrote George Cooke, could never be attained "except while the coolie's ears are hot with the recent application of an Anglo-Saxon palm."[82]

Not surprisingly, few specific cases of master-servant violence survive on record. Except for the most serious of offenses, cases of violence between Chinese and Europeans rarely reached the courts. There is some evidence also that European violence against Chinese that resulted in permanent injury tended to be either resolved through compensation, sometimes with the encouragement of the courts, or simply overlooked.[83] Some successful prosecutions by chair coolies of Europeans for violent behavior were reported in newspapers in the 1860s, and a few cases involving master-on-servant violence appear among the police reports of the late 1840s. On 1 March 1847 Thomas Roberts (whose occupation is not stated) was fined five dollars and ordered to pay one dollar (or the equivalent of about a week's wages) to Hong-a-kum, a carpenter, for assault: Roberts had struck Hong because Hong had refused to work for him until Roberts repaid a debt owed to him. Later that month, Alexander Robertson, a publican, was fined three dollars "for assaulting his Chinese cook and cutting him over the eyes."[84]

The minimal compensation and derisory fines perhaps explain why such prosecutions were so rare. Some could be extremely costly: in October 1846 Yaoung Mea, a carpenter, employed one of the colony's prominent but underemployed lawyers, Norton D'Esterre Parker, to intervene on his behalf against Murdoch Bruce, the Scottish overseer of public works, who had been beating Yaoung about the head with a piece of wood and flogging him with a horsewhip. Parker wrote to Bruce urging him to "arrange" the matter out of court and received a dismissive reply containing a veiled jocular threat of violence against Parker himself. When Bruce refused to withdraw the insult, Parker had him bound over by the chief magistrate under a penalty of $100 to keep the peace. Yaoung's grievance, buried under the lengthy exchanges between Bruce and Parker, resulted in a fine of 50¢ for assault. Parker, who charged Yaoung $7 for his services, had apparently assured his client that he would be able to obtain $50 in damages.[85]

82. Cooke, *China*, 360.

83. In April 1845 a coroner's jury persisted in its verdict of accidental death in the case of a Chinese beaten to death by three drunken Europeans despite the coroner's instruction "that it was contrary to the evidence and that it should be manslaughter against some person unknown." *FC*, 9 Apr. 1845, 740; 14 July 1842, 65.

84. *CM*, 11 Mar. 1847, 15.

85. The *China Mail* dramatized the case and produced several verses on it, one of which was: "But by England's laws, / Than which none can be finer, / You can't assault a man, / Because he's born in China." *HR*, 13 Oct. 1846, 163; *CM*, 15 Oct. 1846, 142–43.

Fifty-cent fines were a standard penalty in cases of minor violence between Chinese during this period: they perhaps formed part of the chief magistrate's policy of encouraging Chinese community leaders to resolve minor cases, "where the injury is only personal," without the intervention of the magistrate.[86] The same fine in Yaoung's case against Bruce was a clear signal that similar cases in which Europeans were at fault were best settled out of court. It may also have been a reflection of concerns that too much encouragement to litigation of this kind would tilt the master-servant relationship too far in favor of Chinese servants. These concerns were underlined less than a year later when the dangers of allowing Chinese servants too much free rein became apparent in a report from Shanghai of a series of prosecutions for assault by Cantonese servants against Europeans in the consular court, which had jurisdiction over Europeans but not Chinese. These cases, the correspondent believed, had been brought forward to squeeze and intimidate employers: they had culminated in the abortive prosecution of a large portion of the European community on charges of assault and breach of the peace following disturbances at a Chinese theatrical performance organized by a servant in the employ of the British vice-consul, to which passing foreigners had been invited.[87]

Servants in Hong Kong may not have had the protection in criminal cases that their comrades in Shanghai enjoyed, but it does appear that they made some use of the courts in disputes over wages. While, as in most other parts of the empire, the employer had the criminal law at his disposal to enforce his side of the contract, the employee could resolve disputes over wages only through a civil suit. Examples of such cases from early British Hong Kong are not very common, but the few that survive suggest that Chinese employees could be successful in their claims against their European employers. Some examples are recorded from 1850, the first full year of operation of the new petty sessions court, which assumed jurisdiction over master and servant disputes. Most involve large sums of more than $20 and possibly originate from contractors of labor or more well-placed employees. Three claims, however, by Leong Ahchaong, Lee Ahkew, and Kwok Ahtie, on 25 September, all against one George Kingston Barton, were each for sums of $2.83, with 49¢ in costs: no details are given, but it is quite possible that Barton's domestic staff, owed arrears of a couple of weeks' wages, had decided that enough was enough.[88]

86. Hillier to Caine, 11 Oct. 1845, CO 129/13, 244.
87. *HR*, 24 Aug. 1847, 136–37.
88. One single case of a claim for wages by one Chinese against another is recorded. In 1851

In some ways association with European employers privileged servants in their relations with other Chinese and with the lesser agents of the colonial authorities. Chinese connected with Europeans were often more likely to take their grievances with others to court: such practices were hinted at in the defense by the painter Wong Akew, on trial in 1866 for the theft of forty-five dollars from John Brown, the master of one of the colonial gunboats, that Brown's Chinese servant had pointed the finger at Wong after a quarrel.[89] The police were chary about interfering with servants walking the streets at night, particularly those who carried the monograms of European employers on their lanterns.[90] Employers even occasionally went out of their way to help servants when they were in difficulties with the authorities. When, late one evening in August 1846, Lieutenant Martin of the 18th Regiment learned that one of his servants had been wounded in a riot and then arrested by the police, he and a colleague interrupted their dinner to go down to the police station to bail him out, since Martin "could not conveniently dispense with the services of his servant who had charge of his wardrobe."[91] Martin and his colleague were themselves confined in jail for the night on a charge of drunk and disorderly behavior. A more solid example appears in 1849, when Mr. Olding, the P. & O. agent, went to the aid of two of his coolies who had been intercepted by an Indian policeman while delivering packages one evening. The policeman had asked to examine their basket and, when they refused, insisted they accompany him to the police station. They refused to do this and said they would go to Olding instead. A scuffle had followed, and the coolies were arrested on a charge of "causing disturbance in the street." The case was tried the following morning and discharged after the intervention of Olding, who threatened to take the matter before a higher court.[92]

The confidence that some Chinese acquired through domestic service helped some navigate their way through the criminal justice system even where their employers were of no help. Early in 1851, in a case before the Supreme Court, Tsoi-hong-chune, the boy employed by Lieutenant Dickenson of the Ceylon Rifles, was implicated by his codefendant, Tung-Ashing, a coolie, as an accomplice in the theft of a watch from Dickenson:

---

a servant was held justified in refusing to fulfill his promise "to allow his wages to go against a loss sustained through his ignorance or neglect." *FC*, 27 July 1850, 238; 29 Sept. 1850, 307; 2 Oct. 1850, 314; *HR*, 9 Sept. 1851, 142.

89. *Hongkong Daily Press*, 27 Feb. 1866.

90. Tronson, *Narrative*, 235.

91. Martin and Graham to Caine, 22 Aug. 1846, Correspondence received by the Chief Police Magistrate, Public Record Office, Hong Kong, HKRS 100, 303–6.

92. *CM*, 2 Aug. 1849, 122.

[T]he boy explained that his fellow-prisoner had said nothing about him to the Magistrate, but had been since advised by his friends to bring the accusation, on purpose to shift the robbery from his own shoulders. He had been several years on the island, during all of which he had borne a good character. If he desired to steal the watch, he could easily have done so, and would never have thought of taking for an accomplice a stranger from another district. He had been out on bail, and if he were guilty, would have left the colony.

The court acquitted Tsoi and sentenced Tung to seven years' transportation.[93] In December 1850 Tam-achuen, an enterprising young servant employed by the American firm Holliday Wise and Co., was caught trying to cash a crudely forged check for $300 on his masters' account at the Oriental Bank.[94] The Supreme Court convicted Tam and awarded him what the newspapers considered to be the mild sentence of two years' imprisonment with hard labor.[95] While in prison, Tam, "so far from being required to work in irons on the roads with his fellow miscreants, was allowed the free run of the gaol yard" and was employed by one of the turnkeys "to act as his table servant, to make his bed, clean his shoes, and mix his gin and water."[96] Early in February 1851, six weeks into his sentence, Tam made the best of his privileges and escaped "just in time to spend New Year's day in his native district of Heangshan."[97]

Regulation and Registration

Some disjunction appears between the padded bourgeois domesticity of Matilda Sharp and Alfred Weatherhead and the more hard-pressed, violent world of the publicans and small tradesmen who appear with their servants before the magistrate's court. Economic distinctions played a part, but a difference in the methods of recruiting and bonding servants may also have been responsible. Sharp appears to have obtained her servants through the bank for which her husband worked, and they would most probably have been vouched for by the comprador of the bank. Weatherhead, though he did not himself employ a

93. *CM*, 6 Mar. 1851, 39. Tung was pardoned after the wreck of the ship which was carrying him and other transported prisoners to Singapore: Bonham to Grey, 25 June 1851, and Tung's petition, 21 June 1851, CO 129/37, 117–23.
94. *CM*, 19 Dec. 1850, 203.
95. *FC*, 5 Feb. 1851, 45.
96. *FC*, 22 Feb. 1851, 64.
97. *FC*, 5 Feb. 1851, 45.

comprador, obtained his servants from a comprador in a merchant house, who sent along a string of candidates and made himself responsible for any losses sustained through them: Weatherhead likened the system to the guarantee societies in England.[98] The practice, known as "Chinese security," was so common in Hong Kong that it was incorporated into some of the early colonial legislation governing the registration of servants.[99] Chinese security was another legacy of the old Canton system: the guarantor provided a certificate insuring the servant in return, not for any direct premium from the employer, but for a commission taken from the servant's wages. Compradors procured servants through family or village connections: this doubtless strengthened the squeezing system organized among compradors and market-stall holders, but European employers probably also benefited from some of the discipline and cohesion that this patriarchal system conferred on labor relations in a purely Chinese setting.

It is not clear exactly where John Wright or Henry Clarke obtained their servants, but it is unlikely that they made use of Chinese security. Since the problems of the various publicans and minor tradesmen who went to the courts to discipline their servants did not relate to the loss of property, no indication is given of whether they made use of compradors or Chinese security. There are, however, suggestions that at some point in the late 1840s or early 1850s the system of Chinese security began to break down. Europeans on lower incomes may have found it easier to bypass the expensive comprador system altogether by recruiting their servants from the labor pool within the colony. Compradors themselves were moving on to larger things: increasingly the term "comprador" came to mean the wealthy, influential, and semi-independent manager-intermediaries of large European firms rather than mere stewards of households or small businesses. The government also made periodic, if unsuccessful, attempts to undermine the squeeze system by regularly publishing the prices of provisions in the markets and, in 1858, by removing the management of markets by monopolists.[100]

The growing concern with servant theft in the late 1840s and 1850s may also have been a reflection of the decline of the system of Chinese security. A case before the Supreme Court in its summary jurisdiction confirmed that Chinese security was not actionable in a court of law. In December 1851, Framjee Jamsetjee, a Parsi landlord, having lost a watch, a telescope, and a barometer, took his servant before the magistrate on a charge of theft. The

98. Weatherhead, "Hong Kong," 18.

99. (Hong Kong) n.7 of 1846; (Hong Kong) n.6 of 1857.

100. (Hong Kong) n.9 of 1858; Bowring to Stanley, 11 June 1858, CO 129/68, 95; *CM*, 9 June 1859, 90.

magistrate dismissed the charge on the ground of insufficient evidence. Framjee then collected additional evidence and sued the comprador who had supplied and guaranteed the servant. The comprador, Wong A-tong, who happened to be the chief justice's own comprador, ran a sideline in providing and guaranteeing servants for Europeans in return for 15 or 20 percent of the servants' wages. Wong had earlier offered to cover half of Framjee's losses but subsequently resisted the claim altogether. The chief justice, despite his connection with Wong and the fact that another servant accused by Framjee had taken refuge in the judge's house, saw no difficulty in ruling on the case, and decided that Framjee had no ground of action because no contract existed between him and Wong. The use of Chinese security continued well into the next decade, as the accounts by Weatherhead and others indicate, but the *China Mail*, in reporting Framjee's case, noted its important implications for the security papers of servants:

> Those who rely upon such documents will now find that they are worthless in our Supreme Court, a fact which will by this time be known to all the Compradors in the place,—the English law having stepped in and relieved them from obligations which have been established by the statute of Old Custom generations before foreign law of any sort was thought of in China. For ourselves, we do not much regret it: having little dependence on compulsory honesty, and knowing from experience that it can be secured more effectually than by the obligations of Compradors.[101]

The decline of Chinese security and the perceived increase in servant crime combined with other trends in the colony that increasingly threatened the confidence and security of its small European population. Although they helped confirm Hong Kong's importance as a British possession, the rapid increases in the Chinese population in the 1850s and 1860s dwarfed and isolated the European community even further and, by making the colony a more crowded, noisier, and more polluted place, increased the friction between communities. The political disturbances of the 1850s, economic problems in the 1860s, and the perception that English methods of justice were simply not working made crime the greatest source of anxiety among Europeans. Hong Kong, commented governor Sir Richard MacDonnell in 1866, had become a magnet for "the migratory refuse of many millions of Chinese."[102] Although cooperation between Chinese and European merchants flourished,

101. *CM*, 11 Dec. 1851, 198.
102. MacDonnell to Carnarvon, 23 Nov. 1866, CO 129/116, 109.

the cultural or economic connections that might exist in other colonial societies between colonial elite and the mass of the population were almost nonexistent, and the apparatus had yet to be built for connecting the power and
influence of the Chinese elite with the interests of the colonial government.
In settlement colonies, local governments could rely on broadly shared cultural, political, and religious values for their legitimacy; in slave and plantation societies, economic domination by Europeans made "every man a magistrate";[103] among settled non-European populations, some use could be made
of precolonial political structures. Hong Kong's colonists possessed none of
these advantages: there was, wrote Bowring in 1855, "an absolute abyss between the governors and the governed"; no more than 500 out of the 120,000
Chinese living under British rule, Governor Robinson estimated in 1862, had
"any idea as to the general nature of the institutions or laws under which
they live."[104]

If 96 percent of the Chinese in Hong Kong might be ignorant of British institutions, the colonial government was equally unclear about the structures
by which the Chinese outside European homes organized their own relationships. These structures consisted of loose dialect groupings, nascent guild
organizations, neighborhood associations centering on temples or bazaars,
and secret societies offering mutual aid. The colonial authorities in these early
years tended to interpret such groupings respectively as clannish conspiracies,
illegal combinations among workmen, dangerous power bases, and outlawed
criminal networks, such as the Triad Society. Although the government made
sporadic attempts to create low-level local structures of power along what
it believed to be traditional Chinese principles, these were not very successful.[105] Of particular concern to the government were the large floating populations—on land and in the harbor—of sojourning, masterless labor. In the
early 1860s, when Robinson made his statement about the gulf between government and people, the colony's boat population accounted for more than a
quarter (around 30,000) of its Chinese population, and a category known as
"street coolies" was estimated at 5,000. Hong Kong's European economy relied on a large sector of the boat population for transport and on cheap casual
labor for portering, chair carrying, and other unskilled work. These coolies
were constantly replenished by the continuous influx of displaced labor from
China. They were deliberately kept in abundant supply in order to keep their
wages low. Because of this, and because their needs were few, they tended to

103. Samaraweera, "Masters and Servants."
104. Bowring to Grey, 1 Mar. 1855, CO 129/49, 197; Robinson to Newcastle, 28 Mar. 1862,
CO 129/85, 270.
105. For a discussion of these policies, see Ting, "Peace Officers."

be underemployed, undernourished, and easily prone to petty, opportunistic crime and collective disorder.

The government resorted to the criminal justice system in an attempt to control and monitor Hong Kong's fluid and unstable population. The police and lower courts increasingly intruded into the daily life of the colony. By the 1860s the equivalent of about a tenth of the population was appearing annually before the magistrates' courts, a large proportion for regulatory or minor property offenses, and only a small proportion leaving the courts without some form of punishment or restraint. Supplementing control by the police and the courts, and adding to their powers and case loads, were the registration and curfew laws consolidated by the mid-1860s and remaining in force for most of the remainder of the century. These laws are interesting because they originated in attempts to control the movement of labor into and within the colony, because they made special provisions for servants in the employ of Europeans and other categories of labor that had contact with Europeans, and because some of them gave rise to large-scale labor protest.

Attempts to pin down Hong Kong's fluid population and foster some kind of permanent Chinese settlement in the colony were a constant preoccupation of the colonial government. Domestic servants were an important target in these schemes. They frequently inconvenienced their employers by leaving for the mainland at a day's notice, complained the *Friend of China*, "and so long as they can come to, and depart from the island unquestioned, having their wives in their native villages, where they find a refuge, when they flee from justice, so long we have no security for their fidelity."[106] The first registration scheme came shortly after the acquisition of the colony. In the summer of 1844 the great sinologist and missionary official, Charles Gutzlaff, then Chinese secretary to the British government in China, almost single-handedly undertook the registration of the whole Chinese population on the island. European householders employing watchmen and other servants were specifically invited to send them to Gutzlaff, who would use his famous understanding of the Chinese character to weed out unreliable employees and certify that the remainder had "sufficient security for their good conduct." Like most of Gutzlaff's schemes, this was a complete failure. The *Friend of China* complained that he had concentrated too much on respectable shopkeepers, who were known to be reliable, and too little on the "thousands of vagrant Chinese in the vicinity, of whom the Reverend Magistrate knows as little as he does of the interior of China."[107]

106. *FC*, 19 Oct. 1844, 545.
107. *FC*, 31 Aug. 1844, 488.

A more serious but disastrous attempt at registration was introduced in October 1844 under the first Registration Ordinance, which required all adult inhabitants to be either registered or removed from the colony, made it an offense for contractors to employ coolies or other workmen who had not obtained registration tickets from the government. In framing the ordinance Governor Davis made two political errors: first, by including Europeans in the ordinance's provisions, he aroused the opposition of the merchant community, who regarded the measure as an assault on their rights as free-born Englishmen; second, by requiring the payment of annual fees for the registration tickets, he inflamed the Chinese population, who saw the measure as a capitation tax.[108] Gutzlaff, in his Chinese proclamation explaining the measure, aggravated the problem by translating the fee for coolies as a dollar a month (between a quarter and a half of their wages) instead of one dollar per year.[109] The European colonial elite mishandled their protests by enlisting the support of their Chinese compradors: the resulting trade stoppages, strikes, and minor riots demonstrated how easily resistance to the colonial government could be organized. Davis suspended the ordinance and produced new legislation, which excluded Europeans from registration and did away with the fees.[110] The effectiveness of the opposition, however, and Davis's rapid capitulation encouraged skilled labor, then hard at work on the buildings for the new colony, to mobilize and organize.

The irresolution of the government in the registration controversy had, the *Friend of China* believed, "imparted to the ignorant natives ideas of their own powers, and of the weakness of the law." The government itself, it reported, had been obliged to pay its contractors and laborers "sums in the shape of gifts" before they would agree to finish contracted work. In other instances "contractors are obliged to throw up contracts; the labourers refusing to work for certain individuals who have incurred their displeasure by informing upon any of their number who may have committed a crime. The stonemasons form one combination, the brick-layers another and the carpenters a third. Each set appear to act independently, but either of them can impede the erection of a building by leaving off work."[111] In early January 1845, a carpenter caught pilfering in the market was handed over to the police; several hundred of his fellow workmen struck work, "and intimated to the Gentle-

108. (Hong Kong) n.16 of 1844; Memorials from English Merchants, 30, 31 Oct. 1844, CO 129/7, 209, 211; Joseph Jardine to David Jardine, 1 Nov. 1844, Jardine Matheson Archives, Cambridge University Library, Private Unbound Correspondence, Hong Kong, P145; *FC*, 2 Nov. 1844, 561.

109. Davis to Stanley, 11 June 1845, CO 129/12, 178.

110. (Hong Kong) n.18 of 1844.

111. *FC*, 11 Jan. 1845, 640.

man under whom they were employed that, unless he bribed the prosecutor to come forward and deny his charge they would cease to labour." [112] In another case later that month a European who replaced his building contractor found that an employee of the first contractor was intimidating the new laborers. He handed the man over to the police, and the chief magistrate sentenced him to a fine of forty dollars and a short imprisonment:

> Upon hearing of this, the stone masons held a meeting, at which it was resolved that the party who obtained the conviction should also obtain the culprit's liberation; that the new contractor should pay all arrears of wages due by the old contractor, who has absconded; and that the four men who appeared as witnesses should be fined by this self constituted court in the sum of $20. Failing the carrying out of this their fiat, labour was to be suspended. We hear that the contractor has submitted to pay men wages whom he did not employ, also that the witnesses have paid their fine, but the man is of course still in prison. [113]

It was perhaps owing to such disturbances that European colonists waited for more than a decade before again making common cause on a political issue with their Chinese counterparts. The experience may also explain why the government came down so heavily on future attempts by labor to combine against Europeans. The case of the washermen to whom European households contracted out their laundry is a good example. In 1854, 40 washermen went on strike in an attempt to force an increase in their charges to reflect the rising cost of charcoal: one was sentenced to jail for refusing to wash shirts at under $2.50 per 100. [114] A further dispute with the washermen arose in August 1857, when the government banned them from using certain streams: 43 washermen were fined $5 each for ignoring the ban. When the tailor and shoemaker guilds held a meeting to raise money to support the washermen, all 243 participants were arrested and remanded to prison before being fined $5 each. "A more outrageous proceeding on the part of a constitutional government we never heard of," declared the *Friend of China*, now in more antiestablishment hands: it predicted that such measures would only drive legitimate Chinese political activities further underground. [115]

---

112. Ibid.

113. *FC*, 22 Jan. 1845, 652; *CM*, 19 June 1845, 71; *HR*, 24 June 1845, 101.

114. Asked why the courts should intervene when similar strikes in England were not subject to the criminal law, the *Friend of China* remarked that the man in question had been charged with threatening the life of a washerman willing to work below that price. *FC*, 13 Sept. 1854, 292.

115. Prosecutions for combinations among workmen or intimidation of workmen were rare in this period: hardly more than one or two per annum for most of the years between 1850 and 1870 for which figures are available. The tendency of Europeans to keep labor at arm's length by

The revised 1844 registration ordinance placed too great a burden on the registrar-general's department, confounded attempts at a census, and failed as a measure of control because registration was so easily obtained by "those who hung loose on the community, and only applied for tickets to make a bad use of them."[116] A new scheme introduced in early 1847 placed the main responsibility for registration on Chinese householders rather than individuals. It included special provisions for Chinese servants of Europeans, which were enacted "for the benefit and protection of the European residents of this colony."[117] Under the scheme, Chinese domestic servants, artificers, and workmen in the employ of Europeans were to be registered individually, on production of certificates from their employers, who were expected to obtain Chinese security. The scheme required such employees to deliver their registration tickets to their employers, who were to return the tickets to them when their term of service expired, or, in case of dismissal or desertion, to the registrar-general. Since the ordinance prescribed fines and prison terms for Chinese persons not in possession of registration tickets, it placed considerable powers in the hands of European employers. Neither this ordinance, however, nor a short-lived revived version introduced during the tense year of 1857 appears to have been especially welcomed by employers.[118] The press criticized the servant provisions for being complex and unnecessary, and an 1858 ordinance, which reenacted most of the other controls of the 1857 ordinance, omitted the sections on servants.[119]

Registration of servants was not implemented again until 1866, when Governor MacDonnell reintroduced it as part of a large and comprehensive system of anticrime measures. His predecessors had already extended control through registration and regulation to boatmen, employees of cargo boats, and sedan chair carriers, the groups of laborers most likely to come into contact with Europeans and believed to be most associated with crime.[120] MacDonnell now deepened control of the population by requiring the licensing

---

working through Chinese contractors may explain this, although this did not always guarantee peaceful labor relations. A strike in August 1867 by eighty stoneworkers, contracted through a Chinese to work on a house belonging to the American firm of Heard & Co., led to the sentencing of eleven of them to fourteen days' hard labor. The cause of the strike is unclear. The contractor employed a barrister to obtain arrest warrants. *FC*, 8, 15 Aug. 1857, 251, 258; *CM*, 2, 3 Aug. 1867.

116. Davis to Grey, 13 Mar. 1847, CO 129/31, 220.

117. (Hong Kong) n.7 of 1846.

118. (Hong Kong) n.6 of 1857.

119. *FC*, 20 Jan. 1847, 23; *HR*, 26 Jan. 1858, 15; (Hong Kong) n.8 of 1858.

120. (Hong Kong) n.15 of 1860; (Hong Kong) n.6 of 1863. Both measures led to strikes and protests. Memorandum by Kingsmill, Acting Attorney General, 28 Nov. 1860, CO 129/78, 327; Mercer to Newcastle, 24 July 1863, CO 129/93, 111–12. Tsai, *Hong Kong*, 58.

of all Chinese junks and reimposing household and servant registration.[121] In welcoming the measure, the *China Mail* noted that a greater number of professional men in the colony were now obliged to recruit their own servants and could not rely on compradors to vet them.[122] The attorney general commended the scheme, predicting that it would "prove a source of safety as well as of great convenience for it is well known that most of the Robberies committed in houses take place through the instrumentality of Chinese Servants, and as the latter will have to produce the list of their former employers at the back of the Certificate of Registration the character of every applicant will easily be obtained."[123]

The scheme was a clear and explicit attempt to replace the declining system of Chinese security with a new arrangement in which Europeans themselves controlled their servants with the backing of the government rather than of Chinese compradors, individually, in the additional leverage registration tickets gave them over their employees, and collectively, in the pool of knowledge available by tracing previous employers on the backs of such tickets. Both employers and their servants quickly took to the system. Within a month of its introduction, on 1 January 1867, 4,343 servants had registered under the ordinance, each paying a fee of fifty cents. So useful were the tickets to employers that the registrar-general had to warn them, in early February, against making extensive remarks about servants' characters on the backs of tickets.[124] Although employers, as well as their employees, were liable for unregistered servants, enforcement seems to have been against servants rather than employers: commenting on the unusual number of registration cases before the magistrates in June 1867, the *China Mail* complained that the prosecution of servants but not employers made " 'fish' of one class and 'flesh' of another" and was "contrary to the spirit of fairness in the light of which we 'Britishers' so delight to regard ourselves."[125]

By the mid-1860s class legislation against the Chinese in Hong Kong was so much a part of the fabric of colonial government that it would have required far more than the prosecution of negligent employers to revive the "spirit of fairness" thought to characterize British rule. MacDonnell's measures against crime, aimed at "self-preservation" by the European community and imposed in the face of explicit Royal Instructions against class legis-

---

121. (Hong Kong) n.6 of 1866; (Hong Kong) n.7 of 1866.

122. *CM*, 22 Feb. 1866, 30.

123. Comment by Julian Pauncefote, attorney general, on (Hong Kong) n.7 of 1866, CO 129/114, 523.

124. *Gazette*, 2 Feb. 1867.

125. *CM*, 19 June 1867.

lation, perfected the system of registering householders and boats, singled out Chinese offenders for corporal punishment, and introduced a tattooing and deportation scheme for some prisoners. Most of these measures merely consolidated the piecemeal efforts of his predecessors to control the Chinese population. Ordinance no. 9 of 1867, for example, in extending a nine-o'clock curfew to Chinese women as well as men, completed a system that had been imposed sporadically since the acquisition of Hong Kong, as an administrative measure of questionable legality in the 1840s, and, from 1857, as one of the measures enacted during the hostilities with China: the curfew was retained after the hostilities were over because it reduced property crime and noise at night.

MacDonnell's controversial and short-lived gambling monopoly, however, was an innovation. Designed to reduce police corruption and improve intelligence on criminal activities, the monopoly legalized gambling in strictly controlled government-licensed establishments. Such a system had been urged unsuccessfully by officials since the mid-1850s as a measure against crime, especially crime by employees of Europeans. Bowring reported in 1858 how "merchants of the colony frequently are subjected to heavy losses from the passion for play of their compradors, while the inhabitants of the island generally would have some security against the misdoings of their native servants, if the places in which they indulge their gambling propensities were not concealed from the public eye."[126] W. T. Bridges, a lawyer and acting government official (who was shortly to be investigated for his involvement in the existing opium monopoly), noted how the government of the neighboring Portuguese settlement of Macao, which already operated the kind of gambling monopoly proposed for Hong Kong, had, within six hours of being informed of his name by the Hong Kong authorities, traced the servant who murdered Glatz's apprentice, and most of the property stolen, through the good offices of the Macao gambling farmer.[127]

MacDonnell's 1867 scheme, smuggled into the colony's legislation against the strong reservations of the Colonial Office, included regulations prohibiting both Europeans and their Chinese servants from entering the licensed gambling houses.[128] MacDonnell claimed that the scheme had led to a decrease in crime between 1868 and 1869 of 22 percent in serious offenses and

126. Bowring to Labouchere, 6 Jan. 1858, CO 129/67, 11.
127. Bridges to Bowring, 8 Feb. 1858, CO 129/67, 124–25.
128. The regulations under (Hong Kong) n.9 of 1867 (*Gazette*, 12 Sept. 1867, 19 Sept. 1868) did not explicitly exclude servants of Europeans from gambling establishments: MacDonnell appears to have achieved this through instructions given direct to the licensees. MacDonnell to Buckingham, 29 May 1868, Parliamentary Papers (hereafter PP) 1869 (409) 43:5, *Hong Kong (Gambling Houses), Copy of Correspondence*.

18.4 percent in minor offenses.[129] He also claimed that larcenies among servants had declined by an even greater amount: "I am not aware," he boasted, "that the criminal statistics of any British colony have ever shown so remarkable a decrease of crime in the same period."[130] The experiment did not last long. The Colonial Office was concerned about the embarrassingly large revenue derived from such a vice and was under pressure from missionary and other organizations to abolish the monopoly. A campaign within Hong Kong in late 1870 and early 1871, when MacDonnell was absent from the colony, urged the recriminalization of gambling. A petition from the Chinese community complained that gambling debts had poisoned business relations and led to embezzlement, bankruptcy, the selling of children, and suicides: it asked why the regulations restrained Europeans but not Chinese from the vice.[131] The chief justice repeatedly denounced the policy in court, and the European Chamber of Commerce argued, contrary to MacDonnell's claims, that legalized gambling had encouraged rather than reduced dishonesty among employees. The decline in crime, it suggested, had been the result of improved policing and the greater use of flogging in punishing criminals.[132] The gambling monopoly was brought to an end in December 1871.

Conclusion

A dark picture has been painted here of MacDonnell's policies in Hong Kong, but his measures to control and monitor the Chinese population were complemented by the more formal involvement of Chinese elites in the colony's political sphere, albeit in a subordinate capacity. The same ordinance that consolidated registration arrangements for Chinese inhabitants also included provisions for voluntary neighborhood watch committees. Proceeds from the gambling scheme (partly because the Colonial Office refused to allow them to enter the general revenue) were donated to a committee formed by the Chinese elite to build a hospital that was to become the center of Chinese political power for the remainder of the century.[133] Undoubtedly repressive

129. MacDonnell to Granville, 12 Apr. 1870, CO 129/144, 256.

130. Ibid., 257. These claims are highly dubious: the incoming assistant superintendent of police, T. Fitz Roy Rice, noted in 1871 that various serious crimes, including some murders, had not been included in the returns and that charge sheets containing many cases occurring in 1869 had been left at an outstation and not discovered until after the returns were submitted. Report by T. Fitz Roy Rice, 5 Oct. 1871, CO 129/152, 259–61.

131. Petition from the Chinese community, Feb. 1871, CO 129/149, 226–29.

132. Whitfield to Kimberley, 10 Dec. 1870, CO 129/146, 289–90, 6 Feb. 1871, in MacDonnell to Granville, 12 Apr. 1870, CO 129/144, 226–29, 130–34.

133. See Sinn, *Power and Charity*.

though they were, the registration and curfew measures placed servants in an advantageous position compared with the rest of the Chinese population and were part of a process of assimilating Chinese servants to the European system. The lists of past employers on the backs of servants' registration tickets were designed to protect European employers against suspect servants, but they could also be an asset to servants with clean records, who, despite the worries of colonists, probably formed the vast majority of employees. Servants could avoid the curfew by using official night passes readily available to European employers, who needed the services of chair coolies and boys after dark.[134] The 1870 ordinance consolidating the now well-established curfew system included provisions for the discretionary issue of annual passes for the trusted Chinese elite of the colony.[135]

All these measures were means of sorting out the respectable and the reliable from the "thieves, pirates, and other bad characters" drawn to Hong Kong from among "the most criminal and desperate classes in the Chinese Empire"; they amounted, in MacDonnell's words, "almost to a social revolution of our relations towards the Chinese population."[136] The 1866 Registration Ordinance, together with the short-lived gambling regulations, also mark the end of a slow revolution in the relations between Chinese servants and their European employers, by which servants were gradually removed from the compradorial system, with its roots in the old Canton trade, and brought more fully under European control. This process was accelerated by the decline of Chinese security and the increasing tendency of Europeans to recruit their own servants. Its results were also a recognition that the standard, judicial methods of controlling servants and servant crime were inadequate in Hong Kong's peculiar situation, where absconding servants could so easily melt into the vast hinterland beyond the colony. As the colonial government consolidated its control over Hong Kong's Chinese population through registration and restrictions on movement in the 1860s, a special status was created for servants. While subjected to more direct surveillance and control by Europeans, their close association with Europeans also set them apart from the bulk of the Chinese population. Twenty-five years of colonial rule and the relaxation of political tensions after 1860 had probably encouraged many servants, particularly those who had grown up in Hong Kong, to identify

134. *Gazette*, 5 Dec. 1857.

135. (Hong Kong) n.14 of 1870.

136. MacDonnell's reply to an address by Chinese residents objecting to recent legislation, Oct. 1866, CO 129/115, 221; MacDonald to Buckingham, 6 Mar. 1869, PP 1869 (409) 43:26, *Hong Kong (Gambling Houses), Copy of Correspondence*; MacDonnell to Buckingham, 29 Oct. 1867, CO 129/125, 104.

themselves more closely with the interests of the colony. As Matilda Sharpe's experience suggests, familiarity appears also to have led many Europeans increasingly to draw the line that divided the domestic from the dangerous, not between them and their servants, but between their servants and the still threatening society beyond the garden gate.

TWELVE

Britain

The Defeat of the 1844 Master and Servants Bill

Christopher Frank

During the winter and spring of 1844, a campaign of petitioning and public meetings by Chartists, trade unionists, and short-time committees throughout England and Scotland forced Parliament to abandon a bill that would have greatly extended the scope of master and servant law. Actively promoted by the home secretary, the bill had the backing of nearly all of the nation's magistrates and judges.[1] Its defeat marked the beginning of the national campaign by workers against the ancient penal characteristics of employment law.

A Bill for Enlarging the Powers of Justices in Determining Complaints between Masters, Servants, and Artificers, and for the More Effectual Recovery of Wages before Justices, was introduced into the House of Commons in February 1844 by three career Tory backbenchers.[2] Their stated purpose was to remedy the illogical jurisdiction conferred by master and servant statutes, which usually contained ambiguous wording in the clauses that defined their scope. During the 1820s and 1830s, the Court of Queen's Bench added to this confusion by ruling that individuals not engaged in trades specifically named in the many master and servant statutes, as well as those hired by the job or piece, were not covered by the provisions of these coercive labor

1. *Hansard's Parliamentary Debates: Third Series* (hereafter *Hansard*), 73:1306-8, 74:526; *Justice of the Peace* (hereafter *JP*) VIII, 2 Mar. 1844, 154-55; *Legal Observer* XXVII, 16 Mar. 1844, 406; *Times*, 3 May 1844, 4; Challinor, *Radical Lawyer*, 144-45; Steinfeld, *Coercion*, 136-41; Frank, "Constitutional Law," chs. 2-3.

2. Engels, *Condition*, 319; *Journals of the House of Commons* (hereafter *JHC*), 99:52 (22 Feb. 1844).

3. *Bramwell v. Penneck* (1827), 7 B&C 627; *Lancaster v. Greaves* (1829), 9 B&C 536; *Hardy v. Ryle* (1829), 9 B&C 224; *Kitchen v. Shaw* (1837), 6 A&E 729; Napier, "Contract of Service," 85-87, 106-12; Steinfeld, *Coercion*, 129-32, 134-41.

laws.[3] By 1844 magistrates and employers alike felt that there was little sense to such distinctions, which limited the usefulness of these statutes to masters and confused justices of the peace. Workers charged with master and servant offenses were increasingly represented by attorneys, who insisted on conformity to the letter of the law. They challenged the validity of contracts of employment that lacked adequate consideration, the failure of employers to adhere to the terms of legal agreements, and the adequacy of warrants of commitment and convictions that did not demonstrate the magistrate's jurisdiction.[4] The proposed legislation would have disposed of these problems by bringing nearly all employment relationships under the umbrella of master and servant law.[5]

The bill was intended to remedy two potential sources of confusion about the magistrates' jurisdiction. The first gray area was the definition of the employment relationship. Did an agreement to perform a specific task for an employer create a relationship of service, subjecting the worker to the master and servant acts? Were individuals who did outwork in their homes servants, though they might take in work from several masters? The element of exclusivity in the master and servant relationship was an issue with which high court judges had wrestled earlier in the nineteenth century.[6] The second source of confusion was the less than clear language in the scope provisions of these statutes. For example, the Statute of Artificers specifically identified sixty-one distinct occupations, but the same clauses also used such broad terms as "any servant," and "all servants and labourers."[7] Did the statute apply to all workers, or only those in the specifically named trades? Similar mixtures of specific and general language were present in many later master and servant acts. To give just one example, the 1747 Act for the Better Adjusting and More Easy Recovery of the Wages of Certain Servants; and for the Better Regulation of Such Servants applied to "artificers, handicraftsmen, miners, colliers, keel-men, pitmen, glass-men, potters, and other labourers, employed for any certain time, or in any other manner."[8] To which "other labourers" did the act apply? Merely those in the named occupations, or anyone who made any type of agreement to perform labor?

In 1801 a parliamentary committee recommended giving magistrates au-

4. Challinor, *Radical Lawyer*; Trainor, *Black Country Elites*, 231; Steinfeld, *Coercion*, 105–7.

5. The only exception being domestic servants.

6. *Lowther v. Earl of Radnor* (1806), 8 East 113; *Hardy v. Ryle* (1829), 9 B&C 224.

7. (Engl.) 5 Eliz. c.4 (1562); Sir H. Calthrop, *Reports of Special Cases Touching Several Customes and Liberties of the City of London* (London, 1670), 20.

8. (G.B.) 20 Geo.II c.19 (1746) s.1; the act also expressly applied to servants in husbandry. Other important master and servant acts with ambiguous scope provisions were (G.B.) 6 Geo.III c.25 (1766) and (U.K.) 4 Geo.IV c.34 (1823).

thority to hear cases involving job and piece workers, as well as other occupations not specifically named in the master and servant statutes.[9] No action was taken, but in 1806 two men employed to dig an irrigation ditch were entitled to sue for their unpaid wages under the 1747 act despite the fact that they were not servants but only employed to perform a task that was not mentioned in any master and servant statute. Lord Ellenborough parsed the provision to find that, "unless the words 'other labourers' mean to comprehend a different description of persons from those before particularly named, it is difficult to account for their insertion at all." The 1747 act extended to laborers employed for "any certain time or in any other manner."[10] Ellenborough thereby temporarily extended the reach of master and servant law beyond anything it had recently known.

However, by the second quarter of the nineteenth century, the Court of Queen's Bench had reversed Ellenborough and severely limited the application of these statutes. Two cases in particular provoked commentary from magistrates and legal journalists hoping to reverse their consequences, and so contributed to the genesis of the 1844 bill: *Hardy v. Ryle* (1829) and *Kitchen v. Shaw* (1837).[11]

Thomas Hardy of Macclesfield had agreed to weave certain pieces of silk for Thomas Hall in his own home. When he neglected to finish the work, he was brought before magistrate John Ryle, who sentenced him to one month in the house of correction under 4 Geo.IV c.34 (1823). Hardy then sued Ryle for trespass and false imprisonment. At stake was not whether silk weavers were regulated by the provisions of master and servant law—several other acts made it clear that they were—but, rather, whether Hardy's relationship with Hall was one of master and servant. The attorneys for Hardy argued successfully that the 1823 act "clearly applies only to contracts of service; and a person cannot be said to become the servant of another, unless he enters into his service exclusively." Hardy had not agreed to work exclusively for Hall, but only to perform a specific task. This case was of considerable importance because it excluded all work that was by the job, piece, or task from the jurisdiction of many master and servant acts.[12]

9. *Report, Select Committee on State of the Laws between Masters and Servants*, Parliamentary Papers (hereafter PP) 1801 (62) 3:135–38.

10. *Lowther v. Earl of Radnor*, 8 East 113–25.

11. 9 B&C 224–28; 6 A&E 729–35; Steinfeld, *Coercion*, 127–30; Napier, "Contract of Service," 111. Also see *Bramwell v. Penneck* (1827), 7 B&C 536; *Lancaster v. Greaves* (1829), 9 B&C 627.

12. Steinfeld notes that though these rulings excluded pieceworkers under "general" master and servant acts (1747, 1766, 1823), those in a small number of specific trades were still covered

Kitchen v. Shaw was an action by a fourteen-year-old domestic servant against the magistrate who committed her to a month's imprisonment for leaving her employer's house after a dispute over wages. At issue was whether domestics fell within the class of "labourers or other persons" in the statute 6 Geo.III c.25 (1766). Lord Chief Justice Denman ruled that the "other persons" did not mean "all persons whatever who enter into engagements to serve for stated periods, but persons of the same description of those before enumerated." The effect of this decision, together with *Hardy v. Ryle*, was to restrict the coverage of master and servant law to those trades specifically named in the statutes and, within those trades, to cases where there was a contract to serve.

Keeping up to date with these developments could be a challenge for magistrates, most of whom lacked formal legal training. One source that magistrates could turn to for assistance in interpreting and understanding the law was the *Justice of the Peace*, an authoritative weekly law journal that dealt with issues pertinent to magistrates, including articles, reports, and commentary on master and servant law.[13] As a service to its readers it also contained a weekly question and answer section, "Practical Points": from 1842 to 1844 (and beyond), questions related to the jurisdiction of magistrates in master and servant cases were among the most common queries.

One constant in these letters was ignorance or confusion about the definition of "servant" settled by *Hardy v. Ryle*.[14] In 1843 one magistrate wrote that he was stunned after reading in a previous issue that master and servant law was only applicable where there was a contract to serve. For years it had been the practice in his region for magistrates to act in cases where there was no contract of service, but only an agreement to do a piece of work.[15] Many magistrates continued to believe that the authority on this subject was *Lowther v. the Earl of Radnor*.[16] These letters reveal that the difference between a contract to serve and an agreement to do a job could be quite subtle. Several queries were similar to one asking the difference between a contract to pro-

---

by the statutes (G.B.) 17 Geo.III c.56 (1777) and (U.K.) 6&7 Vict. c.40 (1843). He concedes, however, that it was widely perceived by magistrates, employers, and workers that job and piece-workers were excluded from the provisions of master and servant law.

13. Daintree, "Legal Periodical," 187–90.

14. *JP* VIII, 29 June 1844, 446.

15. *JP* VII, 19 Aug. 1843, 484.

16. *JP* VI, 26 Mar. 1842, 178; 16 Apr. 1842, 222; 21 May 1842, 304; 2 July 1842, 399; 3 Dec. 1842, 751; VII, 23 Sept. 1843, 569; 4 Nov. 1843, 663; VIII, 14 Dec. 1844, 830; *Potters' Examiner*, 27 Jan. 1844, 72; *Manchester Examiner*, 19 July 1845, 3; *Manchester and Salford Advertiser and Chronicle*, 4 Jan. 1845, 2; 3 May 1845, 5.

vide 18,000 bricks (a contract to do a job) and an agreement to make bricks generally (a contract to serve).[17]

There was considerable misunderstanding about the growing number of agricultural laborers hired by the job.[18] Many correspondents complained that the exclusion of pieceworkers meant that master and servant law was no longer relevant to employment in the countryside.[19] One letter commented that "as nine men out of ten in this district work by the piece, the authority of magistrates can hardly be appealed to."[20] Responding to such queries, the journal acknowledged that in many areas "the statutes relating to master and servant are nearly useless."[21]

In spite of *Kitchen v. Shaw*, the phrase "other labourers" in many master and servant statutes continued to puzzle magistrates, who asked their journal whether it included railway workers, bricklayers, stewards, nursery governesses, butchers, masters and matrons of workhouses, and many others.[22] The answer was always the same: it was not safe for a magistrate to act unless the trade in question was specifically named in a master and servant statute. "Practical Points" also addressed a number of queries about domestic servants, whom *Kitchen v. Shaw* made exempt from master and servant law. Some justices thought that it was unfair that domestic servants lacked an inexpensive remedy for recovering wages, and others felt it was illogical that people who were so clearly in a relationship of master and servant could not be held to their agreements.[23] Even well-informed and good-intentioned magistrates had to cope with hair-splitting anomalies. Could a domestic servant who also milked cows be considered a servant in husbandry and so fall within the statutes? If agricultural servants lived in the master's house, could they be considered domestic servants, and so exempt from master and servant law? Could

17. *JP* VI, 2 Apr. 1842, 190–91; 27 June 1842, 413; 17 Sept. 1842, 574; VII, 26 Aug. 1843, 500–501; VIII, 15 Mar. 1844, 189; 17 Aug. 1844, 558; 28 Sept. 1844, 651.

18. *JP* VI, 16 Apr. 1842, 220; 25 June 1842, 380; 23 July 1842, 449; 10 Sept. 1842, 555; VII, 1 Apr. 1843, 170; 12 Aug. 1843, 470; 26 Aug. 1843, 500–501; 23 Sept. 1843, 569; 28 Oct. 1843, 649; 4 Nov. 1843, 663; VIII, 17 Aug. 1844, 558; 31 Aug. 1844, 591; 28 Sept. 1844, 651; Kussmaul, *Servants in Husbandry*; Snell, *Annals*.

19. *JP* VI, 12 Feb. 1842, 81.

20. *JP* VI, 22 Jan. 1842, 32; 12 Feb. 1842, 81.

21. *JP* VII, 3 Dec. 1843, 751; VIII, 21 Sept. 1844, 636.

22. *JP* VI, 29 Jan. 1842, 45; 26 Mar. 1842, 178; 30 July 1842, 465; 1 Oct. 1842, 608; 31 Dec. 1842, 819; VII, 4 Mar. 1843, 98; 23 Sept. 1843, 570; 21 Oct. 1843, 634; 4 Nov. 1843, 665–66; 25 Nov. 1843, 711; 23 Dec. 1843, 773; VIII, 13 Apr. 1844, 252; 21 Sept. 1844, 636; 12 Oct. 1844, 682; 16 Nov. 1844, 758; 14 Dec. 1844, 830; and see *Ex Parte John Cresswell*, PRO KB 1/125/38.

23. *JP* VI, 31 Dec. 1842, 823; VII, 25 Mar. 1843, 154; VIII, 23 Mar. 1844, 207; 13 Apr. 1844, 253; 12 Oct. 1844, 687.

men who metered coal onto ships be considered keelmen and fall within a magistrate's jurisdiction?[24]

The increasing involvement of attorneys at petty sessions in the 1840s made it harder for justices of the peace to act in cases where they were unsure. Any magistrate who read a law journal or a newspaper from Lancashire, Northumberland, Durham, Staffordshire, or Yorkshire between 1843 and 1848 would have been aware of the victories of William Prowting Roberts before the Court of Queen's Bench in breach of contract cases. Roberts won many of these actions by exposing poorly written warrants of commitment and convictions that failed to establish fully the jurisdiction of the magistrate.[25] For their mistakes, magistrates could be, and were, embarrassed with charges of false imprisonment, charged under criminal informations, and burdened with the costs of defending themselves.[26] Legal commentators warned magistrates to exercise caution in enforcing master and servant law, as the higher courts had "nearly nullified the statutes; they cannot be safely executed."[27] The *Justice of the Peace* advised that "except in cases of absolute certainty, justices should decline to act under statutes which serve only to entrap them, and involve them in costs and damages."[28]

The 1844 bill would have removed many of the grounds on which magistrates' rulings could be questioned, and thus it is hardly surprising that they were among its most loyal supporters, and the most disappointed when the measure had to be dropped.[29] In fact, one of the bill's three cosponsors was Robert Palmer, who had been a justice of the peace in Berkshire and Wiltshire

24. *JP* VII, 24 June 1843, 362; 22 July 1843, 423; 23 Sept. 1843, 362; VIII, 18 May 1844, 358; 8 June 1844, 373; 6 July 1844, 459; 3 Aug. 1844, 521; 21 Sept. 1844, 633. Also see *In Re Ellen Griffith* (1844), *Ex Parte Eli Ormond* (1844), and *Mary Hughes v. Robert Anwyl* (1854), PRO KB 1/120/57, KB 1/117/39, KB 1/225/42; Steinfeld, *Coercion*, 54–56.

25. *Leeds Mercury*, 11 May 1844, 79; *Law Times* II, 20 Jan. 1844, 314–15; III, 4 May 1844, 79; 8 and 15 June 1844, 185, 207; *JP* VIII, 27 Jan. 1844, 56; 11 May 1844, 312; 27 June 1844, 500; 23 Nov. 1844, 774; *Northern Star* (hereafter *NS*), 23 Dec. 1843, 4; 13 Jan. 1844, 1; 20 Jan. 1844, 4; 10 Feb. 1844, 4; 24 Feb. 1844, 4; 2 Mar. 1844, 4, 7; 11 May 1844, 1, 4. Also see *In Re William Sheldon et al.*, PRO KB 1/119/31.

26. In August 1844 a group of Durham magistrates settled eighteen false imprisonment charges by paying Roberts and his clients £200 and all legal costs (PRO HO 43/67, 13 July, 3 Sept., and 19 Oct. 1844). He successfully sued magistrate Colin Lindsay for false imprisonment in 1845, winning £30 and all legal costs (*NS*, 12 Apr. 1845, 4, 8). He pursued a criminal information against stipendiary magistrate Thomas Bailey Rose in 1851, in which the magistrate was forced to pay his own legal costs (PRO KB 1/190/23, KB 1/191/60, and *Staffordshire Advertiser*, 15 June 1850, 5). Welsh attorney John Owen won £120 and legal costs against magistrates who falsely imprisoned seven Rhondda colliers in 1843 (Morris and Williams, *South Wales*).

27. *JP* VI, 20 Aug. 1842; VIII, 8 June 1844, 381–82; 27 July 1844, 498; 21 Sept. 1844, 636.

28. *JP* VII, 18 Feb. 1843, 61–62; VIII, 11 May 1844, 323–24.

29. *JP* VIII, 2 Mar. 1844, 154–55; 4 May 1844, 290; 18 May 1844, 335.

for seven years before entering Parliament.[30] Magistrates who were forced to administer an illogically applied law, and under increasing pressure to administer it correctly, were strongly in favor of its simplification.

Despite the uncertain state of the law and the misgivings of the magistracy, however, employers continued to rely on the penal clauses of the master and servant statutes in fighting trade-union action and maintaining labor discipline. Magistrates, who in many districts were recruited from the employing class, could usually be depended upon to present a striking laborer with the choice between returning to work or the house of correction.[31] In turn, trade unions began to challenge this partnership of magistrates and employers through speeches, pamphlets, newspaper articles, and legal action. The success of union counsel in undermining employers' use of master and servant law was a crucial impetus for the introduction of the 1844 bill.

On 11 August 1843 the miners' union of Northumberland and Durham hired Chartist solicitor William Prowting Roberts to provide its membership with legal representation for a reported salary of £1,000 during his first year, and £500 per year thereafter.[32] Roberts was a skilled and determined representative who dedicated his professional life to labor causes.[33] For three decades he traveled across eight counties, representing miners and laborers prosecuted under master and servant law or the 1825 Combination Act. He also developed an interest in workplace safety, attending several coroners' inquests on behalf of unions, accident victims, or their families.[34] He was involved in the majority of high-profile trade-union conspiracy cases that occurred during his professional life.[35] Although the less confrontational "new model" unions of the late 1850s and 1860s held Roberts at a greater distance, they still hired him to recover misappropriated funds, defend striking workers against intimidation and master and servant prosecutions, and assist in the preparation of appeals.[36] His involvement with the agitation against the penal

30. Stenton, *Who's Who* 1 (1832–85): 298; *Hansard*, 79:530.
31. D. Phillips, "Black Country Magistracy"; Swift, "English Urban Magistracy"; Woods, "Master and Servant"; Zangerl, "County Magistracy"; Foster, "Class and Country Government"; Knipe, "Justice of the Peace"; Godfrey, "Judicial Impartiality."
32. Challinor, *Radical Lawyer*, 21.
33. There were other solicitors who practiced mainly in labor cases, but only Roberts seems to have represented workers and trade unions exclusively.
34. Challinor, *Radical Lawyer*, 79, 133–35, 207; PRO HO 45/1830, 1873, 7007, 7581; *Miners' Advocate*, 19 Oct., 15 Dec. 1844, 193, 195, 197–99; Roberts, *Haswell Colliery Explosion*.
35. These include *R. v. Selsby* (1847), *R. v. Rowlands* (1851), *Walsby v. Anley* (1861), *O'Neill and Galbraith v. Longman and Kruger* (1863).
36. On Roberts's relationship with Alexander MacDonald, see Challinor, *Radical Lawyer*, 205–8, 212; for his work on embezzlement cases, see McIlroy, "Financial Malpractice," and *R. v.*

provisions of master and servant law continued until his death in 1871.[37] His success in court was an important reason for the introduction of the 1844 bill, and his efforts outside were critical in bringing about its defeat.

The penal clauses of master and servant law were a particular grievance for miners in Northumberland and Durham, where mine owners used it to support their system of contracting and labor discipline. Once a year, pitmen signed an unequal eleven-month bond in terms set by an employers' combination. The bond gave owners and their managers a wide freedom to fine miners, and precluded the pitmen from working elsewhere even if their masters could not give them regular work. A breach of the bond meant being hauled before a magistrate, whose interests were often not far removed from the coal trade.[38]

Between 1843 and 1848 Roberts defended scores of miners against master and servant prosecutions. Roberts used a variety of arguments to defend workers in such cases. He sometimes disputed whether the defendant was a servant within the meaning of the act or was engaged in one of the trades it covered. In other cases he argued that the contract of employment was bad for want of sufficient consideration or, if it was valid, that the master had repudiated it by failing to adhere to its terms. Another strategy was to prove that the employer had voided the agreement with illegal activity, such as paying wages in truck or at a public house. Roberts often argued that "variance" between the summons, warrant, or testimony of the prosecutor made the proceedings void. When he lost at petty sessions, Roberts initiated writs of certiorari and habeas corpus to bring the cases before the Court of Queen's Bench, where he often won due to poorly written warrants of commitment or convictions. Between December 1843 and 1846, Roberts had the master and servant convictions of no fewer than thirty-seven miners overturned by Queen's Bench, to say nothing of his clients in other trades.[39] Friedrich Engels wrote that "the miners' attorney general . . . seemed to be everywhere at once, striking

---

Welston and Hickie and *R. v. Ellis*, MSS.78.OS.4.1.33, University of Warwick, Modern Records Centre.

37. Roberts testified twice before the 1866 Select Committee: PP 1866 (449) 13 "Evidence Taken before the Select Committee on Master and Servant," entries for 12 and 19 June 1866.

38. Challinor, *Radical Lawyer*, 80–81; Welbourne, *Miners' Unions*, 68–73; Colls, *Pitmen*, 293–94; Fynes, *Miners of Northumberland*, 54, 65, ch. 8; Webb, *Story of the Durham Miners*, 7–10, 30; Steinfeld, *Coercion*, ch. 4; PRO HO 45, box 644, 15 Apr. 1844.

39. Willibald Steinmetz in his essay exploring the development of labor's instinctive desire "to be left alone by the law" perhaps fails to appreciate fully the level of success unions enjoyed during the 1840s before the courts. Steinmetz, "De-juridification," 269–76; Frank, "Constitutional Law," ch. 4; Challinor, *Radical Lawyer*, ch. 7, 103; *NS*, 14 Feb. 1846, 1.

terror into the hearts of coal owners."[40] Fear of expense and inconvenience caused employers in St. Helens, Preston, and Manchester to drop breach-of-contract charges against workers when they heard that Roberts would defend them.[41]

The reporting of Roberts's victories before Queen's Bench in the *Northern Star*, *Miners' Advocate*, and *Potters' Examiner* had the effect of damaging the legitimacy of magistrates, while at the same time curiously enhancing workers' faith in the institutions of high justice in England. Headlines such as "Constitutional Law versus Justices' Justice," "Constitutional Law versus Coal King Law," "Steam Gaol Delivery: Another Glorious Triumph of Constitutional Law over Magisterial Ignorance," and "More of Labour's Triumphs: The Value of the Law When Honestly Administered" fostered the notion that only through the use of legal counsel could the collusion between magistrates and employers be defeated.[42] After one successful case before Queen's Bench, the *Northern Star* "rejoiced to find that in the real law there is yet protection for the poor. To get the law is the thing, and Mr. Roberts appears to have discovered the magical process by which this . . . is to be achieved." After another victory before Queen's Bench, the journal reported, "Thus a second judge has awarded a triumph to the law and affixed the stamp of ignorance upon 'the great unpaid' of a second county." These sentiments were often repeated.[43]

As the *Northern Star* reported victory after victory, Roberts rapidly became a celebrity among the pitmen. He addressed the miners' public meetings, published articles in the *Miners' Advocate* and *Miners' Monthly Magazine*, and consulted at union delegate meetings. Advertisements in the *Northern Star* promised a free portrait of Roberts with every new three-month subscription.[44] When Roberts arrived in town to defend workers he was often accompanied by parades with bands playing "See the Conquering Hero Comes." Miners wrote a number of ballads and folk songs commemorating the "miners' attorney-general."[45] This publicity was as dangerous for mine owners as his legal victories. This new confidence in their legal standing had the poten-

40. Engels, *Condition*, 289.

41. Ibid., 288–89; Challinor, *Radical Lawyer*, 103.

42. *NS*, 23 Dec. 1843, 4; 20 Jan. 1844, 4; 10 Feb. 1844, 4; 24 Feb. 1844, 4; 11 May 1844, 1, 4; 8 Feb. 1845, 4; 5 July 1845, 8; *Miners' Advocate*, 27 Jan. 1844, 37; 29 Mar. 1844, 68–69.

43. *NS*, 23 Dec. 1843, 3; 20 Jan. 1844, 4; 10 Feb. 1844, 4; 24 Feb. 1844, 4; 2 Mar. 1844, 7; 11 May 1844, 4; 22 June 1844, 5; *Potters Examiner*, 30 Mar. 1844, 137–39; 6 Apr. 1844, 145.

44. *NS*, 2 Sept. 1843; 16 Sept. 1843.

45. *NS*, 15 Feb. 1845, 1; 26 Apr. 1845, 1; 4 Oct. 1845, 1; *Sheffield and Rotherham Independent*, 15 June 1844, 5, 8; 29 June 1844, 5. Machin, *Yorkshire Miners*, 51–52. Challinor, *Radical Lawyer*, 106–7.

tial to lessen pitmen's inhibitions about refusing to work under objectionable conditions.

From the mine owners' perspective, Roberts's victories represented a miscarriage of justice. It was frustrating to watch men who had clearly violated the spirit of the law go unpunished due to technicalities illuminated by "scheming lawyers." Even when the men were punished, Roberts's involvement could turn it into a Pyrrhic victory due to delay, added expense, or negative publicity.[46] Pit owner John Taylor complained to the commissioner of mines that in the first half of 1844, "the pitmen's legal advisor, Mr. Roberts, commenced action after action on points arising out of a bond which was . . . drawn up in good faith, and well understood by the parties concerned." The "vexatious legal proceedings" of the "miners' attorney-general" made "the agreement for twelve months binding upon them [the owners] and not upon their workmen."[47] The Committee of the Coal Trade complained that because of Roberts, "Last year . . . the control of the collieries no longer remained with the viewers or owners."[48] According to one mine owner, Roberts was "specially employed for the purpose of annoying them."[49]

It is likely that the publicity arising from Roberts's victories was a causal factor in the introduction of the 1844 bill. The *Northern Star* certainly suspected there to be a connection:

It would appear that these frequent triumphs of the law, affording, as they do, a sort of protection to labour, though a costly one, have raised the alarm of the capitalists. A bill has been very snugly and quietly introduced into the House of Commons, ostensibly for the purpose of giving increased powers to "Servants and Artificers for the More Effectual Recovery of Wages Before Justices"; yet for the real purpose of conferring additional powers upon masters and their Justices. The bill has been prepared and brought by Mr. William Miles, Mr. Robert Palmer, and Mr. Galley Knight. . . . Can anyone tell us, whether these three Honourable Gentlemen, or any of them, are connected with, or have any interest in mines or collieries?[50]

Perhaps the *Northern Star* was looking for this connection in the wrong place. Although the bill was introduced by Miles, Palmer, and Knight, Home

---

46. Challinor, *Radical Lawyer*, 79.

47. *Report . . . into the State of the Population of the Mining Districts*, PP 1846 (737) 24:392 (hereafter *Mining Districts*).

48. PRO HO 45, box 644, 8 June 1844.

49. *Observations by the Committee of the Coal Trade* (1844), 5–6, in Carpenter, *Labour Disputes*.

50. *NS*, 2 Mar. 1844, 4.

Secretary Sir James Graham rewrote it in committee and actively promoted it in the House. During the spring of 1844, as the miners of Northumberland and Durham drifted toward one of the decade's longest and most bitter strikes, Graham was in regular contact with northern coal owners like Lord Londonderry and the earl of Northumberland, as well as the bishop of Durham and a committee of Durham magistrates.[51] As home secretary, Graham was well aware of Roberts's efforts on behalf of the National Miners' Association. He could not have been pleased about the "legal harassment" of northern mine owners, or the embarrassing proceedings of a "Chartist Demagogue" against those who maintained order in the North.[52]

Graham's office placed him in a position to monitor labor disputes across the nation and to witness the limitations of master and servant law in the face of renewed trade-union aggressiveness. After enduring six years of wage cuts, workers could no longer tolerate deteriorating conditions, and 1842–44 saw a significant rise in the number of strikes. The emergence of national unions in the 1830s and 1840s had raised considerable concern among employers, and their power was frequently exaggerated. For example, the National Miners Association was widely but incorrectly believed to have more than 100,000 members and an annual income of £50,000, making it "one of the most awe-inspiring unions of its time."[53] In 1844 it authorized 33,000 miners in Northumberland and Durham to walk out for more than four months in a strike that cost the northern coal owners an estimated £80,000 in foregone income.[54] As frantic correspondence from magistrates flooded into the Home Office demanding troops and reporting the swearing in of special constables, Graham may well have considered the merits of a stronger master and servant act to curb the power of trade unions.

The miners' aggressive legal resistance to master and servant prosecutions made the current law increasingly unacceptable to magistrates and employers alike. By replacing a large body of disputed statutes that covered only certain categories of workers in specific types of employment relationships with a single act that applied to nearly all workers, they could limit the options available to "crafty attorneys" in defending workers.[55]

On 22 February 1844 Miles, Palmer, and Knight were given leave by the House of Commons to present A Bill for Enlarging the Powers of Justices in Determining Complaints between Masters, Servants, and Artificers, and

---

51. PRO HO 45, boxes 644 and 646.
52. *Times*, 17 July 1844, 6.
53. Challinor and Ripley, *Miners' Association*, 8, 82.
54. *Mining Districts*, 395.
55. *NS*, 13 July 1844, 4.

for the More Effectual Recovery of Wages before Justices.[56] As its title suggests, the bill was promoted as a wage recovery measure for workers who had been outside the scope of the existing acts.[57] Its supporters made little reference to the fact that these same workers would now be exposed to harsh penal sanctions for breaking agreements, neglecting work, or "misbehaving." The bill was intended to clarify doubts about the types of work and agreements covered by the master and servant acts. It extended all the provisions of four existing master and servant acts[58] to every type of employment relationship (save domestic service). This included trades not enumerated in any act, as well as hirings where the relationship was not technically one of master and servant.

One week after the bill's introduction, the *Northern Star* warned its readers that contrary to the bill's title, its primary purpose was not to expedite the recovery of back wages but to give magistrates the power to punish breaches of contract by "every order of labour in the land."[59] A week later it published excerpts from the bill, noting again that it would "affect all classes of labourers."[60] The *Northern Star* was not the only journal to notice the bill in its early stages. The *Justice of the Peace* supported the bill but urged its promoters to go further. For magistrates who were tired of being second-guessed, "the proposal hardly seemed explicit enough." Reviewing recent reversals under 4 Geo.IV c.34, the journal blamed the vulnerability of justices of the peace on poor legislative draftsmanship. It pleaded with Parliament to protect magistrates enforcing the law in good faith from exposure to expensive appeals.[61]

The bill passed second reading without division or debate on 6 March, and a week later it was committed.[62] In committee, Graham rewrote the bill, say-

56. The bill passed first reading the following day. Any connections between the bill's co-sponsors and specific interests are not readily apparent. William Miles was a Tory backbencher from age eighteen to sixty-five. His father made the family fortune in banking and trade with the West Indies. Palmer was a lawyer, magistrate, and career politician who sat in Parliament for thirty-five years without reaching the cabinet level. Their statement before the House of Commons expresses a concern with the anomalies and confusions faced by magistrates in enforcing the law.

57. The bill would have expedited the recovery of back wages by allowing "Stewards, Bailiffs, Foremen, or Managers" to be summoned before magistrates in lieu of the masters themselves. It would also have raised the limit of unpaid wages recoverable by certain types of workers to the ten-pound level that already applied to others. The same laborers could recover under master and servant law. These aspects of the bill were not controversial and attracted little attention.

58. (G.B.) 20 Geo.II c.19 (1746); (G.B.) 31 Geo.II c.11 (1758); (G.B.) 6 Geo.III c. 25 (1766); and (U.K.) 4 Geo.IV c.34 (1823).

59. *NS*, 2 Mar. 1844, 4.

60. *NS*, 9 Mar. 1844, 4.

61. *JP* VIII, 2 Mar. 1844, 131–32, 154–55.

62. *JHC*, 99:90.

ing that he agreed with its object, but "the means that were taken for attaining that object were inexpedient." Graham decided that instead of adding amending legislation to an already large and complex body of law, it would be more sensible to repeal six extant master and servant acts and replace them with a single measure "containing all the portion that was really valuable in those acts," and applying to all forms of labor under all types of agreements. Miles, Palmer, and Knight agreed that Graham's bill was more "clear and precise," and it was printed the same day.[63] Graham, whose "personal unpopularity was extreme" in 1843–44, was later roundly criticized both inside and outside of the House of Commons for refusing to make it a government bill. As public protest grew, Graham was accused by the *Times* of using Miles, Knight, and Palmer as lightning rods to absorb opposition to a measure of his making. If Peel and Graham were to parcel out responsibility for introducing potentially controversial bills to backbenchers, it was argued, the government would lose all accountability.[64]

Although the redrafted bill would have achieved the same objective as the original version, extending master and servant law to job and piece workers of all trades, it was entirely different in form. Because it repealed instead of merely amending the existing master and servant acts, Graham had to reintroduce their common provisions, including the hated penal double standard.[65] The bill's fourth clause provided that any worker who was absent from work, left work unfinished, or was guilty of any "misbehaviour concerning such service or employment" could be sentenced by a magistrate to two months' imprisonment with or without hard labor. This was not new law, but the boldly obnoxious and unambiguous wording led to an unmistakable shift in emphasis. There could now be no pretense that this was primarily a wage recovery bill. This became apparent when the amended bill was debated on 20 March. Duncombe criticized the penal clause, saying it "gave to the magistracy some extremely harsh powers." Graham and Miles argued in vain that under existing law magistrates already had the authority to commit workers to *three* months' imprisonment for the same offenses.[66] They had failed to anticipate the depth of working-class hostility to even the existing state of master and servant law.

Roberts was en route to Glasgow to attend a conference of the National

63. *Hansard*, 73:980.

64. Torrens, *Graham*, 2:272–73, 232–40; *Hansard*, 73:1590; 74:527; *Times*, 3 May 1844, 4; *Morning Chronicle*, 13 Apr. 1844, 2; Gash, *Peel*, 438–44.

65. In addition to the four acts mentioned in the original bill, Graham's version would also have repealed (Engl.) 5 Eliz. c.4 (1562) and (G.B.) 27 Geo.II c.6 (1754).

66. *Hansard*, 73:1306–8.

Miners' Association when he received a letter from Duncombe warning that the bill would have important consequences for his clients.[67] The union, representing as many as 50,000 miners, had a network of local branches held together by traveling lecturers and regional delegates. This apparatus, along with short-time committees and the *Northern Star*, managed to organize public meetings and petitions opposing the bill with remarkable speed. On Monday, 25 March, Roberts told the miners' conference that the bill "struck at the liberties of the working classes." He distributed copies of Graham's version, explaining each of its eleven clauses to the delegates. He reminded his audience that the existing law allowed employers and magistrates "to drag a man from his family and send him to a dungeon" upon the evidence "of any underlooker, viewer, foreman, or deputy."[68] The conference authorized a petition protesting that magistrates operating alone would have powers "more despotic ... than is consistent with the liberty which your petitioners are taught to regard as their birthright," and denying "the most necessary of safeguards against a harsh, or hasty, or capricious exercise of judicial authority." Delegates were asked to sign the petition themselves and to distribute it to their constituents.[69]

Were it not for the fortuitous timing of the conference and the efforts of Thomas Duncombe at Westminster, the protest would not have had time to get under way. On two occasions, Duncombe and the bill's other opponents were able to delay its third reading. The day after the National Miners' Association adopted Roberts' petition, the bill stood as the seventh item on Parliament's orders of the day.[70] Duncombe and Ferrand moved that the bill should be withdrawn and reintroduced for first reading because of the radical alteration in its form. Graham and Sir Robert Peel would have permitted the withdrawal of the bill, but because of the absence of William Miles, the bill's sponsor, the measure was postponed. On 18 April, when a number of petitions protesting the measure had already been received by the House, Duncombe was able to have its third reading postponed until 1 May.[71]

The labor press took full advantage of this reprieve. The *Potters' Examiner*, published by the United Branches of Operative Potters, reprinted the notorious fourth clause on 30 March, warning that the bill's purpose was "to meet the conduct of provincial magistrates in their late and present attempts to destroy the liberty of working men, by acting from their own vindictive minds,

67. *NS*, 30 Mar. 1844, 8.
68. *NS*, 30 Mar. 1844, 4, 8.
69. *NS*, 6 Apr. 1844, 4, 8.
70. *Hansard*, 73:1588.
71. *JHC*, 99:214; *Hansard*, 73:1589–90; *NS*, 30 Mar. 1844, 5.

and not from the letter of the law." It urged members to circulate petitions throughout the potteries, because the bill would make "trades' unions . . . a non-entity, as strikes cannot take place, except in defiance of the dungeon."[72] The *Northern Star* published additional commentary on 6 April, along with excerpts from Roberts's pamphlet warning of the consequences should it become law. It printed the petition, with directions to readers to have it adopted at every public meeting, union gathering, or short-time protest that occurred over the next fortnight.

In its four April issues, the *Northern Star* reported on sixty-six public meetings across Great Britain at which resolutions were passed and petitions circulated against the "damnable bill." This coverage is useful in showing the involvement of trade unions, short-time committees, and Chartists in defeating the measure, as well as the rhetorical strategies that speakers drew upon to ignite the indignation in their audiences. The speeches and resolutions focused as much on current injustices in the substance and procedure of master and servant law, as on the proposed changes in the law. Lecturers most often objected to the bill's potential use against trade unions, its inclusion of women and children in the penal sanctions, its enforcement by magistrates, its failure to provide the "ancient English liberty" of trial by jury, and the harsh and vague wording of its penal offenses. By 1 May the campaign had presented 213 petitions, said to represent the opposition of "nearly two million people."[73]

Of the sixty-six meetings, seventeen were sponsored by trade unions. At these meetings the fourth clause of the act, containing the penal sanctions, was almost always read aloud, often to boos. Master and servant law was perhaps an employer's most effective legal weapon against trade-union activity. If men chose to go on strike without giving proper notice, they could be imprisoned or forced to return to work. In industries with annual hirings (like the miners' bond), there was only one time in the year that strikes could safely take place, making it easier for owners to minimize the effectiveness of turning out. "Let this bill become law, and every trades union in the Kingdom will be annihilated!"[74] William Fleming, the secretary of the Dyers of Glasgow, told his audience that the bill "struck at the root of trade unions, and was intended to prevent the working classes from meeting to protect themselves against . . . the duplicity of tyrannical employers." London shoemaker, W. Clark, worried that his union would dissolve if the bill became law: they "sometimes had to stand out for wages; but let this bill become law, and who would dare come out for them? Where would they get

72. *Potters' Examiner*, 30 Mar. 1844, 138; 6 Apr. 1844, 138, 146, 158.
73. *JHC*, 99:217, 224, 229, 232, 243; *Times*, 2 May 1844.
74. Simon, "Master and Servant," 171; *NS*, 6 Apr. 1844, 4; 20 Apr. 1844, 3.

men to take upon themselves the awful responsibility of being their officers?" Societies representing groups as diverse as seamen, miners, potters, fustian cutters, silk weavers, cordwainers, letter-press printers, shoemakers, painters, sawyers, and tailors came forward to oppose the bill.[75] Some of these unions were directly threatened because their trades were not specifically named in an existing master and servant act, or because they worked by the job or piece. However, trades like the miners and potters that had labored under the oppressive weight of the penal provisions for three centuries were no less vigorous in their opposition. The bill created no new law for them, but their unions welcomed the opportunity to draw attention to the oppressive administration of master and servant.

At twenty-six of the sixty-six meetings, petitions supportive of Lord Ashley's ten-hours amendment were also circulated and signed. The campaign was fortunate to be able to capitalize on the existence of active short-time committees. In April 1844 Richard Oastler and other speakers were traveling across the country and addressing public meetings on the factory issue. They had no difficulty circulating a second petition, as was done throughout Lancashire and Yorkshire. These two campaigns were informed by the same ideas about women's proper relationship with the family, workplace, and the state. Speakers at these meetings treated the bill as a new threat to women, and stressed that men needed to "protect our wives and families," and "weak women and little children."[76] Although women were sometimes prosecuted under these laws, and often used them to recover unpaid wages, the suggestion that the bill was a unique threat to them, and hence all family life, was a useful rhetorical strategy that underscored contradictions in middle-class political economy and domesticity. Factory regulation advocates often justified the interference in women and children's employment contracts with the suggestion that they were "much less free agents than men."[77] By the same logic, opponents of the 1844 bill could emphasize its threat to women and suggest that it was unfair to subject "much less than free agents" to imprisonment for breach of contract.

The leaders of Chartism—Feargus O'Connor, Patrick O'Higgins, Bronterre O'Brien, W. P. Roberts, R. G. Gammage, and Joshua Hobson—also did their part by addressing large public meetings where petitions were signed. The biased administration of master and servant law, the double standard of

75. *NS*, 6 Apr. 1844, 4; 13 Apr. 1844, 5, 8; 20 Apr. 1844, 6–8; 27 Apr. 1844, 8.

76. *Manchester Times*, 20 Apr. 1844, 6, 8; *NS*, 6 Apr. 1844, 4; 13 Apr. 1844, 4, 8; 20 Apr. 1844, 4, 7–8; 27 Apr. 1844, 6–8.

77. Clark, *Breeches*, 215, 220–22, 226, 232–38, 242; Rose, *Limited Livelihoods*, 68. Many women participated in job and piece work; see Alexander, "Women's Work," 73–103.

its sanctions, and Parliament's attempt to extend its scope to workers who wanted no part of it were injustices ideally suited to excoriation by the language and ideology of Chartism. These laws were particularly obnoxious examples of "class legislation." They were unjustly written and enforced because laborers had no role in either process.[78]

At most meetings, speakers played to their audience's general distrust of the magistracy by contrasting the expansion of summary jurisdiction with "our ancient rights of trial by jury."[79] Even though twelve jurors could have all the class bias of a single magistrate, that master and servant law was enforced summarily was one of the most common attacks made on the bill in public meetings. References to the death of the "Palladium of British Liberty" were commonplace in the campaign's speeches and resolutions.[80] This rhetoric was timely because the expansion of magistrates' summary powers was a topic frequently discussed in Parliament during the second quarter of the nineteenth century. Politicians who opposed this expansion often talked about the central place of the jury trial in English liberty.[81]

The operation of master and servant law was made more objectionable by the altered social backgrounds of the "Injustices of the Peace" who enforced this law. In the second quarter of the nineteenth century, in many regions, coal and iron masters were replacing titled landowners as the dominant group among magistrates. Because master and servant cases so often dealt with coal and iron workers, these men were seen to be judging cases in which they had a direct interest. The *Potters' Examiner* objected that "The powers of the manufacturers will become omnipotent, as the magisterial benches are nearly wholly filled by themselves."[82] The coal interest had always dominated the magistracy in Northumberland and Durham, causing the bishop of Durham to complain to Sir James Graham that in the North few men of the standing to be magistrates were outside of the coal interest, so that miners could not rid themselves of the notion that they were before a partial tribunal in master and servant disputes.[83] Even nonlabor journals acknowledged the bias of magistrates in this region. According to the *Non-Conformist*, "All the world is aware of the manner in which the laws are administered by the 'great unpaid,' . . . 'Justices' justice' has become a term of opprobrium throughout the United Kingdom."[84]

78. See the comments of O'Brien, Cuff, and Clark in *NS*, 13 Apr. 1844, 4, 8; 20 Apr. 1844, 7.
79. *NS*, 20 Apr. 1844, 7.
80. *NS*, 20 Apr. 1844, 8; 27 Apr. 1844, 6, 8; *Non-Conformist*, 1 May 1844, 292–93.
81. P. Smith, "Circumventing the Jury"; Sweeney, "Summary Jurisdiction."
82. *Potters Examiner*, 6 Apr. 1844, 146.
83. PRO HO 45, box 644, 15 Apr. 1844.
84. *Non-Conformist*, 1 May 1844, 293.

This was no mere problem of perception. According to Challinor, Roberts "found at Chesterfield they had dispensed with the time consuming procedure of hearing both sides before deciding in favour of an employer."[85] There are many examples between 1842 and 1848 of magistrates denying workers the right to make a full defense, or to have legal counsel.[86]

The flow of petitions into Parliament steadily increased, reaching its crescendo on 1 May when Thomas Duncombe introduced the last of the protests and launched into a scathing attack on the bill and its supporters. He called the measure "one of the most insidious, arbitrary, iniquitous, and tyrannical attempts to oppress the working class that had ever been made." Undaunted by the laughter that his hyperbole provoked, Duncombe accused its promoters of bringing the bill for third reading under "false colours and pretences" because it was not the same bill that had passed its first two readings. Drawing attention to the workers' petitions, he noted that there was not one presented in favor of the bill. Supported by Joseph Hume, he moved to postpone consideration for six months, a virtual death sentence for the "damnable bill."[87]

The bill's promoters expressed surprise at the working-class reaction. Graham, Miles, and Knight felt that the petitioners had been misled: "[N]ever was a grosser deception practiced upon a people; never did a people labour under a more complete mistake." Knight insisted that they wanted only to make it easier for all workers to collect unpaid wages. Graham reminded the House that the penal clauses objected to were "already the law of the land" for many workers. This was a benevolent bill: it made it easier to collect unpaid wages; it allowed magistrates to summon workers in breach-of-contract cases rather than have them arrested under warrant; it lowered the maximum sentence workers faced; it raised the maximum amount of unpaid wages that they could recover. An M.P. countered that if the working classes were asked whether for all of these improvements they would be willing to face imprisonment for absence, neglect, or misconduct, their answer, as the petitions showed, would be a very loud no.[88] Hume suggested that the matter be taken up by the government and be more thoroughly examined, but many other

85. Challinor, *Radical Lawyer*, 103–4.

86. In addition to the cases in note 23 above, see, for example, *R. v. Lewis et al.* (1844), *NS*, 30 Dec. 1843, 4; 20 Jan. 1844, 4; 13 LJ 46; *R. v. Richards et al.* (1844), PRO KB 1/119/31; 13 LJ 147; Challinor, *Radical Lawyer*, 103–4; J. Williams, *Derbyshire Miners*, 90–97; *In Re Capestick et al.* (1844), PRO KB 1/119/30; 8 JP 297; *In Re John Hirbert et al.* (1844), PRO KB 1/119/29; Machin, *Yorkshire Miners*, 47–53; *In Re William Sheldon and others* (1844), PRO KB 1/123/39; *Re Bailey, Re Collier* (1854), PRO KB 1/222/9–10, 30–31, and KB 1/223/46–47; *R v. Biggins*, Modern Records Centre, Coventry, MSS.78.OS.4.1.22. Steinfeld makes reference to many of these cases but fails to investigate the social contexts from which they emerged. Steinfeld, *Coercion*, 154.

87. *Hansard*, 74:523.

88. *Hansard*, 74:524–30.

members felt the bill was unnecessary. As dinner time approached, the cries of "Division! Division!" became so persistent that most of Robert Palmer's speech was drowned out. When the division on the motion to postpone was held, the tellers for the ayes emerged with a nearly two to one victory. The "damnable bill" was dead.[89]

Reactions to the bill's defeat were naturally varied. The *Justice of the Peace* complained that "Never was so harmless a production so unjustly vilified," and observed that because of its failure, "certain persons continue to be subjected to a bad law, and magistrates called upon to execute an almost unintelligible one, simply because some object to be governed by any law at all."[90] The *Non-Conformist* held up the master and servants bill as an argument against pending factory legislation, warning workers to be wary of government interference in relations between capital and labor: "[W]hen interested demagogues urge them to go to parliament for protection, let them point to the master and servants bill as a specimen of the redress they are likely to obtain."[91] The *Northern Star* happily proclaimed the "triumph of labour," over "the government attempt to make him a very slave to his employer."[92]

The campaign against the 1844 master and servants bill confirms the depth of working-class hostility to this body of law. Although workers often made arguments strategically calculated to intersect with important issues of the day, hostility to imprisonment for breach of contract was always present. At numerous meetings workers objected to the one-sided offenses, procedures, and penalties, all of which seemed inconsistent with their concept of British rights and liberties. The demonstrations reveal that laborers had little faith in the knowledge and integrity of the magistracy and opposed its use of the law of master and servant to force men and women to work under objectionable conditions, and to hinder efforts to negotiate better ones.

The benefit of hindsight tells us that the "triumph of labour" was short-lived, for the penal clauses of master and servant law were actually used more frequently against workers over the next twenty years. As late as 1867, nearly 10,000 men and women were prosecuted for master and servant offenses in England and Wales.[93] This increased use of the law at home, as well as its proliferation throughout the British Empire, leaves one to wonder what, if anything, was accomplished by labor in 1844. The defeat of the 1844 bill was

89. *Hansard*, 74:523, 526–28, 530; *Morning Chronicle*, 2 May 1844, 290. The vote was 97 to 54 in favor of withdrawing the bill.
90. *JP* VIII, 4 May 1844, 290.
91. *Non-Conformist*, 1 May 1844, 292–93.
92. *NS*, 4 May 1844, 4.
93. PP 1867–68 (4062) 67:25–32 (*Return of Judicial Statistics of England and Wales*).

important because it was the first, though by no means last, time that labor organized itself on a national scale around opposition to master and servant law. The campaign drew attention to the injustices of the law and its administration and brought labor into ongoing debates about the magistracy. Parliament learned how politically inexpedient it would be to attempt to expand master and servant law in England on such a large scale again. The protest of 1844 is important because it was the earliest large-scale organized working-class expression of discontent with master and servant law; it publicized and clearly articulated the injustices of the current law's administration; and it began a tradition of trade-union opposition which would ultimately culminate in repeal. The defeat of the "damnable bill" had ramifications well beyond 1844.

THIRTEEN

India, 1858–1930

The Illusion of Free Labor

Michael Anderson

It has been argued that "in the field of labour relations the *laissez faire* practised by the Government of India was a policy rather than the absence of one."[1] This is true only to a point.[2] Apart from the abolition of slavery, the ameliorative factory acts, and the supervised recruitment systems on plantations,[3] the machinery of the state played an important role in administering the law of master and servant, both in plantation and industrial employment. The colonial state maintained the penal aspects of the law well into the twentieth century, a half century longer than in England, a delay in reform that is in striking contrast to other changes in the doctrines of Indian law. The significance of master and servant law in India arose from the nature of the labor market in specific sectors of the economy, the demands of employers, and the colonial state's characterization of Indian workers as immature, recalcitrant, and incapable of enjoying full "freedom."

The Labor Market and New Employment

Lack of unskilled labor, most now agree, did not represent an obstacle to the growth of Indian industry during the colonial period.[4] Although true in a sense, this assertion reveals little about the problem of forming a waged

1. Bagchi, *India*, 117.
2. Despite a handful of admittedly outspoken advocates, Indian administrators were never completely enthralled with laissez-faire doctrines. Pragmatic considerations of finance and feasibility were more serious constraints on state action. See Bhattacharya, "Laissez faire," 1–22, and E. Stokes, *Utilitarians*.
3. See the chapter by Mohapatra in this volume.
4. M. Morris, *Bombay Cotton*, ch. 4; Bagchi, *India*, ch. 5.

labor force. In the course of industrialization managers needed to recruit and retain workers willing to exchange labor for wages within new production schemes. Many Indian and most European managers complained vociferously of inadequate labor supplies, particularly in newly established industries in northern India before 1921 but also in other districts.[5] In 1905 European employers at the Conference of the Indian and Ceylon Chambers of Commerce passed a resolution calling on the government to investigate;[6] the resulting study found no general labor shortage in northern India, but labor supply problems associated with strikes, plague epidemics, and, in certain cities such as Kanpur, rapid industrial growth that created bursts of demand.[7] Where the quantity of labor was sufficient, its quality frequently fell foul of colonial complaint. "The labour of the people," wrote one contemporary, "is not strenuously nor successfully exerted, and man to man, an Indian does much less work in a given time than a European."[8] Industrial managers often accused workers of indolence, absence, and inefficiency. Conflicts over discipline and work intensity lay behind many strikes that were called in the name of wages. Although workers could not escape the arbitrary authority relations that characterized Indian factories, they did not surrender. Beatrice Webb noted in 1912:

> What is quite clear is that these old standing European inhabitants of India have not acquired the art of managing the Indians. What is equally clear is that the Indian is sometimes an extraordinarily difficult worker *to sweat*. He does not care enough for his earnings. He prefers to waste away in semi-starvation rather than overwork himself. However low his standard of life, his standard of work is lower—at any rate when he is working for an employer whom he does not like. And his irregularities are baffling.[9]

Views like this are contested,[10] but even if they are exaggerations, they were held widely enough to influence management, government, and trade-union leaders.[11] Pressed by employers, key government officials were also eager to

---

5. Industrialization was slower and later in southern India and experienced fewer problems with labor supply. In 1921 the economic downturn combined with the onset of sustained demographic growth to mark the beginning of marked labor surplus.

6. Quoted in Fremantle, "Indian Labour," 511.

7. Ibid.

8. Temple, *India*, 100.

9. Webb, *Indian Diary*, 95. I am grateful to Elleke Boehmer for this reference.

10. For example, in Datta, "Indian Worker."

11. A passionate proponent of worker discipline was the railway union leader, and later labour minister and president of India, V. V. Giri. See Giri, *Labour Problems*.

devise systems of recruitment and terms of employment that would increase supply without creating high wages or triggering political instability. To understand how the law was used, one must know something of the organization of the labor market.

The nonagrarian labor market in 1875 had six principal components: migrant labor to overseas colonies on an indenture basis; internally migrant labor to plantations; both short- and long-term recruitment for public works, including canals, roads, and miscellaneous construction projects; labor for small-scale artisan production and cottage industries; employment in the large-scale industrial sector, including railways and coal mining; and urban labor in the service sector, including prostitution, domestic service, and municipal work such as sweeping. Each sector had its own means to recruit, transport, and discipline workers, although they also shared some circumstances and modes of organization. Moreover, because labor pathways overlapped, changes in one sector could introduce unforeseen modifications in other sectors. In the 1890s declining demand for indentured labor in Mauritius led to an increase in job seekers in Bengal industries and Assam plantations;[12] in the Punjab, increased demand for public-works labor in constructing canals and reconstructing Delhi not only pulled in migrants from Bikaner state, but also diverted labor from factory employment in Agra.[13] While intersectoral labor mobility was hardly perfect, there was something akin to an all-India labor market that permitted movement.

Each of these markets relied upon a proletarian labor pool of agrarian or tribal origin. As early as the late eighteenth century there existed a reserve army of often low-caste laborers without rights in land, although there were frequently bitter European complaints about wage demands, unwillingness to work, and specific labor shortages, as Ahuja shows for Madras at the turn of the century.[14] The cumulative effects of deindustrialization, commercialization of agriculture, and gradual demographic expansion nonetheless left entire communities with little to sell but their labor, creating rural push factors behind labor migration.[15] Das Gupta has identified a high propensity to migrate among untouchables and low-caste groups, tribals, dispossessed artisans, and landless laborers.[16] Excess agrarian labor made possible the massive

12. Chakravarty, "Industrial Labour," 253.

13. Webb and Webb, *Indian Diary*, 94.

14. Ahuja, "Origins."

15. See the meticulous study by Chakravarty, "Industrial Labour," which examines these developments in the light of ecological constraints.

16. Das Gupta, "Eastern India," 326.

export of indentured workers to overseas colonies (over 1.3 million between 1831 and 1920),[17] and the pressures only increased after 1921 when population figures commenced their unbroken ascent.[18] Although ties to kin and local patrons provided economic security for some landless groups, for most it was no guarantee of subsistence. Becoming a migrant worker was often no choice at all: as Chakravarty has stressed, the two available options were "either to die working with bare hands or die starving."[19] Even in 1931, after five decades in which a stable urban labor force had grown, the Whitley Commission concluded that "few industrial workers would remain in industry if they could secure sufficient food and clothing in the village; they are pushed, not pulled, to the city."[20]

Where possible, employers drew upon local supplies of labor. Most small-scale manufacturing had modest labor demands, met from local sources. Ahmedabad depended on local rather than migrant operatives.[21] Madras and the up-country centers such as Kanpur, Coimbatore, Madura, and Ambasamudram drew upon a mix of existing urban service groups and local agrarian laborers in nearby villages.[22] According to Das Gupta's careful study, even the Hooghly industrial center drew principally upon local Bengali labor for jute mills, railway works, and engineering houses until the late 1880s. However, between 1891 and 1911, when the jute mills nearly tripled their employment rolls, there was substantial migration from Bihar and the Northwestern Provinces. Migration continued, and by 1921 the local Bengalis composed just 24 percent of the Bengal workers in jute mills, 26 percent in cotton mills, and 33 percent in railway workshops.[23] The Bengal coal mines depended heavily on imports of tribal labor.[24] The TISCO steel town of Jamshedpur drew

17. Northrup, *Indentured Labor*, 156.

18. Dyson, *India's Historical Demography*.

19. Chakravarty, "Industrial Labour," 265.

20. Royal Commission on Labour in India (hereafter RCLI) *Report* (London, 1931), 16. Yamin, "Ratnagiri," 489, has rightly cautioned that not all instances of migration can be explained by rural push factors, although her evidence of migration from Ratnagiri district to Bombay as early as 1840, when rates of population growth were low, does not rule out the possibility of distress-motivated movement.

21. "The cotton mills of Ahmedabad draw 65% of their labour from Ahmedabad district and the adjacent State of Baroda, while most of the remainder come from areas not far distant." RCLI *Report*, 10.

22. To say that the labor was partially agrarian in origin does not mean that cultivation was the only or even the main occupational background. For example, Coimbatore laborers were taken from "poor agriculturalists, landless labourers, small traders, village servants and unemployed hand-weavers": E. Murphy, *South Indian Textile*, 27.

23. Das Gupta, "Eastern India," tables 6 and 9.

24. Simmons, "Coal Mining Industry."

migrants from all over India, though much of the initial construction work and subsequent unskilled labor was performed by persons recruited locally in Chotanagpur.[25] In the Bombay labor market, migrants from Ratnagiri first arrived in the 1840s, even before the existence of a factory sector.[26] Although information on the early phase of cotton production is lacking, by 1911 it seems that 63 percent of Bombay mill hands had migrated more than 100 but less than 200 miles.[27] Unlike the overseas indenture system and the regulated migration of the plantations, where the colonial state supervised the recruitment and welfare of migrants, the mills and factories recruited for themselves. (A comparison might be made to the initiatives of the mining industry of the Transvaal before the Boer War.)[28] Similarly, migration for employment in urban services and public works operated through informal networks and jobbers. Nevertheless, a system of migration operated.

There was an intimate link between debt and obligations to work. In an economy where the "availability of land, credit and employment was often concentrated in the hands of the same small groups of agricultural managers and industrial entrepreneurs,"[29] there arose institutionalized links between credit and labor. Creditors exchanged small advances for large quantities of work, while workers shied away from low-waged employment without a nominal sum in advance. These arrangements, which frequently amounted to thinly disguised forms of forced labor, were common throughout the subcontinent and were conveniently available for industrial entrepreneurs assembling their work forces. The labor-loan system was not simply imposed by employers, however. It was one of the ways in which workers molded the labor market, because the demand for advances, particularly where migration was involved, was "so universal and so deeply seated in the habits of the labourers that it is impossible either to ignore it or overthrow it."[30] Although the system attracted humanitarian criticisms, and left employers vulnerable to absconding workers, it was conceded that "[w]henever labour on a large scale has to be organized, it can only be done successfully under the system of advances."[31] Landless workers had a keen appetite for credit, given their poverty, the seasonal nature of their work, and the need to finance wed-

---

25. Das Gupta, "Eastern India," 37; Datta, *Tata Iron*, 27–29, stresses that the local Chotanagpur area also supplied a large number of skilled laborers, but his evidence is sketchy.

26. Yamin, "Ratnagiri."

27. M. Morris, *Bombay Cotton*, 63, table VI. See also Kooiman, *Bombay Textile Labour*, ch. 2; Newman, "Textile Industry."

28. See the chapter by Chanock in this volume.

29. Tomlinson, *Modern India*, 28.

30. G. Stokes, *Madras Legislative Council Proceedings, 1902* (Madras, n.d.), 206.

31. Ibid.

dings and other social obligations. Lacking collateral, they were forced to offer months or years of future labor to repay the loan and to secure the debt. As Prakash has shown, these arrangements were rarely a simple loan-for-labor exchange but were deeply embedded in networks of reputation, contingent deference, and community-regulated norms.[32] Paternalism and reciprocal obligations did exist but cannot justify the romanticized worker-employer idylls that some employers chose to portray. Where indebtedness arose in factory production, a more market-like exchange was inevitable, not only because community standards did not transport easily but also because, as we shall see, law reshaped the relationship.

In early industrialization, migration and subsequent employment were organized by intermediaries—"labour-lords"—who linked employment centers with the agrarian hinterland.[33] The social role of the labor intermediary dated from at least the eighteenth century[34] but was easily incorporated into capitalist systems of production. From a functionalist viewpoint, labor lords performed similar services in each sector: they located individuals within labor catchment areas who were then transported to the place of employment and brought into service.[35] It is likely, however, that their most important function lay not in recruitment but in control and discipline. For industrial workers, the *sardar* or jobber, rather than the manager or owner, was the real employer. Jobbers not only possessed the power to hire or fire at will but often controlled access to credit, housing, shops, and medical care as well.[36] Workers customarily paid the jobber a commission, or *dastoori*, which reflected the strong push factors operating in the labor market and also symbolized the worker's submission to the jobber's authority. Deference to the jobber was essential, not only because he wielded arbitrary and often severe authority but also because he was the only source of protection against the employer or outside depredations. This pattern had important consequences for the nature of the employment relationship in industry, since contact between employers and workers, including the communication of command and dissent, was mediated by jobbers. The jobber system "perpetuated social relations of a feudal

32. Prakash, *Bonded Histories.*

33. The phrase comes from Chakravarty, "Industrial Labour," 251. The labor lord went under a variety of names according to region and type of employment: jobber, sardar, maistry, tindal, muccadam, ticcadar, and so on.

34. Chakrabarty, *Bengal,* 112.

35. In Ahmedabad, where local labor served initial demands, the mukkaddam system developed much later. See Patel, *Making,* 29.

36. See Chakrabarty, *Bengal,* 96, 107–14; Chandavarkar, "Workers' Politics"; Kooiman, *Bombay Textile Labour,* 21–28; M. Morris, *Bombay Cotton,* 142–48; E. Murphy, *South Indian Textile,* 34–36; Newman, "Textile Industry."

kind within the industrial framework,"[37] making it impossible to explain the employment relationship as a bargain between two independently contracting parties. Jobbers were accused of accepting bribes, indulging in gratuitous cruelty, and spurring a high rate of turnover among workers.[38] Yet, as Newman has pointed out, the jobber system served as a flexible and reasonably efficient mechanism for supplying labor.[39]

Discipline and Advances

In this context, the role of law in constituting the new employment relationships was less one of recruitment than of labor discipline in specific sectors. Where strong demographic push factors underpinned the jobber system of discipline, employers did not press for a massive legal intervention. It is true that in 1888 Tata sought a formal recruitment system for factories, but his proposal arose out of anxiety about future strikes rather than a gross shortage of labor.[40] The ready availability of already proletarianized labor obviated the need for the head and hut taxes, expropriation of lands, and widespread systems of conscription that were employed to drive peasants into waged labor, or the pass laws that held them to it, in other nineteenth-century colonies. Apart from overseas indenture and plantations the state in India did not intervene directly to mobilize labor. Employers were left to arrange their own recruiting and disciplining mechanisms. But government enacted, and maintained, a highly penal law of master and servant as an intrinsic part of Indian labor law.

With a basis in English statutory and common law, Indian master and servant law evolved its own distinctive characteristics. Its eighteenth-century history is still little explored, but Ahuja has shown that in Madras there were several attempts late in the century to regulate wages and that in 1811 comprehensive "Police Regulations" were registered at the Supreme Court. They included detailed provisions, borrowed from the eighteenth-century English statutes, for summary enforcement before magistrates and at quarter sessions. There were also significant departures from the English acts. Breach of contract (desertion, disobedience, insolence, neglect of duty) was punishable by up to twenty-four lashes and four months' imprisonment. Masters or mistresses guilty of illegally punishing servants or not paying wages

37. Kooiman, *Bombay Textile Labour*, 25.
38. RCLI *Report*, 23–26.
39. Newman, "Textile Industry."
40. M. Morris, *Bombay Cotton*, 54.

were to be fined. Wage-fixing provisions punished both those demanding and those paying higher wages; other provisions made refusal of work when unemployed an offense, and punished headmen who secreted idle artificers or coolies. As in England and elsewhere in the empire, these provisions were bolstered by broad vagrancy provisions.[41] How common such regulations were in late eighteenth-century India, and how they were enforced, must be a matter of future research. But it seems likely that the laws of 1814 and 1819, by which criminal breach provisions were introduced in Bombay and Calcutta respectively, were parts of an older, continuing practice of the colonial state.[42]

In other parts of the empire similar municipal police regulations were in fact the foundation of master and servant law, including penal sanctions,[43] and we still lack a history of many such local initiatives. It is easier to see the development of policy in later decades, and at the higher levels of the state. Considering the matter in 1837, the Indian Law Commission chaired (and almost entirely dominated) by T. B. Macaulay, agreed "with the great body of jurists in thinking that in general a mere breach of contract ought not to be an offence, but only to be the subject of a civil action."[44] The commission reasoned, however, that there must be exceptions to this rule, most notably when civil damages were unlikely to be paid or when they would provide inadequate recompense. Despite Macaulay's profoundly liberal disposition, the commission shied away from recognizing equality in master and servant contracts. Special criminal punishments were proposed for servants only in a nar-

41. Ahuja, "Origins," 159–95.

42. Bombay Rule, Ordinance, and Regulation 1 of 1814 applied to "household servants, hamauls, or palanquin bearers" on the island of Bombay. It provided for punishment of one month of hard labor, plus loss of wages and discharge from service, for any servant found guilty of a misdemeanor or ill-behavior while in employment, or for being absent from service on false pretenses (art. 2). Similar punishments were provided for a servant leaving before the end of the term of employment (art. 4). However, it also laid obligations upon employers. Article 3 prohibited masters from discharging servants before the end of the term of contract, punishable by a twenty-rupee fine. Provisions for the corporal punishment of servants were repealed by Bombay Rule, Ordinance, and Regulation 1 of 1827. In 1855 a tailor successfully brought a case of wrongful imprisonment against a justice of the peace who had negligently applied the regulation. The case gained much publicity, exposing the blatant abuse of employees possible under the regulation (see *Vithoba Malhari v. Corfield*, 3 Bom. H.C.R. App.). The regulation was repealed the next year (Bombay Regulation 13 of 1856), only four years before the breach-of-contract provisions were reintroduced in Bombay by Act 13 of 1859. Under Bengal Regulation 7 of 1819, section 6 provided for punishment of every menial servant who quit his employer without a certain notice or before the expiry of his term of employment. This was repealed by Act 17 of 1862. Bombay Regulation 12 of 1827 provided in section 18 for punishment for servants who neglected their duty. See also the Calcutta and Madras Police Regulations.

43. Quebec, for example: see the chapter by Craven in this volume.

44. Indian Law Commission, *A Penal Code* (hereafter Draft Code) (Calcutta, 1837), note P.

row range of circumstances where injury was thought likely to arise in consequence of an absent or disobedient servant.[45]

Macaulay's anxiety for the physical and financial vulnerability of masters, as well as the potential for duplicity and skulduggery among servants, revealed his own class position and was an index of European unease in relations with Indian servants. To illustrate the potential dangers of unreliable servants, the commission noted that it was often necessary for "travellers of the upper classes, even for English ladies, ignorant perhaps of the native languages, and with young children at their breasts, to perform journeys of many miles over uninhabited wastes, and through jungles in which it is dangerous to linger for a moment, in palanquins borne by persons of the lowest class."[46] Servants, it was noted, "generally come from the lower ranks of life, and would be unable to pay any thing."[47] Thus, the Draft Code proposed that palanquin bearers and other servants engaged in conveyance, such as baggage carriers, be subject to criminal punishment for breach of contract.[48] Similar provisions were proposed for seamen whose insubordination during a voyage "often produces fatal consequences,"[49] and for servants attending on infants, the sick, or those of "unsound mind."[50] Beyond this narrow range Macaulay was loath to venture, noting that if all petty breaches of contract were made offenses, "we should give not protection to good masters, but means of oppression to bad ones."[51]

When the Draft Code was reconsidered in 1846–47, there was considerable pressure to extend criminal breach to cover all menial servants. But Macaulay's model prevailed, and when the code was promulgated in 1860, it omitted the original section dealing with seamen but retained sections applicable to service during a voyage or journey (s.490) and service to supply the wants of a helpless person (s.491). A new provision (s.492) introduced punishments

45. It was stressed that the criminal provisions would apply only where the contract of employment was lawful, that is, where the servant has not been compelled into service.

46. Draft Code, note P.

47. Draft Code.

48. Draft Code, clause 463. Palanquin bearers had also greatly exercised those drafting the eighteenth-century municipal regulations: Ahuja, "Madras."

49. Draft Code, clause 464.

50. Draft Code, clause 465. Justifying this section, which is the only penal sanction to have survived into the present day, the commission opined that "the misery and distress which their neglect may cause is such as the largest pecuniary payment would not repair." Note P.

51. Draft Code, note P. The commission added that it had been urged to make every menial servant subject to criminal punishment for breach of contract, but "it does not appear to us that in the existing state of the market for that description of labour in India, good masters are in much danger of being voluntarily deserted by their menial servants."

for breach of contract to serve at a distant place to which the servant was conveyed at the master's expense. This last section affected many workers, since some employers commonly paid migration costs. These three sections, rooted in the perceptions and problems of a colonial ruling class, introduced innovations without direct parallel in English law.

Of much greater significance for structuring the Indian labor market was the Workman's Breach of Contract Act of 1859. The act was intended to give employers closer control over "artificers, workmen, and labourers" who absconded or refused to work after receiving advances. It was introduced at the instance of the Calcutta Trades Association, and though applicable initially to the three Presidency towns of Calcutta, Madras, and Bombay, by 1865 it had been extended to cover most of British India.[52] Perhaps more than any other piece of Indian colonial legislation, this act symbolized—or even constructed—the legal inequality of master and servant. An employer who deliberately broke a contract was only liable for civil damages,[53] but the laborer who persisted in breach despite a magistrate's order was not only liable for civil damages but could be punished under the criminal law with either a fine or imprisonment of up three months with hard labor (section 2). In practice, it was virtually impossible for impoverished and illiterate laborers to mount the lengthy process of a civil suit against dishonest masters, but it was relatively simple for employers to complain to the nearest magistrate for police assistance in apprehending a laborer. For employers who made use of the act, it amounted to a substantial subvention from the colonial state. It also provided them with a unique legal tool not otherwise available under the common law. The established common-law principle was that specific performance should not apply to contracts of employment on the grounds that forcing a person to work against his or her consent was tantamount to forced labor.[54] But performance of a service contract could be ordered under the Workman's Breach of Contract Act. A similar order could be made under section 8 of the Employers

52. (India) n.13 (1859). The act was extended by notification to areas including the Punjab (1859), Poona (1859), Jubbulpor and Saugor (1859), all collectorates in the Bombay Presidency (1860), Kanpur (1862), Beerbhum, Darjeeling, Murshidabad, Nuddea, and Rajshahi (1863), all districts of the Madras Presidency, Assam (1864), Sindh (1873), Hazaribagh and other scheduled districts (1881), Nagpur (1906), and Mandala (1907). Application to Singapore, Malacca, and Prince of Wales Island was repealed in 1874 (Act 16). Application of the act to the Punjab was upheld despite a defective government notification; *Crown v. Muhammad Shafi*, 11 PR 1902 Cr.

53. The common-law doctrine was codified in the Indian Contract Act, n.9 of 1872, sections 39 and 73.

54. Freedland, *The Contract of Employment*; the principle was codified in the Specific Relief Act, (India) n.1 of 1877, s.21.

and Workmen (Disputes) Act of 1860, which also provided for criminal punishment of breach of contract.[55]

Many administrators and judges who discussed the criminal breach of contract commented that the 1859 act was based on English law. This was only partly true. The act was modeled on one section of a British statute of 1823, which made a laborer's breach of contract punishable by loss of wages or imprisonment with hard labor up to three months. In Britain the statute played a key role in mobilizing certain types of labor, particularly for small-scale manufacturing, during the middle decades of the nineteenth century.[56] To that extent, the 1859 act in India was simply an application of a British labor model to Indian conditions. But as in many other instances, the metropolitan model was substantially modified when applied to a subservient people: the Indian act introduced the criminal provisions but omitted legal protections for employees that had formed an integral part of the law in England or Scotland. Under British law, for instance, a laborer could lodge a complaint against a master for cruelty, ill-treatment, or refusal to provide basic necessities, and thus secure a magistrate's order for discharge from service.[57] In India neither legislation nor judicial doctrine provided special protections against an employer's physical, emotional, or sexual abuse.[58]

The distinctiveness of the Indian act lay in its emphasis on monetary advances. The main British act was of general application, but the Indian Workman's Breach of Contract Act could only be invoked where contracts involved a monetary advance.[59] In practice, this did little to narrow its application,

---

55. (India) c.9 (1860). The act was passed at the instance of the Bombay government following an uprising among railway workers in 1859 (Das, *History of Indian Labour Legislation*, 257). Applicable to workers on railways and other public works, it was only extended to certain districts and was seldom used before it was finally repealed in 1932 on the recommendation of the Royal Commission on Labour in India: RCLI *Report*, 337. Criminal statistics suggest that its use was confined to the Punjab, principally in the labor unrest of 1920 and again in 1926; otherwise convictions were infrequent: *Report on the Administration of Criminal Justice in the Punjab, Annual Series, 1867–1939*. There is no evidence that the act was ever used on railways: RCLI Evidence, 8 (1) 177.

56. (U.K.) 4 Geo.IV c.34 (1823) s.3, reaffirming and amending (G.B.) 20 Geo.II c.19 (1746) and (G.B.) 6 Geo.III c.25 (1766).

57. (G.B.) 20 Geo.II c.19 (1746) s.2. Although magistrates were probably more sympathetic to employers than employees, this protection was no mere sham. Under (U.K.) 14 & 15 Vict. c.11 (1851) it was a crime to assault a servant or to fail to provide food, clothing, or lodging to a servant. See the chapter by Hay in this volume.

58. Even if special legal protections did exist, their effectiveness would be open to question in a context where most workers had little access to legal institutions and were economically dependent upon their employers.

59. (India) c.9 of 1860 cleaved much more closely to the British model: penal sanctions were

since bonded servitude was prevalent in the nineteenth century and laboring for wages was closely bound up with the demand for credit. A significant proportion of employment contracts involved some species of monetary advance. Even where genuine advances were not forthcoming, employers adopted the practice of advancing nominal sums in order to bring the contract within the ambit of the 1859 act.[60] Since the Indian act, unlike its British and Bombay antecedents, did not require employers to register their complaints under oath,[61] there were no legal protections against perjury or unfounded claims. Employer abuse of the law went unchecked for decades. Only in 1920 was the act amended to require complaint under oath and to hold masters accountable for civil damages in cases of vexatious or frivolous claims.[62]

Penal Contracts in the Workplace

While some scholars have commented on the act's oppressive nature, there has been no systematic study of its interpretation or application outside of the Assam tea gardens.[63] Assessing its importance in constituting employment relationships requires attention to the types of labor involved, comparative rates of complaint and conviction, and judicial decisions. It is possible to assemble a partial picture from administrative reports and high-court judgments.

The 1859 act was more popular among employers than the labor provisions of the Penal Code and generated far more convictions. The criminal breach provisions of the Penal Code were invoked most frequently in Bengal and, to a lesser extent, in the Punjab and the Northwestern Provinces. The number of prosecutions under the code in Assam was not large, though in the tea gardens a substantial number of contacts were executed under section 492 in the late 1890s.[64] The 1859 act was invoked much more frequently. Although

---

not limited to contracts involving advances, and it gave magistrates general powers to adjudicate disputes.

60. See, for example, *Queen-Empress v. Indrajit*, ILR 11 All 262 (1889), where a three-rupee advance was given for a three-year contract, or *Tangi Joghi v. Hall*, ILR 23 Mad 203 (1899), in which both two- and four-year contracts were secured with a one-rupee advance. The consideration in such contracts "is often so grossly inadequate as to suggest that the so-called advance was merely a device for bringing the contract within the Act": *Emperor v. Namdeo Sakharam*, 11 CrLJ 273 (1910).

61. The position was reinforced by (India) c.10 of 1873, s.13, which provided that the failure to take an oath did not invalidate proceedings.

62. (India) n.12 of 1920, sections 2, 3.

63. Studies of Assam include Arnold, "Plantations," and Behal and Mohapatra, "Tea."

64. Such contracts enjoyed a sudden increase in popularity, with nearly 3,400 executed in

its operation came under the greatest official scrutiny in Assam, employers used the act more frequently in Madras, Bombay, and the Punjab. Evidence for the varieties of work involved is sketchy, although it is clear that in Assam contracts with criminal penalties for breach were used almost exclusively in the tea gardens. Similarly in Madras, the largest proportion of complaints arose in the plantation production of tea, coffee, pepper, cardamom, and cinchona. Employment on public works, particularly canal building, represented the most common use in the Punjab, and was probably important in Madras and Bombay as well. Penal contracts for work in government rubber plantations were common in Burma,[65] where the act was also used to discipline workers in tungsten mines during the First World War. To the extent that case law is representative, it appears that another common use of penal contracts was in small-scale production, particularly in textiles, consumer goods, and light engineering. Contrary to Gandhi's idealizations, labor conditions in small-scale production were often worse than in larger undertakings, and frequently assumed the character of semislavery.[66] The act provided a ready resource for small masters who could not mobilize the private policing available to larger employers. Penal contracts were used with servants and carriers during troop movements. So too they were used in the formal factory sector, particularly in Amritsar, Beerbhoom, and Kanpur, although this did not account for a large proportion of all penal contracts. Finally, from the reported judgments it is clear that penal contracts were used to secure a variety of skilled laborers, including carpenters, goldsmiths, clerks, shop assistants, and stonemasons.

Contemporary observers were inclined to see the criminal breach provisions as part of a temporary phase in the transition to a free labor market.[67] The legal developments suggested otherwise, however. In Bombay, Madras, and the Punjab, where the criminal breach laws were most widely used, the number of offenses reported under the Workman's Breach of Contract Act generally escalated between 1890 and 1920. The spectacular increase in Pun-

---

1898, though the reason for their popularity is not explained: *Report on Labour Immigration into Assam* (Calcutta, 1898), 15.

65. In Burma, where the government was a major employer, the question arose whether the government could benefit from an act drafted to benefit "any master or employer." The question was answered in the negative in *Lower Burma by King-Emperor v. Ramiah*, 3 LBR 33 (1905), and in the positive in *Upper Burma by Emperor v. Nga Tun Zan*, 11 CrLJ 58 (1910).

66. The discussion of cottage industries in Mirzapur during the 1850s in Bayly, *Rulers, Townsmen*, 341, is instructive: neither "traditional" nor fully capitalist, small-scale producers were able to rely upon ties of caste and community to enforce systems of semislavery. See further on labor in the small-scale sector RCLI *Report*, 90–106.

67. See, for instance, Fremantle, "Indian Labour," 516.

jabi penal contracts after 1904 can be attributed to increased canal construction[68] and, after 1912, to the building of New Delhi.[69] The increase in Madras did not abate with the Madras Planters Labour Act, 1903,[70] which replaced the Workman's Breach of Contract Act in several plantation districts. In the Northwestern Provinces, the wartime surge in industrial production brought about a shortage of skilled labor that led to a steady increase in penal contracts in factories.[71] Although actual convictions amounted to only a fraction of reported offenses, the figures indicate that employers increasingly relied on the act to control workers. Only after 1920, when the act was substantially amended,[72] did convictions decline.

In those labor markets where demographic push and labor lords solved the problem of recruitment, criminal punishment for breach served principally to retain workers. Workers impressed or lured by false promises often fled.[73] Very frequently the terms of the contract were not properly explained, and it is clear that workers were often misled as to the conditions and nature of the work. As early as 1863 the magistrate of Canara noted the hardship to laborers who found themselves prosecuted under section 492 of the Penal Code for breaking contracts that "they would not have signed" had the terms been properly understood. He proposed that all legal contracts under the section should be signed and executed before a magistrate, but the government of India rejected the proposal.[74] Some contracts were signed under duress. The events of 1903 in Assam were not untypical: 1,792 recruits migrated to the tea gardens on the promise of relatively favorable terms; only after they had traveled hundreds of miles to the work site were their contracts "voluntarily dissolved" and much less favorable contracts under the 1859 act negotiated.[75]

68. *Report on the Administration of Criminal Justice in the Punjab* (hereafter *CJP*), annual series (Lahore, 1904–10).

69. Irving, *Indian Summer*, 135–36.

70. (Madras) n.1 of 1903.

71. *Criminal Statements of the High Court of Judicature at Allahabad, 1918*, 2.

72. (India) n.12 of 1920.

73. Where start-up labor needs were high, jobbers came under pressure to fill their quotas for fresh recruits in short periods of time, and sometimes used coercive means to bring in laborers, particularly when the jobbers themselves were subject to criminal penalties for unfilled quotas. One recruiter for a Madura coffee estate, for example, agreed that if he failed to deliver thirty-five coolies within one month, he would pay compensation, be subject to the criminal penalties for breach of contract, and work as a coolie for five years to repay his advance (*Ramasami v. Kanadasami*, ILR 8 Mad 379 [1885]).

74. National Archives of India, Leg. Proc., Jan. 1864, nos. 10–12.

75. Their original contracts were made under (India) n.6 of 1901. Although the advance provided "was considerably less than the loss of pay entailed by the change in the form of contract," it was probably demanded by some workers looking for credit: *Resolution on Immigrant Labour in Assam for the Year, 1903–1904*, 4.

Another factor that made the criminal breach laws popular with employers in such areas was the highly unstable character of the labor force. Contemporary commentators agreed that industrial laborers in particular were given to absenteeism, high rates of turnover, and departure without notice. The criminal breach provisions, rather than adequate wages and humane conditions, kept laborers in place. The system of advances under penal contract only slightly disguised what often amounted to perpetual servitude. In many cases, the combination of low wages, deductions for basic goods, and advances taken to meet consumption needs made saving extremely difficult, and it became "practically impossible for [the worker] to repay the advance."[76] The act did not require contracts to specify the conditions or duration of employment, and under common law there was no prohibition on a contract of indefinite or lifelong duration.[77]

The act was also popular among employers in areas where recruitment was a problem. For example, in the Assam tea gardens contracts under the act covered 40 percent of the labor force in 1891 despite the existence of a separate labor recruitment regime in the area.[78] In Madras, where the act was used widely to recruit labor for plantations, public works, and miscellaneous semiskilled employment, the police were so overwhelmed with complaints against laborers that the local government was forced in 1863 to create a special corps of legal officers to administer the criminal breach provisions.[79] Together with section 492 of the Indian Penal Code, the act was used extensively to bind laborers who had migrated some distance at the employer's expense. In the Punjab and some areas of Madras, laborers who migrated from the Princely States had a notorious reputation for abandoning work and were made subject to the act even though employers often found it difficult to enforce its provisions in a foreign jurisdiction.[80]

References to the act were written right into the text of many employment contracts. In such cases both parties were keenly aware of the criminal penalties.[81] Employees were led to believe that it was the written agreement that

76. S. K. Bose, Indian Colliery Employees' Association, in RCLI Evidence, 4 (1) 192.

77. On the lifelong employment contract in English law, see Veneziani, "Evolution," 56.

78. Behal and Mohapatra, "Tea," 37.

79. (Madras) n.3 of 1863. The act also introduced a fee for complainants and empowered magistrates to add a fine on top of the criminal penalty in order to cover costs of administration (ss.2, 3). Apart from relieving the call upon police time, the act was designed to shift costs of enforcement onto employers: *Madras Council Proceedings* 1863, 30. The provision was superseded by (India) n.7 of 1870, and repealed by (Madras) n.2 of 1880.

80. See *CJP*, 1906, 4, and *Siddha v. Biligiri*, ILR 7 Mad 354 (1884).

81. Both written and verbal contracts were subject to the discipline of the legislation. In the context of high printing costs and a low level of illiteracy, the common incidence of written

made them subject to criminal punishment if they failed to work.[82] Even if such a contractual provision was legally absurd,[83] it reminded the worker of the employer's power to use the police. The employer could apply to a magistrate, who was empowered to issue either a summons or a warrant to bring an absconding worker before the magistrate for further hearing.[84] The fugitive employees could be tracked down and returned entirely at the state's expense, rather than the employer's. At the hearing, the employer, if successful, enjoyed the option of choosing between two magistrate's orders: either to require the worker to repay the advance in full or to perform the work according to the terms of the contract. (The worker had no such choice).[85] Only if the laborer failed to comply with this order did criminal sanctions apply. Thus, what was punishable under the act was not the refusal to perform work but failure to comply with the magistrate's order.[86] This strictly required two separate and independent proceedings, although employers were sometimes successful in pressing magistrates to order imprisonment at once, in anticipation of noncompliance with the order.[87] In many cases, the magistrate was empowered to pass an order even if the time for performing the contract had elapsed.[88] Although the act explicitly applied where money was advanced for

agreements might seem surprising. For the employer, however, a contract in writing not only provided ready evidence of legal obligation but also served to sacralize the agreement, underscoring the criminal sanctions involved. It was not unknown for contracts to contain other punishments for breach of contract, including the forced sale of personal property. See, for instance, *Tara Doss v. Bhaloo Sheik*, 8 WR CR 69 (1867).

82. Sometimes the act was invoked for disciplinary purposes rather than to simply prevent absconding. A worker in a Saidapet tannery, for instance, signed a contract that stipulated that if he failed to work for one week, or damaged the skins with a knife, or failed to report such damages to his employer, or went to work for other tanneries, his employer could complain to a magistrate under the act. See *Queen v. Tulukanam*, ILR 7 Mad 131 (1884).

83. Application of the criminal law depends solely upon the circumstances and actions of the parties and is not affected by an undertaking to be subject its provisions. Although this point was never made explicit by the courts, it was certainly implicit in several judgments. See *Purna Chandra Nandan v. Tarack Nath Chandra*, ILR 36 Cal 917 (1909). Here again, the point was to draw attention to an already existing threat and to cloak it in the solemnity of a legal agreement.

84. Whether a summons or a warrant was issued was left to the magistrate's discretion.

85. The worker had no right to choose between repayment and returning to work: *Emperor v. Amir Baksh*, 15 CrLJ 423.

86. *Queen-Empress v. Namdeo Rat Un*, Cr C 617 (1892); *King-Emperor v. Takasi Nukayya*, ILR 24 Mad 660 (1901); ILR 28 Mad 37; *Emperor v. Dhondu*, 6 Bom LR 255 (1904), contra *Queen-Empress v. Kattayan*, ILR 20 Mad 235 (1897).

87. Despite the opinion in *Queen-Empress v. Indrajit*, ILR 11 All 262 (1889), which endorsed summary trials for factory labor in Kanpur, the weight of judicial opinion went against summary trials. See *Pollard v. Mothial*, ILR 4 Mad 234 (1881); *Emperor v. Dhondu*, 6 Bom LR 255 (1904); *Emperor v. Balu Saluji*, ILR 33 Bom 25 (1904).

88. *Bharosa v. Emperor*, 15 CrLJ 599 (1914), contra *Khoda Baksh v. Moti Lal Jahori*, 5 CrLJ 66 (1906), and *Narsing Prasad Singh v. Emperor*, 8 CrLJ 134 (1908).

work, before 1914 it was also applied to advances in kind,[89] including working materials.[90]

An initial summons from a magistrate was often enough to compel laborers back to their employers, especially in the Punjab. In the district of Sialkot, for instance, where the 1859 act was widely used to retain workers building the Chenab Canal in 1897, the sessions judge observed that of the 197 persons brought before magistrates during the year, only one was convicted. The mere commencement of legal proceedings "brings the recalcitrant workmen to submission."[91] Similar patterns were reported as early as 1873, and again in the first decade of the twentieth century.[92] This presents a striking contrast with Tezpur district in Assam, where it was reported in 1904 that more than half of the laborers under a magistrate's order preferred to undergo imprisonment rather than return to the garden to complete their contracts.[93]

Workers commonly offered magistrates explanations for their departure from work, alleging unpaid wages, harsh conditions, insult, and physical abuse. English cases in the late 1850s suggested that a servant with a lawful excuse for absence could not be convicted under the principal statute.[94] Because the Workman's Breach of Contract Act made reference to "fraudulent" breaches (preamble) and to refusal to work "without lawful or reasonable excuse" (s.1), it implied a category of nonfraudulent breaches of contract based on lawful or reasonable grounds for departing work. In the same vein, section 492 of the Penal Code explicitly protected the worker from punishment in cases where "the employer has ill-treated him or neglected to perform the contract on his part."[95] A large number of cases before magistrates were sent for review to the high-court judges, but the question arose in only a handful of the reported cases. In an 1867 case, a silk spinner in the employ of Lyall & Co. left work after completing only twelve months of his thirty-six-month contract, having repaid his advance in full. In its judgment, the Calcutta High Court drew upon the wording of the preamble to reason that the act applied only to fraudulent breaches of contract; since no fraud was disclosed on the facts, the complaint was not cognizable under the

89. *Kondadu v. Ramudu*, ILR 8 Mad 294 (1885); *Emperor v. Chiragh*, 15 CrLJ 603 (1914).

90. Anonymous 6 MHC App 24 (1870).

91. *CJP*, 1897, part III, 5.

92. Of the 1,024 persons brought before Punjab magistrates in 1873, only 66 were convicted (ibid., 1873, 17). In the district of Umballa in 1881, proceedings were commenced against 489 persons, but only 1 was convicted for the entire year (ibid., 1881, 10; see also ibid., 1906, 4).

93. *Resolution on Immigrant Labour in Assam, 1903–4*, 5.

94. C. M. Smith, *Law of Master and Servant*, 337.

95. I am unable to find, at any time during the sixty-six-year life-span of this provision, even a single reported case in which it was invoked.

act.[96] In 1889 the Allahabad High Court repudiated this interpretation, holding that fraud was not an essential ingredient of an offense under the act, since the terms of the preamble could not be called in to restrict the language of the enacting section.[97] This judgment was influential—mostly due to its obiter admonition that the criminal law must be used to prevent combinations among factory workers—and may have undermined reliance on the fraudulent breach criterion among magistrates and judges. The fraudulent breach test used in 1867 was followed in one other case where the employer had failed to pay full wages,[98] but there are no other reported cases where unpaid wages, poor treatment, or physical abuse are presented as grounds justifying the worker's breach. In a few cases the judiciary refused to enforce unconscionable contracts—particularly where the agreement amounted to a disguised form of slavery[99]—but where the contracts were not invalid the high courts failed to excuse workers' breaches in circumstances of unpaid wages or ill-treatment.[100]

The judiciary did mitigate the effects of the act by strictly defining what types of contracts could be enforced. In 1872 we see the beginnings of an effort to distinguish among forms of credit in labor contracts. The case involved a laborer in Khandesh District who agreed to work more than eight years to pay off an existing debt of Rs. 195.[101] He left work after three months and the magistrate sentenced him to two months rigorous imprisonment. The high court set aside the magistrate's order on the ground that as a simple agreement to work off an old debt, where no fresh advance had been provided, the contract was not enforceable under the act. Even if the decision probably had little practical effect, it was followed by a string of judgments over the next three decades, particularly in Bombay, that set aside contracts based on loans rather than advances for work. Thus magistrates' orders were set aside where the rate of repayment was not specified,[102] or where the sum advanced was to be recovered from wages, not from work.[103] This distinction

96. *Tara Doss v. Bhaloo Sheik* (1867) (on file with author).

97. *Queen-Empress v. Indrajit* (1889), ILR 11 All 262.

98. *Purna Chandra v. Tarack Nath*, ILR 36 Cal 917 (1909).

99. *R. v. Jethya*, 108 (1872), Anonymous MHCR 7 App 30 (1873); *In re Ambu*, 15 CrLJ 384 (1914).

100. Although in principle, the language of the act "shows plainly that the interference of the Magistrate is limited to cases where the neglect or refusal to perform is wilful and without lawful and reasonable excuse": *Queen-Empress v. Rajab*, ILR 16 Bom 368 (1892), at 370 per Jardine, J.

101. 9 Bom HCR 171 (1872).

102. *Ram Prasad v. Dirgpal*, ILR 3 All 744 (1881).

103. *Queen-Empress v. Ningappa Rat Un*, CrC 754 (1895); *Emperor v. Muhammad Din*, 15 CrLJ 166 (1914); *Sandhi v. Khem Chand*, 21 CrLJ 546 (1920).

permitted the high courts to annul orders enforcing clearly exploitative contracts. For instance, where a one-rupee advance was to be repaid at the end of a two-year period, it was held to be a loan without interest rather than an advance for work.[104] Indeed, any agreement whereby the advance was to be repaid in a lump sum at the end of the specified period, rather than set against a quantity of work to be performed, became unenforceable under the act.[105] Although these legal doctrines only evolved in the late 1890s and the early part of the new century, they were significant in the frequent cases where employers kept workers in constant debt by deducting subsistence items from wage payments.

Judicial Construction of a Working Class

The 1859 act produced a large number of high-court decisions, usually sent up on revision by district magistrates or sessions judges dissatisfied with the judgments of the lower magistrates. The high-court judgments relating to the act are important, not only because the doctrine of precedent gave the courts a quasi-legislative power, but also because in them the judiciary began to confront the most basic questions about the nature of laboring relationships in India. Both the act and section 492 of the Penal Code applied to "artificers, workmen, and labourers." These terms derived from eighteenth-century and earlier British statutes and had little currency in India where caste designations and indigenous terms were more likely to describe occupations. The courts therefore had to decide what workers were covered by the act. In the answers they supplied, the high courts played a role in the much larger process of reclassifying Indian society in the light of new productive relations. And by one of the common perversions of colonial justice, the Indian courts resolved problems of definition in part through a reliance on English judicial precedents, which in turn were informed by English social categories and changing class alignments.[106] What emerged from judicial interpretation of the act was a new social grouping, defined in legal terms, that anticipated the emergence of an industrial working class in India.

It was established by 1869 that the terms "artificer, workman, or labourer" did not apply to domestic or personal servants, despite pressure from the

---

104. *Tangi Joghi v. Hall*, ILR 23 Mad 203 (1899).

105. *Emperor v. Gooroomoondian*, 4 CrLJ 200 (1906).

106. The legal definition of "artificer" was drawn partially from its judicial interpretation under the Truck Act, (U.K.) 1&2 Wm.IV c.37 (1831), which emphasized that the artificer should actually do the work "with his own hands." C. M. Smith, *Law of Master and Servant*, 31.

European residents of Calcutta to apply the act to domestic labor.[107] Still, the courts were consistent in denying such applicability.[108] Thus contracts involving a dhobi, a horsekeeper, and a cook were all held to fall outside the scope of the criminal breach provisions.[109] These decisions offer no reasoning other than the presumed semantic domain of artificer, workman, and laborer, but the operative distinction was one between productive labor and personal service. Despite the explicit provisions of the Penal Code dealing with personal servants (ss.490, 491), the administration of the criminal breach provisions was focused most sharply on laborers engaged in productive relations. "The artificer is an intermediate term betwixt the artist and the artisan; manufacturers are artificers, and in an extended sense any one who makes a thing by his contrivance is an artificer."[110]

If the law of criminal breach did not apply to domestic servants, it did apply to a wide range of manual laborers. In an important early (1867) decision that established that the act applied to both skilled and unskilled labor, the Calcutta High Court held that a "coolie" working in an Assam tea garden fell within the terms of the act.[111] In the context of changing social categories, it remained unclear exactly which skilled and unskilled laborers fell under the act. In a string of often contradictory judgments, it was held that the act did not apply to temple servants, a clerk, a butcher supplying skins, an elephant driver, and a general agricultural worker.[112] By 1904 the class basis of the criminal breach laws was consolidated, and the definitional boundaries were delineated more precisely in a case that excused a stage actor from criminal punishment. The 1859 act and section 492 of the Penal Code involved those who used "muscles and sinews" as an essential element in their work, or who were involved in the "industrial arts."[113] Where workers were not engaged

107. *Queen v. Soobhoi*, 12 WR Cr 26 (1869). The terms of the contract stipulated that it was for *chakri*, which the court interpreted to mean domestic service. The use of indigenous categories of employment in legal documents was common at this time. By the end of the First World War, indigenous terms appeared less frequently and most contracts that came before the high courts expressed the employment relation in legally approved terms.

108. The effects of the ruling were anticipated by the Calcutta Trades Association in 1863, when it was realized that neither the Penal Code nor the Breach of Contract Act would fill the legal vacuum created by the 1862 repeal of the 1819 Regulation which had endowed magistrates with summary jurisdiction over domestic servants (above, n. 42). The association submitted a memorial to the government of Bengal, proposing a new bill for punishing breach of contract by domestic servants: NAI, Leg. Proc., Mar. 1864, no. 18.

109. *Crown v. Kallu*, 20 PR 1876 Cr; 1 Weir 688; 1 Weir 689.

110. *Crabb's English Synonyms*, quoted in *Imam-ud-din v. Hurmazjee*, 28 PR 1904 Cr, at 74.

111. The legislature "advisedly employed the widest terms to designate the person receiving such advance": *Queen v. Gaub Gorah Cacharee*, 8 WR Cr 6 (1867).

112. 1 Weir 689; 1 Weir 689; 7 MHC App 12; 8 CLR 254; 7 B 379.

113. *Imam-ud-Din v. Hurmazjee*, 28 PR 1904 Cr, at 76.

in "manual labour" but performed tasks involving intellectual or managerial skills, the act did not apply.[114] Criminal breach had to be restricted to "physical labour of a certain kind," the court reasoned; otherwise "there is not an office judicial, executive, revenue or ministerial, however high it may be" that could not be brought within the terms of criminal punishment.[115]

In keeping with English jurisprudence, there emerged in India an implicit and often awkward distinction between a contract for a servant's labor and a contract for a particular service rendered by an independent agent. The issue was not articulated in this way but turned on the legal domain of artificer, workman, and laborer. Nevertheless, the rule was that while servants in breach of their contracts could be subject to criminal punishment, independent contractors could not.[116] The difficulty was in drawing the distinction. One key requirement was that the employee had to be involved in some type of manual labor.[117] The second test, drawn from the English common law, was that, unlike an independent contractor, a servant was subject to the employer's right of control and was obliged to follow the lawful orders and directions of the employer.[118] What of cases where the relationship of control and subordination was not so clear?[119] For some years the most influential case involved a boat owner who was given an advance to transport salt from certain factories to Madras.[120] The Madras High Court held that he did not fall within the ambit of the act since there was nothing in the contract to indicate that he would render personal labor.[121] However, where a worker contracted

114. See also *Ramzan v. Noor Mahomed Yacub*, 15 CrLJ 383 (1914), which excluded an attendant in a butcher shop from the scope of the act on the grounds that the attendant had minor accounting responsibilities.

115. *Imam-Ud-Din v. Hurmazjee*, at 73.

116. Against an independent contractor in breach, only a civil suit would lie. Thus criminal penalties could not be ordered against a person who contracts to supply wood (13 WR Cr 1), supply lime (1 Weir 691), or who contracts to have bricks carted, but not by himself (9 CrLJ 107).

117. Thus, where a worker received an advance to supply both materials and labor to build a ghat, his own involvement in the work was sufficient to attract the act: *Queen-Empress v. Amirkhan Rat. Un.*, CrC 204 (1884).

118. The distinction was elaborated in later decades: *Goolbai v. Pestonji*, AIR 1935 Bom 333; *Kondiba Gopal v. Mestregean*, AIR 1928 Bom 91; *Balthazar & Son Ltd v. Municipal Corporation of Rangoon* (1936), ILR 14 Rang 160. See also the Privy Council case, *Bull v. W. African Shipping Agency and Ligherage Co*, AIR 1927 PC 173.

119. The courts encountered greater difficulty with persons who neither contributed capital nor worked, but simply supervised others. In such cases, no clear judicial doctrine evolved. Cf. *Gilby v. Subbu Pillai*, ILR 7 Mad 100 (1884), and *Sein Yin v. Ah Moon Shoke*, 15 CrLJ 235 (1914).

120. *Caluram v. Chengappa*, ILR 13 Mad 351 (1890). From the facts it appears that in Madras the act was commonly applied to boat owners engaged in transport.

121. A similar test was applied to a man who contracted to convey wood but made no express provision to perform any labor personally: *Queen-Empress v. Hanma Rat. Un.*, CrC 537 (1891).

to convey clay in the employer's boat, rather than his own, he was held by the same court to be a workman for the purposes of the act.[122] Although the judges did not make the point explicit, the legal distinction was effectively between property holders who brought some form of capital to the production process and those who had nothing to sell but their labor.[123] In a closely related decision, it was held that a worker entitled to a percentage of the annual profits was not an ordinary laborer but of a much higher status.[124]

The practice of contracting with jobbers rather than directly with workers was common, particularly in Madras and among larger employers. Typically, the jobber would take an advance to supply a number of laborers and supervise their working for a period of months. Although the act made specific provision for such arrangements, the courts were ambivalent about enforcing them. Partly this was due to an English judicial interpretation of the Truck Act, which excluded contracts with intermediaries.[125] Following a group of cases relating to jobbers, the position evolved that, although the act did not apply to a contract merely to supply laborers, it did apply to an undertaking that the work would be executed,[126] though in Bengal it was held that the act did not apply to a recruiter who did not personally labor.[127]

In this process of categorization, the Indian judiciary, like judges elsewhere in the empire, gradually built a law of master and servant that contained the conceptual core of industrial jurisprudence, that is, a distinction between workers and employers that was capable of general application. The relative novelty of this law was located in the abstract quality of its principal categories (artificer, workman, and laborer), which were made to encompass a broad range of occupational positions formerly subject to particularistic obligations. This abstractness, this lack of particularity, addressed laborers in general rather than addressing members of particular castes or occupational groupings.[128]

---

122. *In re Mamu Beari*, 15 CrLJ 651 (1914).

123. For instance, the Allahabad High Court asked: is the relevant contract to supply labor, or to supply bricks? Taking the view that only labor was being supplied, the act was held to apply. *Bharosa v. Emperor*, 15 CrLJ 599 (1914).

124. *Purna Chandra Nandan v. Tarack Nath Chandra*, ILR 36 Cal 917 (1909).

125. Although the distinction between a contract for service and a contract for services was theoretically identical to that in England (see Barwell and Kar, *Law Relating to Service*, 1:1–44), actual practice ignored the distinction almost entirely.

126. See Anonymous 3 MHC App 25 (1867), *Rowson v. Hanama Mestri*, ILR 1 Mad 280 (1877), *Ramasami v. Kanadasami*, ILR 8 Mad 379 (1885).

127. *Khetu Dafadar v. Frederick Dixon*, 6 CrLJ 191 (1907).

128. And yet simultaneously, the colonial legal system reinforced the ascriptive identities of caste and community through family law. See Galanter, *Law and Society*, ch. 7, and M. Anderson, "Classifications and Coercions," 158–77.

If judicial interpretation played a role in delineating the boundaries and essences of working-class formation, what view did it take of relations with employers? The question assumes importance from a comparative perspective since in Britain and the United States the respective judiciaries endorsed varieties of "contractual fundamentalism" that seriously curtailed the rights of workers to strike and organize. The theoretical model of contractual obligation laid out a legal space in which individuals could freely negotiate the terms of their relationship. Thus, workers could work for whomever they pleased, and employers could choose their own workers, so long as the two parties founded their relationship upon a freely negotiated contract. Providing legal technicalities were satisfied, the contract was binding regardless of the social position of the parties. The courts in the main refused to consider questions of substantive justice or fairness. The emphasis was upon mutual agreement to a set of reciprocal obligations, and the law simply enforced them. According to classical contract theory, it was the volition of the parties rather than the fairness of the agreement that required judicial protection.

In India, freedom of contract ideology, while of some influence, never attracted either the enthusiasm or uncompromising adherence to principle displayed by its supporters in Anglo-American jurisprudence. Under the Workman's Breach of Contract Act, the ideology of contractual fundamentalism found strong expression in only a handful of cases relating to factory labor. An 1870 decision involved a silk spinner who had contracted to work under Lyall & Co. in Beerbhoom for four months a year in each of three years, but had left work.[129] The magistrate refused to pass an order against him, on the grounds that the contract forbade him working for other employers but the mill made no undertaking to provide work during the other eight months of the year when employment was scarce. In short, the agreement could lead to starvation and was void as unreasonable. On appeal, the Calcutta High Court rejected the magistrate's reasoning. In what became an influential judgment,[130] Justice Hobhouse maintained that the law was straightforward: where an advance was made, work must be performed, and if it is not performed, then the magistrate must proceed against the laborer. It must be presumed that skilled silk spinners knew that the business was only carried on for a limited season, and where a laborer agreed to work, "he must be held to do so with his eyes open, and knowing well what he was about."[131] In

129. *Koonjobehary Lall v. Raja Doomney* (1870), 14 WR Cr 29.
130. The precedent was followed not only in Bengal (*Lyall & Co v. Ram Chunder Bagdee*, 18 WR Cr 53 [1872]), but also in Bombay (*In re Sehamber Ram Tehal*, 5 CrLJ 337 [1907]).
131. *Lyall & Co.*

other words, the court would not consider the content of the contract; the parties knew their own minds and were the best judges of their own affairs. Besides, the judgment added, such arrangements were necessary for industry: the manufacturer "knows that the business of the factory will stop if he does not arrange beforehand with the labourers to work at the factory in such detail."[132]

The sanctity of contract was emphasized further in an 1889 case in which a carding mistry had received an advance of three rupees upon contracting with Elgin Mills of Kanpur to work for three years.[133] The agreement stipulated that if he was absent, or refused to work, or took up employment with another mill, he should pay ninety-nine rupees to Elgin Mills, but that he could be granted leave "on some emergent occasion" if he gave previous notice. After applications for leave were twice refused, he left the mill, leaving behind nineteen rupees in unpaid salary. The employer complained to a magistrate and the case came before the Allahabad High Court on revision. The court rejected the argument of the sessions judge that criminal sanctions should apply only to fraudulent breaches of contract and disregarded the worker's defense that he had not understood the terms of the contract and had been abused by one of the managers. Instead, Justice Straight focused upon the sanctity of contractual obligations, particularly in the context of workers who might seize the opportunity to organize:

> I need not point out the importance of statutory provisions of this kind, and their being enforced in large commercial centres like Cawnpore, where, by combined action on the part of persons employed in large commercial establishments there, the proprietors of those establishments might be placed not only at very grave and sudden inconvenience, but very serious pecuniary loss.[134]

In a similar case,[135] the same court insisted on enforcing the contractual obligations of a factory worker in Mirzapur whose terms of employment made it virtually impossible ever to repay his advance, thus effectively binding him to work for the remainder of his life. Despite the inequity of the stipulated terms, the court emphasized that the worker must have known both the nature of the contract and the effect of the act when he entered employment. The sanctity of contractual relations was to be upheld: "[W]e are most un-

132. Ibid., 31.
133. *Queen-Empress v. Indrajit* 144 (1889), ILR 11 All 262 (1889).
134. ILR II All 262 (1889), 267.
135. *Lucas v. Ramai Singh*, 15 CrLJ 233 (1914).

willing to interfere in cases of this kind."[136] Even though the criminal punishment of workers made the ideal of free contract farcical, the legal fiction
was still held aloft.

Despite the strong language of these judgments, their logic only informed,
and did not come to dominate, the law of master and servant. Alongside the
relatively new model of free contract, an older model of reciprocal obligations
and substantive entitlements continued to influence judicial thinking. Thus a
more interventionist judicial response evolved, particularly in Bombay, where
the effect of the act was blunted by three politically activist judges who succeeded one another.[137] There were similar decisions in Madras and the Punjab.
In a 1910 case the Bombay court differed sharply from the assumptions of the
1889 Allahabad decision, asserting that magistrates were obliged to determine
the precise terms of the contract before it could be enforced.[138] It declared the
sums involved "so grossly inadequate as to suggest that the so-called advance
was merely a device for bringing the contract within the act" and warned
of abuses by employers and magistrates. In England and the United States,
freedom-of-contract doctrine forbade judicial scrutiny of contractual terms
in order to support a free labor market. But Justice Chandavarkar turned this
logic on its head. He appealed to the ideal of free labor to justify abrogat-
ing five labor contracts, arguing that the act was easily abused "to interfere
with the free competition of labour to secure adequate wages." In some ways,
this was simply the culmination of a longer judicial trend, present in Bombay
from the 1890s, to oppose the act in its technical administration. For example,
workers were made exempt from court fees,[139] allowed an unlimited period
in which to pay off their advance,[140] and exempted from criminal sanction
where their contracts would not be enforceable through civil process. How
far these reported decisions (and the others cited) affected the actual administration of the law is very difficult to determine. In other cases we know that
judicial activism was ignored. In a startling judgment of 1894, Jardine and
Ranade, two judges famous for their activist bent of mind, annulled a magistrate's order on the grounds that the government notification of 1862 that empowered magistrates to enforce the act in Bombay applied only to magistrates
in office at that time and had no prospective effect.[141] The decision should

136. 15 CrLJ, 234.

137. K. T. Telang, M. G. Ranade, and N. G. Chandavarkar.

138. *Emperor v. Namdeo Sakharam* 149 (1910), 11 CrLJ 273 (1910).

139. *Queen-Empress v. Budhu Rat Un*, CrC 534 (1891); *Queen-Empress v. Bhagooji Rat Un*,
CrC 625 (1892).

140. *Queen-Empress v. Bhau Rat Un*, CrC 418 (1888).

141. *Queen-Empress v. Chonia Rat Un*, CrC 701 (1894). It seems that a similar judgment was

have derailed the enforcement of penal sanctions in Bombay, but it went un-
reported and had little impact.

Toward a Formally Free Labor Market

Pressures to legislate a formally free labor market, in the sense that criminal penalties would not apply to workers in breach, gradually increased in
the run-up to the First World War. In part, this reflected a change in politics in the metropole, where the momentum of the labor movement in the
wake of the 1901 Taff Vale decision[142] heightened political and social attention to laboring conditions. This had ripple effects in India. A more powerful
push came from nationalist politicians who denounced the systems of semislavery still operating under British rule.[143] At the same time, magistrates,
judges, and district officers began to criticize some abuses of the act, particularly in the Punjab, where it was condemned as "a modified form of slavery."[144]
Initially, the official reaction was to devise more comprehensive systems of
surveillance to guarantee sanitary conditions and health care. For example,
the Madras Planters Labour Act, 1903, which was designed to replace the
Workman's Breach of Contract Act, actually made the criminal breach provisions more stringent in some ways,[145] but also obliged planters to provide
housing, clean water, sanitary facilities, and medical care.[146] Although planters had been lobbying for an act applicable in the Native States for decades,
they were forced to accept an act that limited contracts to one year and made
ill treatment a reasonable ground for absenting work.[147]

---

delivered in Bombay in the early 1860s, although it was not reported. See R. West, *Presidency of Bombay*.

142. *Taff Vale Railway Co. v. Amalgamated Society of Railway Servants* [1901], AC 426 (HL).

143. K. Perraju Pantulu, for example, condemned the Madras Planters Labour Bill as "class legislation . . . intended for the benefit of the few" and asked why plantation employment "should not be conducted on such principles of contract as are applicable to ordinary trans-actions": Madras Council Proceedings, 1902, 214.

144. Major O'Brien, District Magistrate of Shahpur, in *CJP*, 1913, 6. Similarly, in 1908, the district magistrate of Montgomery wrote that "the Act has in my opinion become antiquated and is now used as a means whereby unscrupulous contracts can obtain complete control over ignorant coolies": *CJP*, 1908, 6. However, his argument presumed the helplessness of coolies, and he argued for their protection rather than their liberation.

145. (Madras) n.1 of 1903 punished the breach of contract, rather than refusal to obey a magistrate's order (ss.28–30); in addition to forfeiting wages, workers were required to pay four annas per day of absence from work (s.28); and the act made provision for executing orders made in Native States (s.44).

146. Planters could be fined for failure to fulfill these obligations (s.15).

147. Ss.5, 28. In practice, the act was only made applicable in Wynaad and the Nilgiris, while the Workman's Breach of Contract Act continued in force throughout the rest of Madras.

The First World War focused attention on India's productive capacity, and the drive to promulgate policies comparable with those of other industrial economies was led by the Indian Industrial Commission. In 1917, one of the commission's members, M. M. Malaviya, proposed to repeal the Workmen's Breach of Contract Act and thus institute a "free market in labour." It met with stiff opposition from the Madras and Assam governments, reflecting the political clout of plantation owners. In the Imperial Council in 1919, Malaviya pressed his argument for repeal, alluding to the forthcoming International Labour Conference in Washington, and asked what the conference representatives might think of imprisonment for failing to perform a contract.[148] Opting to ameliorate and delay, the government of India passed an amendment in 1920, signaling its intention to repeal the act entirely in five years' time. The amendment introduced new limitations, gave magistrates the discretion to refuse to enforce unfair contracts, and provided punishments for employers bringing frivolous or vexatious complaints.[149] Convictions were marginally reduced, but there were still ample opportunities for employer abuse, as the Assam Labour Enquiry Committee pointed out in its blasting criticism of the act in 1922. The committee regarded the act as an anachronism and advocated a system of "free labour."[150] But penal contracts remained popular with many employers until the act and the corresponding sections of the Penal Code were finally repealed in 1925,[151] half a century after the effective abolition of penal sanctions in Britain.

Once the legal framework of a formally free labor market was in place,[152] what impact did it have on employment relations? Arguably very little. Inquiring into the matter in 1930, the Royal Commission on Labour in India received remarkably few complaints from employers about the abolition of

148. Government of India, *Indian Council Proceedings*, 1919, 26 (17 Sept. 1919).

149. See (India) n.12 of 1920, which also required complaints to be brought within three months of breach, excluded advances exceeding Rs. 300, and stipulated that orders to perform work should not exceed one year in duration.

150. Assam Labour Enquiry Committee, 1921–22, *Report*, 92.

151. Section 491 of the Penal Code was left intact.

152. Employers and high-court judges in Burma favored replacing the 1859 act with a local law providing for penal contracts, but the move was successfully opposed by administrative officers (see RCLI Evidence 10 (1) 21). Penal contracts under (India) n.6 of 1901 had been abolished in part by (India) n.11 of 1908, with the remaining penal contracts withdrawn by notification in 1915. (Madras) n.1 of 1903 was repealed by (Madras) n.6 of 1927 with effect from 1929. Penal contracts were revived in the plantations of Coorg under (Coorg) n.1 of 1926, which remained in force until 1931. The Employers and Workmen (Disputes) Act of 1860 was moribund, though it remained on the books until 1932. The only form of penal contract to survive was sec. 491 of the Penal Code, relating to the care of dependent persons, but apart from one early case there is no evidence that it has ever been used.

penal contracts. A few grievances came from large employers such as Kanpur factories and Punjab public-works engineers, but most witnesses reported no serious difficulties.[153] There was in fact only a slow realization that the sixty-six-year-old act was gone. The penal contract had entered the folklore of work. Its threats continued to be effective in practice if not in law.[154] Workers were encouraged in the impression that penal contracts were in place,[155] while employers, particularly in small-scale manufacturing, continued to complain to magistrates until 1940. That convictions continued to be registered under the act as late as 1939 reveals a great deal about the administration of criminal justice at the local level. In the Northwestern Provinces, there were at least 178 convictions under the act between 1926 and 1939. Similarly, the repealed provisions of the Penal Code continued to be invoked.[156] Most employers were able to maintain existing recruitment systems with small adjustments, such as slightly increased wages or reduced numbers of unsecured advances.[157]

Moreover, important sectors such as the railways, the cotton mills of Bombay, and the jute mills of Calcutta had never much relied upon penal contracts. Many factory managers found that agreements under the Workman's Breach of Contract Act "had little effect in holding the workers to conditions which they disliked."[158] Though Fremantle was no doubt wrong when he judged in 1909 that the use of penal contracts had been "almost entirely abandoned" in favor of other means, the creation of a formally free labor market had little effect on employers' systems of control, which relied on the authority of jobbers and on holding wages in arrears. For large-scale industry, compulsion had never really provided a practical solution to labor problems. Not only did it raise humanitarian objections; it was simply too costly. If Indian industry held any hope of competing against foreign imports without absurdly high tariffs, it would need to force the costs of discipline, labor mobility, and social reproduction back upon the work force. This task was

153. On Kanpur, see RCLI Evidence 3, 258. The Punjab government reported that in public works, contractors were now required to show more "indulgence in the treatment of labour" (RCLI Evidence 2, 24), while in most other areas no major difficulties were reported.

154. Oral evidence of Dr. A Mukhtar, in RCLI Evidence 7 (2) 139.

155. RCLI *Report*, 377. In Assam it remained customary to give out advances at the commencement of a contract. Workers were generally not informed that the act had been repealed and were asked to sign contracts easily mistaken for penal contracts. Most workers did not know that they were free of the criminal breach laws (RCLI Evidence 6 (1) 76, 184, 216).

156. Evidence of the Bombay Social Service League, in RCLI Evidence 1 (1), 430; 1 (2), 65.

157. RCLI Evidence 1 (1), 201; 6 (1), 26, 76. In an attempt to reduce their exposure through unsecured advances, some plantations like the Singara Tea Estate offered an extra 5 percent commission to laborers who did not take advances: RCLI Evidence 11, 384.

158. Fremantle, "Indian Labour," 516.

achieved through a formally free labor market, which housed multiple forms of informal coercions.

It can be argued, however, that the state's commitment to a free labor market was only ever passive. The government was not willing to threaten the stability of existing social relations by launching an all-out onslaught on slavery and bondage. Although slavery, forced labor, and the sale of girls into prostitution were punishable under the Indian Penal Code (ss.370–74), enforcement was not vigorous. For instance, in the Lower Provinces of Bengal between 1878 and 1902 there were only two convictions for slavery (ss.370–71) and fifty-three for forced labor (s.374).[159] In Punjab, where the only complete series of disaggregated data is available for the period 1867 to 1940, convictions for slavery averaged fewer than three per year, while those for forced labor averaged slightly more than six per year.[160] Meanwhile, district officials were generally unwilling to intervene against the open sale of wives and sexual servants. Forms of agrestic bondage were tolerated, though the Bihar and Orissa Kamiauti Agreements Act, 1920, declared illegal contracts that engaged laborers for a period longer than one year. The act enjoyed very limited success, since without a dramatic transformation of economic conditions, mere legislation could not break the ties of servitude.[161] India entered into a series of undertakings that committed it to the elimination of forced labor, including the Slavery Convention of 1926 and the ILO Convention on Forced Labour of 1939. Nonetheless, forms of servitude continued and, some have argued, even expanded after 1947.

Where penal contracts were not used, written contracts played a minor role in constituting the employment relationship before the First World War. Formal agreements were almost always used for European workers, and sometimes for highly skilled Indian workers such as engineers. But unskilled laborers, who were often illiterate anyway, were not asked to sign contracts. Even after the war, when the upsurge in trade-union activity encouraged employers to clarify and stabilize legal obligations, many industrial undertakings did not bother with formal covenants. In the large majority of cases, there was nothing more than a verbal agreement or assumed understanding between worker and employer or, often, between worker and jobber.[162] By the 1920s, most larger undertakings had written factory rules relating to hours of work, starting times, absence, leave, bonus, fines, and due notice for resignations.

---

159. *Report on the Administration of Criminal Justice in the Lower Provinces of Bengal*, annual series (Calcutta, 1879–1902).

160. Derived from *CJP*, 1867–1940.

161. See RCLI *Report*, 362; Prakash, *Bonded Histories*, 160.

162. RCLI Evidence 1 (1) 145; 2 (1) 64; 3 (1) 232; 5 (1) 161; 7 (1) 22.

Copies of the rules were made available to workers, who were asked to signify their acceptance with either a signature or thumb mark.[163] Full written contracts were used on the twelve major railway lines, in the plantations of Madras and Assam, and in the factories and mines of the Central Provinces.[164] In these cases, standardized contract forms were printed in large numbers and filled in upon appointment. Where formal contracts were concluded, they were subject to a one anna stamp under the Stamp Act.[165]

Unlike its nearest common-law cognates, the United Kingdom, United States, and Australia, India did not develop a vigorous jurisprudence relating to employment contracts. The basic principles of the law of master and servant were adopted from English precedents, but in India those principles did not resolve key issues of industrial organization, such as job security and the organization of labor processes, as they did in England. Relatively few cases regarding nonpenal employment contracts went to the high courts. When the first Indian treatise on the law of master and servant was published in 1952, it relied heavily on English precedents to fill the perceived gaps in the Indian case law.[166]

There is no compelling economic or social reason why a master and servant jurisprudence should have developed in India. Its growth in the United States and Britain does not mean that it is a necessary concomitant of "mature" industrialization. But the contrast is important, because it reveals a great deal about the involvement of legal institutions in the formation of industrial relations and a working class.

In India, the contract generally did not serve as the common reference point for determining mutual obligations. These derived instead from relations of hierarchy and deference, which were constantly being remade in the workplace. In circumstances of high illiteracy among workers and a preference for paternalistic ma-bap idioms among employers, the terminology of the law found little social use. In working relations, law was only invoked in one of three instances: where the employer found it convenient, where the state was willing to enforce particular measures through monitoring and inspecting, and where workers or trade-union leaders developed the knowledge and expertise to press particular legal claims. Otherwise, the law of contract was largely irrelevant. The point can be demonstrated with refer-

---

163. Upper India Chamber of Commerce, Cawnpore, in RCLI Evidence 3, 258.
164. RCLI Evidence 3 (1) 117, 131; 6 (1) 216; 7 (1) 60–164; 8 (1) 177.
165. (India) n.1 of 1879.
166. Since the jurisprudence of case law is simply the by-product of social and economic conflict, it is not surprising that in the very different socioeconomic conditions of India there arose a different set of jurisprudential concerns.

ence to contractual capacity. Under the Indian Contract Act (s.11) and the Indian Majority Act, workers under seventeen could not enter into a binding contract of service.[167] Following a Privy Council ruling of 1903, a minor in India was absolutely incompetent to contract, and any contract involving a minor was not merely voidable as under English law but absolutely void, and therefore unenforceable.[168] Despite the very clear legal position, minors were widely employed under contracts of service and were even subject to regulation under successive Factories Acts. The anomaly was occasionally noted by legal scholars and was implicit in the Madras Planters Labour Act, 1903, which aimed to reduce the age of majority to sixteen, but it did not generate any case law.[169]

What accounts for the comparative irrelevance of the wider law of contract in the Indian workplace? Part of the answer lies in the role of legal doctrine in political mobilization. In both the United Kingdom and the United States, employers cleaved to the doctrine of freedom of contract to undermine the collective action of trade unions. At the same time, freedom of contract in labor relations stood at the center of an enormous political storm between the legislative and judicial branches of government. The body of relevant case law was enormous in each instance, but two judgments stand out as icons. In Taff Vale (1901), the House of Lords made trade unions liable to be sued for the torts of civil conspiracy and procuring breach of contract. Freedom of contract was the legal weapon that employers could now use against any union. The judgment stirred organized lobbying by labor leaders that not only resulted in the granting of absolute legal immunity to trade unions in the 1906 Trade Disputes Act but also set in motion the events leading to the establishment of the Labour Party.[170] In *Lochner v. New York* (1905)[171] the U.S. Supreme Court struck down a New York statute limiting hours of work for bakers on the grounds that the statute represented an unconstitutional interference with freedom of contract. The judgment had two long-term effects: it chalked out the terrain of struggle between the legislative and judicial branches over labor law that was not resolved until 1937;[172] and it "galvanised Progressive opinion and eventually led to a fundamental assault on the legal thought of

---

167. (India) n.9 of 1872; (India) n.9 of 1875.

168. *Mohori Bibee v. Dharmodas Ghosh* (1903), 30 I.A. 114.

169. W. Stokes, *Codes*, 517; Barwell and Kar, *Law Relating to Service*, 1:11–14; (Madras) n.1 of 1903, s.8.

170. Woodland and Storey, *The Taff Vale Case*.

171. 198 U.S. 45 (1905).

172. *In N.L.R.B. v. Jones & Laughlin*, 301 U.S. 1 (1937), the U.S. Supreme Court upheld the National Labor Relations Act, and thus acquiesced in the supremacy of statutory regulation over the common law.

the old order."[173] In short, the contract of employment was the legal vehicle through which employers could gain the judiciary's assistance in cutting down trade unions and regulating legislation.

In India the picture was different for at least three reasons. First, the judiciary never became a center of political power to rival the legislative branch: the power of the executive-cum-legislative organs remained supreme in successive colonial constitutions.[174] Without constitutional powers to review legislation, the Indian courts could not have produced a judgment along the lines of *Lochner*. Second, employers did not need to rely on the courts to keep workers in check: most had private means of oppression and could usually rely on the more direct route of political influence. Third, no organized trade-union movement arose until after 1918, by which time British jurisprudence had thrown up a ring fence around the doctrine of freedom of contract. By the time that freedom of contract might have been used against trade unions in India, employers were unable to do so, particularly since India's membership in the International Labour Organisation obliged it to recognize trade unions. This history helps explain why employers offered such feeble legal resistance to the rise of trade unions in the interwar period.

Conclusion

The Indian history of master and servant law, and of its penal sanctions, was distinctive. This form of "unfreedom" was only one of many in the subcontinent. In the absence of an agrarian revolution, absolute deprivation and rural push factors continued to generate several forms of servitude. The officers of the raj were not overeager to create the conditions for a free labor market. Although labor was commodified, the concepts and conduct of employment remained embedded in social hierarchies where identity and power intertwined.[175] Recruitment and control depended upon precapitalist mechanisms adapted to capitalist production. Slavery and servitude were banned in law but tolerated in practice. These conditions help to explain why the law of penal contracts continued to operate for a full fifty years after it had been abolished in Britain. This fact is in striking contrast to many other areas of Indian law. Influential legal figures like Thomas Babington Macaulay, Henry Maine, James Stephen, and Whitely Stokes were genuinely committed to founding a

173. Horwitz, *Transformation*, 33.

174. The history of how the courts in colonial India came to have such truncated powers vis-à-vis the executive has yet to be written. Many ordinary common-law powers, such as the judicial review of administrative action, simply did not obtain.

175. The argument has been advanced most forcefully by Chakrabarty, *Bengal*.

legal system largely congruent with British models. Indian legal reforms were based on the "best" British practice, and in some instances legal reforms in India even preceded those in England or Scotland. The long persistence of penal contracts is thus an anomaly in a larger legal pattern.

The strongest underlying cause was the political influence of employers, such as planters, industrialists, and public-works officers, within the colonial state. Penal contracts were enforced against a colonized population with minimal political influence, whose members were viewed through racial categories. The juridical image of Indian unskilled labor emphasized recalcitrance, irresponsibility, and laziness—the qualities derived from class-race stereotypes. These descriptive characteristics justified and made sense of the penal prescription. Even after the repeal of penal contracts, the Indian worker was understood to be dependent, illiterate, and unable to fully grasp his or her legal obligations. Such a person could not be a fully free actor and, hence, could not enjoy full legal capacity. Even where workers were technically entitled to complete contractual capacity, it was understood to be largely out of keeping with their actual conditions. In these circumstances, the contract of employment did not become the legal foundation of formally free labor relations. Employers chose to rely on jobbers and personal relations of authority and deference to constitute the employment relation. A free labor market based on contractual relations existed in theory, but in practice it was distorted by coercive employer policies and ineffective legal reforms. Meanwhile, penal sanctions for breach of contract were widely used in some sectors of the economy over the whole period, and the belief that they could be used was undoubtedly important in some industries or locales even after repeal.

The view of the Indian worker that caused the state to maintain penal sanctions for so long also had important consequences for other kinds of legislation. Because workers were viewed as juridical minors unable to look after their own affairs, the state could justify a more proactive and interventionist role. The enduring image of helpless workers provided the ideological preconditions for what were portrayed as paternalistic state policies. As a result, protective legislation, rather than the recognition of worker demands, became the keystone of state policy in the interwar period, in the same period in which the penal sanctions for breach of contract were repealed.

FOURTEEN

Assam and the West Indies, 1860–1920

Immobilizing Plantation Labor

Prabhu P. Mohapatra

Indentured labor replaced slavery as the predominant form of labor in the British West Indies sugar plantations after 1838. After experimenting with free Africans, Madeirans, liberated African slaves, and Chinese, the planters in British Guiana and Trinidad settled for imported labor from India. The first Indian laborers arrived in British Guiana in 1838, privately recruited on behalf of John Gladstone for his plantations in Demerara. That same year the discovery of indigenous tea plants in Assam in northeast India led to the East India Company's first experimental plantation in Assam. The Assam Tea Company was incorporated in London the next year to cultivate and produce tea in Assam for export.[1]

The newly reconstructed plantation sector in the West Indies and the nascent plantations of India shared a common beginning. Laborers for Gladstone's plantations in British Guiana and the first laborers for the Assam company were recruited from the central Indian Upland of Chotanagpur. For the rest of the nineteenth century, these two plantation complexes, separated by several thousand kilometers, shared many aspects of labor organization. Both recruited labor from Gangetic districts of the United Provinces under five-year indenture contracts, enforced by penal sanctions, and transported that labor over long distances. Further, the colonial governments in India and the West Indies actively recruited labor, regulated employment, and created a process to enforce contracts. These similarities suggest intriguing possibilities for comparative study of the labor regimes in these two regions. Over the seventy years that indenture contracts were enforced, until 1915 in Assam and

1. P. Griffiths, *Tea Industry*, 64; *Papers Relating to the Tea Industry in Bengal* (hereafter *Papers*) (Calcutta, 1873), ii.

1917 in the West Indies, distinct styles of labor management and particular worker identities emerged, both of which hinged on the compulsory nature of the contract. This chapter focuses on the process of enforcing indentures in the West Indies and Assam. How did indentures, backed by penal sanctions, operate to immobilize labor after it had been mobilized over long distances? And how effective was such immobilization? The legal framework guided the immobilization, raising questions about the efficacy of law in the extraction of labor power, and of the resistance it evoked.

In the three sections that follow, I provide an overview of indentured labor in the plantation systems of Assam and the West Indies, describe the origin and development of the penal contract provisions in the labor laws of both regions, and address the legal and extralegal means by which the planters sought to control, discipline, and exact labor from a bound labor force. I try to account for the different deployment of the penal provisions in the indenture law of these two plantation complexes, distinguished by high rates of prosecution in the West Indies and comparatively low rates in Assam. Of special significance were differences in the place of penal contract provisions, and divergences in the roles of the colonial state, in the machinery of labor control. I also take up the theme of the efficacy of law and explore it briefly in the operation and eventual demise of the criminal breach of contract law[2] that replaced indenture in Assam between 1908 and 1926.

Indentured Labor and the Plantation System

Between 1838 and 1917, 239,000 indentured laborers arrived to work on the plantations of British Guiana, and another 145,000 arrived in Trinidad.[3] Except for sporadic immigration in the decade following 1838, and a halt for a few years after 1851, there was continuous annual importation of Indian labor. During the peak of immigration in the 1870s, an average of 5,000 laborers arrived every year in British Guiana and 3,000 in Trinidad. Their pay was set by statute at one shilling a day for a term of five years, with provision for repatriation after ten years residence in the colony.

Indentured labor resuscitated the flagging sugar industry. Both West In-

2. (India) n.13 of 1859.
3. British Guiana and Trinidad received the bulk of the indentured immigrants from India to the West Indies. Jamaica received 40,000 immigrants and a few thousand were shared among St. Lucia, St. Vincent, Grenada, and Nevis. The French colonies Guadaloupe and Martinique and the Dutch colony Surinam also received Indian immigrants. Much of the legal apparatus of enforcement in these non-English colonies shared features of British indentured ordinances and a comparison between the systems would be instructive although I have not attempted it here.

dian colonies experienced spectacular and sustained growth in acreage under cane, production, and sugar exports. Buoyed by favorable prices, British Guiana sugar exports increased from 36,000 tons in 1845–48 to a peak of 120,000 tons in 1884, while acreage under cane tripled. In Trinidad, exports increased from 19,000 tons in 1845–48 to 64,000 in 1884–85.[4] After 1884, declining sugar prices, in part the result of increased beet sugar production, eventually reduced production, exports, and acreage under cane in both colonies, and this continued until the First World War. The Caribbean sugar industry is thus characterized by two distinct phases: growth from 1850 to 1883, followed by stagnation and crisis from 1884 until the end of indenture in 1917. The number of indentured immigrants arriving in these colonies, however, was roughly the same in both periods. They were crucial to the early growth, and their low wages enabled planters to maintain sugar production at precrisis levels when declining prices reduced profits.

The tea plantations of Assam followed a slightly different trajectory. From their commencement in 1839, they were plagued by shortages of capital and labor until a speculative boom in 1860 led to the rapid development of gardens and the importation of thousands of laborers through native recruiting agencies. "Tea mania" collapsed in 1865 with a series of bankruptcies, mergers, and consolidations. The restructured tea industry grew steadily, aided by many imported indentured laborers from the central Indian uplands and the congested districts of the Gangetic plains, recruited through state-regulated agencies. In 1882 the government deregulated emigration and strengthened penal sanctions by special labor legislation. One million indentured laborers (including children) arrived in Assam in the next twenty years as tea acreage, production, and exports grew spectacularly. Acreage more than doubled, production tripled, and India surpassed China as the world's largest exporter of tea.[5] This expansion took place under conditions quite the opposite of the West Indies as tea prices had slumped to half the level of the 1880s by the beginning of the 1900s. After a decade of stagnation and slump the war years saw another surge in the growth of production and acreage.

Before analyzing the effect of indenture laws and penal contracts, let me point to some similarities and differences between indentured labor in these two plantation complexes. Most indentured laborers were between fifteen and thirty years of age, but there was a marked difference in the gender composition of the work force in the two regions. In Assam the work force was equally male and female; in the West Indies, fewer than three in ten

4. Laurence, *Question of Labour*, appendix I.
5. Behal and Mohapatra, "Tea," 143–45.

laborers recruited from northern India were women. In spite of this differ-ence, both regions relied on imported labor rather than internal reproduc-tion to build and maintain the labor force. Annual imports of labor remained crucial through periods of growth and stagnation. Although planters in both regions reproduced their labor force by importing laborers, the scale was radi-cally different. In Assam, the average annual importation reached 50,000 per year between 1880 and 1905. The average for both the Caribbean colonies did not exceed 8,000 laborers per year in any decade, and no more than 9,000 arrived in British Guiana in any single year. These differences reflected the size of the total labor force. At their height in 1919, the Assam tea plantations employed 900,000 laborers, which was double the number at the beginning of the twentieth century. The combined labor force on the sugar plantations in both the Caribbean colonies (as well as cocoa in Trinidad) was never more than 110,000.[6]

A second feature of both plantation complexes was the remarkably stable nominal wage. The so-called statutory minimum wage—one shilling per day or task in the West Indies and five rupees per month in Assam for adult male labor—remained constant throughout seventy years of indentured labor. It enabled the plantations to grow phenomenally in production and profits in favorable years and to survive during prolonged slumps. It also depressed the wages of free labor. The penal sanctions of indenture law, by immobilizing a substantial section of the labor force, allowed planter control over the labor market.[7]

The other main effect of indenture in both regions was to substitute con-tractual penalties for market discipline. Planters and colonial officials argued that the local labor force, whether recently freed slaves in the West Indies or the local Assamese, demanded exorbitant wages and in any case were un-willing to participate regularly in plantation work.[8] This justified import-ing workers. However, when imported labor was made available, planters de-manded restrictions on the labor market in order to guarantee that workers were not only present in sufficient numbers but also were "reliable" in that they did not "wander about" testing the market. In other words, the plant-ers demanded a labor force bound to the employer for long terms. The colo-nial states obliged by introducing a series of special labor laws and an institu-tionalized system of "voluntary servitude" that remained in place for nearly

6. Employment peaked at 72,000 in British Guiana and 38,000 in Trinidad.

7. Rodney, *Guyanese Working People*, 34. In Assam statutory wages under the special labor laws were Rs. 5.50 in the last two years of the indenture.

8. See P. Griffiths, *Tea Industry*, 73, 101–3. For West Indian planter complaints about high wages and irregular work habits of freed slaves, see Brereton, *Trinidad*, 75–80.

a century both in India and the West Indies. A brief review of the origins and evolution of the penal sanctions and their incorporation in legislation reveals the paradoxical process by which the contract institutionalized a form of servitude.

Penal Contract Legislation in Assam and the West Indies

Initially imported labor was not subject to special penal contract in either region. In the West Indies planters complained that imported workers were "too uncivilised" to honor normal agreements (usually renewable one-month contracts). Laborers were naturally inclined to frequent changes of employment, claimed the planters; their ability to make and honor contracts could only be slowly acquired through a period of apprenticeship. In 1846 Lord Harris, governor of Trinidad, described recently imported Indian workers as "naturally dissolute and depraved in their habits if left to themselves and much inclined to fall into habits of drinking and of wandering idly about the country, and therefore require close supervision of Government, in order to correct, if possible—but at all events to prevent—any evident cases of vagabondage and licentiousness."[9]

Such views justified planters' demands for more stringent labor controls in response to mass desertions and the high cost of importing workers. The colonial state acquiesced in the institution of long-term contracts and penal provisions on the solicitous ground of preserving the health of the immigrants. High mortality on plantations was blamed on unrestrained mobility. If planters were to be held responsible for the health of imported laborers, they must be bound to the plantation for a sufficient term.

The West Indian colonies introduced penal legislation gradually. In the immediate aftermath of abolition, and given the vigilance exercised by the Anti-Slavery Society, the Colonial Office was under pressure not to accede to demands for penal contracts. The need to distinguish indenture from slavery was paramount. As early as 1836, British Guiana promulgated a master and servant ordinance to enable justices of the peace to enforce three-year contracts. It did not apply to imported workers as a Colonial Office order of 1838 limited their contracts to one year and only if contracted in the colony.[10] An 1846 Code of Regulations for Coolie Labour in Trinidad marked the first effort to impose penal contracts on imported Indian labor. It allowed im-

9. Lord Harris to Gladstone, July 1846, cited in D. W. D. Commins, *Note on Emigration from India to Trinidad* (hereafter Commins Report) (Calcutta, 1893), 6.

10. For more on the British Guiana legislation and the Colonial Office role, see the chapters by DeBarros and Banton in this volume.

prisonment for absence from work and instituted a pass law that effectively confined laborers to their allotted plantation.[11] The Colonial Office, however, disallowed the Trinidad code in 1847. A series of ordinances followed allowing voluntary contracts for up to three years; those unwilling to contract were to pay a monthly tax. Failure to collect the taxes, and planters' demands for stricter control and longer-term contracts, led to further enactments between 1851 and 1854 that substantially reproduced the 1846 regulations.

Long-term penal contracts, anathema to the Colonial Office in the late 1830s and 1840s under Stephen, were finally allowed in 1852 in Trinidad and 1853 in British Guiana. Henceforth five-year contracts at statutory wage rates became the standard for Indian laborers.[12] Laborers were required to live on plantations and could be arrested by policemen without warrant if found without a ticket of leave or a certificate exempting them from labor. Initially, absence from work was punishable by fine, but the penalty was soon changed to imprisonment for fourteen days. Desertion, defined as absence from the plantation without leave, was also punishable by imprisonment. Subsequent refinements included imprisonment for such offenses as malingering, "wilful indolence," and "habitual idleness"[13] and fines or imprisonment for disobedience, neglecting work, refusing to amend work, insolence, and insubordination.[14] Breach of hospital regulations (introduced in 1864 in British Guiana and Trinidad) was punishable by imprisonment. Periods of imprisonment and desertion were to be added to the term and endorsed on the indenture.[15] Thus the principal features of the penal legislation for immigrant labor in the West Indies were established between 1850 and 1870.[16] The context in

11. Lord Harris to Gladstone, July 1846, cited in Commins Report, 4.

12. Laurence, "Labour Contracts," gives a narrative account of changes in Colonial Office policy regarding labor contracts after emancipation. See also Trotman, *Crime in Trinidad*, 185–87. These conditions were codified in (British Guiana) n.7 of 1854 and (Trinidad) n.24 of 1854.

13. Defined as absence from work for twelve days in a month.

14. Many of the penal provisions relating to performance of work were borrowed from the apprenticeship period legislation, replacing corporal punishments by imprisonment and fines. See the chapter by Turner in this volume for an analysis of postemancipation labor legislation in the West Indies.

15. In British Guiana this applied only to imprisonment for offenses other than labor offenses.

16. British Guiana enactments for Indian indentured immigration in this period included n.20 and n.21 of 1850, n.20 and n.21 of 1851, n.3 and n.16 of 1853, n.7 of 1854, n.8 of 1855, n.22 and n.25 of 1856, n.1 and n.7 of 1857, n.2 and n.26 of 1858, n.5 of 1859, n.1 and n.19 of 1860, n.28 and n.30 of 1862, n.3 of 1863, n.4 and n.13 of 1864, n.5 of 1865, n.13 and n.15 of 1866, n.3 of 1867, and n.9 of 1868. Trinidad enactments for Indian indentured immigration in the period included n.5 of 1850, n.11 of 1851, n.11 and n.12 of 1852, n.24 of 1854, n.7 of 1855, n.13, n.14, and n.27 of 1859, n.6 of 1860, n.16 and n.23 of 1862, n.3 of 1865, n.6 of 1866, n.26 of 1869, and n.13 of 1870. Both colonies also legislated for immigrant labor from China and elsewhere.

which this legislation developed demonstrates the connection between the labor needs of the plantations in a phase of explosive growth and the need for stringent control and restrictions on the bargaining power (through desertion and workplace resistance) of newly recruited immigrant workers.

Several amendments followed the British Guiana Enquiry Commission in 1871. The most significant involved raising the reindenture fee to stop the practice of continuous reindenture with payments of bounty. A second change introduced the "livret" system, which was designed to keep track of the days worked by each laborer in the colony so as better to police the extension of indentures for days lost to unlawful absence.[17] To reduce the frequency of imprisonment for mere absence from work, extension of indenture became the main punishment. In British Guiana an ordinance of 1876 empowered the immigration agent to endorse the number of days lost to absence and to extend the indenture. In Trinidad, magistrates had the equivalent authority. Nevertheless, when planters came to realize that merely extending indentures gave them little control over workers, they framed prosecutions under other offenses for which fines and imprisonment were provided. The extension of indentures for absence from work fell into disuse and was removed from the lawbooks at the end of the century.[18]

At the end of the nineteenth century, both colonies possessed a large number of consolidated ordinances, perfected over the preceding fifty years, to regulate relations between indentured workers and their employers.[19] A variety of punishable offenses were available to planters in enforcing penal contracts. During this period the colonial state also developed apparatus to "protect" labor: an official known as the protector of immigrants, provisions for hospitals, standards for dwellings, a statutory minimum wage, and protection against gross physical abuse. Laborers could complain to the protector about excessive tasks, low wages, or other breaches by the planters. Imprisonment for a laborer's breach of contract was thought to balance these protections by compensating the planter for the costs of labor. Thus the British Guiana Commission of 1871 defended indenture on grounds of both cost and protection:

> An indenture, as it seems to us, is justifiable, however contrary to English ideas, to insure payment by the immigrant for services rendered, that is for his passage out, which payment, it seems can be insured in no

17. (British Guiana) n.7 of 1873. Because of procedural difficulties the system was little used. It was removed when the immigration ordinances were revised in 1897.

18. Thus in British Guiana only twelve estates bothered to claim lost days for endorsement in 1882. Laurence, *Question of Labour*, 143.

19. For example, (Trinidad and Tobago) n.19 of 1899.

other way. It may also be defended on the ground of his helplessness on arrival in a new country; for if a man must necessarily be dependent on others for the preservation of his health, there is no harm in recognising the fact by law.[20]

The defense of indenture assumed, on the one hand, freely contracting parties and, on the other, that one of those parties was dependent. The myth of indenture as a paternalistic and caring system persisted throughout the period. As the governor of British Guiana put it in 1909, "Indenture means care in sickness, free medical attendance, free hospital accommodation, morning rations in early days, sanitary dwellings, habits of industry gained, a guaranteed minimum daily wage, and general supervision by Government officials."[21] What he failed to mention was that indenture could mean jail for minor breaches of employment discipline, or that, in 1909, nearly 30 percent of indentured immigrants were subject to legal proceedings. The governor's remarks nevertheless managed to convey the overwhelming involvement of the colonial state in the organization and functioning of the labor system.

In Assam, the legislation of penal contract followed a similar trajectory. Between 1840 and 1861, a period marked by interrupted, sporadic growth of tea acreage and production, there was little government involvement in recruiting and employing laborers. Laborers committed to three-year contracts, though they were seldom enforced through court action. The first legislation to regulate recruitment and employment appeared during the expansion of the early 1860s. Indian labor contractors, paid so much per head, "considered their duty and responsibility discharged when the living are landed and the cost of the dead are adjusted." High mortality rates among the workers they recruited led the colonial state to enforce registration of laborers and sanitary regulations en route in 1863.[22] The combined impact of death and desertion resulted in the introduction of indenture in Assam. Between 1863 and 1866, 35,000 of the 85,000 workers transported to Assam died or deserted. Section 492 of the India Penal Code, enacted in 1860, allowed employers to prosecute defaulting laborers whom they had conveyed over long distances. The maximum penalty under the act was one month's im-

20. *Report of the Commissioners of Enquiry on the Treatment of Immigrants in British Guiana*, Parliamentary Papers (hereafter PP) 1871 (393) 20:558, para. 249.
21. *Reports of the Committee on Emigration from India to the Crown Colonies and Protectorates* (hereafter Sanderson Report), PP 1910 (5192 to 5194) 27:568.
22. "Statement of objects and reasons" prefixed to (Bengal) n.3 of 1863 in Government of India (hereafter GOI), Legislative Department "A" Proceedings no. 28–36, Apr. 1865. National Archives of India (hereafter NAI).

prisonment; prosecution terminated the contract. Planters complained that deserting workers courted imprisonment to escape the contract. Citing examples of immigration ordinances in overseas colonies, planters demanded heavier penal provisions.[23] In January 1863, the Workman's Breach of Contract Act of 1859[24] was extended to Assam. Originally enacted for the Presidency towns of British India, it empowered magistrates to order workers who were in breach of contract after receiving an advance to perform their obligations. Nevertheless, the planters considered this act inadequate because prosecution could terminate the employment contract, imprisonment was limited to three months, and there was uncertainty whether the cost of transporting workers to Assam constituted an advance.

The Bengal Council responded to the planters' demands for penal contracts by passing the first of several special labor acts, which allowed extensive powers of private arrest. Act 6 of 1865 also provided for three-year contracts with a statutory minimum wage, a nine-hour working day, and a government inspector empowered to cancel contracts for mistreatment of laborers. Desertion, refusal to work, and unlawful absence from work were punishable by imprisonment. Planters and their agents could arrest absconders without warrant. However, the act required that the contract be executed before a magistrate in the recruiting district rather than in the district where labor was to be performed. Laborers who had already finished a contract term or local laborers could not contract under this act: they were either employed without a penal contract or, more commonly, contracted under the 1859 act. Although Bengal Act 7 of 1873 was subsequently to permit recruitment outside the provisions of the 1865 legislation, it was hardly ever used as planters favored long-term penal contracts.[25]

From 1865 to 1882 the government regulated labor recruitment and established a wide-ranging penal contract system. In 1882, after persistent complaints from the planters about high recruitment costs and inadequate penalties, the colonial state substantially deregulated emigration and strengthened penal powers. The term of indenture increased from three to five years. Contracts could be signed before a magistrate in the labor districts rather than in the recruiting districts. The act allowed contracts of similar duration with local workers, effectively increasing the hold of the planters over time-expired

23. For planters' complaints, see *Reports on the Working of Act III of 1863*, GOI Legislative Department "A" Proc. no. 30–38, Nov. 1865. Planters had resorted to large-scale illegal detentions of laborers during 1861–64. They called for flogging of recalcitrant laborers, special police, and return of deserters to plantations.

24. (India) n.13 of 1859. See also Michael Anderson in this volume.

25. (Bengal) n.6 of 1865; (Bengal) n.7 of 1873.

laborers.[26] It expanded the power of private arrest and simplified the procedure for endorsing and extending indentures for unlawful absence from work. Deregulated recruitment and strengthened penal powers expedited the massive importation of labor and subsequent expansion of the tea industry.

Strong opposition to the special labor acts emerged during this period, focusing largely on recruitment abuses. In 1893 the term of indenture was reduced to four years and the maximum term for local labor contracts (used mainly for time-expired laborers) to one year.[27] These changes, however, prompted planters to bind time-expired workers under the 1859 act instead; this also enabled them to evade the requirement under the special acts to maintain registers and account for employee mortality. Until the twentieth century both sets of penal contract laws were widely used in Assam. New recruits were hired under the special labor legislation as modified in 1882 and 1893, while the 1859 act was used mainly for reengaging laborers whose indentures had expired.[28]

The turn of the twentieth century was a period of acute crisis marked by overproduction. High labor mortality, increased recruitment costs, and a rising incidence of labor disturbances prompted substantial changes to the penal contract system. In 1901 the government intervened to further regulate recruitment under the special legislation. Penal powers were substantially reduced in 1908 when private power of arrest was revoked in Assam.[29] Without the key provision for private arrest, planters preferred to make their contracts under the 1859 breach-of-contract act, which involved fewer regulatory requirements. After 1915, when the special labor legislation and its recruiting system were dismantled, planters employed laborers largely under the 1859 act, which was amended in 1920 and finally abolished in 1925.[30]

In this account of penal labor legislation in Assam and the West Indies, certain similarities stand out. In both regions, the formative period of legislation coincided with phases of rapid plantation expansion: 1850–75 in the Caribbean, and 1865–1901 in Assam. The primary function of the legislation was to restrict the wage increases that a burgeoning demand for labor

26. (India) n.1 of 1882. Control over time-expired laborers, who had substantial bargaining power, was a major concern of the planters. The practice of awarding them large bonuses to reengage for a year was stopped, and bonuses drastically reduced, after the passage of this act.

27. (India) n.7 of 1893.

28. In the more accessible Surma Valley, (India) n.13 of 1859 was predominantly used for both new recruits and reengagements, while planters in the more remote Brahmaputra valley favored (Bengal) n.6 of 1865.

29. (India) n.6 of 1901; (India) n.11 of 1908. See Behal and Mohapatra, "Tea," for a fuller account of the dismantling of the penal contract regime in Assam.

30. (India) n.8 of 1915; (India) n.12 of 1920; (India) n.3 of 1925.

would create in an open market. A second function of the legislation was to immobilize the laborer, thereby regulating competition among the planters themselves. The penal labor contract was thus crucial in fueling expansion of plantations. Five-year penal contracts were common to both plantation complexes, ensuring predictability and control over labor costs over extended periods. The most important function of the penal legislation, however, was to ensure "labour discipline," minimizing the likelihood that workers would withdraw their labor.

Enforcing the Penal Contract

To be effective, penal contracts had to be enforced. In both regions, the colonial state claimed the role of neutral arbiter, enforcing contracts voluntarily entered into by two equal parties. It was true that only one of the parties risked imprisonment for breach of the contract, but this was regarded merely as an incident of his or her inability to pay civil damages for want of property. At the same time, though, the state assumed the role of protector, treating the immigrant laborer as a dependent. These contrary assumptions—that the laborer was competent to contract but not to look after his or her own interests—were reconciled uneasily in the special indentured labor legislation.

Employers could enforce the contract against laborers through self-help as well as with state assistance. Planters had the right to arrest "absconders" in Assam and (with more restrictions) in the West Indies. A less obvious form of employer self-help was the planters' power to set tasks, to compel workers to work, to impose fines for bad or short work and minor misdemeanors and, especially in Trinidad, to keep a week's wages in arrears to ensure attendance, the "trust week."[31] The mechanism of enforcement, although theoretically the sole preserve of the state, comprised a spectrum of practices that ranged from the legal to the quasi-legal and completely illegal, enforced both privately and by the state.

Assam and the West Indies had much in common with respect to enforcement, but the state's role was somewhat different in the two regions. Both Trinidad and British Guiana financed one-third of the cost of labor imports out of public subsidies. In Assam, although the colonial state regulated recruitment, it never directly financed labor immigration. In the West Indies, vigorous abolitionist agitation had made planter authority suspect and led to state intervention to protect slaves and apprentices. In contrast, Assam had

---

31. Commins Report, Diary. Surgeon General Commins found the imposition of fines for minor misdemeanors a common practice in Trinidad as also withholding wages to ensure attendance in the following week.

no previous history of plantation slavery. In consequence, the West Indian colonial states took a more active part in enforcement than the state in Assam.

In the West Indies, employers or their representatives filed complaints before stipendiary magistrates for breaches of the immigration ordinances. The magistrate then issued a summons to the laborer, and the case would be heard by summary procedure. Managers could withdraw complaints by paying the cost of the summons, which they recovered from the laborer. The threat of conviction was often enough to discipline recalcitrant workers. On conviction, the laborer could be ordered to pay a fine or undergo imprisonment from seven days to three months depending on the breach. In both British Guiana and Trinidad, a large proportion of the total cases heard in magistrates courts resulted in convictions and committals.[32]

In Assam, planters were not required to seek warrants for deserters unless there was a magistrate close by; otherwise, they could arrest the laborer and bring him or her before the magistrate afterward. This applied only to laborers under the special labor acts and not to those under the 1859 breach-of-contract act or free laborers. Offenses under both legislative schemes were prosecuted summarily before magistrates, who would issue summons on receipt of complaints. Offenders under the breach of contract act were required to perform their contract or face three months' imprisonment. As we shall see, though, these formal aspects were honored mostly in the breach in Assam. Deserters were often arrested without warrants and not produced before magistrates, and the power of arrest was used indiscriminately against free laborers and those covered by the 1859 act as well as those whose indentures came under the special legislation.

The proportion of indentured labor prosecuted annually for breach of contract is a potentially useful indicator of enforcement, especially in the comparative context.[33] The base line for any such comparison is the number of workers covered by penal contracts in each region. There were, on average, 10,000 indentured laborers in Trinidad between 1876 and 1916, with little change from year to year. In British Guiana there were 33,000 in 1871, constituting the overwhelming bulk of plantation labor, but that number declined

32. David Trotman's calculation shows that offenses under indenture and master and servant ordinances averaged between 16 and 20 percent of offenses, between 19 and 25 percent of convictions, and between 18 and 23 percent of committals in Trinidad from 1875 to 1899, by quinquennium, and 16 percent of offenses but 30 percent of committals in the first decade of the twentieth century: Trotman, *Crime in Trinidad*, 188, 295.

33. However, it must be used with care. Does a high rate of prosecution indicate the failure of the penal legislation to work economically, or a rigid labor regime? Does a low rate indicate successful management of labor relations and low labor resistance, or merely sluggish enforcement?

steadily with each decade, reaching a low of 7,000 in 1916.[34] In Assam, on the other hand, there were 20,000 laborers under the special labor acts in 1881, or 22 percent of the total adult labor force. Coverage increased rapidly under Act 1 of 1882, both in numbers and as a proportion of the labor force, reaching 150,000, or 55 percent of the labor force, in 1900. Thereafter the numbers declined rapidly so that by 1913 only 5,000 laborers were indentured under the special legislation. However, these numbers do not include laborers with penal contracts under the 1859 act,[35] which in 1886 covered about 40 percent of the total adult labor force under penal contract.[36] This proportion increased until, by 1910, the 1859 act had replaced the special legislation as the principal source of penal contracts in Assam.

Tables 14.1 and 14.2 indicate the number of prosecutions as a proportion of the indentured labor force. They reveal several interesting differences between the use of the state legal structure in the West Indies and Assam.

The rate of prosecutions for labor offenses was high in the West Indies, where between one-fifth and one-third of indentured workers faced prosecution annually. Prosecution rates in both these colonies rose from the mid-1880s to the end of indenture period. This secular trend coincided with the crisis in the sugar industry and reflected planters' attempts to extract more labor, and the increasing resistance of the indentured workers. Many prosecutions were withdrawn; for those that were pursued, about 65 percent resulted in convictions. One in three convicted offenders was sentenced to imprisonment in Trinidad and more in British Guiana. Others found themselves in jail when they defaulted on fines.[37] In both colonies, about 7 percent of all indentured workers were imprisoned for breach of contract annually in the late nineteenth century, and about 6 percent in the first decade of the twentieth century. In sum, the penal labor regime in the West Indies between 1880 and 1917 had an average annual prosecution rate above 20 percent, a conviction rate above 15 percent, and an imprisonment rate of about 7 percent. This represents tens of thousands of prosecutions instituted by managers and overseers against laborers. By way of contrast, 17 complaints were laid against

34. There were 23,000 in 1881; 17,000 in 1891; 14,000 in 1901; and 9,000 in 1911.

35. Statistics of the labor force covered by (India) n.1 of 1882 were collected and reported every year, but labor under (India) n.13 of 1859 was seldom counted.

36. *Special Report on the Working of the Inland Emigration Act I of 1882 in Assam for 1886–89* (hereafter Assam Special Report) in GOI Emigration, "A" Proc. no. 6–14, Nov. 1891, para. 111.

37. In Trinidad, 397 sentences of imprisonment were imposed in 1911–12, and 523 fines. The total number of indentured immigrants imprisoned was 840, indicating that the majority of those fined were subsequently jailed in default of payment: *Report to the Government of India on the Conditions of Four British Colonies and Surinam* (hereafter McNeill's Report), PP 1914–16 (7744) 47:592.

TABLE 14.I.

Offenses, Convictions, and Committals of Indentured Immigrants,
Trinidad and British Guiana, 1880–1917 (five-year average)

	Offenses	Convictions	Committals	Prosecutions as Percentage of Indentured Population[a]
Trinidad				
1880–84	3,357	2,296	885	22.1
1885–89	2,911	2,135	743	21
1890–94	3,554	2,554	839	24
1895–99	3,315	2,417	1,047	24
1900–1905	3,769	2,889	1,512	26
1906–10	3,913	2,830	1,362	27
1911–17	3,012	2,191	970	28
British Guiana				
1880–84	4,049	2,466	1,562	20.5
1885–89	2,902	1,702	1,272	16.5
1890–94	4,121	2,320	1,822	22.8
1895–99	3,654	2,259	2,086	23.6
1900–1904	4,017	2,163	1,921	28.5
1905–9	3,441	1,735	—	33.7
1910–14	2,176	1,327	—	23.4

SOURCES: *Blue Books* for Trinidad and British Guiana; *Annual Report of Immigration Agent General of British Guiana* (*ARIAG*) for the relevant years.

[a]Numbers for Trinidad apply the British Guiana ratio of offenses under the immigration ordinances to the total breach of contract offenses, as these were not distinguished in the Trinidad immigration reports.

managers and overseers in British Guiana between 1905 and 1910, six of which resulted in convictions. In many years, virtually no complaints by indentured immigrants against managers were recorded. In Trinidad, such complaints were so rare that the immigration department did not keep records.[38]

In contrast to the West Indies, the prosecution rate in Assam under the Special Labour Acts of 1882 and 1901 was extremely low. The raw number of prosecutions increased from about 500 a year in the early 1880s to about 1,400 in 1895, keeping pace with the increasing number of laborers. After 1895 the number declined steadily. On average, barely more than 6 laborers in 1,000 were prosecuted under these acts, and never more than 1 percent. Convictions as a proportion of prosecutions were high: 80 percent on average, of which

38. *Annual Report of Immigration Agent General Of British Guiana* (hereafter *ARIAG*) for relevant years. See also McNeill's Report, 29.

TABLE 14.2.

Offenses Committed and Persons Convicted for Criminal Breach of Contract,
Assam, India, 1879–1922 (five-year average)

	Special Labour Legislation			Breach of Contract Act		
	Offenses	Convictions	Coverage	Offenses	Convictions	Coverage
1879–82	373	448	35,000	595	534	87,000
1883–87	808	689	81,000	300	192	106,000
1888–92	1,046	934	102,000	442	185	152,000
1893–97	1,268	901	128,000	858	249	215,000
1898–1902	782	373	105,000	611	194	288,000
1903–7	640	292	78,000	1,057	346	340,000
1908–12	373	137	28,000	915	362	452,000
1913–17	125	22	6,500	1,218	305	535,000
1918–22	125	7	300	852	177	601,000

SOURCES: *Report on the Administration of Criminal Justice in Assam*; *Annual Report on Labour Immigration into Assam* for the relevant years.

Note: The Special Labour Legislation was (India) n.1 of 1882 (from 1882 to 1901) and (India) n.6 of 1901 (from 1901 to 1915). From 1880 to 1900, about 60 percent of the laborers not covered by the special legislation were contracted under (India) n.13 of 1859, while the rest were so-called free laborers. After 1908 it would seem that this proportion increased, but there are no reliable statistics of the number formally contracted under the 1859 act.

three-quarters resulted in imprisonment. Under the 1859 act, there were still fewer prosecutions before the late 1890s. Thereafter, prosecutions increased as rapidly as those under the special acts declined. Even so, the rate of prosecution remained below 1 percent.

How do we explain the high rates of prosecution for breach of contract in the West Indies and the low rates in Assam?

One set of explanations links high prosecution rates to low earnings. In 1892–94, Charles Mitchell, Trinidad's protector of immigrants, attempted unsuccessfully to enforce legislation barring low-wage plantations from further allotments of indentured workers.[39] The planters argued that earnings were low because Indian immigrants were habitually idle. They inadvertently drew attention to the prosecution rate by demanding that periods of unlawful absence, imprisonment, and hospitalization be excluded from the calculation of annual earnings.[40] In 1897 an articulate Indian indentured laborer named

39. By (Trinidad) n.13 of 1870, s.66, estates were to be denied allotments where more than 15 percent of indentured men earned less than forty-three dollars annually.

40. The government succumbed to planter pressure. It raised the limit to 30 percent of the adult male indentured population, allowed discretionary allotment to defaulting estates, and forced the protector to retire on grounds of failing "mental faculties." See Governor's dispatches for 1895–96, Public Record Office (hereafter PRO) CO 384/192.

Bechu told a Royal Commission that high rates of prosecution were caused by low earnings and by the planters' strategy of prosecuting during the off-season to relieve their wage burden.[41] In Trinidad during the sugar crisis of 1894–95, low-wage estates had higher rates of desertion and prosecution than those where earnings were above average.[42]

In 1904 the Colonial Office asked the governor of Trinidad to investigate whether low earnings contributed to high rates of prosecution. He reported that prosecutions were high because of the habitual indolence of the workers, while earnings were low because workers deserted and spent their time working on small farms belonging to former indentured laborers rather than working on the estates. Besides this paradoxical vision of the indentured laborer as a lazy entrepreneur, he noted that wages on the sugar estates were at most about 70 percent of the statutory minimum. High rates of absenteeism might be because neither the work nor the environment were attractive to the laborer, "and the workers get tired of them, go stale and do as little as they can manage to do."[43]

In 1910, when the Sanderson Committee remarked unfavorably on the prosecution rates for labor offenses in Trinidad and British Guiana, planters and officials argued that the rates were high because the indenture laws compelled estate managers to prosecute deserters. (The clause at issue was intended to prevent managers from forcing indentured laborers off the plantation whenever there was insufficient work.) The planters attributed the prosecution statistics to multiple complaints against a few recalcitrant individuals who were usually "habitual idlers" (legally defined as laborers absent from work for more than twelve days in two consecutive months) and to the presence of "returnees" or "refractory groups like Punjabis" who instigated laborers to "defy authority." That high rates of desertion, defined as seven days' absence from the plantation in British Guiana and three days' in Trinidad, could be caused by ill treatment, low wages, and indeed by high rates of prosecution was never fully admitted. In one unguarded moment, however, W. H. Coombes, Trinidad's new protector of immigrants and a champion of the planters, admitted that "bad management" was a cause of high rates of prosecution, "on some estates, by young and overbearing overseers, unaccustomed to command and discipline, who treat the immigrants harshly and without

41. *Report of the Royal West Indian Commission*, PP 1898 50:471, evidence of Bechu, in Minutes of Evidence, appendix C, part II.

42. Governor of Trinidad to Secy. Colonies, 1 Sept. 1896, 286, and the minute on it by Lord Stanmore, PRO CO 295/374.

43. Governor of Trinidad to Secy. Colonies, 2 May 1905, 121, PRO CO 295/433.

tact, provoking them to breaches of the Ordinances, for which they at once bring them up [before magistrates]."[44]

One important cause of high prosecution rates was the elaborate penal provisions that facilitated quick recourse to magistrates for enforcement of discipline. The ordinances specified a remarkable number of punishable offenses, many of them not strictly related to work performance. The British Guiana and Trinidad ordinances contained five distinct penal offenses related to keeping dwellings clean, and six more under the hospital regulations. Social offenses (adultery, harboring or enticing wives, or threatening a wife) were also punishable with hefty fines and imprisonment, as was drunkenness.[45] A multiplicity of offenses bore more directly on the performance of work: refusal or neglect to amend work that the manager judged badly done; cheating on work; "wilful disobedience"; abusing or insulting persons in authority; damage to property through carelessness; inciting other laborers to stop work or stopping others from working. Another set dealt with absence and desertion, including compulsory residence on the estate and its corollary, arrest and imprisonment if found outside without ticket of leave by any police constable or the manager. Unlawful absence from work was punishable by imprisonment and endorsement on the indenture. Leaving the plantation to lay a complaint before the protector was allowed, unless it was to make a trivial complaint, or done in the company of five persons, or the worker carried an agricultural implement or weapon.

Detailed records of prosecutions for breach of the indenture laws are available only for the years 1909 to 1915. In Trinidad, as Table 14.3 shows, about half of the prosecutions of indentured workers were for desertion, vagrancy, or absence from estate without leave. Most of the rest involved work-related offenses on the estates. These were relatively evenly split between work-avoidance offenses (habitual idleness, absence from work without lawful excuse, or malingering) and direct defiance of authority (refusing to begin or finish work, refusal of lawful orders, using abusive and threatening language or gestures against managers or overseers, damaging or endangering estate property). Prosecutions for social offenses were far less numerous. In British Guiana fewer than 14 percent of the prosecutions were for desertion, while nearly two-thirds were for workplace offenses (other than habitual idleness).

44. W. H. Coombes to Governor of Trinidad, 29 Aug. 1910, Encl. no. 2 in Governor to Secy. Colonies, 1 May 1911, PRO CO 885/21.

45. (British Guiana) n.18 of 1891; (Trinidad and Tobago) n.19 of 1899. In addition, Indian immigrant laborers had a "criminal conversation" (adultery) action in damages against their wives' paramours.

TABLE 14.3.
Offenses by Immigrants, Trinidad and British Guiana

	Trinidad, 1909–12	British Guiana, 1912–15
Offenses committed off the estate	5,073	984
Desertion	2,517	713
Absence without leave	1,075	264
Vagrancy	1,481	—
Found without pass	—	7
Malingering and related offenses	2,650	3,390
Habitual idling	412	713
Absence from work	1,975	2,677[a]
Malingering	263	—
Insubordination and related offenses	2,710	716
Refusal to start or finish work	1,507	—
Refusal to obey, improper work	682	489
Dissuading others from working	71	—
Threats, gestures against overseers	367	227
Damaging employer's property	73	—
Drinking while at work	10	—
Social offenses	777	177
Hospital regulations	457	110
Domestic offenses	320	67
All other offenses	19	—
Total offenses	11,229	5,271

SOURCES: McNeill's Report for Trinidad; *ARIAG*, 1912–15, for British Guiana.
[a] Includes refusal to begin or finish work.

These data undermine the planters' contention that high prosecution rates resulted from the statutory requirement to prosecute for desertion. Similarly, records of imprisonment for British Guiana in 1873–81 show that only 20 percent of incarcerated indentured workers had been committed for desertion, while nearly three-quarters had been jailed for work avoidance or insubordination.[46]

Nevertheless, desertion remained a persistent problem in both colonies and seems to have increased over time, especially in the last two decades of the operation of the indenture system.[47] Deserters tended to be repeat

46. Calculated from *ARIAG*, 1881.

47. Laurence, *Question of Labour*, 150–51. The proportion of deserters in British Guiana to the total indentured population averaged 2.34 percent between 1875 and 1884, 2.7 percent in the next decade, and rose to 4.5 percent in the decade 1895–1904 and slightly less in the last decade of indenture. Calculated from *ARIAG* for relevant years.

offenders. Between 1908 and 1912, 40 percent of the more than 7,000 indentured laborers charged with desertion from ninety-eight Trinidad estates were prosecuted more than once.[48] Planters and officials regularly despaired at these "habitual offenders" who were not deterred by prison sentences.

If these high rates of prosecution signified the inability of the system to reproduce itself without recourse to legal coercion, they also demonstrated how pervasively workers resisted the system of compulsory labor. Resistance took other more overt forms, including strikes and violent attacks on plantation authorities, but these were relatively isolated and sporadic events in contrast to the steady stream of daily resistance evident in such widespread offenses as insolent behavior, insulting and threatening gestures, or damage to employer property. An experienced immigration agent in Trinidad described these "grossly provocative" insolent gestures:

> The most common is this: the immigrant, when ordered to do work that is not congenial, will point to, or hold his private parts and say in Hindustani, "This may do it; I won't" . . . [or] a man will hold his cutlass or his agricultural fork or hoe in a threatening manner and tell his manager or overseer that if he is compelled to do again what is not congenial to him, he will kill him as he can't "see him in the eyes" *i.e.* that there is no room above the ground for both of them.[49]

This semiotic of defiance and refusal opposed the crux of the system, the planter's need for complete control over a work force whose statutory wages were barely sufficient for survival. Bechu attributed the high rates of prosecution not to the innate laziness or incapacity of the workers but to their desperate attempts to resist the planters' drive to push wages below the point of starvation. In his analysis, this led to continuous struggle over tasks, scamping of work, and finally to acts of collective defiance that periodically broke out, only to be suppressed by the armed intervention of the state.[50]

From the planters' point of view, though, high prosecution rates reflected the "civilising" aspect of indenture. Only through the imposition of criminal sanctions could imported labor be taught the value of steady work, industrious habits, and the sanctity of contract. Missionaries waxed eloquent about the moral effect of indenture as late as 1910.[51] If the natural inclination of the

48. McNeill's Report, 25–26.

49. "Note of Emigration Agent of Trinidad A De Boissiere," in GOI Emigration, "A" Proc. no. 13–22, Nov. 1912.

50. Bechu wrote many letters to the press about indenture conditions. See in particular *Georgetown Daily Chronicle*, 10 Nov., 29 Dec. 1900.

51. For instance Reverend John Morton testified in 1909 that under indenture the worker is "restrained from influences until they know what the influences are." Sanderson Report, 2:338.

laborer was to dishonor the contract and "the only independence which they would desire is idleness" (as Trinidad governor Lord Harris put it in 1846), high rates of prosecution were both necessary and unavoidable. Until the very end of the indenture system, planters and officials in the West Indies colonies remained complacent about the prosecution rate. The criminalization of plantation labor had become institutionalized in the West Indies, where the planters imagined themselves as locked in a desperate struggle against malingerers, habitual idlers, absconders, and vagrants, compelled by the laborers' natural inclinations to use the law against them.

That law, weaving myriad prohibitions around the workplace, residence, hospitals, and the plantations, in its baroque regard for detail, was not only the result of this culture of criminalization but actively reinforced it. Planters and officials relied on punishment meted out by the magistrate as their main instrument for enforcing contracts and imposing labor discipline. Although it began in the anxiety of the colonial state to distance indenture from slavery and to restrain the planters' private authority, by the end of the nineteenth century the indenture laws had acquired their own raison d'être, an over-elaborate machinery that churned out what it was supposed to eradicate. This in turn stiffened worker resistance to the compulsory labor regimes, putting considerable strain on the system, raising the cost of supervision, requiring increased state support for the enforcement of discipline, and thereby providing grist for the mill of those opposed to indentured immigration.[52]

Enforcement in Assam

The relatively low prosecution rates in Assam corresponded to a much simpler legal code than in Trinidad or British Guiana. Where the West Indian labor laws contemplated twenty-five distinct classifications of offenses, Assam's specified just three. Workers could be imprisoned for fourteen days if they were absent from work for more than seven days. Desertion (not defined in law, but meaning more than seven days' absence from work and absence from the plantation) was punished with a fine and one month in prison for a first offense, and three months' imprisonment and a fine equivalent to twenty months' wages for repeated convictions. Habitual drunkenness at work was punishable by a week's imprisonment. Compared with the extravagances of

52. The main opponents of indentured immigration within the colony were the nascent creole workers' organization and the articulate creole middle class. These strongly opposed state subventions to a labor system that lowered the wages of free laborers and served only the planter interest. See the evidence of C. P. David in Sanderson Report, 1:219–25, and the association memoranda in the appendix, 15–22, 113–15.

the West Indian laws, this was legal minimalism. The Assam laws created no punishable offenses related to the actual performance of work. Moreover, between 1882 and 1908, no less than 95 percent of convictions in Assam were for desertion. Most of the remaining prosecutions were for enticing laborers to desert, directed against leaders of groups of workers who were arrested while attempting to leave the plantation.[53]

Low rates of prosecution and no performance offenses suggest that the indenture laws were relatively less important for labor discipline in Assam. This does not mean that the labor regime on the tea plantations was more relaxed. On the contrary, the labor regime in Assam was every bit as strict as that of the West Indies. The state may have been less involved in enforcing labor contracts, but the planters disciplined labor more actively. Assam's indenture laws privatized the enforcement of the labor contract.

The keystone of the penal contract system in Assam was the private power of arrest. When it was introduced in 1865, this power was intended to help planters combat desertions in a province where there were too few magistrates to enforce indentures, particularly in the remote parts. Some planters had already been independently detaining and capturing absconders.[54] This illegal form of labor control was legalized by granting planters the private power of arrest. The commissioner of Assam, comparing planters with a ship's master in high seas, had recommended they be given magisterial powers.[55] Under the 1865 legislation, anyone authorized by a planter could arrest a laborer indentured under the special labor legislation. Planters were allowed to arrest an absconder without warrant if found more than ten miles from the nearest magistrate.[56]

Revelations of horrible excesses of this authority, including severe corporal punishment, prompted some limitations on the right of private arrest in 1873.[57] In 1904 the commissioner of Assam was shocked to discover ferry

53. Calculated from the *Report on the Administration of Criminal Justice in Assam* for the years 1879–1922.

54. See Superintendent of Assam Tea Company to Commissioner of Assam, enclosure in Commissioner to Government of Bengal, 4 July 1864, GOI (Legislative Department) "A" Proc. no. 30–38, Nov. 1865, referring to the "organised establishment of Chaprassies and Barkandazes for the purpose of pursuing and capturing such of the company's coolies as absconders and as also for preventing coolies from absconding." In another enclosure, the deputy commissioner of Sibsagar district mentions the system of placing chowkidars on all ghats (river crossings) and roads leading to the district to catch runaways and the practice of paying them two rupees per head for runaways.

55. Letter of Commissioner of Assam to Secy., Government of Bengal, 6 Oct. 1864, in ibid.

56. The distance requirement was reduced, in the planters' interest, to five miles by (India) n.1 of 1882.

57. P. Griffiths, *Tea Industry*, 22. Several planters openly admitted that they flogged workers

masters, boatmen, and station masters in railway stations all exercising the power of arrest at the planters' behest.[58] The private power of arrest operated through an elaborate private machinery of watchdogs, watchmen, and informers. This apparatus was used not only to prevent "absconding" but also to regulate labor on the plantation by compelling laborers to work, or punishing short work and other breaches of contract. The private "Coolie catching" machinery of labor control obviated recourse to indenture law except when prosecuting deserters.[59] Many deserters were arrested and brought back to the plantation without being prosecuted and so never entered the statistics.[60]

Low prosecution rates were trumpeted as an index of satisfactory labor relations on the plantations. The privatization of enforcement blurred the limits of legality. Planters were forbidden to assault laborers on pain of severe fines and other punishments, but there were many such acts, probably only the worst cases emerging in the record of the late nineteenth century. The Colonial Office dismissed protests by the emergent nationalist intelligentsia against the planters' arbitrary exercise of power. The prevalent view within official circles was that "the tea planter as master of a large and irregular labour staff must enforce discipline by occasional severe measures which need not be looked into too closely, because these are substantially just and for the general good of the coolies."[61] As one deputy commissioner put it in responding to complaints about corporal punishment on the plantation, "As a rule the coolie is not caned unless he has committed some offence for which the punishment would be far more severe if he were tried and convicted before a court of law . . . and the coolie as a rule is not an undue sufferer from these illegal actions."[62]

---

to compel adherence to the contract; some suggested that they would cease to do so if the government took over the administration of corporal punishment. See letters of W. Stoddart, C. Eglinton, and A. R. Spier, managers of tea estates in Assam and Cachar, in P. Griffiths, *Tea Industry*, 45, 151, 152.

58. "Coolie is detained at every ferry he comes to; he can not obtain a ticket and I have lately discovered that the station masters are subsidized by the planters to arrest on suspicion in their interests. Managers exercise their power of arrest whether the coolie is under Act VI, under Act XIII or under no act at all." B. Fuller, Chief Commissioner of Assam to Governor General Curzon, 2 Sept. 1903, 4 Jan. 1904, Curzon Collection MSS Eur. F 111/204, India Office Library (hereafter IOL).

59. "At the present time if we were to send every coolie that ought to be punished before a magistrate, about one third of our coolies would be in court daily as complainants, prisoners and witnesses" — planter C. A. Alexander to Deputy Commissioner Cachar in P. Griffiths, *Tea Industry*, 148.

60. Assam Special Report, para. 238–39.

61. Note of the Governor of Bengal, para. 4 in GOI, Emigration Department, "B" Proc. no. 1–3, Sept. 1893, NAI.

62. Assam Special Report, para. 239.

Many managers admitted that flogging was common, and in 1894 a delegation of tribal headmen from the recruiting districts witnessed the flogging of a young woman for wrongly plucking four leaves instead of three in her baskets.[63] Another official wrote that the laborers themselves exaggerated when they designated every form of "punishment however mild and done for coolies good" as *phatak* (literally meaning confinement or jail).[64] Laborers used the term to designate the punishment as well as the penal contract system as a whole. The power of private arrest was applied not only to new recruits under the indenture legislation but was used as well against workers contracted under the 1859 act and those whose time had expired, giving planters the power to immobilize practically the whole labor force.[65]

Thus the limited recourse to the magistrates for enforcement of the contract in Assam was a direct consequence of the provisions that allowed private arrest without warrant. The main effect of the penal contract legislation was to suppress wage levels. It also enabled the extremely unhealthy gardens to retain their work force, in effect increasing the mortality rates as laborers were prevented from fleeing. Elsewhere I have argued that the indenture system and penal contract legislation were substantially transformed between 1901 and 1908 when the high cost of cheap labor plunged the industry into an acute crisis of overproduction and declining profits. The colonial state considered penal contract and the private power of arrest to be responsible for the high cost of recruitment and low natural reproduction of the labor force. The system had ensured low wages, but the exploitation of the labor force resulted in high mortality and resistance in the form of desertion and, increasingly, violent protests, riots, and disturbances.[66] Assam's penal contract system was gradually dismantled over the next two decades and was completely repealed in 1915. The 1859 breaches-of-contract act, amended in 1920, remained in force until 1926.[67]

The planters resisted the dismantling of the penal contract system, arguing that tea could not be produced without it and that its abolition would ruin the industry. After 1908, most planters placed their laborers (both new recruits and those whose terms had expired) on three-year contracts under the 1859 act. They lobbied for a local enticement act to punish those who enticed or harbored absconding laborers while returning the runaway to the garden

63. *Papers,* and "Note of the Santhal Headmen on their visit to Assam," in GOI Emig. "B" Proc. no. 3, Sept. 1893.

64. D. C. of Lakhimpur in Assam Special Report, para. 240.

65. Fuller to Governor General, in GOI Emig. "A" Proc. no. 12–14, Dec. 1904.

66. Behal and Mohapatra, "Tea," 156–58, 168–70.

67. (India) n.8 of 1915; (India) n.13 of 1859; (India) n.12 of 1920; (India) n.3 of 1925.

from which he or she had escaped. Its object was to bind the laborer to the employer in the same manner as the special legislation. The secretary of state rejected the bill—the first time that London disallowed an Indian bill.[68] The planters fought to retain the 1859 act even after a massive uprising in 1921 resulted in a huge exodus of laborers from Chargola in Assam.[69]

The planters argued that the penal contract system was essential not only for tea but also for the health and the moral well-being of the laborers. It taught them cleanliness and hygiene; it counteracted the "frequent desire for change," which labor market conditions promoted; it kept them "from the clutches of money lenders."[70] But their major justification for retaining some form of penal contract was that it taught laborers the value of making and obeying contracts. Planters denied that the penal contract imposed any hardship on the laborers. Actual recourse to its provisions was minimal, as low rates of prosecution proved. The penal contract worked, they argued, not by physical compulsion or enforcement but by its symbolic power or moral effect. "I like Act XIII," one plantation superintendent told an official enquiry; "I know it is not very binding but the coolie seems to have an idea that by touching the pen he has to carry out his part of the agreements when he takes money."[71] In responding to the labor committee's queries, another manager maintained that the 1859 act was "more or less a shadow":

A: It is only the power behind that shadow that make it worth having at all.

Q: What is the power behind the shadow?

A: The mere fact that they make an agreement.

Q: Do you mean putting the thumb impression?

A: It amounts to that. Morally he has given his word that he would stay on the garden for the three years.

Q: Was this explained to him?

A: I do not know.[72]

What was the power behind the shadow? One district officer maintained that the successful use of Act 13 of 1859 was directly attributable to widespread private arrests under Act 6 of 1865:

---

68. For tea industry lobbying, see the voluminous correspondence of the Indian Tea Association in IOL ITA Papers Eur/Mss/174/1017 (IOL). The enticement bill and its rejection by the secretary of state is to be found in the file IOL "Assam Labour Enticement Bill" L\E\7\903.

69. *Report of the Assam Labour Enquiry Committee, 1921–22* (hereafter *ALE*).

70. Evidence of L. Church and W. Nicholls, *ALE* Proc. VI, 18.

71. *ALE*, 44.

72. Evidence of D. Simmon, Supt. Jorahat Tea Company, *ALE*, 185.

The Coolie is utterly ignorant of the distinctions between the Act VI and Act XIII. He merely knows that he has executed an agreement for a year or two and received bonus which is usually the same in either case. The stamped paper in his eyes is the same. It is the existence of Act VI and the fact that the coolie sees his fellow labourers sent to jail for desertion and refusal to work that enables the planter to work Act XIII successfully.[73]

The power behind the shadow of Act 13 was nothing but the private power of arrest in Act 6. The moral effect of penal legislation was argued before the 1906 Assam Labour Enquiry Committee by virtually all the planters as well as many provincial officials. The committee, concerned with the extreme unpopularity of Assam in the recruiting districts, refuted the planters' position and recommended the abolition of private arrest:

[I]t is urged that the sections (195 and 196) authorising private arrest have a moral effect on the labour force which enables the planter to keep his labour on the garden. . . . But the "moral effect" which seems so valuable to employers is understood in recruiting districts. It is known that Assam is a country where labour is not free and where the employer is more powerful than elsewhere and the knowledge is one of the factors of the distaste of the country which is so marked. The more importance the employers attach to the "moral effect" of these sections, the more important it is that the section should be withdrawn, because it is evidence that they are *really* effective and their effect is to perpetuate a state of affairs which so long as it lasts will render a free flow of labour to Assam impossible.[74]

That private arrest continued long after its repeal in 1908 was well known to the colonial officials and of course to the laborers as well. Many planters did not think it was illegal to "persuade" their laborers to return. The Assam Labour Enquiry Committee found in 1921 that the shadow of Act 6 lingered on in Act 13, that illegal arrests of absconders continued. As late as 1930 the Royal Commission on Labour in India could see visible traces of the penal contract system on the backs of a few flogged laborers. Contract-making practices had changed. Instead of a signed agreement paper laborers were now asked to affix their thumb mark in a "bonus book." Many laborers told the Royal Commission that taking *girmit* money rendered them liable

73. (India) n.13 of 1859; (Bengal) n.6 of 1865. Deputy commissioner of Sibsagar in Assam Special Report, 154.
74. *ALE*, 1906, 106.

to be detained. The penal legislation may have been abolished, but the huge unrelenting apparatus of surveillance and detention, carefully crafted since 1860, remained.[75] So did labor resistance, reflected in high rates of desertion throughout the period, and in violent conflicts that broke out every year between the planters and the coolies. Assam had the most such conflicts of all the Asian plantation systems.

The penal contract systems of the West Indies and Assam differed in the elaboration of their penal provisions and in the agencies of enforcement. One depended overwhelmingly on state administration of penal law, while the other relied on private enforcement. In both systems, breaches of contract were caused largely by the operation of the law designed to prevent them. In both systems the "recalcitrance" of labor remained the major problem; desertion and breaches of contracts could not be stopped, nor could the labor force be completely pacified.

75. See evidence of laborers Shamkumar, Chuttan, Khudiram, and others in *Report of the Royal Commission on Labour in India* (London: H.M.S.O., 1931) Evidence 6: 63, 116–18, 154. For the practice of managers taking "agreement," see pp. 69, 71, 75, 154.

FIFTEEN

West Africa, 1874-1948

Employment Legislation in a Nonsettler Peasant Economy

Richard Rathbone

Misleading generalizations have dominated popular perceptions of Africa, but specialists have long recognized that the peoples of so massive and varied a continent cannot have had a single common history. Africa's precolonial regions were diverse and distinct. Although in the colonial period there was a greater convergence of experience through agencies of imposed change and the patchy insinuations of what we call (but seldom explicate) modernization, the distinctions remained significant; one of the reasons for this was the imbrication of precolonial realities in the processes of colonialism and modernization. While these interactions of precolonial histories and the particularities of colonial rule produced distinctive colonial and postcolonial states, the differences between settler and nonsettler states arguably provide the most significant comparative taxonomy for generalizing recent African history. Put very crudely, areas in which there was a significant white settler presence, or where the export economy rested in large measure on mineral extraction, were strikingly different in almost every respect from those areas of Africa in which national income and individual accumulation depended, as they did in West Africa, on peasant production.[1]

Somewhat ironically West Africa, having borne the brunt of the Atlantic slave trade, almost everywhere escaped white settlement for a variety of reasons.[2] In the British-ruled sections of this region[3] most whites and those

---

1. In this region, most notably reliant upon cocoa, palm oil, and oil seed production.

2. In a rare moment of whimsy, Kwame Nkrumah advocated the erection of a statue of a mosquito in Accra to honor one of the major causes of European disinclination to settle in the region.

3. The Gambia, the Gold Coast, Nigeria, and Sierra Leone.

others frequently categorized as "non-natives" in colonial censuses, were almost invariably officials, teachers, or *commerçants* and hence birds of passage rather than permanent residents or landowners.[4] Where "non-natives" did represent the interests of either mining or commerce, their influence on policy appears to have been slight,[5] and certainly it weakened very considerably in the last twenty-five years of colonial rule.[6] Compared with the impact of settlers and of mining interests on policy generally and on labor legislation in particular in East and Central Africa,[7] those whites classified as being outside the very limited numbers of those involved in the immediate work of administration in West Africa were relatively uninfluential.[8]

But the mirror image rather than an exact explanation of this is the relatively slight inputs of capital investment in nonsettler states even if the actual figures are hard to extract with confidence. Although total investment in the cluster of mining opportunities can look impressively large on paper, only a very small proportion of overall nominal capital ever found its way to the colonies in the form of actual investment and local spending.[9] Looking at capital more broadly also makes clear that a particularly high proportion of overall expenditure was dedicated to bursts of railway construction.[10] Between a third and a quarter of all capital investment in Africa up to the Second World War was devoted to railway building.[11] Taken together, these data

4. This is apparent in census data even if these are an imprecise guide. In 1935–36 there were about 9,000 Europeans in the four British West African territories whose combined populations were about 24.5 million. Comparable figures for the three British East African territories give a rough ratio of 28,500 whites to an African population of just under 12 million.

5. Part of the context of this was refusal of colonial governments to grant William Lever land for palm oil plantations in Nigeria and Sierra Leone. Such concessions and plantations themselves were held to be contrary to the ideal of "trusteeship." Similarly, the Colonial Office resisted the clamor of mining concerns to replicate the South African style of labor control, including compounds, in West Africa.

6. See Fieldhouse, *Merchant Capital*, and for further evidence, Stockwell, *Business of Decolonization*.

7. As well as in Algeria and even more obviously South Africa. For a contrasting case, see D. Anderson, "Master and Servant," and his chapter in this volume.

8. This did not stop them trying in the early years and they had some successes. In the Gold Coast, the Chamber of Mines prevailed upon government to use its Transport Department for labor recruitment in 1910. District Officers in the Gold Coast's Northern Territories certainly intervened in labor recruitment. But worrying evidence of the high en route mortality of migrants led to an order by the secretary of state for the colonies in 1924 forbidding future assistance. See *House of Commons Debates*, 23 June 1924, vol. CLXXV, c.8.

9. Even the combined nominal figures for mining investment in the Gold Coast, Nigeria, and Sierra Leone look puny in comparison with the extensive flows to South Africa and the Rhodesias.

10. The figures are from Frankel's still valuable *Capital Investment in Africa*.

11. In turn, something close to 75 percent of all government loans in British African territories were raised for railway construction.

accurately suggest minimal industrialization outside the borders of the Union of South Africa.[12] In turn this implied a small industrial wage-labor force in proportion to overall populations and, so far as British West Africa was concerned, episodic and reactive rather than linear or exponential patterns of labor demand.

By the end of the interwar period fewer than 200,000[13] Africans in these West African British territories were employed by European concerns. That estimate includes just under 90,000 employed in mining and about 20,000 employed on the railways. The admittedly shaky estimates of the overall numbers of wage labor, which include artisans, petty traders, and those employed by the usually small African, Lebanese, and Syrian trading concerns, provide a figure of under 500,000 direct wage earners out of a global population of the four territories of about 25 million.

Different colonial systems were shaped by the interaction of precolonial verities[14] and the frequently ill-judged (and no less often frustrated) intentions of the new European rulers. Outside West Africa and especially where colonial governments came to be politically dominated by settlers, colonial states began to exhibit a number of basic similarities irrespective of the nationality of the colonial metropole. The common feature of states as superficially dissimilar as Angola, Algeria, Kenya, and Southern Rhodesia seems to have been the centrality of concerns about the supply of relatively cheap manual labor.[15] These states shared two major elements of colonial policy: direct taxation and land reservation. The levying of direct taxes was intended not merely to provide state revenue but also to force Africans to earn cash incomes to pay the taxes. Land reservation redirected Africans away from rural self-employment and the cash sale of any agricultural surplus or craft products manufactured during "slow" periods in the agricultural cycle and toward wage labor.

While not entirely missing from British West Africa, neither policy was of great significance there.[16] By the 1930s direct taxation by central govern-

12. A point made vigorously in Havinden and Meredith, *Colonialism and Development*.

13. These numbers (like many colonial statistics before the late 1940s) are inexact and should be regarded as approximations. That they were collected unscientifically and haphazardly is clear in the incompatibility between official sources like censuses, *Annual Reports*, and *Blue Books*.

14. Including sharply differentiated factor endowment and demography, stressed throughout in Iliffe, *Africans*.

15. The argument about whether such colonial labor was in fact "cheap" or expensive was probably initiated in Orde Browne, *African Labourer*, 31. The ascent or descent into linguistic philosophy in recent discussions of the issue leads me to use the qualifier "relatively" for safety's sake.

16. The virtual absence of pass laws is another significant dissimilarity, although (Sierra

ments in British West Africa was a comparatively slight burden. In the Gold Coast its application to Africans was successfully resisted until 1943 and most inefficiently collected thereafter. Although poll tax was levied in 1856, it was never seriously collected: the Poll Tax Ordinance was formally repealed in 1866.[17] In Nigeria direct taxes[18] of varying kinds in each of the state's constituent provinces yielded about 18 percent of overall government revenue; the average burden upon adult Africans was nine pence per annum. In the Gambia, where it provided just over 6 percent of revenue, Africans, again on average, paid seventeen pence per year.[19] In Sierra Leone[20] just over 19 percent of revenue derived from direct tax but the burden on Africans was less than eleven pence per annum.[21]

Also, land reservation was relatively rare. Where it occurred, as it did in the Gold Coasts Concessions Ordinance of 1900, for example,[22] it was mostly driven by concerns about hardwood forest conservation in the face of over-energetic felling during logging booms and the control of ruthless concession hunting in potentially auriferous or diamondiferous areas. It is fair even if unfashionable to conclude that in these areas, and for most of the colonial period, most Africans were not driven to wage employment by the manipulation of successfully orchestrated labor policies.[23] No less important, through-

Leone) Laws (Part VII) c.170 (1924) stipulated that Protectorate "natives" could not leave their chiefdoms without the permission of the chief. This was widely ignored. By contrast, in French Equatorial Africa (and Madagascar) workers were obliged to carry *livrets de travail* and in French West Africa *livrets d'identité*, which combined current and past contracts and identity documents.

17. Attempts were made to levy income tax, but these, like many other intended colonial policies, were frustrated by fervent and very successful African middle-class opposition campaigns.

18. Extension of the Native Revenue Ordinance in 1927 provides a partial explanation of the "Aba riots" in 1929 when the first attempts to collect this tax were made in the southeast: (Nigeria) n.17 of 1927.

19. A "yard tax" of five shillings per yard of up to four huts.

20. The imposition of Hut Tax in 1896 led to violent resistance in 1898, usually known as the "Hut Tax War." A more limited house tax of five shillings per household was substituted and was collected at that rate for about forty years.

21. Compare this with Kenya where the figures suggest nearly a third of revenue came from direct tax with Africans paying three shillings, six pence per annum or Southern Rhodesia where over 33 percent of revenue rested on direct tax and Africans paid over six shillings per year.

22. Until the postindependence government vested mineral rights in the state, there was no major challenge to the notion that land rights lay with local communities. The much later discovery of mining opportunities in Sierra Leone in 1926 led to the passage of (Sierra Leone) n.36 of 1927, which gave control over mining rights to the crown. Its major impact fell upon Kono District. But there were (so far as I can see) no large-scale evictions.

23. But, of course, some were, especially where the immediate interests of government were concerned. For example, for a brief period, the Nigerian government used chiefs, agents of

out the colonial period and beyond, wage earners formed a minority of the adult, economically active population in these states. Given the reliance of the state upon the revenue generated by rural production and rural production's reliance upon labor,[24] governments' apparent lack of interest in facilitating labor's role is striking. Only in the course of the two world wars is there hard evidence of local administrative concern with the seduction, by alternative and better employment opportunities, of available labor away from agriculture; and that was by no means general in all parts of the region.

Wage earners were, rather, impelled by factors that often derived from the region's long history of combined but decidedly uneven development resulting from starkly differentiated factor endowment[25] and very varied microclimates and ecologies.[26] Manual wage labor in the region's mines and even in the almost exclusively African-owned cash crop enterprises[27] was disproportionately drawn from areas of comparative and often dreadful seasonal, cyclical, or endemic poverty. With some exceptions like the tin mines of Nigeria[28] and the diamond[29] and hematite industries of Sierra Leone, much labor was undertaken by long-distance migrants driven by the whip of hunger and the absence of local alternatives.[30] Obviously such workers had often to endure painful extended separations from family, arduous travel, and frequently unpleasant, poorly paid, and sometimes health-threatening work.[31] Some of this migration involved considerable travel on foot, across borders that were distinctly permeable except in wartime. In Nigeria and especially in the Gold Coast, many migrant workers in farming as well as in industry[32] were drawn from the poorer French territories that surrounded them.[33]

---

colonial rule, for labor recruitment for the government-owned coal mines at Enugu when the labor supply was tight.

24. Despite the mythology, only some of this could be properly described as family labor.

25. And no less important, proximity to coasts, ports, and prime cities.

26. The area ranges from the very poorly watered Sahelian fringes to the rain-rich remnants of the tropical rain forest.

27. Plantations were very few in number and small in size. The Rose's Lime Juice citrus plantation of the southern Gold Coast was perhaps the most extensive but during its short life employed very few workers.

28. Admirably described in Freund, *Capital and Labour*.

29. By 1937 the Sierra Leone diamond industry's labor force consisted of 59 percent Kono and 25 percent Mende workers from the locality.

30. The impact of periodic drought in sub-Sahelian areas is very apparent on the size and composition of the manual labor market throughout the region over time.

31. See, for example, *Gold Coast Government Report to Medical and Sanitary Department* (Accra, 1924).

32. And, intriguingly, in the colonies' armed forces too.

33. For the suggestion that push-factors included the comparatively lighter tax regimes of the British colonies compared with the heavy dependence upon direct taxation and prestation

This was not a static picture. So far as the Gold Coast is concerned, the best data come from the mining sector. In 1911 something close to three-quarters of mine labor came from the Gold Coast. By 1921 that figure had fallen to well under 60 percent and the bulk of these workers were to be found in the better paid and physically safer surface occupations. Local labor was not being undercut by less demanding, poorer migrants; instead, it was increasingly engaged in more lucrative, less life-threatening, and of course more proximate cash-crop production, especially cocoa.

A system of government as well as an economy that rested on indirect taxation and significant interregional and intercolonial labor migration speaks volumes about the comparative success and the domination of the peasant-led economies of these territories.[34] Those who were obliged or, more rarely, wished to rely upon wage labor were relatively few in number.[35] The reasons for this are obvious enough. Until the mid-twentieth century, these remained thinly populated regions even if their density was far greater than in the French West African territories.[36] The most notable economic opportunities throughout the period following the abolition of the Atlantic slave trade by the British in 1807 had occurred in the agricultural domain; even in the depressed interwar years there was still a niche for those with access to and rights over land and especially for those who could also command family labor or the capital for wage labor[37] to clear bush for new farms. Despite, and

by the French, see Asiwaju, *Northern Yorubaland*. Burkinabe and Nigeriennes also migrated into richer French colonies like Côte d'Ivoire for work on farms, the docks, and harbors. These are the stars of Jean Rouch's magical film *Moi, un noire*.

34. Most indirect taxation was levied on imports and exports at the ports of entry or exit. The absolute value of this "take" tended to rise other than at the height of the Depression. There is no doubt that peasant production adapted wonderfully to the exigencies of the export market. The contribution of the mineral sector to the total export basket was seldom more than about 25 percent.

35. If one uses the recovery year of 1936 as a datum, the following very sketchy figures emerge. The Gambia had an estimated population of 200,000. The Gold Coast, with a population of 3.2 million, had 135,000 wage earners, of whom fewer than 25,000 worked in the mines. Nigeria had 227,000 wage earners in a total population of 19 million, while Sierra Leone had 9,500 miners in a population of less than 2 million. Compare this with figures from colonies to the east and south: Kenya, with a population of 3.1 million, had about 200,000 wage earners; S. Rhodesia, population 1.3 million, had 225,000 wage earners (including inward migrants); Nyasaland, population 1.6 million, had 120,000 wage earners (including migrants working in the Union or Southern Rhodesia).

36. A brief glance at any vintage atlas confirms that the spatial extent of the French territories was far greater than the four British territories. But in the laconic words of the film-maker-novelist Ousmane Sembene, a good deal of the French territory was *beaucoup de sable*.

37. Or labor which share-farmed. This was and is common in Akan cocoa-growing areas where it is called *abusa*. Many farmers gained access to long-term usufructs in this manner.

perhaps because of, the depression in farm-gate prices which began as early as 1922 in the area, more and more land fell under cultivation.[38]

The counterattractions to urban or mine labor were accordingly to be found in the rural sector. It was no coincidence that in 1917, gold exports from the Gold Coast stood at nearly 450,000 ounces and cocoa exports at 91,000 tons; by 1927 gold exports had fallen to under 200,000 ounces and those of cocoa had risen to over 200,000 tons.[39] To this one must add the growth in private trading and small-scale service industries.[40] As early as 1931 something like 15 percent of southern Nigerians classified themselves as traders or craftsmen and this proportion was to increase.[41] In 1921 the number of those who classified themselves as clerical workers in the Gold Coast was nearly double the number of those employed at the mines.

Labor and Its Regulation

In many parts of the region, tribute labor had been extracted by traditional leaders before the colonial era. Although we know far too little about precolonial economic history, it seems that in some cases this had probably been not much more oppressive than the reciprocal and sometimes informal, local cooperation of neighbors and kinsfolk.[42] In others it had been part of more extensive and complex systems of control, taxation, and slavery.[43] In the colonial period much of the British-controlled part of the region was administered by varying systems of what came to be called "indirect rule," rule through chiefs. In the period before chiefs were given government salaries,[44] it is clear that many collected local tax in the form of labor as well as tribute in kind.[45]

38. Many farmers survived falling prices by increasing their acreages and yields. Nonetheless very considerable misery was an everyday rural experience in the period 1925–35.

39. It was estimated that at the height of the 1919–20 cocoa boom, carriers carrying cocoa to markets and railheads could sometimes earn between ten and fifteen shillings a day. Underground mine work, much hated for obvious reasons, paid significantly less than this. Only by 1937 did the top day-rate for the most skilled tradesmen on the mines in the Gold Coast reach ten shillings a day.

40. The transport revolution and especially the ubiquity of the Ford truck gave particular prominence to those with the flair to practice "make do and mend" engineering, for example.

41. Many traders were, of course, selling their and their family's agricultural surplus.

42. The two linkages are not exclusive; neighbors were more often than not obliged to co-operate in this fashion because of the ties of kinship.

43. We know enough about the precolonial history of Asante to be able to say that its gold-mining industry could be regarded as a good exemplar of a premodern command economy. See Wilks, *Asante*, and Wilks, "Land, Labour and Capital."

44. Recognized chiefs were almost universally paid salaries by the 1930s, although most complained, often with good reason, that these were insufficient.

45. And by using fines, licensing fees, and other imposts collected in their native authority

Following the Geneva Convention on forced labor (1930),[46] local legislation came to specify the limits of such exactions. In Sierra Leone, the Forced Labour Ordinance of 1932 contains detailed provisions defining what "personal services" recognized chiefs might call upon. The same is true of the Ashanti Labour Ordinance and the Gold Coast Territories Labour Ordinances of 1935, the Gambian Forced Labour Ordinance of 1934, and the Nigerian Forced Labour Ordinance of 1933.[47]

The colonial state's use of forced labor and its equivalents in these territories is much less marked than it was in many other parts of Africa.[48] This provides perhaps another element in the more general argument about these territories' comparative economic well-being.[49] There was, however, a history of the exploitation of forced labor for large capital works[50] and, more regularly, for maintaining the increasingly important road systems as well as during wartime.[51] As already suggested, the Geneva Convention had initiated some reforms but its numerous exceptions and generally permissive tone[52] allowed the retention of selective areas of forced labor. The Nigerian Ordinance of 1933 prohibited all forced labor as defined in the convention other than for somewhat vaguely specified "transport purposes"[53] or when such labor could be described as legitimate "personal services" for chiefs. At the same time, however, the Native Authority Ordinance allowed these indirect

---

courts. The oppressive use of these powers was an argument advanced for the formal payment of chiefly salaries.

46. The convention allowed chiefs with administrative responsibilities and who were not adequately paid to enjoy "personal services." While it sought the eventual ending of all forced labor, it commended the use of communal labor for the public good. This amounted to a significant weakening of its general definition of forced labor as all work or services, extracted from any person under the menace of penalty and for which the individual had not offered himself voluntarily.

47. (Gold Coast) n.32 and n.33 of 1935; (Gambia) n.8 of 1934. Interestingly chiefs were forbidden from extracting labor in these ways in Kenya and Tanganyika and, for reasons about which I am less clear, in the Gambia, too.

48. But in the Northern Territories of the Gold Coast before 1932 Africans had been obliged to provide unpaid labor on roadworks in lieu of part of the local tax burden.

49. In nonsettler territories such as the more arid areas of French West Africa, the imposition of a labor tax tells us a great deal about a region's relative poverty.

50. A Nigerian example was the Baro-Kano and Eastern Railways. Labor was provided by the use of "political" labor. A contingent of laborers was provided for the purpose by each province. An attempt to substitute voluntary labor in 1924 failed and "political labor" was again resorted to. See *Report* by W. G. A. Ormsby Gore on his visit to West Africa, Cmd. 2744 (1926), 133.

51. See R. Thomas, "Forced Labor."

52. The result of shrewd, cynical, and successful lobbying by the colonial powers.

53. This seems largely to have concerned requisitioned head-porterage for the extensive baggage of officials "on trek."

rule bodies to requisition labor for "public purposes" and for any other purpose approved by the governor.[54]

In the Gold Coast, forced labor was regulated in Ashanti and the Northern Territories by the two ordinances mentioned and by the Gold Coast Colony Labour Ordinance of 1935.[55] Under these, provincial commissioners could "require" native authorities, local traditional rulers and their councils, to maintain their roads and to comply with the health and sanitation regulations spelled out in legislation such as the ubiquitous Towns Ordinances.[56] Under this heading, able-bodied men were annually liable for up twenty-four days of such work (outside harvest seasons) at the prevailing local day rate.[57]

In Sierra Leone, the Forced Labour Ordinance of 1932 regulated chiefs' rights to labor. Laborers used by chiefs in personal or public services could be employed for no more than thirty days per year.[58] Personal services could be commuted for cash, and payment could be made in harvest share. By the 1930s, however, forced labor was in temporary retreat. To credit either the Geneva Convention or progressive colonial policy with this would ignore the imperatives of the labor market: during the Depression, impoverished "voluntary" labor was far more easily recruited from a large, needy labor pool. The return to forced labor—for example, in the Nigerian tin mining industry in 1942—accompanied a resurgence of cash crop prices, which reinforced the considerable attractions of rural wage labor and bush clearing for new farms for the best part of a generation.[59]

It is frequently claimed that government was, throughout the colonial period, the single largest employer of labor. Teasing out the numbers to substantiate that proves to be a difficult project. Many of those employed as manual, "blue-collar" workers by government were casually and occasionally employed by the day and hence are seldom to be found in annual statistics. For those at higher wage levels, the census data until the 1940s are open to many criticisms. For our purposes, the notable imprecision of occupational descriptions is a particular problem. But again for the Gold Coast the proportions

54. The key point here is surely that government put the onus of works and hence recruitment on to the shoulders of chiefs. Orde Browne was almost certainly correct in saying that "forced labour is . . . intensely unpopular with all administrative officers." *African Labourer*, 40.

55. (Gold Coast) n.21 of 1935.

56. This included antimalarial work, some of which was epidemiologically absurd, the digging of public latrines and collection of night-soil and garbage. The burden of enforcement in this and many other ordinances fell upon chiefs. Failing regular inspections resulted in communal punishments, in effect.

57. These rates were regularly gazetted and, I am told, widely known.

58. Especially work on the farms of chiefs.

59. Freund, *Capital and Labour*, ch. 5.

become a little clearer. In 1921 close to 80 percent of those employed as artisans and laborers by the Railways and Public Works Departments alone amounted to just below 10,000 men; the mining industries at the same time employed less than 8,000. White-collar employment in the government service increased throughout the colonial period. In the Gold Coast, these clerical grades, a work force of nearly 800 employees in the early data, had swelled to nearly 5,000 by 1931 and to over 6,000 by 1948.

In the absence of industry beyond the very limited mining sectors, it is logical that government should have been the largest employer. But British West African colonial governments were slow to create specific labor departments.[60] The first came into being in the Gold Coast in 1938. Nigeria's Labour Department was not to operate before 1942. When they were created, their functions were to be many and various; they were, for example, to play a major role in attempting to ensure that nascent, sometimes militant, and, by the 1940s, legally recognized labor organizations concerned themselves with economistic "wages and conditions" issues rather than with radical nationalist politics. In wartime unions were called upon to prevent vital work being interrupted by "wild-cat" strikes and walkouts[61] and to create what government would regard as orderly wage and condition bargaining mechanisms.[62] But as regulators of employers as well as employees, they were to be among the major irritants of expatriate companies in a period of encroaching state regulation.[63]

The picture is therefore one that contrasts very considerably with East, Central, and South Africa. Wage labor constituted throughout all but the very late colonial period a relatively and absolutely small element in the overall work force. The vast majority of workers remained in agriculture or agriculturally related occupations. Until late in the colonial period, the contribution of anything that might conceivably be classified as "industry" to export revenue was consistently dwarfed by that of agricultural commodities.[64] What

60. This emerged from a dispatch from the secretary of state, W. Ormsby Gore, in July 1937, which resolved to make what W. M. Macmillan described at the time as "benevolent plans" leading to the growth of wage boards, conciliation, workman's compensation, and trade unions. See Meek et al., *Europe and West Africa*. Labor departments had, suggestively, much longer histories in East and Central Africa.

61. West African colonial governments had, in Macmillan's opinion, an "exaggerated dread of strikes." That was particularly notable in wartime. The anxiety went all the way to 10 Downing Street: see my *Ghana*, 1:xxi n. 16, for example.

62. Colonial governments in the region were encouraging the formation of labor unions by the late 1930s. The intention was largely the creation of abiding wage agreements, worker education, and the establishing of clear contact points among labor.

63. See, for example, Fieldhouse, *Merchant Capital*.

64. This somewhat altered in the case of gold after Britain left the gold standard.

then explains the battery of legislation that dealt with labor in these colonies? No less important, how was the legislation used and with what regularity? Some of it undoubtedly reached the statute book because of the enormous complexity of handling slave populations freed under the emancipation ordinances that almost everywhere accompanied the formal imposition of colonial rule in West Africa. For a variety of reasons, the earliest pretensions to emancipation in West Africa, and most especially in Nigeria,[65] initially abolished the legal status of slavery while neither actually abolishing slavery nor emancipating slaves.[66] In the settlement following the conquest of Northern Nigeria in the first decade of the nineteenth century, the British evolved a compact with the old rulers of the area, who were major slave owners. This involved recognizing much of the authority of the precolonial Shari'a courts of the region.[67]

The economy of the region hung vitally upon slave production, especially of cotton. Consequently, the emancipation of slaves was a "jerky" process[68] whereby slavery survived for decades in a variety of modified forms. While colonial intervention justified itself with antislavery sloganeering, colonial policy actually sought to protect the local economy and hence the slave masters from the collapse that might have been produced by rapid, root-and-branch emancipation. The transition from slavery to wage labor was viewed as a gradual, largely organic process. This was recognized in 1905 when Lugard wrote that "had the Government not taken steps to discourage the too rapid transition from the old to a better labour contract, a complete dislocation of the social conditions of the country might . . . have taken place."[69]

The "better labour contract" to which Lugard referred included the Nigerian Master and Servant Proclamation of September, 1902, which distinguished between paid servants and domestic slaves.[70] But the burden of gov-

---

65. Where the huge extent of slavery—"one of the largest slave societies in modern history," according to Lovejoy and Hogendorn, *Slow Death*, xiii—presented particular problems. According to them, the Sokoto Caliphate alone had between 1 and 2.5 million slaves in its population by the end of the nineteenth century.

66. See ibid.

67. Which, under the developing system of indirect rule, retained the right to regulate domestic slavery.

68. In the words of Lovejoy and Hogendorn, *Slow Death*, 7.

69. *Northern Nigeria Annual Report*, 1905–6, 409, quoted in Lovejoy and Hogendorn, *Slow Death*, 62.

70. The proclamation had the force of law. Much of the rest of the emerging labor code in Nigeria (Proclamation no. 3 of 1901, the ordinance to regulate and control the recruiting of native labor for foreign service of 1913, and the similarly named ordinance of 1916, for example) appear to be measures to regulate and police the recruitment of Nigerians to work on the plantations of Principe and São Thomé.

ernment—and slave owners'—concern was the problem of the large-scale movement of ex-slaves, or at least slaves whose legal status was no longer that, senso strictu, of slaves. To control this "problem" the colonial government pressed into service a vagrancy law, which became part of the Northern Nigerian Criminal Code in 1904.[71] Far more significant was the maintenance of the Shari'a courts' control over individual cases and the colonial government's continuing faith in gradual transition. The policy essentially aimed at keeping slaves in place while their status changed from unfree to free labor. In that process few slaves had sufficient capital or earning power to do other than remain, at best, clients of their masters and, at worst, slaves in all but name.

More of the region's early legislation undoubtedly sought to bridge the huge gap between European and African expectations and legal norms. It is a commonplace observation in the historiography of nineteenth-century West Africa that the absence of mutually agreed notions of contract, debt recovery, and liability was a constant source of friction and a restraint of trade. More specifically, the very limited amount of "modern" employment in the course of the starkly pre-industrial nineteenth century was conducted in a rapidly changing universe still dominated in large measure by "domestic slavery" and customary obligations to traditional hierarchy. There was some concern to create a body of legislation that mirrored what were seen as desirable controls on labor. Masters and servants legislation was first passed, for example, in the Gold Coast three years after the annexation of the colony in 1874 and the abolition of slavery there in the same year.[72] It was not occasioned by labor shortage: forced recruitment and long service contracts were rarities in these territories.[73] It was instead intended to erode slavery by compelling "masters" to forgo ideas of "ownership" of labor in favor of contract. Under this law, employers could not use the courts to recall "deserters" without proof of contract.

There were prosecutions under these ordinances. There is, however, little uniformity in the data across British West Africa. Employers and employees in Nigeria appear to have made very little use of the legislation. The number of summonses in both the Southern and Northern Nigerian jurisdictions appears to have been consistently in single digits by the twentieth century. By the 1920s the legislation appeared to be dead in Southern Nigeria; with the exception of a single summons in 1925, which was dismissed, there are no cases

71. (Northern Nigeria) n.23 of 1904.

72. (Gold Coast) n.16 of 1877 was amended on several occasions, notably by (Gold Coast) n.1 of 1912 and n.11 of 1921. The penal provisions were repealed by n.20 of 1931.

73. I have encountered many examples of contracts on the mines being as short as one month but none of longer than one year.

recorded for the years 1923–30. The annual figures for the Northern jurisdiction provide further evidence of a dying sanction; while there had been twelve convictions in 1912, the figures for the 1920s show that in many years there were no convictions and never more than two in any year.[74] In Sierra Leone a similar pattern of decline is notable as is another tendency in all three colonies, the strikingly high rate of discharge or dismissal of such cases. In several years there were more cases dismissed than convictions. For example, in 1894, forty-three cases were brought and thirty-one dismissed. In 1925 of the fifty-five cases brought, twenty-eight were dismissed; and in 1926, twenty-one of the thirty-one cases brought were dismissed.[75] At the same time there were years in which there were no cases brought. As seems to be the case in Nigeria, the legislation appears to be very little used by the mid-1920s.[76]

In the case of the Gold Coast there is slight but inexplicably uneven evidence of diminution in cases as the economy expanded. For example, while there were 123 cases recorded in 1912 there were only 41 in 1925.[77] But there is much that remains unexplained and problematic in the Gold Coast data. These matters were, of course, heard in magistrates courts which, tragically for the historians, were not courts of record. It is impossible to discover whether it was employers or employees who initiated individual cases and, as important, what kinds of employers were using the legislation.[78] Some of the data are, however, suggestive. There can be little doubt that summonsing was used to intimidate recalcitrant employees. In 1911, for example, of the 105 cases brought, only 2 resulted in convictions; the rest were discharged. Disposals could be profoundly influenced by the inclinations of individual magistrates. For example, in the Gold Coast, the years 1913 to 1915 appear to be the only ones in which whipping rather than small fines or short terms of imprisonment was the fate of those convicted.[79] While individual magis-

74. Source: Blue Books for Northern Nigeria and the Lagos Colony and Protectorate and after amalgamation those for Nigeria.

75. Sierra Leone Blue Books.

76. Twenty-eight convictions in 1925, eight in 1926, three in 1927, four in 1928, and none in 1929. Ibid.

77. There are for example unexplained peaks and troughs; in 1921 there were 128 summonses (76 of which were discharged or dismissed). Gold Coast Blue Books (hereafter GCBB).

78. Because of the nature of the Gold Coast economy in the late nineteenth century, some employers would almost certainly have been African. But it is impossible to tease out big firms from singleton employers, or government from the private sector from the available data.

79. In 1913, of 99 cases recorded 27 resulted in discharges; 72 were convicted, 33 imprisoned, 16 fined, 14 whipped, and 9 bound over. In 1914 of 122 cases brought, 38 were discharged or dismissed; 84 were convicted, 42 fined, 33 imprisoned, 7 whipped, and 2 bound over. In 1915 of 90 cases brought, 11 ended in discharge/dismissal; of the 79 convicted, 39 were fined, 18 imprisoned, 6 whipped, and 16 bound over. GCBB.

trates might have been enthusiastic about physical punishment, others appear to have favored greater leniency and in some years there is a far greater, if also unexplained, use of binding over.[80] In some years, all the cases brought were dismissed or discharged.[81]

Somewhat mysteriously, labor legislation, unlike virtually every other element in the gradually elaborated colonial criminal and civil codes was only rarely challenged by the growing number of highly politicized African lawyers in the region. Interpreting this is problematic. African lawyers were to make most of their money and reputations out of land and succession matters. But lawyers were also bourgeois, in the more extensive sense of that word, and were themselves considerable employers in both their professional and domestic lives.[82] By the 1940s it was a frequent complaint of early trades unionists that it was hard to attract the interest and support of these rather grand, important people. That accusation is borne out by some decidedly elitist commentary by lawyers of the time on the subject of the *menu peuple*; but this hardly satisfies as a complete answer to the question of their apparent lack of concern.

Part of the explanation of an elaborated but not that intensively used legislation was its utility in handling the transition from unfree to nominally free labor and initially its leverage with masters in its insistence upon contract rather than rights in people. But in common with much of the imperial project in the region, some of its construction was anticipatory. There were assumptions on the part of "forward imperialists" of rapid growth, greater levels of wage employment, and the rest for which legislation would be needed. These predictions were in large measure to be disappointed by the interwar years.[83] Much of the legislation was the borrowed clothes, the legal hand-me-downs of earlier colonial and metropolitan experiences. But inasmuch as, in the early colonial period, the bulk of the extremely limited amount of wage labor was to be found in government employment, this legislation was in part specific and carefully targeted "housekeeping." As very limited industrial, mostly mining, development emerged around the turn of the twentieth

80. For example, in 1891 the magistrate(s) dismissed 17 cases, fined 24 offenders and bound over a further 24. In 1892 dismissals or discharges outnumbered convictions by 33 to 23. In 1893 of 196 cases brought, 26 were discharged or dismissed and 147 were bound over. In 1894, 7 of the defendants in the 10 cases brought were bound over and 2 of the cases were dismissed. GCBB.

81. In 1922 all 57 cases brought were withdrawn or thrown out. GCBB.

82. Clerks, messengers, office cleaners on the one hand and grooms, house servants, drivers, cooks on the other. Some of the Accra houses of the top lawyers were mansions, and some lawyers owned more than one carriage. Many lawyers came from business families and some conducted business as well as their profession.

83. See Havinden and Meredith, *Colonialism and Development*.

century, the firms were no doubt delighted to find such legislation at their disposal. They were much less delighted to confront colonial governments and the Colonial Office, which obdurately resisted being cajoled into legislating for the elaboration of a system of recruitment, residence, and contract, including pass laws, which would have imitated the South African example. So far as the redressive aspects of master and servant legislation were concerned, it is unlikely that these were open to many in the industrial let alone rural work force, who, as we have seen, were frequently "foreign" and accordingly all too often excluded, both socially and formally, from many legal rights. Nor were they in a position to pay for legal representation to bring such matters before the colonial courts. The relative reticence, if such it was, of employers to use the other side of this legislation in British West Africa has ultimately, I believe, more to do with the politics of labor supply and demand in the period. Although there are the usual complaints about labor shortage, these appear to have been more frequently incantatory than real.

Certainly there were occasional hiccoughs in recruitment. For example, the combination of the influenza epidemic and a meningitis outbreak[84] on the Gold Coast in 1919 undoubtedly impeded recruitment temporarily. There was a similar minor crisis about 1937 in both the Gold Coast and Sierra Leone, when the strong recovery of cash-crop prices lured many laborers back to their own farms or to those of others. The limited evidence on the regimes of both governments and the firms suggests that dismissal, or refusal to reemploy government day workers, largely met their control objectives.[85] Worker resistance to poor wages, frequently appalling conditions, and a total lack of security up to and beyond the interwar period are most evident in remarkably high figures of absenteeism[86] and whatever one makes of the constant carping by management about negligent work and indifference to the tasks at hand, although this should not minimize the significance of more obvious forms of resistance such as strikes.

It is noteworthy that the contemporary view of W. M. Macmillan, an outspoken liberal opponent of many contemporary South African policies or practices, found West African employers "far less considerate and 'conservative' of their labour."[87] His concerns rested largely on a somewhat bizarre

84. A very serious epidemic, which appears to have killed at least 60,000 people.

85. As did violent treatment of workers, of which there are numerous reports.

86. Where those figures exist. What little available evidence there is on West African mining concerns suggest that some managements scarcely knew who or how many they employed on any given day.

87. In Meek et al., *Europe and West Africa*, 44. "West Africa," he writes later, "has a great deal to learn from the practice and experience of the Witwatersrand Native Labour Association" (55).

faith in the putative quality of life bestowed by a "stabilised" rather than a migrant work force, which, rather eccentrically, included praising elements of the "compound" system. Nevertheless his testimony is interesting as a contemporary radical-liberal denunciation of what he regarded as a lack of labor policy and of labor laws that lay on the statute book rather than being used, tested, and reformulated.

Orde Browne's justly famous *The African Labourer* surveys the legislation governing labor in the period up to the beginning of 1931. The long, useful section devoted to summarizing labor legislation colony by colony was, in large measure, history by the time the book was published in 1933. For each of the territories with which this piece is concerned, he lists a raft of legislation in which breach of contract is a criminal matter and under which penal sanctions could be imposed. These sanctions included whipping for offenders under the age of sixteen and fines of up to twenty pounds and/or imprisonment of up to three months.[88] Without exception, these ordinances were already being repealed and replaced with new legislation that was more in harmony with the Geneva Convention and with the more liberal sentiments of the first and second National Governments of the United Kingdom (August 1931 to June 1935).[89] In essence, breach of contract was leaving the criminal for the civil jurisdiction. But just as the earlier legislation had resulted in few prosecutions, the new laws also led to very few actions.

The enhanced value of tropical production during the Second World War ensured that laissez-faire would give way to solid government intervention and direction.[90] This would almost certainly have happened without the outbreak of war. The Colonial Office took very seriously the implicit message of Lord Moyne's West Indies Royal Commission, whose report was submitted only days before the outbreak of war.[91] That message was that neglect and illtreatment of labor was the begetter of serious unrest and underproduction. As never before, bureaucracy intervened to supervise labor and its welfare and to impose minimum wages. As part of that project, labor unions were, for the first time in these colonies, both encouraged and recognized. Much of the currently fashionable criticism of the overmighty postcolonial state lacks

88. Under the Gold Coast Ordinances 11 of 1921 and 1 of 1924.

89. And to be fair, in concert with the feelings of the Colonial Office, which for decades had been uncomfortable if weak when it came to action about the use of penal sanctions for labor offenses in West Africa.

90. This, rather than "the unintended arrival of an African working class," was what ultimately transformed the colonial state. A. Phillips, *Enigma of Colonialism*, from where this quotation comes, contains much of value but also much that is asserted rather than proved.

91. Some of the complexity of this can be examined in Cooper's long and sometimes bewildering *Decolonisation and African Society*.

the historical understanding to recognize that, for these territories at least, the command economy was born in the 1940s and its parents were not the Marxian sympathies of African leaders and their advisers but a treasury-led Colonial Office. Contingent history ensured that before the end of the 1940s, these colonial states were shortly to be independent. Despite and possibly because of the close identity of the separate trade-union movements with early radical nationalism, labor legislation maintained a propensity to paternalistically patrol conditions while strictly controlling wages, making labor action unlawful, and limiting workers' rights.

SIXTEEN

Kenya, 1895–1939

Registration and Rough Justice

David M. Anderson

The recruitment of African labor at poor rates of pay and under primitive conditions of work was characteristic of the operation of colonial capitalism in Africa during the nineteenth and twentieth centuries. The implications of these conditions have been generalized very widely in the historiography of colonial Kenya.[1] Where capital was centered upon extractive industries or upon settler agriculture as in Kenya, historians have found much evidence to indicate that colonial states (and the metropolitan government) readily colluded with capital in providing the legal framework necessary for the recruitment and maintenance of labor in adequate numbers and at low cost to the employer. Dependence on revenues from the enlargement of the tax base gave the colonial state sufficient incentive for such policies, but a direct interest in the provision of cheap labor can also be inferred from the fact that the state itself was commonly the largest single employer of labor in territories throughout British colonial Africa. The colonial state therefore shared the desire of the European settler to encourage Africans into the labor market, while also sharing a concern to moderate the wages paid to workers. Criticisms of labor conditions prevailing in any colony were thus likely to be interpreted as criticisms of the state itself.[2]

These general economic imperatives were bolstered by moral strictures: the "gospel of labor" was a central element in the civilizing mission of Euro-

---

1. The key works are Clayton and Savage, *Government and Labour*; van Zwanenberg, *Colonial Capitalism*; Stichter, *Migrant Labour*; Kitching, *Class and Economic Change*; Berman, *Control and Crisis*, ch. 2; and Berman and Lonsdale, *Unhappy Valley*, 1: ch. 5.

2. For contemporary surveys of the subject, the first of their kind, see Buell, *Native Problem*, and Orde Browne, *African Labourer*. For a more recent introduction, see Freund, *African Worker*.

pean rule, frequently referred to by settler farmer and government official alike as the justification for stringent labor laws. But any simplistic formulation of a uniform "European view" on African labor ignores the fissiparous nature of settler society and the heterogeneity of the colonial state itself. As Clayton and Savage recognized in what was the first (and remains the best) of the now several studies of labor in colonial Kenya, the legislation governing labor evolved out of the conflicts between the various factions.[3] Kenya's settler colonialism was always a house divided, its voices as discordant as they were clamorous. Larger employers of African labor, often wealthier and better capitalized, blamed the mistreatment of labor upon "the small settler" who lacked the resources and experience to manage his farm appropriately. At the level of the state, a gulf existed between the legislative devices advocated by the Nairobi administration and those thought appropriate by officials in London, while on the ground in Kenya some officials willingly contrived to increase labor recruitment for settler employers while others worked to expose the many employers who abused their African labor. It is around these disputes within European colonialism in Kenya that the problems of labor come most sharply into focus.

This essay examines the range of labor law operating under colonial jurisdiction in Kenya, with a particular emphasis on the place of master and servant legislation. Despite the prominence given to master and servant statutes in the early establishment of the colonial legal system in East Africa (prior to 1914), thereafter a wider variety of law came to be used in the regulation of employment offenses. Statistical evidence on the prosecution of workers and employers in colonial Kenya is far from adequate for any meaningful discussion of changing patterns over the longer term, but other evidence, drawn from court proceedings and colonial archival sources, suggests that master and servant ordinances were relatively little used and that what use there was diminished over time. Labor disputes of the sort normally covered by master and servant laws more often emerged in the courts for prosecution under other ordinances as the colonial state developed a body of overlapping law in the area of employment regulation. However, any definition of the legal position, no matter how precise, can tell us relatively little about the social experience of African laborers, especially African farm workers and domestic servants. In these important areas of employment, African workers were seldom able to use the law to secure their interests. Moreover, employers who vociferously demanded sterner laws to regulate labor commonly ignored the provisions of the justice system by "settling" disputes out of court. Evidence

---

3. Clayton and Savage, *Government and Labour*, xiii–xxii.

on judicial punishments handed out in relation to labor offenses shows that corporal punishments remained the norm for African workers until the 1930s, but this was not the case for other races. For African workers labor law became more sophisticated and less overtly oppressive over time, but it is to be doubted that reforms in place by the early 1950s brought any significant additional protections for African employees.

Master and Servants Legislation in Kenya, 1895–1923

Twenty years before British imperial interests extended a protectorate over East Africa in 1895, the old penal employment laws had been repealed in the seat of empire. The application of master and servants legislation to East Africa after 1900 was therefore not merely a consequence of the transplantation of English law to the colonies; it arose from a deliberate decision to impose a particular type of legislation that was by then already considered outmoded in the metropole. Writing in the early 1930s, Orde Browne still found a defense for the retention of penal sanctions in Africa on the grounds that colonial legislation comprised "omnibus laws" better suited to the primitive state of colonial political economy and the peculiarities of colonial labor markets. His Whiggish notion was that economic development would bring legal reform but that, until such separate legislation evolved, the interests of the employer had to be protected.[4] As we shall see, labor laws in Kenya surely protected the rights of the employer but they were perilously slow to reform; and when new legislation was invoked it did not necessarily mean that the worst excesses of the old would be removed.

The first master and servants legislation enacted in the East African Protectorate was introduced in 1906, to update and improve earlier labor regulations of 1898 and 1902. The 1898 regulations related to what was then the largest field of employment, the use of porters in the transportation of goods throughout the protectorate. This law was loosely framed around the usual terms of master and servants legislation, but it is apparent that some practices of the indigenous labor market were also codified. For example, the statutes allowed for advance payments to porters once engaged and stipulated monthly payments, both norms for the engagement of porters from coastal East Africa throughout the second half of the nineteenth century.[5] This aside, the legislation was designed principally to deal with the matter of desertion. Porters absconding after an advance of wages were liable to a fine of sixty

4. Orde Brown, *African Labourer*, 81–86.
5. The insight is Stephen Rockel's; see his "Caravan Porters," ch. 6, and "Nation of Porters," 173–95.

rupees under these regulations, along with six months' imprisonment and twenty-five lashes. The lesser offense of "desertion without warning" brought only the fine but gave the employer the option of forcibly imposing the terms of service.[6] The emphasis of the law was to protect the contractual interests of the employer rather than the employee, and the penal sanctions were designed to act as a strong deterrent against workers who were thought to be largely ignorant of the burden of contract law. The tone of these early regulations was to characterize all of Kenya's labor laws until the later 1930s.

The 1898 regulations were repealed with the introduction of a broader ordinance in 1902, the Native Porters and Labour Regulation.[7] The act encompassed all forms of employment in the protectorate covered by contracts of greater than two months' duration. At this time larger groups of porters and laborers were typically gathered together by labor recruiters, sometimes with the assistance of chiefs or headmen. Coercion was commonplace. Most such laborers were taken into the employ of government, and this was reflected in the terms of the regulations. Such contracts were supposed to be prepared in front of a magistrate, whose duty it was to explain the terms to each worker individually. This was intended to act as a deterrent to coercion, but in reality its more practical purpose was to alert laborers to the penalties for desertion.[8]

The arrival of European settler farmers in the protectorate from 1902 enlarged the demand for labor and altered the character of employment. By 1906 there were more than 600 white settlers, most of whom were seeking to employ "native labour" on their farms and in their homes. The initial pressure for legislation to regulate this labor was brought by the settlers themselves, not by government. The Colonists' Association, representing the interests of the colony's European community, presented a draft ordinance to the government in 1906. It was accepted largely unaltered and forwarded to London for approval as the Master and Servants Ordinance.[9]

The Colonists' Association committee had based its draft on the Gold Coast master and servant ordinance of 1893[10] and the Transvaal master and servant ordinance of 1880.[11] Officials in London noted the somewhat dated nature of the legislation but considered that the East African ordinance was probably necessary "in order to obtain reasonable service from the natives

6. Clayton and Savage, *Government and Labour*, 32.

7. Ibid., 30.

8. Ibid., 32.

9. (E.A.P.) n.8 of 1906; *East Africa Gazette*, 15 Apr. 1906; Ghai and McAuslan, *Public Law*, 83.

10. (Gold Coast) n.8 of 1893.

11. (Transvaal) n.13 of 1880.

who are unused to the benefits and obligations of continuous labour."[12] Labor at a "primitive" stage of development was thought to require "primitive" forms of labor law. What this meant in practice was that the rights of the master were enforced in draconian terms, whereas relatively few protections were offered to the servant.

The terms of the East African Ordinance of 1906 made this abundantly clear. As Mandy Banton shows, the character of the ordinance was strongly influenced by recent South African experience.[13] Under the 1906 ordinance no unwritten contracts were to last more than one month, but if the servant remained the verbal contract was impliedly renewed.[14] This gave little incentive to the employer to move toward written contracts. By this means, a laborer who was unfamiliar with a European reckoning of time might find himself bound to remain merely through ignorance. Breaches of contract were to be dealt with by civil proceedings, but the Transvaal model of allowing criminal penalties was followed. Offenses were separated into "major" and "minor" categories, again following the practice in the Transvaal. Minor offenses included failure to work, intoxication or absence during working hours, careless or improper work, and using insulting language to the master or his agent. The maximum fine for such offenses was one month's wages, or a term of imprisonment lasting one month. Major offenses included any willful breach of duty; drunkenness leading to loss, damage, or risk to property of the master; failure to report death, loss, or injury to animals; and desertion from service without lawful cause. For these offenses the maximum fine was two months' wages or two months' imprisonment.

Not a single specific clause in the 1906 master and servant ordinance protected the worker, yet by 1908 Governor Sadler felt able to claim that the law operated "as much for the protection of the natives as for the benefit of the white settler, between whom the government in the person of the various DOs [district officers] stands in the position of arbitrator."[15] But for the master and servant codes to be effective, this role of arbitration had to be accepted and understood by all sides. This clearly was not the case. Sadler himself went on to admit that district officers were inclined to use the ordinance "to punish the native" on behalf of the master. Cases arose generally at the instigation of the European employer, and there is no evidence to suggest that African employees saw the courts as offering any protections. Mandy Banton has noted that colonial officials expressed the worry that aggrieved laborers

12. See above, p. 273 n. 63.
13. Ibid.
14. Clayton and Savage, *Government and Labour*, 70 n. 36.
15. Above, p. 274 n. 67.

were unlikely to go to law: "[A] labourer who has been ill-treated generally prefers to return to his home, rather than wait and take proceedings against his employer."[16] To address this problem, magistrates were circularized to encourage them to properly investigate disputes and to reach settlements, and warned that the power to inflict punishment should be resorted to only in "those cases in which other adjustment is impossible, or which obviously call for punishment."[17] These directives, however, had little impact.

The 1910 amendment to the master and servant ordinance did bring some improvements, with a specific clause setting down basic requirements to be met by employers in regard to the welfare of the employees.[18] But it also separated workers into racially designated categories by narrowing the terms of the ordinance to apply only to "Arab and Native" workers. This innovation again reflected the claims of European settlers that African labor was at a less advanced stage of development than Asian or European labor, and so needed to be treated differently under the law.[19] Isolating African labor in this way made it easier to enforce categories of offense and—more important—punishments thought "appropriate" to that category of labor. None of the punishments provided under the law were reduced by the 1910 amendment, and imprisonment with hard labor for absence from work was added. Lest African laborers should be in any doubt as to whom this legislation was intended to benefit, the amendment reduced the fine against the employer for withholding wages, a very common practice on Kenya's European farms at this time.[20]

Further minor amendments were introduced in 1912, 1915, 1916, 1918, and 1919.[21] Those imposed during the First World War were considered as emergency acts, and so needed no approval from London. These changes served to tighten the constraints upon employees and to add to the severity of the punishments imposed, making desertion a cognizable offense, allowing the police to arrest deserters without a warrant, and increasing the penalties for breach of contract. These measures were deemed necessary to maintain recruitment for the dreaded Carrier Corps, whose levels of mortality from disease and malnutrition vastly exceeded the casualties inflicted upon African combatants during the campaign in East Africa.[22] But none of the provisions brought in during the war as "emergency measures" to retain labor were subsequently

---

16. Ibid.
17. Above, p. 274 n. 69.
18. (E.A.P.) n.4 of 1910.
19. Chapter by Banton in this volume.
20. Clayton and Savage, *Government and Labour*, 43–44 and n. 67; M. Ross, *Kenya*, 90–103.
21. (E.A.P.) n.4 of 1912; (E.A.P.) n.3 of 1915; (E.A.P.) n.1 of 1916; (E.A.P.) n.30 of 1918; (E.A.P.) n.27 of 1919.
22. Clayton and Savage, *Government and Labour*, 91–97.

repealed after 1918. The amendment of 1919 was of greater significance in the longer term, setting up a system of inspectors of labor (within the Department of Native Affairs), empowered to inspect workplaces and make rules governing workplace practices. This development, prompted in part by the grim experience of Carrier Corps recruitment during the war, marked the beginning of a structure for the protection of the employee, including some limited provision for the medical examinations of recruits. Throughout the 1920s this small office, with a maximum of five inspectors, was responsible for overseeing all African employment in the colony.[23]

By the 1920s, half a century since the introduction of the Employers and Workmen Act, 1875, in England,[24] master and servant legislation remained the central element in the structuring of colonial labor law in Kenya and throughout much of British Africa. Far from any tendency toward legal reform in favor of employees' rights, between 1900 and 1923 penal sanctions under the Kenyan master and servant ordinances had been widened and strengthened. As the economy had developed, so too had the political power of European employers, and it was their interests that continued to shape the law. McGregor Ross, Norman Leys, and other critics of Kenya's settler community often presented the circumstances of the colony as exceptional, yet Kenya's master and servant ordinance was used as the basis for the drafting of an ordinance for neighboring Tanganyika in 1923.[25] Ironically, given British criticism of the treatment of Africans under German administration, this enactment replaced German laws of labor contract after the transfer of the territory to British mandate under the League of Nations. The Tanganyika ordinance was to be the last example of the implementation of a new master and servant code in Britain's African colonies.[26]

The justification for imposing upon the colonies law that was considered outmoded in the metropole evidently owed more to prevailing views of the primitive development of the African labor force than to Orde Browne's faith in legal evolution. The retention of punitive sanctions in law enacted in the 1920s might be defended in economic terms, but it was underpinned by overtly racist attitudes. This becomes clearer when we set the master and servant ordinances in a wider legal context.

23. Ibid., 147.
24. (U.K.) 38&39 Vict. c.90 (1875).
25. (Tanganyika) n.32 of 1923.
26. Chapter by Banton in this volume. Cooper, *Slaves to Squatters*, 88, notes that the ordinance "was not implemented in Zanzibar until 1925 and then had little effect."

Overlapping Legislation, 1910–1939

The provisions of the master and servant regulations were augmented by a range of other laws affecting labor. Some of these were enacted to enable government to secure labor for its own purposes, but for the most part they arose at the specific request of the European settler community, whose representatives felt the need to bolster the legal position of the employer. An important accumulated effect of the imposition of these additional labor regulations was to shift the burden of prosecution away from the master and servant ordinance.

Under the Native Authority Ordinance (1912) the government regulated the powers devolved upon appointed chiefs and their agents. An amendment to this ordinance in 1919 provided for the compulsory recruitment by local chiefs of paid labor for specified government works, such as porterage or road construction, up to a limit of sixty days per annum. Any African who had been in wage employment for three of the previous twelve months was exempt from compulsory recruitment, a mechanism quite explicitly aimed at "encouraging" workers into wage labor. This ordinance was widely used throughout the colony during the interwar years. A total of 10,547 workers were ordered out under this proviso in 1922, rising to 25,501 in 1923. Numbers averaged 13,693 workers per annum during the 1920s but fell to an average of 4,421 workers per annum during the 1930s.[27]

In a similar measure, the Native Followers Recruitment Ordinance (1915), introduced as a wartime contingency to secure adequate labor for the detested Carrier Corps, provided for the compulsory conscription of 3,000 laborers per month. Only those already employed by Europeans were exempt from recruitment, so again this act was framed in such a way as to encourage more Africans into employment on the European farms. As a direct consequence, recruitment of farm workers increased markedly during the war, and many more workers accepted longer contracts. Whereas a three-month contract had been the norm before 1914, by the end of the war the average duration of contract in Kiambu was approaching twelve months. When the fear of Carrier Corps recruitment was removed in 1919, the average length of labor contracts in Kiambu quickly dropped back to six months, contributing to a sharp rise in settler anxieties that a major labor crisis was looming with the slackening of wartime controls.[28]

Other legislation was of a more permanent nature, and more obviously

27. Clayton and Savage, *Government and Labour*, 153 and 200.
28. Ibid., 87; Savage and Munro, "Carrier Corps"; Watkins, *Watkins*, is an account of the man who commanded the Carrier Corps.

worked to the longer-term benefit of the settler employer. The Registration of Natives Ordinance (1915) had first been mooted in the recommendations of the Native Labour Commission of 1912–13, although its imposition was suspended by the Colonial Office until 1919.[29] This act introduced what was, in effect, a set of pass controls for African males of working age. Instituted over the whole territory by 1920, the act required every male over fifteen years to register before his local administrative officer and to be issued with a fingerprinted certificate of identity.[30] This document, known as a *kipande*, provided basic personal details and acted as a record of employment. A central registry was established to hold the records, and by 1931 nearly 2 million *kipande* had been issued. John Ainsworth, a senior official in Kenya and staunch defender of African interests, had argued that this would protect Africans by providing greater job security and making it harder for settlers to defraud them of their wages. This was surely the case, but in effect this law restricted the workers' freedom of mobility to a far greater degree than had any provision under the master and servant ordinance. Unless a laborer was signed off from his previous employment, it was not legal for another employer to engage him. Any laborer leaving employment without being formally signed off was considered to have deserted, and forms were provided for employers to notify the police of such cases. The pass system then allowed such individuals to be more easily traced: any inspection of the *kipande* by an official, or even by a prospective employer, could reveal a discrepancy in the record that might result in prosecution if reported. Not surprisingly, native registration was highly popular among settlers but deeply unpopular among Africans.[31]

The ordinance had an immediate and widespread impact on the control of labor. There were 2,220 successful prosecutions of African laborers under the Registration Ordinance in 1921, representing some 62 percent of the 3,595 desertions reported during the year,[32] and by the following year reported desertions had fallen to fewer than 3 per 1,000 laborers.[33] The system placed considerable powers in the hands of employers, and this gave opportunities

29. *Report of the Native Labour Commission, 1912–13* (hereafter *RNLC*) (Nairobi, 1913); Clayton and Savage, *Government and Labour*, 61.

30. (Kenya) n.19 of 1920, notified in the *Gazette*, 18 Aug. 1920. The legislation was reissued fifteen months later with some minor changes to penalties, including increased fines for employers who failed to comply: (Kenya) n.56 of 1921.

31. Clayton and Savage, *Government and Labour*, 132. For another account, see van Zwanenberg, *Colonial Capitalism*, 183–89.

32. *Native Affairs Department Annual Report 1931* (hereafter *NADAR* 1931), Public Record Office (hereafter PRO) CO 544/34, for prosecution figures, and N. Leys, *Kenya*, 198, for total numbers of reported cases. Leys estimates the prosecution rate at 77 percent, which would imply a fairly high rate of acquittal.

33. Clayton and Savage, *Government and Labour*, 132.

for abuse. By failing to sign a *kipande*, or by noting derogatory remarks on the document, an employer might entrap the worker or prevent him from moving to new employment. Such abuses were acknowledged to be common.[34] The majority of those prosecuted under the registration ordinance would have been liable to prosecution for desertion under the master and servant ordinance, but the simplicity of the process involved, which even allowed the employer to claim expenses if asked to appear in court at the prosecution of a laborer, in contrast with the provisions under the master and servant ordinance, which required that the master apply to a magistrate for a summons against the alleged deserter, indicates the advantages to the employer. Alarmed by the large number of prosecutions and the amount of police work and court time this was taking up, in 1925 the Colonial Office compelled the Kenya administration to remove desertion under the ordinance from the list of offenses cognizable to the police, once again necessitating employers to take out a summons. Despite this reform, in 1929 there were still more than 4,000 Africans convicted under the ordinance, representing some 2.7 percent of all those Africans in employment.[35]

Aside from the 130,000 or so Africans contracted to work as wage laborers by the early 1920s, more than 100,000 others were resident on European-owned farmlands as "squatters." In return for the use of the land, these African squatters provided labor, services, or rent-in-kind to the landowner. This system, similar in form to that described as "kaffir farming" in southern Africa, worked to the benefit of undercapitalized settler farmers who, in the early years of settlement, commonly lacked the resources to develop properly the large farms they owned.[36] The Resident Native (Squatters) Ordinance (1918) sought to regulate these practices by formally defining squatters as "labour tenants" rather than as tenants paying a cash rent, thereby bringing them under closer legal control and giving employers rights of contract.[37] Under the ordinance, squatters had to be attested on a labor contract of not less than 180 days per annum (although this was not immediately enforced in every district).[38] At this point it was assumed that squatters were in effect servants, therefore falling within the jurisdiction of the master and servant regulations. It is certain that many squatters were prosecuted accordingly. In

34. The evidence before the Native Punishment Commission, below, provides many examples. See also the discussion in M. Ross, *Kenya*, ch. 7, and some additional examples in van Zwanenberg, *Colonial Capitalism*, ch. 7.

35. Figures calculated from *NADAR* 1931, PRO CO 544.

36. For a history of squatting, see Kanogo, *Squatters*, and van Zwanenberg, *Colonial Capitalism*, ch. 8.

37. (E.A.P.) n.33 of 1918.

38. Ghai and McAuslan, *Public Law*, 83.

1923, however, this came to a dramatic halt when the Supreme Court ruled that a resident laborer on an estate was not, after all, a servant under the master and servant ordinance.[39] This meant that the criminal penalties attached to desertion under the master and servant regulations could not be applied to squatters, nor could remedies be sought for minor complaints.[40]

The European settler community quickly acted to try to reverse the effect of this decision, proposing that the provisions of the master and servant ordinance be extended to squatters. This would have diminished the squatter's rights as a labor tenant and was accordingly disallowed by the secretary of state.[41] However, remarkably similar provisions became law in 1925 under the Resident Native Labourer's Ordinance, which replaced the 1918 ordinance and was approved by the new Conservative administration in London.[42] This effectively replicated many of the terms of the master and servant ordinance in specific relation to resident laborers but once again enhanced the power of the employers in certain critical respects. The most significant one was the removal of the requirement that a magistrate attest the contract, which had the effect of allowing the employer to set conditions and wages at below normal levels. The Resident Native Labourers Ordinance, implemented in 1939, took this a step further by finally expunging any remaining tenancy rights held by squatters, giving district councils the authority to limit the numbers of livestock held by squatters and to restrict the land available to them, and ultimately empowering magistrates to order evictions.[43] At the same time landlords could require squatters to work up to 270 days per annum.[44] The evolution of the ordinances governing resident laborers chart the shift toward the proletarianization of farm labor in Kenya.

Domestic servants also took employment with Europeans, some resident on farms and members of squatter families, others temporary migrants to Kenya's colonial towns. These workers were regulated by the master and servant laws and were, of course, affected by the pass laws. The Registration of Domestic Servants Ordinance, introduced in 1926, specifically targeted these workers. Modeled on Hong Kong legislation, it was intended to regulate the movement of servants between employers, ensuring that those lacking satisfactory references would be denied labor permits and forced to return to

39. *Thathi wa Mbati v. R.*, Kenya Law Reports 1923.
40. Ghai and McAuslan, *Public Law*, 95.
41. Clayton and Savage, *Government and Labour*, 173.
42. (Kenya) n.5 of 1925.
43. (Kenya) n.30 of 1937.
44. Stichter, *Migrant Labour*, 100–101; Clayton and Savage, *Government and Labour*, 128–31; Kanogo, *Squatters*, 35–40; van Zwanenberg, *Colonial Capitalism*, 253–55.

their home areas. It was prompted in part by mounting anxieties about social control in Nairobi, where it was estimated that six Africans were seeking work for every job available in domestic service in the town. On the one hand, settlers argued for influx controls to reduce crime in the city, but on the other hand this surplus of labor ensured that wages remained low and that there was little pressure on settler employers to improve conditions of work for African domestic servants. The more immediate impetus for the enactment of the ordinance in 1926 was a spate of assaults on European women and children in which domestic servants were implicated.[45]

Other more central elements of the criminal law also impinged upon the domain of the master and servant regulations. Kenya's Stock and Produce Theft Ordinance was among the most punitive of its kind anywhere under British jurisdiction, imposing statutory fines at ten times the value of the stock or produce stolen, along with imprisonment and flogging. These punishments, which vastly exceeded the norms under the master and servant acts, could be extended to the convict's family if he or she was found unable to meet the fine. In the case of a stock theft prosecution, such a draconian level of punishment might easily have the effect of wiping out the entire capital resources of an African family.[46] The choice as to whether a farm laborer caught stealing a bag of maize meal from his master's barn would be prosecuted under the master and servant regulations or the theft ordinance lay with the European employer. Where the employer wished to be rid of the laborer without contractual complications, summoning the police to the farm to instigate a prosecution for theft was by far the easiest option.[47]

Prosecution and Punishment[48]

For the European settlers who agitated for the introduction of the master and servant ordinance of 1906, their principal motive had been to lessen the incidence of desertion by creating legal sanctions to bind employees more closely to the workplace. What settler employers wanted was the ability to enforce contract. But it appears that the law had little real impact on desertion. Instead, what resulted was a steady increase in the prosecution of workers for

45. For the relevant papers, see Kenya National Archive (hereafter KNA) Pol/5/561, "Indecent assaults 1920–44." For Hong Kong, see the chapter by Munn.

46. D. Anderson, "Stock Theft," and "Policing, Prosecution."

47. Until the 1940s, it was very uncommon for police to visit a European farm except at the explicit invitation of the owner. See D. Anderson, "Policing, Prosecution."

48. Changes in the organizational structure and powers of the courts are described in the *Judicial Department Annual Reports*, PRO CO 544.

petty disciplinary offenses. As a consequence, the legal system itself, and the magistrate's courts in particular, became the butt of criticism from European employers who felt that the state should assist them more directly in securing and maintaining labor, whether through fiscal policies or judicial decree. This was the political context within which magistrates dealt with cases between 1906 and the 1920s. Over these years the assumption prevailed among all sections of the European community that the courts were there principally to punish African laborers—all part of the process of instilling the civilizing discipline of labor.

The majority of cases under the master and servant regulations were heard before magistrates who were members of the colonial administration. Every district officer of whatever rank held magisterial powers, and all first- and second-class magistrates were empowered to hear master and servant cases. Rural justices of the peace, drawn from the European settler community, had no authority to hear cases under the 1906 or the 1910 legislation.[49] Keeping these justices out of the sphere of labor disputes was thought to be in the wider interests of African workers, but to say that the magistracy was overeager in enforcing punitive sanctions against the African employee in master and servant cases would be no exaggeration. As Ghai and McAuslan have noted, the high court repeatedly issued circulars to magistrates reminding them of the need to establish that a labor contract actually existed before taking action against a laborer.[50]

The statistics we have on prosecutions under the master and servant ordinance are far from complete. Although only occasional aggregate figures are available for the earliest years, it is evident that a "large number were proceeded against" under the ordinance.[51] From the 1920s, the annual reports of the Native Affairs, Judicial, Police and Prisons Departments provide better statistics on prosecutions. Apart from the statistical abstracts, case records of Kenya's subordinate courts do not survive, so we have no body of case material from which to work.[52] Aspects of the legal process relating to master and servant regulations come to light in other judicial sources, however, such as cases of serious crime where trial records survive, and most notably in the testimony given before government commissions of inquiry into questions affecting labor. The evidence provided in these sources is discussed first,

49. (E.A.P.) n.8 of 1906; (E.A.P.) n.4 of 1910.
50. Ghai and McAuslan, *Public Law*, 142.
51. For the quotation, see *East African Protectorate Annual Report, 1912–15*, Cd. 7050 (1914). For an informative survey of the earlier colonial labor recruitment, see report on *Slavery and Free Labour in East Africa*, Cd.1631 (1903), written by W. J. Monson.
52. A few papers relating to revision cases do survive in the Kenya National Archive. See Clayton and Savage, *Government and Labour*, 32 n. 36, for two examples from 1907.

giving a more detailed context for the statistical analysis that concludes this section.

The fullest and most informative account of labor relations in the early years of colonial rule in Kenya is to be found in the papers of the Native Labour Commission of 1912–13.[53] Set up explicitly to investigate the anxieties of European employers regarding the labor supply, this commission took oral and written evidence from 284 witnesses, mostly European employers, but including 64 Africans. The evidence of European witnesses was dominated by complaints about the law's inadequacy in drawing Africans into the labor market.[54] In the face of labor shortage, many settlers admitted resorting to forms of coercion, a fact corroborated by the 40 African witnesses who alleged that they had been coerced into wage labor. The vast majority of the Europeans appearing to give evidence advocated that some further form of incentive to labor be supported by the state, whether through the indirect means of greatly increased taxation and the reduction of lands available for subsistence cultivation, or more direct methods of forced labor through quotas, levies, or even conscription.[55]

Among the welter of complaints voiced by employers, considerable attention focused on the burdens placed on them by the existing labor legislation. The master and servant ordinance of 1910 was roundly criticized as "a lamentable failure."[56] European employers particularly disliked the requirement for employer testimony about servants' misdemeanors; employers were too busy to go to court on such trivial matters. Could not the court accept an affidavit from the employer and punish the laborer accordingly?[57] The inadequacy of the police made it pointless to report desertions: "When a boy deserted now it was a hopeless matter to expect his being brought back again; neither the labour agent nor the police seemed able to do anything," commented a settler from Athi River.[58] In most cases the police would not even search for

53. The following section draws upon the *RNLC* which includes a summary of the evidence of all witnesses. See also M. Ross, *Kenya*, 92–98.

54. *RNLC* witness No. 91 (Lord Delamere), 108–11, for a notable example.

55. By M. Ross's estimate (*Kenya*, 92–93), sixty-eight witnesses urged an increase in taxation to encourage labor supply, seventy-six suggested that some remission of tax be awarded to those who fulfilled a minimum number of days in waged labor, and forty-nine witnesses wanted the area of land reserved for Africans to be reduced so as to force more people off the land and into employment.

56. *RNLC* written evidence, Malindi Planter's Association, 24 Nov. 1912, 275–76.

57. *RNLC* witness No. 107 (A. Cartwright), 121, and written evidence of G. Stanley, 4 Jan. 1913, both settler farmers. See also witness No. 61 (G. Blain, an engineer with the Public Works Department), 84, for comments on his time wasted taking "petty cases" before the magistrate.

58. *RNLC* witness No. 9 (Stocker), 15–16; witness No. 187 (J. J. Drought), 171–82; and witness No. 46 (P. W. Redford), 66–67.

the deserter unless the employer first went before the magistrate to lodge the case, as the ordinance required. Even when a case was notified, the police were very unlikely to apprehend the deserter.[59] The registration of laborers under the ordinance, supposedly "the panacea" for the employers' constant troubles over desertion, had proved worthless because it provided no means of identification: "[T]he native found it just as easy to run away after registration as before. He did so with impunity then and does so now."[60]

None other than the government's own inspector of labour, J. M. Pearson, supported many of these complaints in a general attack upon the operation of the master and servant legislation:

> The main criticisms of the system of 1910 that seem to deserve the most serious consideration are those which point to the inequality of the parties to the contract. In effect, any wrongs of the employee (bad food, blows, wages withheld, etc) can be remedied by complaint to any government post, and the whole force of the administration lies behind the complainant. Wrongs of the employer, however (desertion, bad work, insolence, neglect, etc) are very seldom capable of redress . . . because the other party to the contract has left the jurisdiction and cannot be found. A summons, and then a warrant, is issued without result. The police are unable to find him.[61]

The high rate of desertion was the real issue underlying the many grumbles about enforcement of contract. Under the 1910 ordinance, the principal duty of the magistrate was to attest that contracts of labor were voluntarily made. This had been seen as a protection against coercion, labor recruiters having to bring newly contracted workers before the magistrate before leaving the district. But, in contradiction of employers who thought government was not doing enough to encourage the labor supply, Dr. Norman Leys reported that this "protection" was widely abused by magistrates who were too keen to assist in bringing labor out: "Some magistrates, when labourers object to the terms of the contract, send them away to give the recruiter the chance of arguing them round, others use a less fair way of getting them to agree." As a consequence, Leys argued, Africans did "not believe magistrates to be impartial between black and white," but rather saw them as part of the system of labor recruitment. It was hardly surprising, therefore, that they were reluctant to turn to the magistrate when they had been wronged. In his view, only

59. *RNLC* witness No. 107 (A. Cartwright), 121.
60. *RNLC* written evidence, J. E. Jones, chairman of Malindi Planter's Association, 4 Jan. 1913, 276–78.
61. *RNLC* written evidence, J. M. Pearson, 14 Oct. 1912, 253.

an end to coercion coupled with the proper enforcement of the protections of labor enshrined in the 1910 ordinance would bring an end to desertions.[62]

Even when the successful prosecution of a worker was obtained under the 1910 legislation, there was general dissatisfaction among employers with the punishments delivered. Many employers reminded the commission that labor was in short supply. If the court imprisoned the worker, then another had to be found to replace him. Even just sending the worker to court withdrew his labor from the farm and was therefore unwelcome. A popular solution, endorsed by Nakuru's town magistrate, was for the appointment of European employers as justices of the peace in each district, which would both bring the court closer to the farms and plantations, thereby entailing less loss of employer's time appearing for cases, and put legal authority in the hands of those who were familiar with local labor conditions.[63] Whereas the master and servant ordinance placed the magistrate properly in the role of arbitrator of labor disputes, to most settlers he was an impediment. Many argued that there was no need at all for legal process in labor matters, asking to be given "plenary powers" over their labor to settle disputes in the workplace with corporal punishments. J. K. Watson, a labor contractor in Nairobi, considered that "an employer should have the right of treating his labour in the way that an officer treated his soldiers."[64] More often, the analogy drawn was with the disciplining of children. The owner of a huge 15,000-acre estate at Nakuru, Captain A. H. James, thought that African laborers "were as children and should be treated as such," flogging being the best means of instilling "reasoning power and a sense of discipline" in what he termed "the raw native population."[65] Even the government's district officer, who was also the local magistrate at Eldoret, where desertion was especially prevalent, wanted all deserters summarily flogged on recapture.[66]

These comments reveal a great deal about the social climate in which the 1910 master and servant legislation operated, and there was much in the evidence presented before the commission to support the view that employers gave scant regard to those provisions in the legislation that safeguarded the rights of workers. Some employers openly admitted to a flagrant disregard

62. *RNLC* written evidence, Dr. Norman Leys, 26 Dec. 1912, 270–74.

63. *RNLC* witness No. 92 (A. Donald, Nakuru Town Magistrate), 111; witness No. 60 (C. Hirtzel), 82; witness No. 107 (A. Cartwright), 121; witness No. 187 (J. J. Drought), 171–82; written evidence, A. C. Ward, 27 Nov. 1912, 251–52.

64. *RNLC* witness No. 45 (J. K. Watson), 66.

65. *RNLC* witness No. 113 (Capt. A. H. James), 125–26. Others who argued along similar lines included No. 14 (Charles Anderson), 23–24; No. 29 (D. Beaton), 47–49; No. 40 (E. A. Bool), 58–59; and No. 59 (C. H. Reynolds), 81–82.

66. *RNLC* witness No. 195 (N. E. F. Corbett), 185–86.

for the terms of the existing labor legislation, and missionaries and officials
cited numerous examples of illegal practices. It was apparently common, for
example, for part of a laborer's wages to be withheld each month in order to
ensure that he recontracted for a further period. Other employers exploited
the laborer's ignorance of contract to prolong duration or to deduct wages,
while infringement of servants' rights to food, adequate housing, and medical
treatments was widespread.[67] Mervyn Beech, a district officer at Dagoretti,
close to Nairobi, recounted a case that he had investigated:

> One European had a system of giving a chit for each day's work but
> seldom gave chits for more than 28 days. He then beat and flogged
> indiscriminately so that the natives ran away without completing the
> month's work, refusing to pay anything unless thirty days were com-
> pleted. When he [Mr. Beech] looked into the case a string of natives
> came up with calabashes containing chits, and no one could produce
> thirty.[68]

In another example cited by Beech, a farmer had brutally flogged a squatter for refusing to work and then, when he ran away, caught him and sued
him for breach of a verbal contract. Despite the limited protections afforded
to African laborers under the law, few such cases came to the attention of
the courts. The district officer at Nakuru, Crewe-Read, informed the inquiry
that he had had three complaints of Africans being mistreated by employers
over the previous few weeks, "but in two out of the three the complainants
had disappeared."[69] Neither masters nor servants, it seems, saw much point
in seeking redress before a magistrate.

Over the decade following the deliberations of the Labour Commission,
Kenya's labor question became embroiled in further controversies. First, the
high mortality of labor recruited for service in the Carrier Corps during
the 1914–18 war reached scandalous proportions and did little to encourage Africans into waged employment. Second, when labor recruitment fell

67. Among the most outspoken witnesses were A. C. Hollis (No. 1, 1–3), McGregor Ross
(No. 28, 42–47), Charles Dundas (No. 42, 61–62), Mervyn Beech (No. 51, 71–75), John Ainsworth (No. 129, 135–38), Rev. W. Chadwick (No. 137, 143–44), C. R. W. Lane (No. 214, 194–96),
Dr. H. R. A. Philp (No. 226, 203–7), Ruffell Barlow (No. 227, 207–10), and Dr. Norman Leys
(written evidence, 270–74). This body of evidence should be contrasted with that of Drought,
a European settler farming at Londiani, who was harshly critical of the practices of "bad employers" among government officials (witness No. 187, 171–82).

68. *RNLC* witness No. 51 (Mervyn Beech), 72.

69. *RNLC* witness No. 110 (E. C. Crewe-Read), 123. Norman Leys, in written evidence,
26 Dec. 1912, 270–74, gives further examples of brutality by employers that did not come before
the courts.

sharply with the ending of wartime pressures, the military-minded Governor Northey issued a circular urging government officials to assist local settlers in recruiting labor. Encouraged and welcomed by settlers struggling to secure labor in a market savagely curtailed by the ravages of wartime recruitment, the circular was speedily withdrawn by an embarrassed governor after intervention from London. This was a great setback to European employers, who greeted the reversal as an act of betrayal. From 1920, the debarring of officials from any role in labor recruitment finally removed the ambiguity from the government's position on the compulsion of labor.[70]

Commenting on Kenya's master and servant laws in the wake of the fuss surrounding the Northey circulars, Milner, then secretary of state for the colonies, reassured those critical of labor practices in the colony that "it would be difficult to find a more comprehensive set of regulations to secure the well-being of natives employed outside their reserves. I am satisfied that if these Ordinances are made more widely known they will have the effect of removing much of the anxiety felt by those who are interested in the Native labour question."[71] By the early 1920s there was indeed some evidence that African employees were beginning to use the provisions of the law to protect their own interests against abuses. Nonpayment of wages by employers allegedly dissatisfied with a worker was a common grievance on the part of employees, and between 1921 and 1923 the total sums of money recovered from employers on behalf of employees by the Native Affairs Department labour inspectorate more than doubled. And in each year during the 1920s more than 400 Africans sought compensation from employers through the courts.[72] The law was evidently being more used than in the past.

But Milner's assumption that comprehensive regulations necessarily made for good law was ill-founded. Over the same period, between 1917 and 1923 to be precise, a series of incidents was reported in Kenya in which African employees died or suffered serious injuries at the hands of their European masters. In the investigation of these cases it became clear that settlers commonly resorted to ad hoc corporal punishments of laborers on the farm, seldom took the trouble to invoke the terms of the master and servant ordinance when a laborer committed an offense, and frequently infringed the law themselves by withholding wages, destroying labor cards and passbooks, and brutally beating Africans.[73] Nothing much, it seemed, had changed since the Labour

70. For the best account of the Northey labor scandal, see van Zwanenberg, *Colonial Capitalism*, 104–36, but see also Clayton and Savage, *Government and Labour*, 108–21.

71. Quoted above, p. 277 n. 75.

72. Bookbinder, "Black Man's Burden," 24.

73. D. Anderson, "Master and Servant," 472.

Commission of 1912–13: "rough justice" was still the norm on the European-owned farms; settler farmers were often unwilling to resort to the master and servant regulations; and African laborers were denied, or chose not to invoke, what protections the law may have afforded them.

Although these events provided the political backcloth to the Native Punishments Commission, set up by Kenya's Legislative Council in 1921, the inquiry was in fact prompted by a different set of concerns about the overcrowding of prisons with petty offenders, most especially those convicted for labor offenses.[74] The commission was charged to investigate the general system of judicial punishments in the colony and to make specific recommendations for the more effective treatment of labor offenses: in effect, to seek means of keeping offenders against the master and servant and native registration ordinances out of jail.[75]

Like the Labour Commission of 1912–13, this inquiry brought forward a flood of European witnesses keen to give their views on the whole question of African labor. Once again, employers expressed their dissatisfaction with the operation of the master and servant regulations. Court proceedings were time-consuming and drew labor away from the farm; the courts were slow and cumbersome in handling cases; magistrates were too ready to give workers the benefit of doubt and there were accordingly far too many cases discharged; and—the point made with greatest force—the courts were too lenient in the punishments handed out to convicted offenders.[76]

The testimony of the thirty or so magistrates among the seventy-four witnesses who gave evidence before the commission was less predictable and altogether more interesting.[77] It was clear that all magistrates felt overburdened by the sheer number of labor offenses that appeared before them as criminal charges, and that there was great uncertainty as to how such cases should be disposed of. Francis Isaac, senior commissioner and first-class magistrate at Nakuru, reported that in his district, over a nine-month period in 1921–22, there had been 235 cases heard under the master and servant ordinance

74. Motion of the Prisons Committee of Legislative Council, 11 May 1920, KNA, Attorney General (hereafter AG) deposit 5/243.

75. Transcript of the evidence laid before the Native Punishments Commission (hereafter NPC) along with a copy of the report can be found in KNA AG 5/241. The commission was established by Government Notice No. 205, *Kenya Government Gazette*, 25 May 1921. For the full terms of reference, see KNA AG 5/243. Some seventy-four witnesses appeared but among them were only eight Africans.

76. Among the critics were W. B. Brook, resident commissioner at Kitale, and E. N. Millington, manager of Kambala Estates at Molo: NPC evidence.

77. NPC evidence. Twenty-five of these were district officials invested with the powers of first- or second-class magistrates, the remainder being resident magistrates based in urban centers and other legal officers with experience of magisterial duties.

and 168 cases under the newly enacted Registration of Natives Ordinance. These two ordinances thereby accounted for 47 percent of all criminal cases heard, took up the lion's share of magisterial time, and were extremely costly to the court in the payment of expenses to the many witnesses who had to be called.[78] In the smaller and less developed district of Lumbwa fewer Africans were engaged under contract, but even here the magistrate, Senior Commissioner Tate, calculated that over the past year 14 percent of the cases heard at the Kericho court were registration offenses, and more than 20 percent came under the master and servant ordinance. "I am of the opinion," wrote Tate, "that these cases do not represent more than 50% of the charges which would be brought against native employees had every labour employer a Court of Law at his back door."[79] As courts became more accessible, and the country more developed, the burdens upon the magistrate would increase.

Isaac saw the greater empowerment of justices of the peace as the only practical solution to the problem, although he felt it would be safer for them to sit as a bench and not as individuals, and to hear cases under the registration and master and servant ordinances only where the employer had lodged the complaint, such as desertion. He did not think that justices of the peace should preside over remedies sought by the laborer, such as nonpayment of wages.[80] His doubts over giving justices full authority in labor cases reflected Tate's comment that European employers tended to regard the master and servant ordinance as binding only on the employee, and that the magistrate inevitably found himself adjudicating "the word of the master against that of the native." Tate had little confidence that justices drawn from the settler community would be impartial in such cases, a view reiterated by several other magistrates.[81]

Like many other magistrates, Tate regretted that so many trivial labor offenses under these ordinances necessarily appeared before the courts as criminal cases, when they might more reasonably be treated as civil matters.[82] C. S. Hemsted, the district commissioner for Embu, noted that the majority of convicted Africans on these petty charges found themselves imprisoned through their inability to pay the fine imposed by the court. It was almost inevitable that this should occur in numerous master and servant cases, as laborers were unlikely to have been paid wages while in dispute with their

78. NPC evidence of Francis Isaac.
79. NPC evidence of H. R. Tate (senior commissioner, Nyanza).
80. NPC evidence of Francis Isaac.
81. For example, H. R. Montgomery, the district commissioner at Kakamega, was "adamant the JPs should not be allowed authority over labour case"; NPC evidence.
82. NPC evidence of Tate and S. H. Carnelly.

employer, and were most probably attending a court far distant from their home areas, where they might have looked to raise the fine.[83] In contrast to the courts in European farming districts and in urban areas, when magistrates at courts in the African reserves imposed similar fines they were generally paid promptly.[84]

The question of punishments raised the greatest division of opinion among the magistracy. The Indian Penal Code operating in Kenya up until 1930 gave first- and second-class magistrates considerable discretion in deciding the punishments to be imposed, particularly with regard to flogging. The commission had been set up to reduce the numbers of convicts being impris-oned; recognizing that nonpayment of fines was a significant cause of impris-onment, many magistrates defended judicial flogging as the only alternative. Some were less wary of this recourse than were others. One magistrate, the resident commissioner in Nairobi, Joseph Wightman, stated that he had "fre-quently been asked by natives to award them lashes rather than a sentence of imprisonment," and this he had done. Eric Johnson, a barrister since 1902 and resident magistrate since 1915, and therefore one of Kenya's most experienced legal officers, reported that he had customarily given convicts at Nakuru a choice between imprisonment and a flogging, and that out of forty cases in only two had the African elected to go to jail. He assured the commission that all these cases were "comparatively trivial matters such as desertion under the master and servant ordinance." Johnson stoutly defended the practice, on the grounds that African wages were so low that fines would all too often result in the convict being incarcerated through inability to pay.[85]

The majority of magistrates giving evidence to the Punishments Com-mission advocated flogging as the most appropriate punishment for labor of-fenses, although they were more inclined to see the reason in the primitive stage of development of the African work force than in Johnson's economic pragmatism. Baringo's district commissioner Bamber lambasted those lib-erals who "misunderstood" the salutary effects of "a good thrashing" upon native labor, stating that he "thoroughly believed in it for all minor offences and especially for offences under the Master and servants Ordinance."[86] One of Nairobi's senior police officers and the town's resident magistrate were among the many who took the same view.[87] Several senior and experienced magistrates, such as de Wade, Palethorpe, and Fazan, worried about the ef-

83. NPC evidence of C. S. Hemsted, 27 Oct. 1921.
84. NPC evidence of R. F. Palethorpe (assistant district commissioner, Nairobi).
85. NPC evidence of Eric T. Johnson.
86. NPC evidence of F. J. Bamber.
87. NPC evidence of Wollesley-Bourne, R. F. Hamilton, and R. W. Hemsted.

fects of flogging but saw it as a necessary evil given the circumstances of the colony.[88] A much smaller minority, of whom Tate was the most articulate spokesperson, argued against corporal punishments for adult offenders of whatever race on moral grounds. Quoting at considerable length from a pamphlet entitled "Hints to Magistrates," by Kenya's former chief justice, Sir Robert Hamilton, Tate declared that flogging was "not for every day use but is a power in reserve for exceptional cases which call for sharp and stern punishment." This was in fact the line taken by the high court, but few of Kenya's magistrates appeared sympathetic to the policy. Only Tate and his close colleague S. H. Carnelly, the resident magistrate at Kisumu, followed through the logic of the argument that the many offenses under the master and servant codes that were not criminal should not be subject to corporal punishments.[89]

If magistrates were deeply divided over the efficacy of flogging, almost to a man they condemned any notion that employers should be given power to administer corporal punishments directly to laborers. However, it was widely acknowledged that "few settlers hesitate to flog their servants for petty offences,"[90] and most magistrates appear to have been little concerned by this practice, illegal though it was. Among employers it was generally argued that "employees prefer to be dealt with by their employers rather than be taken before a magistrate,"[91] this being presented as a just reason to give them plenary powers. Magistrate's objections were grounded primarily in their awareness of the dangers of excesses, a view perhaps sharpened by the several very brutal cases of beatings by Europeans that came before the courts while the Punishments Commission was sitting.[92]

When the Punishments Commission finally reported in 1923, three of its recommendations had a direct bearing upon the prosecution of master and servant cases. First, it was decided not to grant justices of the peace magisterial powers over labor offenses on the grounds that they lacked the necessary linguistic skills to hear cases effectively, that they were inadequately trained in the law, and that they would be in a difficult position in dealing with labor disputes among their neighbors and friends. Second, the commission made a general recommendation that offenders under the master and servant ordinance should be not be sent to jail and that first offenders in the case of trivial offenses should be cautioned. On the third recommendation, concern-

88. NPC evidence of de Wade, Palethorpe, and Fazan.
89. NPC evidence of Tate and Carnelly.
90. NPC evidence of R. W. Hemsted.
91. NPC evidence of Henry C. Stanning, a sisal planter from northern Nakuru.
92. The most notorious of these was the prosecution of Jasper Abraham for the murder of one of his African farm laborers: see PRO CO 533/305/46261 (1923).

ing flogging, the commissioners were unable to reach a unanimous verdict. The majority came out in favor of flogging as an acceptable form of punishment for African labor and preferable to imprisonment for petty offenders, although they were evidently aware that this was unlikely to meet with approval from the Colonial Office.[93]

The Native Punishments Commission had been established to find means of significantly reducing the numbers of Africans serving prison sentences for petty offenses against the labor legislation, but the statistics on prosecutions and punishments covering the interwar years show that no such effect was achieved. Table 16.1 presents the total number of convictions obtained for all cases heard under the master and servant ordinance from 1922 to 1939, along with convictions obtained under the native registration ordinance over broadly the same period. After the enactment of the latter ordinance it is safe to assume that relatively few laborers would have been prosecuted for desertion under the master and servant regulations, as detection and successful prosecution were easier and more likely under the registration ordinance. The vast majority of registration offenses concerned desertion, although a few employers were also prosecuted for failure to properly sign off laborers. These figures need to be treated merely as indicating the general trend of prosecutions. It can be seen that master and servant convictions showed no marked change, averaging around 1,600 per year. By contrast, convictions under the registration ordinance show a generally rising trend. For both ordinances, convictions show a peak over the recession years of 1929 to 1931, when the wages of African farm laborers and domestic servants were reduced.[94] Setting this in the wider context of the Kenyan court system, the overall number of convictions in all the courts of the colony shows a sharply rising trend over this period, reflecting the extension of colonial authority and the maturation of the legal system. In this respect, the master and servant convictions go against the general trend, suggesting that relatively fewer prosecutions were being pursued under these regulations over time.[95]

For the 1930s improvements in the court returns make it possible to break these aggregate figures down by race and gender and to begin to say something about rates of conviction, acquittal, and discharge, and about patterns of punishments. Table 16.2 presents an analysis of the combined prosecutions under the Employment of Natives Ordinance (which incorporated the master and servant codes from 1930) and the Domestic Servants Ordinance from

93. *Report of the Native Punishments Commission*, KNA AG 5/243.
94. Van Zwanenberg, *Colonial Capitalism*, 52–56.
95. For additional figures and a general analysis, D. Anderson, "Policing, Prosecution," 183–201.

TABLE 16.1.

Convictions under Master and Servants Ordinance, 1922–1939,
and Native Registration Ordinance, 1920–1938, Kenya

Year	Master and Servant Convictions	Native Registration Convictions	Male Africans in Registered Employment[a]
1920	n/a	206	n/a
1921	n/a	2,220	n/a
1922	2,187	2,494	119,170
1923	1,839	2,335	138,330
1924	1,387	2,240	133,890
1925	1,533	2,277	152,400
1926	1,417	2,956	169,000
1927	1,620	4,114	147,893
1928	1,312	3,121	152,274
1929	1,492	4,244	160,072[b]
1930	1,614	4,697	157,359
1931	2,434[c]	5,293	141,473
1932	1,626	4,610	132,089
1933	1,417	3,092	141,085
1934	2,095	3,605	n/a
1935	1,082	4,767	n/a
1936	1,447	4,567	173,000
1937	1,195	4,182	183,000
1938	1,754	3,527	182,964
1939	1,593	n/a	n/a

SOURCES: Compiled from Judicial Department Annual Reports in PRO CO 544 and Clayton and Savage, *Government and Labour*, 153 and 200, their primary source being the statistics presented in the NADAR. The third column, presenting average monthly numbers of Africans in registered employment, should also be treated with considerable caution, owing to the many irregularities from year to year in the collection of the figures. See van Zwanenberg, *Colonial Capitalism*, 73–75.

[a] Figures are monthly averages. In addition, a minimum of 150,000 African squatters were resident on European-owned farms by the 1930s, and the majority of these would have engaged in some form of employment on the farm for part of the year in lieu of rent.

[b] Taking 1929 as a sample year, African employment can be broken down into the following major subcategories: agricultural laborers, 76,830 (40%); domestic servants, 22,400 (12%); railway work, 15,000 (8%); and other government departments, 12,890 (7%).

[c] Increase in 1931 partly due to inclusion of convictions under Domestic Servants Ordinance (see Table 16.2 for breakdown).

TABLE 16.2.

Combined Prosecutions under Employment of Natives and
Domestic Servants Ordinances, 1931-1938, Kenya

	Europeans				Asians			
	Convicts		Acquitted/ Dismissed		Convicts		Acquitted/ Dismissed	
	M	F	M	F	M	F	M	F
1931	475	18	100	4	529	2	95	1
1932	242	16	54	14	202	1	79	—
1933	362	11	145	15	171	—	78	—
1934	691	193	50	18	46	1	30	—
1935	121	30	35	7	98	—	21	—
1936	440	12	210	4	110	2	28	1
1937	111	22	46	5	132	—	29	—
1938	150	26	18	5	104	—	45	—

	Africans				Totals			
	Convicts		Acquitted/ Dismissed		Convicts		All Cases	
	M	F	M	F	M	F	M	F
1931	1,407	3	335	2	2,411	23	2,941	30
1932	1,160	5	301	—	1,604	22	2,038	14
1933	865	8	286	1	1,398	19	1,907	35
1934	1,158	6	147	1	1,895	200	2,122	219
1935	825	8	232	—	1,044	38	1,332	45
1936	880	3	124	1	1,430	17	1,792	23
1937	928	2	180	—	1,171	24	1,426	29
1938	1,471	3	211	2	1,725	29	1,999	36

1931 to 1938, by race and by gender.[96] The relatively high total of cases for
1931, almost 3,000, represents a peak that is most probably linked to the impact of the depression upon labor relations. The low point in prosecutions,
1935, comes as the Kenyan economy was finally emerging from recession, but
the substantial fluctuation in rates of prosecution from year to year makes it
difficult to interpret the overall figures.

The prosecution figures reflect the racial division of Kenya's labor market. Over the period 1931-38, Africans were prosecuted in 65 percent of the

96. The figures have been gathered from the *Judicial Department Annual Reports*, 1931 to
1938, PRO CO 544/34 (1931), 38 (1932), 40 (1933), 44 (1934), 46 (1935), 49 (1936), 53 (1937),
and 55 (1938).

cases heard, Europeans in 22 percent, and Asians in 13 percent. Virtually all the Europeans prosecuted were employers, and it is perhaps surprising, given the general nature of Kenya's legal system at this time, that they represent 22 percent of the total convictions over the eight-year period. Many fewer Asians found themselves before the courts, and those who did were mostly either employers or domestic servants. By far the majority of those convicted were African, and most of these were laborers: of the 1,410 Africans convicted in 1931, 143 were domestic servants, 1,182 were laborers of various kinds, and only 85 were employers. Once brought before the courts, African laborers were more likely to be convicted than Asian or European employers. From 1931 to 1938, 23 percent of Asians and 20 percent of Europeans prosecuted were acquitted or dismissed, while only 17 percent of Africans escaped conviction.

The very small number of cases involving women probably fairly reflects the limited extent to which women then engaged in contractual labor: only 7 Asian women and 45 African women came before the courts between 1931 and 1938. Those European women prosecuted were all employers, numbering 400 over the eight-year period. The statistics on acquittals and dismissals suggests that the magistrates showed no greater leniency to European female employers than to male employers.

If we then look at the punishments enforced in these cases, a clearer picture emerges. Table 16.3 gives a breakdown of punishments of convicts by race. Beginning with an analysis of Europeans prosecuted, we see that of the 493 Europeans convicted in 1931, no less than 50 percent were simply bound over, and that none at all were given custodial sentences. The 23 Europeans who ended up in jail in 1931 did so as a result of their failure to pay the fines imposed by the courts. This reflects the general pattern of sentencing over the 1920s, when magistrates tended to treat European employers leniently. The replacement of the Indian Penal Code in 1930 with new regulations based on English law, along with the revision of much legislation that had been based on Indian laws, marked the beginnings of a change in the character of punishments imposed by the courts. After 1931 the effects of these changes can be seen as magistrates imposed sterner sentences against European employers.[97] Between 1931 and 1938 the greater majority of Europeans convicted were fined (70 percent of total sentences). More surprisingly, half of these convicts, 993 cases over the 1931–38 period, went to jail in default for nonpayment of fines. The obvious explanation for this is the impact of economic recession. No fewer than 598 Europeans were imprisoned for nonpayment of

97. H. Morris and Read, *Indirect Rule*, ch. 4.

TABLE 16.3.
Punishments by Race under Employment of Natives and
Domestic Servants Ordinances, 1931–1938, Kenya

	1931	1932	1933	1934	1935	1936	1937	1938
Europeans								
Fine	169	79	194	67	100	257	68	120
Prison in default	23	124	103	598	4	115	26	
Fine and prison					1			
Prison						1		
Whipping								
Bound over	247	5	1	176			2	6
Other punishment	54				1			
Cautioned	a	16	32	44	22	10	16	10
Damages or wages	a	34	43	9	23	69	47	14
Total	493	258	373	884	151	452	133	176
Asians								
Fine	274	110	65	33	58	91	68	80
Prison in default	170	19	37	4	6	7		2
Fine and prison	3		2			1		
Prison	1	1	2					
Whipping								
Bound over	72	2		1	1	2	2	1
Other punishment	11							
Cautioned	a	56	24	1	17	5	16	13
Damages or wages	a	15	41	8	16	6	47	8
Total	531	203	171	46	98	112	132	104
Africans								
Fine	275	153	121	117	150	141	148	274
Prison in default	169	198	204	183	118	140	243	443
Fine and prison	52	23	9	66	27	33	35	20
Prison	751	655	471	693	419	420	380	598
Whipping	19	15	3	3	5	4	27	2
Bound over	116	58	6	7	25	59	21	47
Other punishment	28	2	1	8	1	2		10
Cautioned	a	34	27	65	72	72	61	72
Damages or wages	a	27	31	22	16	14	15	8
Total	2,434	1,165	873	1,164	833	883	930	1,474

[a] Included within "other punishments" for 1931.

fines in 1934, the severest year of the recession when prices of coffee, maize, and sisal were lowest.[98] Labor department reports from the same year indicate that nonpayment of wages by employers to African laborers was a very serious problem, and so although we do not know the nature of the cases, we can infer that economic factors may have been at the root of a majority.[99] The numbers of Europeans serving custodial sentences for charges under these ordinances declined very sharply after 1936, as the economy, and especially the coffee price, recovered.

The court's treatment of Asian offenders conformed to a clearer and more consistent pattern, with only 6 percent of convicts being bound over while 73 percent received fines. Like Europeans, Asians were seldom awarded custodial sentences—only nine were handed down over this eight-year period. A much smaller proportion of Asian convicts—18 percent of the total as compared with 34 percent of European convicts—finished up in jail through nonpayment of court fines. Despite the European-cultivated image of the Asian as a bad employer, more than twice as many Europeans than Asians were convicted, and the number of Asians appearing before the courts was significantly lower as a proportion of their total population.

For Africans, the range of punishments imposed was considerably wider, although once again magistrates showed a distinct preference for a particular kind of punishment. As we have already noted, under the Indian Penal Code in the 1920s magistrates had enormous latitude in determining punishments, having the power to issue a whipping sentence in addition to other punishments under a very wide range of ordinances, including the master and servant ordinance. It was a principal complaint of the Bushe Commission, set up in the early 1930s to investigate the operation of the judicial system, that magistrates in the past had African convicts whipped almost as a matter of course.[100] Flogging had been endorsed by the Native Punishments Commission of 1921–23, and it was clearly supported by a wide cross-section of European public opinion in the colony throughout the 1920s. But where corporal punishments had been the norm for African convicts up to the 1920s, in the 1930s they were dramatically reduced; thereafter, most Africans were still sentenced to terms of imprisonment, albeit without a flogging. Between 1931 and

---

98. D. Anderson and Throup, "Agrarian Economy," 8–28.

99. *Native Affairs Department Annual Report*, 1934, "Labour Section Report," PRO CO 544/44.

100. *Report (Bushe) of the Commission of Enquiry into the Administration of Justice in Kenya, Uganda and the Tanganyika Territory in Criminal Matters*, May 1933 (London, 1934); H. Morris and Read, *Indirect Rule*, 119–20.

1938, no less than 48 percent of Africans convicted were awarded custodial sentences, and more than half of those fined were subsequently imprisoned for defaulting on payment. In total, 65 percent of those Africans convicted finished up in jail, while only 3 percent were bound over. This is precisely what many magistrates had feared when giving evidence to the Punishments Commission on the likely effect of replacing corporal punishments with fines for labor offenses.

More generally, this all suggests that the courts operated a highly differentiated pattern of sentencing that appears to have been racially determined: Europeans, all of whom were employers, could expect to be bound over or, at worst, fined; Asians, including both employers and employees, but with a high proportion of the cases relating to domestic servants, could expect to be fined by the court; Africans, the vast majority of whom were employees, could expect to be given custodial sentences. To some extent this reflected the differences between the courts' treatment of masters (Europeans and most Asians) and servants (Africans), but it was a difference heavily reinforced by the courts' racial attitude toward punishment.

Discussion

Analysis of these prosecutions under the master and servant legislation and other laws regulating labor can tell us relatively little about the social experience of the workplace, but a number of points can be made about the workers' experience of the law. Most significantly, the evidence before the Labour Commission and the Punishments Commission suggests that most infractions by workers or employers did not come to court at all. The vast majority of incidents were settled with "rough justice" on the farm. The assertion of many European settlers that this course of action was "welcomed" by African laborers should not be too hastily dismissed as an apologist's defense of the unethical. Few Africans were aware of their rights under labor law, and it is very likely that those who were had little faith in the colonial courts to uphold those rights. Although the magistrates became more moderate in their treatment of labor after 1930, largely because changes in the law limited their powers, it remains apparent that even after the abolition of the worst punitive provisions imposed under the Indian Penal Codes the courts were still inclined to act on behalf of the employer. That said, employer testimony suggests that the actions of colonial courts did not meet with their approval either, partly for bureaucratic reasons, but more substantively because court proceedings kept labor from the workplace and might also reveal the many dubious practices carried out on the farms by employers in breach of the labor laws. For employee and employer alike, summary justice on the farm may have appeared more attractive than the roulette wheel of the courtroom.

The wide range of legislation under which labor might be prosecuted for offenses relating to the workplace, especially breaches of contract, illustrates that the master and servant laws cannot be viewed in isolation. Social attitudes among European settlers supported the kind of master and servant regulations that had prevailed in England in the early nineteenth century, and their clamor for "better" laws was invariably linked to more rigorous punishments. But it is also notable that Kenya's European settlers were successful in obtaining a wide set of laws, within and beyond master and servant, that allowed them to continue to control and coerce labor in ways no longer politically or socially acceptable in England.

The history of labor legislation in Kenya may be best understood as an example of "delayed" legal reform, but the question remains as to why this was so. The history of labor law reform in nineteenth-century England is perhaps instructive here. Workers' rights were altered in the English reforms of 1875, by which time larger industrial employers no longer required the provisions for adjusted settlements that master and servant legislation had so long provided. Increasingly they faced labor in combination, negotiating settlements to workplace disputes with groups of workers or with the nominated representatives of workers. By contrast, small businesses employing less labor, and not wishing to confront labor in combination, preferred to remain with the master and servant regulations. The formulation of Kenya's labor laws might therefore be viewed as a product of the primitive development of capitalist forces within what was still, up to 1940, a predominantly rural and underdeveloped economy. Significantly, the transformation of the Kenyan economy wrought by the impact of the Second World War and its aftermath, which witnessed the emergence of growing service, commercial, assembly and manufacturing sectors, heralded an era of rapid labor law reform. Even in the agrarian sector this coincided with the increased commercialization of production on European-owned farms, with greater investment in mechanization as acreage under cultivation increased.[101] European settler farmers were themselves propelled into a different phase of capitalist development in this process. They quickly came to see less advantage in a casual labor force, employed ad hoc and paid in kind, but instead pushed hard for a shift to full wage labor and the increased proletarianization of the African work force.[102] Coupled with these changes, the legalization of African trade unions in the

101. Mosley, *Settler Economies*, chs. 5 and 6.

102. C. Leys, *Underdevelopment*, chs. 2 and 3, still offers the best general account of this process.

late 1930s and their dramatic growth in the later 1940s fundamentally altered the terrain on which Kenya's labor disputes were conducted. Even then, the principal of punitive sanctions against workers were not removed from the Kenyan labor statutes until the 1950s.[103]

To this extent, the evolution of master and servant regulations in colonial Kenya between the early 1900s and the 1950s would appear to have resembled that of England before the 1870s. If the reasons can be identified as partly linked to the evolution of the political economy, it must also be realized that the underpinnings of Kenya's labor laws were predominantly racial. The allowance of labor law in Kenya that was no longer acceptable in England had been argued on grounds of the "type" of labor to be employed. In the traditions of British imperial paternalism, African workers were to have a labor law suited to their status and stage of development. By this argument, the "rights" of labor were not negotiable by labor, but were defined by the laws of a state in which those laborers resided but had no participatory political role. As in England in an earlier era, it was to be a combination of economic development and political struggle that would see Kenya's workers escape from the worst punitive criminal sanctions of the master and servant regulations after 1940.[104]

103. Clayton and Savage, *Government and Labour*, ch. 11.
104. See Cooper's *Waterfront* for the best study of labor struggles in postwar Kenya yet published. But see also Hyde, "Plantation Struggles."

Bibliography of Secondary Works Cited

Adamson, Alan. *Sugar without Slaves*. New Haven, 1972.

Ahuja, Ravi. "The Origins of Colonial Labour Policy in Late 18th-Century Madras." 44 *International Review of Social History* 159 (1999).

Aiton, Grace. "The Selling of Paupers by Public Auction in Sussex Parish." 16 *New Brunswick Historical Society Collections* 93 (1961).

Alexander, Sally. "Women's Work in 19th-Century London." In *The Rights and Wrongs of Women*, edited by Juliet Mitchell and Ann Oakley, 59–111. Harmondsworth, 1976.

Allen, Carleton Kemp. *Law in the Making*. 7th ed. Oxford, 1964.

Allen, Richard B. *Slaves, Freedmen, and Indentured Labourers in Colonial Mauritius*. Cambridge, 1999.

Altink, Henrice. "Slavery by Another Name: Apprenticed Women in Jamaican Workhouses in the Period 1834–8." 26 *Social History* 40 (January 2001).

Anderson, David M. *Colonial Crimes: Law and Society in Kenya, 1895–1952*. Oxford, 2005.

———. "Master and Servant in Colonial Kenya, 1895–1939." 41 *Journal of African History* 459 (2000).

———. "Policing, Prosecution and the Law in Colonial Kenya, c. 1905–39." In *Policing the Empire: Government, Authority and Control, 1830–1940*, edited by David M. Anderson and David Killingray. Manchester, 1991.

———. "Policing the Settler State: Colonial Hegemony in Kenya, 1900–52." In *Contesting Colonial Hegemony: State and Society in Africa and India*, edited by Dagmar Engels and Shula Marks. London, 1994.

———. "Stock Theft and Moral Economy in Colonial Kenya." 56 *Africa* 399 (1986).

Anderson, David M., and David Killingray, eds. *Policing the Empire: Government, Authority and Control, 1830–1940*. Manchester, 1991.

Anderson, David M., and David W. Throup. "The Agrarian Economy of Central Province, Kenya, 1918–39." In *The Economies of Africa and Asia in the Inter-War Depression*, edited by Ian Brown. London, 1989.

Anderson, M. R. "Classifications and Coercions: Themes in South Asian Legal Studies in the 1980s." 10, no. 2 *South Asia Research* 158 (1990).

Arber, Edward, and A. G. Bradley, eds. *Travels and Works of Captain John Smith*. Edinburgh, 1910.

Armitage, David. *Ideological Origins of the British Empire*. Cambridge, 2001.

Arnold, David. "Plantations, Factories and Labour Law in Colonial India." Mimeograph, Institute of Commonwealth Studies. London, 1988.

Arthurs, H. W. *Without the Law: Administrative Justice and Legal Pluralism in Nineteenth-Century England.* Toronto, 1985.

Asiwaju, A. *Northern Yorubaland under French and British Rule.* Oxford, 1976.

Atiyah, Patrick. *The Rise and Fall of Freedom of Contract.* Oxford, 1979.

Atkinson, Alan. *Camden: Farm and Village Life in Early New South Wales.* Melbourne, 1988.

———. "Four Patterns of Convict Protest." 37 *Labour History* 28 (1979).

Baayen, R. Harald. *World Frequency Distributions.* Dordrecht, 2001.

Baehre, Rainer. "Paupers and Poor Relief in Upper Canada." *Historical Papers* 57 (1981).

Bagchi, A. K. *Private Investment in India, 1900–1939.* Cambridge, 1972.

Bain, 'Atu. "A Protective Labour Policy?: An Alternative Interpretation of Early Colonial Labour Policy in Fiji." 23 *Journal of Pacific History* 119 (1988).

Baker, J. H. *An Introduction to English Legal History.* 3rd ed. London, 1990.

Banner, Stuart. "When Christianity Was Part of the Common Law." 16 *Law and History Review* 27 (1998).

Bannister, Jerry. "The Campaign for Representative Government in Newfoundland." 5 *Journal of the Canadian Historical Association* 19 (1994).

———. "Crime and Criminal Justice in Eighteenth-Century Newfoundland." Ph.D. diss., University of Toronto, 1999.

———. *The Custom of the Country: Law and Naval Government in Newfoundland, 1699–1832.* Toronto, 2003.

———. "Irish Transportation in 1789 and Government in Newfoundland." Paper presented to the Canadian Historical Association annual meeting, St. John's, June 1997.

———. "The Naval State in Newfoundland, 1749-1791." 11 *Journal of the Canadian Historical Association* 17 (2000).

———. "Surgeons and Criminal Justice in Eighteenth-Century Newfoundland." In *Criminal Justice in the Old World and the New: Essays in Honour of J. M. Beattie,* edited by Greg T. Smith, A. N. May, and S. Devereaux. Toronto, 1997.

Barker, Anthony J. *Slavery and Antislavery in Mauritius, 1810–33.* London, 1996.

Barker, C. B. *Pilkington Brothers and the Glass Industry.* London, 1960.

Barnes, Thomas Garden. *Somerset, 1625–1640: A County's Government during the "Personal Rule."* Cambridge, 1961.

———, ed. *Somerset Assize Orders, 1629–1640.* Frome, 1959.

Bartrip, P. W. J., and S. B. Burman. *The Wounded Soldiers of Industry: Industrial Compensation Policy, 1833–1897.* Oxford, 1983.

Barwell, Noel Frederick, and Sudhansu Sekhar Kar. *The Law Relating to Service in India.* 3 vols. Bombay, 1952–57.

Bayly, C. A. *Imperial Meridian: The British Empire and the World, 1780–1830.* London, 1989.

———. *Rulers, Townsmen and Bazaars: North Indian Society in the Age of British Expansion, 1770–1870.* Cambridge, 1983.

Beattie, J. M. *Crime and the Courts in England, 1660–1800.* Princeton, 1986.

———. *Policing and Punishment in London, 1660–1750: Urban Crime and the Limits of Terror.* Oxford, 2001.

Beckett, J. C. *The Making of Modern Ireland, 1603–1923.* London, 1981.

Beckles, Hilary. "'Black Men in White Skins': The Formation of a White Proletariat in West Indian Slave Society." 15 *Journal of Imperial and Commonwealth History* 5 (1986).

———. "Rebels and Reactionaries: The Political Responses of White Labourers to Planter-Class Hegemony in Seventeenth-Century Barbados." 15 *Journal of Caribbean History* 1 (1981).

———. "A 'Riotous and Unruly Lot': Irish Indentured Servants and Freemen in the English West Indies, 1644–1713." 47 *William and Mary Quarterly* 503 (October 1990).

———. *White Servitude and Black Slavery in Barbados, 1627–1715.* Knoxville, 1989.

Behal, R. P., and Prabhu P. Mohapatra. "'Tea and Money versus Human Life': The Rise and Fall of the Indenture System in the Assam Tea Plantations." 19 *Journal of Peasant Studies* 142 (April–June 1992).

Beier, A. L. *Masterless Men: The Vagrancy Problem in England, 1560–1640.* London, 1985.

Bell, David Graham. "A Note on the Reception of English Statutes in New Brunswick." 28 *University of New Brunswick Law Journal* 195 (1979).

———. "Slavery and the Judges of Loyalist New Brunswick." 31 *University of New Brunswick Law Journal* 9 (1982).

Ben-Amos, Ilana Krausman. *Adolescence and Youth in Early-Modern England.* New Haven, 1994.

Benson, Adolph B. *Peter Kalm's Travels in North America: The English Version of 1770.* New York, 1987.

Benton, Lauren. *Law and Colonial Cultures: Legal Regimes in World History, 1400–1900.* Cambridge, 2002.

Berlin, Ira, and Philip D. Morgan, eds. *The Slaves' Economy: Independent Production by Slaves in the Americas.* London, 1991.

Berman, Bruce. *Control and Crisis in Colonial Kenya: The Dialectic of Domination.* London, 1990.

Berman, Bruce, and John Lonsdale. *Unhappy Valley: Conflict in Kenya and Africa.* London, 1992.

Bhattacharya, S. "Laissez faire in India." 2 *Indian Economic and Social History Review* 1 (1965).

Billings, Warren M. "The Law of Servants and Slaves in 17th-Century Virginia." 99 *Virginia Magazine of History and Biography* 45 (1991).

Bindon, Kathryn M. "Hudson's Bay Company Law: Adam Thom and the Institution of Order in Rupert's Land, 1839–54." In *Essays in the History of Canadian Law I,* edited by David H. Flaherty. Toronto, 1981.

Birch, Alan. *The Economic History of the British Iron and Steel Industry, 1784–1879.* London, 1967.

Bittermann, Rusty. "Farm Households and Wage Labour in the Northeastern Maritimes in the Early 19th Century." In *Contested Countryside: Rural Workers and Modern Society in Atlantic Canada, 1800–1950*, edited by Daniel Samson. Fredericton, 1994.

Blair, S. "The Revolt at Castle Forbes." 64 *Journal of the Royal Australian Historical Society* 78 (1978).

Boa, Sheena. "Experiences of Women Estate Workers during the Apprenticeship Period in St. Vincent, 1834–38: The Transition from Slavery to Freedom." 10 *Women's History Review* 381 (2001).

Boeyens, Jan C. A. "'Black Ivory': The Indenture System and Slavery in Zoutpansberg, 1848-1869." In *Slavery in South Africa: Captive Labor on the Dutch Frontier*, edited by Elizabeth A. Eldredge and Fred Morton. Boulder, Colo., and Pietermaritzburg, South Africa, 1994.

Bolland, Nigel O. "The Politics of Freedom in the British Caribbean." In *The Meaning of Freedom: Economics, Politics, and Culture after Slavery*, edited by Frank McGlynn and Seymour Drescher. Pittsburgh and London, 1992.

———. "Systems of Domination after Slavery: The Control of Land and Labour in the British West Indies after 1838." 23 *Comparative Studies in Society and History* 591 (1981).

Bookbinder, Jeff. "Black Man's Burden: An Analysis of Labour Legislation in Four British African Colonies." Unpublished manuscript, Osgoode Hall Law School, York University, Toronto, 1985.

Bowen, Lynne. "Independent Colliers at Fort Rupert: Labour Unrest on the West Coast, 1849." 69 *Beaver* 25 (April–May 1989).

Bradford, H. "The Industrial and Commercial Worker's Union of Africa in the South African Countryside, 1924-1930." Ph.D. diss., University of the Witwatersrand, 1985.

Brand, I. *The Convict Probation System: Van Diemen's Land, 1839–1854*. Hobart, 1990.

Brass, Tom, and Marcel van der Linden, eds. *Free and Unfree Labour: The Debate Continues*. New York, 1997.

Brereton, Bridget. "Family Strategies, Gender and the Shift to Wage Labour in the British Caribbean." In *The Colonial Caribbean in Transition: Essays on Post-Emancipation Social and Cultural History*, edited by Bridget Brereton and Keven A. Yelvington. Barbados, 1999.

———. *A History of Modern Trinidad, 1783–1972*. Kingston, 1981.

Brode, Patrick. "Simcoe and the Slaves." 73 *Beaver* 17 (1993).

Brooks, C. "Apprenticeship, Social Mobility and the Middling Sort, 1550-1800." In *The Middling Sort of People*, edited by J. Barry and C. Brooks. New York, 1994.

Brophy, Alfred L. "Law and Indentured Servitude in Mid-Eighteenth Century Pennsylvania." 28 *Willamette Law Review* 69 (1991-92).

Brown, Kathleen M. *Good Wives, Nasty Wenches, and Anxious Patriarchs: Gender, Race, and Power in Colonial Virginia*. Chapel Hill, 1996.

Brunet, Michel. *Les Canadiens après la conquête, 1759–1775: De la révolution canadienne à la révolution américaine*. Montreal, 1969.

Buell, Raymond Leslie. *The Native Problem in Africa*. New York, 1928.

Burley, Edith I. *Servants of the Honourable Company: Work, Discipline, and Conflict in the Hudson's Bay Company, 1770–1879*. Toronto, 1997.

Burn, W. L. *Emancipation and Apprenticeship in the British West Indies*. London, 1937.

Byrne, Cyril, ed. *Gentlemen-Bishops and Faction Fighters: The Letters of Bishops O Donel, Lambert, Scallan, and Other Irish Missionaries*. St. John's, 1984.

Byrne, P. J. *Criminal Law and the Colonial Subject: New South Wales, 1810–1830*. Cambridge, 1993.

Cadigan, Sean Thomas. *Hope and Deception in Conception Bay: Merchant-Settler Relations in Newfoundland, 1787–1855*. Toronto, 1995.

Cahill, Barry. "'How Far English Laws Are in Force Here': Nova Scotia's First Century of Reception Law Jurisprudence." 42 *University of New Brunswick Law Journal* 113 (1993).

———. "Slavery and the Judges of Loyalist Nova Scotia." 43 *University of New Brunswick Law Journal* 73 (1994).

Cairns, John W. "Employment in the Civil Code of Lower Canada: Tradition and Political Economy in Legal Classification and Reform." 32 *McGill Law Journal* 673 (1987).

Campbell, Alan B. *The Lanarkshire Miners: A Social History of Their Trade Unions, 1775–1974*. Edinburgh, 1979.

Canny, Nicholas P. "The Permissive Frontier: The Problem of Social Control in English Settlements in Ireland and Virginia, 1550–1650." In *The Westward Enterprise: English Activities in Ireland, the Atlantic, and America, 1480–1650*, edited by K. R. Andrews, N. P. Canny, and P. E. H. Hair. Liverpool, 1978.

Carpenter, Kenneth E., series ed. *Labour Disputes in the Mines: Eight Pamphlets, 1831–1844*. New York, 1972.

Carter, Marina. *Lakshiv's Legacy: The Testimonies of Indian Women in 19th-Century Mauritius*. Stanley, Mauritius, 1994.

———. *Servants, Sirdars and Settlers: Indians in Mauritius, 1834–1874*. Delhi, 1995.

Cashen, J. "Masters and Servants in South Australia, 1837–1860." 10 *Journal of the Historical Society of South Australia* 34 (1982).

Castles, A. *An Australian Legal History*. Sydney, 1982.

Chakrabarty, D. *Rethinking Working Class History: Bengal, 1890–1940*. Princeton, 1989.

Chakravarty, L. "Emergence of an Industrial Labour Force in a Dual Economy—British India, 1880–1920." 15 *Indian Economic and Social History Review* 249 (1978).

Challinor, Raymond. *Radical Lawyer in Victorian England: William Prowting Roberts and the Struggle for Workers' Rights*. London, 1990.

Challinor, Raymond, and Brian Ripley. *The Miners' Association: A Trade Union in the Age of Chartists*. London, 1968.

Chalmers, George. *Opinions of Eminent Lawyers on Various Points of English Jurisprudence*. London, 1858.

Chandavarkar, R. S. "Workers' Politics and the Mill Districts in Bombay between the Wars." 15 *Modern Asian Studies* 603 (1981).

Chanock, Martin. *The Making of South African Legal Culture, 1902–1936: Fear, Favour and Prejudice*. Cambridge and New York, 2001.

Chase, Ashton. *A History of Trade Unionism in Guyana, 1900 to 1961*. Ruimveflt, n.d.

Clairmont, Donald H., and Dennis W. Magill. *Nova Scotian Blacks: An Historical and Structural Overview*. Halifax, 1970.

Clark, Anna. *The Struggle for the Breeches: Gender and the Making of the British Working Class*. Berkeley, 1995.

Clarke, D. G. *Domestic Workers in Rhodesia: The Economics of Masters and Servants*. Salisbury, 1974.

Clayton, Anthony, and Donald C. Savage. *Government and Labour in Kenya, 1895–1963*. London, 1974.

Coghlan, T. *Labour and Industry in Australia*. Melbourne, 1969.

Colls, Robert. *The Pitmen of the Northern Coalfield*. Manchester and Wolfeboro, 1987.

Commins, D. W. D. *Note on Emigration from India to Trinidad*. Calcutta, 1893.

Commons, J. R., and J. B. Andrews. *Principles of Labor Legislation*. New York, 1915.

Connell, R. W., and T. H. Irving. *Class Structure in Australian History*. Melbourne, 1980.

Conrad, Robert Edgar. *The Destruction of Brazilian Slavery, 1850–1888*. Malabar, 1993.

Cooke, George Wingrove. *China: Being the Times' Special Correspondence from China in the Years 1857–1858*. London, 1858.

Cooper, Frederick. *Decolonisation and African Society*. Cambridge, 1996.

———. *From Slaves to Squatters: Plantation Labour and Agriculture in Zanzibar and Coastal Kenya, 1890–1925*. New Haven, 1980.

———. *On the African Waterfront: Urban Disorder and the Transformation of Work in Colonial Mombasa*. New Haven, 1987.

Copp, Terry. *The Anatomy of Poverty: The Condition of the Working Class in Montreal, 1897–1929*. Toronto, 1974.

Coquillette, Daniel R. "Radical Lawmakers in Colonial Massachusetts: The 'Countenance of Authoritie' and the Lawes and Libertyes." 67 *New England Quarterly* 179 (1994).

Crais, Clifton. *White Supremacy and Black Resistance in Pre-Industrial South Africa: The Making of the Colonial Order in the Eastern Cape, 1770–1865*. Cambridge, 1992.

Craven, Paul. "Automatic Detection and Visualization of Domain-Specific Similarities in Documents: DWIC Analysis and Its Application in the Master and Servant Project." In *La Historia en una Nueva Frontera/History in a New Frontier: Proceedings of the XIII International Conference of the Association for History and Computing, Toledo, 1998*, edited by F. J. A. Perez. CD-ROM. Cuenca, 2000.

———. "A General Purpose Conceptual Clustering Engine." In *Structures and Contingencies in Computerized Historical Research: Proceedings of the IXth International Conference of the Association for History and Computing, Nijmegen, 1994*, edited by Onno Boonstra, G. Collenteur, and B. van Elderen. 9 *Cahier Vereniging voor Geschiedenis en Informatica* 33 (1995).

————. "Law and Ideology: The Toronto Police Court, 1850–80." In *Essays in the History of Canadian Law II*, edited by David H. Flaherty. Toronto, 1983.

————. "The Law of Master and Servant in Mid-Nineteenth-Century Ontario." In *Essays in the History of Canadian Law I*, edited by David H. Flaherty. Toronto, 1981.

————. "Master and Servant Legislation of Atlantic Canada in Imperial Context." Paper presented at the Atlantic Law and History Workshop II, Dalhousie Law School, 1995.

————. "'The Modern Spirit of the Law': Blake, Mowat and the Breaches of Contract Act, 1877." In *Essays in the History of Canadian Law VIII, in Honour of R. C. B. Risk*, edited by Blaine Baker and Jim Phillips. Toronto, 1999.

————. "Workers' Conspiracies in Toronto, 1854–72." 14 *Labour/Le Travail* 49 (1984).

————, ed. *Labouring Lives: Work and Workers in Nineteenth-Century Ontario*. Toronto, 1995.

Craven, Paul, and Douglas Hay. "The Criminalization of 'Free' Labour: Master and Servant in Comparative Perspective." 15 *Slavery and Abolition* 71 (1994). Also in *Unfree Labour in the Development of the Atlantic World*, edited by Paul Lovejoy and Nicholas Rogers. London, 1995.

Creighton, W. B., W. Ford, and R. Mitchell. *Labour Law*. Sydney, 1993.

Crowley, F. "Master and Servant in Western Australia, 1829–1851." 4–5 *Journal and Proceedings of the Western Australian Historical Society* 94 (1953).

————. "Working Class Conditions in Australia, 1788–1851." Ph.D. diss., University of Melbourne, 1949.

Crowley, John. "Empire versus Truck: The Official Interpretation of Debt and Labour in the Eighteenth-Century Newfoundland Fishery." 70 *Canadian Historical Review* 311 (1989).

Crowley, Terry. "Rural Labour." In *Labouring Lives: Work and Workers in Nineteenth-Century Ontario*, edited by Paul Craven. Toronto, 1995.

Cunliffe, Marcus. *Chattel Slavery and Wage Slavery: The Anglo-American Context, 1830–1860*. Athens, 1979.

Cushing, John D., ed. *The Earliest Printed Laws of Pennsylvania*. Wilmington, 1978.

Daintree, Donald. "The Legal Periodical: A Study in the Communication of Information." M.A. thesis, Librarianship and Information Science, University of Sheffield, 1975.

Daniels, Christine. "Liberty to Complaine: Servant Petitions in Maryland, 1652–1797." In *The Many Legalities of Early America*, edited by Christopher L. Tomlins and Bruce H. Mann. Chapel Hill and London, 2001.

Darnell, M. "Law and the Regulation of Life: The Case of Indentured Chinese Labourers." Paper presented at the Ball and Chain Conference, University of New South Wales, December 1996.

Das, R. K. *History of Indian Labour Legislation*. Calcutta, 1941.

Das Gupta, Ranajit. "Factory Labour in Eastern India: Sources of Supply, 1855–1946 — Some Preliminary Findings." 13 *Indian Economic and Social History Review* 277 (1976).

Datta, S. B. *Capital Accumulation and Workers' Struggle: The Case of Tata Iron and Steel Company, 1910–1970.* Stockholm, 1980.

———. "Role of the Indian Worker in the Early Phase of Industrialization: A Critique of the Established View, with Special Reference to Tata Iron and Steel Co., 1910–1930." 20 *Economic and Political Weekly* M-130 (1985).

Davidoff, L., and C. Hall. *Family Fortunes: Men and Women of the English Middle Class, 1780–1850.* London, 1987.

Davidson, A. P. "An Analytical and Comparative History of Master and Servant Legislation in Tasmania." LL.M. thesis, University of Tasmania, 1975.

Davis, Mike. *Late Victorian Holocausts: El Niño Famines and the Making of the Third World.* London, 2001.

Deakin, S. "Contract, Labour Law and the Developing Employment Relationship." Ph.D. diss., Cambridge University, 1989.

———. "The Contract of Employment: A Study in Legal Evolution." 11 *Historical Studies in Industrial Relations* 1 (2001).

Dean, Warren. *Rio Claro: A Brazilian Plantation System, 1820–1920.* Stanford, 1976.

Deane, Phyllis, and W. A. Cole. *British Economic Growth, 1688–1959.* Cambridge, 1969.

Dechêne, Louise. *Habitants and Merchants in Seventeenth Century Montreal.* Translated by Liana Vardi. Montreal, 1992.

Dening, Greg. *Mr. Bligh's Bad Language: Passion, Power and Theatre on the Bounty.* Cambridge, 1992.

Diamond, C. R. "The Native Grievances Enquiry, 1913-14." 36 *South African Journal of Economics* 211 (1968).

Dictionary of Canadian Biography. 14 vols. to date. Toronto, 1966–.

Dixon, C. H. "Seamen and the Law: An Examination of the Impact of Legislation on the British Merchant Seaman's Lot, 1588–1918." Ph.D. diss., University of London, 1981.

Dobson, C. R. *Masters and Journeymen: A Prehistory of Industrial Relations, 1717–1800.* London, 1980.

Doxey, G. *The Industrial Colour Bar in South Africa.* Cape Town, 1961.

Drescher, Seymour. "Free Labor vs. Slave Labor: The British and Caribbean Cases." In *Terms of Labor,* edited by Stanley L. Engerman. Stanford, Calif., 1999.

Duman, Daniel. *The English and Colonial Bars in the Nineteenth Century.* London, 1983.

Dumett, Raymond, and Marion Johnson. "Britain and the Suppression of Slavery in the Gold Coast Colony, Ashanti and the Northern Territories." In *The End of Slavery in Africa,* edited by Suzanne Miers and Richard Roberts. London, 1988.

Dupont, Jerry. *The Common Law Abroad: Constitutional and Legal Legacy of the British Empire.* Littleton, Colo., 2001.

Dyson, Tim, ed. *India's Historical Demography: Studies in Famine, Disease and Society.* London, 1989.

Dyster, B. "Why New South Wales Did Not Become Devil's Island (or Siberia)." In *Beyond Convict Workers,* edited by B. Dyster. Sydney, 1996.

Dyster, B., and D. Meredith. *Australia in the International Economy in the 20th Century.* Cambridge, 1990.

Edgar, A. "On the Jurisdiction of Justices of the Peace in Disputes between Employers and Employed Arising from Breach of Contract." In *Transactions of the National Association for the Promotion of Social Science, 1859* 687 (1860).

Ekirch, A. Roger. *Bound for America: The Transportation of British Convicts to the Colonies, 1718–1775.* Oxford, 1987.

Elbourne, Elizabeth. "Freedom at Issue: Vagrancy Legislation and the Meaning of Freedom in Britain and the Cape Colony, 1799 to 1842." In *Unfree Labour in the Atlantic World*, edited by Paul Lovejoy and Nicholas Rogers. London, 1994.

Ellis, Henry. *Hong Kong to Manilla and the Lakes of Luzon, in the Philippine Isles in the Year 1856.* London, 1859.

Elphick, Richard, and Hermann Giliomee, eds. *The Shaping of South African Society, 1652–1840.* Middleton, Conn., 1988.

Elphick, Richard, and V. C. Malherbe. "The Khoisan to 1828." In *The Shaping of South African Society, 1652–1840*, edited by Richard Elphick and Hermann Giliomee. Middleton, Conn., 1988.

Eltis, David. "Europeans and the Rise and Fall of African Slavery in the Americas: An Interpretation." 98 *American Historical Review* 1399 (1993).

———. "Labour and Coercion in the English Atlantic World from the Seventeenth to the Early Twentieth Century." 14 *Slavery and Abolition* 207 (1993).

———. *The Rise of African Slavery in the Americas.* Cambridge, 2000.

———. "Slavery and Freedom in the Early Modern World." In *Terms of Labor*, edited by Stanley L. Engerman. Stanford, Calif., 1999.

Engels, Friedrich. *The Condition of the Working Class in England.* London, 1845.

Engerman, Stanley L. "Coerced and Free Labor: Property Rights and the Development of the Labor Force." 29 *Explorations in Entrepreneurial History* 1 (1992).

———. "Economic Adjustments to Emancipation in the United States and British West Indies." 13 *Journal of Interdisciplinary History* 191 (1982).

———. "The Economic Response to Emancipation and Some Economic Aspects of the Meaning of Freedom." In *The Meaning of Freedom: Economics, Politics, and Culture after Slavery*, edited by Frank McGlynn and Seymour Drescher. Pittsburgh and London, 1992.

———. "Servants to Slaves to Servants: Contract Labour and European Expansion." In *Colonialism and Migration: Indentured Labour before and after Slavery*, edited by P. C. Emmer. Boston, 1986.

———, ed. *Terms of Labor: Slavery, Serfdom, and Free Labor.* Stanford, Calif., 1999.

English, Christopher. "The Development of the Newfoundland Legal System to 1815." 20 *Acadiensis* 89 (1990).

E.N.N. [Anon.] "The Growth of Centipedism in British Guiana." *Georgetown Vignettes* 14 (1917).

Etherington, Norman. "Criminal Law and Colonial Fiji, 1875–1900." 31 *Journal of Pacific History* 42 (1996).

Fergusson, Charles Bruce, ed. *The Diary of Adolphus Gaetz*. Halifax, 1965.

Fieldhouse, David. *Merchant Capital and Economic Decolonization: The United Africa Company, 1929-1989*. Oxford, 1994.

Fingard, Judith. *Jack in Port: Sailortowns of Eastern Canada*. Toronto, 1982.

Fischer, David Hackett. *Albion's Seed: Four British Folkways in America*. New York, 1989.

Fleming, Roy F. "Negro Slaves with the Loyalists in Upper Canada." 45 *Ontario History* 27 (1953).

Fletcher, Ian, C. L. E. Nym Mayhall, and Philippa Levine, eds. *Women's Suffrage in the British Empire: Citizenship, Nation, and Race*. London and New York, 2000.

Forster, G. C. F. "The North Riding Justices and Their Sessions, 1603-1625." 10 *Northern History* 102 (1975).

Foster, D. "Class and County Government in Early-Nineteenth Century Lancashire." 9 *Northern History* 48 (1974).

Frank, Christopher. "Constitutional Law versus Justices' Justice: Trade Unions, Lawyers, and Magistrates, 1842-1857." Ph.D. diss., York University, Toronto, 2003.

———. " 'He Might Almost as Well Be without Trial': Trade Unions and the 1823 Master and Servant Act—the Warrington Cases, 1846-47." 14 *Historical Studies in Industrial Relations* 3 (Autumn 2002).

Frankel, S. H. *Capital Investment in Africa*. London, 1938.

Freedland, M. R. *The Contract of Employment*. Oxford, 1976.

Fremantle, S. H. "The Problem of Indian Labour Supply." 57 *Journal of the Royal Society of Arts* 510 (1909).

Freund, Bill. *The African Worker*. Cambridge, 1988.

———. *Capital and Labour in the Nigerian Tin Mines*. London, 1981.

Fudge, Judy, and Eric Tucker. "Law, Industrial Relations, and the State: Pluralism or Fragmentation?: The Twentieth-Century Employment Regime in Canada." 46 *Labour/Travail* 251 (Fall 2000).

Fynes, Richard. *The Miners of Northumberland and Durham: A History of Their Social and Political Progress*. Sunderland, 1873.

Fyson, Donald. *The Court Structure of Quebec and Lower Canada, 1764 to 1860*. Montreal, 1994.

———. "Criminal Justice, Civil Society and the Local State: The Justices of the Peace in the District of Montreal, 1764-1830." Ph.D. diss., Université de Montréal, 1995.

Gadd, Ian A., and Patrick Wallis, eds. *Guilds, Society and Economy in London, 1450-1800*. London, 2002.

Galanter, M. *Law and Society in Modern India*. Delhi, 1989.

Galenson, David W. "Labor Market Behavior in Colonial America: Servitude, Slavery, and Free Labor." In *Markets in History: Economic Studies of the Past*, edited by David W. Galenson. Cambridge, 1989.

———. *White Servitude in Colonial America*. Cambridge, 1981.

Gardiner, F., and C. Lansdown. *South African Criminal Law and Procedure*. Cape Town, 1924.

Gash, Norman. *Sir Robert Peel: The Life of Sir Robert Peel after 1830*. Totowa, N.J., 1972.

George, Staughton, B. M. Nead, and T. McCamant, eds. *Charter to William Penn, and Laws of the Province of Pennsylvania.* Harrisburg, 1879.

Ghai, Y. P., and J. P. W. B. McAuslan. *Public Law and Political Change in Kenya.* London, 1970.

Gilmour, James M. *Spatial Evolution of Manufacturing: Southern Ontario, 1851–1891.* Toronto, 1972.

Girard, Philip. "The Rise and Fall of Urban Justice in Halifax, 1815–1886." 8 *Nova Scotia Historical Review* 57 (1988).

Giri, V. V. *Labour Problems in Indian Industry.* Bombay, 1972.

Godfrey, Barry. "Judicial Impartiality and the Use of Criminal Law against Labour: The Sentencing of Workplace Appropriators in Northern England, 1840–1880." 3(2) *Histoire et Sociétés/Crime, History and Societies* 57 (1999).

Goldring, Philip. "Employment Relations in the Fur Trade, 1821–1892." Paper presented at the Canadian Historical Association annual meeting, Halifax, 1981.

Goodrich, C. L. "The Australian and American Labour Movements." 4 *Economic Record* 193 (1928).

Graves, A. "From Truck to Gifts: The Trade Box System in a Colonial Economy, 1863–1906." Paper presented at the Commonwealth Labour History Conference, Warwick University, September 1981.

Green, William A. "The Apprenticeship System in British Guiana, 1834–38." 9 *Caribbean Studies* 49 (1969–70).

———. *British Slave Emancipation: The Sugar Colonies and the Great Experiment, 1830–1865.* London, 1976.

———. "Emancipation to Indenture: A Question of Imperial Morality." 22 *Journal of British Studies* 98 (1983).

Greer, Allan. *Peasant, Lord, and Merchant: Rural Society in Three Quebec Parishes, 1740–1840.* Toronto, 1985.

———. *The People of New France.* Toronto, 1997.

Griffiths, P. *A History of the Indian Tea Industry.* London, 1967.

Griffiths, Paul. "Masterless Young People in Norwich, 1560–1645." In *The Experience of Authority in Early Modern England*, edited by Paul Griffiths, Adam Fox, and Steve Hindle. London, 1996.

———. *Youth and Authority: Formative Experiences in England, 1560–1640.* Oxford, 1996.

Gritt, A. J. "The Survival of 'Service' in the English Agricultural Labour Force: Lessons from Lancashire, c. 1650–1851." 50 *Agricultural History Review* 25 (2002).

Grubb, Farley. "Does Bound Labour Have to Be Coerced Labour? The Case of Colonial Immigrant Servitude versus Craft Apprenticeship and Life-Cycle Servitude-in-Husbandry." 21 *Itinerario* 115 (1997).

———. "The End of European Immigrant Servitude in the United States: An Economic Analysis of Market Collapse, 1772–1835." 54 *Journal of Economic History* 796 (1994).

———. "Immigration and Servitude in the Colony and Commonwealth of Pennsylvania: A Quantitative and Economic Analysis." Ph.D. diss., University of Chicago, 1984.

————. "The Long-Run Trend in the Value of European Immigrant Servants, 1654–1831: New Measurements and Interpretations." 14 *Research in Economic History* 167 (1992).

————. "The Market for Indentured Immigrants: Evidence on the Efficiency of Forward-Labor Contracting in Philadelphia, 1745–73." 45 *Journal of Economic History* 855 (1985).

————. "Servant Auction Records and Immigration into the Delaware Valley, 1745–1831: The Proportion of Females among Migrant Servants." 133 *Proceedings of the American Philosophical Society* 157 (1989).

Guild, Purcell June. *Black Laws of Virginia: A Summary.* New York, 1936. Reprint, 1969.

Hahlo, H., and E. Kahn. *South Africa: Its Laws and Constitution.* London, 1960.

Hall, Douglas G. *Five of the Leewards, 1834–1870: The Major Problems of the Post-Emancipation Period in Antigua, Barbuda, Montserrat, Nevis and St. Kitts.* Barbados, 1971.

Hamilton, Gilian. "Contract Incentives and Apprenticeship: Montreal, 1791–1820." Ph.D. diss., Queen's University, 1993.

Hammond, J. L., and Barbara Hammond. *The Skilled Labourer.* Edited by John Rule. London, 1975.

Hancock, David. "'A World of Business to Do': William Freeman and the Foundation of England's Commercial Empire, 1645–1707." 57 *William and Mary Quarterly*, 3rd ser., 3 (2000).

Handcock, Gordon. "Benjamin Lester." In *Dictionary of Canadian Biography*, 5:490–92. Toronto, 1983.

————. "The Lester Diaries and the Summer of 1767." Paper presented to the Wessex Society, St. John's, 1995.

————. *Soe Longe as There Comes Noe Women: Origins of English Settlement in Newfoundland.* St. John's, 1989.

————. *The Story of Trinity.* St. John's, 1997.

Hansen, Karen Tranberg. *Distant Companions: Servants and Employers in Zambia, 1900–1985.* London, 1989.

Hardy, Jean-Pierre, and David-Thiery Ruddel. *Les apprentis artisans à Québec 1660–1815.* Montreal, 1977.

Harring, Sidney L. *White Man's Law: Native People in Nineteenth-Century Canadian Jurisprudence.* Toronto, 1998.

Harris, Douglas Colebrook. *Fish, Law, and Colonialism: The Legal Capture of Salmon in British Columbia.* Toronto, 2001.

Harris, J. "The Struggle against Pacific Island Labour, 1868–1902." 15 *Labour History* 40 (1968).

Harrison, Brian, gen. ed. *Oxford Dictionary of National Biography.* 60 vols. Oxford, 2004.

Hartlen, Gary. "Bound for Nova Scotia: Slaves in the Planter Migration, 1759–1800." In *Making Adjustments: Change and Continuity in Planter Nova Scotia, 1759–1800*, edited by Margaret Conrad. Fredericton, 1991.

Hassell Smith, A. *County and Court*. Oxford, 1974.

———. "Labourers in Late Sixteenth-Century England: A Case Study from North Norfolk: Part I." 4 *Continuity and Change* 11 (1989).

Hassell Smith, A., Gillian M. Baker, and R. W. Kenny, eds. *The Papers of Nathaniel Bacon of Stiffkey*. 3 vols. Norwich, 1979–.

Havinden, Michael, and David Meredith. *Colonialism and Development: Britain and Its Tropical Colonies, 1850–1960*. London, 1993.

Hay, Douglas. "Dread of the Crown Office: The English Magistracy and King's Bench, 1740–1800." In *Law, Crime and English Society, 1660–1840*, edited by Norma Landau. Cambridge, 2002.

———. "Judges and Magistrates: High Law and Low Law in England and the Empire." In *The British and Their Laws in the Eighteenth Century*, edited by David Lemmings. London, 2005.

———. "The Laws of God and the Laws of Man: Lord George Gordon and the Death Penalty." In *Protest and Survival: Essays for E. P. Thompson*, edited by John Rule and Robert Malcolmson. London, 1993.

———. "Master and Servant in England: Using the Law in the Eighteenth and Nineteenth Centuries." In *Private Law and Social Inequality in the Industrial Age: Comparing Legal Cultures in Britain, France, Germany and the United States*, edited by Willibald Steinmetz. Oxford, 2000.

———. "The Meanings of the Criminal Law in Quebec, 1764 to 1774." In *Crime and Justice in Europe and Canada*, edited by Louis Knafla. Montreal, 1981.

———. "Patronage, Paternalism, and Welfare: Masters, Workers, and Magistrates in Eighteenth-Century England." 53 *International Labor and Working-Class History* 27 (1998).

———. "The State and the Market: Lord Kenyon and Mr. Waddington." 162 *Past and Present* 101 (1999).

———. "Time, Inequality, and Law's Violence." In *Law's Violence*, edited by Austin Sarat and Thomas R. Kearns. Ann Arbor, 1992.

Hay, Douglas, and Paul Craven. "Master and Servant in England and the Empire: A Comparative Study." 31 *Labour/Le Travail* 175 (1993).

Hay, Douglas, and Nicholas Rogers. *Eighteenth-Century English Society: Shuttles and Swords*. Oxford, 1997.

Head, Grant C. *Eighteenth Century Newfoundland: A Geographer's Perspective*. Toronto, 1976.

Hecht, J. J. *The Domestic Servant Class in England*. Westport, Conn., 1981.

Helmcken, John Sebastian. *The Reminiscences of Doctor John Sebastian Helmcken*. Edited by Dorothy Blakey Smith, with an introduction by W. Kaye Lamb. Vancouver, 1975.

Hening, William Waller. *The Statutes at Large; Being a Collection of all the Laws of Virginia, from the First Session of the Legislature, in the Year 1619*. 13 vols. in various editions beginning New York, 1823; facsimile reprint of selected editions Charlottesville, Va., 1969.

Heron, Craig. "Factory Workers." In *Labouring Lives: Work and Workers in Nineteenth-Century Ontario*, edited by Paul Craven. Toronto, 1995.

Herrick, Cheesman A. *White Servitude in Pennsylvania: Indentured and Redemption Labor in Colony and Commonwealth*. New York, 1969.

Higgins, H. B. "A New Province for Law and Order (Part 1)." 29 *Harvard Law Review* 13 (1915).

Higman, Barry W. *Slave Populations of the British Caribbean, 1807–34*. Baltimore, 1984.

———. "Urban Slavery in the British Caribbean." In *Perspectives on Caribbean Regional Identity*, edited by Elizabeth M. Thomas-Hope. Liverpool, 1984.

Hill, Bridget. *Servants: English Domestics in the Eighteenth Century*. Oxford, 1996.

Hilton, G. W. *The Truck System: Including a History of the British Truck Acts, 1465–1960*. Cambridge, 1960.

Hirst, J. B. *Convict Society and Its Enemies*. Sydney, 1983.

Hoe, Susanna. *The Private Life of Old Hong Kong: Western Women in the British Colony, 1841–1941*. Hong Kong, 1991.

Hogg, Grace Laing. "The Legal Rights of Masters, Mistresses and Domestic Servants in Montreal, 1816–1829." M.A. thesis, McGill University, 1989.

Hogg, Grace Laing, and Gwen Shulman. "Wage Disputes and the Courts in Montreal, 1816–1835." In *Class, Gender and the Law in 18th- and 19th-Century Quebec: Sources and Perspectives*, edited by Donald Fyson, C. M. Coates, and K. Harvey. Montreal, 1993.

Holdsworth, W. S. *A History of English Law*. 17 vols. London, 1903–72.

Holman, H. T. "Slaves and Servants on Prince Edward Island: The Case of Jupiter Wise." 12 *Acadiensis* 100 (1982).

Holt, Thomas C. *The Problem of Freedom: Race, Labor and Politics in Jamaica, 1832–1938*. London, 1992.

Hooker, M. B. *Legal Pluralism: An Introduction to Colonial and Neo-Colonial Laws*. Oxford, 1975.

Hornby, Jim. *Black Islanders: Prince Edward Island's Historical Black Community*. Charlottetown, 1991.

Horwitz, Morton J. *The Transformation of American Law, 1870–1960: The Crisis of Legal Orthodoxy*. New York, 1992.

Houston, Cecil, and William Smyth. *Irish Emigration and Canadian Settlement: Patterns, Links, and Letters*. Toronto, 1990.

Hyde, David. "Plantation Struggles in Kenya: Trades Unions on the Land, 1945–63." Ph.D. diss., SOAS, University of London, 2001.

Iliffe, John. *The Africans: The History of a Continent*. Cambridge, 1995.

———. *A Modern History of Tanganyika*. Cambridge, 1979.

Illick, Joseph E. *Colonial Pennsylvania: A History*. New York, 1976.

Innes, Joanna. "Prisons for the Poor: English Bridewells, 1555–1800." In *Labour, Law and Crime: An Historical Perspective*, edited by Francis Snyder and Douglas Hay. London, 1987.

———. "Statute Law and Summary Justice in Early Modern England." 52 *Bulletin of the Society for the Study of Labour History* 34 (1987).

Innes, Stephen. *Creating the Commonwealth: The Economic Culture of Puritan New England*. New York, 1995.

———. "Fulfilling John Smith's Vision." In *Work and Labor in Early America*, edited by Stephen Innes. Chapel Hill, 1988.

Innis, Harold Adams. *The Fur Trade in Canada: An Introduction to Canadian Economic History*. Toronto, 1956.

International Confederation of Free Trade Unions. *Internationally-Recognised Core Labour Standards in Canada: Report for the WTO General Council Review of the Trade Policies of Canada*. Geneva, 2000.

Ireland, Willard E. "The Appointment of Governor Blanshard." 8 *British Columbia Historical Quarterly* 213 (1944).

Irving, Grant. *Indian Summer: Lutyens, Baker and Imperial Delhi*. New Haven, 1981.

Jack, Isaac Allen. "The Loyalists and Slavery in New Brunswick." 4 *Proceedings and Transactions of the Royal Society of Canada*, Section II, 137 (1898).

Janson, Charles William. *The Stranger in America*. London, 1807.

Janzen, Olafe Uwe. "Newfoundland and the International Fishery." In *Canadian History: A Reader's Guide*, vol. 1, *Beginnings to Confederation*, edited by M. Brook Taylor. Toronto, 1994.

———. "Showing the Flag: Hugh Palliser in Western Newfoundland in 1764." 3 *Northern Mariner/Le Marin du Nord* 3 (1993).

———. "'They Are Not Such Great Rogues as Some of Their Neighbours': A Scottish Supercargo in the Newfoundland Fish Trade, 1726." Paper presented to the Canadian Historical Association annual meeting, St. Catharines, 1996.

Jenkins, Edward. *The Coolie, His Rights and Wrongs*. London, 1871.

Jenkins, J. G., ed. *A History of the County of Stafford*. Vol. 8. London, 1963.

Jewell, Joseph. "Autobiographical Memoir of Joseph Jewell, 1763-1846." Edited by A. W. Slater. 22 *Camden Miscellany* 1964.

Johnstone, F. A. *Class, Race and Gold*. London, 1976.

Jones, Alice Hanson. *American Colonial Wealth: Documents and Methods*. 3 vols. New York, 1978.

Jordaan, B. "Employment Relations." In *Southern Cross: Civil and Common Law in South Africa*, edited by R. Zimmerman and D. Visser. Oxford, 1996.

Junior, Osmond Tiffany. *The Canton Chinese; or, The American Sojourn in the Celestial Empire*. Boston, 1849.

Kahn-Freund, Otto. "Blackstone's Neglected Child: The Contract of Employment." 93 *Law Quarterly Review* 508 (1977).

Kanogo, Tabitha. *Squatters and the Roots of Mau Mau*. London, 1987.

Karsten, Peter. *Between Law and Custom: High and Low Cultures in the Lands of the British Diaspora—The United States, Canada, Australia, and New Zealand, 1600-1900*. Cambridge, 2002.

Kealey, Gregory, ed. *Canada Investigates Industrialism: The Royal Commission on the Relations of Labor and Capital, 1889*. Toronto, 1973.

———. *Toronto Workers Respond to Industrial Capitalism, 1867-92*. Toronto, 1980.

Kelly, J. D. "Coolie as a Labour Commodity: Race, Sex, and European Dignity in Colonial Fiji." 19 *Journal of Peasant Studies* 246 (April–June 1992).

Kelly, Kevin P. "A Demographic Description of Seventeenth-Century York County, Virginia." Unpublished manuscript, Colonial Williamsburg Foundation, n.d.

Kelsall, R. K. "Wage Regulation under the Statute of Artificers." In *Wage Regulation in Pre-Industrial England*, edited by W. E. Minchinton. Newton Abbot, 1972.

Kennedy, William, Paul McClure, and Gustave Lanctot, eds. *Reports on the Laws of Quebec, 1767–1770*. Ottawa, 1931.

Kent, Joan. *The English Village Constable, 1580–1642*. Oxford, 1986.

Kercher, B. "Commerce and the Development of Contract Law in Early New South Wales." 9 *Law and History Review* 299 (1991).

King, Peter. *Crime, Justice, and Discretion in England, 1740–1820*. Oxford, 2000.

———. "The Summary Courts and Social Relations in Eighteenth-Century England." *Past and Present* (forthcoming).

Kitching, Gavin. *Class and Economic Change in Kenya: The Making of an African Petite-Bourgeoisie*. New Haven, 1980.

Klein, Herbert, and Stanley L. Engerman. "The Transition from Slave to Free Labor: Notes on a Comparative Economic Model." In *Between Slavery and Free Labor*, edited by Moreno Fraginals, Moya Pons, and Stanley L. Engerman. New York, 1985.

Knaplund, Paul. "James Stephen on Granting Vancouver Island to the Hudson's Bay Company, 1846–1848." 9 *British Columbia Historical Quarterly* 259 (1945).

Knipe, John Richard. "The Justice of the Peace in Yorkshire, 1820–1914: A Social Study." Ph.D. diss., University of Wisconsin, 1970.

Kolish, Evelyn. "The Impact of the Change in Legal Metropolis on the Development of Lower Canada's Legal System: Judicial Chaos and Legislative Paralysis in the Civil Law, 1791–1838." 3 *Canadian Journal of Law and Society* 1 (1988).

———. "Imprisonment for Debt in Lower Canada, 1791–1840." 32 *McGill Law Journal* 603 (1987).

Kooiman, Dick. *Bombay Textile Labour: Managers, Trade Unionists and Officials, 1918–1939*. New Delhi and Amsterdam, 1989.

Kussmaul, Ann. *Servants in Husbandry*. Cambridge, 1981.

Lacey, M. *Working for Baroko*. Johannesburg, 1981.

Lahey, Raymond. "Catholicism and Colonial Policy in Newfoundland, 1779–1845." In *Creed and Culture: The Place of English-Speaking Catholics in Canadian Society, 1750–1930*, edited by T. Murphy and G. Stortz. Toronto, 1993.

Lai, Walton Look. *Indentured Labor, Caribbean Sugar: Chinese and Indian Migrants to the British West Indies, 1838–1918*. Baltimore and London, 1993.

Lal, Brij V. "'Nonresistance' on Fiji Plantations: The Fiji Indian Experience, 1870–1920." In *Plantation Workers: Resistance and Accommodation*, edited by Brij V. Lal, Doug Munro, and Edward D. Beechert. Honolulu, 1993.

Lamb, W. Kaye. "The Governorship of Richard Blanshard." 14 *British Columbia Historical Quarterly* 1 (1950).

Lancaster, Alan. "Proposals for Hinterland Settlement and Development of British Guiana, 1884-1890." 59 *History Gazette* 1 (1993).

Landau, Norma. *The Justices of the Peace, 1679-1760*. Berkeley, 1984.

———. "The Trading Justice's Trade." In *Law, Crime and English Society, 1660-1840*, edited by Norma Landau. Cambridge, 2002.

Lane, Joan. *Apprenticeship in England, 1600-1914*. London, 1996.

Lane, W. *The Workingman's Paradise: An Historical Novel*. Brisbane, 1892.

Larose, Michel. "Les contrats d'engagement des travailleurs forestières de la Mauricie." 13 *Material History Bulletin* 69 (1981).

Laurence, K. O. "The Evolution of Long-Term Labour Contracts in Trinidad and British Guiana, 1834-1863." 5 *Jamaican Historical Review* 9 (1965).

———. *A Question of Labour: Indentured Immigration into Trinidad and British Guiana, 1875-1917*. Kingston and London, 1994.

Leechman, A. *The British Guiana Handbook*. London, 1913.

Lemon, James T. *The Best Poor Man's Country: A Geographical Study of Early Southeastern Pennsylvania*. Baltimore, 1972.

Levine, David, and Keith Wrightson. *The Making of an Industrial Society: Whickham, 1560-1765*. Oxford, 1991.

Levy, Barry. *Quakers and the American Family: British Settlement in the Delaware Valley*. New York, 1988.

Levy, Norman. *Transvaal: The Foundations of the South African Cheap Labour System*. London, 1982.

Leys, Colin. *Underdevelopment in Kenya: The Political Economy of Neo-Colonialism*. London, 1975.

Leys, Norman. *Kenya*. London, 1924.

Ligon, Richard. *A True and Exact History of the Island of Barbados*. 1673. Reprint, London, 1970.

Linebaugh, Peter, and Marcus Rediker. *The Many-Headed Hydra: Sailors, Slaves, Commoners, and the Hidden History of the Revolutionary Atlantic*. Boston, 2000.

Lipson, E. *The Economic History of England*. Vol. 3, *The Age of Mercantilism*. 6th ed. London, 1956.

Loades, David. *The Mid-Tudor Crisis, 1545-1565*. London, 1992.

Louis, William Roger, gen. ed. *The Oxford History of the British Empire*. 5 vols. Oxford, 1998-99.

Lovejoy, Paul E., and Jan S. Hogendown. *Slow Death of Slavery: The Course of Abolition in Northern Nigeria, 1897-1936*. Cambridge, 1993.

Lucassen, Jan. "Free and Unfree Labour before the Twentieth Century: A Brief Overview." In *Free and Unfree Labor: The Debate Continues*, edited by Tom Brass and Marcel van der Linden. New York, 1997.

Lutz, John. "After the Fur Trade: The Aboriginal Labouring Class of British Columbia, 1849-1890." 3 *Journal of the Canadian Historical Association* 69 (1992).

Machin, Frank. *The Yorkshire Miners: A History*. Barnsley, Yorks., 1958.

Mackenzie, John M. *The Empire of Nature: Hunting, Conservation and British Imperialism*. Manchester, 1988.

Mackie, Richard. *Trading beyond the Mountains: The British Fur Trade on the Pacific, 1793–1843*. Vancouver, 1997.

Madden, Frederick, and David Fieldhouse. "Imperial Policy and Legislation, 1689–c. 1760." In *The Classical Period of the First British Empire, 1689–1783: The Foundations of a Colonial System of Government*, edited by F. Madden and D. Fieldhouse. Westport, Conn., 1985.

Makahonuk, Glen. "Wage-Labour in the Northwest Fur Trade Economy, 1760–1849." 41 *Saskatchewan History* 1 (1988).

Mandelbrote, H. J. *Cambridge History of South Africa*. Vol. 8, *Constitutional Development, 1834–58*. 2nd ed. Cambridge, 1959.

Mandle, Jay R. *The Plantation Economy: Population and Economic Change in Guyana, 1838–1960*. Philadelphia, 1973.

Manley Smith, C. *The Law of Master and Servant*. London, 1860.

Mannion, J. J. "The Maritime Trade of Waterford in the Eighteenth Century." In *Common Ground: Essays on the Historical Geography of Ireland*, edited by W. Smyth and Kevin Whelan. Cork, 1988.

———, ed. *The Peopling of Newfoundland: Essays in Historical Geography*. St. John's, 1977.

Marquis, Greg. "State or Community? Criminal Justice in Halifax, 1815–1867." Paper presented at the Atlantic Law and History Workshop II, Dalhousie Law School, 1995.

Marshall, John George. *The Justice of the Peace and County and Township Officer in the Province of Nova Scotia*. Halifax, 1846.

Marshall, P. J. "Britain without America — A Second Empire?" In *The Oxford History of the British Empire*, vol. 2, edited by P. J. Marshall. Oxford, 1998.

Marshall, W. K. "The Termination of Apprenticeship in Barbados and the Windward Islands: An Essay in Colonial Administration and Politics." 5 *Journal of Caribbean History* 1 (1971).

Martin, Robert Montgomery. *Reports, Minutes and Despatches on the British Position and Prospects in China*. London, 1846.

Masters, Betty R. *The Chamberlain of the City of London, 1237–1987*. London, 1988.

Mathieson, William Law. *British Slavery and Its Abolition, 1823–1838*. New York, 1967.

Matthews, Keith. *Lectures on the History of Newfoundland, 1500–1830*. St. John's, 1988.

Maxwell-Stewart, H. "The Bushrangers and the Convict System of Van Diemen's Land, 1803–1846." Ph.D. diss., University of Edinburgh, 1990.

McCalla, Douglas. *Planting the Province: The Economic History of Upper Canada*. Toronto, 1993.

McCusker, John J., and Russell R. Menard. *The Economy of British America, 1607–1789*. Chapel Hill, 1985.

McGowan, Don C. *Grassland Settlers: The Swift Current Region during the Era of the Ranching Frontier*. Victoria, 1983.

McGrath, Ann, and Kay Saunders, eds. *Aboriginal Workers: Special Issue*. 95 *Labour History* (1995).

McIlroy, John. "Financial Malpractice in British Trade Unions, 1800–1930: The Background to, and Consequences of, Hornby v. Close." 6 *Historical Studies in Industrial Relations* 1 (1998).

McKay, A. "The Assignment System of Convict Labour in Van Diemen's Land, 1824–1842." M.A. thesis, University of Tasmania, 1958.

McQueen, H. "Convicts and Rebels." 15 *Labour History* 3 (1968).

McQueen, R. "Master and Servant as 'Social Control': The Role of Law in Labour Relations on the Darling Downs, 1860–1870." 10 *Law in Context* 123 (1992).

———. "Master and Servants Legislation in the 19th Century Australian Colonies." Unpublished manuscript, School of Social and Industrial Administration, Griffith University, n.d.

Meek, C. K., W. M. Macmillan, and E. J. Hussey. *Europe and West Africa*. Oxford, 1940.

Mensch, Betty. "Freedom of Contract as Ideology." 33 *Stanford Law Review* 753 (1981).

Merritt, A. "The Development and Application of Masters and Servants Legislation in New South Wales—1845–1930." Ph.D. diss., Australian National University, 1981.

Merritt, J. *The Making of the AWU*. Melbourne, 1986.

Metcalf, Thomas R. "'Hard Hands and Sound Healthy Bodies': Recruiting 'Coolies' for Natal, 1860–1911." 30 *Journal of Imperial and Commonwealth History* 1 (September 2002).

Miller, C. "Master and Man: Farmers and Employees in Nineteenth-Century Gloucestershire." In *Conflict and Community in Southern England*, edited by Barry Stapleton. New York, 1992.

Minchinton, W. E., ed. *Wage Regulation in Pre-Industrial England*. Newton Abbot, 1972.

Mohamed, Khalleel. "The Establishment of a Portuguese Business Community in British Guiana." 60 *History Gazette* 2 (1993).

Mohapatra, P. "Coolies and Colliers: A Study of the Agrarian Context of Labour Migration from Chotanagpur, 1880–1920." 1 *Studies in History* 247 (1985).

Moher, James. "From Suppression to Containment: Roots of Trade Union Law to 1825." In *British Trade Unionism, 1750–1850: The Formative Years*, edited by John Rule. London and New York, 1988.

Mommsen, W. J., and J. A. de Moor, eds. *European Expansion and Law: The Encounter of European and Indigenous Law in 19th- and 20th-Century Africa and Asia*. Oxford and New York, 1992.

Moogk, Peter N. "Apprenticeship Indentures: A Key to Artisan Life in New France." *Historical Papers* 65 (1971).

———. *Building a House in New France: An Account of the Perplexities of Client and Craftsmen in Early Canada*. Toronto, 1977.

Morgan, Edmund S. *American Slavery, American Freedom: The Ordeal of Colonial Virginia*. New York, 1975.

Morris, H. F., and James S. Read. *Indirect Rule and the Search for Justice: Essays in East African Legal History*. Oxford, 1972.

Morris, J. H., and L. J. Williams. *The South Wales Coal Industry, 1841–1875*. Cardiff, 1958.

Morris, M. D. *The Emergence of an Industrial Labour Force in India: A Study of the Bombay Cotton Mills, 1854–1947*. Berkeley, 1965.

Morris, Richard B. *Government and Labor in Early America*. Boston, 1981.

Morse, Hosea Ballou. *The Chronicles of the East India Company Trading to China, 1635–1834*. 5 vols. Oxford, 1926–29.

———. *The International Relations of the Chinese Empire*. 3 vols. London, 1910–18.

Mosley, Paul. *The Settler Economies: Studies in the Economic History of Kenya and Southern Rhodesia, 1900–63*. Cambridge, 1983.

Muir, James. "Structures, Symbols and Servants: Authority and the Maintenance of Discipline in the Hudson's Bay Company, 1713–1763." Unpublished major research paper, History Department, York University, 1994.

Mumewa E., and D. Fesl. "For the Unknown God, Queen and Big Business." Paper presented at the Ball and Chain Conference, University of New South Wales, December 1996.

Munn, Christopher. *Anglo-China: Chinese People and British Rule in Hong Kong, 1841–1880*. London, 2001.

Munro, Doug. "The Historiography of the Queensland Labour Trade." In *Free and Unfree Labor: The Debate Continues*, edited by Tom Brass and Marcel van der Linden. New York, 1997.

———. "The Labor Trade in Melanesians to Queensland: An Historiographical Essay." 28 *Journal of Social History* 609 (1995).

———. "Patterns of Resistance and Accommodation." In *Plantation Workers: Resistance and Accommodation*, edited by Brij V. Lal, Doug Munro, and Edward D. Beechert. Honolulu, 1993.

Murdoch, Beamish. *Epitome of the Laws of Nova Scotia*. 3 vols. Halifax, 1832–33.

Murphy, Eamon. *Unions in Conflict: A Comparative Study of Four South Indian Textile Centres, 1918–1939*. New Dehli, 1981.

Murphy, Terrence, and Gerald Stortz, eds. *Creed and Culture: The Place of English-Speaking Catholics in Canadian Society, 1750–1930*. Montreal and Kingston, 1993.

Murray, D. J. *The West Indies and the Development of Colonial Government, 1801–34*. Oxford, 1965.

Napier, Brian William. "The Contract of Service: The Concept and Its Application." Ph.D. diss., University of Cambridge, 1975.

Nash, Gary B. *Quakers and Politics: Pennsylvania, 1681–1726*. Princeton, 1968.

———. *The Urban Crucible: Social Change, Political Consciousness, and the Origins of the American Revolution*. Cambridge, 1979.

Neal, D. "Law and Authority: The Magistracy in New South Wales, 1788–1840." Paper presented at the Law and History Conference, La Trobe University, May 1983.

———. *The Rule of Law in a Penal Colony*. Cambridge, 1991.

Neale, R. S. *Bath, 1680–1850*. London, 1981.

Newman, R. "Recruitment of an Industrial Labour Force through Intermediaries: A

Comparative Study of the Cotton Textile Industry." In *Arrested Development in India*, edited by C. J. Dewey. Delhi, 1988.

Newsome, Eric. *The Coal Coast: The History of Coal Mining in B.C., 1835–1900*. Victoria, 1989.

Newton-King, Susan. "The Labour Market of the Cape Colony, 1807–28." In *Economy and Society in Pre-Industrial South Africa*, edited by Shula Marks and Anthony Atmore. London, 1980.

———. *Masters and Servants on the Cape Eastern Frontier, 1760–1803*. Cambridge, 1999.

Nichol, W. "Malingering and Convict Protest." 47 *Labour History* 18 (1984).

Nicholas, S., ed. *Convict Workers: Reinterpreting Australia's Past*. Cambridge, 1988.

Northrup, David. *Indentured Labor in the Age of Imperialism, 1834–1922*. Cambridge, 1995.

Oberwittler, Dietrich. "Crime and Authority in Eighteenth-Century England: Law Enforcement on a Local Level." 15 *Historical Social Research* 10 (1990).

Offutt, William M., Jr. *Of "Good Laws" and "Good Men": Law and Society in the Delaware Valley, 1680–1710*. Urbana, 1995.

O'Flaherty, Patrick. *Old Newfoundland: A History to 1843*. St. John's, 1999.

Oldmixon, John. *The British Empire in America*. London, 1708.

Oliver, Edmund Henry, ed. *The Canadian North-West, Its Early Development and Legislative Records: Minutes of the Councils of the Red River Colony and the Northern Department of Rupert's Land*. 2 vols. Ottawa, 1914-15.

Olivier, Sydney. *White Capital and Coloured Labour*. London, 1929.

Orde Browne, G. St. J. *The African Labourer*. London, 1933.

———. *Labour in Tanganyika Territory*. London, 1926.

Orren, Karen. *Belated Feudalism: Labor, the Law, and Liberal Development in the United States*. Cambridge, 1991.

Orth, John V. *Combination and Conspiracy: A Legal History of Trade Unionism*. Oxford, 1991.

———. "Contract and the Common Law." In *The State and Freedom of Contract*, edited by Harry Scheiber. Stanford, Calif., 1998.

Örücü, Esin. "Mixed and Mixing Systems: A Conceptual Search." In *Studies in Legal Systems: Mixed and Mixing*, edited by Esin Örücü, Elspeth Attwooll, and Sean Coyle. London, 1996.

Owen, William. *Narrative of American Voyages and Travels of Captain William Owen, R.N., and Settlement of the Island of Campobello in the Bay of Fundy, 1776–1771*, edited by Victor Hugo Paltsis. New York, 1942.

Oxley, D. *Convict Maids: The Forced Migration of Women to Australia*. Cambridge, 1996.

Pachai, Bridglal. *Beneath the Clouds of the Promised Land: The Survival of Nova Scotia's Blacks*. Halifax, 1987.

Palley, Clair. *The Constitutional History and Law of Southern Rhodesia, 1888–1925*. Oxford, 1966.

Palmer, Colin A., ed. *The Worlds of Unfree Labour: From Indentured Servitude to Slavery*. Aldershot, 1998.

Palmer, Robert C. *English Law in the Age of the Black Death, 1348–81: A Transformation of Governance and Law.* Chapel Hill, 1993.

Parthasarathi, Prasannan. "Rethinking Wages and Competitiveness in the Eighteenth Century: Britain and South India." 158 *Past and Present* 79 (1998).

Patel, Sujata. *The Making of Industrial Relations: Ahmedabad Textile Industry, 1918–1939.* Delhi, 1987.

Paton, Diana. "The Penalties of Freedom: Punishment in Post-Emancipation Jamaica." In *Crime and Punishment in Latin America: Law and Society since Late Colonial Times*, edited by Ricardo D. Salvatore, Carlos Aguirre, and Gilbert M. Joseph. Durham and London, 2001.

———. "Punishment, Crime, and the Bodies of Slaves in Eighteenth-Century Jamaica." 34 *Journal of Social History* 923 (2001).

Pentland, H. Clare. *Labour and Capital in Canada, 1650–1860.* Edited by Paul Phillips. Toronto, 1981.

Perkins, J. "Convict Labour and the Australian Agricultural Company." In *Convict Workers: Reinterpreting Australia's Past*, edited by S. Nicholas. Cambridge, 1988.

Perkins, Simeon. *The Diary of Simeon Perkins, 1804–1812.* Edited by C. B. Fergusson. Toronto, 1948.

Phillips, Anne. *The Enigma of Colonialism: British Policy in West Africa.* London, 1989.

Phillips, David. "The Black Country Magistracy, 1835–1860: A Changing Elite and the Exercise of Its Power." 3 *Midland History* 161 (1976).

Pilarczyk, Ian. "The Law of Servants and the Servants of Law: Enforcing Masters' Rights in Montreal, 1840–1845." 46 *McGill Law Journal* 779 (2001).

———. "'Too Well Used by His Master': Judicial Enforcement of Servants' Rights in Montreal, 1830–1845." 46 *McGill Law Journal* 491 (2001).

Piva, Michael J. *The Condition of the Working Class in Toronto, 1900–1921.* Ottawa, 1979.

P.L.I.S. (Public Legal Information Services). *Manners, Morals and Mayhem: A Look at the First 200 Years of Law and Society in New Brunswick.* Fredericton, 1985.

Podruchny, Carolyn. "Unfair Masters and Rascally Servants? Labour Relations among Bourgeois, Clerks and Voyageurs in the Montréal Fur Trade, 1780–1821." 43 *Labour/Le Travail* 43 (1999).

Poos, L. R. *A Rural Society after the Black Death: Essex, 1350–1525.* Cambridge, 1991.

———. "The Social Context of Statute of Labourers Enforcement." 1 *Law and History Review* 27 (Spring 1983).

Prakash, Gyan. *Bonded Histories: Genealogies of Labor Servitude in Colonial India.* Cambridge, 1990.

Preyer, Kathryn. "Crime, the Criminal Law and Reform in Post-Revolutionary Virginia." 1 *Law and History Review* 53 (Spring 1983).

Prowse, D. W. *A History of Newfoundland, from the English Colonial and Foreign Records.* 1895. Reprint, Belleville, 1972.

Pue, W. Wesley. "British Masculinities, Canadian Lawyers: Canadian Legal Education, 1900–1930." 16 *Law in Context* 80 (1999).

Putnam, Bertha. *The Enforcement of the Statutes of Labourers during the First Decade of the Black Death*. New York, 1908.

Quinlan, M. "Balancing Trade with Labour Control: Imperial/Colonial Tensions in Relation to the Regulation of Seamen in the Australian Colonies, 1788–1865." 9 *International Journal of Maritime History* 1 (1997).

———. "Industrial Relations before Unions: NSW Seamen, 1810–1852." 38 *Journal of Industrial Relations* 264 (1996).

———. "Pre-Arbitral Labour Law in Australia and Its Implications for the Adoption of Compulsory Arbitration." In *Foundations of Arbitration*, edited by S. Macyntire and R. Mitchell. Melbourne, 1989.

Quinlan, M., and C. Lever-Tracy. "From Labour Market Exclusion to Industrial Solidarity: Australian Trade Union Responses to Asian Workers, 1830–1988." 14 *Cambridge Journal of Economics* 159 (1990).

Radforth, Ian. "The Shantymen." In *Labouring Lives: Work and Workers in Nineteenth-Century Ontario*, edited by Paul Craven. Toronto, 1995.

Ragatz, Lowell James. *The Fall of the Planter Class in the British Caribbean, 1763–1833*. New York, 1977.

Ralston, H. Keith. "Miners and Managers: The Organization of Coal Production on Vancouver Island by the Hudson's Bay Company, 1848–1862." In *The Company on the Coast*, edited by E. Blanche Norcross. Nanaimo, 1983.

Randall, Adrian. *Before the Luddites: Custom, Community and Machinery in the English Woollen Industry, 1776–1809*. Cambridge, 1991.

———. "The Industrial Moral Economy of the Gloucestershire Weavers in the 18th Century." In *British Trade Unionism, 1750–1850: The Formative Years*, edited by John Rule. London and New York, 1988.

Rathbone, Richard, ed. *Ghana*. London, 1992.

Ravi, Ahuja. "The Origins of Colonial Labour Policy in Late 18th-Century Madras." 44 *International Review of Social History* 159 (1999).

Raymond, William Odber. "The Negro in New Brunswick." 1 *Neith* 1 (1903).

Rediker, Marcus. *Between the Devil and the Deep Blue Sea: Merchant Seamen, Pirates and the Anglo-American Maritime World, 1700–1750*. Cambridge, 1987.

Reid, K. "Contumacious, Ungovernable and Incorrigible: Convict Women and Workplace Resistance, Van Diemen's Land 1820–1839." In *Representing Convicts: New Perspectives on Convict Forced Labour Migration*, edited by I. Duffield and J. Bradley. London, 1997.

Renteln, Alison Dundes, and Alan Dundes. "What Is Folk Law?" In *Folk Law: Essays in the Theory and Practice of Lex Non Scripta*, edited by Alison Dundes Renteln and Alan Dundes. Madison, 1995.

Rich, Edwin Ernest. *The Fur Trade and the Northwest to 1857*. Toronto, 1967.

Roberts, Michael Frederick. "Wages and Wage-Earners in England, 1563–1725: The Evidence of the Wage Assessments." Ph.D. diss., Oxford, 1981.

Roberts, S. H. *The Squatting Age in Australia, 1835–1847*. Melbourne, 1964.

Roberts, William Prowting. *The Haswell Colliery Explosion . . . 28th September, 1844.* Newcastle-upon-Tyne, 1844.

Robertson, Allen B. "Bondage and Freedom: Apprentices, Servants and Slaves in Colonial Nova Scotia." Paper presented at the Royal Nova Scotia Historical Society, January 1992.

———. "Tenant Farmers, Black Labourers and Indentured Servants: Estate Management in Falmouth Township, Nova Scotia." Paper presented at the Third Planter Studies Conference, Acadia University, October 1993.

Robertson, Marion. *King's Bounty: A History of Early Shelburne, Nova Scotia.* Halifax, 1983.

Robin, Martin. *Radical Politics and Canadian Labour, 1880–1930.* Kingston, 1968.

———. *The Rush for Spoils: The Company Province, 1871–1933.* Toronto, 1972.

Rockel, Stephen. "Caravan Porters of the *Nyika*: Labour, Culture and Society in Nineteenth Century Tanzania." Ph.D. diss., University of Toronto, 1997.

———. "A Nation of Porters: The Nyamwezi and the Labour Market in Nineteenth Century Tanzania." 41 *Journal of African History* 173 (2001).

Rodger, N. A. M. *The Wooden World: An Anatomy of the Georgian Navy.* London, 1986.

Rodney, Walter. *A History of the Guyanese Working People, 1881–1905.* Baltimore, 1981.

Rodway, James. *Stark's Guide-Book and History of British Guiana.* Boston, 1907.

Rogers, Nicholas. "Vagrancy, Impressments and the Regulation of Labour in Eighteenth-Century Britain." In *Unfree Labour in the Development of the Atlantic World,* edited by Paul E. Lovejoy and Nicholas Rogers. Ilford, Essex, 1994.

Roll, Eric. *An Early Experiment in Industrial Organisation.* London, 1930.

Rose, Sonya O. *Limited Livelihoods: Gender and Class in Nineteenth-Century England.* Berkeley, 1992.

Ross, McGregor. *Kenya from Within.* London, 1927.

Ross, Robert. *Beyond the Pale: Essays on the History of Colonial South Africa.* Hanover and London, 1993.

———. *Cape of Torments: Slavery and Resistance in South Africa.* London, 1983.

———. "'Rather Mental than Physical': Emancipations and the Cape Economy." In *Breaking the Chains: Slavery and Its Legacy in the Nineteenth-Century Cape Colony,* edited by Nigel Warden and Clifton Crais. Johannesburg, 1994.

———. *Status and Respectability in the Cape Colony, 1750–1870: A Tragedy of Manners.* Cambridge, 1999.

Rule, John. "Employment and Authority: Masters and Men in 18th-Century Manufacturing." In *The Experience of Authority in Early Modern England,* edited by Paul Griffiths, Adam Fox, and Steve Hindle. London, 1996.

———. *The Experience of Labour in Eighteenth-Century Industry.* London, 1981.

———, ed. *British Trade Unionism, 1750–1850: The Formative Years.* London and New York, 1988.

Rushton, Peter. "The Matter in Variance: Adolescents and Domestic Conflict in the Pre-Industrial Economy of Northeast England, 1600–1800." 25 *Journal of Social History* 89 (1991).

Ryan, Shannon. "Fishery to Colony: A Newfoundland Watershed, 1793–1815." In *The Cadiensis Reader*, vol. 1, *Atlantic Canada before Confederation*, edited by P. A. Buckner and D. Frank. 2nd ed. Fredericton, 1990.

Salinger, Sharon V. "Labor, Markets, and Opportunity: Indentured Servitude in Early America." 38 *Labor History* 311 (spring–summer 1997).

———. *"To Serve Well and Faithfully": Labor and Indentured Servants in Pennsylvania, 1682–1800*. New York, 1987.

Samaraweera, Vijaya. "Masters and Servants in Sri Lankan Plantations: Labour Laws and Labour Control in an Emergent Export Economy." 18 *Indian Economic and Social History Review* 123 (1981).

Sasaki, Masaya, ed. *Ahen Senso No Kenkyu-shiryohenhen*. Tokyo, 1964.

Saunders, Kay. *Workers in Bondage: The Origins and Bases of Unfree Labour in Queensland, 1824–1916*. St Lucia, 1982.

———, ed. *Indentured Labour in the British Empire, 1834–1920*. London, 1984.

Savage, Donald C., and J. Forbes Munro. "Carrier Corps Recruitment in the British East Africa Protectorate, 1914–1918." 7 *Journal of African History* 313 (1966).

Schuler, Monica. *"Alas, Alas, Kongo": A Social History of Indentured African Immigration into Jamaica*. Baltimore, 1980.

———. "The Recruitment of African Indentured Labourers for European Colonies in the Nineteenth Century." In *Colonialism and Migration: Indentured Labour before and after Slavery*, edited by P. C. Emmer. Dordrecht, 1986.

Schweitzer, Mary M. *Custom and Contract: Household, Government, and the Economy in Colonial Pennsylvania*. New York, 1987.

Scott, Benjamin. "The Custom of Apprenticeship in the City of London." In *Transactions of the National Association for the Promotion of Social Science, 1862*. London, 1863.

Scott, James C. *Domination and the Arts of Resistance*. New Haven, 1990.

Scully, Pamela. *Liberating the Family? Gender and British Slave Emancipation in the Rural Western Cape, South Africa, 1823–1853*. Portsmouth, 1997.

Sharp, Buchanan. *In Contempt of All Authority: Rural Artisans and Riot in the West of England, 1586–1660*. Berkeley, 1980.

Sharpe, J. A. *Crime in Seventeenth-Century England: A County Study*. Cambridge, 1983.

Shivji, Issa G. *Law, State and the Working Class in Tanzania*. London, 1986.

Shlomowitz, Ralph. "The Transition from Slave to Freedmen Labor in the Cape Colony, the British West Indies, and the Postbellum American South." In *Free Labor: The Debate Continues*, edited by Tom Brass and Marcel van der Linden. New York, 1997.

Shoemaker, Robert. *Prosecution and Punishment: Petty Crime and the Law in London and Rural Middlesex, c. 1660–1725*. Cambridge, 1991.

Sider, Gerald. *Culture and Class in Anthropology and History: A Newfoundland Illustration*. Cambridge, 1986.

Simmons, C. P. "Recruiting and Organising an Industrial Labour Force in Colonial India: The Case of the Coal Mining Industry." 13 *Indian Economic and Social History Review* 455 (1976).

Simon, Daphne. "Master and Servant." In *Democracy and the Labour Movement*, edited by J. Saville. London, 1954.

Sinn, Elizabeth. *Power and Charity: The Early History of the Tung Wah Hospital, Hong Kong*. Hong Kong, 1989.

Slee, J. "Alexander Nisbet's Nonaversive Approach to Reforming Convict Boys under Transportation to VDL, 1836–1837." Paper presented at the Ball and Chain Conference, University of New South Wales, December 1996.

Smandych, Russell C. "William Osgoode, John Graves Simcoe, and the Exclusion of the English Poor Law from Upper Canada." In *Law, Society and the State: Essays in Modern Legal History*, edited by Louis A. Knafla and Susan W. S. Binnie. Toronto, 1995.

Smandych, Russell C., and Rick Linden. "Administering Justice without the State: A Study of the Private Justice System of the Hudson's Bay Company to 1800." 11 *Canadian Journal of Law and Society* 21 (1996).

Smith, Abbott Emerson. *Colonists in Bondage: White Servitude and Convict Labour in America, 1607–1776*. Chapel Hill, 1947.

Smith, Adam. *An Inquiry into the Nature and Causes of the Wealth of Nations*. Vol. 1. Edited by R. H. Campell, A. S. Skinner, and W. B. Todd. Oxford, 1976.

Smith, C. M. *A Treatise on the Law of Master and Servant*. London, 1860.

Smith, Carl T. "Protected Women in 19th-Century Hong Kong." In *Women and Chinese Patriarchy: Submission, Servitude and Escape*, edited by Maria Jaschok and Suzanne Miers. Hong Kong, 1994.

Smith, Joyce Stevens, and Joyce Savidge. *Matilda: Her Life and Legacy*. Hong Kong, 1988.

Smith, Kevin D. "Fragmented Freedom: The Historiography of Emancipation and Its Aftermath in the British West Indies." 16 *Slavery and Abolition* 101 (1995).

Smith, Philip. "Circumventing the Jury: Petty Crime and Summary Jurisdiction in London and New York City, 1790–1855." Ph.D. diss., Yale University, 1996.

Snell, K. D. M. *Annals of the Labouring Poor: Social Change and Agrarian England, 1660–1900*. Cambridge, 1985.

Somers, Margaret R. "Rights, Relationality and Membership: Rethinking the Making and Meaning of Citizenship." 19 *Law and Social Inquiry* 63 (1994).

Spence, W. G. *Australia's Awakening: Thirty Years in the Life of an Australian Agitator*. Sydney, 1909.

Spray, William A. *The Blacks in New Brunswick*. Fredericton, 1972.

Steedman, Carolyn. "Lord Mansfield's Women." 176 *Past and Present* 105 (2002).

Steele, Ian K. "The Anointed, the Appointed, and the Elected: Governance of the British Empire, 1689–1784." In *The Oxford History of the British Empire*, vol. 2, *The Eighteenth Century*, edited by P. J. Marshall. Oxford, 1998.

Steinberg, Marc W. "Capitalist Development, the Labor Process, and the Law." 109 *American Journal of Sociology* 445 (2003).

Steinfeld, Robert J. *Coercion, Contract and Free Labor in the Nineteenth Century*. Cambridge, 2001.

———. *The Invention of Free Labor: The Employment Relation in English and American Law and Culture, 1350–1870.* Chapel Hill, 1991.

Steinfeld, Robert J., and Stanley L. Engerman. "Labor—Free or Coerced? A Historical Reassessment of Differences and Similarities." In *Free Labor: The Debate Continues,* edited by Tom Brass and Marcel van der Linden. New York, 1997.

Steinmetz, Willibald. "Was There a De-juridification of Individual Employment Relations in Britain?" In *Private Law and Social Inequality in the Industrial Age: Comparing Legal Cultures in Britain, France, Germany and the United States,* edited by Willibald Steinmetz. Oxford, 2000.

Stenton, Michael. *Who's Who of the British Members of Parliament: A Biographical Dictionary of the House of Commons.* 4 vols. Atlantic Highlands, N.J., 1976–81.

Stephen, James. *The Slavery of the British West Indies Delineated: As it Exists both in Law and in Practice and Compared with the Slavery of Other Countries both Ancient and Modern.* London, 1824.

Stevens, Robert. *Law and Politics: The House of Lords as a Judicial Body, 1800–1976.* Chapel Hill, 1978.

Stichter, Sharon. *Migrant Labour in Kenya: Capitalism and African Response, 1895–1975.* Harlow, 1982.

Stockwell, Sarah. *The Business of Decolonization: British Business Strategies in the Gold Coast.* Oxford, 2000.

Stokes, E. *The English Utilitarians and India.* Delhi, 1959.

Stokes, W. *The Anglo-Indian Codes.* Oxford, 1887.

Stone, Arthur J. "The Admiralty Court in Colonial Nova Scotia." 17 *Dalhousie Law Journal* 363 (1994).

Stone, Thomas. "The Mounties as Vigilantes: Perceptions of Community and the Transformation of Law in the Yukon." In *Historical Perspectives on Law and Society in Canada,* edited by Tina Loo and Lorna R. McLean. Toronto, 1994.

Story, G. M., W. J. Kirwin, and J. D. A. Widdowson, eds. *Dictionary of Newfoundland English.* 2nd ed. Toronto, 1990.

Strange, Carolyn, ed. *Qualities of Mercy: Justice, Punishment, and Discretion.* Vancouver, 1996.

Stuart, Julian. *Part of the Glory: Reminiscences of the Shearers' Strike Queensland, 1891.* Sydney, 1967.

Sturge, Joseph, and Thomas Harvey. *The West Indies in 1837, being the Journal of a visit to Antigua, Montserrat, Dominica, St. Lucia, Barbados and Jamaica Undertaken for the Purpose of Ascertaining the Actual Condition of the Negro Population in the Islands.* London, 1838.

Svenson, S. *The Shearers' War: The Story of the 1891 Shearers' Strike.* St. Lucia, 1989.

Sweeney, T. "The Extension and Practice of Summary Jurisdiction in England, 1790–1860." Ph.D. diss., Cambridge University, 1975.

Swift, Roger. "The English Urban Magistracy and the Administration of Justice during Early Nineteenth Century Wolverhampton, 1815–1860." 17 *Midland History* 75 (1992).

Swinfen, D. B. *Imperial Control of Colonial Legislation, 1813–1865: A Study of British Policy towards Colonial Legislative Powers*. Oxford, 1970.

Sylvester, Dorothy. *A History of Cheshire*. London, 1971.

Tambila, Anso. "A History of the Tanga Sisal Labour Force, 1936–1964." M.A. thesis, Dar es Salaam, 1974.

Temple, R. *India in 1880*. London, 1880.

Thomas, L. *The Development of the Labour Movement in the Sydney District of New South Wales*. Canberra, 1962.

Thomas, Roger. "Forced Labour in British West Africa: The Case of the Northern Territories of the Gold Coast, 1906–1927." 14 *Journal of African History* 73 (1973).

Thompson, E. P. "The Crime of Anonymity." In *Albion's Fatal Tree: Crime and Society in Eighteenth Century England*, edited by Douglas Hay, Peter Linebaugh, and E. P. Thompson. New York, 1975.

———. "Folklore, Anthropology, and Social History." 3 *Indian Historical Review* 255 (1977).

Tighe, W., and F. A. Russell. *The Law as between Master and Servant and the Law of Employers' Liability in New South Wales Comprising the Masters and Servants Act, Truck Act, Employers' Liability Act, Factories and Shops Act and Coal Mines Regulation Acts with an Account of the Rights and Duties of Master and Servant at Common Law and with Copious Annotations and References*. Sydney, 1905.

Ting, Joseph S. P. "Native Chinese Peace Officers in British Hong Kong, 1841–1861." In *Between East and West: Aspects of Social and Political Development in Hong Kong*, edited by Elizabeth Sinn. Hong Kong, 1990.

Tinker, Hugh. *A New System of Slavery: The Export of Indian Labour Overseas*. Oxford, 1974.

Tomlins, Christopher L. "In Nat Turner's Shadow: Reflections on the Norfolk Dry Dock Affair of 1830–31." 33 *Labor History* 494 (1992).

———. *Law, Labor, and Ideology in the Early American Republic*. Cambridge, 1993.

———. "Perspectives on the Historical Significance of Indentured Servitude: The Early American Case." Unpublished manuscript, n.d.

———. "Reconsidering Indentured Servitude: European Migration and the Early American Labor Force, 1600–1775." 42 *Labor History* 5 (2001).

———. "Subordination, Authority, Law: Subjects in Labour History." 47 *International Labor and Working Class History* 56 (1995).

Tomlins, Christopher L., and Bruce H. Mann, eds. *The Many Legalities of Early America*. Chapel Hill and London, 2001.

Tomlinson, B. R. *The Economy of Modern India, 1860–1970*. Cambridge, 1993.

Torrens, McCullagh. *The Life and Times of the Right Honourable Sir James R. G. Graham, Bart. GCB, MP*. London, 1863.

Trainor, Richard. *Black Country Elites: The Exercise of Authority in an Industrial Area, 1830–1900*. Oxford, 1993.

Tronson, J. M. *Personal Narrative of a Voyage to Japan, Kamtschatka, Siberia, Tartary and Various Parts of Coast of China; in HMS Barracouta*. London, 1859.

Trotman, David. *Crime in Trinidad: Conflict and Control in a Plantation Society, 1838–1900*. Knoxville, 1986.

Trudel, Marcel. *L'esclavage au Canada français: Histoire et conditions de l'esclavage*. Quebec, 1960.

Tsai, Jung-fang. *Hong Kong in Chinese History: Community and Social Unrest in the British Colony, 1842–1913*. New York, 1993.

Turner, J. W. "Coalmining and Manufacturing in Newcastle, 1797-1900." Ph.D. diss., University of Newcastle, 1977.

———. "Newcastle Miners and the Master and Servant Act, 1830–1862." 16 *Labour History* 30 (1969).

Turner, Mary. "The 11 O'clock Flog: Women, Work and Labour Law in the British Caribbean." In *Working Slavery, Pricing Freedom: Perspectives from the Caribbean, Africa and the African Diaspora*, edited by Verene Shepherd. New York, 2002.

———. *Slaves and Missionaries: The Disintegration of Jamaican Slave Society, 1787–1834*. Urbana, 1982.

———. "Slave Workers, Subsistence and Labour Bargaining: 'Amity Hall', Jamaica 1805–1832." In *The Slaves' Economy: Independent Production by Slaves in the Americas*, edited by Ira Berlin and Philip D. Morgan. London, 1991.

———, ed. *From Chattel Slaves to Wage Slaves: The Dynamics of Labour Bargaining in the Americas*. London, 1995.

Ulrich, Laurel Thatcher. *Good Wives: Image and Reality in the Lives of Women in Northern New England, 1650–1750*. New York, 1982.

van der Horst, Sheila T. *Native Labour in South Africa*. Oxford, 1972.

Van Kirk, Sylvia. *Many Tender Ties: Women in Fur-Trade Society in Western Canada, 1670–1870*. Winnipeg, 1980.

van Onselen, Charles. *Chibaro: African Mine Labour in Southern Rhodesia, 1900–1933*. Johannesburg, 1976. Reprint, London, 1980.

———. "Worker Consciousness in Black Miners: Southern Rhodesia, 1900-1920." In *Studies in the History of African Mine Labour in Colonial Zimbabwe*, edited by I. R. Phimister and C. van Onselen. Salisbury, 1978.

van Zwanenberg, Roger M. *Colonial Capitalism and Labour in Kenya, 1919–1939*. Nairobi, 1975.

Venables, Josephine Liardet. "Account of the Rebellion in China in the Early Fifties." Unpublished manuscript, 1854.

Veneziani, B. "The Evolution of the Contract of Employment." In *The Making of Labour Law in Europe: A Comparative Study of Nine Countries up to 1945*, edited by B. A. Hepple. London, 1986.

Vickers, Daniel. *Farmers and Fishermen: Two Centuries of Work in Essex County, Massachusetts, 1630–1850*. Chapel Hill, 1994.

Walker, James W. St. G. *The Black Loyalists: The Search for a Promised Land in Nova Scotia and Sierra Leone, 1783–1870*. Toronto, 1992.

Walker, Michael J. "The Extent of the Guild Control of Trades in England, c. 1660–

1820: A Study Based on a Sample of Provincial Towns and London Companies." Ph.D. diss., Cambridge University, 1985.

Walker, R. J., and M. G. Walker. *The English Legal System*. 3rd ed. London, 1972.

Walker, Timothy. *Introduction to American Law*. Philadelphia, 1837.

Ward, J. R. *British West Indian Slavery, 1750–1834: The Process of Amelioration*. Oxford, 1988.

Ward, W. Peter. "The Administration of Justice in the North-West Territories, 1870–1887." M.A. thesis, University of Alberta, 1966.

Watkins, Elizabeth. *Oscar from Africa: The Biography of O. F. Watkins*. London, 1995.

Weatherhead, Alfred. "Life in Hong Kong, 1856–1859." Unpublished manuscript lecture, n.d. Typescript in the Hung On-to Memorial Collection, University of Hong Kong.

Webb, Sidney. *The Story of the Durham Miners (1662–1921)*. London, 1921.

Webb, Sidney, and Beatrice Webb. *Indian Diary*. Edited by Niraja Gopal Jayal. Oxford, 1990.

Webber, Jeremy. "Labour and the Law." In *Labouring Lives: Work and Workers in Nineteenth-Century Ontario*, edited by Paul Craven. Toronto, 1995.

Welbourne, Edward. *The Miners' Unions of Northumberland and Durham*. Cambridge, 1923.

West, J. *The History of Tasmania*. 1852. Reprint, London, 1971.

West, R. *The Acts and Regulations in Force in the Presidency of Bombay*. Bombay, 1867.

Whatley, Christopher A. "Scottish 'Collier Serfs'? British Coal Workers? Aspects of Scottish Collier Society in the Eighteenth Century." 60 *Labour History Review* 66 (1995).

Whitely, William. "Governor Hugh Palliser and the Newfoundland and Labrador Fishery, 1764–1768." 50 *Canadian Historical Review* 141 (1969).

Whiting, J. R. S. *Prison Reform in Gloucestershire, 1776–1820: A Study of the Work of Sir George Onesiphorus Paul, bart.* Chichester, 1975.

Wilkinson, W., and F. Wilkinson. *The Australian Magistrate*. Sydney, 1903.

Wilks, Ivor. *Asante in the 19th Century*. Cambridge, 1989.

———. "Land, Labour and Capital and the Forest Kingdom of Asante." In *The Evolution of Social Systems*, edited by M. Rowlands and J. Friedman. Pittsburgh, 1977.

Williams, Griffith. *An Account of the Island of Newfoundland, with the Nature of its Trade, and Method of Carrying on the Fishery, with Reasons for the great Decrease of that Most Valuable Branch of Trade*. London, 1765.

Williams, James Eccles. *The Derbyshire Miners: A Study in Industrial and Social History*. London, 1962.

Willis, John. "Statute Interpretation in a Nutshell." 16 *Canadian Bar Review* 1 (1938).

Willoughby, W. P. *Race Problems in the New Africa*. Oxford, 1923.

Winks, Robin W. *The Blacks in Canada: A History*. Montreal, 1971.

———, ed. *The Oxford History of the British Empire*. Vol. 5, *Historiography*. Oxford, 1999.

Wood, Horace Gray. *Treatise on the Law of Master and Servant*. Albany, 1877.

Woodland, C., and R. Storey, eds. *The Taff Vale Case*. Warwick, 1978.

Woods, D. C. "The Operation of the Master and Servants Act in the Black Country, 1858–1875." 7 *Midlands History* 93 (1982).

Woodward, D. "The Background to the Statute of Artificers: The Genesis of Labour Policy, 1558–63." 33 *Economic History Review*, n.s., 32 (1980).

———. *Men at Work: Labourers and Building Craftsmen in the Towns of Northern England, 1450–1750*. Cambridge, 1995.

Worden, Nigel. "Between Slavery and Freedom: The Apprenticeship Period, 1834–1838." In *Breaking the Chains: Slavery and Its Legacy in the Nineteenth-Century Cape Colony*, edited by Nigel Worden and Clifton Crais. Johannesburg, 1994.

———. "Slave Apprenticeship in Cape Town, 1834–1838." 7 *Studies in the History of Cape Town* 32 (1994).

———. *Slavery in Dutch South Africa*. Cambridge, 1985.

Worger, W. *South Africa's City of Diamonds: Mineworkers and Monopoly Capitalism in Kimberley, 1867–1895*. New Haven, 1987.

Worsfold, W. B. *The Reconstruction of the New Colonies under Lord Milner*. London, 1913.

Wrigley, E. A., and R. S. Schofield. *The Population History of England, 1541–1871: A Reconstruction*. Cambridge, 1989.

Wynn, Graeme. *Timber Colony: A Study in the Historical Geography of Early New Brunswick*. Toronto, 1981.

Yamin, G. "The Character and Origins of Labour Migration from Ratnagiri District, 1840–1920." 9 *South Asia Research* 33 (1989).

Yen-p'ing, Hao. *The Comprador in Nineteenth Century China: Bridge between East and West*. Cambridge, 1970.

Zangerl, Carl. "The Social Composition of the County Magistracy in England and Wales, 1831–1887." 11 *Journal of British Studies* 113 (1971).

Contributors

DAVID M. ANDERSON is University Lecturer in African Studies at the University of Oxford and a Research Fellow of St. Antony's College, Oxford. His most recent publications include *Eroding the Commons: Politics of Ecology in Baringo, Kenya, 1895–1963* (2002) and *Histories of the Hanged: Britain's Dirty War in Kenya and the End of Empire* (2004). He is currently researching the history of illicit drugs in Africa.

MICHAEL ANDERSON is Senior Governance Adviser at the U.K. Department for International Development and Fellow in Law at the London School of Economics. His research interests include comparative legal history, the laws of South Asia, human rights, and environmental law.

JERRY BANNISTER is an assistant professor in the Department of History at Dalhousie University, Halifax, and author of *The Rule of the Admirals: Law, Custom, and Naval Government in Newfoundland, 1699–1832* (2003).

MANDY BANTON (B.A., Ph.D. [London]) is a senior archivist at the National Archives of the United Kingdom (formerly the Public Record Office) and an expert on the records of the Colonial Office. From her appointment in 1984 she has specialized in document research and cataloging and in providing advice on using the public records.

MARTIN CHANOCK is Professor of Law and Legal Studies at La Trobe University in Melbourne and author of *The Making of South African Legal Culture: Fear, Favour and Prejudice* (2001). His main interests are in the fields of legal history and legal anthropology. He is currently part of a group working on issues related to customary law and sustainable development and is working on a project on law and state capacity in the colonial successor states.

PAUL CRAVEN teaches in the Social Science Division at York University in Toronto. His publications include *An Impartial Umpire: Industrial Relations and the Canadian State* (1980), *Labouring Lives: Work and Workers in 19th-*

Century Ontario (1995), and articles and book chapters about Canadian industrial and legal history and labor relations. He is codirector, with Douglas Hay, of the Master and Servant Project at York University.

JUANITA DE BARROS is a professor of history at McMaster University, Hamilton, Ontario, and author of *Order and Place in a Colonial City: Patterns of Struggle and Resistance in Georgetown, British Guiana, 1889–1924* (2002).

CHRISTOPHER FRANK is currently a research affiliate at the Institute for the Humanities and teaches history at the University of Manitoba. His 2003 York University dissertation, "Constitutional Law versus Justices' Justice: English Trade Unions, Lawyers, and the Magistracy, 1842–1862," examines labor's legal and political campaign against penal employment law and magistrates' summary powers. He is currently working on a social and legal history of the truck system in Great Britain.

DOUGLAS HAY is a professor in Osgoode Hall Law School and the Department of History, York University, Toronto. He is an author or coeditor and contributor to *Labour, Law and Crime: An Historical Perspective* (1987), *Policing and Prosecution in Britain, 1750–1850* (1989), *Eighteenth-Century English Society: Shuttles and Swords* (1997), and articles on English and Canadian legal, social, and labor history. He is codirector, with Paul Craven, of the Master and Servant Project at York University.

PRABHU PRASAD MOHAPATRA is Reader, Department of History, Faculty of Arts and Social Sciences, Delhi University, Delhi, India. His research interests include labor/social history, long-distance migration, and ecological history. His book, *Displaced Destinies: A History of Indian Labour Diaspora in the West Indies*, was published in 2004. He is currently researching early colonial labor laws and the history of industrial relations in postindependent India.

CHRISTOPHER MUNN served as an administrative officer in the Hong Kong government between 1980 and 1992. He currently works for the Hong Kong Monetary Authority and is an honorary research fellow of the Centre of Asian Studies at the University of Hong Kong. His publications include *Anglo-China: Chinese People and British Rule in Hong Kong, 1841–1880* (2001).

MICHAEL QUINLAN is a professor in the School of Industrial Relations and Organisational Behaviour at the University of New South Wales, Sydney. His major research interests are the history of worker organization and labor regulation in Australia and occupational health and safety. He has written a number of articles on the regulation of merchant seamen and whalers in the nineteenth century and is currently compiling a database on worker organization in Australia, 1788–1900.

RICHARD RATHBONE was Professor of Modern African History in the University of London and taught at that University's School of Oriental and African Studies until his early retirement in 2003. He is currently Honorary Professor in history at the University of Wales, Aberystwyth. His recent books include a two-volume documentary study of Ghana's decolonization (1992), *Murder and Politics in Colonial Ghana* (1993), and *Nkrumah and the Chiefs: The Politics of Chieftaincy in Ghana, 1951–60* (2000).

CHRISTOPHER TOMLINS is Senior Research Fellow at the American Bar Foundation in Chicago, where he has been since 1991. Formerly he was Reader in Legal Studies at La Trobe University, Melbourne. He is author of *The State and the Unions: Labor Relations, Law and the Organized Labor Movement in America* (1985) and of *Law, Labor and Ideology in the Early American Republic* (1993). He is also editor or coeditor of several essay collections, the most recent being *The Many Legalities of Early America* (2001). He is currently writing a book on the legal economy of English colonization of the North American mainland, parts of which have been appearing in articles and essays since 1995.

MARY TURNER, Caribbean historian, is Senior Research Fellow at the Institute of Commonwealth Studies, London University. She pioneered the modern study of British Caribbean slave rebellions, contributed to studies of slave culture and religion, and added a new strand to labor history by establishing, in association with colleagues, that slave workers throughout the Americas developed collective bargaining procedures: *From Chattel Slaves to Wage Slaves: The Dynamics of Labour Bargaining in the Americas* (1995). She is currently researching the relationship between changes in legal status and labor conditions on Caribbean sugar plantations.

Index of Statutes

This is a highly condensed index to most of the British and British colonial statutes (including ordinances, proclamations, and Imperial orders-in-council [O-in-C], as well as enactments of representative legislatures) mentioned in the text and footnotes. It is organized by enacting jurisdiction and year, within broad geographical regions. Abbreviations used in the text and notes are shown in parentheses following the name of the jurisdiction. In compiling the list of colonies and their dates, we have used Anne Thurston, *Sources for Colonial Studies in the Public Record Office*, Volume 1 (London: HMSO, 1995).

There was no standard method of identifying statutes within the British Empire. Methods included sequential numbering, numbering within calendar years, numbering within regnal years, and variants of these. In this index, we use the most economical identification found on the copy we have seen (in almost every case). A few statutes are identified by title, and some others by date of passage or promulgation. British statutes are identified in this book according to the *Chronological Table of the Statutes*, which is not uniformly consistent with other schemes.

General Index

Abbreviations used:

CJ   Chief Justice
CO   Colonial Office
CO Sec.   Secretary of State for the Colonies, Colonial Secretary
DC   District Commissioner
Gov.   Governor
HC   High Commissioner
J   Judge, Justice of court of record
JP   Justice of the Peace
Mag.   Magistrate
parlt.   parliamentarian, member of a legislature (including cabinet ministers)